MITCHELL'S BUILDING SERIES

Components

Derek Osbourn   *Dip Arch (Hons) RIBA MCSD*

Mitchell   London

© Derek Osbourn 1989

First published 1971
Second edition 1979
Reprinted 1987
Third edition 1989

Typeset by Latimer Trend & Company Ltd, Plymouth
and printed in Great Britain by
The Bath Press, Bath
Published by The Mitchell Publishing Company Limited
a subsidiary of B T Batsford Limited
4 Fitzhardinge Street, London W1H 0AH

A CIP catalogue record for this book is
available from the British Library

ISBN 0 7134 5653 1

Contents

CONTENTS

Acknowledgment to the 1989 edition

This edition is a further updated version of the original work of Harold King. Although his style of presentation for the subjects covered has been retained whenever possible, the format of the text has been revised to align with that of the more recent volumes in the *Mitchell's Building Series*. The *Roofing* chapter, which appeared in the original edition of this book, has been reinstated in this latest edition. A new chapter has also been incorporated, *Economic Criteria*. This has been written by Steven Gruneburg BSc (Social Science), to whom I am grateful for such a well informed and lucid account of an involved subject area.

The publishers and I again acknowledge with thanks the Controller of Her Majesty's Office for permission to quote the Building Regulations 1985 and Amendments, the British Standards Institute, and the research and development associations for permission to quote from their publications. My gratitude also goes to those already listed in the Acknowledgment to the two previous editions for their continued support, as well as to those companies who have suplied information and drawings for inclusion in this edition. These latest contributions have been credited in the new text and/or drawings.

In updating this work it has been necessary to draw upon much accumulated data supplied by others as documents, articles from trade and professional journals, or during discussions over many months. The excellent feature articles in the *Architects Journal* are in example of such an information source. I apologise to others not credited and offer my sincere thanks.

Jean Marshall prepared the new drawings and made the alterations to those of the earlier editions where necessary. I am very grateful for her patient interpretation of my drafts. My sincere gratitude goes to Rosemary Glanville, a colleague and friend, who cheerfully undertook that worst of all tasks involved in the production of a book, the proof reading! I also owe thanks to the staff of the Polytechnic of North London library for their help in the research, and particularly to Tricia Noble who spent many hours on the indexing.

Lastly, thanks must go to my family, friends and colleagues for my absence and pre-occupations during the production of the book, and to Thelma Nye for her encouragement, patience and very able editorial direction.

London 1989   D O

1 Component design

1.1 Introduction

The definition of a **building component** is given in BS 6100: Building and civil engineering terms Part 1 *General and miscellaneous* Subsection 1.5.1: 1984 *Co-ordination of dimensions, tolerances and accuracy* as a 'product manufactured as a distinct unit to serve a specific function or functions'. Components of various shapes and sizes, colours and texture are provided by the skills of many trades to fulfil the various functional requirements of a building suitable for human needs. The relationship of these various components to one another, as well as the components themselves, gives the visual character of the building and combines with other criteria to form aesthetic expression. So far in our technological development the act of building requires a vast number of these separate parts or components because we have not yet evolved an entirely monolithic form of construction, using one material and an erection process employing a single technique.

For example, a conventional house requires bricks or blocks for walls; concrete, steel or timber beams for floor and roof structure; and tiles or sheets of various materials for the roof finishes. Sections of timber, metal and glass are required for windows and doors; carpet sheets and clay tiles for floor finishes; various metal and earthenware forms for kitchen and bathroom fittings; sheets of timber for shelving and screens; complicated shapes of metal and plastics for door handles, window fasteners, coat hooks, etc. Other types of building require similar components, perhaps of different sizes and/or proportion, but all requiring to fit together satisfactorily to ensure the resulting enclosure provides an adequate physiological and psychological environment for its users. Components for a building, therefore, include every article used in its construction, or for use in the building and its surroundings.

Of the time spent on a site by a contractor using this method of construction, only about one-third is involved with actual erection processes and the remainder goes on preparation. This is because much reliance is placed on cutting and shaping materials on site to ensure they fit together reasonably well according to the design intention. Nevertheless, small components, such as bricks or blocks, provide great flexibility during erection because of their ease of cutting, both horizontally and vertically, and a covering of plaster or other applied finish helps to mask any poorly formed joints. Timber sections have the inherent facility for cutting and scribing to juxtapose surfaces and can be covered over by plasterboard or panelling. This, in itself, tends to be labour intensive and can result in costly wastage. Sometimes, it also results in an excessive amount of 'making good' in order to achieve dimensional adjustment.

The example of the introduction of standard parts for fixings, such as the nail and the screw, was paralleled in terms of achievement by Sir Joseph Paxton's production of factory standardized components to effect a seemingly impossible building programme for the building to house the 1851 Great Exhibition. These mechanisms for speeding construction were followed by the development of standard parts for cladding, such as the standard window and door. With the more advanced technology of today, involving rapid mass-production processes and sophisticated handling equipment, larger units can be made and components previously considered separately can be grouped together. Examples include: a door with door frame and door furniture delivered to the site pre-hung and pre-finished; factory glazed windows; composite wall panels either in timber, steel or concrete; trussed rafters and roof trusses which fold up for transportation; and hot and cold water systems and associated pipework to form complete units for use as service cores.

A vast amount of time is capable of being saved by the use of standard rationalized component design which also results in labour efficient jointing techniques and fewer on site operations.

However, the *design* and formation of these components are normally the responsibility of manufacturers, and this has often given rise to deep rooted fears in building designers. There is not only a concern that the mass-production of standard parts of a building under automated factory conditions gives rise to monotonous, straight-jacketed design concepts, but also that the site erection processes necessary to bring these individual parts together reduce the possibility of real craftsmanship and creativity. Although these fears relate mainly to the impact larger size components have on the design of a building, similar concerns exist about the smaller components where inadequate consideration has been given to their context within a building. Nevertheless, the use of mass produced components is well established and they will be increasingly employed as conventional site operations fail to meet the need for higher technical standards of performance. In order to meet this challenge, the designer must combine skills in design with other skills allowing communication of ideas to draw upon the parallel expertise of specialists in technical performance, material properties and manufacturing techniques.

Industrialization is not exclusively concerned with changes of method on site or in the factory, but involves a new attitude to design and construction which concerns client, designer (architect), administrator, manufacturer and contractor. Traditionally, it is generally true – perhaps surprisingly – that the construction industry is the only major industry where design and construction are carried out under different management control. Industrialization breaks down these traditional divisions of responsibility in the building process and favours a mutually dependent organization.

1.2 System building

The incorporation of many forms of components to form the whole design of a building should not be confused with **system building**, as this involves the use of a few specially related components in a much more restrictive way to create a particular form of building. For example, a system built factory employs larger scale components of one main material (eg concrete or timber) to form complete constructions of wall, floor and roof elements designed to fit together as a series of repetitive units with little scope for variation in appearance or distances between joints. System building manufacturers produce their components independently of most other building component manufacturers, and the buildings resulting from their particular range of components are referred to as *closed system* buildings. The manufacturers who supply components for use with those of other manufacturers are responsible for *open system* building. One of the most important features of the difference between 'open' and 'closed' building systems involves the on site construction techniques employed for each. Open systems still employ a great deal of craft skill which may vary for each type of component used, albeit modified to match developments in their designs, whereas closed systems frequently rely on single techniques peculiar to a chosen system and form a complete building package for the client. Chapter 3 deals with system building based on independent large scale factory processes for the production of components.

1.3 Requirements of components

Every building component will have to fulfil a number of requirements in respect of a minimum standard of performance to be expected. These must be first set down, and from more detailed analysis, the **performance specification** for the component can be devised to provide exact data about requirements and function. This form of specification lists the measurable terms of expected achievement and differs from the conventional **production specification** which describes the materials, standard of workmanship and method of manufacture in absolute terms without recourse to the expertise of the manufacturer. By not stating the performance standard required, a performance specification allows the manufacturer to select suitable materials and production methods. Thus, the incentive to develop economic methods of production lies with the manufacturer.

In devising a suitable solution to the problems posed by a performance specification the manufacturer is expected to consider current (and often, modified or innovatory) manufacturing techniques, user requirements, anthropometric and ergonomic data, the properties and behaviour of appropriate materials, and analyse cost data so that conclusions may be reached which lead to the design of a component to give satisfactory technical performance. To these criteria must be added the aesthetic considerations imposed by the designer, who may require the assistance of the manufacturer or other specialists – depending on the precise nature of the component design.

The aesthetic considerations of component design could be partly influenced by prevailing fashions, attitudes or styles. However, it should not be forgotten that the aesthetic appeal must never be subject to pure whim, since technological considerations relating to purpose must have equal weight of influence. Likewise, the dictates of technology must be skilfully moulded to produce an aesthetically pleasing component.

The performance specification first describes the component and its use in general terms, giving information sufficient to allow an intending manufacturer to decide whether they are able to submit a price or tender. The inclusion of CI/SfB Classification for the component (see page 396) will be useful for this purpose. The manufacturer can then be invited to state the type and quality of components already manufactured by them which they consider satisfies the specification. Reference should be made to any appropriate publication of the British Standards Institution which applies to the component and further reference must be made to the governing regulations which may be relevant. The specification documentation should state the desired maximum and minimum life of the component. Manufacturers should also be required to state the delivery period and their requirements for storage of the component on site, as well as give details about the planned life of the component and recommended methods of maintenance. Any guarantees required to be provided by the manufacturer and the nature of any insurance cover must be specified.

The success of the performance specification as a descriptive method depends on an agreed list of terms or headings upon which a description of the performance of a component may be based. This will then form the basis of a common means of communication between the building design team (architects, interior designers, technicans, structural engineers, services engineers, quantity surveyors, and others (see *Mitchell's Introduction to Building*, chapter 15) who are concerned with description of components. Reference can be made to *Performance Specification Writing for Building Components: DC 9*, published by HMSO, which provides guidance notes on the content of the technical aspects of performance specifications. Figure 1.1, based on DC 9, provides a summary of the main properties relative to a check list of some specific components. It will depend upon the particular requirements to be met whether a property should be specified or not. In certain cases the user of a performance specification will be unable to set quantified values for the properties, but may request the component manufacturer to furnish details in respect of a component offered in response to a performance specification. It is important to note that the numbering system is based on the *Master List of Properties* (CIB Report No 3 1964) published by the International Council for Building Research Studies and Documentation. Thus, it provides a direct link between component and material properties.

1.4 Component testing and Quality Assurance

The **British Board of Agrément** employs the resources of the Building Research Establishment and other organizations to help bring into general use in the building industry new materials, products, components and processes. The Board offers an assessment service based on examination, testing and other forms of investigation. The aim is to provide the best technical opinion possible within the knowledge available, and those innovations satisfying critical analysis relative to their intended performance are issued with an *Agrément Certificate*. Products or processes already covered by a *British Standard* do not normally fall within the scope of this Board, and items to be subsequently covered by a British Standard are issued with an Agrément Certificate which is renewable after three years.

DIMENSIONAL SUITABILITY

This is a check list and it will depend upon particular requirements to be met whether a property should be specified or not. In certain cases the performance specification writer will be unable to set quantified values for the properties but may request the component manufacturer to furnish details in respect of a component offered in response to a performance specification.

Heading	CIB No.	Window	Roof finish	Partition	Internal door set	Ceiling	Floor finish
GENERAL INFORMATION	1.1						
Description of component	1.1.01	×	×	×	×	×	×
Type and quality		×	×	×	×	×	×
Identification of standards,	1.1.02						
quality mark	1.1.03	×	×	×	×	×	×
Purpose and use	1.1.04	×	×	×	×	×	×
Accessories	1.1.05	×	×	×	×	×	×
COMPOSITION and MANUFACTURE	1.2						
Composition	1.2.01	×	×	×	×	×	×
Manufacture and assembly	1.2.02	×	×	×	×	×	×
SHAPE, DIMENSION, WEIGHT	1.3						
Shape	1.3.01	×	×	×	×	×	×
Dimension	1.3.02	×	×	×	×	×	×
Geometric properties	1.3.03	×	×	×	×	×	×
Volume	1.3.04	−	−	−	−	−	−
Weight	1.3.05	×	×	×	×	×	×
GENERAL APPEARANCE	1.4						
Character of visible face	1.4.01						
Evenness	1.4.01.1	×	×	×	×	×	×
Appearance	1.4.01.2	×	×	×	×	×	×
Transparency, translucency	1.4.02	×	−	×	×	×	×
PHYSICAL, CHEMICAL AND BIOLOGICAL PROPERTIES	1.5						
Specific weight	1.5.01	×	×	×	−	×	×
Internal structure	1.5.02	×	×	×	×	×	×
Chemical formulation and material specification	1.5.03	×	×	×	×	×	×
Penetration of air and gases	1.5.04	×	×	×	×	×	×
Properties relating to the presence of water	1.5.05						
Moisture content	1.5.05.1	×	×	×	×	×	×
Solubility in water	1.5.05.2	×	×	×	×	×	×
Capillarity	1.5.05.3	×	×	×	×	×	×
Drying and evaporation	1.5.05.7	×	×	×	×	×	×
Moisture movement	1.5.05.8	×	×	×	×	×	×
Water absorption	1.5.05.4	×	×	×	×	×	×
Water penetration	1.5.05.5	×	×	×	×	×	×
Water vapour penetration	1.5.05.6	×	×	×	×	×	×
Thermal properties	1.5.06.1						
Thermal movement	1.5.06.1	×	×	×	×	×	×
Specific heat	1.5.06.2	−	×	×	−	×	×
Freezing and melting point	1.5.06.3	−	−	−	−	−	−
Radiation coefficient	1.5.06.4	×	×	×	−	×	×
Thermal conductance	1.5.06.5	×	×	×	×	×	×

1.1 *Component properties to be considered when preparing a performance specification with reference to a selected list of components* *Continued . . .*

Continued

Heading	CIB No.	Window	Roof finish	Partition	Internal door set	Ceiling	Floor finish
Thermal properties—continued							
Warmth to touch	1.5.06.6	−	−	×	×	−	×
High and low temperatures	1.5.06.7	×	×	×	×	×	×
Thermal shock	1.5.06.8	×	×	×	×	−	×
Strength properties	1.5.07						
Tension	1.5.07.1	×	×	×	×	×	×
Compression	1.5.07.2	×	×	×	×	×	×
Shear	1.5.07.3	×	×	×	×	×	×
Bending	1.5.07.4	×	×	×	×	×	×
Torsion	1.5.07.5	×	×	×	×	×	×
Impact	1.5.07.6	×	×	×	×	×	×
Hardness	1.5.07.7	×	×	×	×	×	×
Resistance to fatigue	1.5.07.8	×	×	×	×	×	×
Mechanical properties	1.5.08						
Resistance to mechanical wear	1.5.08.1	×	×	×	×	×	×
Resistance to the insertion and extraction of nails and screws	1.5.08.2	×	×	×	×	×	×
Resistance to splitting	1.5.08.3	−	×	×	×	−	×
Resistance to tearing	1.5.08.4	−	−	×	−	−	×
Resistance to bursting	1.5.08.5	−	−	−	−	−	−
Rheological properties (flow and deformation)	1.5.09	×	×	×	×	×	×
Frictional resistance	1.5.10						
Coefficient of friction	1.5.10.1	−	×	−	−	−	×
Degree of slipperiness in use	1.5.10.2	−	×	−	−	−	×
Adhesion	1.5.11	−	×	−	−	−	×
Acoustic properties	1.5.12						
Sound absorption, sound reflection	1.5.12.1	×	−	×	×	×	×
Sound transmission	1.5.12.2	×	−	×	×	×	×
Optical properties	1.5.13						
Light absorption, light reflection	1.5.13.1	×	×	×	×	×	×
Light transmission	1.5.13.2	×	−	×	×	×	−
Light refraction and dispersion	1.5.13.3	×	−	×	×	×	−
Optical distortion	1.5.13.4	×	−	×	×	×	−
Electrical properties	1.5.14						
Electrical conductivity (electrical resistance)	1.5.14.1	×	×	×	×	×	×
Dielectric constant	1.5.14.2	−	−	−	−	−	−
Liability to develop and shed electro-static charges	1.5.14.3	×	×	×	×	×	×
Effect of sunlight	1.5.15	×	×	×	×	×	×
Effect of electro-magnetic and particle radiation	1.5.16	−	−	×	×	×	×
Effect of freezing conditions	1.5.17	×	×	×	×	×	×

1.1 *Component properties*

Continued . . .

Continued

Heading	CIB No.	Window	Roof finish	Partition	Internal door set	Ceiling	Floor finish
Effect of fire	1.5.18						
Combustibility	1.5.18.1	×	×	×	×	×	×
Fire-resistance	1.5.18.2	×	×	×	×	×	×
Surface spread of flame	1.5.18.3	×	×	×	×	×	—
Effect of chemicals	1.5.19	×	×	×	×	×	×
Effect of impurities	1.5.20	×	×	×	×	×	×
Effect of fungi, micro-organisms and insects	1.5.21	×	×	×	×	×	×
Effect of other building materials	1.5.22	×	×	×	×	×	×
Changes of behaviour during use	1.5.23	×	×	×	×	×	×
Setting time	1.5.23.1	—	×	—	—	×	×
Heat evolution in preparation and application	1.5.23.2	—	×	—	—	×	×
Change in volume	1.5.23.3	×	×	×	×	×	×
Properties important from the point of view of hygiene	1.5.24						
Toxicity	1.5.24.1	×	×	×	×	×	×
Odour	1.5.24.2	×	×	×	×	×	×
Taintability	1.5.24.3	×	×	×	×	×	×
Tendency to deposit dust	1.5.24.4	—	×	×	—	×	×
Injury to skin	1.5.24.5	×	×	×	×	×	×
Liability to vermin infestation	1.5.24.6	×	×	×	×	×	×
Liability to become dirty, ease of cleaning	1.5.24.7	×	×	×	×	×	×
Safety	1.5.24.8	×	×	×	×	×	×
Tendency to deposit dust	1.5.24.4	—	×	×			
DURABILITY	1.6						
Durability of the component or assembly	1.6.01	×	×	×	×	×	×
Durability of specified component parts	1.6.02	×	×	×	×	×	×
Guarantee of durability	1.6.03	×	×	×	×	×	×
PROPERTIES OF THE WORKING PARTS, CONTROLS, ETC.	1.7						
Method of operation	1.7.01	×	—	×	×	—	—
Connection data	1.7.02						
Mechanical connection	1.7.02.1	×	—	×	×	—	—
Connection to power supply	1.7.02.2	×	—	×	×	—	—
Performance data	1.7.03						
Mechanical data	1.7.03.1	×	—	×	×	—	—
Capacity	1.7.03.2	—	—	—	—	—	—
Other performance data	1.7.03.3	×	—	×	×	—	—

1.1   *Component properties*

Continued . . .

Continued

Heading	CIB No.	Window	Roof finish	Partition	Internal door set	Ceiling	Floor finish
Consumption of energy and ancillary materials	1.7.04						
Supplied energy	1.7.04.1	×	−	×	×	−	−
Ancillary materials	1.7.04.2	×	−	×	×	−	−
Efficiency	1.7.05	−	−	−	−	−	−
Manoeuvrability and control	1.7.06	×	−	×	×	−	−
Other technical data	1.7.07						
Mechanical	1.7.07.1	−	−	−	−	−	−
Thermal	1.7.07.2	−	−	−	−	−	−
Electrical	1.7.07.3	−	−	−	−	−	−
Secondary effects and disturbances during operation	1.7.08	×	−	×	×	−	−
WORKING CHARACTERISTICS	1.8						
Ease of handling	1.8.01	×	×	×	×	×	×
Consistence, workability, working time	1.8.02	−	−	−	−	−	−
Ease of cutting, sawing, bending, etc	1.8.03	−	×	×	×	×	×
Capability of being jointed to other components	1.8.04	−	×	×	×	×	×
Fixing	1.8.05	×	×	×	×	×	×
Surface treatments	1.8.06	×	×	×	×	×	×
Capability of withstanding rough handling	1.8.07	×	×	×	×	×	×
Capability of withstanding storage	1.8.08	×	×	×	×	×	×

1.1   *Properties to be considered when preparing performance specifications for typical components and finishes*

The Building and Engineering Section of the British Standards Institution (BSI) offer testing services for a wide range of building materials and components, including: windows and doors, wall claddings, ironmongery, and plumbing units. Testing facilities enable the following forms of testing to be carried out: weathertightness and simulated wind gust loading; mechanical strength and related characteristics of metallic and plastics components and materials; impact, pressure, endurance and corrosion; artificial weathering; and assessment of finishes on components or materials. The primary purpose of the testing service is to assist manufacturers in the development and marketing of the products, and to provide building designers and specifiers with data on performance of products being considered for specific building projects. In addition, it assists standard bodies, trade associations, government departments and manufacturers in the development of performance based product specifications. Items are tested against national or international performance standards, government department specifications, manufacturers' or users' own specific requirements.

Having completed a satisfactory test, the material or component receives a BSI *Test Report* as well as a *Kitemark*. This Kitemark is a registered trade mark owned by BSI and may only be used by manufacturers licensed by them. The appearance of this symbol (figure 1.2) on a product indicates the BSI has independently tested samples of the product against the appropriate British Standard and confirmed that the standard has been complied with in every respect. When appropriate, tests can also be carried out on a product for conformity with British Standards concerned with safety or to the safety requirements of standards. Products satisfying such tests receive a *Safety Mark*.

The manufacturer is also required to produce and maintain other qualities based on BS 5750: 1979 *Quality Systems*. These are assessed by BSI as part of their **Quality Assurance Services' Certification and Assessment** scheme which sets out the organization, responsibilities, procedures and methods involved in manufacturing the product. Where a firm's *design capability* is to be included in the assessment, BS 5750: Part 1 is used. Of great significance in an increasingly competitive world for consultancy organizations pursuing fewer project commissions, firms offering professional design services – such as architects – are also seeking certification under this scheme. Otherwise, where a firm works to a published specification or the customer's specification, BS 5750: Part 2 is used.

Firms registering for the scheme are required to have a documented quality system which complies with the appropriate Part of BS 5750 and a related *Quality Assessment Schedule*. Before an assessment is arranged, a detailed appraisal of the applicant's documentation for compliance with these requirements is undertaken. The applicant is then notified of any significant omissions or deviations from the requirements in order that suitable amendments can be made prior to the assessment. Once the applicant's documented procedures are considered to be satisfactory, an assessment visit is arranged.

The assessment itself involves an in-depth appraisal of the firm and a requirement to demonstrate the practical application of the documented procedures. Where an assessor discovers a deviation from the requirements or witnesses a non-compliance with the documented procedures, a *Discrepancy Report* is given. After any deviations have been answered or rectified, or if no deviations are discovered, initial registration is granted and a *Certificate of Registration* can be issued. The registration assessment programme continues subsequent to granting the initial registration to confirm that the Quality System is operating effectively throughout the lifetime of individual projects falling within the scope of Registration. Post-Registration assessment visits are carried out at pre-agreed intervals, normally at the rate of two visits within the first six months

and a minimum of two visits per annum thereafter. Any later and acceptable alterations to the details shown on the Certificate of Registration can be made by endorsements. Registration entitles the firm to use the *Registered Firm Symbol* (figure 1.2) on letter headings, in advertisements and for other promotional purposes relating to the *organization and management* of the firm, ie not for products.

1.2 *British Standard Kitemark and Quality Assurance Registered Firm Symbol*

1.5 Methods of manufacture

It is necessary for the designer of a component to understand the discipline of factory production so that collaboration with the manufacturer at design stage will be more useful. Two methods of factory production are appropriate to the manufacture of building components, namely, flow line production and batch production.

Where **flow line production** is in operation, a stream of component parts in various stages of completion travel by conveyor belt through a number of work positions to completion. At each work position one or more operations are carried out until at the final work position, at the end of the assembly line, the component is complete. The operations are standardized at each work position and careful organization is required so that the necessary materials are always available. Flow line production methods can be highly automated, which means a high level capital investment in automatic machinery with a minimum of labour.

With this type of manufacturing process it is not easy for alternative operations to be carried out at a particular work position although, providing alternative work can be done in the same space of time as the standard operation, the system can be modified. An example would be the fitting of different types of opening light in a standard frame surround.

However, a flow line system is most efficient when uninterrupted by alternative operations. This presupposes complete standardization, which in its turn requires the development of a co-ordinated system of sizes and dimensions. Flush doors are normally produced by a flow line system. It is obvious from this example that where a large number of components are involved and the quality of the raw material can be carefully controlled, then factory production and factory applied finishes produce an article of better quality and value than traditional methods.

Batch production involves the setting up of machinery to manufacture a batch of components. An example of this would be the moulding of jambs and rails for a timber window, followed by the manufacture of a batch of sill sections after the machines have been reset. Batch production is not only adopted for machinery operations. It is also used for the assembly of parts where quantities, in mass production terms, are comparatively small, or where there is too much variety to allow the efficient use of flow line techniques.

Batch production is also the appropriate method where the cost of processing is low in comparison to the cost of setting up the process. In connection with the production of timber components, woodworking machines have a high rate of production in relation to the time taken to set the machine up. The relationship of the cost of production to the cost of setting up can, however, be made more economical if the variety of sections and mouldings can be reduced for a particular component. Thus, where the same moulded cross section of timber can be used for the various parts of, say, a glazed window wall, then the cost of one machine setting will be spread over the cost of the total length of the moulded section for the job.

In practice, **combinations of both flow line and batch methods** are used. For example, in the factory production of timber components the machining will probably be done by batch production and the assembly of the timber sections into the completed component will be carried out by flow line techniques. However, it must always be remembered that production techniques are continuously being examined, modified, and improved in an effort to overcome difficulties and disadvantages. It is essential that the consultation at design stage should be fully developed to facilitate this process.

A simple production line would be a single and continuous operation with the input of raw materials at one end and the output of finished goods at the other. At the start of production line there will be a store of raw materials which will allow certain fluctuations in delivery. Where one operation takes longer to perform than the others the line will have to be split, or additional machines and/or men introduced at this point. Storage will also have to be provided at the end of the production line to absorb fluctuations in demand. The theoretical layout of a production line will almost certainly be inhibited by physical limitations of factory space.

The proportion of overheads is not so high with mass production when compared with the production of a small number of components on a small scale. The percentage of the working year during which the factory is operating to full capacity is also a significant consideration in the cost per unit of the component. Machinery should be capable of being modified so that improvements in the design of a component can be incorporated without undue capital expenditure.

In order to produce components economically there is an optimum output in terms of the number of components produced relative to the nature of component and type of plant used. However standardized a production system is, it is inevitable that some components will be required to be non-standard, or may be required in such small numbers as to make them uneconomic to produce on the standard production line. The higher the degree of automation the more difficult it is to produce non-standard items, and it must be expected that they will be more expensive and have an extended delivery period. It follows from this that manufacturing techniques which can produce related components economically over the widest possible range will be more acceptable in the long term.

To allow a manufacturer greater control over the production and detailing, it is a good system to invite quotations for components on the basis of a performance specification which indicates the parameters within which the product must perform. The successful contractor, at this stage, can then be consulted in respect of detail and development work.

The various processes in the factory production of a range of standard timber windows are detailed in chapter 4, pages 83 to 86. It is very important that production can proceed efficiently without delays caused by imprecise information from the designer or the management personnel of the factory. Various *computer programs* are now available which ensure that precise details are made available for this purpose and a typical example for the production of a modular uPVC window is shown in figure 1.3. For most components, such *programs* are available from computer specializing companies which can be run on a large range of computers, or can be written by a component production specialist. They provide instruction about overall controlling sizes (see page 24); materials; quantity, dimension and price of each part of the component; works cutting schedule; special features of the component; a list of sub-components in stock which could be used; and sometimes the time needed for manufacture and delivery. When this range of information can be available to the designer speedily at an early stage in the design process, he or she can work

Continued on page 20

```
WINDOWLINK  LTD

WORKS  ORDER


DATE:           22.11.87
CUSTOMER:       WESTERN WINDOWS
REFERENCE:      12345/1
NOTES:


SYSTEM:         SLIMLINE UPVC
FINISH:         WHITE              HANDLE COLOUR:  WHITE
BEAD COLOUR:    WHITE              CILL COLOUR:    WHITE
HANDLE TYPE:    LOCKING            CILL REQUIRED:  150MM CILL
STYLE:          60 S.F.S
QUANTITY:       2
```

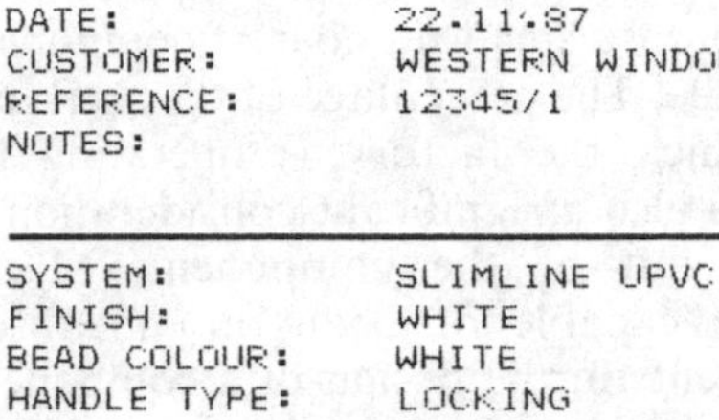

```
 - - E - -        - - E - -
 |        |      |        |
 |         \    /         |
 B          \  /          |
 |          /  \          |
 |         /    \         |
 - - - - - - - A - - - - - -
```

```
A: 1800 B: 1000 E:   600
```

PART DESCRIPTION	QTY	WIDTH	HEIGHT
150MM CILL (WHITE)	2	1900.0	
F01/11 OUTER FRAME (WHITE)	4	1805.0	
RPR05 OUTER FRAME REINFORCING	4	1686.0	
F01/11 OUTER FRAME (WHITE)	4		965.0
ZOO SASH (WHITE)	8	573.0	
ZOO SASH (WHITE)	8		907.0
TOO TRANSOM/MULLION (WHITE)	4		893.0
RPR12/18 TRANSOM REINFORCING	4		788.0
SIDE HUNG HINGE (PAIR)	4		
ESPAGNOLETTE 150MM	4		
4:12:4/CLEAR/STANDARD	4	474.0	808.0
4:12:4/CLEAR/STANDARD	2	568.0	874.0

1.3 *Computerized schedule for the production of a uPVC window (Windowlink Ltd)*   *Continued . . .*

Continued . . .

WINDOWLINK LTD

COSTING ANALYSIS — TRADE

```
DATE:            22.11.87
CUSTOMER:        WESTERN WINDOWS
REFERENCE:       12345/1
NOTES:
```

```
SYSTEM:          SLIMLINE UPVC
FINISH:          WHITE               HANDLE COLOUR:   WHITE
BEAD COLOUR:     WHITE               CILL COLOUR:     WHITE
HANDLE TYPE:     LOCKING             CILL REQUIRED:   150MM CILL
STYLE:           60 S.F.S
QUANTITY:        2
```

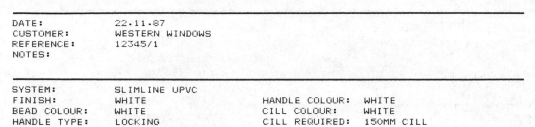

A: 1800 B: 1000 E: 600

PART DESCRIPTION	LENGTH	QTY		PRICE	TOTAL
150MM CILL (WHITE)	3.99		METRE	10.16	40.55
FO1/11 OUTER FRAME (WHITE)	12.19		METRE	5.10	62.20
ZOO SASH (WHITE)	12.43		METRE	4.58	56.88
TOO TRANSOM/MULLION (WHITE)	3.75		METRE	4.58	17.16
RPRO5 OUTER FRAME REINFORCING	7.42		METRE	1.80	13.38
RPR12/18 TRANSOM REINFORCING	3.31		METRE	2.42	8.00
RPBOO 24MM BEAD (WHITE)	17.33		METRE	1.56	27.09
3.5MM GREEN GLAZING WEDGE	17.33		METRE	0.33	5.64
RPGO4 SASH SEAL	12.43		METRE	0.37	4.65
RPGO4 SASH SEAL	12.43		METRE	0.37	4.65
SIDE HUNG HINGE (PAIR)		4	OFF	5.49	21.96
4.8 * 23 C/S S/T SCREW		48	OFF	0.04	1.92
LOCKING HANDLE (WHITE)		4	OFF	6.15	24.60
ESPAGNOLETTE 150MM		4	OFF	0.00	0.00
HANDLE SCREW		16	OFF	0.02	0.32
RPR10 80MM * 8 C/S POZI SCREW		16	OFF	0.04	0.64
180MM CILL END CAP (WHITE)		4	OFF	0.00	0.00
FABRICATION TIME		8	HOURS	0.00	0.00
GLAZING TIME		1.50	HOURS	0.00	0.00
4:12:4/CLEAR/STANDARD		2.52	SQ.M.		109.07

TOTAL: £   398.71

1.3 *Computerized schedule*

Continued . . .

DIMENSIONAL SUITABILITY

Continued

WINDOWLINK LTD

WORKS CUTTING SCHEDULE

```
DATE:           22·11·87
PAGE:           1
SYSTEM:         SLIMLINE UPVC


DESCRIPTION / ORDER REFERENCE                QTY LENGTH      TOTAL

150MM CILL (WHITE)
WESTERN WINDOWS          12345/1               2   1900 W
                                    TOTAL:         3800        1 BAR

F01/11 OUTER FRAME (WHITE)
WESTERN WINDOWS          12345/1               4   1805 W
WESTERN WINDOWS          12345/1               4    965 H
                                    TOTAL:        11080        2 BAR

ZOO SASH (WHITE)
WESTERN WINDOWS          12345/1               8    907 H
WESTERN WINDOWS          12345/1               8    573 W
                                    TOTAL:        11840        2 BAR

TOO TRANSOM/MULLION (WHITE)
WESTERN WINDOWS          12345/1               4    893 H
                                    TOTAL:         3572        1 BAR
```

WINDOWLINK LTD

REINFORCEMENT CUTTING SCHEDULE

```
DATE:           22·11·87
PAGE:           1
SYSTEM:         SLIMLINE UPVC


DESCRIPTION / ORDER REFERENCE                QTY LENGTH      TOTAL

RPR05 OUTER FRAME REINFORCING
WESTERN WINDOWS          12345/1               4   1686 W
                                    TOTAL:         6744        2 BAR

RPR12/18 TRANSOM REINFORCING
WESTERN WINDOWS          12345/1               4    788 H
                                    TOTAL:         3152        1 BAR
```

1.3 *Computerized schedule*   *Continued . . .*

Continued

WINDOWLINK LTD

STOCK REQUIREMENTS SCHEDULE

```
DATE:            22.11.87
PAGE:            1
SYSTEM:          SLIMLINE UPVC
```

DESCRIPTION / ORDER REFERENCE	QTY	LENGTH	TOTAL
150MM CILL (WHITE)			
TOTAL:		3800	1 BAR
FO1/11 OUTER FRAME (WHITE)			
TOTAL:		11080	2 BAR
ZOO SASH (WHITE)			
TOTAL:		11840	2 BAR
TOO TRANSOM/MULLION (WHITE)			
TOTAL:		3572	1 BAR
RPRO5 OUTER FRAME REINFORCING			
TOTAL:		6744	2 BAR
RPR12/18 TRANSOM REINFORCING			
TOTAL:		3152	1 BAR
RPB00 24MM BEAD (WHITE)			
TOTAL:		16504	3 BAR
3.5MM GREEN GLAZING WEDGE			
TOTAL:		16504	1 COIL
RPG04 SASH SEAL			
TOTAL:		23680	1 COIL
SIDE HUNG HINGE (PAIR)			
TOTAL:	4		4 OFF
4.8 * 23 C/S S/T SCREW			
TOTAL:	48		48 OFF
LOCKING HANDLE (WHITE)			
TOTAL:	4		4 OFF
ESPAGNOLETTE 150MM			
TOTAL:	4		4 OFF
HANDLE SCREW			
TOTAL:	16		16 OFF
RPR10 80MM * 8 C/S POZI SCREW			
TOTAL:	16		16 OFF
180MM CILL END CAP (WHITE)			
TOTAL:	4		4 OFF

1.3 *Computerized schedule*

Continued . . .

```
WINDOWLINK  LTD

GLASS  REQUIREMENTS  SCHEDULE
```

```
DATE:            22.11.87
PAGE:            1


                                        SPACER BAR   GLASS UNIT
DESCRIPTION / ORDER REFERENCE      QTY    W    H      W    H   AREA


4:12:4/CLEAR/STANDARD

WESTERN WINDOWS        12345/1       2                568  874  0.50
WESTERN WINDOWS        12345/1       4                474  808  0.38
                       TOTAL:        6                          2.52


END OF REPORT
```

1.3 *Computerized schedule for the production of a uPVC window (Windowlink Ltd)*

closely with the manufacturer and perhaps make small adjustments to achieve an optimum design solution.

1.6 References and terminology

The most relevant BSs which give detailed information on dimensional co-ordination and modular co-ordination are:

BS 4606: 1970 *Recommendations for the co-ordination of dimensions in building*. Co-ordinating sizes for rigid flat sheet material used in building.

BS 4643: 1970 *Glossary of terms relating to joints and jointing in building*.

BS 5568: — *Building construction*

Part 2: 1978 Modular co-ordination. Specification for co-ordinating dimensions for stairs and stair openings.

BS 5606: 1987 *Accuracy in building*.

BS 6100: — *Glossary of building and civil engineering terms*.

Part 1: *General and miscellaneous*.

Section 1.5: *Operations; associated plant and equipment*.

Subsection 1.5.1: 1984 Co-ordination of dimensions, tolerances and accuracy.

BS 6222: — *Domestic kitchen equipment*.

Part 1: 1982 Specification for co-ordinating dimensions.

BS 6750: 1986 *Specification for modular co-ordination in building*.

PD 6446: 1970 *Recommendations for the co-ordination of dimensions in building*. Combinations of sizes.

DD 22: 1972 *Recommendations for the co-ordination of dimensions in building*. Tolerances and fits for building. The calculation of work sizes and joint clearances for building components.

An understanding of the various terms used in connection with dimensional co-ordination in building is necessary, since descriptions which previously have been used loosely now have specific meanings. The following definitions have been taken from BS 6100: *Building and civil engineering terms* Part 1 *General and miscellaneous* Subsection 1.5.1: 1984 *Co-ordination of dimensions, tolerances and accuracy*:

Building element Major functional part of a building, eg foundation, floor, roof, wall, services.

Component Product manufactured as a distinct unit to serve a specific function or functions.

Assembly A set of building components used together.

Dimensional co-ordination Convention on related sizes for the co-ordinating dimensions of components and the structures incorporating them, for their design, manufacture and assembly.

20

Module   Unit of size used as an incremental step in dimensional co-ordination.

Basic module   Fundamental module, the size of which is selected for general application to building and components. Its value has been standardized as 100 mm.

Modular size   Size that is a multiple of the basic module (100 mm).

Modular component   Component whose co-ordinating sizes are modular.

Multimodule   Module whose size is a selected multiple of basic module (100 mm).

Submodular increment   Increment of size the value of which is a selected fraction of the basic module (100 mm).

Modular co-ordination   *Dimensional co-ordination* employing the basic module (100 mm) or a multimodule.

Accuracy   Quantitative measure of the magnitude of error.

Tolerance   Permissible variation of the specified value of a quantity.

Grid   Rectangular co-ordinating reference system.

Modular space grid   Three-dimensional grid in which the distance between consecutive planes is the basic module or multimodule. This multimodule may differ for each of the three dimensions of the grid.

Modular line   Line formed by the intersection of two modular planes

Modular plane   Plane in a modular space grid.

Planning module   Multimodule adopted for specific applications.

Preferred modular size   Modular size or multimodular size which is selected in preference to others.

Work size   Target size of a building component specified for its manufacture.

Reference system   A system of points, lines and planes to which the sizes and positions of a component, assembly or building element may be related.

Reference space   Space assigned in a structure to receive a component, assembly or building element including, where appropriate, allowances for tolerances and joint clearances. The space is bounded by reference planes which are not necessarily modular.

Co-ordinating plane   Plane by reference to which one component is co-ordinated with another.

Co-ordinating space   Space bounded by co-ordinating planes, allocated to a component including allowances for tolerances and joint clearances.

Co-ordinating dimension   A dimension of a co-ordinating space.

Co-ordinated size   The size of a co-ordinated dimension.

Zone   Modular or non-modular space between modular planes, which is provided for a component or group of components which do not necessarily fill the space, or which may be left empty.

1.7 Dimensional co-ordination

As stated earlier, the traditional pattern of trade following trade with materials cut to fit together on site made it possible for later trades to make good any inaccuracies in completed work. Rationalization of this building process involves the use of an increasing range of factory produced components which avoids the waste arising from cutting on site. For this to be most effective, it is essential that the component dimensions are co-ordinated by reference to an agreed range of sizes.

In accepting agreed dimensional standards for components, the use of non-standard or *purpose-made* components is largely avoided, thereby assisting design decisions and speeding the production of working details. Manufacturers can make more effective use of their production resources (materials, labour and plant) and on site processes can be speeded up because of familiarity with the components and erection permutations. However, it is important that manufacturers co-operate with the real world of building and accept a dimensional framework for their components that not only recognizes the process by which they are made, but also an industry wide discipline. In essence, this means that special consideration must be given by all parties concerned to the *joints and jointing methods* between the components. This is the point where, on a building site, production methods meet realities of construction techniques.

Dimensional co-ordination, therefore, is a system of arranging the dimensional framework of a building so that standardized components can be used within the framework in an inter-related pattern of sizes. In this way it can be closely connected with the overall development of building technology and the evolution of new building processes.

1.8 Modular co-ordination

It is necessary to establish a rectangular three-dimensional grid of *basic modules* into which the component will fit – see figure 1.4. A **module** is the basic dimension of a unit from which all other measurements can be derived. The term *module* comes from the Latin *modulus* (small measure) and has been used in building ever since the first century BC. In a classical Greco-Roman temple the module was the diameter of the column: it was not an absolute measurement, but varied according to the size of individual temples. Most importantly, it was meant to provide the basis of visually acceptable proportions for each component and, unlike today, was not as dependent upon the inter-relationship of different material characteristics, ease of manufacture and transport, or ease of erection of the component.

Notwithstanding the comments made under *Dimensional Co-ordination* concerning the acceptability of standardized component sizes between manufacturer and the actualities of the building site, there is now an **internationally agreed basic modular dimension of 100 mm.** This is used to give guidance to designers and manufacturers about the fundamental unit of size for the horizontal and vertical co-ordinating dimensions of buildings, their spaces, components, and materials. This basic module is denoted by the letter **M**.

The precise overall *modular dimension* for a particular component will depend upon the function of the component as well as the materials from which it is made, the manufacturing processes involved, the most appropriate method of transportation from the factory to site and the ease of storage and/or subsequent positioning in a building. BS 6750: 1986 recommends that components should be manufactured in **multimodular increments** of 3 M, 6 M, 12 M, 15 M, 30 M, and 60 M; and in **submodular increments** (fractions of

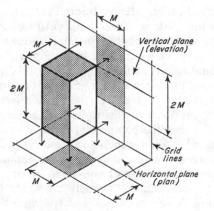

1.4 *Three-dimensional grid of basic modules*

Multi-modules	Preferred modular sizes in multiples of M																											
	3	6	9	12	15	18	21	24	27	30	33	36	39	42	45	48	54	60	66	72	75	78	84	90	96	105	108	120
3 M	3	6	9	12	15	18	21	24	27	30	33	36	39	42	45	48												
6 M		6		12		18		24		30		36		42		48	54	60	66	72		78	84	90	96			
12 M				12				24				36				48		60		72			84		96		108	120
15 M					15					30					45			60			75			90		105		120*
30 M										30								60						90				120*
60 M																		60										120*

*See note 3
Note 1 The preferred modular sizes that are selected in preference to other sizes for horizontal and vertical coordinating dimensions are primarily intended for the sizing of components, groups of components and spaces.
Note 2 The sizes derived from 3 M and 6 M have been restricted in the table to the limits shown.
Note 3 The 15 M, 30 M and 60 M series correspond to the series in a system of preferred numbers which contain the factor five. These series can also be extended to use larger increments in the series such as 120 M or larger.
Note 4 In the selection of sizes from the table, preference should be given to the series of the largest multimodule compatible with functional requirements and economic design.

1.5 *Preferred modular sizes based upon the multimodules for horizontal and vertical dimensions (BS 6750: 1986 table 1)*

the basic module) of either 50 mm as first preference or 25 mm as second preference – see figure 1.5. The adaptation of the basic module in this way permits internationally supplied components to be used with those from the UK. Modular sizes do not give the actual or working size of the component but only allots space for it in a building.

Figure 1.6 shows basic modular spaces for standard steel windows. Increased flexibility in respect of modular sizes can be obtained in several ways; for example, it is possible by using

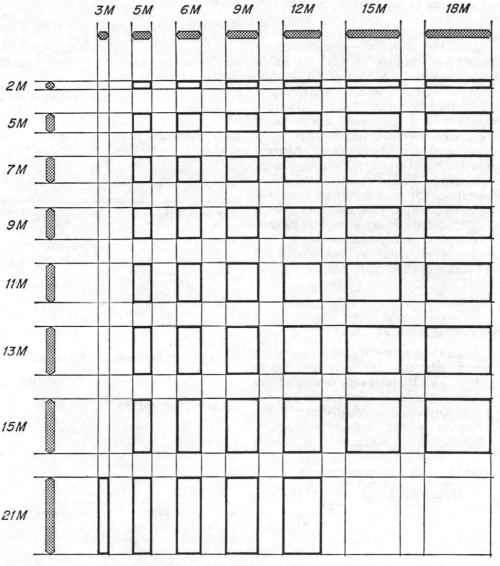

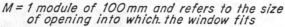

M = 1 module of 100mm and refers to the size of opening into which the window fits

1.6 *Basic spaces for standard steel windows (domestic type)*
see also figure 6.35 for purpose made steel windows

one or more pressed steel box mullions to add 100 mm to the length of the assemblies. Alternatively, using a wood surround will add 100 mm both to the length and height of the assembly. It is also possible to use a combination of basic units to obtain intermediate dimensions. By this means, all modular lengths and heights from 900 mm (3M) upwards can be achieved in increments of 100 mm.

Modular components are often required to be used in conjunction with components which are non-modular. An example of this is given in figure 1.6, taken from BS 6750. This indicates the use of modular windows with BS size bricks, ie 65 mm high with 10 mm joint. Used in an appropriate number of courses, overall modular sizes can be obtained for the brickwork or for a combination of window and brickwork. Alternatively, as in figure 1.7 (4) and (5) on facing page, a filler section can be used to obtain overall modular co-ordination. The Brick Industry's attempt at producing *modular bricks* (200 and 300 × 100, or even 200 × 75) did not meet with great success, perhaps because of a combination of the cost needed for new moulding equipment and the resulting break from the traditional appearance of brickwork.

1.9 Co-ordinating planes and zones

The use of modular grids for the setting out of the spaces occupied by components is described in BS 6750: 1986. This BS makes use of vertical and horizontal **co-ordinating dimensions** to define a regular framework within which to design and to which components and assemblies may be related. The dimensions define *controlling planes*

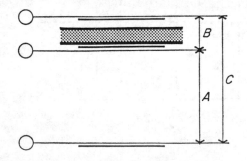

1.8 *Floor to ceiling heights*

Dimension/space	Range of space	Multiples of size
	mm	
Zones for columns and loadbearing walls	100 to 600	3 M or 1 M
Centres of columns and wall zones	from 900	3 M or 1 M
Spaces between column and wall zones	from 600	3 M or 1 M
Openings in walls (eg for windows and doorsets)	from 600	3 M or 1 M

Note   The first preference for the multiple of size in each case is 3 M

1.9(a) *Modular sizes for horizontal coordinating dimensions of spaces (Source*: BS 6750: 1986 table 2)

Dimension/space	Range of space	Multiples of size
	mm	
Floor to ceiling and floor to floor (and roof)	up to 3600	1 M
	from 3600 to 4800	3 M
	above 4800	6 M
Zones for floors and roofs	100 to 600	1 M
	above 600	3 M
Changes of floor and roof levels	300 to 2400	3 M
	above 2400	6 M
Openings in walls (eg for windows, including sills and/or sub-sills, and for doorsets)	300 to 3000	3 M or 1 M

Note 1   For application of 75 mm sizes for bricks and 200 mm sizes for blocks, see A.2.3.3.
Note 2   Where the option of 3 M or 1 M is given, the first preference for the multiple of size is 3 M.

1.9(b) *Modular sizes for vertical coordinating dimensions of spaces (Source*: BS 6750: 1986 table 3)

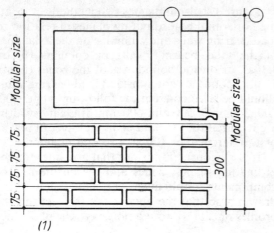

(1)

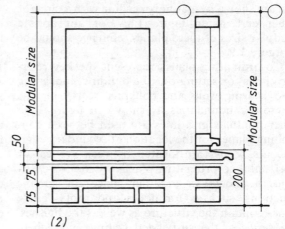

(2)

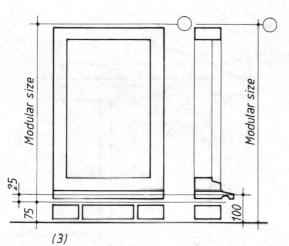

(3)

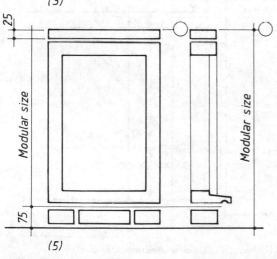

(4)

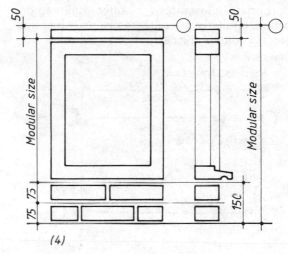

(5)

1.7 *Brick coursing and modular sized windows (BS 6750: 1986)*

and are shown by an unbroken line with a circle at either end, as in figure 1.8. For appropriate modular sizes of these planes reference should be to figure 1.9.

Co-ordinating planes represent the key reference lines for setting out the building, indicating load bearing walls and columns, storey heights and other boundaries as shown in figure 1.10; other modular grid lines are used between controlling planes for the location of secondary components. *Zones* are located between vertical or horizontal co-ordinating planes where it is desirable to allocate a modular space for specific functions, such as for floors and roofs. These zones contain the structure as well as the finishes, the services, the suspended ceiling and, where appropriate, allowances for camber, fall and deflection. Similarly, zones for walls, partitions and columns contain their structure and finishes.

Figure 1.9 also indicates two methods of locating horizontal co-ordinating planes in relation to load bearing walls and columns: on the axial lines of the load bearing walls or columns (figure 1.10a), or on the boundaries of the zones (figure 1.10b). Zones for columns and load bearing walls should be selected from the following range: 100, 200, 300, 400, 500 and 600 mm. If greater widths are required they should be in multiples of 300 as first preference, or 100 as a second preference.

It is obviously important that grid lines for co-ordinating planes, zones and the positioning of components should always be shown on working drawings so that the builder can then set out the profiles on site without ambiguity. The phenome-

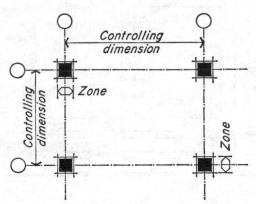

1.10(a) *Horizontal controlling dimensions by axial lines*

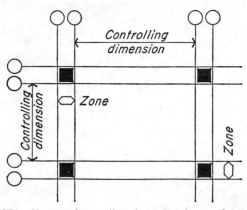

1.10(b) *Horizontal controlling dimensions by zoned boundaries*

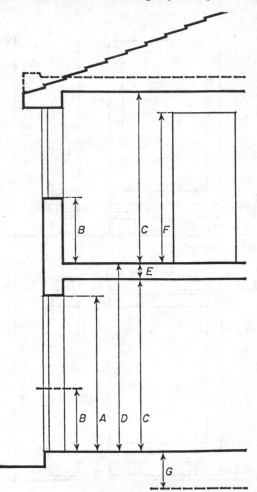

1.11 *Vertical controlling dimensions for housing*

Continued . . .

Continued

A	Window head height		E	Floor thickness
	2300 I			200
	2100 II			250
				300

B Window sill height

0	1000
200	1100
600	1200
700	1400
800	1800
900	2100

F Door set height
2100

C Floor to ceiling height

2500
2400
2350
2300
2100–garages only

G Change of level

300	1700
600	1800
900	2000
1200	2100
1300	2300
1400	2400
1500	

D Floor to floor height
2600–mandatory height
for public sector housing 2700

1.11 *Vertical controlling dimensions for housing*

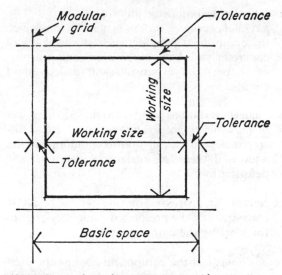

1.12(a) *Space relationship component to grid*

non of one component infringing on the space which should be occupied by its neighbour and this effect becoming cumulative, is known as *creep*, and is avoided by the use of these grid lines.

The range of modular co-ordinating dimensions and zones applicable to housing is shown in figure 1.11.

1.10 Working sizes of components

The basic size of a component is bounded by the modular grid (either between co-ordinating planes or a modular part thereof). From this basic size the **working size** of the component can be established as indicated in figure 1.12.

In order to enable components to fit together without the need for cutting down to size on site or using excessively wide joints and cover strips to make up undersized units, it is necessary that they are manufactured so that their maximum and minimum sizes do not fall outside predetermined limits. As indicated in figure 1.12(a), for a component to fit correctly within its allocated modular grid it will always need to be slightly smaller than its basic size. The theoretical basic size established for a component, useful for planning and design purposes, will have to be reduced to achieve a **working size** to take into account inherent and induced deviations between specified and actual size as follows:

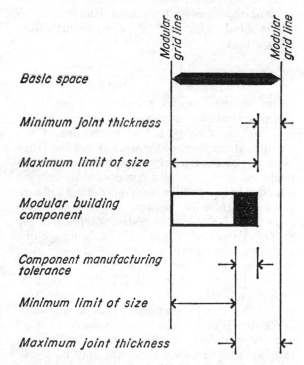

1.12(b) *Relationship of a modular building component to a planning grid*

27

- **inherent deviations** arising from:
  physical characteristics of materials from which the component is made, such as shrinkage of concrete; shrinkage, expansion, and warping of timber; the expansion and deflection of metals;

- **induced deviations** arising from:
  manufacturing processes which give rise to discrepancies in overall finished component size and/or flatness of surface, squareness and deformation;

  setting-out processes on site which result in inaccuracy of the prescribed guidelines or grids for locating the components;

  positioning of the component against the prescribed guideline or grid (or adjoining surfaces) so that slight misplacement occurs in height, length, verticality and/or angularity;

  fixings or seals between components, where these do not form an integral part of the component design (increased inaccuracy with size and quantity of components fixed together).

1.11 Tolerance and fit

Owing to the complex nature of variability in dimensions of components, the problems of tolerance and fit must be solved at the design and manufacturing stage of the work rather than on a building site. A relatively simple method of calculating the work size of a component by relating one edge to the grid line (or co-ordinating plane), or to the centre-line between two grid lines was given in BS 3626: 1968 *A system of tolerances and fits in building* – see figure 1.13. In the design of a component using this method, the designer must first select the basic size *B* or modular space within which the component is to fit and then the manufacturing tolerance *t* must be agreed. Following this, the designer determines the minimum gap *g* that is practicable between the component and the grid line, bearing in mind the jointing technique to be used. This joint may be a butt joint in the case of built-in furniture placed next to each other, or may be a mastic joint between

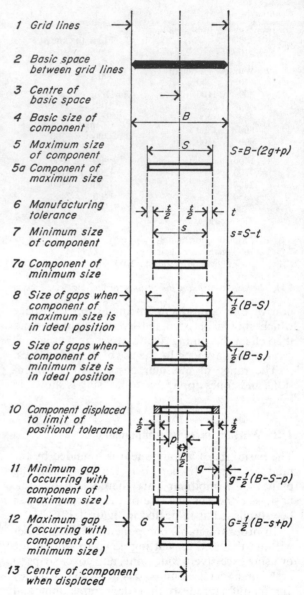

1. Grid lines
2. Basic space between grid lines
3. Centre of basic space
4. Basic size of component — B
5. Maximum size of component — S — $S=B-(2g+p)$
5a Component of maximum size
6. Manufacturing tolerance — $\frac{t}{2}$ $\frac{t}{2}$ — t
7. Minimum size of component — s — $s=S-t$
7a Component of minimum size
8. Size of gaps when component of maximum size is in ideal position — $\frac{1}{2}(B-S)$
9. Size of gaps when component of minimum size is in ideal position — $\frac{1}{2}(B-s)$
10. Component displaced to limit of positional tolerance — $\frac{t}{2}$ $\frac{t}{2}$ — p $\frac{p}{2}$
11. Minimum gap (occurring with component of maximum size) — g — $g=\frac{1}{2}(B-S-p)$
12. Maximum gap (occurring with component of minimum size) — G — $G=\frac{1}{2}(B-s+p)$
13. Centre of component when displaced

1.13 *The size of a jointed component and setting out by reference to centre line (BS 3626: 1963 withdrawn)*

window and structural frame. The minimum practical positional tolerance must next be decided *p*, that is to say the amount of space for manoeuvring into position that can be allowed. Having ascertained the three fundamental allowances, the component size can be established

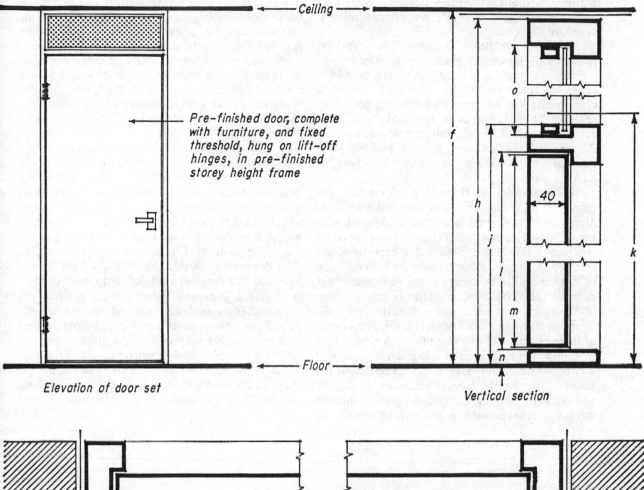

Pre-finished door, complete with furniture, and fixed threshold, hung on lift-off hinges, in pre-finished storey height frame

Elevation of door set

Vertical section

Horizontal section

		mm			mm
a	Actual opening—		*h*	Floor to ceiling set frame	
	tolerances: −zero; +10 overall			overall	*f* − 15
b	Nominal opening co-ordina-		*j*	Door height set frame overall	2090
	ting plane	900	*k*	Door height set opening	2100
c	Frame overall	890	*l*	Door and clearances	2045
d	Width between rebates	830	*m*	Door height fitted	2040
e	Door width fitted	826	*n*	Threshold thickness	15
f	Floor to nominal ceiling	for housing:	*o*	Over panel rebate	for housing:
		2300, 2350,			177, 227, 277
		2400			

Dimension *f* and *b* are grid line (or basic space) dimensions

1.14   *Dimensions for standard door set*

within a theoretical tolerance range t. Figure 1.14 provides a typical example for dimensioning a standard door set.

Although the BS 3626 method may still be useful as an elementary guide, it cannot be recommended in practise because the plus or minus range of tolerance (t) for the work size of a component has not proved to be economically realistic. It has now been replaced by a more accurate method of calculation contained in *DD 22: 1972 Tolerance and fits for building. The calculation of work sizes and joint clearances for building components*.

In providing mathematical formulae for resolving the many inherent and induced deviations in dimensional accuracy associated with the sizing of components (beyond the scope of this book), DD 22 emphasizes that experience has resulted in 'considerable refinement to the theory of tolerances in building which recognises that because the various inaccuracies in manufacture and construction arise independently from different operations, they are most unlikely to occur at their extremes at any one place'. A simple plus or minus tolerance range for a given work size of component does not give information about the number of slightly larger, accurate or slightly smaller size components being supplied within the overall tolerance range. A majority of any one of these sizes can give serious setting out problems on site, especially when a successful joint (with all its own collection of variables) between two components can only be achieved within a very narrow range of tolerances. DD 22 defines *tolerance* as 'the difference between the limits within which a size or position should lie', and goes on to state, 'Tolerance is an absolute value without sign, but the dimension or axis to which it applies has to be stated'.

The aims of DD 22 include providing component manufacturers with a method of more accurately deriving component sizes, providing designers with a method of calculating maximum and minimum clearances for particular assembly situations, and providing factors to be taken into account in determining tolerances for purpose-made components. It is important, therefore that this document should be consulted by those involved in a detailed study of component design. A Building Research Establishment publication entitled, *Graphical aids for tolerance and fits. Handbook for manufacturers, designers and builders*, is also helpful because it removes the need for complex and repetitive calculations and hence minimizes the time and effort at the design stage in considering all factors affecting jointing and fit of components.

2 Economic criteria

2.1 Introduction

The economic framework which may assist designers in their choice of components involves established economic techniques, such as *life cycle costing* and *linear programming*. Without such techniques, decisions would ignore much of modern management theory, which in practice uses scientific method, while allowing for predictable and unpredictable patterns of human behaviour. Adopting a scientific approach involves making deductive use of measurements where possible and appropriate. Systems analysis is concerned with the development of a simplified model of the real world, consisting of a set of mathematical functions or formulae, which Loomba defines as 'a particular representation of reality'. (LOOMBA, N. P., *Linear Programming: A Managerial Perspective*, 2nd ed, Macmillan 1976.)

Thus, models of a specific problem or situation will vary depending on different points of view, different aspects of the system examined and the different questions raised. A systems approach enables the decision maker to see the relationship between different parts of a project as well as the interaction of a project with its environment. A systems approach can, therefore, be applied to components which are the integral parts of a structure and have consequences for the building as a whole.

The aim of this chapter is to outline some of these economic techniques and describe the contribution economic theory can make to systematic and consistent decision making. The approach used by economists involves a framework of concepts including *opportunity costs* and *indifference analysis*, *incremental costs* and *the law of diminishing returns*. These will be dealt with first, followed by a brief summary of the techniques.

2.2 Opportunity cost

The price of a component is determined by the interaction of buyers and sellers in the market for a given product. The price is simply the amount of money required to carry out a transaction to transfer ownership of the component from one party to the other. Money is the means used to allocate resources between the different components of a building. The real cost of a component, the 'opportunity cost', is the cost of a component in terms of the next best foregone alternative. As finance for buildings is usually a major constraint, there is a need to make choices, and decisions have to be taken. The choice of one component means foregoing another. Thus, selecting a particular quality of window frame may mean sacrificing the quality of the balustrading. The foregone component is the real or opportunity cost of the component actually selected.

To apply the concept of opportunity costing to practical economic decision making, it is necessary to consider the possible alternatives available. Only by making comparisons can one establish the best solution for a given set of objectives. Ideally, all reasonable options should be considered and compared. However, because of cost and time constraints, this is seldom possible. Indeed, given the vast number of combinations of different variables, it is usually only feasible to investigate relatively few options in depth. Judgement is still very much required, especially during the shortlisting process.

For example, as far as heating a building is concerned, different costs will be associated with different systems. Only by making comparisons of products can one know that one is opting for the most cost effective solution. Clearly broader issues are involved than pure cost or energy consumption. Aesthetics and the preferences of clients also have to be taken into account. If, from an economic or, for that matter, a financial point of view, a second best option is chosen perhaps for aesthetic reasons, then the economic or financial cost of such a decision can nevertheless be established.

2.3 Indifference analysis

The purpose of decision making in economics is to increase utility. *Utility* is the usefulness or

31

satisfaction derived from the goods and services provided. For rational decision making, it may be assumed that the aim is to maximize utility. Indifference analysis presents a basic understanding of the decision process involved. Different combinations of components will generate the same or different levels of utility. An *indifference curve* is the locus of points showing the combination of components which generate the same total utility. For that reason, any point on the curve will be as acceptable to the client as any other.

In figure 2.1, the horizontal and vertical axes represent two specific types of fixed and opening windows respectively. The curve, I′, is an indifference curve, showing different combinations of the two types of window, which produce equal utility. Point P is a point of preference in that it represents a combination of doors and windows, which would generate greater satisfaction than any of the combinations on I′. Thus I″ is an indifference curve which yields higher utility than I′. It will be noticed that the curves are convex to the origin. Moreover, as indifference curves represent different levels of utility, they cannot intersect each other or touch. Figure 2.1 illustrates three indifference curves. In any situation there would in fact be an infinity of such curves representing increasing levels of satisfaction. The aim of maximizing utility is therefore achieved by reaching the highest possible indifference curve. This curve is found by drawing a budget line, which is dealt with next.

The *budget line* AB represents the boundary of maximum expenditure on the graph. If the total budget allowed for all windows were allocated to fixed windows, then A fixed windows could be purchased. Likewise, if funds were spent on opening windows alone, then B opening windows could be purchased. The triangle ABO represents the region of affordable solutions. The combination of x fixed and y opening windows produces maximum possible utility, given the budget constraint. At point Q the budget line is tangential to an indifference curve, I′. Lower indifference curves are feasible but do not generate as high a level of utility, while higher indifference curves are not financially feasible.

2.4 Incremental cost

Incremental cost is the increase in total cost when a more expensive component is used instead of a cheaper or standard version. Hence, the incremental cost of triple glazing is the extra cost over the price of double glazing. Incremental cost is also the difference extra units of a component make to total cost, for instance, in a high rise building it may be necessary to consider the extra cost of one more lift shaft. The importance of this exercise is to establish if the extra cost is worth the extra benefit. Although very often the choice will remain a subjective design decision, it will nevertheless have economic implications.

2.5 The law of diminishing returns

The law of diminishing returns states that, assuming everything else remains unchanged, as the amount of a component used is increased the returns from extra units of the component eventually decline. For instance, the U-values associated with single, double and triple glazing, namely 5.7, 2.8 and 2 respectively, do not decline steadily as glazing units increase, assuming the

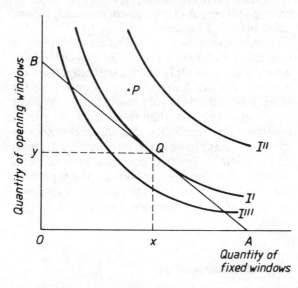

2.1 *Indifference curves and the budget line: showing the derivation of the quantities of fixed and opening windows used*

wall construction remains the same. Increasing from single to double glazing reduces the U-value by 2.9. Whereas triple glazing only reduces U-values by 0.8, in spite of the extra costs involved. Thus the extra return per extra pound spent eventually declines.

The law of diminishing returns also relates costs to the extra benefits derived from the purchase of extra units, which may be glazing units, the number of coats of paint or the quantity of non-load bearing demountable partitions of a given quality or type. Benefits may be measured in terms of revenue, output or one of the performance requirements referred to above, whichever is most appropriate. Components will therefore produce benefits. *Marginal Product* (MP) refers to the increase in total benefits derived from the adoption of one more unit. Thus in determining the quantity of a component to use, the extra benefit must be set against the extra cost. The greater the cost, the greater the extra benefits would have to be to justify the purchase of one more unit.

To ensure the optimum distribution of resources between components, the MP of each component should be proportional to its cost. This is consistent with the result shown in figure 2.2 above. Thus,

$$\frac{MP_a}{P_a} = \frac{MP_b}{P_b} = \frac{MP_c}{P_c} = \ldots \frac{MP_n}{P_n}$$

where MP = marginal product
a, b, c and n = various components
P = cost of component.

This equation demonstrates that the last £1 spent on component 'a' provides an increase in benefits equal to the last £1 spent on component 'b' and so on. If, however, it were possible to gain a greater benefit from expenditure on component 'c', then money should be spent on 'c', until £1 spent on the last unit of 'c' is equal to the MPs of all other parts. This may be achieved either by increasing expenditure on component 'c', if this is a possibility, or by reducing expenditure on all other components to release funds for more of 'c', until the money spent on each component is directly proportional to its cost. The law of diminishing returns determines that as less of the other components are purchased their MPs will rise and

as more of component 'c' is purchased its MP will decline. Thus, increasing the use of one component at the expense of others also affects the value placed on the other components.

The relationships between cost and marginal product and marginal and total product are illustrated in figure 2.2.

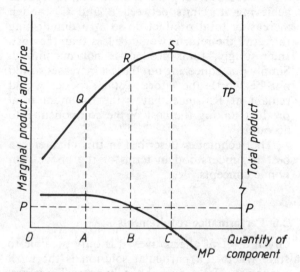

2.2 *Total and marginal product curves and the price of a component: showing the derivation of the quantity of the component used and the effect on total product*

It can be seen that when the increase in total product is constant, the total product curve is a straight line and the marginal product curve is horizontal until A units are used. Thereafter, the rate of increase in total product declines as more units are used. This is shown by the downward slope of the marginal product curve and a lower gradient in the total product curve from Q to S. At S the total product curve is at its maximum, indicating that the total product reaches a maximum and further units of a given component will in fact be counter-productive. This would occur if more than C units of the component were used. Hence the negative marginal product curve beyond C.

It can be seen, however, that in this example, the price level of the component is, say, PP. From O up to B units, the extra product as a result of using one more unit is greater than the cost of acquiring it. As long as subsequent units generate more than they cost, extra units will be purchased. At price P, B units of the component should be purchased, since this quantity ensures that every unit increases total product more than the cost of achieving it. Units between B and C, though increasing total product do so at a diminishing rate, and the returns would be less than the cost. Interestingly, total product is **not** maximized. Simply put, squeezing out the last increases would not be worth the effort. Total product would remain at R, since that is the optimum total product, taking the cost of the component into account.

The techniques described in this chapter can best be understood in terms of the above economic concepts.

2.6 Performance requirements

Given a set of alternatives, it is only possible to state whether a particular solution is the most economic, if its purpose is known. Therefore, before any appraisal techniques can be applied, there must be a clear statement of the performance requirements, namely the aims and objectives for which particular components are needed. Once these have been defined, then, and only then, can decisions be taken concerning the most economic option.

As noted in the performance specification in 1.3 (figure 1.1), component properties, such as combustibility, energy consumption, sound absorption and durability vary to meet different performance requirements. The choice of each component is therefore restricted by its specification. The selection of components should be seen in the context of the overall purpose of the building, be it a theatre, office development or dwelling, as the selection of each integral part will have consequences for the eventual occupants and the functions they wish to carry out. Anticipating the number of individuals likely to use a given space within a building will help to define the economic requirements of components, especially in terms of durability and maintenance. The choice of a component should also take into account total cost, which consists not only of the price and installation costs but also maintenance or annual running charges.

2.7 Techniques

A building is a form of investment. The costs incurred in one period are justified by reference to gains in later periods. Every structure consists of a set of inputs including the site, the labour, the management team and, of course, the components used in its construction. As these resources are usually paid for at the beginning of the life of a project, they are initial costs. However, other inputs are required to run a building, including services, energy, staffing and specialist and routine maintenance engineers. Periodic refurbishment may be needed when individual components reach the end of their expected useful life, even before the building itself is considered obsolete. Components may have some residual value on disposal and this expected value should also be taken into account. Recurring costs are called *annual costs* and are incurred throughout the life of the project. It is necessary to take initial and annual costs into account to establish the total costs of the alternatives in option appraisal.

As buildings consist of combinations of components, different combinations will require systematic examination, using discounted cash flow (DCF) techniques. The need to discount future cash flows arises because it is not possible to add values in one period to values in another without taking into account the time value of money. Individuals invariably prefer immediate payment to payment at some point in the future. Cash in the future is not the same as cash in the hand. Money in the future is worth less than the same amount of money in the current period. The longer the delay in payment the less a given future amount is worth at present. To equate the value of future sums they must be discounted back to a given period, usually the present. This would be the case even in a world without inflation in which money earned no interest.

The benefits of one component compared to another arise in the form of a stream of future gains. These may be measured in terms of rent, levels of safety or savings in labour or energy costs. The value of these future gains must also be discounted back from the period in which they occur. If the total of all discounted future benefits is greater than the discounted cost of the component, then the component is acceptable. However, finding that one particular component is feasible does not exclude the possibility that an alternative would not be even more viable. One must attempt to establish that the chosen option is the best solution compared to the other possibilities.

Several criteria are available to assist in comparing options, each throwing a slightly different light on the problem. None offers an objective criterion which replaces human judgement. They are only tools on which to base a decision.

The criteria most commonly used are:
Net discounted present value
Annual equivalence or costs-in-use
Payback period

In practice the application of any of the above methods is simplified by the fact there is no need to include figures in the calculations which apply equally to all options. If one is making a choice, interest is focused on differences between the options rather than their similarities.

(a) Net discounted present value
Compounding expresses the future value of a present sum of money. For instance, the value of £100 at present at 10% interest per annum, will be worth £121 after two years. The calculation is as follows:

$$£100 \times (1 + 1/10) = £110 \text{ after 1 year} \dots \dots \text{Equation 1}$$

The interest in the second year is 10% of the amount at the beginning of the year, namely £110.

$$£110 \times (1 + 1/10) = £121 \text{ after 2 years} \dots \dots \text{Equation 2}$$

Alternatively, since £110 = £100 × (1 + 1/10), from Equation 1, we may substitute in Equation 2 as follows:

$$£100 \times (1 + 1/10) \times (1 + 1/10) = £100 \times (1 + 1/10)^2 = £121$$

The general formula for compound interest is therefore:

$$PV \times (1 + i)^n FV \dots \dots \dots \text{Equation 3}$$

where PV = present value,
i = interest rate,
n = number of periods
and FV = future value.

Discounting is the converse of compounding and simply expresses the present value of a future sum of money. Thus, if £100 @ 10% per annum is worth £121 after 2 years, then £121 after 2 years is worth £100 currently. The discounted figure may be calculated by transposing the terms in equation 3. Thus:

$$PV = \frac{FV}{(1 + i)^n} \dots \dots \dots \text{Equation 4}$$

The net discounted present value (NDPV) is calculated by subtracting costs from revenues for each period and discounting each result back to the present. Each period is thus expressed in present values which can then be summed. The higher the NDPV, the higher the value of the asset. If £10 m were invested in a project with an NDPV of £1 m at a given discount rate, the value of the investment to the investor would be £11 m, assuming the client's target rate of return on money invested were equal to the discount rate.

NDPV is the most useful method of comparing components. It establishes the current value of a component by calculating its costs and benefits over its expected life. If the NDPV is positive, the value represents the size of the excess of benefits over the cost of acquiring them. It is a measure of the increase in the value of an asset, in this case a building, as a result of using a given component over its entire life. If the NDPV is negative, the initial and annual costs outweigh the future gains and the option should be rejected. The actual value of the NDPV will depend on the discount rate chosen which, in turn, depends on target rates of return chosen by the client, the cost of borrowing and the risk associated with a given project. The same rate of discount would then be applied to each option. The NDPV of each option may then be calculated before choosing the option with the highest NDPV, namely the highest margin of benefits over costs.

Option appraisal of components is simplified by taking advantage of the fact that in making any comparison between components, similarities may be ignored. As components are needed for specific purposes and each component shortlisted must comply with very similar performance requirements, it is usual to ignore the benefit side of the analysis. Thus, the lowest cost option, given similar performance requirements provides the most cost effective solution.

In *Rebuild*, edited by Derricott and Chissick (John Wiley and Sons, 1982), H. F. STAVELEY gives an example of decision making by discounting the renewal and maintenance costs back to the initial cost period of different materials for rainwater goods. This provides a figure of total costs over the different expected lives of the various systems. The discount rate is assumed to be 7%.

1 Polyvinyl chloride (PVC)

	£	£
gutters and rainwater pipes		
Initial cost		450
Renewal at 20 years		
(PV of £450 in 20 years)		
= £450 × 0.2584 =	116	
Renewal at 40 years		
(PV of £450 in 40 years)		
= £450 × 0.0667 =	30	
		146
Total cost		£596

2 Fibre cement gutters and rainwater pipes

Initial cost	500
Renewal at 30 years	
(PV of £500 in 30 years) = £500 × 0.1317 =	66
Total cost	£566

3 Cast iron gutters and rainwater pipes

Initial cost	600
Painting at 10 years (PV of £150 in 10 years) = £150 × 0.5084 =	76
Painting at 20 years (PV of £150 in 20 years) = £150 × 0.2584 =	39
Painting at 30 years (PV of £150 in 30 years) = £150 × 0.1314 =	18
Painting at 40 years (PV of £150 in 40 years) = £150 × 0.0668 =	10
Painting at 50 years (PV of £150 in 50 years) = £150 × 0.034 =	5
	148
Total cost	£748

Thus the option with the lowest discounted PV is the system in the second option. However, STAVELEY points out, considerations other than financial or economic criteria may in the end have greater influence over the final decision. Nevertheless, if, say, cast iron gutters (in this case the most costly solution) were chosen, the extra cost over and above the cheapest acceptable method (option 1), could then be appreciated. The question is, then, whether or not the appearance or some other benefit would be worth the extra cost in any given situation. The decision, whether or not the extra is worthwhile will, bearing in mind the law of diminishing returns, often be a subjective matter related to the brief.

(b) Annual equivalence
Annual equivalence is the cost expressed in terms of the amount needed each year to retrieve the capital invested in a component by the end of its expected life, together with annual interest payments, maintenance and running costs. This method of comparing options may be preferred when annual costs form a high proportion of the total cost of a component, such as a ducted warm air raised floor system. Moreover, if the expected

useful lives of the options vary greatly with each other, the discounted present value criterion will tend to favour those components with shorter lives to those with longer lives, especially when the discount rate used is above 8 to 10%. Annual equivalence is therefore an appropriate method of comparing components with different lives.

As stated above, annual equivalence includes an allowance for a *sinking fund*, which is the amount that must be set aside each year during the life of the component to replace the capital invested in it in the first place. The sinking fund, at least in theory, provides the capital needed to replace a component at the end of its useful life. The sinking fund is similar to a depreciation allowance, though the basis for calculating the sinking fund is very different. The sinking fund account is a cumulative fund, which itself earns interest.

The formula for the annual sinking fund is:

$$SF = \frac{i}{(1 + i)^n - 1} \quad \dots\dots\dots\dots\dots\dots\dots\text{Equation 5}$$

where SF = sinking fund factor
      i = compound interest rate applied to sinking fund
and n = number of periods to end of life of component.

Sinking fund factors can be found in tables. The tables require the user to select the expected life of a given component and the compound interest rate that the sinking fund may be expected to earn. The rate of interest chosen should be pessimistic to ensure that the fund will be able to serve its purpose and replace the component at the end of its life. Clearly, the lower the rate of interest the more would have to be set aside each year to accumulate to the capital required.

A sinking fund table and an example of a comparison of components using annual equivalence appears in *Cost Planning of Building* by FERRY and BRANDON, who compare the annual costs associated with two heating systems. Thus:

Automatic gas-fired heating system	£	£
Annual fuel costs	5,000	
5% interest on capital cost of system (including building work) £30,000	1,500	
Sinking fund to repay capital cost after 20 years at 3% £30,000 @ 3.7p	1,110	
	£7,610	7,610
Electric storage heating system		
Annual fuel costs	6,800	
5% interest on capital cost of system £15,000	750	
Sinking fund to repay capital cost after 15 years at 3% £15,000 @ 5.4p	810	
	£8,360	8,360
Annual saving on costs in use of gas fired system		£750

(c) Payback period
The payback period is the period of time needed to recover the capital costs of a component. It is found as follows:

$$PP = \frac{K}{R} \quad \dots\dots\dots\dots\dots\dots\dots\dots\dots\dots\dots\text{Equation 6}$$

where PP = payback period in years, K = capital cost of component and R = net annual savings or revenue attributable to component.

The payback period criterion is useful for managers and decision makers insofar as it assists in gauging their exposure to the risk that a component may not generate sufficient savings to be worth the capital cost of its purchase. Payback periods are based on actual cash flows without any discounting, in spite of the recognized need to take the time value of money into account. Moreover, just because a component has a shorter payback period than an alternative is not necessarily a good reason for choosing it. For instance, if a component, which has a payback period of two years, requires replacement in the third, then it may be inferior to another with a payback period of five years, which requires less maintenance and lasts for twenty years. Clearly, the whole life of a project has to be considered. Finally the payback period does not assist in establishing the profitability of a component, which must take into account the whole life of a component and not just the first few years. For these reasons, the payback period is not a good criterion to use for making decisions concerning best options.

2.8 Linear programming

Linear programming in economics is concerned with allocating scarce resources between competing requirements. The optimum solution, however, will depend on a set of financial and non-financial constraints. The technique or a variation of it can be applied whenever it is necessary to maximize or minimize an objective, such as minimizing the U-values of fenestration or maximizing the load bearing capacity of a roof for car parking or minimizing costs.

The usefulness of linear programming is that it employs the constraints which operate in any given situation to find the range of possible solutions. Each constraint states that the combination of components should produce a result not more or less than a given value. Each constraint is given an algebraic form, such as:

$$7 \times 7x + 2y \geqslant 140 \dots\dots\dots\dots\dots\dots \text{Equation 7}$$
where x = quantity of component A
and y = quantity of component B.

Linear programming is an iterative mathematical technique used to find the optimum combination of components, which in linear programming terms are called decision variables. Linear programming assumes linear relationships exist between decision variables, the values of which must be non-negative. The technique establishes functions or mathematical relationships between components, as in Equation 7. When only two or three components are under consideration, such as two heating systems within say a hospital complex, it is possible to plot the functions on a graph to define an area referred to as the region of feasible solutions. If several components are involved, graphical presentation is not possible.

However, a technique known as the simplex method using matrix algebra or vectors may be applied to solve the problem, but a discussion of these methods lies beyond the scope of this book.

A client may require several simultaneous objectives, for instance, to provide the minimum thickness of glazing units with the lowest U-values at the lowest cost. One of these objectives must be selected as the objective function, the value of which is to be maximized or minimized. The other aims are then restated as structural constraints. The redefinition of the problem depends on judgement in selecting the objective function and setting the constraints. The problem could be restated as follows. The objective function may be to minimize the cost, while the structural constraints require that the thickness of glazing unit be no greater than (say) 10 mm and a U-value no more than 4.5 W/m²K. Furthermore, all values must be greater than or equal to zero.

FERRY and BRANDON demonstrate the method based on an example in *Building Magazine* of March 1969, concerning two types of cladding panels for a modular factory. The two types of panel (Type A and Type B) varied in terms of glazing and corresponding U-values. Linear programming was used to 'determine the number of each type to provide an external wall of at least 3.5 W/m²K and a glazing area of at least 140 m² for a minimum cost. (FERRY, D. J. and BRANDON, P. S., *Cost Planning of Buildings*, Granada, 1984, pp 322–323). The dimensions of both types of panel were 4 m high × 3 m wide and either could be used in any situation. The area requiring the cladding was 480 m². Type A panels cost £500 and Type B, £400. The figures were used to obtain a graphical representation of the area bounded by the constraints within which the solution could be found. This is shown in figure 2.3.

Since the glazing area should exceed 140 m² and Type A panels contained 7 m² of glazing and Type B, 2 m², this constraint may be shown as:

$$7xA + 2yB \geqslant 140 \dots\dots\dots\dots\dots\dots \text{Equation 8}$$

The function states that x A type panels with 7 m² of glazing and y B type panels with 2 m² of glazing must be greater than or equal to 140 m². This can be plotted by letting x = 0. Then the minimum value of y is 70. If y = 0, then the

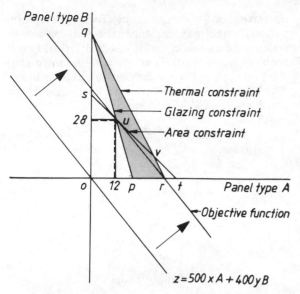

Panel type B

q

s

28

u

Thermal constraint

Glazing constraint

Area constraint

v

o   12 p   r   t   Panel type A

Objective function

$z = 500 \times A + 400\, yB$

2.3 *Linear programming: showing the derivation of the quantities of A and B panels used, given various constraints (after Ferry and Brandon)*

minimum value of x is 20. Since the function is linear, the constraint may be plotted, as in figure 2.3. Thus the values for 'x' and 'y' must lie outside the line 'pq', in the shaded area.

Similarly, the thermal constraint in this example was reduced in algebraic terms:

$$2xA + yB \leqslant 70 \dots\dots\dots\dots\dots\dots Equation\ 9$$

This function states the mathematical relationship between A and B, which must be observed to satisfy the thermal constraint. Again a linear relationship is assumed and this constraint may be plotted, as shown by the line 'qr' in figure 2.3. The line 'qr' shows the maximum combination of A and B panels permitted by the thermal constraint. The triangle pqr is therefore the region of feasibility.

The final constraint in this example is the number of panels required. Since the total number required is 40, the formula for this structural constraint is:

$$xA + yB = 40 \dots\dots\dots\dots\dots\dots Equation\ 10$$

The linear relationship in Equation 10, 'st', is

drawn in figure 2.3, to comply with this constraint. However, only part of the line 'st', namely 'uv', lies within the region of feasibility, which accommodates the glazing and thermal constraints. The combination of panels, which complies with all the above constraints, must lie on 'uv'.

The objective function, Equation 11 in this instance, is concerned with the combination of the two panels which minimizes costs while complying with all the constraints imposed. This objective function calls for the budget line to be minimized, that is, the line should be as close to the origin as possible. Since A panels cost £500 and B panels £400, the objective function may be written as:

$$500xA + 400yB = z \dots\dots\dots\dots\dots Equation\ 11$$
where z lies at or between points u and v on the line st.

To find the gradient of the objective function,

$$let\ z = 0,$$
$$then\ 500x = -400y$$
$$and\ \frac{x}{y} = \frac{-400}{500}$$
$$Thus,\ if\ x = 40$$
$$then\ y = -50$$

This provides sufficient information to establish the gradient of the objective function, which can now be moved up until it intersects the line st, where the value of z will be minimized. The point of intersection is at u, providing the solution of 12 units of Type A and 28 Type B panels.

2.9 Conclusion

The purpose of the economic techniques described in this chapter is to throw light on the nature of a systematic approach to decision making. It is better to know the opportunity cost of a decision than to base decisions on pure intuition. Even when, from an economic point of view, the second best is chosen, if the best option is known, then the designer may ascertain what has been sacrificed in order to make a particular selection. The techniques help to clarify the cost implications of certain design changes and may be used to assist designers to keep within the budgets available.

Moreover, as was stated above, it is not possible to study all options, because of the time and cost involved. It follows that only a few options can be selected for appraisal. The process of shortlisting proposals for investigation is itself intuitive and often subjective. Therefore, although one may establish the best option in terms of economic criterion used, shortlisting still requires judgement. There is no guarantee that the preferred option is the best possible solution. The best solution may not have been selected for consideration in the first place.

3 Industrialized system building

3.1 Introduction

The industrialization of the building process involves the increasing utilization of factory techniques of production in relation to the total process of building. The ultimate of these techniques results in various components being joined together, also in the factory, to form the larger parts of a building, such as composite wall or roof panels with exterior and interior surfaces incorporating structure, weather and fire resistance, sound modulation and thermal control. Freed from the constraints of the actual building site – its unsocial working conditions and effects of cold, heat and dampness – construction in the factory is able to achieve many of the sophisticated performance requirements of a successful modern building with a greater degree of certainty. Subject to fulfilling certain manufacturing criteria, it is possible for a whole building to be constructed in the factory somewhat like cars are manufactured using a 'conveyor belt' system of assembly. Then, after the completed building has been delivered to a prepared site and the required service connections made, it is ready for immediate use.

After the Second World War the number of skilled and semi-skilled workers available to the building industry was inadequate to meet the total volume of new building required. Therefore it became necessary for industrial techniques of design and construction to be applied, particularly in respect of those building types which had come to be recognized as a social necessity, such as housing, hospitals and school buildings.

The methods and materials used in the industrialized systems during their peak of development in the 1960s were derived from rationalized traditional construction techniques organized to the point where prefabricated factory-made components were a dominant feature. Thus, by this time, a great proportion of building work could be carried out in the controlled environment of the factory and there was a more efficient use of manpower with increased productivity under a socially more acceptable working environment. It was considered that the controlled production typified by factory rather than site techniques also resulted in a higher standard of finished component.

3.2 Economic and social factors

For the production of large scale components or buildings using factory techniques to be commercially successful, there must be an *assured long term market with continuity of demand* backed by sufficient investment capital. There must also be a feasible development programme based on sensible cost limits. Pre-ordering and the bulk purchase of materials is an integral part of industrialized building and an important characteristic of the manufacturing process is an increase in economy in direct proportion to the length of production run. Efficient industrialization is achieved by the co-ordinated development of design procedures, production processes and erection techniques. Handling equipment for components fulfilling particular functions (walls, floors, roofs, etc) assumes special importance on the assembly line, particularly in respect of heavy units both within the factory, factory to site and on the site. The limits of road and rail transport assume growing importance as the problems associated with the use of large assemblies increase with the degree of off-site erection and packaging for transit.

Owing to the reliance on pre-planning, it is necessary that instructions should be given on as long a term as possible. Project approval should be reached at least two years in advance of the starting date and, in the public sector, an advance programme should indicate the likely level of approval for periods of five years. Uncertainties and delays are very serious since the system is less flexible than traditional methods. The Agrément

Board method of approval of new components has much to commend it, in that the objective information is provided at an early stage to enable designers and manufacturers to consider the incorporation of new products. In this respect the *Building Regulations 1985* can also assist with the use of industrialized systems as they are now in the form of performance specifications which give more freedom of choice in meeting the requirements for future building projects.

Industrialized system building requires large investment in research covering the specialist knowledge of techniques for factory production, site organization and mechanization. In addition, investigation continues into new ways of assessing user requirements, the development of computer aided drafting and specification techniques, and optimum economic levels for the production of the building components used in forming a complete building.

It must be stated that, with other than a few notable exceptions, industrialized building systems in the UK have not met with consistent success. The essential direction and motivation of the building industry mentioned above did not occur, perhaps because of inconsistencies in approach by succeeding governments. The ideas of developing an industrialized vernacular based on a new factory based technology received much social criticism because concepts of quantity outstripped those of quality. In many cases designers failed to tackle the effects of mechanization on both technical and aesthetic performance. Furthermore, general dissatisfaction with the high rise tower blocks – the most dramatic outlet for system building – coupled with the all too frequent adoption of prefabricated panels to form vast housing estates, the planning of which was almost solely dependent upon the economic positioning of tower cranes and/or runs for gantry cranes, compounded the growing concern about the social consequences of mechanistic design solutions. In particular, some of the anonymously bleak local authority housing estates have been blamed by many for the tenants' loss of identity with the environment and, in part, this has led to depression, vandalism, crime and even riot. These concerns extended to the 'conveyor belt' factory production techniques themselves. The well known socio-economist and author of *Small is*

Beautiful, Dr Fritz Schumacher stated in 1975: 'Modern technology has deprived man of the kind of work that he enjoys most; useful, creative work with hands and brains. And it has given him plenty of work of a fragmented kind, most of which he doesn't enjoy.'

Research based on the analysis of the various remaining commercially viable industrialized building systems indicate little evidence that they are cheaper and quicker than the use of alternative systems. Nevertheless, the main advantages of system building lie in *quality of component production* which results from the current greater understanding of factory techniques and the integration of precise performance requirements, as well as the involvement at inception of designers with a central concern for aesthetic issues (see chapter 1, page 8).

Perhaps the most recent significant work on industrialized building systems, its history, developments, decline in importance, and its future is, *Building Systems, Industrialization and Architecture* by BARRY RUSSELL, published 1981 by John Wiley and Sons.

3.3 'Open' and 'Closed' systems

The terms *open systems* and *closed systems* are used in connection with different approaches to industrialized system building.

An **open system of building** is where components manufactured by one company are usable with those produced by a different company. The purpose of this is to allow the designer a choice of a vast range of components, perhaps from abroad as well as those having been home produced, which are interchangeable over a wide selection of building types. However, the success of an open system industrialized building design is directly proportional to the degree to which internationally agreed dimensional co-ordinated techniques of component manufacture and universal methods of jointing are accepted. If the designer's choice is limited only by his experience and knowledge of the market, technical and aesthetic criteria can be met with reasonable precision to suit specific problems. Although dimensional co-ordination is the key to this freedom, the agreed sizes of components must conform to **international** standards rather than those of any particular country. Therefore, in order to allow the desired flexibility, simplicity and extendability in the use of components across countries the basic dimension or module to which they can be made is 100 mm – see chapter 1, page 22.

In a **closed system of building** the components are not interchangeable with any other system and thus the building is formed from components specifically designed for and applicable to a particular building type, for example, schools or housing. Although a closed building system is carefully developed to meet precisely the requirements of its users, the designer's choice of components is governed by the variations allowed within the particular system. The idea of client participation at the design stage (as in local authority school programmes) and close co-operation with the component manufacturers should produce a *closed* building system which fulfils its function within exacting economic limits.

Both *open* and *closed* systems can incorporate traditional forms of construction such as brickwork, but this tends to detract from the efficiency of the system as such. Since site works take up a large proportion of construction time and effort (preparation as well as actual building), these operations should be rationalized as far as possible. Many systems of building which were initially *closed* are likely to become *open*, mainly through the increased application of dimensional co-ordination, where it is an obvious advantage to combine various systems in respect of the supply of components and fittings. Often a limited number of component manufacturers are formed into a consortium of suppliers for a particular building project. Although this can give rise to contractual responsibility problems, this system results in a little more flexibility than a strictly closed system and is sometimes referred to as *method building*.

3.4 Contractor sponsored and client sponsored systems

Systems of building have been developed and sponsored by both *contractor organizations* and *client organizations*.

In the case of **contractor sponsored systems**,

sometimes referred to as proprietary systems, the contractor provides a building of their speciality and also an erection service. Examples of these are timber framed housing systems; industrial/commercial, structural and building fabric systems, specifically, agricultural, office and educational buildings; and smaller scale prefabricated and/or temporary 'volumetric' systems used for toilets and site offices, etc. Also included in the latter category are air-supported and tent structures. Some examples are illustrated and described in figures 3.1 to 3.6.

In the case of **client sponsored systems**, because of the necessity for a large and continuing building programme and in order to make a particular system viable, various local authorities (which may include new towns as well as government departments) have created between themselves associations for the development of a particular system of building. An association of this kind is called a **consortium** and its members are able to exchange information on building problems, engage in bulk purchase of materials and support the joint use of a particular building technique. The resulting building design can be the subject of competitive construction tenders in the normal manner, or subject to a negotiated contract with a 'specialist' contractor. Examples of *client sponsored systems* are those of the various consortia of local authorities for schools and similar buildings, such as CLASP (Consortium of Local Authorities Special Programme) and the now disbanded SEAC (South East Architects Collaboration), SCOLA (Second Consortium of Local Authorities) and MACE (Metropolitan Architectural Consortium for Education).

The proportion of each building contract employing consortium purchased components varied considerably: CLASP and SCOLA tended towards as large a proportion as possible, to about 40% of the project, whereas SEAC used between 20 and 30%.

3.5 Consortium of Local Authorities Special Programme (CLASP)

This system was originally established in 1957 in the Nottinghamshire county architect's office when eight local authorities agreed to combine in

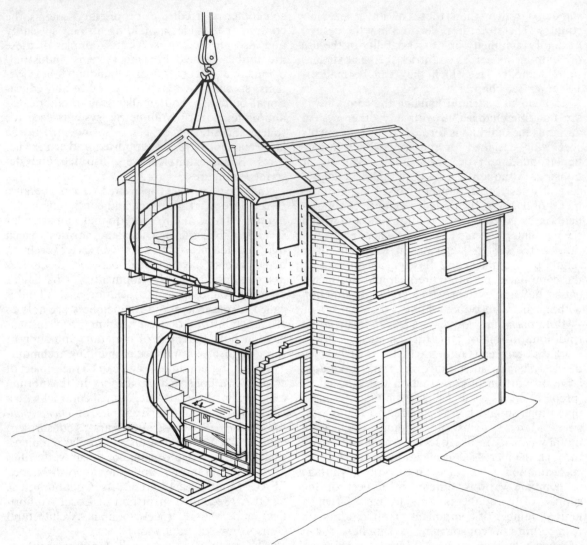

3.1 *Vic Hallam Volumetric Housing System: timber frame construction, highly insulated low energy units, complete with plumbing, electric wiring, central heating, and kitchen, bedroom and bathroom fittings. External brick cladding is applied after units stacked and fixed in position*

the first building consortium in order to develop and control a prefabricated system of school building. Their aim was to *exploit the advantages of economy, quality and speed which are inherent in industrialized building* for a programme of school buildings. Initially, the system to be evolved was also required to solve a specific constructional problem, namely the design of school buildings for sites which were liable to mining subsidence. CLASP received widespread recognition in 1960 which instigated a commercial venture to market it abroad and also provided the impetus for the development of other client sponsored systems in the UK, such as SCOLA and SEAC.

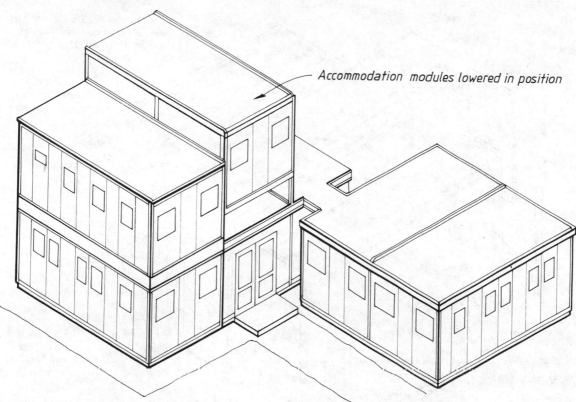

Accommodation modules lowered in position

3.2 *Vic Hallam Linpac Building System: pre-fabricated units with fully insulated walls, floors and roofs used for two storey offices, classrooms and light industry buildings. Walls factory finished in 'Colorcoated Steel' cladding*

CLASP utilizes a light steel frame with lattice floor and roof beams. The Mark 1 to 4 versions used a roof deck of prefabricated timber, and floors also of timber construction either prefabricated or in situ. In common with the later versions of the system, the cladding materials included precast concrete slabs with exposed aggregate facing, and tile hanging, protected metal sheeting or timber boarding on timber cladding frames. Also, the window frames were factory glazed which later incorporated gasket glazing. Opening lights were in metal frames.

In 1971 CLASP introduced the Mark 5 version with a number of modifications, including a steel deck diaphragm roof instead of timber panels and much enhanced precautions against the spread of

fire. In 1973–74 brick was introduced as a standard option to the already available range of external claddings, and in 1977 pitched roofs became available using a timber trussed rafter construction (later changed to steel trusses). The requirement that the system should fully meet the new version of the Building Regulations led to a complete evaluation by the Agrément Board and the National Building Agency. This resulted in CLASP Mark 5 being given an Agrément Certificate in 1979.

The Mark 5 version was introduced in 1971 to deal with an annual building programme of £70 m. Since then there has been a gradual decline in the use of systems building which caused other

Continued on page 47

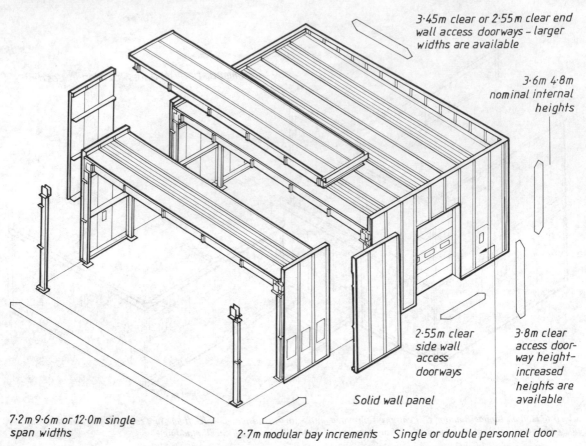

3·45m clear or 2·55m clear end wall access doorways – larger widths are available

3·6m 4·8m nominal internal heights

2·55m clear side wall access doorways

Solid wall panel

3·8m clear access door-way height-increased heights are available

7·2m 9·6m or 12·0m single span widths

2·7m modular bay increments

Single or double personnel door

3.3 *Terrapin Matrex Light Industrial Building System: mass produced modules which can be transported in 'packs' and then erected and linked on site. Modules of lightweight galvanized cold-rolled steel sections, with cladding and roof panels of rigid polyurethane of isocyanurate foam insulation between steel facing sheets (U = 0.6 W/m²K) finished with PVC 'Plastisol'. Window and door frames are of extruded aluminium alloy sections, satin anodised finish. Each roof unit can incorporate 900 mm wide translucent double-skinned glass fibre panel to provide daylighting*

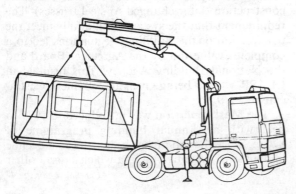

3.4 *Glasdon Modular Building System: small scale factory made module being off-loaded to site*

3.5 *Glasdon Modular Building System: available in a range of sizes from 1.2 × 1.2 up to 18 × 5.4 m composed of grp panels (see figure 3.6). Suitable for a range of building types, including offices, gatehouses, security posts, car park kiosks and sheds*

less successful consortia to cease operation. In 1984 CLASP launched a **Mark 6** version (see figure 3.7) of the system in recognition of a new attitude towards purchasing components which, while recognizing the need to maintain bulk purchase of components for planned economy, took into account the increasing availability of a range of high quality components available to designers and their clients on the open market. The *Sketch Planning Handbook* for the Mark 6 version states:

'The basic objective is to increase the value of CLASP to its Members by recognizing that the current national economic and social factors are very different from those which the Mark 5 system was designed to meet. In particular, the volume of public building programmes has declined substantially and fashions in architectural design have turned away (wrongly in our view) from the modern movement, with its concern for efficiency, user requirements and social need, which have greatly influenced the direction of architecture since the war.

'To meet this objective and take account of these two main changes it has been agreed that the Mark 6 system should have:

● Components and procurement arrangements appropriate to the size of the current building programmes without precluding an increase in capacity should this be required.

47

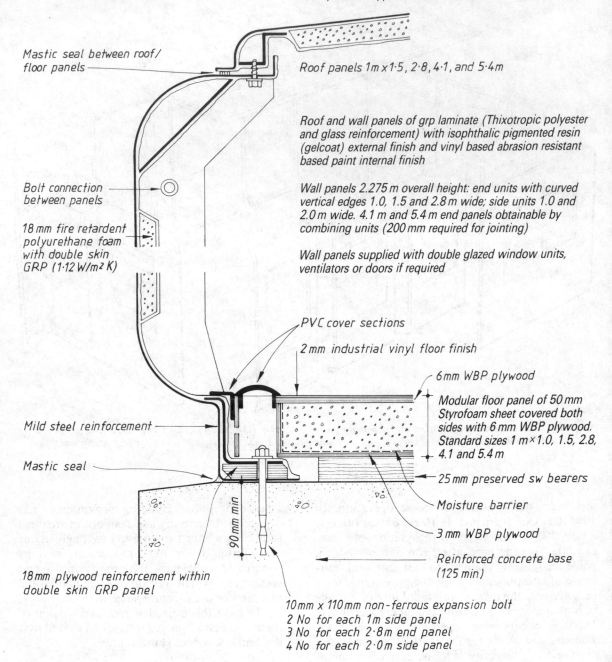

Roof panels supplied with ventilators if required

Mastic seal between roof/
floor panels

Roof panels 1m x 1·5, 2·8, 4·1, and 5·4m

Roof and wall panels of grp laminate (Thixotropic polyester
and glass reinforcement) with isophthalic pigmented resin
(gelcoat) external finish and vinyl based abrasion resistant
based paint internal finish

Wall panels 2.275 m overall height: end units with curved
vertical edges 1.0, 1.5 and 2.8 m wide; side units 1.0 and
2.0 m wide. 4.1 m and 5.4 m end panels obtainable by
combining units (200 mm required for jointing)

Bolt connection
between panels

Wall panels supplied with double glazed window units,
ventilators or doors if required

18 mm fire retardent
polyurethane foam
with double skin
GRP (1·12 W/m² K)

PVC cover sections

2 mm industrial vinyl floor finish

6mm WBP plywood

Modular floor panel of 50 mm
Styrofoam sheet covered both
sides with 6 mm WBP plywood.
Standard sizes 1 m ×1.0, 1.5, 2.8,
4.1 and 5.4 m

Mild steel reinforcement

25 mm preserved sw bearers

Moisture barrier

Mastic seal

3 mm WBP plywood

90 mm min

Reinforced concrete base
(125 min)

18 mm plywood reinforcement within
double skin GRP panel

10 mm x 110 mm non-ferrous expansion bolt
2 No for each 1m side panel
3 No for each 2·8 m end panel
4 No for each 2·0 m side panel

3.6   *Glasdon Modular Building System: construction details*

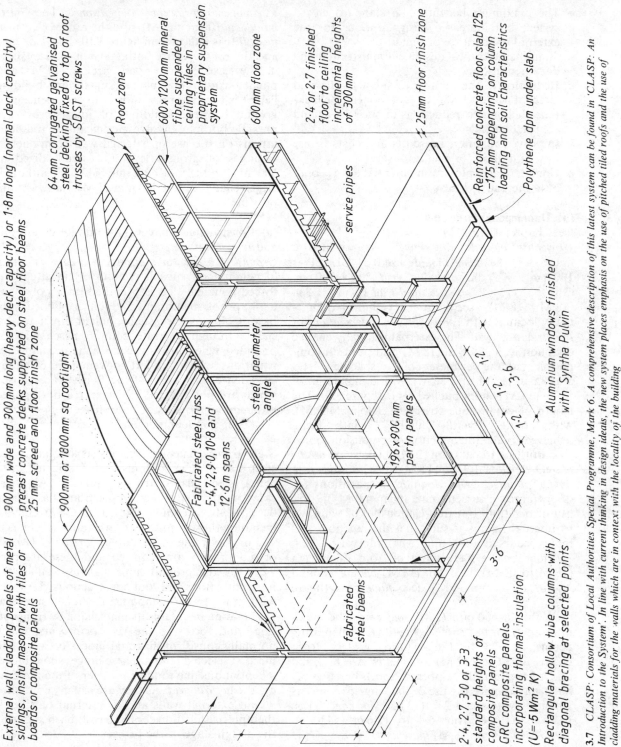

External wall cladding panels of metal sidings, insitu masonry with tiles or boards or composite panels

900mm wide and 900mm long (heavy deck capacity) or 1·8m long (normal deck capacity) precast concrete decks supported on steel floor beams 25mm screed and floor finish zone

64mm corrugated galvanised steel decking fixed to top of roof trusses by SDST screws

Roof zone

600×1200mm mineral fibre suspended ceiling tiles in proprietary suspension system

600mm floor zone

2·4 or 2·7 finished floor to ceiling incremental heights of 300mm

25mm floor finish zone

Reinforced concrete floor slab 125 –175mm depending on column loading and soil characteristics

Polythene dpm under slab

service pipes

Aluminium windows finished with Syntha Pulvin

steel perimeter angle

Fabricated steel truss 5·4,7·2,9·0,10·8 and 12·6m spans

900mm or 1800mm sq rooflight

196×900mm partn panels

fabricated steel beams

2·4, 2·7, 3·0 or 3·3 standard heights of composite panels

GRC composite panels incorporating thermal insulation (U=·5 Wm² K)

Rectangular hollow tube columns with diagonal bracing at selected points

3.7 CLASP: Consortium of Local Authorities Special Programme, Mark 6. A comprehensive description of this latest system can be found in 'CLASP: An Introduction to the System'. In line with current thinking in design ideas, the new system places emphasis on the use of pitched tiled roofs and the use of cladding materials for the walls which are in context with the locality of the building

- The maximum benefits of a standard closed system but increased design options for the external appearance of buildings.
- Simplified technical design, administration and documentation.
- Reduction in the number of site activities and interference and shorter component delivery times leading to reductions in site labour and contract periods.
- Improved maintenance costs and costs in use including those of energy.
- Commercial exploitation potential for use both at home and overseas.'

(a) Dimensional co-ordination
(see chapter 1: 1.6–11)

Horizontal co-ordinating planes As indicated in figure 3.7, the *basic module* used by CLASP is **100 mm** (M), the *planning grid* **300 × 300 mm** (3M × 3M) and the *structural grid* **1.8 m × 1.8 m** (**18 M × 18 M**) – see figure 3.8. Columns are normally located with *centre-lines on intersections of the structural grid*. The external wall may change direction at any 1.8 m (18 M) grid position compatible with the perimeter column spacings of 1.8 and 3.6 m (18 M and 36 M), with a maximum of 5.4 m (54 M) under pitched roofs (figure 3.9). The length of continuous structure is 45 m (450 M), with greater overall building length being achieved by the introduction of expansion joints.

Partitions are 200 mm (2 M) thick *centre on the planning grid* or 100 mm (1 M) thick with *one face on the planning grid*. Openings in partitions for door frames or screens have 100 mm (l M) flexibility of position, but the relationship of windows to internal linings is such that the junction normally occurs at a 300 mm (3 M) interval.

Floor beams have spans of from 1.8 to 9 m (18 M to 90 M), in 1.8 m (18 M) *increments* and within a 600 mm (6 M) deep *floor zone* (figure 3.9).

Within a 600 mm (2 M) *roof zone*, the maximum span for flat roofs is 9 m (90 M) when using beams, or 12.6 m (126 M) using girders. Roof beams of 3.6 m (12 M) and below are flat, and above are generally cambered. Sports or assembly halls may require the use of the long-span girders which fit within a 1.2 m (12 M) *roof zone*. Pitch roof spans are from 5.4 to 12.6 m (54 M to 126 M), in 1.8 m (18 M) *increments*.

Vertical co-ordinating dimensions. The *basic module* is 100 mm (1 M), and the range of *vertical flexibility* is indicated in figure 3.10. The *floor zone* and the *roof zone* are both 600 mm (6 M), except in the case of long-span girders (12 M) and pitched roofs. The normal maximum building height is three storeys, subject to subsidence and ground bearing. Buildings of four storeys are possible but may involve modifications and limitations on the use of external wall components. Changes of ground level are standardized at 600 mm (6 M) and 1.2 mm (12 M), although larger changes on a 300 mm (3 M) *increment* are possible.

(b) Construction (may vary with site conditions and/or project)

Ground slab and foundations A 125 or 175 mm (depending on subsoil conditions) in situ reinforced concrete slab is provided on a polythene damp-proof membrane laid on a blinded sub-base. Columns are usually bolted direct to this slab, although separate column bases may be provided when loading conditions are high. In situations where ground movement created by subsidence may occur, floor finishes are chosen which are not affected by damp (eg hot applied bitumen compounds or asphalt). The *floor finish zone* is 25 mm (submodular).

Steel frame The frame consists of galvanized steel hollow tube columns with fabricated horizontal steel beams, trusses and ties. All these components and their connections have been designed to accommodate ground movements, including those resulting from mining subsidence.

For the frame to be stable, *horizontal bracing* or diaphragms are required and these are provided by the ground floor slab as well as the horizontal floor and roof constructions. Together with other frame components, they ensure that the building maintains its plan shape by transmitting wind forces to the *vertical bracing*, which normally consist of diagonal braces between columns at selected points. These braces should form a continuous line to the perimeter of the building on a *structural grid*. As they are usually contained within external walls and/or internal partitions, their precise location should be established during the design stage of the project.

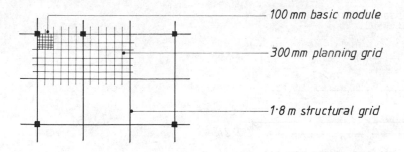

- 100 mm basic module

- 300 mm planning grid

- 1·8 m structural grid

REFER TO STEEL FRAME AND PITCH ROOF FOR BEAM SPANS

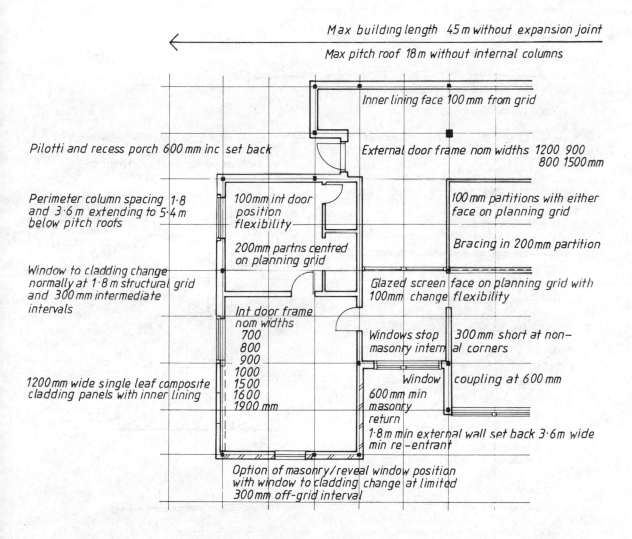

Max building length 45 m without expansion joint

Max pitch roof 18 m without internal columns

Inner lining face 100 mm from grid

Pilotti and recess porch 600 mm inc set back

External door frame nom widths 1200 900 800 1500 mm

Perimeter column spacing 1·8 and 3·6 m extending to 5·4 m below pitch roofs

100 mm int door position flexibility

200 mm partns centred on planning grid

100 mm partitions with either face on planning grid

Bracing in 200 mm partition

Window to cladding change normally at 1·8 m structural grid and 300 mm intermediate intervals

Glazed screen face on planning grid with 100 mm change flexibility

Int door frame nom widths
700
800
900
1000
1500
1600
1900 mm

Windows stop 300 mm short at non-masonry internal corners

1200 mm wide single leaf composite cladding panels with inner lining

Window coupling at 600 mm

600 mm min masonry return

1·8 m min external wall set back 3·6 m wide min re-entrant

Option of masonry/reveal window position with window to cladding change at limited 300 mm off-grid interval

3.8 *CLASP: horizontal co-ordinating planes using basic module of 100 mm*

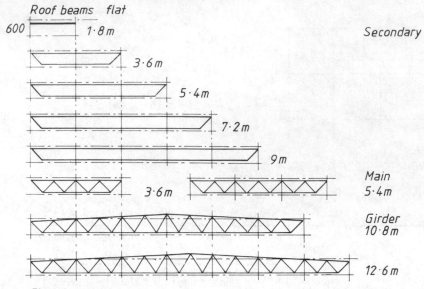

Roof beams flat

600   1·8 m   Secondary

3·6 m

5·4 m

7·2 m

9 m

3·6 m   Main 5·4 m

Girder 10·8 m

12·6 m

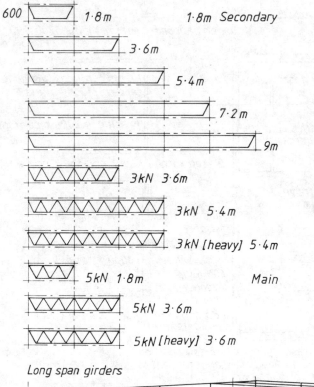

Floor beams

600   1·8 m   1·8m Secondary

3·6 m

5·4 m

7·2 m

9 m

3kN 3·6 m

3kN 5·4 m

3kN [heavy] 5·4 m

5kN 1·8 m   Main

5kN 3·6 m

5kN [heavy] 3·6 m

Pitched roof steelwork — standard trusses [truncated, half, and tied trusses available as well as hip and valley members

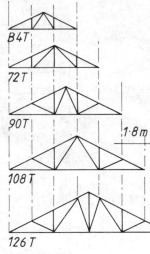

B4T

72T

90T

108T

126T

1·8m

Ridge members [to support valleys at odd grid spans] 18 R

36 R

54 R

Eaves beams [may be 2 ranges]

E18

E36

E54

Long span girders

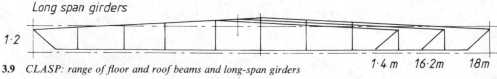

1·2

1·4 m   16·2 m   18 m

3.9 *CLASP: range of floor and roof beams and long-span girders*

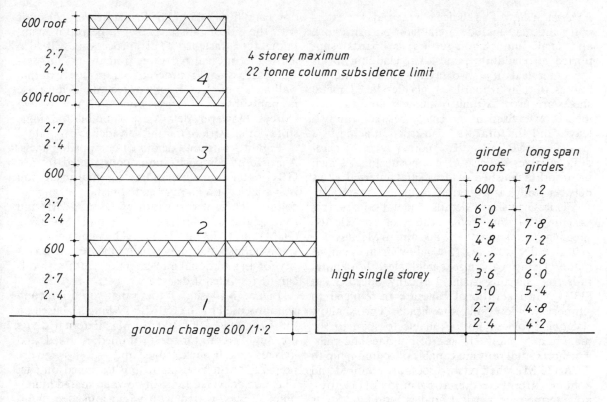

4 storey maximum
22 tonne column subsidence limit

high single storey

	girder roofs	long span girders
	600	1·2
	6·0	
	5·4	7·8
	4·8	7·2
	4·2	6·6
	3·6	6·0
	3·0	5·4
	2·7	4·8
	2·4	4·2

ground change 600/1·2

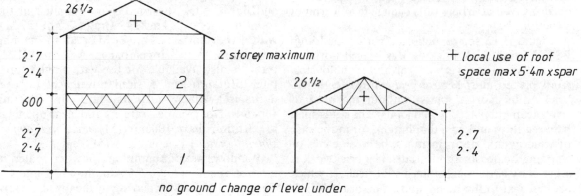

2 storey maximum

+ local use of roof space max 5·4m x spar

no ground change of level under the same roof

3.10 *CLASP: vertical co-ordinating dimensions using basic module of 100 mm. Floor and roof zones are both 600 mm, except in the case of long-span girders (12 m) and pitched roofs*

External walls The choice of materials for external walls may include metal sidings, brickwork and small unit cladding (tiles or boards) supported on cladding frames. The cladding forms the outer leaf of a two layer wall and internal linings of plasterboard, or plastics faced metal sheets are used. A quilt of mineral fibre thermal insulation is fixed in the cavity between the two leaves and the total wall construction achieves a 'U'-value of $0.5 \, W/m^2 K$. Another form of cladding involves the use of composite units which incorporate finished external and internal skins between which is a thermal insulation material.

Figure 3.11 shows details of metal sidings. It is essential that the profile centres of the selected sheeting complies with the 300 mm (3 M) *planning grid* at which cladding-to-window changes can be made. Using galvanized mild steel horizontal rails, the sheeting spans vertically up to 3.3 m (33 M), and additional rails are introduced to support window sills and heads. Too shallow sheeting profiles may be unable to span to the maximum without the use of intermediate rails. The horizontal rails are capable of spanning up to 3.6 m (36 M): when pitched roofs are required and columns are, therefore, at 5.4 m (54 M) centres, an intermediate vertical stud is required. Studs will also be required where windows and doors occur as well as where rails change level within a structural bay.

Figure 3.12 shows details of brick cladding. BS 102.5 mm thick brickwork is braced horizontally between the vertical galvanized mild steel studs placed at *structural grid* centres (eight BS bricks plus mortar joints) without the need of reinforcement placed in bed joints. The studs span between floor and roof diaphragms, or in the case of window and door openings, between eaves or cladding beams as appropriate. The brickwork is secured by twisted galvanized mild steel ties which are screwed to the metal studs. The brickwork is divided into panels on the line of each *structural grid* by vertical movement joints which are weather sealed by bitumen impregnated compressible plastics tubes. So as to ensure a completely dry interior face, a reinforced polythene damp proof membrane is then fixed on the inside of the brickwork.

In order that building the brickwork does not delay the overall production of the project, windows and doors should be fixed into vertical studs with the aid of rails, and a weatherproof membrane then fastened. This procedure will also allow the internal partition framework and service carcassing to proceed before the external walling is complete. Brickwork is intended for use in non-subsidence areas only and up to two storeys. However, details are available for single storey brickwork of mining subsidence capability.

Figure 3.13 shows details of composite panels. A range of composite units constructed from a GRC outer skin surrounding thermal insulation is available with an aggregate finish in a range of colours. There is one width of 1.2 m (12 M) and four heights of 2.4 m (24 M), 2.7 m (27 M), 3.0 m (30 M) and 3.3 m (33 M). The units have a smooth finish internally which obviates the necessity for an additional internal lining, although this can be provided if desired.

Figure 3.14 shows the range of doors and windows used by the CLASP system, all based on the *basic module* of 100 m (M). External doors are supplied in timber – framed, framed and louvred, and framed, ledged and braced – and are prepared for a final paint finish applied on site. They are delivered hung in powder-coated aluminium frames, glazed with wired annealed, laminated or toughened glass, and morticed for locks and flush bolts. The frames are supplied in the room heights of 2.4 m (24 M) and 2.7 m (27 M), with a transom at 2.1 m (21 M) and an opening for glazing in the upper panel. A 2.1 m (21 M) frame is also available for use with single-storey pitch roof projects. A similar range of internal doors is available, also half-hour fire resisting versions. Door frames, screens and clear openings in partitions have 100 mm (M) *horizontal dimensional flexibility* (see figure 3.15).

Windows are of aluminium, powder-coated in a range of colours (see 6.5 Aluminium windows). They are designed for glazing by means of a wrap-around glazing channel system incorporating a vinyl gasket for vertical sliders and clip-on beads, and non-setting glazing mastic to seal glass in fixed lights or top-hung vents. The window units are available as: fixed glazing, clear or obscure, for normal impact or fire resisting situations; top-hung vents; vertical sliders; and solid infill panels. They have a 300 mm (3 M) *horizontal dimensional flexibility*.

Figure 3.15 shows typical arrangement of internal 200 mm (2 M) partitions, which consist of galvanized metal stud framing which supports sheets of either PVC faced steel and/or plasterboard. A half-thickness partition (M) is used for inner linings of double leaf external claddings. The partition is braced at its top to roof or floor diaphragms, or to horizontal members at bottom chord level of trusses forming pitched roofs. The plasterboard only version is of lower cost/performance than the PVC faced steel/plasterboard version which is intended as a fire/sound/service wall (ie pipes, ducts, etc, contained within thickness).

The 100 mm (M) thick partition may be offset on either side of any 300 mm (3 M) *planning grid* line, with one face nominally on that grid line. The 200 mm (2 M) version may be centred on the grid line but the minimum offset is 600 mm (6 M).

Intermediate floors are constructed of ribbed pre-cast reinforced concrete decks, nominally 50 mm (submodule) thick, supported on steel floor beams. The decks are located clear of their projecting ribs by shear connectors on the top chord of floor beams. The joints at beam supports are then grouted up so that the floor performs as a structural diaphragm. At the perimeter, the decks extend beyond the grid line to support external wall components. Floor decks are 900 mm (9 M) wide, and either 1.8 m (18 M) long for normal loads (3 kN/m^2) or 900 m (9 M) long for heavy loads (5 kN/m^2). The loading determines the spacing of the secondary floor beams, but not the spacing of columns on the *structural grid*. The decks, which provide half-hour fire resistance, are located below the upper floor *co-ordinating plane* by 25 mm (submodule) to allow for a *floor finish zone*, and can have 'knock-out' holes to permit penetration of service pipes. Larger holes through the floor may be provided by using beams of trimming angles in galvanized mild steel.

Standard staircase arrangements are contained within a bay size of 5.4 × 3.6 m (54 M × 36 M), but reductions in the well size to 3 m (30 M) or 2.4 m (24 M) are possible by using additional staircase steel components giving limited 600 mm (6 M) flexibility. Two types of staircase are available: those used on sites liable to mining subsidence are constructed of steel channel strings with steel tray treads and landings; those on non-subsidence sites are similar but are constructed using flat plate strings. The staircase bay must directly relate to the *structural grid* and a column must occur at each corner of the bay enclosing the staircase which carries vertically through for the full height of the building. Intermediate columns may occur on the grid lines forming the bay, at 1.8 m (18 M) or 3.6 m (36 M) spacing. The long side of a staircase should not form part of an external wall in buildings over two storeys as intermediate perimeter columns will require the use of additional stiffening components. Tread and landing trays are designed to accept a standard non-slip or other finish. Balustrades can be fixed to the inside staircase string, at landing returns and half-landings. Elsewhere, they should be fixed directly to external wall linings, partitions or screens.

When a flat roof is required, it is provided by corrugated galvanized steel decking which is fixed to the top of roof beams. The decking follows the camber of the roof beams by warping within the deck, and constitutes a structural diaphragm to assist in keeping the frame stable. The decking supports a vapour barrier, insulation, built-up felt finish and solar reflecting chippings.

Details of roof lights are given in 8.4 Plastics dome and figure 8.5. Permanently ventilated and unventilated rooflights are available in two sizes: 900 mm (9 M) and 1.8 m (18 M) square. It is possible to locate them in any position relative to the *planning grid*, although they may not be closer than 200 mm (20 M) to centre-lines of beams. As the apertures for the roof lights have an effect on the roof deck diaphragm, the smaller version must not be positioned closer together than 900 mm (9 M) and the larger version not closer together than 1.8 m (18 M). For the same reason, there are some limitations on the number of roof light apertures occurring within a given area of roof.

A pitched roof structure is an integral part of the steel frame, consisting of galvanized mild steel trusses (figure 3.9), hips and valley members supported on perimeter columns linked by a beam at the eaves. Timber rafters span between cold formed galvanized mild steel 'Z' purlins supported by the trusses, hips and valley members.

Continued on page 58

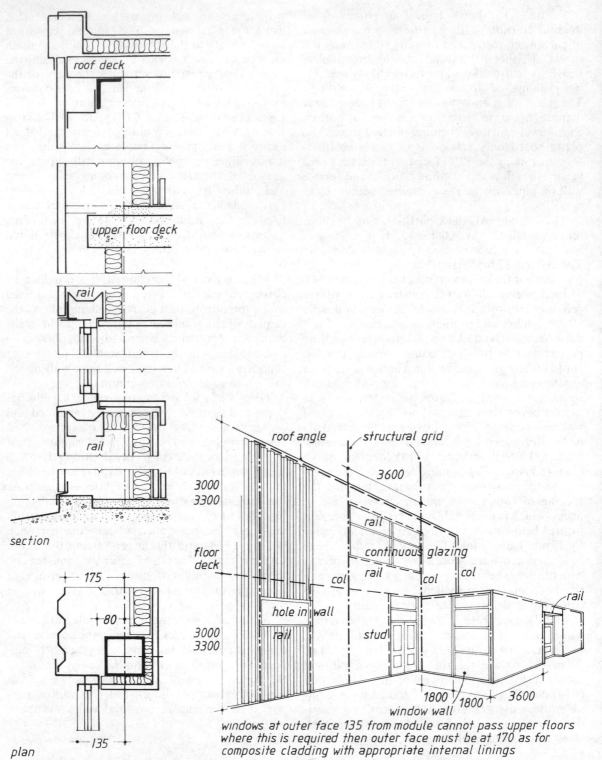

roof deck

upper floor deck

rail

rail

section

175

80

135

plan

roof angle   structural grid

3600

3000
3300

rail

continuous glazing

floor
deck

col   rail   col   col

hole in wall   rail

rail

3000
3300   stud

1800   1800   3600

window wall

windows at outer face 135 from module cannot pass upper floors
where this is required then outer face must be at 170 as for
composite cladding with appropriate internal linings

3.11 *CLASP: construction details of metal sidings*

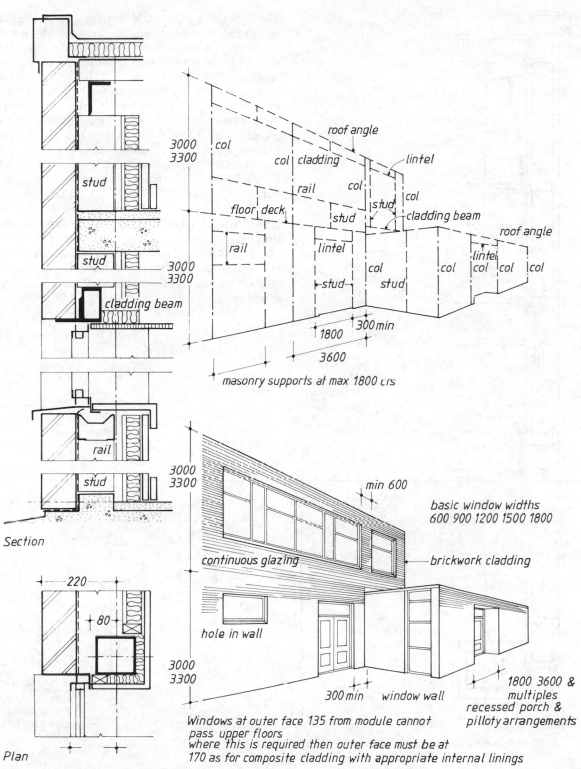

Section

Plan

3.12 *CLASP: construction details of brick cladding*

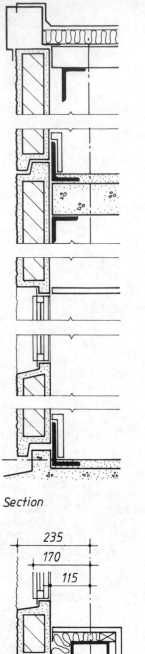

Section

235

170

115

Plan

3.13 *CLASP: construction details of composite panel cladding*

The roof has a pitch of 26 degrees and is suitable for interlocking tiles weighing between 45–50 kg/m²: finishes of greater *or lesser* weight cannot be used without modification to the design of certain structural steel components. Horizontal wind bracing is normally located throughout the ceiling level, but may be raised locally into the inclined plane of the roof. This bracing enables the roof to span between vertical wind braces provided to the perimeter columns at its ends.

Thermal insulation to both the flat roof and the pitched roof constructions gives a 'U'-value of not more than 0.6 W/m²K. A 1.2 m × 600m (12 M × 6 M) lay-in grid type suspended ceiling is also provided using mineral fibre tiles in suspension tees, normally relating to the *structural grid* of 1.8 m (18 M). This system provides one-hour fire resistance. Cavity barriers can be incorporated for smoke and fire compartmentation, or for sound control.

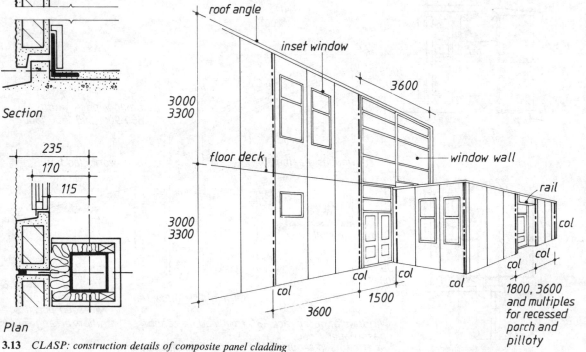

roof angle

inset window

3600

3000
3300

floor deck

window wall

3000
3300

rail

col

col

col

col

col

col

col

1500

3600

1800, 3600 and multiples for recessed porch and pilloty

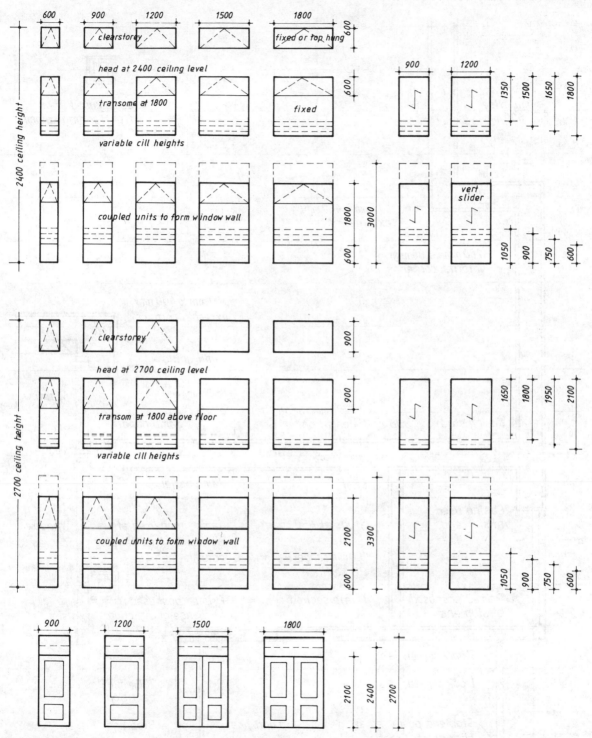

3.14 *CLASP: range of doors and windows using basic module co-ordinating dimension of 100 mm*

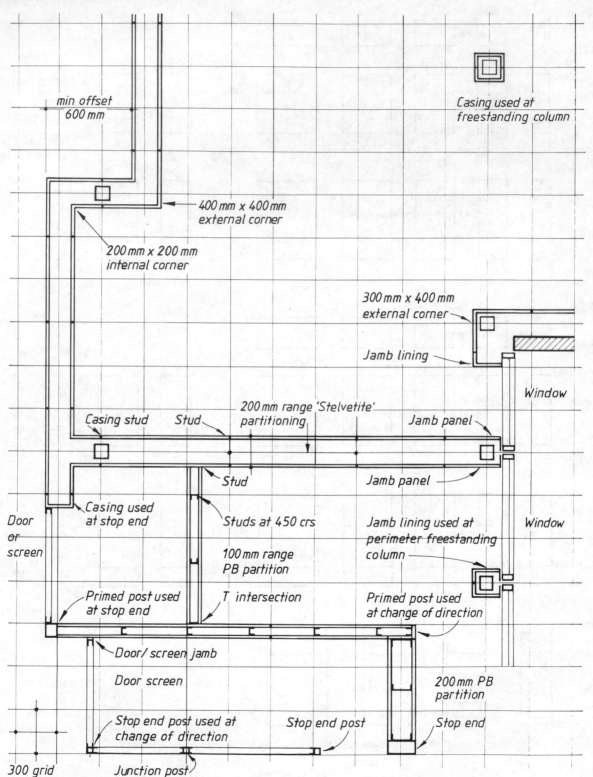

3.15 *CLASP: typical arrangement of internal 200 mm and 100 mm thick partitions*

4 Joinery

4.1 Introduction

General references
The design and practice of joinery, J. Eastwick-Field and J. Stillman, Architectural Press Ltd
Joinery, C. H. Tack, PRL, HMSO.
Handbook of Fixings and Fastenings, Bill Launchbury, Architectural Press Limited.
Windows: Performance, Design and Installation, Beckett and Godfrey CLS/RIBA

Joinery is generally understood to be the fabrication and fixing of timber components such as windows, doors, stairs, built-in fittings, and of external items such as gates, the surfaces of all of which are planed (ie *wrot*), and usually sanded. The ease of working timber, and its 'warm' and interesting appearance, encourage its use.

The quality of joinery work depends upon design, materials and workmanship. The designer must, therefore, understand the principles of design, specify exactly the type and quality of timber and other materials, and the standard of workmanship required and bear in mind the available facilities for manufacture and fixing.

Internally, unprotected wood soon becomes dirty and dull so exposed surfaces are often stained and/or treated with a natural or synthetic resin varnish, or with french or wax polish – clear finishes which considerably enhance the natural appearance of timber. Alternatively, wood is painted. It is important to note that the smoothness of the wood surface determines that of applied finishes.

Externally, all unprotected timbers 'weather' to a uniform grey. Clear finishes can preserve the new appearance of timber, but they require frequent maintenance. See *MBS: Finishes*, chapter 2.

Timber is often used as a strong and inexpensive core, so that metal faced plywood, and metal drawn on wood sections, are economical means of obtaining the appearance of metals. Timber windows are available with sections encapsulated in pvc sheet.

Increasingly, 'solid' timber is being used in conjunction with plywood, blockboard, chipboard, hardboard, plastics laminates and metal sheets and sections. Although sliced wood veneers, often having exotic grain patterns, continue to be glued to surfaces internally, plastics impregnated paper laminates simulating wood are now commonly used. These can be easily cleaned but they are not resistant to scratching and abrasion and are, therefore, not suitable for counter tops and working surfaces.

Principles of good joinery design can be deduced from knowledge of the properties of the materials to be used and the intended conditions of use, eg light or heavy duty, internally or externally. Designs can invariably be improved by careful observation of the behaviour of prototypes.

The limitations of hand and of machine work must be taken into account. For example, a spindle cutter cannot form a square end to a groove; either a separate machine operation or hand work is required. Although joinery can be remarkably accurate, inaccuracies are inevitable in fixing, and more so in refixing removable sections such as glazing beads, so these should be either recessed or projected in relation to the sashes to which they are attached, see figure 6.16, page 163 and 7.28, page 227.

Arrises (ie corners) are better slightly rounded, since sharp arrises are difficult both to obtain and maintain, and the tendency for paint and clear finishes to 'run away' from such corners is undesirable particularly externally.

The choice of the correct timbers requires knowledge of the characteristics and properties of timbers in general, of the available species, and of the conditions to which specific joinery components will be subjected – see page 63. Nomenclature, anatomy and properties of timbers, and causes and means of avoidance of deterioration, are dealt with in *MBS: Materials*, chapter 2.

Traditional naming of timbers is confusing. It will be noted, for example, that the unqualified description *deal* does not relate to any particular species, and the need to use the names given in BSs 881, 589: 1974 *Nomenclature of commercial timbers, including sources of supply* for hardwoods and softwoods respectively, is emphasized.

All timber for building must be dried slowly (ie *seasoned*), if only to avoid too rapid drying and consequent splitting, or to make it receptive to preservatives. Twenty five maximum moisture content is advised for vacuum/pressure impregnation and 22% for organic solvent type preservatives. Timber for joinery must be dried to levels as near as possible to the relatively low moisture contents it will assume, which normally necessitates *kiln seasoning*. This minimizes shrinkage in service, and sometimes expansion, remembering that timber can be too dry. It also reduces thermal conductivity and vulnerability to fungal attack and makes surfaces suitable for gluing and surface finishes. Seasoning is not irreversible, so that priming of joinery 'at works' and protection from the weather in transit to the site and on the site, are necessary. Ideally, timber would not be installed until buildings are heated and 'dried out' and buildings are maintained at constant relative humidities, but normally joinery must be designed and fixed to permit some moisture movement in service, eg by using narrow widths and tongued and grooved joints, or where widths are glued together, as in 'solid' table tops, by employing fixings which allow the overall widths of tops to change with changes in the moisture content of the wood resulting from variations in the humidity of the surrounding air. Incidentally, paint and clear finishes can only delay such movements.

The extra cost of radially cut timber is justified where the smaller movement in its width, and freedom from the 'cupping' of plain sawn timber are critical – as in drawing boards, and/or where an interesting appearance is desired – as that given by 'silver grain' rays in oak.

The low thermal conductivity and capacity of timber and the low thermal movement in its length favours its choice for various uses. Timber retains its strength at high temperatures, and in appropriate thicknesses which allow for losses due to charring, it can provide useful degrees of *fire resistance*, eg even in encasures to protect steel structures. Intumescent strips, which expand in fires, are valuable in sealing gaps around and between fire-resisting doors, and as beads for fire-resisting glazing. The *spread of flame*[1] classification of timbers can be effectively improved by impregnation with, or by surface applications of, fire retardants, although these cannot make timber *non-combustible*[1] and adhesives and surface treatments may not be compatible with them.

As timber changes dimensions to differing extents, tangentially and radially, and longitudinal movement is negligible, some distortion such as cupping, diamonding, and twist of boards having twisted grain, is inevitable with changes in moisture content, but it must be emphasized that conformity with BS 1186: *Timber and workmanship in joinery*, Part 1: 1986 Specification for timber, will minimize such tendencies. 'L' shapes cut out of solid timber should be avoided and complex shapes are best 'built-in' by gluing together mutually compensating pieces into a balanced laminate. Plywood, which has an uneven number of plies with their grain running in opposed directions, demonstrates these principles.

Although timber tends to expand when it is wetted and to return to its former size when it dries again, it must be remembered that if it is restrained while it absorbs water, when it dries it shrinks from the restrained size and becomes smaller than it would have been had it not been restrained – a phenomenon known as *stress setting*. The effects of this permanent shrinkage are obvious where gaps form between timber flooring after flooding (and indeed, when wooden tool handles loosen when they dry after having been wet).

Unless timber is an inherently durable heartwood, or has been impregnated with preservative and the effects of wetting and drying are acceptable, joinery should be designed to minimize the likelihood of wetting by rain or other causes. All such timber should be protected by damp-proof courses and membranes and flashings, and it should be kept above splash rising from pavings and projecting surfaces. Joinery should be designed to be self-draining with no horizontal surfaces and with devices such as lined channels and weep tubes to remove condensation from glass on the inside of windows. Defective joints,

[1]BS 476 terms – see *MBS: Materials*

and cracks must be avoided where they would allow water to flow or be blown into, or to enter timber by capillary action.

A common defect has been the rotting of the lower rails of sashes. Condensation from the inner face of glass enters the wood through defective back putties, the wood swells and cracks the outside paint at a joint, and further water enters. Paint is not a preservative, and in this case it only serves to retain water and fungal decay follows, particularly if sapwood which has not been treated with preservative is present – the sapwood of all species is *non-durable* or *perishable*. Because most softwoods contain sapwood it is now considered essential to preserve them where they are used in windows and external doors and frames and cladding, even if these are to be painted.

A Norwegian method for protecting the lower members of windows is described on page 163.

The National House Builders' Registration Council requires timber for claddings, window frames, casements and sashes and external door frames to be treated with preservative, or a preservative and paint system (NHBRC *Practice Note* No. 1 describes acceptable preservative treatment), unless one of the following *durable* timbers is used:

Afrormosia	Keruing	Sapele
Agba	Makoré	Sweet chestnut
Afzelia	American White oak	Teak
Gurjun	European oak	Utile
Idigbo	Japanese oak	Western Red cedar
Iroko	Red meranti	Yang
Kapur	Red seraya	

The Practice note states, however, that the sapwood of these timbers should be treated with preservative.

End grain is especially vulnerable and if it is cut on site the NHBRC advises that ends should be immersed in preservative for at least one minute, or if this is not practicable, two brush coats should be applied. It must be noted that preservatives should be applied liberally, unlike paint which is 'brushed out'.

Preservatives may adversely affect putties, mastics, window and door furniture and paints. Generally, forty-eight hours must be allowed before applying a primer on a surface which has been treated with preservative and three–four days may be necessary where copper naphthenate preservatives are used. Internally, even *perishable* woods, such as beech, do not require preservative if they are kept 'dry'.

Although timber has a high strength:weight ratio it must not be forgotten that some joinery members are highly stressed, if only occasionally, and eventualities such as persons standing on tables must be foreseen. Concentrations of stress at joints as, in those in side hung, double glazed casement windows, determine jointing methods and these in turn may determine the minimum sizes of the members to be joined.

The economical use of the *standard sizes* of sawn timber is dealt with under 4.5 *Sizes of softwoods*.

4.2 Choice of timbers for uses

If the properties of available timbers are systematically matched to known performance requirements it is often possible to use a timber which is more suited, and yet less costly, than the conventional choice. For example, members in stronger timbers can be smaller and may cost less, than those in 'cheaper' but weaker timbers.

The botanical descriptions: *hardwood* and *softwood* are rarely helpful. Thus, although most hardwoods are denser and therefore stronger than most softwoods, hardwoods are not necessarily hard and softwoods are not always soft, eg yew. Also, hardwoods include species with heartwood having both the greatest and least resistance to fungal attack, and softwoods include species having both 'small' and 'large' moisture movements.

Timbers vary considerably in their properties and appearance, between species, and even between parts of one tree. Hence, information can relate only to average specimens of any species and this, including reference to properties such as: strength, nailing, gluing and resistance to cutting, blunting effect on tools, drying characteristics, durability and resistance to impregnation, and suitability for bending is found in:

MBS: Materials chapter 2
Timber selection by properties, Part 1: Windows,

doors, cladding and flooring, PRL, HMSO. (Further parts will deal with other uses.)

A handbook of hardwoods, PRL, HMSO

A handbook of softwoods, PRL, HMSO

BS 373: 1957 *Testing small clear specimens of timber*

BS 1186: — *Timber and workmanship in joinery*
Part 1: 1986 *Specification for timber*
Part 2: 1971 *Quality of workmanship*

BS 4978: 1973 *Timber grades for structural use*

BS 5268: — *Code of practice in the structural use of timber*
Part 2: 1984 *Code of practice for permissible stress design, materials and workmanship*
Part 4: — *Fire resistance of timber structures*

BS 5756: 1980 *Specification for tropical hardwoods graded by structural use*

BS 5820: 1979 *Methods of test for determination of certain physical and mechanical properties in structural size*

BS 6100: — *Glossary of building and civil engineering terms*
Part 4: — *Forest products*
Section 4.2: 1984 *Sizes and qualities of solid timber*

BS 1186: Part 1 gives the suitability of thirty-six hardwoods and ten softwoods which are available in this country, for twelve joinery applications.

The Building Regulations 1985 Approved Documents A: A1/2 Part B table B1

The National House-Builders Registration Council Handbook

4.3 Specification of timber for joinery

Timber can never be 'free from all defects' and a requirement that it must be 'reasonably free', requires interpretation for various types of joinery. Some guidance is given in:

BS 459 *Doors* Part 4: 1965

BS 1576 *Wood door frames and linings*: 1953

BS 1186: *Timber and workmanship in joinery*
Part 1: 1986 Specification for timber
Part 2: 1971 Quality of workmanship

BS 4471: 1987 Specification for sizes of sawn and processed softwood

BS 1186: Part 2: 1971 details quality requirements for timber in four 'use classes', ie Class 1S – joinery for clear finishing and Classes 1, 2 and 3

for painting. Rules are given for 'concealed' and 'semi-concealed' surfaces. The Standard must be consulted for details, but the following notes will give guidance:

1 Timber must be free from fungal decay, and from insect damage other than pinhole borer (ambrosia) holes which are permitted in concealed and semi-concealed surfaces, and if the holes are filled, also in Class 1, 2 and 3 surfaces.
2 Sapwood is not allowed in hardwood surfaces exposed to the weather.
3 Unsound, dead, and loose knots are restricted to concealed and semi-concealed surfaces and knot sizes are limited.
4 Laminating, finger jointing and edge jointing must not be unduly conspicuous and may be disallowed by the purchaser for Class 1S use. For this use also, the species and character of grain must be the same on all surfaces and be matched as far as possible.
5 For Class 1 timber, checks and shakes are restricted in size and depth. Not less than 8 growth rings per 25 mm are specified and the slope of grain is restricted to not more than 1 in 8 in hardwoods and 1 in 10 in softwoods.
6 Sapwood (except 2), including discoloured sapwood, is allowed.

The recommended moisture contents for all class of joinery are given in figure 4.1.

	Moisture content percent + or − 2
External joinery	
Heated or unheated buildings	17
Internal joinery	
Heated buildings	
(i) intermittent	15
(ii) continuous, with room	
temperatures of 12–18°C	12
20–24°C	10
(iii) timber in close proximity to	
sources of heat	8

4.1 *Moisture contents for joinery when handed over to the purchaser*

4.4 Workmanship

The traditional craftsman had great pride in providing a high standard of workmanship, and the expression: 'the work is to be performed in a workmanlike manner' was generally understood in a given context. Today, more precise descriptions are necessary and these are provided by – BS 1186: Part 2: 1971 (amended 1976), *Quality of workmanship in joinery*. Requirements are specified for fit of parts and the degree of care in forming joints, including glued joints. At present, only a simple definition is given of an acceptable surface finish. The BS includes: tolerances for joints which permit movement; dimensions of gaps around painted and unpainted doors and sashes; requirements for fit of drawers; laminated wood, and descriptions of *finger joints* which reduce waste by joining short lengths of timber.

Joinery must be protected from exposure and damage during transport and storage on site and during the course of the work. Protection on the site is usually done by the use of strips of hardboard, covering by polythene sheet, or in the case of special work, by 'boxing in' behind a plywood or hardboard covered frame. The contractor should also, in good quality work, ensure that the heat and humidity conditions in the building are suitable for the joinery to be delivered and fixed, so that the conditions are commensurate with the required moisture content of the timber.

Clear seals are available which can be applied to joinery work at the time of manufacture, and which prevent moisture penetration and so protect the work from moisture movement before the final finish is applied.

When timber is framed up, the faces of all the members joined should be perfectly fitted together, with true and flush surfaces in alignment throughout the joint.

Sizes of so-called 'structural' members, the collapse of which would endanger lives, are calculated. However, the sizes of other joinery members whether acting as beams, cantilevers, columns or struts have traditionally been based on 'experience'. Actual sizes were then often increased for extra 'safety', for convenience in jointing, or even just to 'fill in spaces'.

To minimize waste, where possible sizes should be based on the standard sawn sizes.

Due to differences in tangential and radial moisture movements, sections which deviate too widely from rectangles are liable to distort, and for this reason built-up sections may be preferred, even for simple sections like door frames with stops. Built-up sections may also be more economical, and complex profiles must be built-up to minimize waste. Externally however, joints which are not glued with waterproof glue present opportunities for water to enter.

The costs of grinding cutters and setting up machines are high, and a large number of operations can only be justified by a very large order.

4.5 Sizes of softwoods

Metric sizes have been agreed by all the major softwood producing countries and the principal European importing countries. Figure 4.2 shows the relevant data from BS 4471: Part 1:

Normal sources	Thickness[2]	Width[2]								
	mm	75	100	125	150	175	200	225	250	300
Europe	16	X	X	X	X					
	19	X	X	X	X					
	22	X	X	X	X					
	25	X	X	X	X	X	X	X	X	X
	32	X	X	X	X	X	X	X	X	X
	36[1]	X	X	X	X					
	38	X	X	X	X	X	X	X		
	40[1]	X	X	X	X	X	X	X		
	44	X	X	X	X	X	X	X	X	X
	50	X	X	X	X	X	X	X	X	X
	63		X	X	X	X	X	X		
	75		X	X	X	X	X	X	X	X
America	44[3]	X	X	X	X	X	X	X	X	X
	100		X		X		X		X	X
	150				X		X			X
	200						X			
	250								X	
	300									X

[1]These thicknesses are unlikely to be available
[2]The sizes given are for 20% moisture content. For every 5% additional moisture content up to 30% sizes must be 1% greater and for every 5% moisture content less than 20% sizes may be 1% less.
[3]Canadian commercial hemlock (*Hem-fir*)

4.2   BS 4471: 1987 Basic cross-sectional sizes of sawn softwoods at 20% moisture content

Minus deviations permitted on up to 10% of the pieces in any sample are 1 mm on widths and thicknesses up to 100 mm, and 2 mm on greater sizes.

The standard provides for *precision timber* produced by machining (*regularizing*) at least one face and edge of a section to give a uniform thickness and/or width throughout 1 mm less than the basic sawn size.

Figure 4.3 gives the reductions allowed for planing sawn sections to accurate sizes, ranging in the case of joinery form 7 mm to 13 mm, according to sizes of pieces.

Purpose	Reduction from basic size to finished size for sawn width and/or thickness (mm)				
	15 to and incl. 22	Over 22 to and incl. 35	Over 35 to and incl. 100	Over 100 to and incl. 150	Over 150
Constructional timber, surfaced	3	3	3	5	6
Floorings[1]	3	4	4	6	6
Matchings and interlocking boards[1]	4	4	4	6	6
Planed all round					
Trim	5	5	7	7	9
Joinery and cabinet work	7	7	9	11	13

[1]The reduction of width is overall the extreme size exclusive of any reduction of the face by the machining of a tongue or lap joint

4.3 *Reductions from basic sizes to finished sizes to accurate sizes by processing of two opposed faces of softwoods*

Plus or minus 0.5 mm is allowed on all finished sizes. Lengths of softwoods are from 1.8 m to 6.3 m rising by 300 mm increments.

Finished thickness mm	Finished widths mm				
	22	30	36	44	48
6	X		X		
14			X		X
17	X		X		X
22	X	X	X	X	X
30			X	X	X
36			X		X
44					X
48					X

4.4 *Finished widths and thicknesses of small resawn softwood sections*

Minus 0.5 mm is permitted off not more than 10% of the pieces in any parcel and plus 3 mm on any proportion of a parcel.

4.6 Sizes of hardwoods

BS 5450: 1977 Specification for sizes of hardwoods and methods of measurement gives *Sizes of hardwoods and methods of measurement* – as follows:

Thickness mm	Width mm				
	50, 63	75	100, 125	100, 175	200, 225, 250, 300
19		X	X	X	
25	X	X	X	X	X
32		X	X	X	X
38		X	X	X	X
50			X	X	X
63				X	X
75				X	X
100					X

4.5 *Basic cross-sectional sizes of sawn heartwoods having 15% moisture content*

Hardwoods are not necessarily imported in BS sizes. Availability in any particular species should be checked.

Permitted deviations from the basic sizes are:

Basic size mm	Minus mm	Plus mm
Under 25	1	3
25–75	2	6
76–125	3	9
126–300	4	12

4.6 *Permissible deviations from basic thicknesses or widths of hardwoods at 15% moisture content*

Sizes will be similar for moisture contents less than 15% and greater for moisture contents up to 30% to an extent which can be estimated using the values for radial and tangential movements given in *The Handbook of Hardwoods* PRL, HMSO.

Hardwood in one of the specified thicknesses is often in random widths with either square or waney edges.

The following table gives the reductions allowed for planing sawn sections to accurate sizes, ranging in the case of joinery from 7 mm to 14 mm according to the sizes of the pieces.

End use or product	Reduction from basic size to finished size for basic sawn sizes of width or thickness (mm)				
	15 to 25 mm	26 to 50 mm	51 to 100 mm	101 to 150 mm	151 to 300 mm
Constructional timber, surfaced	3	3	3	5	6
Floorings, matchings and interlocked boarding, planed all round	5	6	7	7	7
Trim	6	7	8	9	10
Joinery and cabinetwork	7	9	10	12	14

4.7 *Reductions from basic sawn sizes to finished sizes by processing two opposed faces of hardwoods*

Finished sizes after processing are allowed plus or minus 0.5 mm deviation.

Lengths of imported hardwoods vary according to species and origin. BS *basic lengths* are any integral multiple of 100 mm but not less than 1 m. No minus deviations are allowed.

4.7 Building boards

Plywood, blockboard, laminboards, densified laminated wood, particle boards, fibre building boards and other boards which may be used in the manufacture of components are discussed in *MBS: Materials*, chapter 3. Over recent years the use of medium density fibreboard (MDF) has gained importance in use for the manufacture of furniture and BS 1105: *Fibre building boards* Part 2: 1971 *Medium board and hardboard* was amended in 1985 for its inclusion. The main characteristics of MDF are homogeneity and ease and precision of machining. Both faces are smooth and the density is of the same order as the high density medium board. MDF is essentially a high quality interior board for furniture, decorative panelling and similar manufacturing purposes, although moisture-resistant boards are available which extend its uses.

4.8 Joints

BS 1186: *Quality of timber and workmanship in joinery* Part 2: 1971 *Quality of workmanship* gives detailed requirements for fit, tolerances and general workmanship for the more common joints used in joinery.

The choice of joints depends upon the relationships and shapes of members to be joined. Joints may require to be designed to relate to rebates and mouldings in the members, see figure 4.51. Other factors include: strength, appearance (including 'secret' methods, see figure 4.13), need for demounting, see figures 4.22 and 4.24, ease of making and cost.

In recent years, the smaller sizes of many members and the greater cost of forming framed joints, have led to increased use of mechanical methods for jointing.

Strength requirements for joints vary considerably in degree, from those which locate members during construction only, to those which are heavily stressed in service in compression, tension, shear and/or torsion, and in one or more directions. The strength of unglued interlocking joints such as mortice and tenon, is related to the reduced sectional area of the weaker member. Nails, screws, bolts and dowels have the disadvantage of concentrating stresses in a limited number of small areas, whereas adhesives, which are generally stronger than the wood they join, distribute stresses more evenly. Combinations of these forms may be beneficial in service, or in assembly where interlocking shapes or inserts hold members together while glue is setting.

Figure 4.8 suggests examples of types of joints appropriate for stated typical situations. The types are listed in the table, and described under the following headings:

Interlocking, eg tongued and grooved
Inserts, eg dowels, nails and screws
Demountable connectors
Adhesives

4.9 Interlocking joints

(a) Mortice and tenon (figure 4.9(a) to (j))
This is the most common means of joining 'flat' rectangular sections of joinery at right angles. The

Types of joints	Stile – top rail of panelled door	Stile – middle rail of panelled door	Stile – intermediate rail of panelled door	Shelf – upright	Drawer side – front and back	Door lining – head – jamb	Framing	Boards edge – edge	End – end	Moulded sections	Architraves – angles	Post – cill	Curved – straight	Handrails and cills end-end	Other sections end – end	Window sills – angles	Movement joints	Demountable joints	'Secret' joints
	'Flat' sections eg Boards									'Thick' sections eg Window frames									
Mortice and tenon	16 (b)	16 (c)-(e)	16 (a)-(d)				16(d) (f)-(i)					40	16 (j)						16 (k)
Tongued and grooved								17 (a)-(f)											
Housed				18 (a)-(e)			18 (f)-(j)												
Combed					19 (a)		19 (b)												
Dovetailed					18 (e) 20 (a)-(c)		18 (j)												22 (d)
Lapped						21 (a)-(c)									21 (d)	21 (e)-(f)			22 (a)-(d)
Mitred and scribed										55	22 (a)					22			
Finger									23						23				
Dowelled	24 (b)	24 (b)		24 (a)				24 (b)											
Loose tongue	25 (a)	25 (a)						25 (a)											
Nails, pins and screws																	43 45	28	28
Bolts													29	29					29
Demountable connectors																		30	
Adhesives								31											

(Interlocks: Mortice and tenon, Tongued and grooved, Housed, Combed, Dovetailed, Lapped, Mitred and scribed, Finger. Inserts: Dowelled, Loose tongue, Nails, pins and screws, Bolts.)

4.8 *Common joints for typical joinery applications (figure numbers)*

Interlocks may require to be supplemented by Inserts and/or adhesives, but Inserts, demountable connectors and adhesives may be the sole method of fixing.

mortice is a slot cut in (usually through) one of the members to receive a tenon projecting from the end of the other member. The tenon is glued in the mortice, and in hand work, it is wedged. The tenon and wedges project initially, but when the glue has set the surplus timber is cut off to give a flush face. For mass production, instead of wedges, the joint is secured by non-ferrous metal star-shaped dowels driven from the face through the joint. This, of course, restricts the finishing work which can be done later and hardwood dowels are better in this respect.

The thickness of a tenon should not be more than one-third of that of the section, and its depth should not exceed five times the thickness.

(a) *Through tenon* In its simplest form this joint is used for joining intermediate rails and stiles in doors. The top and bottom edges of the mortice should be cut so that the slot is slightly dovetailed, thus increasing the strength of the joint. This dovetailing effect is obtained by moving the timber slightly from side to side during the machine cutting process.

Joints may be additionally secured by dowels, particularly in large sections of timber.

(b) *Haunched tenon* This joint is used to connect the stile and top rail of a door, since in order to wedge the joint it is necessary to retain a thickness of timber above the tenon. The cutting away of the front part of the tenon at the top does this, whilst the retention of the haunch minimizes any loss of strength. In making the joint, the stile is cut so a 'horn' projects beyond the top rail in order to resist the pressure from the wedges when the joint is made. The 'horn' is then cut off level with the top of the door and the wedges trimmed to size.

(c) *Twin tenon* Where the mortice and tenon joint is to be made in a deep rail, say 230 mm and over, there would be a tendency for a single deep tenon to shrink and become loose. To avoid this, two tenons are cut one above the other out of the depth of the rail. In good class work the joint is dowelled as well as being wedged.

(d) *Double tenon* Where a rail is more than, say, 65 mm thick two tenons are cut side by side.

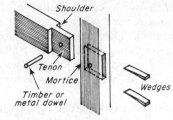

(a) *Through tenon*

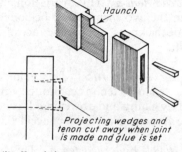

(b) *Haunched tenon*

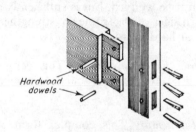

(c) *Twin tenon*

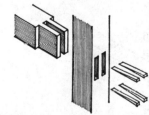

(d) *Double tenon*

4.9 *(a)–(j)*

Continued . . .

(e) *Twin double* A combination of twin and double tenons is used where the rail is deep and over 50 mm thick. Double and twin tenons can be haunched by leaving shoulders of timber at top and bottom of tenons. This joint allows a mortice lock to be fitted with less weakening of the framework.

Confusion must be guarded against in naming tenons. For example, twin tenons are sometimes called a pair of single tenons and the terms twin and double are interchanged!

(f) *Barefaced tenon* This variation, which is used when the two members to be connected are of different thickness, allows one face of the work to be flush.

(g) *Open or slot mortice* This joint is easily made. The tenon or tenons cannot be wedged and is secured by gluing and dowelling. It is often used where the framework will be concealed.

(h) *Twin double haunched tenon* This is a locating joint only, and therefore it is not wedged.

(i) *Stub tenon* Like the open mortice joint this joint cannot be wedged, but is sufficiently strong where both sides of the frame are strengthened by plywood or hardboard.

(j) *Hammer head key tenon* This very strong joint is used to connect curved members to uprights.

(k) *Fox-tail tenon* This complex form of stub tenon used in high class hand work is a 'secret' joint, wedges being (permanently) incorporated in the joint during assembly.

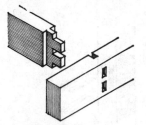

(h)   *Twin double haunched tenon*

4.9 *Mortice and tenon joints*

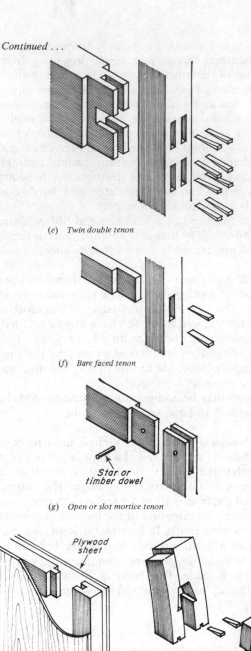

Continued . . .

(e)   *Twin double tenon*

(f)   *Bare faced tenon*

Star or timber dowel

(g)   *Open or slot mortice tenon*

Plywood sheet

(i)   *Stub tenon*

(j)   *Hammer head key tenon*

(b) Tongued and grooved (figure 4.10(a) to (f))
This joint is used principally for joining boards edge to edge, a tongue cut on the edge of one board fitting into a groove cut into the edge of the other. Without glue the joint allows boards to move in their width. With glue the joint locates boards while the glue is setting, although at the cost of extra width equal to the extent of penetration of tongues into grooves. Grooves are often cut slightly deeper than the projection of tongues to ensure a tight joint on the face. Where the reverse face will not be seen and where boards are not to be glued and cramped, the back shoulder can also be cut to remain slightly open.

(a) shows a *square edge tongue*, characteristic of hand work and (b) and (c) show **splayed and rounded tongues** which are more suitable for machine work.

(d) *Lindermann* This machine-made joint with an offset dovetail has been used for the strong joints needed for forming deep stair strings.

(e) and (f) *Square and splayed double tongued and grooved machine made joints* give a larger gluing surface and are suitable for joining boards of 40 mm and more in thickness.

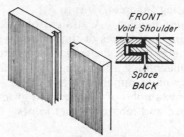

(a)　*Tongued and grooved – square edge tongue*

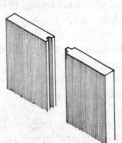

(b)　*Tongued and grooved – splayed tongue*

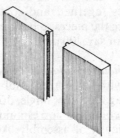

(c)　*Tongued and grooved – rounded tongue*

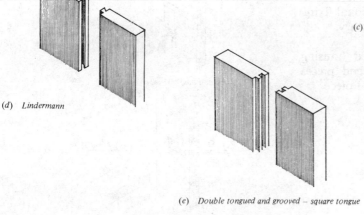

(d)　*Lindermann*

(e)　*Double tongued and grooved – square tongue*

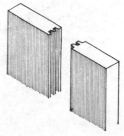

(f)　*Double tongued and grooved – spayed tongue*

4.10　*Tongued and grooved joints*

(c) Housing (figure 4.11(a) to (j))

(a) *Square housing* A straightforward method of locating two pieces of timber being jointed at right angles as in shelving. The joint requires careful machining and gluing, and/or fixing with screws or nails, punched in and filled.

Other examples of tongued and grooved joints are lapped and rebated corner joints.

(b) *Shouldered housing* The groove here is less than the thickness of the horizontal member; and will require additional fixing through the face of the vertical member.

(c) *Stopped housing* The groove is stopped back from the face of the upright. This is done where the improvement in appearance is considered to justify the increase in cost.

(d) *Dovetail housing – single* The groove is cut square on one side and given an upward chamfer to form a single dovetail on the other. The key profile so formed helps to prevent the joint pulling out. This joint can only be assembled by sliding the two parts together, and so the joint is not suitable where the pieces to be connected together are wider than say 300 mm.

(e) *Dovetail housing – double* The groove is fully dovetailed with a corresponding increase in strength as against the single dovetail housing. There is, of course, a corresponding increase in cost and difficulty of assembly. Additional fixing by screwing or pinning is not so necessary.

(f) *Rail housing* A form of stopped housing used in framing between rails and end pieces where the rail is not as wide as the end piece.

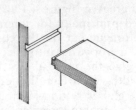

(b) *Shouldered housing*

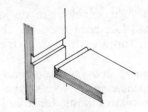

(c) *Stopped housing*

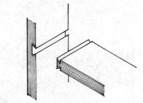

(d) *Dovetail housing – single*

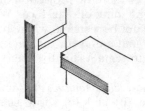

(e) *Dovetail housing – double*

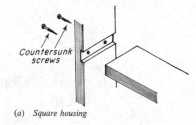

Countersunk screws

(a) *Square housing*

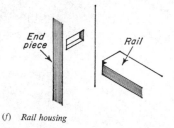

End piece   Rail

(f) *Rail housing*

4.11 *Housing joints*

Continued . . .

Continued

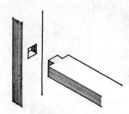

(g) *Double stopped housing*

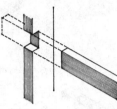

(h) *Face housing*

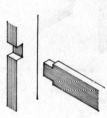

(i) *Shouldered face housing*

(j) *Dovetailed face housing*

4.11 *(a) to (j) Housing joints*

(g) *Double stopped housing* Used in skeleton framing where a neat appearance is required; this joint is principally a *locating* joint not having the strength of the other type of housings.

(h) *Face housing* This easily made joint is used in skeleton framing which is subsequently concealed. In these positions the fixing can be by nails or screws.

(i) *Shouldered face housing* This modification of the simple-faced housed joint provides additional area of contact whilst reducing the amount of timber to be cut away from the vertical member.

(j) *Dovetailed face housing* A housed joint incorporating the strength of the dovetail profile.

Another common housed joint is that used to join stair treads and risers to strings. In this case, the underside of the treads is usually concealed, and the housings are tapered to receive wedges.

(d) Combed (figure 4.12(a) and (b))
These are simple machine cut joints which have a larger gluing surface than butt joints. They should have a push fit. In thicker sections the number of tongues and slots can be increased with advantage.

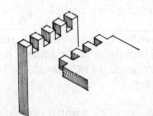

(a) *Corner locking joint*

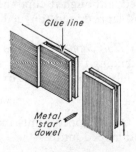

(b)

4.12 *Combed joints*

(e) Dovetailed (figure 4.13(a) to (c))
The parts of these joints are cut to give a mechanical 'lock' in one direction.

(a) is a hand-made *common dovetail* used in high quality joinery, particularly in joints between the sides and backs of drawers.

(b) shows a hand-made *stopped (and lapped) dovetail* joint suitable for joints between the sides and front of drawers. It is hand-made and would be used for high quality work only.

(c) In this typical version, a special machine cuts tails and sockets together in timber up to about 225 mm wide. All machine cut dovetails are stopped and lapped.

Other examples of dovetails shown in this chapter are: the hammer head key joint, the lindermann joint, square and face housing joints and a mitre with secret dovetail.

(f) Lapped (figure 4.14(a) to (f))
This principle is used in various forms, including the stopped dovetail joints.

(a) *Rebated* A lapped joint which allows the joining of two pieces of timber at right angles and at the same time conceals the end grain on one face. As with all lapped conditions the joint is secured by pinning or screwing and gluing.

(b) *Lapped and tongued* A joint commonly used between head and jamb of a door lining, it is stronger than the rebated joint but does not conceal the end grain.

(c) *Rebated and tongued* This joint is not much used, although it combines the merits of rebated and lapped, and tongued joints.

(d) *Half lapped* This is the most usual way of extending the lengths of members where the joint is fully supported. The overlap should be screwed and glued.

Other lapped joints include stopped dovetails and lapped mitres.

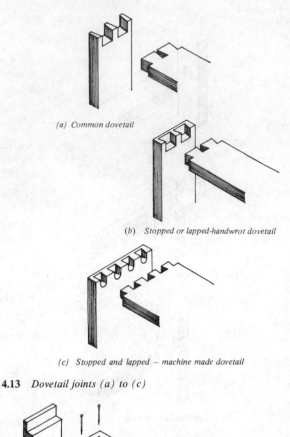

(a) Common dovetail

(b) Stopped or lapped-handwrot dovetail

(c) Stopped and lapped – machine made dovetail

4.13 *Dovetail joints (a) to (c)*

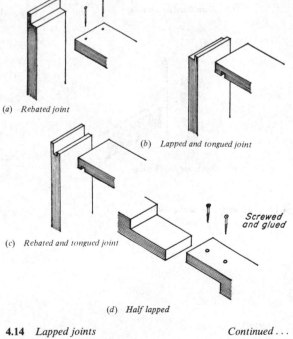

(a) Rebated joint

(b) Lapped and tongued joint

(c) Rebated and tongued joint

Screwed and glued

(d) Half lapped

4.14 *Lapped joints* Continued . . .

(e) *Notched joints* These simple joints provide single or double interlocks between lapped rectangular sections.

(f) *Cogged joints* are similar to notched joints and are used in the same circumstances. For joinery, notched and cogged joints would normally be glued while for carpentry they would probably be nailed.

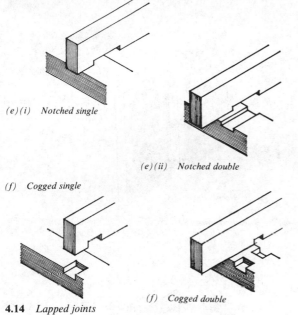

(e)(i) Notched single

(e)(ii) Notched double

(f) Cogged single

(f) Cogged double

4.14 *Lapped joints*

(g) Mitred (figure 4.15(a) to (d))
Mitres conceal end grain, the grain runs continuously around the exposed faces and the appearance is symmetrical. They are used to connect boards at their edges.

(a) is a *plain* mitred joint strengthened with a square block screwed to the boards.

(b) *Lapped* A mitred joint which gives a greater gluing area for increased strength. The shoulders ensure an angle of 90 degrees.

(c) *Mitre with loose tongue* The tongue, preferably of plywood, locates and strengthens the joint. The groove can be stopped so the tongue is not

seen on the surface, although this involves hand work. To ensure a tight fit, the tongue is slightly narrower than the combined width of the grooves.

(d) *Mitre with secret dovetail* This mitred joint has the added strength provided by a secret dovetail, but it cannot be cut by machine.

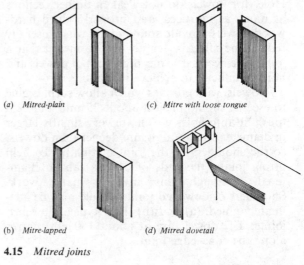

(a) Mitred-plain   *(c)* Mitre with loose tongue

(b) Mitre-lapped   *(d)* Mitred dovetail

4.15 *Mitred joints*

(h) Finger
(a) *The finger joint* This is a strong end–end joint which can reduce waste of costly timber, by joining short pieces together. The proportions of the fingers vary according to the stresses expected – see BS 1186: Part 2.

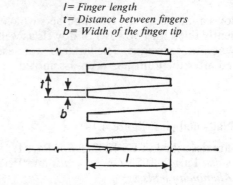

l= Finger length
t= Distance between fingers
b= Width of the finger tip

4.16 *Finger joint (BS 1186)*

4.10 Inserts

These joints employ wood or metal connecting devices such as dowels, loose tongues, nails, screws and bolts either as primary fixings, to reinforce interlocking or glued joints, or to retain members while glue is setting.

(a) Dowelled (figure 4.17(a) and (b))
Holes for dowels do not weaken timber sections as much as mortices, and properly glued hardwood dowels provide sound joints which usefully reduce the effective length of one member in a joint. The necessary true alignment of dowels and holes is difficult to achieve by hand.

Dowels, with grooves which allow surplus glue to escape, should project about 25 mm, and be a 'push fit' into holes which are very slightly larger in diameter and about 4 mm deeper than dowels, so the shoulders of the joint fit tightly. To help fitting joints, the ends of dowels can be chamfered, although this involves hand work. Shoulders of dowelled joints should also be adequately glued. (a) and (b) show typical dowelled joints. The dowels are at about 150 mm centres along the edge–edge joint.

(b) Loose tongue (figure 4.18(a) and (b))
(a) *Loose tongue*   Both pieces of timber forming the joint are grooved and a so called hardwood or preferably a plywood 'loose' tongue is glued in place on one side of the joint to strengthen it. The whole of the joint is then glued and 'cramped up' until the glue is set. This joint is commonly used in table and bench tops.

(b) shows a joint between two members which are sufficiently thick for two rows of dowels as well as a plywood loose tongue. The latter is more easily inserted after the joint has been assembled.

4.11 Nails and pins (figure 4.19)

Nails are described in BS 1202: *Nails* Part 1: 1974 *Steel nails*, Part 2: 1974 *Copper nails* and Part 3: 1974 *Aluminium nails*.

The more common nails used in joinery are illustrated in figure 4.19 with a guide to the metric sizes.

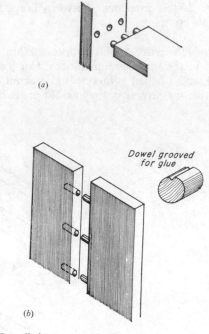

(a)

Dowel grooved for glue

(b)

4.17   *Dowelled joints*

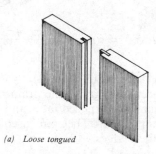

(a)   Loose tongued

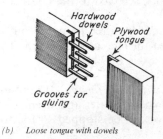

Hardwood dowels

Plywood tongue

Grooves for gluing

(b)   Loose tongue with dowels

4.18   *Loose tongue joints*

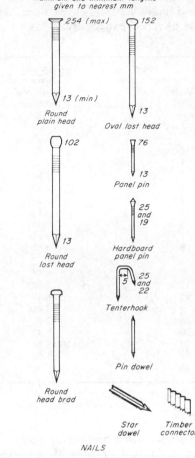

Maximum and minimum lengths
given to nearest mm

254 (max)   152

13 (min)
Round   13
plain head   Oval lost head

102   76

13
Panel pin

25
and
19

13   Hardboard
Round   panel pin
lost head

25
5   and
22
Tenterhook

Pin dowel

Round
head brad

Star   Timber
dowel   connector

NAILS

4.19 *Nails and pins*

Nails are described by methods of forming and by types of heads and shanks, materials and finishes.

Some nails were cut from sheet, but today wire nails are most common.

Lost-head nails have small heads so they can be punched below surfaces.

Improved nails, including *annular ring* and *helically threaded* types, resist withdrawal better than round wire nails.

Automatic nails These nails, which are often resin coated to improve withdrawal resistance, are provided in strips or coils for use in pneumatic guns or manual nailing machines.

Nail heads, in timber which is to be painted or to receive clear treatment, are usually punched below the surface and the hole is filled with proprietary filler. Where a surface is to have a clear finish the filler should be of matching colour.

Externally, steel nails should be zinc coated, but they should be well punched in, as the coating may be damaged. *Panel pins* are used for purposes such as securing sheet materials until non-contact adhesives have set. *Timber connectors* are often called *corrugated wedge fasteners*.

4.12 Wood screws (figure 4.20)

Screws are made in plain, sherardised or galvanized steel, or where corrosion is likely and/or where the screw head will be seen, stainless steel, brass or even bronze screws may be used – the latter metals, however, being less strong than steel.

Screw heads include:

countersunk   the heads are shaped to fit 'flush' in counter-sinkings in wood, or in metal components such as butt hinges.

countersunk and raised   the raised heads reduce the danger of damaging surrounding surfaces in driving the screws.

round particularly suitable for fixing metals which are too thin to countersink.

mirror   for fixing glass and other panels, the slots being concealed by screw-on or snap-on domes.

square   for heavy duty *coach screws*, usually 6 mm diameter or larger, driven with a spanner.

Driving profiles are:

slot   the standard type

clutch   the profile prevents removal

recessed   the *Phillips* and *Pozidriv* heads allow greater purchase to be applied in driving and the specially designed screwdrivers are less likely to slip. Recessed head screws are particularly suitable for mechanical driving.

Thread patterns are:

single spiral   these traditional screws have two-thirds of their length tapered and threaded

double spiral   twin parallel threads on cylindrical shanks have greater holding power, and they extend over a greater proportion of the length of the screw.

For access panels, glazing beads and similar removable items round or raised head, slotted or recessed heads are appropriate, and brass or other metal, or plastics cups allow screws to be withdrawn and re-driven without damaging the surrounding wood, see figure 4.20.

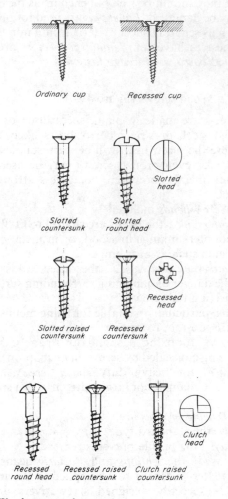

Ordinary cup   Recessed cup

Slotted head

Slotted   Slotted
countersunk   round head

Recessed head

Slotted raised   Recessed
countersunk   countersunk

Clutch head

Recessed   Recessed raised   Clutch raised
round head   countersunk   countersunk

4.20 *Wood screws and cups*

Where screw heads are to be concealed, they may be recessed below the surface and the hole filled with a proprietary filler. If the surface is to be clear finished, a *pellet* of the same timber with the direction of the grain following that of the surrounding timber may be glued in, providing a virtually 'secret', but permanent, fixing.

Screws are described in BS 1210: 1963 *Wood Screws* and figure 4.20 shows examples. Approximate sizes of screw gauges are:

Screw gauge	Nominal diameter of screw and unthreaded shank
	mm
0	1.52
1	1.78
2	2.08
3	2.39
4	2.74
5	3.10
6	3.45
7	3.81
8	4.17
9	4.52
10	4.88
12	5.59
14	6.30
16	7.01
18	7.72
20	8.43
24	9.86
28	11.28
32	12.70

4.21 *Screw gauges*

Turn-button Turn-buttons of wood or metal illustrated in figure 4.39, page 88, are used to fix tops to tables and benches while allowing moisture movement to take place in one direction without attendant distortion or cracking of the tops or frames. In addition, tops can be removed if repolishing or renewal is required.

Slotted angle This method, see figure 4.41, page 90, also allows movement in one direction but tops cannot be removed so easily.

Slot screw Uses for this joint include joining board edges to form table tops, fixing panelling to framing and hanging cupboards on walls.

A projecting screw on one member is inserted in the circular hole of a 'keyhole' cut in a plate which is fixed to a second member. The members are slid so the screw passes along the slot in the 'keyhole'. The plate then holds the screw head securely, and 'secretly', although, as glue is not used the joint is demountable. See figure 4.22.

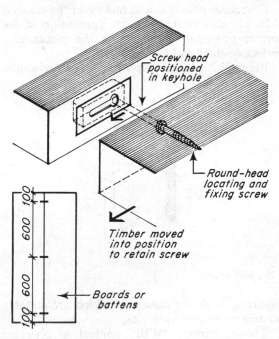

4.22 *Keyhole joint*

Bolts with suitable washers are used for heavy-duty work.

Handrail bolt (figure 4.23)   This joint secures the ends of timber to make up a continuous handrail. A bolt threaded at both ends when tightened produces a very strong joint which is difficult to detect in use. The slots on the underside of the timber are filled with matching timber and cleaned off smooth.

4.13 Demountable connectors

These enable preformed members to be rapidly located and joined. In addition to angle plates which allow moisture movement (figure 4.41) and 'keyhole plates' which allow dismantling (figure 4.22), connectors include the following types:

Corner plates with slots shaped so they draw parts together.

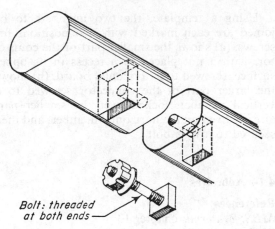

4.23 *Handrail bolt*

Two-part components which clip together, but which can be dismantled, others which draw parts together by a cam action, and plates fixed to table tops with wood screws, threaded for metal screws in the tops of table legs.

Figure 4.24 shows a two-part plastics connector which holds members, usually boards, rigidly at right angles without the need for a housing or other framed joint, or for glue. If required, these joints are easily 'knocked down', although in fact their chief use is for rapid assembly of furniture components by purchasers.

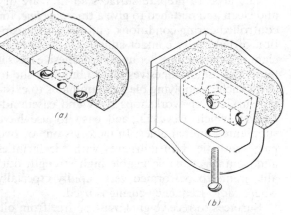

4.24 *Connector*[1]

[1]Plasplugs Ltd, Burton-on-Trent, Staffordshire
(Patent no. 1912/73)

79

Using a template, the two members to be joined are each marked with two positions for screws. (a) shows the smaller part of the connector, with a nut placed in a recess in its upper surface, screwed to a horizontal board. (b) shows the larger part of the connector screwed to a vertical member, locked over the smaller part already fixed on the horizontal member, and then secured to it by a bolt.

4.14 Adhesives

References
MBS: Materials chapter 13
BRE Digest 175 *Choice of glues for wood*
BRE Digests 211 and 212 *Site uses of adhesives*
PRL Bulletin 20: 1971 HMSO
Requirements and properties of adhesives for wood

There is an extremely wide range of adhesives available, having very different properties, suitable uses, and requirements for their use.

Adhesives must be suited to both the substrate and adherent, eg, in relation to their perviousness. Resins and oils in timber and preservative and fire retardant salts can present problems in adhesion. Some adhesives stain wood, and synthetic resin adhesives tend to blunt cutting tools.

It is interesting to note that BRE Digest 212 has a checklist of thirty-four items! Manufacturers' recommendations should be followed.

The need to prepare surfaces so they are dry and clean and matched to give a thin *glue line*, for controlled curing conditions, and with the exception of light duty contact adhesives, the need to clamp members together until the adhesive has set limits the use of adhesives on the building site to work such as applying plastics laminates to existing surfaces. In workshops PVA and casein adhesives which are clean and easy to use have supplanted animal glues. In factories one or two part synthetic resin adhesives with the facilities and control available enable high strength durable joints to be formed very rapidly especially where radio frequency curing is used.

Surfaces to receive glue must be free from oil, grease or dust, and the glue film must be evenly applied. The manufacturer's particular recommendations should be followed. The moisture content of the timber and the temperature of the room and of the glue are of paramount importance. To attempt to joint wet timber in a cold damp workshop is to invite failure.

Correct application and mixing of the catalyst glues are also vital, as is the observation of the correct procedure in bringing the pieces into perfect contact and cramping up.

Figure 4.25 shows simple *butt* or *rubbed* joints.

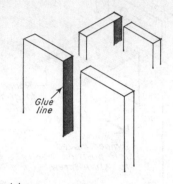

Glue line

4.25 *Butt joints*

Figure 4.26 shows adhesives which are suitable for five exposure categories.

The description 'WBP' applied to plywood refers only to the bonding agent and although the adhesive is suitable for hazardous exposures, for equivalent durability the timber must either be heartwood of a durable species or be treated with a compatible preservative.

4.15 Joiners' shop production

In addition to mass-production joinery factories, joinery workshops are run by specialist firms and by contractors. Specialist firms and the larger contractors maintain substantial timber stocks, and in some cases drying kilns. Some firms specialize in very high quality work for prestige buildings. In such workshops timber is thicknessed, planed, moulded, sanded, and the joints are cut by machine. The parts will then be fitted together, wedged, glued, cramped and finished by hand.

A typical sequence of operations in the manufacture of timber components in a well-equipped joiner's shop will be as follows: The shop foreman

Category	Examples of exposure	Recommended adhesives	Durability of adhesive
Exterior high hazard	Full exposure to weather	RF RF/PF PF (cold setting)	WBP WBP WBP
low hazard	Inside roofs of porches	RF, RF/PF, PF MF/UF	WBP BR
Interior high hazard	Laundries	RF, RF/PF, PF MF/UF	WBP BR
low hazard	Inside dwelling houses, heated buildings, halls and churches	RF, RF/PF, PF MF/UF UF Casein	WBP BR
Chemically polluted atmospheres	Swimming baths	RF, RF/PF, PF	WBP

Key		
	MF	melamine-formaldehyde
	PF	phenol-formaldehyde
	RF	resorcinol-formaldehyde
	UF	urea-formaldehyde
	WBP	weather and boil proof
	BR	boil resistant
	MR	moisture resistant and moderately weather resistant
	INT	interior

4.26 *Adhesives for exposures*
(Information from BRE Digest 175)

'takes off' the quantities of timber required for a component, from the architect's large scale working details or from the workshop setting out rod, and from these quantities prepares a cutting list. The information contained in the cutting list for each project is used when choosing the timber required from the storage racks. The amount of timber used will be set down on a *cost/value sheet*.

See chapter 1, page 16, regarding computerized working schedule for window production. The example of plastics window shown in figure 1.3 could similarly apply to the production of a wood window.

Machining

The basic processes are illustrated in figures 4.27 to 4.37.

(a) The timber is first cut to length by means of a *circular cross cut saw*. Then a *circular rip saw* is used to cut the timber to width and thickness. The timber is cut 'oversize', allowance being made at this stage for planing the finished timber, say 3 mm on each face. The *Standard Method of Measurement* allows a maximum of 3 mm. The sawn timber then passes to the *surface planer* to provide a true *face* and *edge*, and to remove any twist or irregularity. The timber then passes to a *thicknesser* which reduces the timber to the right size.

(b) The *surface planer* and a *thicknesser* is often combined as one machine as illustrated in figure 4.28.

At this stage the timber goes either to the site for fabrication, or to the setting-out bench for further machining.

The setting out is done by the shop foreman, who draws the vertical and horizontal sections of the components full size on a plywood sheet or setting-out board, say 225 mm wide × 12 mm thick. This board is also known as a *setting-out rod*.

As an alternative to drawing direct on to plywood, full size drawings can be prepared in negative form on transparent material such as tracing paper. This has the advantage that prints can be taken to provide a record of the work.

The setting-out rods, being full-size working drawings conventionalized by the shop foreman, go to the marker out, who transfers the relevant lines on to the timber. The dimensions from the setting-out rod can also be used by the shop foreman to produce the cutting list.

Lines of joints, and cuts with depths and type are marked on the timber from the setting-out rod. Since proportions and types of joints should be to accepted standards, it is not always necessary to specify setting out details of joints on working drawings.

From the *setting-out bench* (4.30) the timber travels to the *morticer* (4, 31) or the *tenoner* (4.32), then to the *spindle moulder* (4.33).

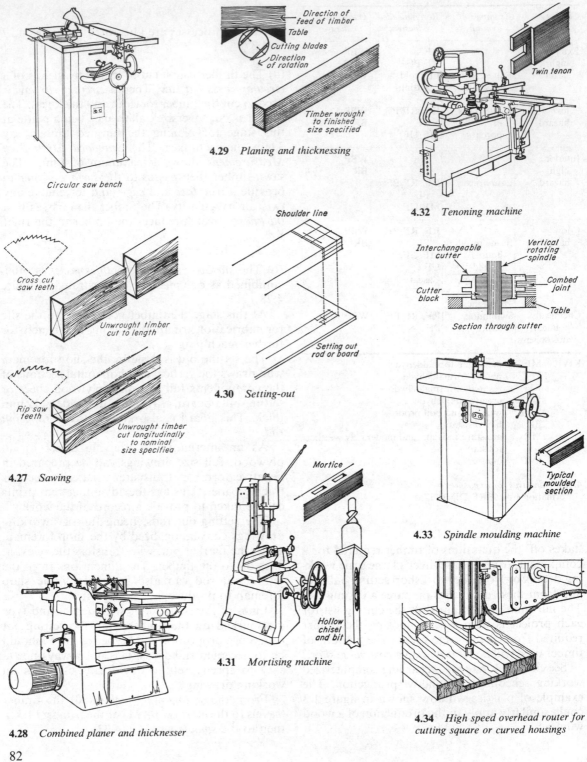

Circular saw bench

4.29 *Planing and thicknessing*

Direction of feed of timber
Table
Cutting blades
Direction of rotation

Timber wrought to finished size specified

Twin tenon

4.32 *Tenoning machine*

Cross cut saw teeth

Unwrought timber cut to length

Rip saw teeth

Unwrought timber cut longitudinally to nominal size specified

4.27 *Sawing*

Shoulder line

Setting out rod or board

4.30 *Setting-out*

Interchangeable cutter
Vertical rotating spindle
Cutter block
Combed joint
Table

Section through cutter

Typical moulded section

4.33 *Spindle moulding machine*

Mortice

Hollow chisel and bit

4.31 *Mortising machine*

4.34 *High speed overhead router for cutting square or curved housings*

4.28 *Combined planer and thicknesser*

82

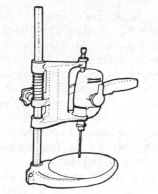

(a) Drill and stand

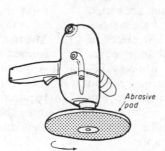

Abrasive pad

(c) Disc sander

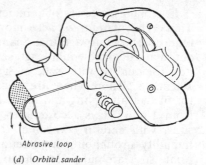

Abrasive loop

(d) Orbital sander

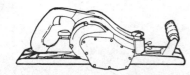

(b) Planer

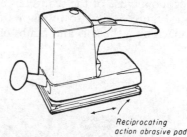

Reciprocating action abrasive pad

(e) Reciprocal sander

4.35 *Portable electric power tools*

The timber can be rebated, moulded, grooved or chamfered on the spindle moulder. Standard profiles are available but cutters can be specially made to any reasonable profiles, and circular work can be carried out.

Surface planer, thicknesser and spindle moulding operations can be combined on a *planer and moulder*. If this machine is used, the mortice and tenon operations are carried out later.

The following machines are ancillary to the main production line machinery:

Router for recessing to any profile as shown in figure 4.34.

Boring machine for drilling holes in series.

Dovetail machine for fabrication of dovetail joints, mainly used for drawer construction. It cuts front and sides together.

Panel saw (or dimension saw) for cutting sheet materials, such as hardboard, plywood, etc, to size.

Band saw for cutting circular work.

Sanding machines
(a) *Belt sander*, which consists of a belt of abrasive sheet under which the timber is passed.

(b) *Drum sander*, which consists of a number of drums covered with abrasive sheet over (or under) which the timber passes, on a moving bed.

After machining, the timber passes forward for fabrication. Portable power tools, such as a planer, drill and hand sanding machines – disc or orbital – will be used during this part of the work. See figures 4.35 (a) to (e).

4.16 Factory production

Large firms mass-produce windows, doors and door sets, cupboard fittings, staircases and sections such as skirtings and architraves. Machinery is similar to that used in joiners' shops, but handwork is almost eliminated and production is large and rapid. There is likely to be an increasing demand for fully finished components, glazed, painted and complete with locks, hinges and fastenings. See chapter 1, page 16 regarding computerized working schedule for window production in a factory. The example of plastics window shown in figure 1.3 could similarly apply to the factory production of a wood window.

The main processes of production are briefly: Timber, brought up to twelve months in advance, requires a large storage area. Scantlings are sorted automatically into equal lengths, and after selection for quality, into 'sets' of say 160 pieces of 100 mm × 50 mm. These are stacked under cover for further air drying and then kiln drying takes from 2 to 18 days according to the species and sizes, with careful control of temperature and humidity throughout. Sawn sections of the appropriate sizes are cut to lengths to make the most economic use of the scantlings available.

Figure 4.36(a) to (c) shows the processes for machining the sills and jambs of windows:

(a) The cut lengths passed on a conveyor, are planed to size and the initial cuts are made to form the required profile. Sill and jamb sections then go on separate lines.

(b) Mortice slots are cut in sills, and tenons are formed on the ends of jambs.

(c) A moulder completes the cutting of the profile, with grooves, throats and chamfers, as required. Sections are batched so as to minimize the changing of cutters. The maintenance and repair of woodworking machinery and the sharpening of cutters is done, wherever possible, automatically, in a separate workshop.

Sill section

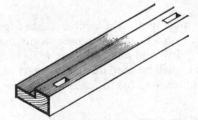

(a) Planer and moulder to face and edge

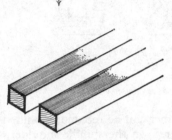

(a) Scantling, cut into section size and passed through planer and moulder to face and edge

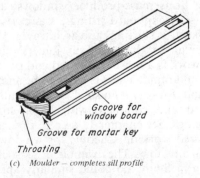

(b) Morticer – cuts mortice slots as required

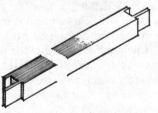

(b) Double end tenon cutter shapes tenons at each end of section

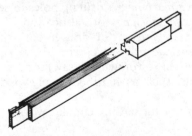

(c) Moulder – completes sill profile

(c) Moulder completes jamb profile

4.36 *Machine fabrication of sill and jamb sections*

84

Random lengths of moulded sections can be cut to non-standard lengths to form 'special' windows, which being out of the main production line are more expensive, although not always prohibitively so.

Sections for external joinery may be vacuum impregnated with preservative before assembly. See *MBS: Materials* chapter 2.

In addition to random checks, parts are inspected at several stages:
1 Length sorting
2 Cross cutting
3 Cleaning off
4 Finishing moulder

Figure 4.37(a)–(k) shows stages in the manufacture of the standard window shown in figure 4.37.

The frames, sashes or casements and vents, are fabricated separately.

(a) The timber sections are machined to form rebates to receive the glass, and then cut to length. The ends of the top rails, stiles and bottom rails of the casement are then machined to form combed joints. The loosely assembled casement is placed in a jig with a cramping device which squares and lines up the joints, glues them with synthetic resin glue and automatically drives a pin or star down at the corners.

(b) The assembled casement is passed through a *drum sander* and then through a *moulder* which profiles the outer edges.

(c) Recesses are cut for cadmium plated hinges. The hinge consists of two interlocking cranked portions, and a separate pin. The single knuckle part of the hinge is dropped in place in the recess and machine screwed into position by zinc plated screws.

The casement is dipped in preservative. The vacuum process cannot, in this instance, be used since the face profile is cut after assembly.

(d) The double knuckle part of the hinge is screwed into position on the jambs of the frame.

(e) The transoms are fitted into the jambs to form H frames, which are then glued.

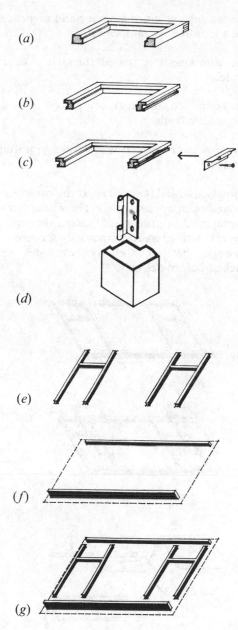

(a)
(b)
(c)
(d)
(e)
(f)
(g)

(f) The head and sill are placed in position on an automatic cramp bed.

(g) The H frame is set down, on the cramp bed, the joints between the H frame and the head and sill being open and spaced slightly apart.

85

(h) The tenons are glued from a hand dispenser and the frame is cramped up.

(i) The component is passed through a drum sander.

(j) Pre-assembled casements are placed in position on the frame.

(k) Hinge pins are driven home by a vibrating hammer.

(l) Knots are sealed (*knotted*) and the casements wedged open by metal dogs. The whole frame is immersed in primer and passed through a dryer. Casements are temporarily secured by plywood battens and the windows are stacked before delivery.

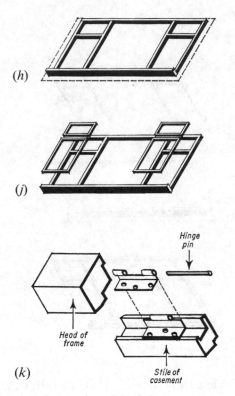

4.37 *Manufacture of standard window*

Figure 4.38 shows a typical standard timber window with the parts and joints named.

4.17 Joinery fittings

Fittings such as benches and cupboards can either be made mainly from suitably thick boards which provide general solidity and make for easily formed joints, or with frames infilled with, or covered with, relatively thin sheets. The first method may be economical for 'one-offs' but for batch or mass production the second method is likely to be more economic and it is illustrated here with three-dimensional drawings which, incidentally, are best able to show the implications of three-way intersections between members.

Fittings should be designed so as much fabrication as possible can be carried out in the joiner's shop and site labour and time in fitting is minimized.

In public buildings special consideration must be given to wear on table tops and the effect of kicks and floor cleaning operations on bases to fittings, for which timber is not always a suitable finish.

(a) Cupboard units

It is best to consider a framed fitting as comprising vertical frames in one direction joined by members in the other direction. Thus, figure 4.39 shows front and back frames joined by cross members. These frames stand on a base, part of which is infilled to form the bottom of a cupboard. A top of cross-tongued boards or veneered blockboard would be fixed, either with 'buttons', or with screws in slotted angles – methods of fixing which allow differential movement. Buttons also permit easy removal and replacement of the top. Ends and vertical divisions are formed by panels with stiles and rails either infilled with plywood or covered with plywood to give a 'flush' appearance.

Figure 4.40 shows (1) cross section frames to receive longitudinal rails and drawer sides, (2) separate units below a top.

A further method shown in figure 4.41 is to make the fitting with solid ends and panels, out of 19 mm or 25 mm nominal blockboard with edges lipped by machine or veneered, with a thin plywood back for bracing. A light framework is made for the front and back. The cupboard units to be fitted complete with all furniture in the joiner's shop.

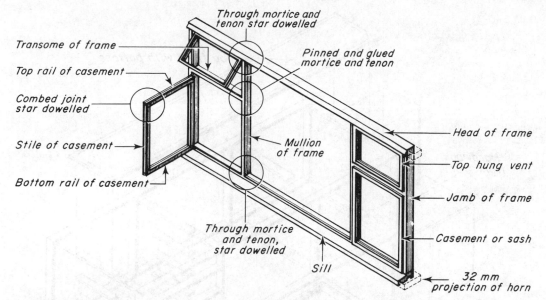

Through mortice and tenon star dowelled

Transome of frame

Top rail of casement

Combed joint star dowelled

Stile of casement

Bottom rail of casement

Through mortice and tenon, star dowelled

Pinned and glued mortice and tenon

Mullion of frame

Sill

Head of frame

Top hung vent

Jamb of frame

Casement or sash

32 mm projection of horn

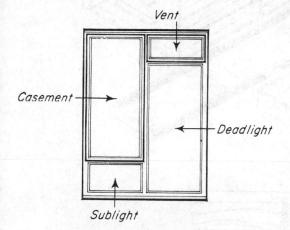

Vent

Casement

Deadlight

Sublight

4.38   *Standard casement windows*

(b) Standard kitchen units

Many joinery manufacturers make a standard range of cupboards and fittings which can be supplied from stock for kitchen units. The British Woodwork Manufacturers issue standards for this type of fitting which is manufactured under licence. A typical fitting is shown in figure 4.42.

(c) Cupboard fitting

The cupboard and drawer fitting shown in figure 4.43 is a single item of joinery for fixing *in situ* after fabrication in the joiner's shop. It is built up of blockboards with all exposed edges lipped and cupboards and door faces of a veneered blockboard. The blockboard horizontal members would be housed and glued to the side panels.

(d) Counter fitting

The counter with glass screen shown in figure 4.44 is an example of a basic framework built out of 75 × 50 mm softwood and covered with 18 mm plywood. The top is also of 18 mm plywood veneered with plastics sheet. The framing of small members under the counter will give support to the hardwood nosing which itself helps to stiffen the construction.

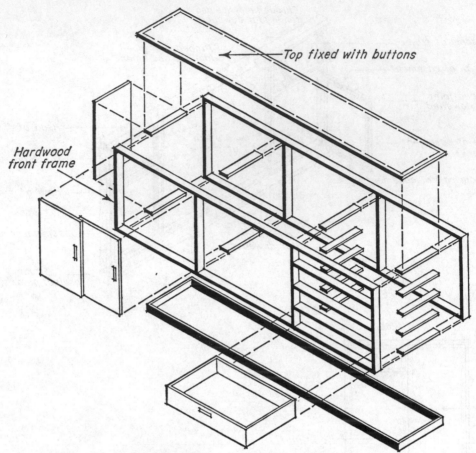

Top fixed with buttons

Hardwood
front frame

FRONT AND BACK FRAMES

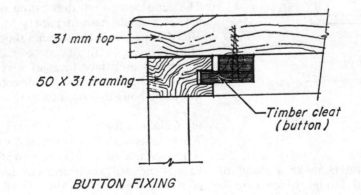

31 mm top

50 X 31 framing

Timber cleat
(button)

BUTTON FIXING

4.39 *Cupboard units – with front and back frames*

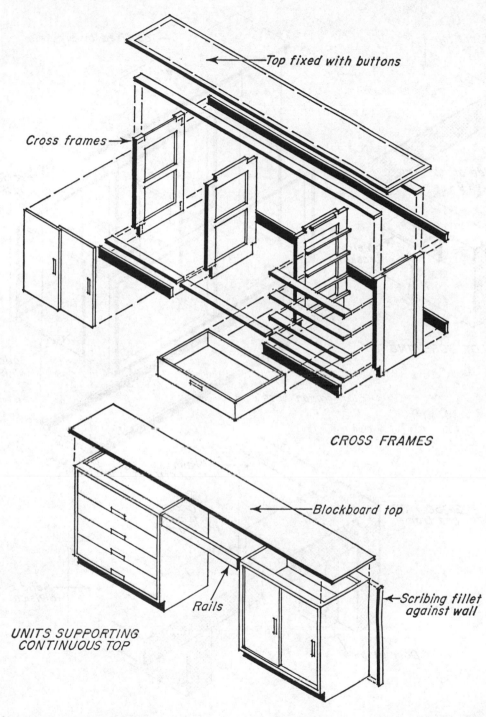

Top fixed with buttons

Cross frames

CROSS FRAMES

Blockboard top

Scribing fillet
against wall

Rails

UNITS SUPPORTING
CONTINUOUS TOP

4.40 *Cupboard units (1) – with cross frames*
(2) – with units below top

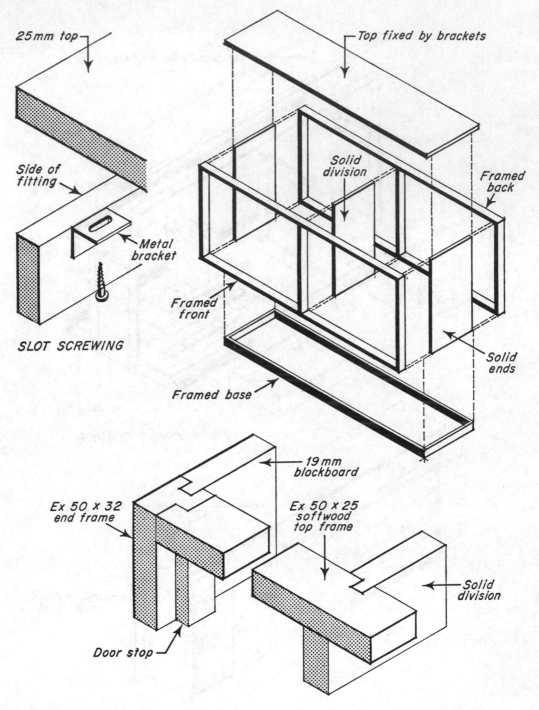

25mm top

Top fixed by brackets

Side of fitting

Solid division

Framed back

Metal bracket

SLOT SCREWING

Framed front

Framed base

Solid ends

19 mm blockboard

Ex 50 x 32 end frame

Ex 50 x 25 softwood top frame

Solid division

Door stop

4.41 *Cupboard units*

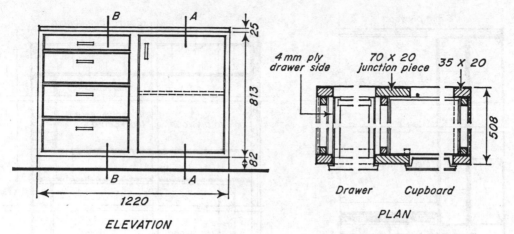

ELEVATION

PLAN

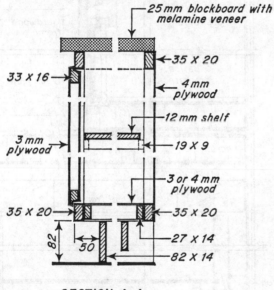

SECTION A-A

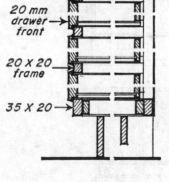

SECTION B-B

4.42 *Standard kitchen cupboard unit*

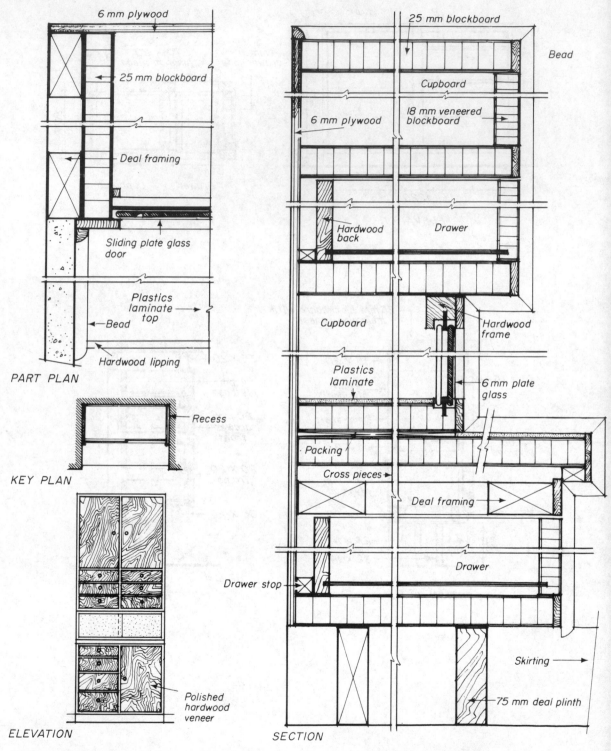

6 mm plywood

25 mm blockboard

Deal framing

Sliding plate glass door

Plastics laminate top

Bead

Hardwood lipping

PART PLAN

Recess

KEY PLAN

Polished hardwood veneer

ELEVATION

25 mm blockboard

Bead

Cupboard

6 mm plywood

18 mm veneered blockboard

Hardwood back

Drawer

Cupboard

Hardwood frame

Plastics laminate

6 mm plate glass

Packing

Cross pieces

Deal framing

Drawer stop

Drawer

Skirting

75 mm deal plinth

SECTION

4.43 *Cupboard fitting*

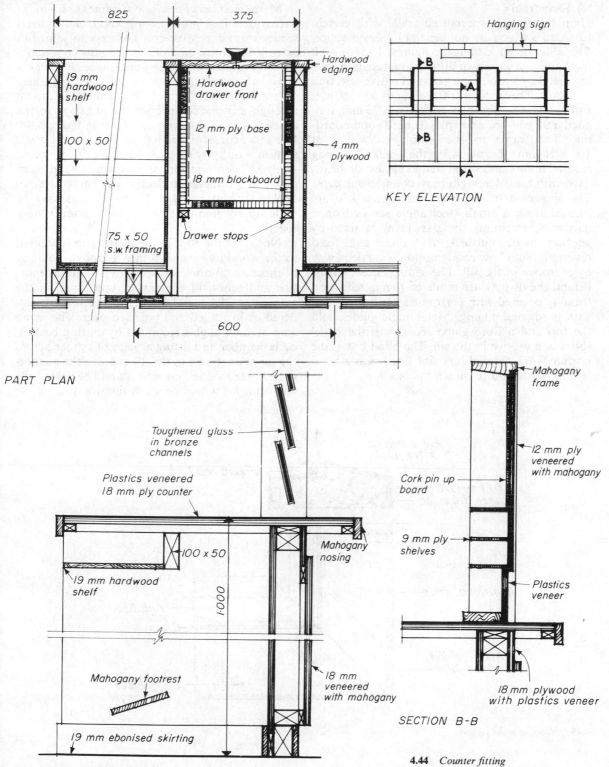

825

375

19 mm
hardwood
shelf

Hardwood
edging

Hardwood
drawer front

12 mm ply base

100 x 50

4 mm
plywood

18 mm blockboard

75 x 50
s.w. framing

Drawer stops

600

PART PLAN

KEY ELEVATION

Hanging sign

B

A

B

A

Toughened glass
in bronze
channels

Plastics veneered
18 mm ply counter

100 x 50

Mahogany
nosing

19 mm hardwood
shelf

1,000

Mahogany footrest

18 mm
veneered
with mahogany

19 mm ebonised skirting

SECTION A-A

Mahogany
frame

12 mm ply
veneered
with mahogany

Cork pin up
board

9 mm ply
shelves

Plastics
veneer

18 mm plywood
with plastics veneer

SECTION B-B

4.44 *Counter fitting*

(e) Shop fronts

Shop fitting is a specialized trade with certain techniques which are not general joinery practice. The shop front details in figures 4.45 to 4.50 incorporate a variety of different materials including metals, to produce a comprehensive selection of details. The fascia is framed out of 50×50 mm soft wood and finished with 100×25 mm tongued and grooved and splayed hardwood boarding. The frame to the shop windows is of 100×50 mm hardwood, the glazing being secured in this case with internal hardwood beads fixed with brass screws in brass countersunk cups. The showcase frames shown in figure 4.50 are formed from a small steel angle screwed on a hardwood surround, the glass being retained by another angle finished in bronze and fixed reversed. Note how condensation is carried away by a groove in the sill. The sliding access panels behind the display are made of 19 mm softwood framing covered with perforated hardboard, and with hardwood edging. Metal angle guides hold the top and a fibre guide secured to the panel slides in a groove in the sill. The blind box is the normal wood framed box zinc lined with a blind lath in hardwood to match the fascia.

Metal members for window frames and similar parts, are often preferred to wood. Solid metal sections are expensive and not easy to joint but extruded aluminium sections are now commonly used for shopfronts. The appearance of metal is provided by brass, bronze or stainless steel sheet on moulded wood cores. The section is drawn through a die which presses the metal on to the timber. A typical section is shown in figure 4.45. It is less expensive and lighter than a solid metal section, but rigid and comparatively easily jointed. There are limits, however, to the complexity of profiles, and clearly, very sharp external angles are not possible. Large sections may be built up by joining two or more smaller ones together.

Note that the edge of the metal strip is secured to the wood by turning it into a groove. Jointing of these metal-on-wood sections is done by mortice and tenon in the timber core, but on the external angles metal is mitred and brazed, soldered or just filled and polished over. The wood core at such angles is jointed by cutting back in each member and fitting a piece of timber across the mitre as shown in the diagram. If the metal is to be brazed a shielding strip should be behind the face and this would be set in the wood block.

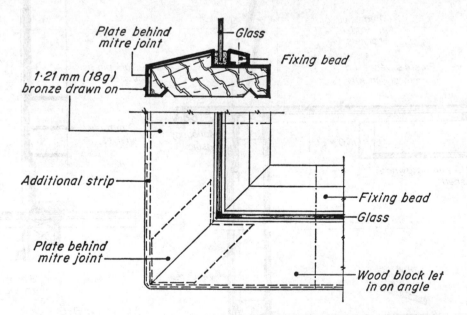

4.45   *Metal on wood sections*

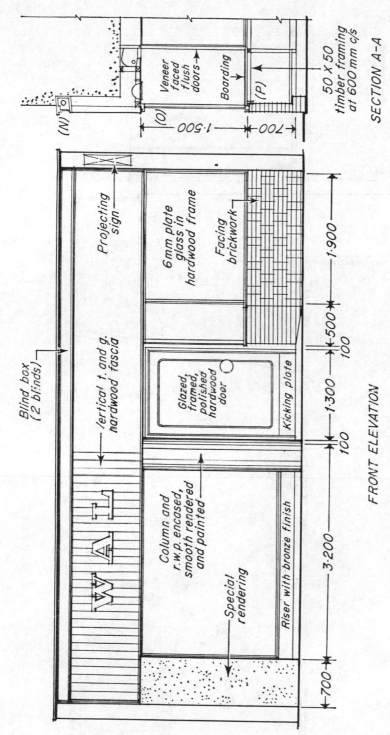

4.46 Shopfront (1)

SECTION A-A

Veneer faced flush doors

Boarding

(P)

(O)

(N)

1·500

700

50 x 50 timber framing at 600 mm c/s

FRONT ELEVATION

Projecting sign

Blind box (2 blinds)

Vertical t. and g. hardwood fascia

6mm plate glass in hardwood frame

Facing brickwork

Glazed, framed, polished hardwood door

Kicking plate

Column and r.w.p. encased, smooth rendered and painted

Special rendering

Riser with bronze finish

WALL

1·900

500

100

1·300

100

3·200

700

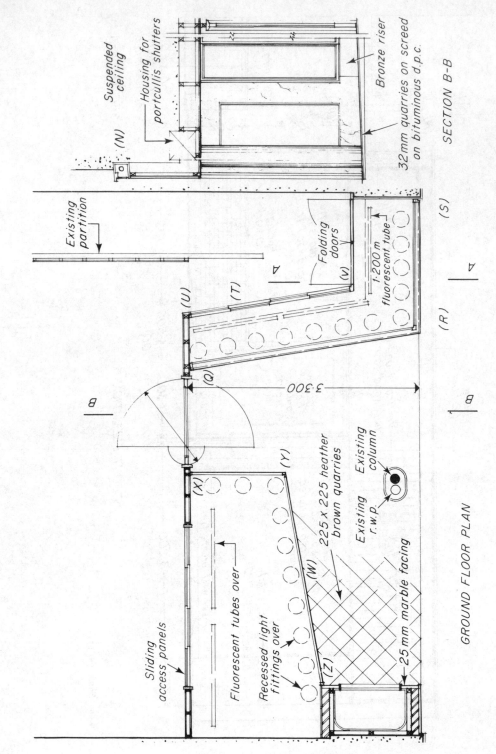

Suspended ceiling

Housing for portcullis shutters

(N)

Bronze riser

32 mm quarries on screed on bituminous d.p.c.

SECTION B-B

Existing partition

Folding doors

1·200 m fluorescent tube

(S)

(U)

(T)

A

(V)

A

(R)

3·300

B

B

(Q)

Sliding access panels

(X)

(Y)

Fluorescent tubes over

Recessed light fittings over

225 x 225 heather brown quarries

Existing column

Existing r.w.p.

(W)

(Z)

25 mm marble facing

GROUND FLOOR PLAN

4.47 Shopfront (2)

96

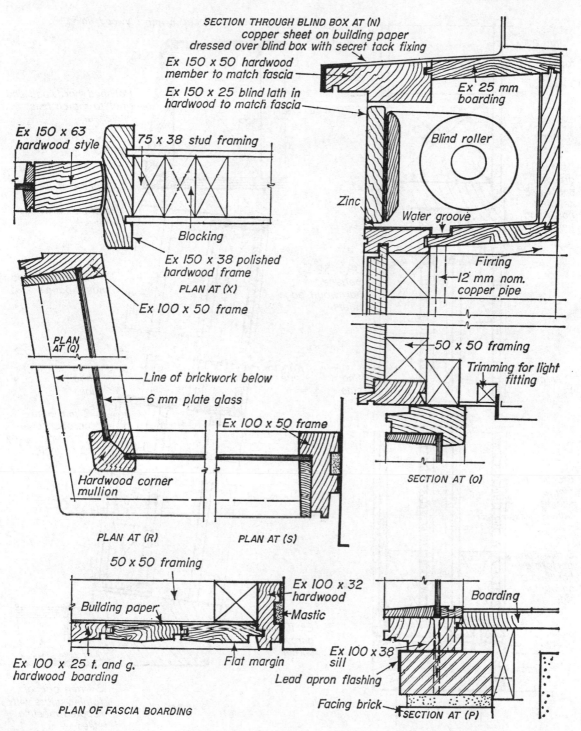

SECTION THROUGH BLIND BOX AT (N)
copper sheet on building paper
dressed over blind box with secret tack fixing

Ex 150 x 50 hardwood
member to match fascia

Ex 150 x 25 blind lath in
hardwood to match fascia

Ex 25 mm
boarding

Blind roller

Ex 150 x 63
hardwood style

75 x 38 stud framing

Zinc

Water groove

Blocking

Ex 150 x 38 polished
hardwood frame
PLAN AT (X)

Ex 100 x 50 frame

Firring

12 mm nom.
copper pipe

PLAN
AT (Q)

Line of brickwork below

6 mm plate glass

Ex 100 x 50 frame

50 x 50 framing

Trimming for light
fitting

Hardwood corner
mullion

SECTION AT (O)

PLAN AT (R)

PLAN AT (S)

50 x 50 framing

Ex 100 x 32
hardwood

Boarding

Building paper

Mastic

Ex 100 x 25 t. and g.
hardwood boarding

Flat margin

Ex 100 x 38
sill

Lead apron flashing

Facing brick

SECTION AT (P)

PLAN OF FASCIA BOARDING

4.48 *Shopfront (3) – details*

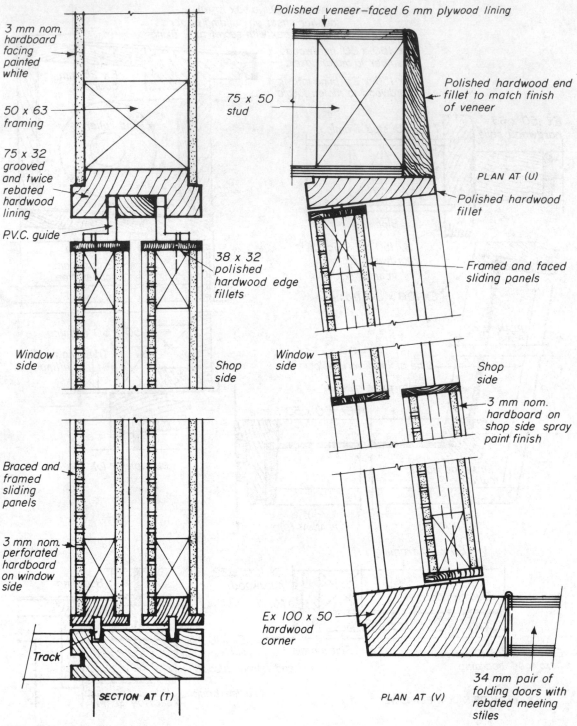

3 mm nom. hardboard facing painted white

50 x 63 framing

75 x 32 grooved and twice rebated hardwood lining

P.V.C. guide

Window side

Shop side

Braced and framed sliding panels

3 mm nom. perforated hardboard on window side

Track

SECTION AT (T)

Polished veneer-faced 6 mm plywood lining

75 x 50 stud

38 x 32 polished hardwood edge fillets

Polished hardwood end fillet to match finish of veneer

PLAN AT (U)

Polished hardwood fillet

Framed and faced sliding panels

Window side

Shop side

3 mm nom. hardboard on shop side spray paint finish

Ex 100 x 50 hardwood corner

34 mm pair of folding doors with rebated meeting stiles

PLAN AT (V)

4.49 *Showcase details (1)*

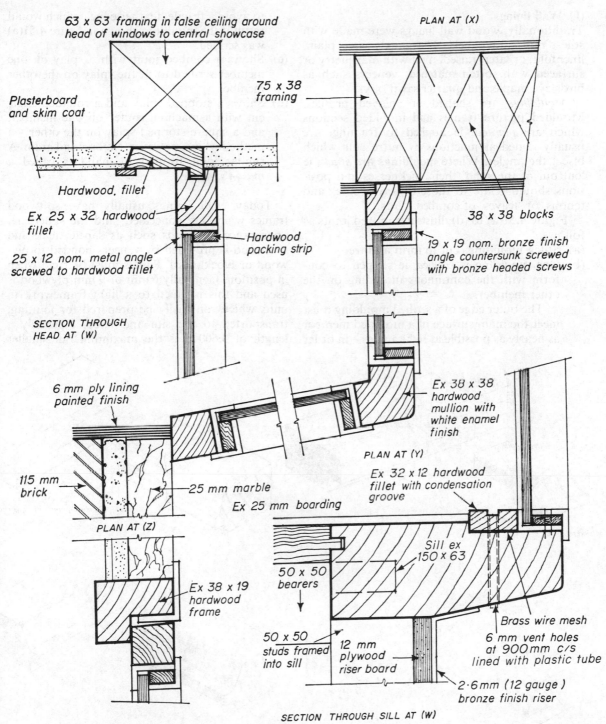

63 x 63 framing in false ceiling around head of windows to central showcase

PLAN AT (X)

75 x 38 framing

Plasterboard and skim coat

Hardwood, fillet

Ex 25 x 32 hardwood fillet

25 x 12 nom. metal angle screwed to hardwood fillet

Hardwood packing strip

SECTION THROUGH HEAD AT (W)

38 x 38 blocks

19 x 19 nom. bronze finish angle countersunk screwed with bronze headed screws

Ex 38 x 38 hardwood mullion with white enamel finish

6 mm ply lining painted finish

PLAN AT (Y)

Ex 32 x 12 hardwood fillet with condensation groove

115 mm brick

25 mm marble

Ex 25 mm boarding

PLAN AT (Z)

Ex 38 x 19 hardwood frame

Sill ex 150 x 63

50 x 50 bearers

50 x 50 studs framed into sill

12 mm plywood riser board

Brass wire mesh

6 mm vent holes at 900mm c/s lined with plastic tube

2·6mm (12 gauge) bronze finish riser

SECTION THROUGH SILL AT (W)

4.50 *Showcase details (2)*

(f) Wall linings

Traditionally, wood wall linings were made with stiles, rails and panels. The panels were plain, linenfold, or later, raised, inset with marquetry or surfaced with, often matched, veneers such as birds eye maple and quarter sawn oak.

Mouldings are shaped or splayed profiles. Moulded picture frames and moulded sections which are *planted*, ie applied to framing, are usually joined at junctions by mitre cuts which bisect the angles. Where mouldings are *stuck*, ie 'cut out of the solid' their thicknesses and positions should relate to those of any rebates and tenons, or 'leaves' of combed joints.

Figure 4.51(a) to (d) illustrates mitred joints as follows:

(a) Stuck mouldings cut to form a mitre.
(b) One moulding is *scribed*, ie shaped to conform with the continuous moulding on the other member.

The outer edge of a scribed moulding must meet the main surface of a moulded member as nearly as possible at right angles – in order to avoid a fragile 'feather edge', which would result if the moulding shown in figure 4.51(a) was scribed.

(c) Shows a combed joint with a splay on one member scribed to fit the splay on the other member.
(d) Shows a stopped splay and a rounded angle cut with a machine router on one member, and a square stopped splay on the other – a method which, however, exposes end grain. A similar joint formed by hand is called a *mason's mitre*.

Today, wall linings usually have softwood frames which are concealed, and the superficial appearance of woods such as sapele, teak and rosewood is provided by veneers bonded to plywood or blockboard. Panels must be rigid when in position. Generally 6 mm or 9 mm plywood is used and this is glued to a light framework in units which can easily be prepared for jointing, transported to the site and fixed. Normally a length of 3,600 m is the maximum but smaller

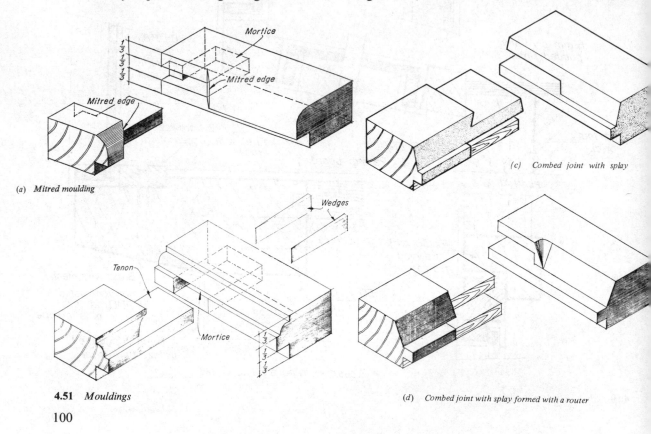

(a) *Mitred moulding*

(c) *Combed joint with splay*

4.51 *Mouldings*

(d) *Combed joint with splay formed with a router*

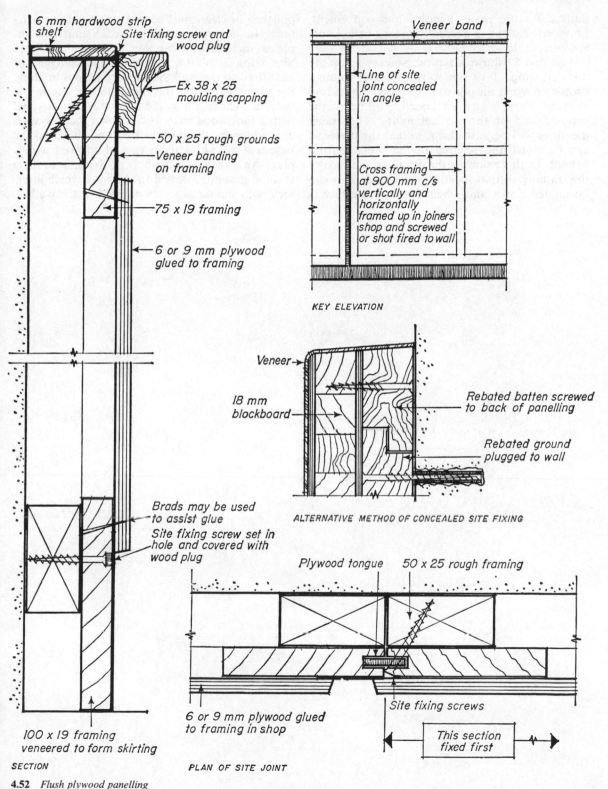

6 mm hardwood strip shelf

Site fixing screw and wood plug

Ex 38 x 25 moulding capping

50 x 25 rough grounds

Veneer banding on framing

75 x 19 framing

6 or 9 mm plywood glued to framing

Brads may be used to assist glue

Site fixing screw set in hole and covered with wood plug

100 x 19 framing veneered to form skirting

SECTION

Veneer band

Line of site joint concealed in angle

Cross framing at 900 mm c/s vertically and horizontally framed up in joiners shop and screwed or shot fired to wall

KEY ELEVATION

Veneer

18 mm blockboard

Rebated batten screwed to back of panelling

Rebated ground plugged to wall

ALTERNATIVE METHOD OF CONCEALED SITE FIXING

Plywood tongue

50 x 25 rough framing

Site fixing screws

This section fixed first

6 or 9 mm plywood glued to framing in shop

PLAN OF SITE JOINT

4.52 *Flush plywood panelling*

units are more easily handled and convenient, provided that the increased number of site joints are acceptable.

Figure 4.52 shows a typical panel of 9 mm ply on a framing of 19 mm softwood. The framing projects beyond the plywood to form a recess and skirting. There is also a recessed band below the capping and at the vertical joints. The frame members will be jointed up, so that the plywood can be glued and secured to the framing from behind. In this example the ply is on the face of the framing so that its edge is exposed. This can be sanded down and when the whole surface is polished or clear finished will give a neat appearance. In the example shown each unit is completed, including the capping, in the joiner's shop. Site fixing is to 50 × 25 mm grounds plugged or shot-fired to the wall. Screws are driven in along the top edge, down the free side and along the bottom. Those along the top edge are covered with a hardwood strip, those down the free sides are hidden by the next section and those on the base will not show if set in and covered with a plug. An alternative method of fixing is to have rebated grounds screwed to the back which interlock with similar grounds plugged to the walls.

5 Doors

CI/SfB (31.5) + (32.5)

5.1 Introduction

A door is a moving part of a building and will be subjected to constant use and often abuse throughout its life. Therefore it must be carefully designed and detailed and well made from good materials. It must also be remembered that conditions of temperature and humidity will often be different in the rooms or spaces on each side of the door, which will produce a tendency for the door to warp or twist. The detailing must counteract this.

A door will either be of unframed, framed, or flush construction. The unframed door consists of tongue and grooved boarding suitably jointed. Framed construction consists of an outer frame of timber, with infill either solid or glazed, to the various panels outlined by the framing. A flush door is formed by the application of sheet material such as hardboard or plywood on a suitable core.

5.2 Performance requirements

A door is a movable barrier to an opening in a building. Doors may be hung to swing, to slide, to fold or to revolve and the various arrangements are shown in plan form in figure 5.1.

(a) Appearance

The appearance of a door into a building or within a building forms an important factor contributing towards the character of the enclosure. Proportion and scale are important considerations, as well as the materials used in the construction method. The relationship of the door to the total wall area, its positioning in a wall and the influence of other openings, such as windows, must be carefully considered. Detailing of architraves and frames are also important.

(b) Durability

Proper maintenance allied to the choice of good materials with good design and workmanship will ensure satisfactory durability throughout the life of the building, and these criteria also apply to all building components, including doors. Timber doors may need special consideration, in particular, external doors, and regular painting or clear treatment is necessary.

(c) Weather protection

In the case of an external door, there is concern with the exclusion of air and water. Penetration tests are often carried out by manufacturers and new British Standards are under consideration which will include this requirement. The top and bottom of the door is particularly vulnerable and special precautions in the form of throating and provision of weather bars should be taken. Figure 5.2 shows details of an external, pre-hung door set suitably detailed.

Outward opening doors should, wherever possible, be set back into the opening and be provided with a projecting weather fillet at the head of the frame. Where practical the edges of the meeting styles of doors hung in pairs should be rebated. Doors should, as far as possible, be draught proof, and the use of some form of additional protection in the form of weatherstripping at the rebate is a wise precaution.

Apart from the weather stripping details illustrated in the drawings, figures 5.3 to 5.6 show further applications of this technique which is a valuable method of reducing air filtration (draughts) at the threshold and closing style of a door. A point to bear in mind is that as buildings in general become better heated the occupants tend to feel draughts where previously there was no discomfort.

The particular type of weather stripping shown consists of extruded aluminium sections secured to the door or threshold which grip a neoprene strip or pad which in turn is compressed into the gap between the frame or threshold and door.

103

DOORS

For side hung doors, determine the inside and outside faces, then, in relation to this, describe the direction of opening as clockwise or anti-clockwise.

For sliding doors, many variations are possible, the arrangement being determined by the choice of track as indicated.

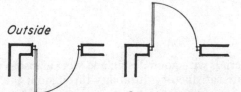

Outside

*Opening inward
–clockwise*   *Opening outward
–anti-clockwise*

Side hung–single leaf–single swing

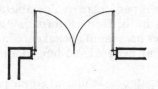

Side hung–single leaf–double swing

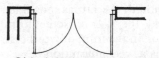

*Side hung–double leaf–single swing
–opening outwards*

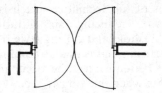

*Side hung–double leaf–single swing
–opening inwards*

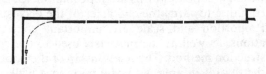

Side hung–double leaf–double swing

(a) *Pass doors*

5.1 *Methods of hanging doors (1)*

104

Outside

*Straight run–single track
–top hung with bottom guide*

*Straight run–single track
–sliding in cavity*

Straight run–double track–top hung

Straight run–triple track–top hung

Curved track–sliding on return wall

The sliding door can also be arranged to fold by pivoting the doors in pairs. A range of sliding, folding, internal doors is sometimes referred to as a folding partition.

(b) *Sliding doors*

Outside

Curved track sliding on return wall
—with pass door

Three leaf—sliding folding door

Four leaf—sliding folding door

Centre hung folding sliding door
with half leaf

Folded
position

Collapsible; on top track and bottom guide
as for a metal folding shutter gate

Flexible; on top track—used as an
internal partition or space divider

(c) Folding doors

5.1 *Methods of hanging doors (2)*

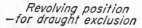
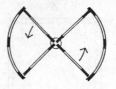

1   Revolving position
—for draught exclusion

2   Leaves folded flat
to give clear passage

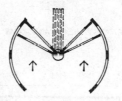

3 Leaves collapsing against
pressure from crowd

*Revolving doors are used to form a draught-proof
lobby and are collapsible by hand to form a clear
opening. They can also be made automatically
collapsible by pressure from a crowd in case of
panic through fire or disturbance.*

(d) Revolving doors

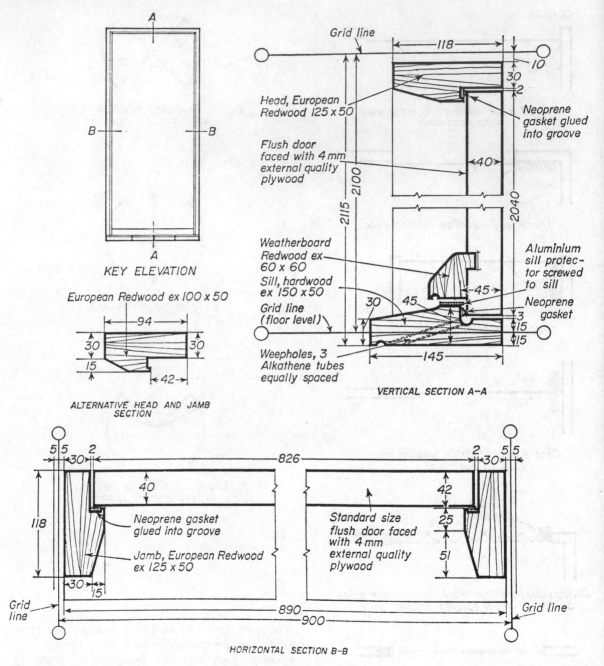

KEY ELEVATION

European Redwood ex 100 x 50

ALTERNATIVE HEAD AND JAMB
SECTION

Head, European Redwood 125 x 50

Flush door faced with 4 mm external quality plywood

Neoprene gasket glued into groove

Weatherboard Redwood ex 60 x 60

Sill, hardwood ex 150 x 50

Grid line (floor level)

Weepholes, 3 Alkathene tubes equally spaced

Aluminium sill protector screwed to sill

Neoprene gasket

VERTICAL SECTION A–A

Neoprene gasket glued into groove

Jamb, European Redwood ex 125 x 50

Standard size flush door faced with 4 mm external quality plywood

Grid line

Grid line

HORIZONTAL SECTION B–B

5.2   *External prehung door set to satisfy air and water penetration test*

A double swing external door presents a particularly difficult situation since the weather stripping must not impede the smooth action of the door. Figure 5.3 shows a method of weather stripping the meeting styles of a pair of double swing timber doors. The neoprene insert is available with tongues suitable to seal gaps from 4 mm to 10 mm wide. The neoprene tongue closes and compresses against a strip of PVC in a similar extruded aluminium channel section, both extrusions being fitted into a groove in the face of the styles. Weather stripping on the top rail of the door can also be carried out by using this type of weather stripping. Figure 5.4 shows a method of weather stripping at the threshold. This will withstand very heavy foot traffic and is ideal provided the 13 mm upstand is not inconvenient. An alternative is shown in figure 5.5 where the upstand is reduced by cutting a rebate in the threshold. This detail gives a small underdoor gap and gives an unobstructed threshold. Toughened glass doors can be weather stripped by fixing an extruded channel with neoprene insert around the closing edges of the doors. The channel is secured by adhesive and is cut away to accommodate locks or a kicking plate to the base of the door. The neoprene tongue would seal against the glass, but the plain channel provides a symmetrical detail, as shown in figure 5.6.

A combined stop and compression seal is shown in detail in figure 5.7. This type of seal is used where an airtight or dust proof seal is required as in a computer room. The door must be sealed all round and top and bottom bolts should be fitted to hold the doors close against the seal.

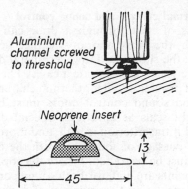

5.4 *Timber door with flush threshold*

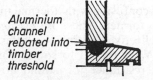

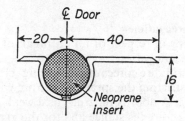

5.5 *Timber door with rebated threshold*

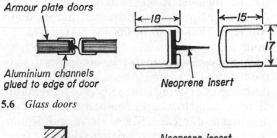

5.6 *Glass doors*

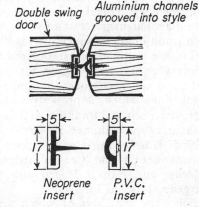

5.3 *Timber swinging doors*

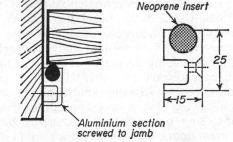

5.7 *Timber door stop*

(d) Thermal control and sound control

The loss of heat through a door can be high although the provision of weather seals may improve the situation. However, metal doors are available which incorporate a cavity filled insulation and provide excellent thermal characteristics. For good sound control doors must be 'solid' with tight seals at all edges. Special doors are required if the criterion is high, and more important, the passage of sound between the door and frame must be restricted. Where the specification requirements are high for both sound control and thermal insulation then two sets of doors with an intervening space, or vestibule, will be necessary.

The term 'sound insulation' should be avoided so as to avoid confusion with 'thermal insulation'. Whereas the former relies on *greater* density (weight) for effective control, the latter relies on less density. With regard to sound control, the terms 'sound resistance' or 'sound attenuation' are better.

(e) Fire precautions

Precautions in respect of an outbreak of fire fall into three categories:

1 Structural fire precautions: being concerned with restricting the spread of the fire within the building. A door is regarded as a weak point in respect of fire resistance and for this reason the position and construction of doors is controlled by the *Building Regulations* in respect of fire resistance. Specially constructed timber doors will resist the spread of fire for periods up to 1 hour.
2 Means of escape: to enable the occupants to leave the building in safety. Adequate width, correct direction of opening and method of hanging are all relevant factors in the consideration of a door as a means of escape. There are various legislative requirements appropriate to different types of buildings and the Local Fire Officer will always advise on any particular situation.
3 To restrict the movement of smoke throughout a public building during an outbreak of fire, it will be necessary to install *smoke-stop* doors (and screens) at strategic points, and in particular at the top of stairways. These doors must be self-closing but need not necessarily be *fire resistant* doors; they must have a good fit in the rebates. See also Fire doors, page 120.

(f) Strength and stability

A door is called upon to resist a number of stresses that will vary according to its use and position. Normal closing and opening, banging, slamming, bumping from articles being carried through and even kicking are to be expected.

In addition to these factors, the door must withstand stresses due to the variations in humidity that occur through changes in weather conditions and artificial conditions within the building.

The strength of the door is dependent on its method of construction and in respect of framed timber doors the strength is dependent on the joints used. Large sections of timber will give general solidity but the jambs will have to withstand greater internal stresses due to moisture movement. Flush doors on the other hand depend upon their total construction, since the facing is in the form of a *stressed skin*.

In addition to the air and water penetration tests already mentioned further research is being carried out with a view to devising tests for a future British Standard. The tests are concerned with resistance to torsion, heavy body impact, hard body impact, slamming and sound reduction. It is likely that a future BS will define four strength standards: light, medium, heavy and severe.

5.3 Unframed doors

These are doors made from a number of vertical tongued and grooved V jointed boards, known as *matchboarding*, which is held firm by means of horizontal members called *ledges* and strengthened by diagonal members known as *braces*. They are a traditional and much used method of construction for inexpensive exterior doors and for temporary doors. Framing, in the form of styles and a top rail, strengthens the construction and gives a door which, if properly made, has further proved itself by tradition and is much used for factory type buildings. BS 459 — *Doors*, Part 4 1965 *Matchboarded doors* specifies the quality, construction and sizes of ledged and braced doors, and framed ledged and braced doors for general use, as follows:

Specification The matchboard which must be

tongued and grooved and jointed on both sides to be 16 mm thick and in the case of the ledged and braced doors there must be three horizontal ledges and two parallel (diagonal) braces nailed or stapled together. When nailing is used, two 50 mm nails, staggered at each ledge, and one at each brace driven below the surface and clinched tight, must be used. Alternatively the boards may be stapled to the ledges and braces with 1.63 mm (16 gauge) clinching staples 32 mm long driven below the surface by mechanically operated tools. The width of the matchboard (excluding the tongues) must be not less than 70 mm and not more than 114 mm.

Where the door is framed, the rails must be through tenoned into the styles, with haunched and wedged tenons to top and bottom rails, pinned by a hardwood dowel or non-ferrous metal star dowel. The joints must be additionally secured by adhesive or by bedding in red or white lead paint. Where weather resistant adhesive is used, the pin or dowel may be omitted. A manufacturing tolerance of 2 mm is allowable in the finished size of the door. The vertical tongued and grooved timbers forming the matchboard are also known as *battens*. Figures 5.8(a) and (b) shows a ledged braced and battened door and a framed ledged braced and battened door to BS 459: Part 4.

(a) Ledged and battened
This is the simplest form of door, being in effect a number of vertical tongued and grooved boards (or battens) strengthened by horizontal timber *ledges*.

The ledged and battened door is mostly used for temporary work since after a time, if subjected to heavy use, it would tend to distort diagonally. This type of door is shown in figure 5.9 in heavier construction than the minimum laid down in the British Standard.

(b) Ledged, braced and battened
This is a more satisfactory form of construction since the diagonal braces prevent the distortion of the door. Figure 5.10 shows this type of door, which is often used for outbuildings. The direction of the brace must be upwards from the hanging style, so that the outer end of the brace supports the top free corner of the door. This is because the brace works in compression (not in tension) and if it is put on the other way round the joints between the battens would tend to open and the door would drop on its hinges. Since there is not enough thickness of timber on the edge of the door to accommodate the screws for butt hinges, this type of door is hung on tee hinges over the face of the battens.

5.4 Framed doors

(a) Framed, ledged, braced and battened
This is a refinement of the ledged and battened type and has the addition of styles, framed to top, bottom and middle rails. An example is shown in figure 5.11. The styles and top rail are the same thickness. Bottom and middle rails plus the thickness of the *battens*, are the same total thickness as the styles. The bottom and middle rails are cut with barefaced tenon, the top rail being fixed with a through, haunched tenon. The battens extend from the top rail to the ground over the middle and bottom rails in order to shed water from the face of the door. The door can be hung on strap or tee hinges, but since there is an outer frame the door can also be hung on butt hinges. Large garage or warehouse doors are made using the same principles of framing, battening and bracing shown for this type of door. The illustrations of these types of doors are of heavier construction than the minimum specified in the British Standard.

(b) Framed panelled
A framed or panelled door is a traditional form of construction. Its success depends on the correct proportions of the framing, the use of good quality well seasoned timber, and accurate framing up with properly made joints. The proportions of the panels must be carefully considered so that the door contributes to the architectural qualities of the building.

The door illustrated in figure 5.12 has a *composite* elevation to illustrate the various forms of panel to be found in doors of this type. The horizontal rails are framed into the styles using various types of mortice and tenon joints fully illustrated in figure 4.9 and described on page 67.

The vertical middle rail or *muntin* is stubtenoned into the horizontal rails. To prevent any

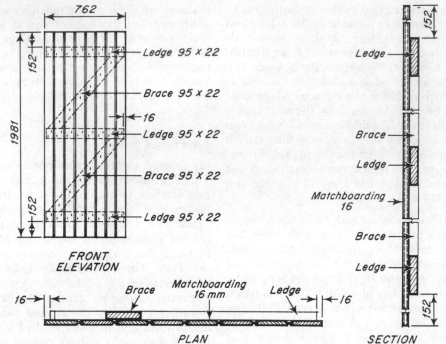

5.8(a) *Details of ledged, braced and battened door to BS 459: Part 4*

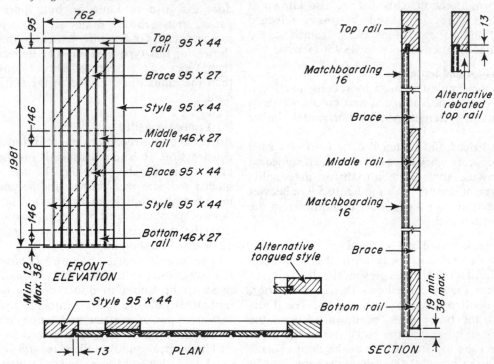

5.8(b) *Details of framed, ledged, braced and battened door to BS 459: Part 4*

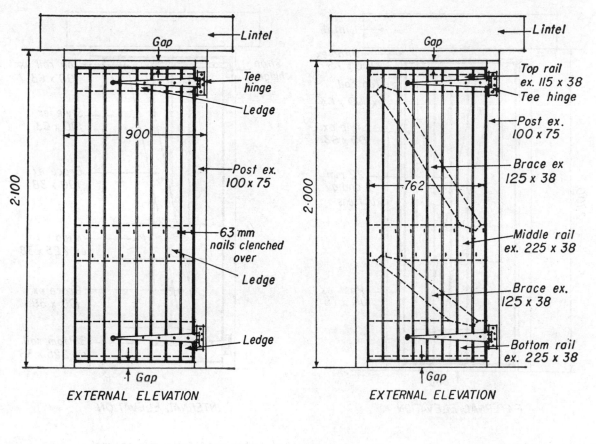

EXTERNAL ELEVATION

Lintel
Gap
Tee hinge
Ledge
900
Post ex. 100 x 75
63 mm nails clenched over
Ledge
Ledge
Gap
2·100

Lintel
Gap
Top rail ex. 115 x 38
Tee hinge
Post ex. 100 x 75
Brace ex. 125 x 38
762
Middle rail ex. 225 x 38
Brace ex. 125 x 38
Bottom rail ex. 225 x 38
Gap
2·000

EXTERNAL ELEVATION

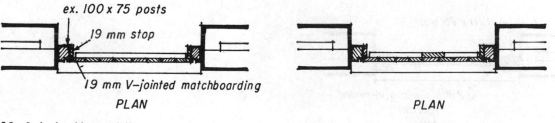

ex. 100 x 75 posts
19 mm stop
19 mm V–jointed matchboarding
PLAN

PLAN

5.9 *Ledged and battened door*

5.10 *Ledged, braced and battened door*

DOORS

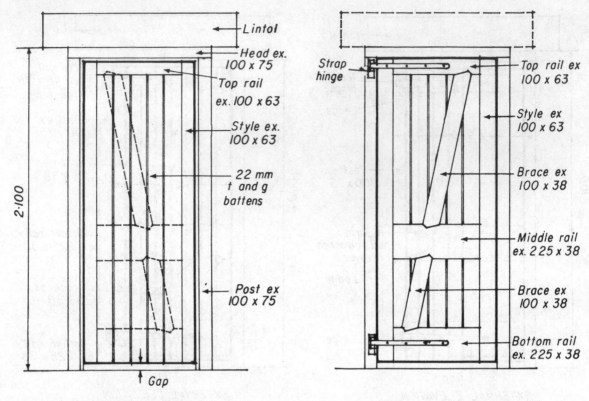

EXTERNAL ELEVATION

Lintol

Head ex.
100 x 75

Top rail
ex. 100 x 63

Style ex.
100 x 63

22 mm
t and g
battens

Post ex
100 x 75

Gap

2·100

Strap
hinge

INTERNAL ELEVATION

Top rail ex
100 x 63

Style ex
100 x 63

Brace ex
100 x 38

Middle rail
ex. 225 x 38

Brace ex
100 x 38

Bottom rail
ex. 225 x 38

The timber sizes shown are nominal

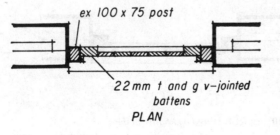

ex 100 x 75 post

22 mm t and g v-jointed
battens

PLAN

5.11 *Framed, ledged and braced door*

tendency for the rails to deform, the styles are grooved and the tenons haunched into them.

The styles (or stiles) should not be too narrow, or difficulty may be experienced in fitting suitable furniture without destroying the framing effect, and the bottom rail must be deep enough to allow proper jointing. Any excessive cutting away of the framing, particularly at the joints to fit bolts and locks, will seriously weaken the construction and these points should be checked at the design stage, by the designer considering the application of the furniture, at the same time as the method of framing.

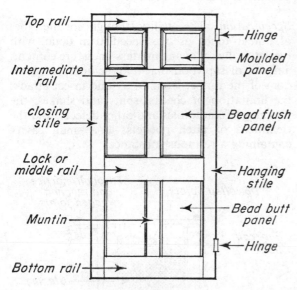

Top rail

Hinge

Moulded panel

Intermediate rail

closing stile

Bead flush panel

Lock or middle rail

Hanging stile

Bead butt panel

Muntin

Hinge

Bottom rail

ELEVATION

5.12 *Panelled door*

(c) Standard panelled and glazed

The specification provides for the patterns, dimensions and construction of the doors as follows:

Specification Timber for framing and the plywood for panels to conform with BS 1186: Part 2: 1971 *Quality of Timber in Joinery. Exterior* quality plywood to be used for exterior doors in accordance with BS 6566: 1985 *Plywood.*

Sizes A guide to the types and sizes of the doors covered by the standard specification is given in figure 5.13.

Type	Height	Width	Finished thickness
Stable, framed ledged and braced	1981	610	44
		686	
		762	
		838	
	2000	807	44
	2032	813	44
	2040	726	
		826	
Ledged and braced	All as above		16/22
Garage doors	2135	2135	44
	1981	2135	

5.13 *Typical range of sizes for framed doors. Doors comply with BS 1186 Parts 1 and 2:* Quality of Timber and Workmanship. *Tolerances to BS 4787 Part 1. For all sizes approximate metric equivalents correct to nearest mm are given*

Framing The option of dowelled or mortice and tenon joints is given for framing. The Standard specifies the finished sizes of the framing and the thickness of the plywood panels for all the types listed in the schedule. Where dowels are used they are to be of hardwood, minimum 16 mm diameter, equally spaced at not more than 57 mm centre to centre, with a minimum of three dowels in bottom and lock rail and a minimum of two for the top rail.

Where the framing is morticed and tenoned the doors must have through haunched and wedged tenons to top and bottom and one other (middle) rail. If there are more intermediate rails these are stub-tenoned (minimum 25 mm) into the styles.

For solid panels, the plywood is framed into grooves to fit tightly, the panels being cut to fit, 2 mm less in width than the grooved opening.

For glazed panels for exterior doors the opening is rebated out of the solid one side; with mitred glazing beads loosely pinned in position for delivery. All mouldings are scribed at the joints.

The adhesive used must comply with BS 5442: Part 3 1979 *Adhesives for use with wood.* A manufacturing tolerance of 2 mm is allowed on the heights and widths of the finished sizes of component parts. The diagrammatic form of each of the joints mentioned is discussed in 4.8 *Joints* starting on page 67.

Furniture Doors should be fitted with butt hinges to BS1227 — *Hinges* Part 1A: 1967 Hinges for general building purposes; locks and/or latches to BS 5870: 1980 *Specification for locks and latches for doors in building*, and BS 3621: 1980 *Specification for thief resistant locks*; and letter plates to BS 2911: 1974.

Finish The British Standard relates to joinery 'in the white', and if the doors are delivered unprimed they should be handled carefully and stored in dry conditions. Knotting and priming should be carried out as soon as possible and before fixing in position.

Figure 5.14 illustrates the BS designs for single panel interior door and a standard exterior glazed door. In addition to the two types illustrated the Standard includes three and four panelled doors and exterior doors with glazing bars. The standard garage doors have six panels.

It will be seen that the British Standard specifies minimum requirements and the panelled and framed doors described are used generally for low cost buildings.

5.5 Flush doors

BS 459: Part 2: 1962 (amendments to 1968) sets down the requirements for exterior and interior factory-made flush doors in timber, in terms of standard strength or stability, since the Standard does not require any particular form of construction. Thus the reputation of, and method of construction used by the manufacturer is all important in respect of quality.

Specification The quality (though not the type) of timber to be used is specified in detail with regard to the following matters: moisture content, amount of sapwood that may be accepted; freedom of the timber from decay and insect attack; the limitation of checks, splits and shakes; the plugging of knot holes and other defects, and the treatment of pitch pockets, ie a small cavity containing a resinous substance.

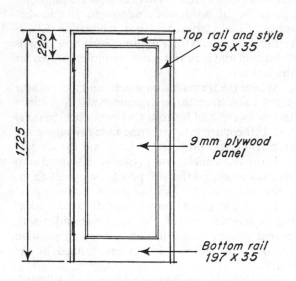

INTERIOR UNGLAZED DOOR No. 1

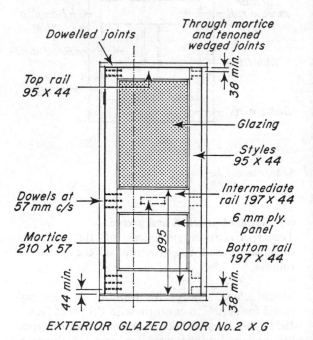

EXTERIOR GLAZED DOOR No. 2 X G

5.14 *Panelled and glazed wood doors: BS 459*

It is useful to note that pin-worm holes are permissible – under certain circumstances, providing that it can be established that the holes are made by the pinhole borer (ambrosia) beetle and no other insect. To make the diagnosis, reference should be made to the *Forest Products Research Leaflet No. 17*. The plywood facing must be in accordance with BS 1186: Part 1 *Specification for Timber*: with Moisture Resistant exterior type for both sides of exterior doors. The direction of grain on the face veneer will normally be vertical. This is important where the door is to receive a clear finish.

Hardboard for facings must be to the requirements of BS 1142: *Fibre building boards*: adhesive to BS 5442: Part 3 1979 *Adhesives for use with wood*.

Where lippings are provided, they are to be solid, fixed to both vertical edges of the door, and measure at least 7 mm on face.

Sizes　The standard sizes are given in given 5.14.

Furniture　Provision for locks, letter plate and hinges are standardized.

Finish　The Standard specification relates to the doors, at the time of despatch from the factory, with an untreated surface. The doors should be protected from exposure to the weather to prevent deterioration during transport and storage, as well as after fixing. When flush doors have to be stored on site, they must be kept from exposure to the weather, in dry conditions – stacked horizontally on level bearers, not less than 3 cross bearers to each pile of doors. Doors should not be stacked leaning at an angle.

The use of flush doors is now almost universal in all types of buildings and there is a large range of types available reflecting considerable variation in price, quality and finish. Flush doors are a component which can be manufactured by methods using a high degree of mechanization with flow-line production techniques and automation.

(a) Solid core

The laminated solid core door is the most expensive form of construction but gives a quality door of high sound insulation which will withstand

	Hardboard flush	Unlipped sealed	Paint Ply	Gaboon
838 × 1981 × 35 mm	●	●	●	●
813 × 2032 × 35 mm	●	●	●	●
762 × 1981 × 35 mm	●	●	●	●
711 × 1981 × 35 mm	●	●	●	●
711 × 1930 × 35 mm	●	●	●	●
686 × 1981 × 35 mm	●	●	●	●
610 × 1981 × 35 mm	●	●	●	●
533 × 1981 × 35 mm	●	●	●	
457 × 1981 × 35 mm	●	●	●	
610 × 1829 × 35 mm	●	●	●	●
381 × 1981 × 35 mm	●	●	●	
533 × 1829 × 35 mm	●	●	●	
457 × 1829 × 35 mm	●	●	●	
838 × 1981 × 40 mm	●	●	●	
813 × 2032 × 40 mm	●	●	●	
762 × 1981 × 40 mm	●	●	●	
686 × 1981 × 40 mm	●	●	●	
610 × 1981 × 40 mm	●	●	●	
762 × 1981 × 35 mm with G.O. 457 × 457	●			
826 × 2040 × 40 mm	●	●	●	
726 × 2040 × 40 mm	●	●	●	
626 × 2040 × 40 mm	●	●	●	
526 × 2040 × 40 mm	●	●	●	

Typical range of standard exterior flush doors

838 × 2057 × 44 mm	
838 × 1981 × 44 mm	
813 × 2032 × 44 mm	
762 × 1981 × 44 mm	All faced with hardwood ply for
686 × 1981 × 44 mm	painting. With or without
610 × 1981 × 44 mm	glazed openings
826 × 2040 × 44 mm	
726 × 2040 × 44 mm	
807 × 2000 × 44 mm	

5.15　*Typical range of standard exterior flush doors. Doors comply with BS 1186 Part 1 and 2:* Quality of Timber and Workmanship. *Tolerances to BS 4787 Part 1: For all sizes approximate metric equivalents correct to nearest mm are given*

heavy use over a long period of time. It is illustrated in figure 5.16. The core laminations are laid alternately to balance stresses, and thus reduce the risk of distortion. Western red cedar is a suitable timber for use in the core since it has a small moisture movement which is an important advantage where the door is subjected to changing temperature and humidity. Hardwood veneers for this class of door would be specially selected and matched for figure of grain.

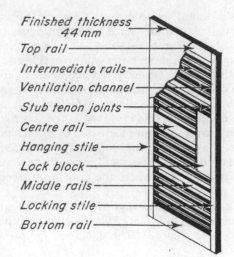

Finished thickness 44 mm
Top rail
Intermediate rails
Ventilation channel
Stub tenon joints
Centre rail
Hanging stile
Lock block
Middle rails
Locking stile
Bottom rail

5.17 *Semi-solid flush door*

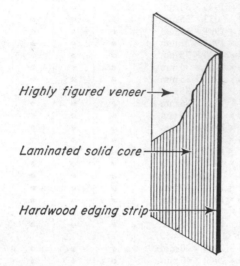

Highly figured veneer

Laminated solid core

Hardwood edging strip

5.16 *Solid core flush door*

(b) Semi-solid core

The semi-solid framed core medium cost door should contain 50% timber, and is best constructed on the *stressed skin* principle, using the plywood to give a construction of great strength and rigidity. The edges of the door are normally lipped in hardwood to protect and cover the edges of the plywood. This type of door will also probably be veneered in hardwood, and a typical example is shown in figure 5.17.

(e) Skeleton frame

The skeleton frame door shown in figure 5.18 is a less expensive method of framing which produces a door suitable for low cost contracts. This class of door would be faced with hardboard or plywood for painting.

(d) Cellular core

There are various proprietary methods of producing a suitable cellular core such as a hardboard 'eggbox' or lattice construction. Both of these are illustrated in figures 5.19 and 5.20. Expanded cellular paper-board, extruded wood chipboard,

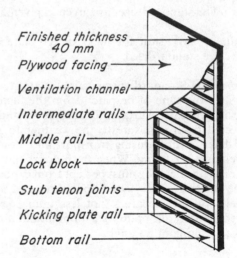

Finished thickness 40 mm
Plywood facing
Ventilation channel
Intermediate rails
Middle rail
Lock block
Stub tenon joints
Kicking plate rail
Bottom rail

5.18 *Skeleton framed flush door*

flaxboard, and a method of utilizing timber 'shavings' in the form of precision cut spirals, are also commonly used for the core. Whichever form of construction is used it must avoid the defect of surface undulation where the 'ripple effect' reflecting the construction of the core is seen on the face of the door. The cost of these doors is related

116

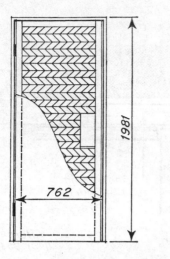

35 MM INTERIOR FLUSH DOOR
–expanded cellular board infill

5.19 *Cellular core*

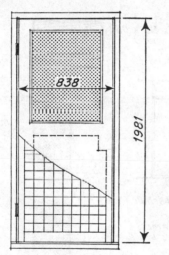

44 MM EXTERIOR FLUSH DOOR
– hardboard lattice core

5.20 *Lattice core*

3 A medium cost plywood facing finished at the factory with a clear finish. This type of clear finish has the double advantage of sealing the timber and enhancing the grain of the facing.
4 A sliced cut figured hardwood veneer plywood of timbers such as sapele, teak, oak, walnut and afrormosia, finished and protected at the factory by a clear lacquer.

The technique of utilizing a grain printing process to reproduce hardwood figure, either on hardboard or an inexpensive plywood is now also used in the manufacture of flush doors. The technique is also used in the furniture industry. The method and type of lipping is also a guide to the cost of the door; the cheapest range will be unlipped, the medium range will be lipped on the vertical edges, either with parana pine or hardwood, and the most expensive range will have a matching hardwood lipping to all edges. It is in any case necessary to lip exterior doors on all edges for weather protection. It is important that a highly finished component such as a flush door, manufactured under strictly controlled conditions, should be carefully stored and handled on site. Manufacturers will not usually guarantee doors unless they are stored flat and dry, protected until ready for use, and not hung in a damp or freshly plastered building.

5.6 Door frames and linings

Doors are hung on either frames or linings within an opening, the difference being that a lining provides a covering to the reveals (sides) and soffit (upper surface) of an opening. A frame should always be strong enough to support the door without help from the main structure of the building; a lining on the other hand is supported to a certain extent by the construction surrounding the opening. Neither frame nor lining must support any construction other than the door.

The size of the opening within the frame should allow between 2 mm and 3 mm clearance for hanging and adjusting the door. Rebates to receive the door should be minimum 12 mm deep, the rebate can either be recessed into a frame from the solid, or more usually formed by a planted stop on the surface of a lining. A planted stop has the following advantages:

to the type of facing that is used, and in ascending order of cost the range is as follows:
1 Painted hardboard.
2 Inexpensive plywood facing for painting.

117

- it makes a more economical use of timber;
- providing it is only temporarily pinned in position it can be adjusted on site to suit the door after it is hung;
- doors can be hung on either side of the stop, making the 'handing' of linings unnecessary;
- linings can be prefabricated in two separate halves, loosely dowelled together so that they can be adjusted on site to fit varying widths of partition. The planted stop fixed on site will then cover the gap between the two parts of the lining. An example of this construction is shown in figure 5.21.

Frames and linings appropriate to panelled and flush standard doors are described in BS 1567: 1953 *Wood doors frames and linings* and standard sections for an inward opening external door shown in figure 5.22.

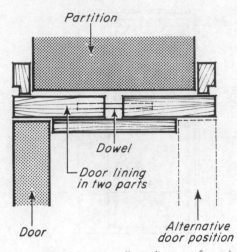

5.21 *Dowelled door lining to allow adjustment for various thicknesses of partition*

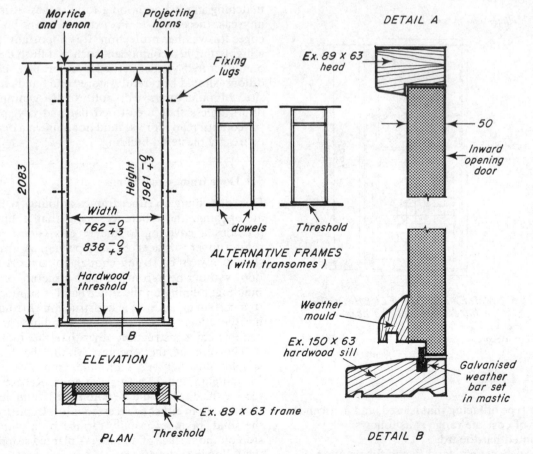

5.22 *Timber door frames*

The backs of frames should be protected against moisture penetration by priming paint before fixing.

Frames are now usually 'built in' as the work proceeds. Temporary strutting is necessary until the walling is built and metal cramps or lugs, as shown in figure 5.23, should be screwed to the back of the frame so as to coincide with the joints in the masonry, say three lugs to each side of the opening. Projecting 'horns' on the frame can also be built in to assist in restraining the frame. If a threshold is not fitted, metal dowels protruding from the foot of the post should be let into the step. The joint between door frame and masonry opening should be raked out to a depth of say 12 mm and pointed with a suitable mastic. The mastic will probably be gun applied, and the width of mastic filling to the joint should be at least 6 mm or it will be ineffective. A detail is shown in figure 5.24.

Linings, on the other hand, must be fixed after the opening is formed. Timber pallet pieces (elm is preferable) are built into the brickwork or block-work joints and the lining screwed or nailed to these. In good class work the screws would be countersunk and pelleted in timber matching the frame to conceal the screw head. It may be necessary, particularly if the opening is wide, to fix the lining at the soffit also.

If the wall is plastered it is necessary to provide architraves (cover strips) to cover the joint between the lining and the plasterwork.

5.7 Standard trim

For low cost contracts *standard trim* sections as covered by BS 584: 1967 (1980) *Specification for wood trim (softwood)* would be of suitable section. The architrave sections are shown in figure 5.25.

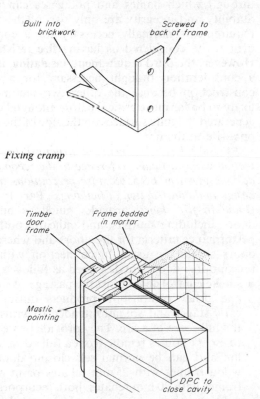

5.23 *Fixing cramp*

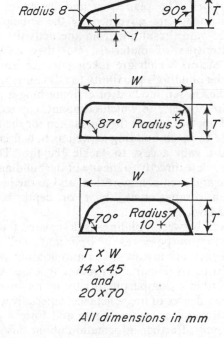

5.25 *Standard architraves: BS 584*

5.24 *External door in timber frame*

119

Architrave details are shown in figures 5.41 and 5.42. Care should be taken to ensure that the thickness of the architrave is greater than the thickness of the skirting in order to avoid an awkward detail at the architrave–skirting junction. Traditionally a block of timber known as an architrave block was fixed at this point, against which both architrave and skirting butted.

The BS trim can be specified to be delivered at one of two alternative levels of moisture content, (a) 14 to 17% where the conditions are such that the moisture content can be substantially maintained until completion of the building, or (b) not greater than 20%.

The lower moisture content will be preferable since it will reduce the risk of movement and twisting of the trim after fixing.

5.8 Fire doors

The spread of fire through buildings may be limited by dividing them into horizontal or vertical compartments by fire resisting construction. Walls and floors forming these compartment are referred to as *compartment walls* and *compartment floors*. The plan area and height of the compartments are governed by the anticipated calorific value resulting from the activities and characteristics of materials, etc, they enclose. Other factors which are taken into account include the building's proximity to adjoining buildings, the chosen method of extinguishing a possible fire, the ease to which occupants can escape should one occur, and the time taken for the Fire Brigade to reach building as well as how firemen can best gain access to tackle the fire. These factors relate directly to the use of the building, its volume and area configuration, and to the height of each compartment above or depth below ground level.

A wall between buildings is designated for fire protection purposes as a *separating wall* and similar factors must be taken into account when considering its potential for retaining a fire. Also, walls within a compartment may be required to provide a degree of fire resistance, especially when they surround an escape route and form a *protected shaft*. Further information about this subject can be obtained from BS 5588 Parts 1–5 *Fire precautions in the design and construction of buildings*.

Openings required for doors, shutters, hatches, ducting, pipes and the like provide a weak link through which smoke and fire can pass any fire resisting wall, thereby causing hazard to adjoining parts of the building or to another building close by. For this reason there are precise rules about the size and construction of such openings and their infills – of which doors are likely to be the largest and, because they must open freely, the most dangerous. Nevertheless, fire doors have at least one of two functions to perform: to protect escape routes from the effect of fire so that occupants can safely reach a final exit, and to protect the contents and/or the structure of a building by limiting the spread of fire.

To act as an effective barrier, a door and its frame must provide **stability** against collapse or excessive deflection, and **integrity** against the development of cracks and other openings through which flames and hot gases can pass. Stability and integrity are only two of the three requirements normally necessary for a component to be considered as having **fire resistance**. However, the third requirement, **insulation**, is not a consideration thought necessary for a door construction because the other two factors are likely to be far more critical before enough heat is generated to ignite surfaces on the side of the door opposite to the fire.

PD 6512 *Use of elements of structural fire protection with particular reference to the recommendations given in BS 5588 'Fire precautions in the design and construction of buildings'*, Part 1: 1985 *Guide to fire doors*, provides guidance on fire doors, including shutters, and indicates both the performance criteria for fire doors and where fire doors should be used. In connection with fire precautions, doors are described as follows:

● **smoke control doors** resist the passage of smoke and other combustion products during the early stages and are not intended to withstand the full force of a fire. They provide protection to escape routes remote from a fully developed fire and can be normal self closing doors in wood frames with 25 mm rebates or in metal frames with 20 mm rebates, both incorporating nylon brushes or synthetic rubber seals held in grooves, or metal or plastic draught strips;

120

- **fire check doors** to provide integrity against transfer of fire for a stated time, without allowing excessive quantities of smoke to escape. They are used to keep the protected escape routes sufficiently free from smoke for such time as is considered reasonable for all the occupants at risk to become alerted to a fire situation and to safely reach a final exit;
- **fire resisting doors** to provide a higher standard of *integrity* than fire check doors but the same standard of *stability*. As fire will penetrate the smallest of gaps, the enhanced fire resisting period is now generally provided by the addition of *intumescent strips* set in the edges of the door and/or the frame rebates. These foam at high temperatures and seal gaps. Fire resisting doors are provided for fire compartmentation and isolation of special risk areas. The doors should be capable of achieving a period of fire resistance appropriate to the structural requirements. When these doors are provided to protect a means of escape route they also need to provide smoke control.

Fire doors (FD) are designated by the amount of *integrity* they provide. Therefore, a fire door providing 30 minutes *stability* is designated as FD20 if it is a **fire check door** in recognition of its reduced *integrity*, and as FD30 for a **fire resisting door** because it provides both *stability* and *integrity* for 30 minutes. Similarly, a one hour fire check door is designated FD45, a one hour fire resisting door FD60; and a four hour fire check door as FD120 with the equivalent fire resisting door as FD240. Doors which must also provide smoke control are designated by adding suffix S; for example, FD20S, FD60S.

To be designated as a fire door, samples must be tested according to the procedures laid down in BS 476 1972: *Fire tests on building materials and structures*, Part 8: *Test methods and criteria for the fire resistance of elements of building construction*. This BS does not specify how elements should be constructed, but requires a door specimen to be representative of that used in practice, including all *essential ironmongery*. This means that the door should be fitted with a suitable latch which, together with the butts, retains the door in its frame.

Special care must be taken to ensure that any ironmongery morticed into the door does not reduce the fire stopping capabilities of the door. A failure in fire resistance can occur when heat is conducted through morticed ironmongery and causes the ignition of the non-fire side of the door. The use of intumescent material in the form of plugs, for insertion at hinge, latch and striking plate positions, and paste to be packed around latches, locks etc, largely overcomes this conduction problem. Figure 5.26 indicates a typical arrangement of ironmongery on a single leaf fire door.

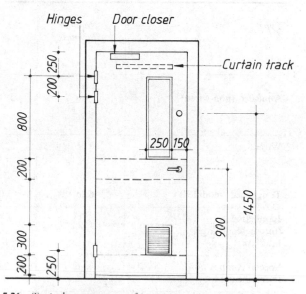

5.26 *Typical arrangement of ironmongery on a single leaf fire door (Courtesy of Castlecomer Woodwork Company Ltd)*

Self closing devices, an essential feature of all fire doors (including smoke control doors), should be able to close a door fully and engage the latch because it may not be capable of subsequently functioning against pressure exerted by the fire. In less hazardous conditions, such as in housing, special rising butts (eg stainless steel with brass bushes) may be allowed as a substitute for a door closer, although one of the many concealed door closers are likely to be cheaper. A pair of double doors should have rebated meeting stiles and be fitted with a door selector (figure 9.19 page 225) to ensure proper closing. The selector must be able to resist the pressure of the fire.

Further details regarding the use of appropriate ironmongery for fire doors can be obtained from *Code of Practice for hardware essential to the optimum performance of fire-resisting timber doorsets* published by the Association of Builders Hardware Manufacturers; and *Code of Practice: Architectural ironmongery for use on fire resisting self closing timber and emergency exit doors*, as well as *Fire and escape door hardware: Part 1 General notes*, and *Part 2 Products*, published by the Guild of Architectural Ironmongers. An additional reason for the growing interest in ironmongery used for fire doors involves the potential conflict which could arise between the need for ease of escape in the event of a fire, and the need to provide adequate security against unlawful entry into a room or a building. For further information see chapter 9 *Ironmongery*.

Fire doors can have **glazing** providing the sizes and construction of its surround comply with PD 6512: Part 3 1987 *Guide to the fire performance of glass* – see figures 5.27 and 5.28. Further guidance will also be available from PD 6512: Part 2 *Examples of two designs of FD rated doors*,

Type	Nominal thickness	Size of pane†	Type of system	Test results†	
				For stability and integrity only	For stability, integrity and insulation
Annealed (non-wired)	mm 6	m 0.10 × 0.15	Multiple paned copperlight panel, max. 0.4²	h 1	h —
Wired	6	2.0 × 0.8 1.6 × 1.4 2.0 × 1.4	Single pane Multiple pane Multiple pane	1.5 1 0.5	— — —
Toughened (modified)	6 to 12	2.0 × 2.85	Single pane	0.5	—
Laminated (intumescent or gel interlayer)	11 20 72	1.98 × 0.8 2.0 × 1.4 1.2 × 1.6	Single pane Multiple pane Single pane	— — —	0.5 1 1.5
Special composition (borosilicate)	6	2.0 × 1.0	Multiple pane	2	—
Glass blocks	80	2.438 × 2.438	Blocks 240 mm × 240 mm with mortar joints and steel rod reinforcement	—	0.5‡

* Results should not differ substantially when tested in accordance with BS 476 : Part 22.

† This table is based on publicly available data. The levels of performance given do not represent the maximum that can be achieved, but do indicate levels of performance which have been achieved using a specific glazing system and which can be substantiated by test evidence available from either the glass or glazing system manufacturer. The use of a different glazing system may result in an increased or reduced level of performance.

‡ Tested in accordance with BS 476 : Part 1; insulation criterion met for approximately 15 min only. BS 476 : Part 1 was withdrawn in 1972 on the publication of BS 476 : Part 8.

NOTE 1 Conventional toughened glass will not usually achieve the minimum (30 min) performance level for fire resistance.

NOTE 2 The use of PVB laminates to combine one or more of the above glasses may increase or decrease the performance depending on the glass(es) combined and the installation.

NOTE 3 There is no information available on performance where resin interlayers are used for combining glasses.

5.27 *Fire performance properties of glass: test results in accordance with BS 476: Part 8* when glazed vertically in suitably designed systems*

which is in the course of preparation. As for any other door, glazing in a fire door is useful for transference of light from one area to another as well as providing a means of vision through a closed door, thereby avoiding collisions. The glass should generally be 6 mm thick wired glass and be adequately retained: timber doors and beads need particular attention in that failure in a fire is deemed to have occurred when ignition starts by heat transfer through the glass to the side opposite to the fire. Care must also be exercised when an opening is cut in a solid fire door, ie not a purpose-made glazed fire door, to receive the glazing as this may ultimately decrease the ability of the door to withstand deformation in a fire. For further information see 7.2(d) *Fire precautions* (*Glazing*).

Where fire doors are required to be FD60 and above, metal doors protected by glass fibre-reinforced gypsum are generally used. Doors of this nature are likely to be very heavy to close, and assistance can be given by hanging them on an inclined overhead track. The door will normally be held open by a counter-weight connected to a cable incorporating a fusible link. The link breaks when a critical temperature is reached, allowing the door to slide to a closed position.

Figure 5.29 illustrate typical fire door construction details for different fire ratings. All timbers should comply with BS 1186 Part 1: 1986 *Specification timber*, and Part 2: 1971 *Quality of workmanship*; adhesives to BS 5442: Part 3 *Adhesives for use with wood*; and plywood to BS 6566: Parts 1–8 1985 *Plywood*, for internal (with moisture resistant resins) and external (with weather and boil proof resins). Manufacturers produce fire doors to different specifications and are required to obtain a test certificate for a sample door. Following this each door is required to have a colour coded plastic plug inserted in the hanging style of the door, approximately 600 mm from the top or bottom. Also, many manufacturers now have a *Quality Assurance Schedule* (chapter 1 page 14) which confirms that their production processes are to agreed standards.

The *Building Regulations 1985: Approved Document B; Sections 1 Dwelling houses, 2 Flats, 3 Institutional, 4 Other residential, 5 Assembly*, and *6 Offices, shops, industrial and other non-residential*, as well as *Appendix A* of the *Approved Document* give precise requirements for buildings with compartment and separating walls, including for doors (and for suspended ceilings). These documents refer to all fire doors as being fire resisting doors. External doors and frames are designated as **unprotected areas** whatever their construction and are not considered as providing fire resistance.

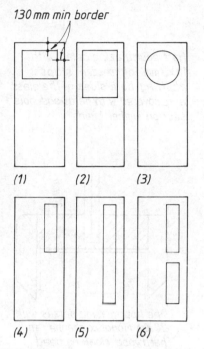

Examples of glazed apertures in fire doors

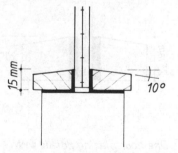

Half hour glazing detail with 15 mm hardwood bole section timber beads, bedded in intumescent putty

5.28 *Typical glazing details in fire doors*

Continued . . .

Continued

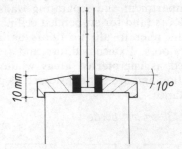

Half hour glazing detail with
10x3mm intumescent strips
abutting both sides of the glass
and covered with hardwood bole
section timber beads

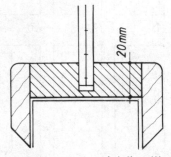

One hour glazing details with
20mm Monolux channel and
hardwood cloaking bead

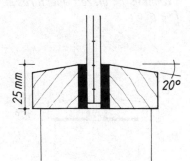

One hour glazing details with
25x3mm intumescent strips
abutting both sides of the glass
and covered with hardwood bole
section timber beads

5.28 *Typical glazing details in fire doors (Courtesy of Castlecomer Woodwork Company Ltd)*

5.9 Sound resistant doors

Sound waves can travel from one room to another by *flanking transmission* along and through the fabric of the building, *impact transmission* by vibration directly through the thickness of the separating construction, or by *airborne transmission* through gaps in any part of the construction (see *Mitchell's Introduction to Building* chapter 7 *Sound control*). Rather like fire resistance, a single door and its frame usually provides an easier path for transmission of sound between two rooms when compared with an imperforate wall of almost any construction. This is because the door is likely to be of much *lighter unit weight* than its surrounding wall, and also because of the possibility of *air gaps* between door and door frame. For these reasons the net resistance to sound through a wall with a door (or window) will be limited to only about 7 dB above that of the door itself, no matter how heavy the surrounding wall (see figure 5.30).

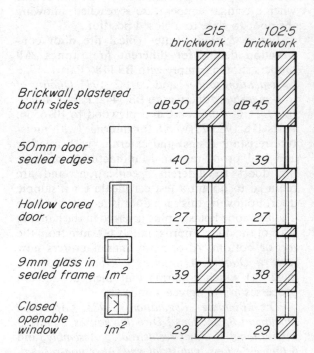

5.30 *Effect of openings in walls have on sound attenuation performance (BDA)*

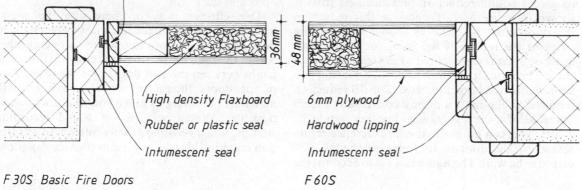

PVC coated intumescent strip with integral brush pile to provide smoke stop

36mm

48mm

High density Flaxboard

Rubber or plastic seal

Intumescent seal

6mm plywood

Hardwood lipping

Intumescent seal

F 30S Basic Fire Doors
BS 476: Part 8

F 60S
BS 476: Part 8

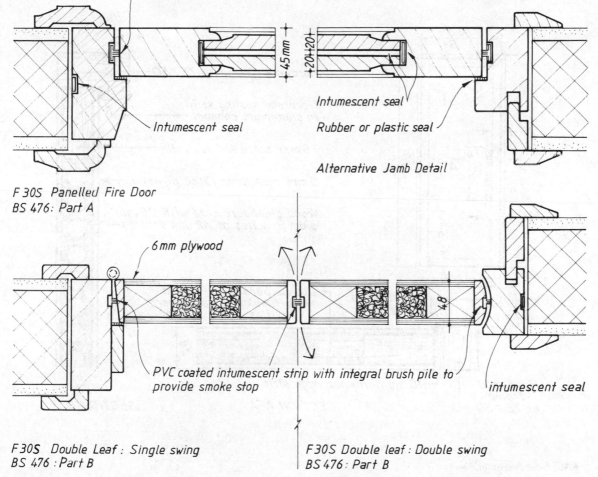

PVC coated intumescent strip with integral brush pile to provide smoke stop

45mm

20+20

Intumescent seal

Intumescent seal

Rubber or plastic seal

Alternative Jamb Detail

F 30S Panelled Fire Door
BS 476: Part A

6mm plywood

4.8

PVC coated intumescent strip with integral brush pile to
provide smoke stop

intumescent seal

F 30S Double Leaf : Single swing
BS 476 : Part B

F 30S Double leaf : Double swing
BS 476 : Part B

5.29 *Typical fire door construction details for different fire ratings (Courtesy of Castlecomer Woodwork Company Ltd)*

A type of flush door which would be expected to give a sound reduction of 3 decibels (dB) is shown in figure 5.31. To achieve this reduction the door must be hung as shown with sealing strips at the rebate of the frame, and the frame must be adequately secured to the walling, which should be at least 190 mm thick solid masonry to achieve the reduction indicated. The dB reduction required to eliminate a normal conversation from one side of a construction to another would be 27 dB. This is a normalized level difference represented by the door in its frame as shown, well fitted in the wall. The figure takes into account the combination of, and the different dB ratings for door and wall.

One effective way of increasing the sound resistance of a wall requiring a door opening is to provide a pair of doors opposite to one another within the thickness of the wall construction. The jambs between the two doors and the inside face of the doors themselves should be lined with materials providing as much sound absorption as possible. Alternatively, as in sound recording studios, *sound resisting lobbies* filled with absorption materials should be used to provide isolation.

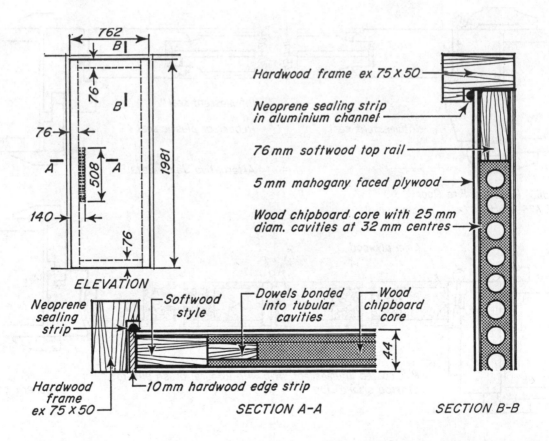

5.31 *Sound resistant door*

5.10 Specialist doors

Figure 5.32 indicates doors suitable for dark-rooms, where photographic processes take place, and for resisting X-rays, as would be used for medical buildings.

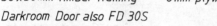
6 mm dia flexible seal on 10 x 4 mm PVC Intumescent carrier

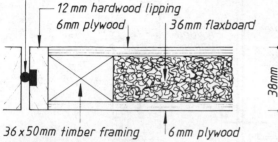

36 x 50mm timber framing   *6 mm plywood*

Darkroom Door also FD 30S

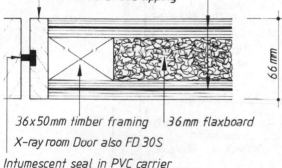

X-ray room Door also FD 30S

Intumescent seal in PVC carrier

5.32 *Darkroom and X-ray room door details (Courtesy Castlecomer Woodwork Company Ltd)*

5.11 Glazed doors

In addition to the standard panelled glazed door previously described, purpose-made glazed doors are mostly much used so that persons passing through can see if anyone is coming from the opposite direction. Where these doors are used in entrances, as they often are, very heavy use is made of them and appropriate construction is essential. Figure 5.33 shows an example of a pair of glazed doors in hardwood as part of a glazed entrance screen detail. Points to emphasize are the weather stripping by neoprene gaskets in extruded aluminium sections at the threshold, and the extruded aluminium weather stripped door stops. Further details of this type of weatherstripping are given on pages 103 and 106–7.

Since this type of door will be in constant use it is sensible to use a floor spring as a means of controlling the movement. The floor spring can be fitted with a device which checks the doors open at 90 degrees.

Another example of glazed door construction is shown in figure 5.34. This is a range of doors formed from extruded aluminium sections and is suitable for an hotel or department store entrance. The profiles are neat and points to note are the draught-proofing by woven pile strips and the different methods of securing the glazing in the door and fanlight.

5.12 Glass doors

Figure 5.35 illustrates a toughened plate glass door and side screen of the type fitted at the entrance to shops and showrooms. The door is controlled by an adjustable top centre pivot hung on a double action floor spring. A special lock will be fitted in the top and bottom metal rails with the lock keepers set into the hardwood frame and concrete floor. The attractive feature of this type of door is its transparency, but it is sometimes difficult to know when the door is open, and for this reason some form of decoration may be fixed to the door to indicate its position.

5.13 Louvred doors

This is a form of door which is now much used both internally for decorative purposes and externally where permanent ventilation is required. In the example shown in figure 5.36 the louvres are housed into a vertical louvre style which is then shop glued within the panel formed by the main framing of the door. The edges of the louvres, because of their projection in front of the face of the door, are chamfered off at the corners. The louvre slats are set at 45 degrees and fixed so that there is a minimum overlap of 3 mm. The door is shown closing against an extruded aluminium threshold.

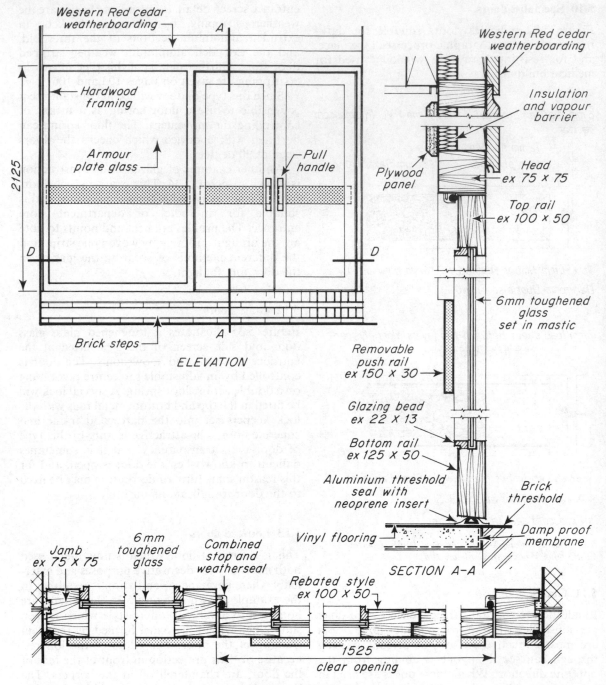

Western Red cedar
weatherboarding

Western Red cedar
weatherboarding

Hardwood
framing

Insulation
and vapour
barrier

Armour
plate glass

Pull
handle

Plywood
panel

Head
ex 75 x 75

2125

Top rail
ex 100 x 50

D — D

6mm toughened
glass
set in mastic

Brick steps

ELEVATION

Removable
push rail
ex 150 x 30

Glazing bead
ex 22 x 13

Bottom rail
ex 125 x 50

Aluminium threshold
seal with
neoprene insert

Brick
threshold

Vinyl flooring

Damp proof
membrane

SECTION A-A

Jamb
ex 75 x 75

6mm
toughened
glass

Combined
stop and
weatherseal

Rebated style
ex 100 x 50

1525
clear opening

PLAN AT D-D

5.33 *Hardwood glazed doors*

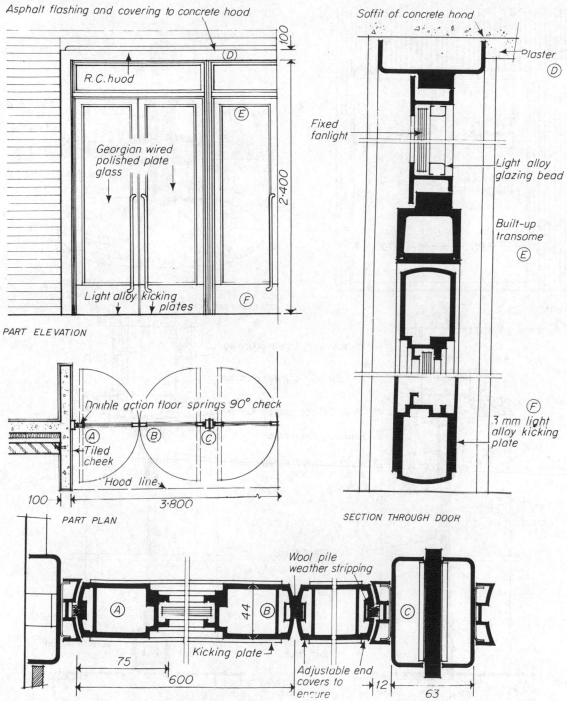

Asphalt flashing and covering to concrete hood

R.C. hood

Georgian wired polished plate glass

Light alloy kicking plates

100

2·400

D

E

F

PART ELEVATION

Double action floor springs 90° check

Tiled cheek

Hood line

100

3·800

A

B

C

PART PLAN

Soffit of concrete hood

Plaster

D

Fixed fanlight

Light alloy glazing bead

Built-up transome

E

F

3 mm light alloy kicking plate

SECTION THROUGH DOOR

Wool pile weather stripping

A

B

C

44

Kicking plate

Adjustable end covers to ensure alignment

75

600

12

63

PLAN THROUGH DOORS AND FRAME

5.34 *Glazed aluminium doors*

129

DOORS

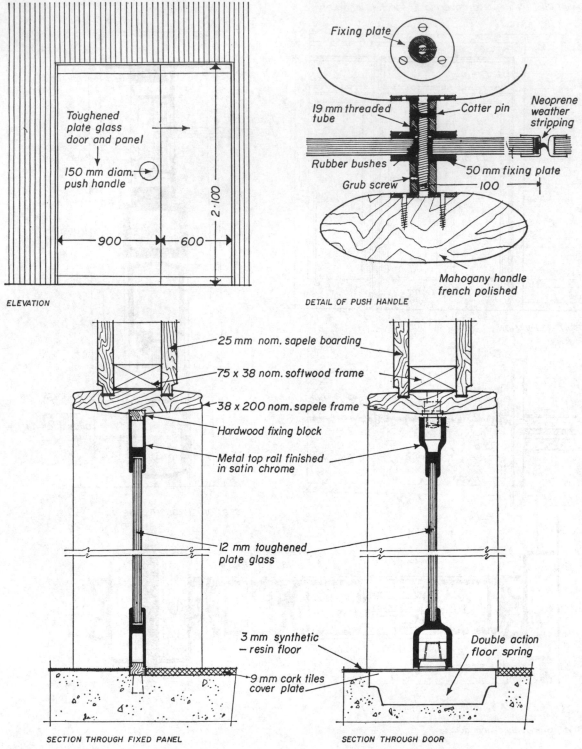

Toughened
plate glass
door and panel

150 mm diam.
push handle

2·100

900   600

ELEVATION

Fixing plate

19 mm threaded
tube

Cotter pin

Neoprene
weather
stripping

Rubber bushes

50 mm fixing plate

Grub screw

100

Mahogany handle
french polished

DETAIL OF PUSH HANDLE

25 mm nom. sapele boarding

75 x 38 nom. softwood frame

38 x 200 nom. sapele frame

Hardwood fixing block

Metal top rail finished
in satin chrome

12 mm toughened
plate glass

3 mm synthetic
– resin floor

9 mm cork tiles
cover plate

Double action
floor spring

SECTION THROUGH FIXED PANEL

SECTION THROUGH DOOR

5.35 *Glass door*

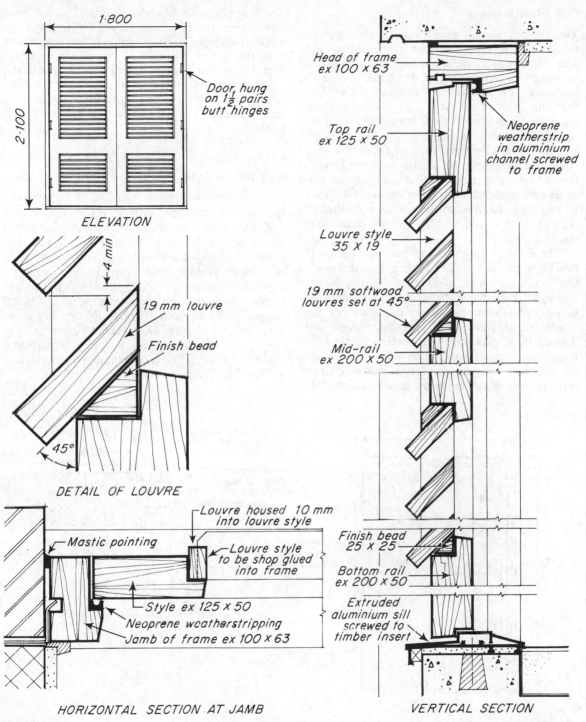

1·800

2·100

Door, hung on 1½ pairs butt hinges

ELEVATION

4 min

19 mm louvre

Finish bead

45°

DETAIL OF LOUVRE

Head of frame
ex 100 × 63

Top rail
ex 125 × 50

Neoprene
weatherstrip
in aluminium
channel screwed
to frame

Louvre style
35 × 19

19 mm softwood
louvres set at 45°

Mid-rail
ex 200 × 50

—Louvre housed 10 mm
into louvre style

—Mastic pointing

—Louvre style
to be shop glued
into frame

—Style ex 125 × 50

Neoprene weatherstripping

Jamb of frame ex 100 × 63

HORIZONTAL SECTION AT JAMB

Finish bead
25 × 25

Bottom rail
ex 200 × 50

Extruded
aluminium sill
screwed to
timber insert

VERTICAL SECTION

5.36 *Timber louvre door*

5.14 Flexible doors

This type of door is used where it is not possible for the user to open the door in the normal way. The most usual applications are in industrial buildings, warehousing or hospitals where the user may be pushing or driving a trolley or carrying bulky packages. It is a comparatively inexpensive alternative to installing automatic opening and closing devices. The door is composed of a flexible membrane of either reinforced rubber or neoprene, or where complete vision is desired for safety in operation, and the use is not excessive, transparent or translucent plastic sheet. In any case, because of the risk of collision, this type of door would be fitted with a clear plastic vision panel.

The door is designed to open on impact, the flexibility of the sheeting taking the force out of the 'collision', and allowing the user to pass through. The doors then close automatically, being controlled by jamb spring hinges. The door illustrated in figure 5.37 is a lightweight door formed by a steel angle supporting frame at the head and hinged side, from which is hung a flexible sheet of 8 mm reinforced rubber clamped into the heel of the angle by means of a steel flat.

The hinges are double action vertical spring type. For larger doors up to say 4.000 m high by 4.000 m wide the framing would be of steel tubing with the spring mechanism made as a separate detachable unit, and arranged to slide inside the vertical tube framing from the top. The heaviest doors are suitable for openings which are used by large vehicles and other heavy industrial transport.

5.15 Bronze doors

In complete contrast a pair of purpose-made, monumental cast bronze doors is shown in figures 5.38 and 5.39. The doors are set round a rolled steel channel framing which is *bolted* into the main structure of the building. The doors swing on single action floor springs. The separate moulded sections forming the door frame are clipped back to the main steelwork by metal straps, and are also 'tucked in' to the stone surround to the opening. These doors are examples of fine craftsmanship in a traditional setting and would be a dominant element in any architectural composition.

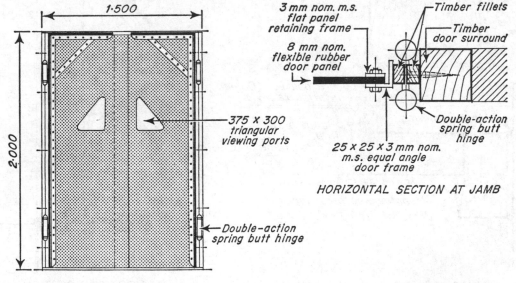

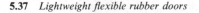

5.37 *Lightweight flexible rubber doors*

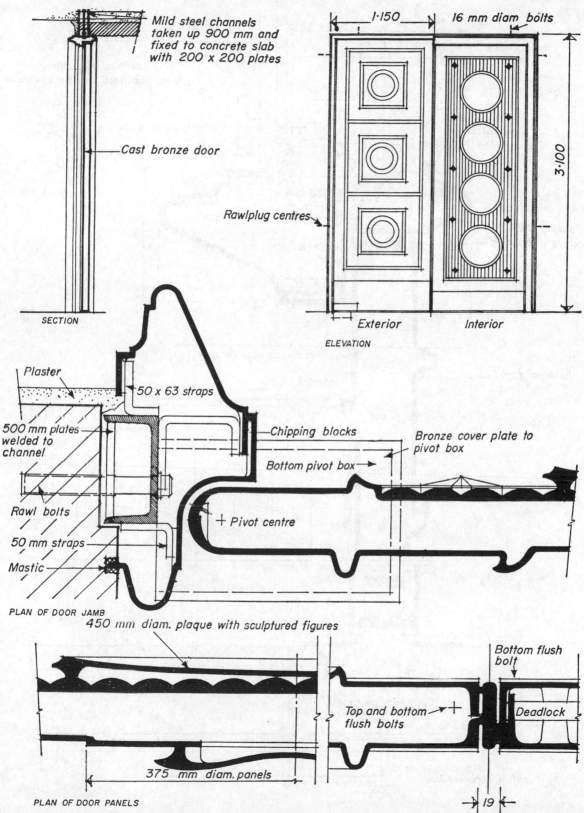

Mild steel channels taken up 900 mm and fixed to concrete slab with 200 x 200 plates

Cast bronze door

SECTION

1·150   16 mm diam bolts

Rawlplug centres

3·100

Exterior   Interior

ELEVATION

Plaster

50 x 63 straps

500 mm plates welded to channel

Chipping blocks

Bronze cover plate to pivot box

Bottom pivot box

+ Pivot centre

Rawl bolts

50 mm straps

Mastic

PLAN OF DOOR JAMB

450 mm diam. plaque with sculptured figures

Bottom flush bolt

Top and bottom flush bolts

Deadlock

375 mm diam. panels

PLAN OF DOOR PANELS

19

5.38 *Cast bronze doors (1)*

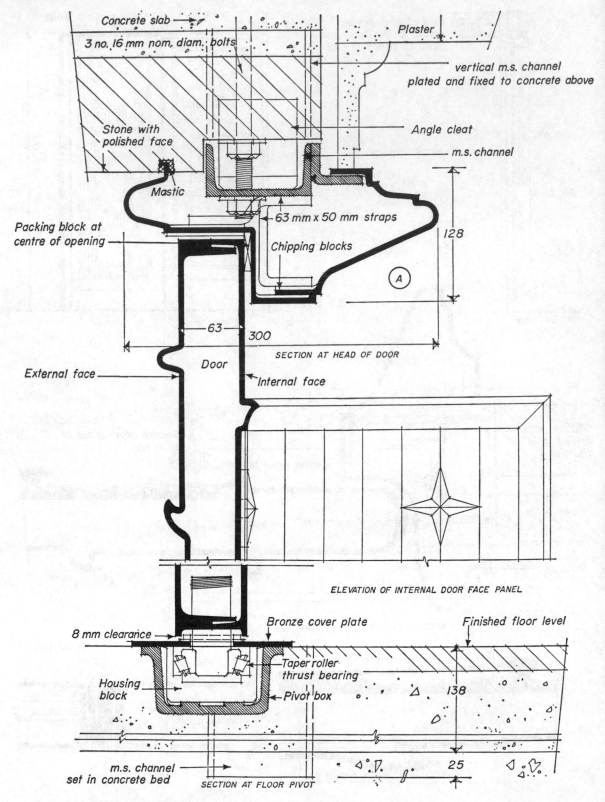

Concrete slab

3 no. 16 mm nom. diam. bolts

Plaster

vertical m.s. channel
plated and fixed to concrete above

Stone with
polished face

Angle cleat

m.s. channel

Mastic

63 mm x 50 mm straps

Packing block at
centre of opening

Chipping blocks

A

128

63

300

SECTION AT HEAD OF DOOR

Door

External face

Internal face

ELEVATION OF INTERNAL DOOR FACE PANEL

Bronze cover plate

Finished floor level

8 mm clearance

Taper roller
thrust bearing

Housing
block

138

Pivot box

m.s. channel
set in concrete bed

25

SECTION AT FLOOR PIVOT

5.39 *Cast bronze doors (2)*

5.16 Vestibule doors

Figures 5.40 and 5.41 show the application of a pair of purpose-made hardwood doors to close off a vestibule for extra security when the building is shut up for the night. Teak would be a suitable timber to use in this instance. A pair of hardwood glazed doors form the main entrance doors to the building. A special feature of these doors is the *rounded corner* detail at the junction of the styles and rails. Toughened glass should, of course, be used in this situation. The *night doors* are a form of folding door. Each side of the opening having a pair of doors hung leaf on leaf. Note that the method of hanging is devised so that the edges of the doors do not show and the outer door forms a decorative hardwood lining to the sides of the vestibule during the day. The entrance doors are hung on double action floor springs to allow the doors to act as a means of escape in the case of fire during the time that the building is in use, and the fact that the line of swing impedes the outer doors does not matter since the two sets of doors will not be in use at the same time. Each of the night doors will be hung on $1\frac{1}{2}$ pairs (3 to each door) of substantial brass hinges. The doors are an example of good class joinery work and will have to be carefully made and well hung to avoid trouble in use, since the stress on the hinges to the outer doors will be considerable.

5.17 Sliding and sliding-folding doors

These types of doors are now much more used and providing that the problems of manipulation and maintenance are understood the doors will work satisfactorily throughout their life. It must be emphasized, however, that the working parts of the doors must be treated like machinery and must be regularly maintained. It should also be borne in mind that the more complex the mechanism the greater chance of failure. A straight sliding single leaf door is the simplest and cheapest but takes up most space when open. Increasing the number of leaves saves space but complicates the mechanism. Folding systems take up the least space of all but require the most complex hanging gear. The weight of the doors can be taken on wheels or rollers at the base or alternatively suspended from hangers on a track at the head of a door. A neater finish can usually be obtained by the bottom rollers but general opinion is that top track is the most efficient method of hanging.

(a) Straight track sliding: single leaf

The track system chosen as an example of this type of action is suitable for interior doors not exceeding a width of 1200 mm and operating on a 'ball runner' principle. The details are shown in figure 5.42. The linear ball bearing motion is provided by a sliding inner bar grooved to receive chrome steel ball bearings and running between a vee section galvanized steel outer track. The ball bearings are located by a retainer cage. This type of gear, which will operate on doors weighing between 55 kg and 90 kg, is very reliable and prevents lifting or rocking of the doors when in use. The illustration shows an internal door in a house and this type of gear is often used where there is not sufficient space to allow a door to swing. The bottom of the door is controlled by a small nylon guide screwed to the floor at one side of the opening, so that a floor channel is not required and the fixing is suitable for carpeted interiors. It is also possible to fix this gear in the cavity of a double partition which makes a very neat detail.

(b) Straight track sliding: double leaf

Figure 5.43 shows a simple two leaf arrangement for garage doors with double top track. Note that each leaf requires two hangers each having four wheels and running in a steel track of box-like section. The track is supported on special brackets of malleable iron or forged steel. The heavier the door the larger the track. The biggest being 150 mm by 125 mm, nominal, which would be capable of supporting doors weighing up to about 1500 kg. There should be about 13 mm clearance between the doors and between the door and the wall. The bottom of the doors is held in place by malleable iron guides running in a steel channel let into the floor. The design of the track should prevent outward movement and so avoid any tendency for the doors to jam. The bottom rollers should also be so arranged that any dirt that gets into the channel will be ploughed out rather than pressed down. There are many alternative designs for track and channel guides. The leaves of the

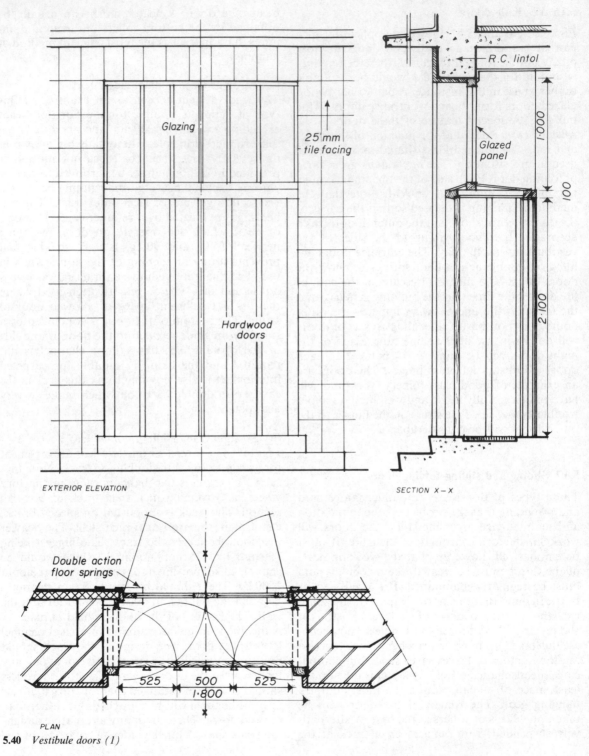

Glazing

25 mm tile facing

Hardwood doors

EXTERIOR ELEVATION

R.C. lintol

Glazed panel

1·000

100

2·100

SECTION X – X

Double action floor springs

525   500   525

1·800

PLAN

5.40 *Vestibule doors (1)*

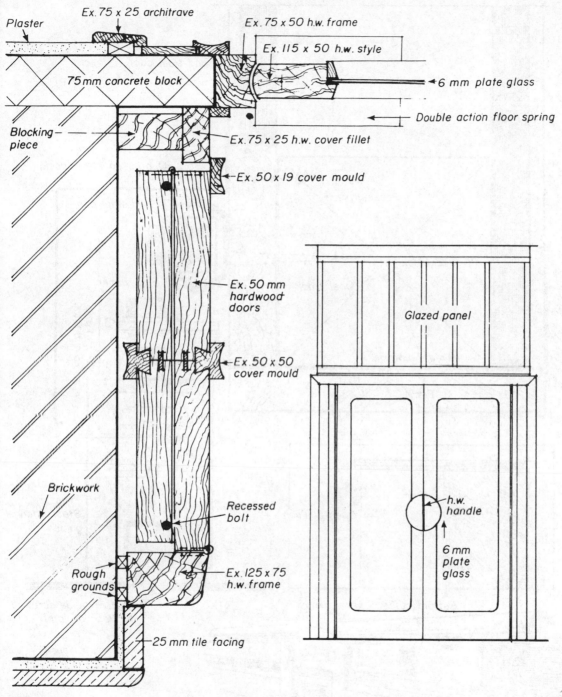

Plaster

Ex. 75 x 25 architrave

Ex. 75 x 50 h.w. frame

Ex. 115 x 50 h.w. style

75 mm concrete block

6 mm plate glass

Double action floor spring

Blocking piece

Ex. 75 x 25 h.w. cover fillet

Ex. 50 x 19 cover mould

Ex. 50 mm hardwood doors

Ex. 50 x 50 cover mould

Brickwork

Recessed bolt

Ex. 125 x 75 h.w. frame

Rough grounds

25 mm tile facing

Glazed panel

h.w. handle

6 mm plate glass

PART PLAN

INTERIOR ELEVATION

5.41 *Vestibule doors (2)*

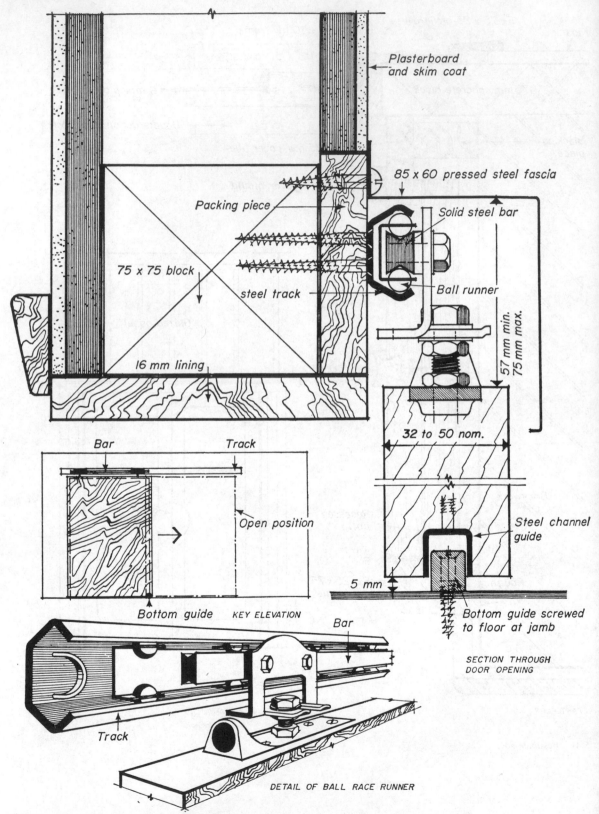

Plasterboard and skim coat

85 x 60 pressed steel fascia

Packing piece

Solid steel bar

75 x 75 block

steel track

Ball runner

16 mm lining

57 mm min.
75 mm max.

32 to 50 nom.

Bar

Track

Open position

Steel channel guide

5 mm

Bottom guide screwed to floor at jamb

Bottom guide   KEY ELEVATION

SECTION THROUGH DOOR OPENING

Bar

Track

DETAIL OF BALL RACE RUNNER

5.42 *Sliding gear for internal door. Straight track, single leaf*

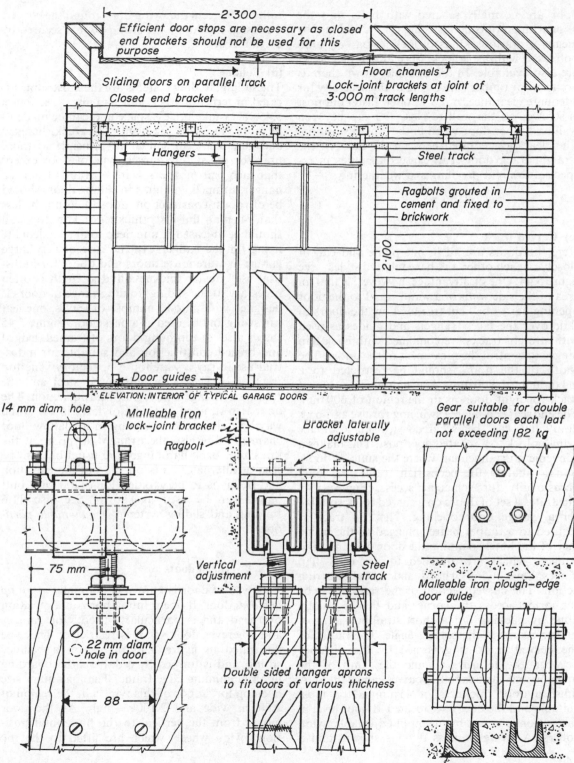

2·300

Efficient door stops are necessary as closed end brackets should not be used for this purpose

Sliding doors on parallel track

Closed end bracket

Floor channels

Lock-joint brackets at joint of 3·000 m track lengths

Hangers

Steel track

Ragbolts grouted in cement and fixed to brickwork

2·100

Door guides

ELEVATION: INTERIOR OF TYPICAL GARAGE DOORS

14 mm diam. hole

Malleable iron lock-joint bracket

Ragbolt

Bracket laterally adjustable

Gear suitable for double parallel doors each leaf not exceeding 182 kg

75 mm

22 mm diam. hole in door

Vertical adjustment

Steel track

Malleable iron plough-edge door guide

88

Double sided hanger aprons to fit doors of various thickness

Easy clean floor channel

DETAILS OF DOOR GEAR

5.43 *Sliding garage doors. Straight track, double leaf*

door are normally secured with bolts into the floor with an outside fastening on the end leaf by means of various kinds of locking bar or jamb bolt used with a padlock. Special cylinder locks are also available. In the example shown there is no frame or timber trim owing to the necessity for adequate clearance, but a wooden fastening post is screwed to the wall to close the gap between wall and inner door when in the closed position. The clearance required between the faces of the straight track doors can cause difficulties in respect of draught proofing and weathering.

(c) Curved track

Here the doors are all in one plane and can fit closely to each other and have rebated styles – see figure 5.44. One disadvantage, however, is that an area of the side walls of a width equal to the door opening has to be kept free to allow the doors to slide over the face. Hangers and guides as used with straight tracks are combined with back flap hinges to control the movement of the doors. The width of the doors should be restricted to a maximum of 900 mm. The minimum curve of track for light doors is in the region of 600 mm. The end leaf can be free swinging for use as a pass door and can be secured with an ordinary cylinder lock to a rebated door post. This makes a convenient arrangement where the suite of doors is used mainly for pedestrian traffic and only occasionally for vehicular access. Figure 5.43 illustrates a set of doors on a curved track suitable for a garage door opening. The top track is secured to a timber bearer plugged to the inside face of the lintel spanning the door opening. The hangers which are attached to the back flap hinges have nylon wheels and a ball bearing action. The curved section of the track must be supported across the corner and this is usually done by packing out a short straight length of timber bearer at the correct angle. The radius of the curved track is governed by the distance between the return wall and the jamb of the opening and various radius curves can be fitted. A finished door thickness of 45 mm is the most suitable and the doors are located at floor level in the bottom channel by means of adjustable nylon rollers. A swing or pass door is shown, and a

roller bolt steers the swing door round the corner. To fasten the doors, the swing door is secured by a cylinder lock.

(d) Folding

The sliding, folding systems are the most sophisticated in terms of track and hanging – see figure 5.45. They take up less space and can be made to fit more closely at the head. The track, hangers and guides are all similar in principle to those used for the sliding curved type of door except that each pair of doors swings inwards from the hanger. Framed and filled in sliding doors should be of robust construction and should not be less than 45 mm finished thickness. The top rail should be at least 150 mm deep to allow adequate fixing for the hangers. In the case of very large garage or warehouse doors and doors for industrial use, greater thickness and strength is often necessary. If the sliding, folding range of doors is designed with an odd number of leaves, one leaf can swing and be used as a pass door. Figure 5.45 shows a set of top hung doors of framed, ledged and braced construction and suitable for industrial use in say a warehouse or factory. The top track is of U section galvanized steel and the runners or hangers have ball bearing action. The door is restrained at the floor level in the usual way by nylon rollers running in a shallow floor channel. Note also the draught stripping at the threshold. Back flap hinges are usual but will be seen at alternate joints on the outside elevation and if this is to be avoided then (100 mm) butt hinges can be used as shown. See also 11.6 Folding and sliding system (*Demountable partitions*).

5.18 Overhead doors

This type of door is known colloquially as an *up and over* door. It opens into a horizontal position overhead and is particularly useful for garages and wherever floor space is restricted. The type illustrated in figure 5.46 pivots on a balance spring, and is formed by cedar weatherboarding in an aluminium edge frame. The maximum size opening for a door of this type is in the region of 2.500 m wide and 2.100 m high. As the door moves from the vertical to the horizontal position, nylon wheels which are fitted to the top

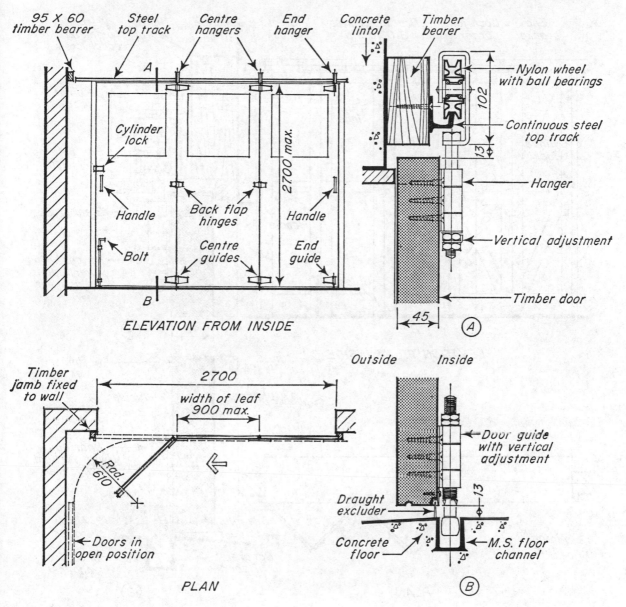

ELEVATION FROM INSIDE

PLAN

5.44 *Top hung sliding doors*

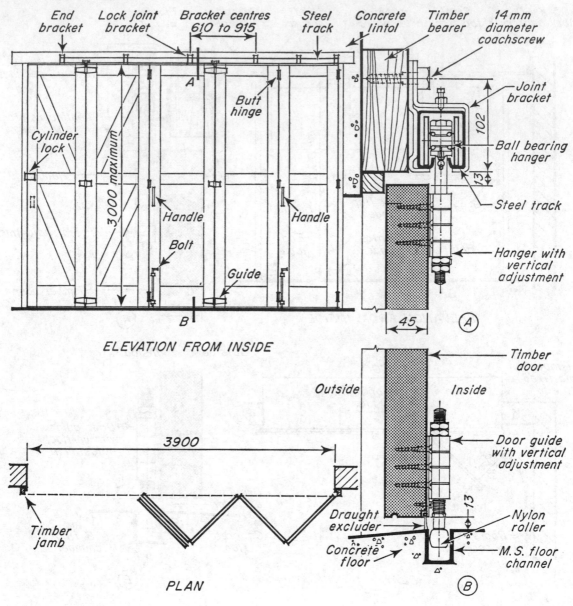

ELEVATION FROM INSIDE

PLAN

5.45 *Top hung folding doors*

142

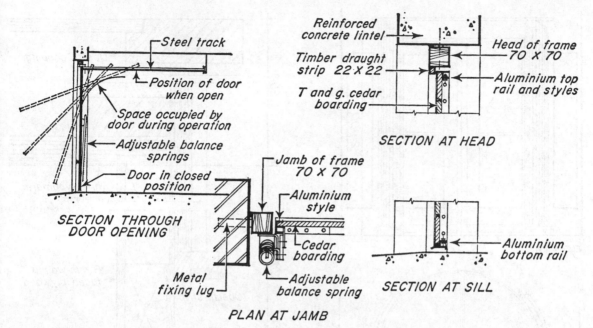

5.46 *Overhead door*

corners of the door run along the steel track at high level, the action of the door being balanced by special springs positioned as shown.

5.19 Revolving doors

Since this type of door requires special fittings and mechanism it is manufactured by specialist firms. The designer has freedom in the design of the leaves of the door and the curved casing. There are various patent methods of collapsing these doors so that a direct through access is possible when desired. The leaves should always be made to collapse in an outward direction in an emergency, and the door should be glazed, using safety glass. For a four compartment door an overall diameter of 1.800 m to 2.100 m is usual. Where luggage has to pass through the doors as in hotel entrances the large diameter is essential. A four compartment door with associated joinery work is shown in figure 5.47. Where space is limited a three compartment revolving door can be used and in this case the diameter can be reduced to 1.500 m. It is good practice to place an auxiliary swing door in close proximity to the revolving

door and where the revolving doors are used in association with steps at an entrance the first riser should be at least 1.000 m away from the sweep of the doors.

5.20 Patio doors

Increasing use of the garden as additional living space has brought about the need for a well designed and draught-proof sliding door for domestic use. Figure 5.48 gives an example of a reversible sliding door of aluminium construction produced to manufacturers' standard sizes for economy.

The illustration shows a combination of fixed light and sliding door in anodized extruded aluminium section. The doors are 'reversible' when fixing for either right or left hand opening, and are factory glazed with a sealed double glass unit set in vinyl glazing channel. The sliding portion rolls on nylon ball bearing rollers and the door is weather stripped with silicone treated woven wool pile. The fixed panel is sealed with a vinyl membrane, and the aluminium frames are bedded and

Continued on page 145

143

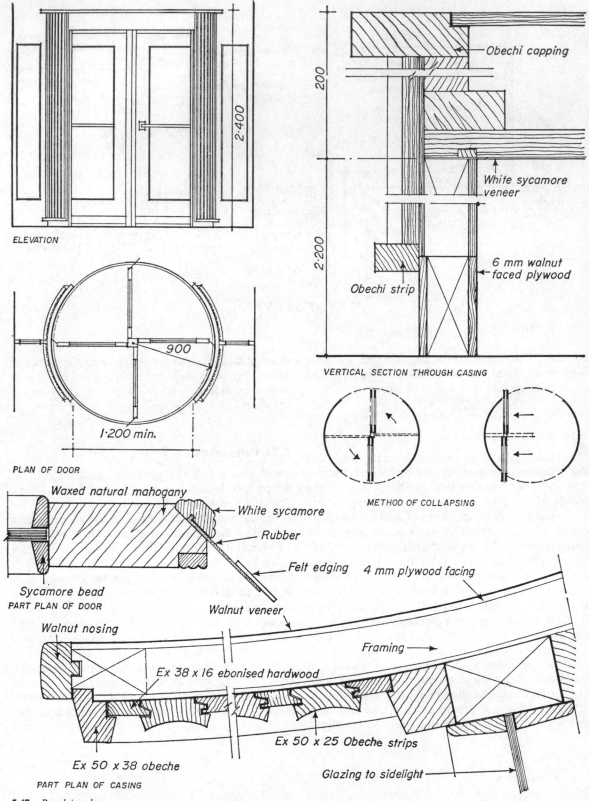

ELEVATION

2·400

200

2·200

Obechi capping

White sycamore veneer

6 mm walnut faced plywood

Obechi strip

VERTICAL SECTION THROUGH CASING

900

1·200 min.

PLAN OF DOOR

METHOD OF COLLAPSING

Waxed natural mahogany

White sycamore

Rubber

Felt edging

Sycamore bead

PART PLAN OF DOOR

Walnut veneer

4 mm plywood facing

Walnut nosing

Framing

Ex 38 x 16 ebonised hardwood

Ex 50 x 25 Obeche strips

Ex 50 x 38 obeche

PART PLAN OF CASING

Glazing to sidelight

5.47 *Revolving door*

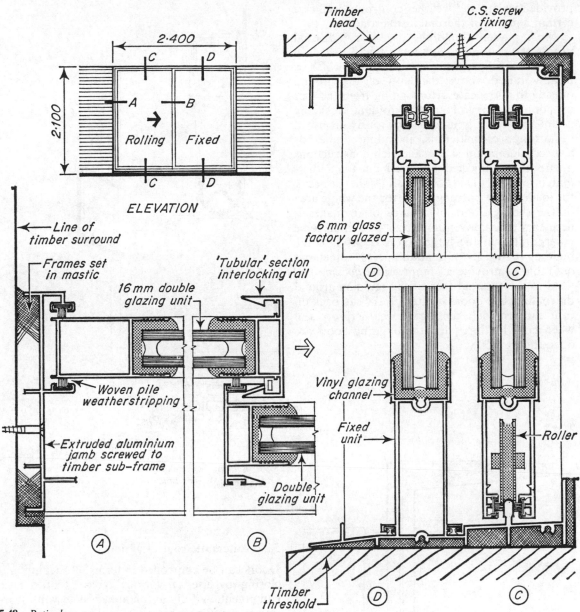

5.48 *Patio door*

sealed into timber subframes by a suitable gun applied mastic.

Security is always an important consideration, in particular with a door which slides to open, and this particular example has an adjustable plate which prevents the door being lifted out, in addition to cylinder lock and pull handle.

5.21 Loading bay doors

Loading bay doors are generally required to provide access for loading or unloading to or from a carrier (lorry), into or out of a building. These doors need to be easily operable from both inside and outside of the building, but must also

145

provide security and weather control as well as a certain amount of thermal insulation.

Most modern buildings used for industrial processes or storage have the outside wall flush with the face of a *loading platform*, which is usually raised above the level of the ground outside to allow ease of unloading from the rear or side of a lorry. Top hung folding or sliding doors are generally used as previously described in a range of materials, including timber or pressed aluminium sheet sandwich constructions incorporating injected polyurethane foam thermal insulation (U = 0.3 W/m²K). The necessity for loading bay openings to cover the whole area of the sliding doors of a lorry often makes it necessary for a conventional size 'pass door' to be incorporated in the large access doors into the building (figure 5.49). In addition, it is sometimes desirable to provide a compressible *docking pad* fixed to the external face of the building around the loading bay doors so that a lorry can back on to it and provide a temporary weatherproof seal when both the lorry and the building doors are open (figure 5.50).

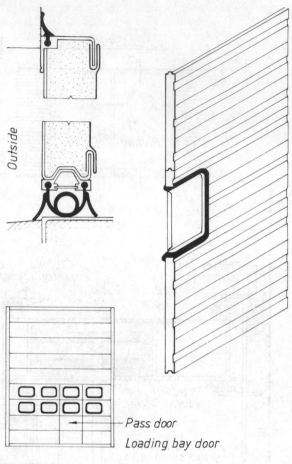

5.50 *Loading bay docking pad (R.S. Stokvis & Sons Ltd)*

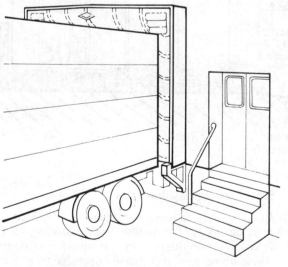

5.49 *Loading bay door*

5.22 Automatic control of doors

Doors can be controlled in terms of opening and closing by use of various types of automatic equipment. A fully automated system will incorporate a device which acts as the initial sensing control such as a push-button, a sensitized mat or a photoelectric beam. This initial sensor will be followed by a timing device connected to the motorization apparatus which causes the doors to move. Alternatively the motorization can be operated by remote control from a central point such as a security cabin. The timing apparatus can vary from a simple cut-out to complex electronic control with programmed instructions to incorporate variable time delays for closing and opening doors in series as circumstances or security requires. It is essential that all automatic control devices allow the doors to be moved by hand in the event of a power failure. The motor gear usually takes its initial power from electricity which is then used to generate hydraulic or pneumatic pressure to cause the doors to move as signalled. The equipment should be capable of incorporating a checking action which slows the doors down towards closing in order to avoid clashing and rebound. A further refinement should be a repeat cycle of opening and closing should the door meet any obstruction.

Specialist advice should be sought on this type of gear since automation techniques are rapidly developing, and more sophisticated control is possible.

Automatic control may be required in hospitals, hotels, shops, offices or security buildings, and both swing doors and sliding doors can be controlled. Briefly, for the swing door the control will be as follows, a master control with time delay for setting the time that the door is held open, and a regulating resistance for setting the speed of movement for the sliding doors. The leaves may be driven electromechanically by a driving wheel attached to a moving rail at the top of each leaf. The rail regulates the width of opening, brakes the door before the end of its movement, and makes electrical disconnection at the end of the movement. The maximum speed of opening for a sliding door will be in the region of 1 m per second.

6 Windows

6.1 Introduction

A window is an opening designed primarily to let light and/or air into a building. It will also provide a view of what is outside, or inside if this is part of the design requirements. A window opening will normally be fitted with glass or similar transparent material – usually in a frame – to keep out the weather. The following list gives, in broad outline, the main points to be considered in connection with window design:

- Choosing the correct positions of the opening with due regard to both aesthetic and functional needs.
- Choosing the correct materials and proportions for the frame, so that it fulfils satisfactorily both technical and aesthetic requirements.
- Complies with the requirements of the *Building Regulations 1985* with regard to thermal insulation and fire protection of the external wall in which it is located; and, if opening, supplies the required amount of ventilation (to habitable room, kitchen, bathroom, common space or sanitary accommodation).
- Choosing correctly the weight and type of glass for the infill.
- Arranging the right part of the window to open, both in respect of proportion of opening and position and type of sash in order to admit any desired amount of fresh air for adequate ventilation.
- Determining whether or not the window opening when glazed will have any special requirements in respect of sound or heat insulation.
- Making sure that the method of manufacture and jointing will satisfactorily withstand the elements for an agreed period of time.
- Ensuring that the junction between the fixed and moving parts of the frame, and the junction between the outer frame and the window opening will remain weathertight throughout their expected life (which should be defined).

- Ensuring that the completed product will fulfil all the current applicable statutory regulations and requirements.
- Doing all this within an agreed cost limit.

It will be seen that a large number of technical and aesthetic decisions must be correctly taken to produce a satisfactory component and that windows are a most important building element in respect of giving architectural character to a façade, and controlling the comfort conditions in the room which they light and ventilate. The more important design points are summarized in the following paragraphs.

6.2 Performance requirements

(a) Appearance

The pattern of windows on the façade is known as the *fenestration*, and this is a very important element in the design of a building being second only in architectural importance to the overall form or mass of the building. Important factors in the fenestration pattern are the subdivision of the window, the proportion of the panes and the recessing or the projection of the window opening. It is important to remember that the lines of sight from windows which afford a good prospect or view should be unobstructed. There should also be clear lines of sight from standing or sitting positions unobstructed by transoms or mullions.

(b) Lighting

The matter of lighting, both natural daylight and artificial lighting, is part of the fundamental design procedure for a building. Work should be carried out in greater detail at each stage of the design so that the lighting effect of each window has been fully considered before production drawings are made.

The window must light a room efficiently by

Limit of daylight penetration useful
in the performance of tasks

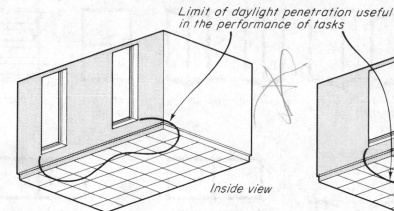

Inside view

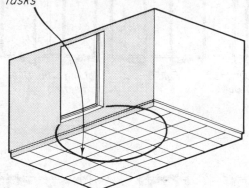

A

Tall narrow windows generally give better daylight
penetration to rear of room although uneven patterns
will result when windows are widely spaced

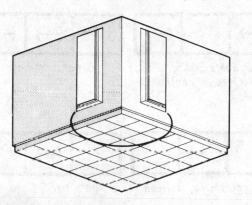

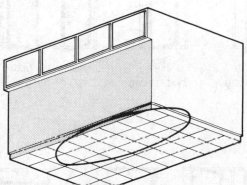

C

High level windows generally result in glare
and poor illumination of window wall

B

Windows in adjoining walls of square rooms
generally provide good daylight penetration
although this depends on their closeness
and comparative widths

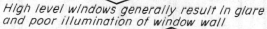

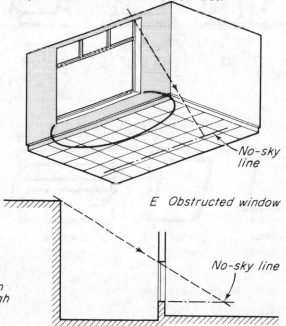

No-sky
line

E Obstructed window

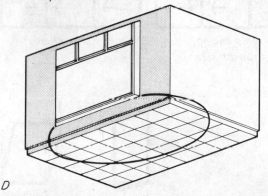

No-sky line

D

Unobstructed window: daylight penetration in room
will be influenced by external obstruction although
overall results will be modified by shape of
obstruction and reflectance of room surfaces

6.1 *Effects of window shape and position on penetration and distribution of daylight. From: Window: Performance, Design &*
Installation by Beckett and Godfrey CLS/RIBA 1974

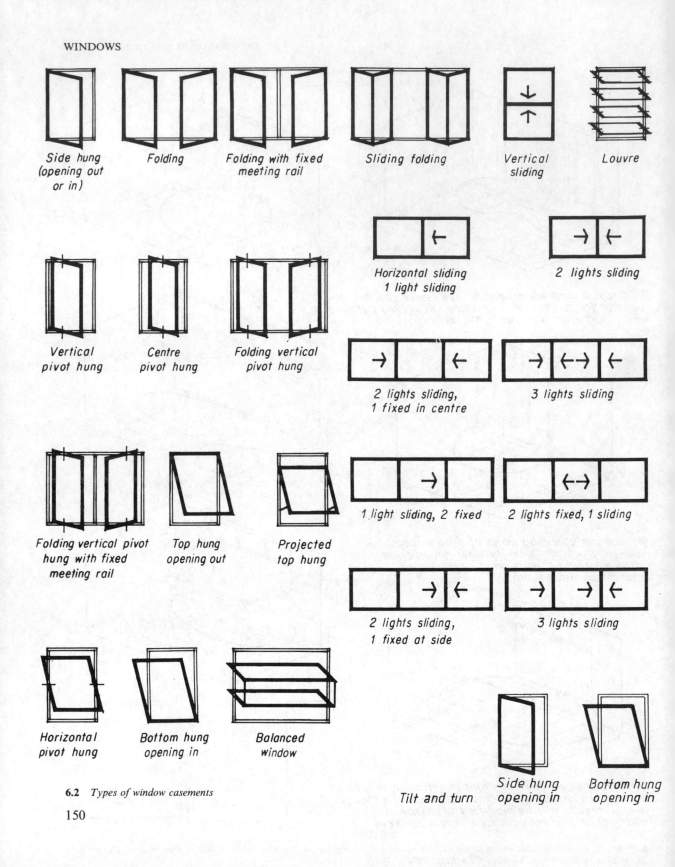

Side hung (opening out or in)

Folding

Folding with fixed meeting rail

Sliding folding

Vertical sliding

Louvre

Vertical pivot hung

Centre pivot hung

Folding vertical pivot hung

Horizontal sliding 1 light sliding

2 lights sliding

2 lights sliding, 1 fixed in centre

3 lights sliding

Folding vertical pivot hung with fixed meeting rail

Top hung opening out

Projected top hung

1 light sliding, 2 fixed

2 lights fixed, 1 sliding

2 lights sliding, 1 fixed at side

3 lights sliding

Horizontal pivot hung

Bottom hung opening in

Balanced window

Tilt and turn

Side hung opening in

Bottom hung opening in

6.2   *Types of window casements*

providing the right amount of daylight in the right place with due regard to the use of the room. Where illumination of the room is a critical factor, the amount of light falling on the working surface at any point should be calculated. Calculation of illumination levels in respect of daylight is a complex matter and students are referred to *MBS: Environment and Services* chapter 4 *Daylighting*.

It is however, not only a matter of providing the right area of window, but the shape and position also affect the distribution of light in the room, together with the amount of obstruction caused by the mullions and transoms. See figure 6.1, page 149.

The contrast between the light area of the window and the dark area of the wall in shadow, in which the window is placed, is an important factor. Too sharp a contrast creates glare. A good illustration of these points, which may be helpful, is to consider the traditional Georgian arrangement of tall windows with wide-splayed internal reveals painted a light colour, which reflect the light well and lessen the contrast between the window and wall. The windows, if they go down to the floor, distribute light over a large area of floor, which again gives valuable reflection into the room. Similarly, when they are carried up to near the ceiling, the same effect is produced at high level. Rather than concentrating the window area into one wide opening, a number of openings are used, spaced out so as to avoid areas of deep shade in the corners of the room. Glazing bars of narrow section are also splayed, so that the inclined surfaces are lighted and only a thin edge is in complete shade and dark. The good illumination given by these windows, without an excessive window area, should be noted.

(c) Ventilation

Window openings should be arranged to give an amount of ventilation most suited to the use of the room or space served by the window. This may require a large amount of opening, to give a very rapid change of air or alternatively a small opening which gives a regulated and controlled slow change of air. The question of air movement is considered in more detail in *MBS: E and S* chapter 3. It may be desirable to provide one or more types of ventilation in the same window.

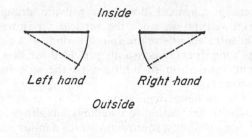

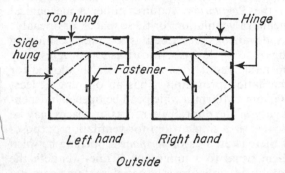

6.3 *Handing of casements*

Figure 6.2 shows the alternative ways of providing opening lights, or casements in a window.

In *handing* a side hung casement window the following convention is followed:
The opening casement is right or left hand according to the side on which the casement occurs looking from the *outside*. The casement is always hinged on the outside of the frame. Most working drawings show a view of the casement as seen from the outside as shown in figure 6.3. Note that the apex of the triangle showing the convention for opening always indicates the hinged side of the opening light.

In terms of ventilation the vertical sliding sash window is efficient. The opening which is variable according to the position of the sash gives ventilation at high level by letting out the used air and is normally protected by an arch or lintel at this point. The sash can also be opened at the bottom for letting in fresh air, the opening being up to half the total area of the window. The opening is easy to operate provided that the window is well made and well balanced. Bottom hung, *opening in* and top hung, *opening out* windows are also an efficient means of ventilation. The side hung opening casement does not provide draught-proof ventilation since the vertical slit causes a concentrated air stream. In most windows a small top hung opening is usually provided for slow or night ventilation in addition to the side hung casements.

The Building Regulations 1985 are concerned only with ventilation to dwellings; buildings containing dwellings; rooms containing sanitary conveniences; and bathrooms. *Approved Document F* of the *Regulations* requires either a mechanical means of ventilation for these spaces, or openable windows of prescribed size and positioning (figure 6.4), louvres, airbricks or progressively openable ventilators. A door is also allowed for ventilation providing it has an opening at least 100 mm × 100 mm which can be opened independently of the door. Two rooms or spaces may be treated as a single room for ventilation purposes if there is an area of *permanent* opening between them equal to a minimum of one-twentieth the combined floor areas. Special requirements are stipulated when a ventilating window opens on to a courtyard. Alternative approaches to the provision of natural ventilation to those given in the Regulations are provided in BS 5925: 1980 *Code of practice for design of buildings: ventilation principles and designing for natural ventilation*; and of

Room or space	Ventilation to be provided

Dwellings
  habitable rooms,
  kitchens and bathrooms
	1 At least one ventilation opening with an area at least 1/20th of the floor area of the room or space
	2 Some part of the ventilation opening to be at least 1.75 m above floor level

Buildings containing dwellings *common spaces*	1 At least one ventilation opening with an area of at least 1/20th of the floor area of the space

Any building
  sanitary
  accommodation
	1 At least one ventilation opening with an area of at least 1/20th of the floor area of the room or space

6.4 *Natural ventilation provided by openable window* (Building Regulations 1985 Approved Document F Table 1)

mechanical ventilation in BS 5720: 1979 *Code of practice for mechanical ventilation and air conditioning in buildings*.

Apart from empirical data quoted in the *Building Regulations 1985* it is not easy to say in precise terms how much opening should be provided to give a certain ventilation rate because this is dependent on wind pressure and *stack effect*. Stack effect occurs mainly in winter, when warm air escapes from the upper part of the room and is replaced by cold, and therefore heavier air from outside.

(d) Weather resistance

An important function of an external wall is its ability to provide weather resistance in order to maintain the intended thermal control and durability during its life. Openings in the wall, such as those provided by windows, need special consideration in this respect as they result in the juxtapositioning of different materials and a corresponding change in the way performance requirements are to be fulfilled. Wind and rain penetration often occurs at these openings as a result of poor detailing or inadequate installation of the window. Careful analysis of construction methods which achieves a reasonable degree of weather resistance, an example of which is given in figure 6.5, will indicate that the window itself – including its cross-sectional profiles – plays an important part in achieving protection to the inside of a building.

Standard tests for assessing the weather resistance performance of windows are laid down in:
BS 5368 *Methods of testing windows*
        Part 1: 1976 *Air permeability test*
        Part 2: 1980 *Watertightness test under static pressure*
        Part 3: 1978 *Wind resistance tests*
        Part 4: 1978 *Form of test report*
BS 6375 Performance of windows
Part 1: 1983 *Classification for weathertightness*
Part 2: 1987 *Specification for operation and strength characteristics*

BS 6375 lays down the criteria against which the results obtained from BS 5368 are classified, and includes methods to facilitate the selection and specification of windows in terms of exposure categories based on design wind pressures. The test apparatus comprises a chamber with an open-

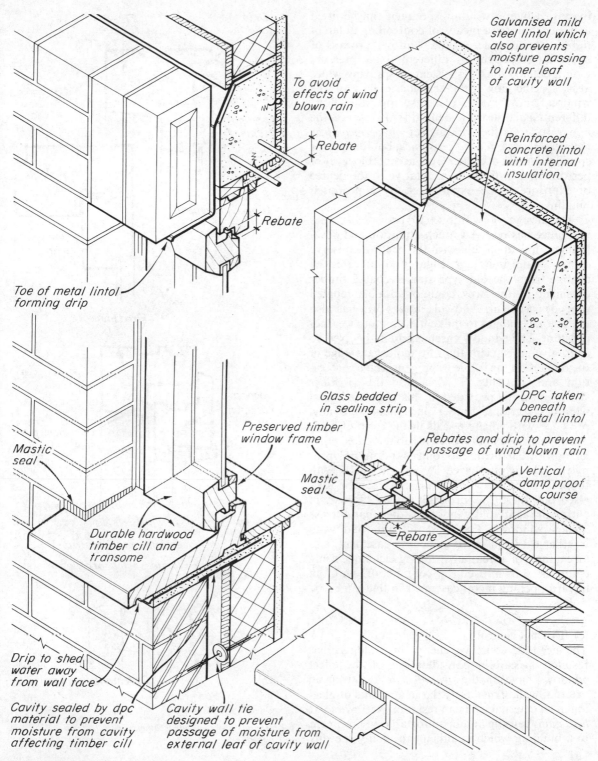

To avoid effects of wind blown rain

Rebate

Rebate

Galvanised mild steel lintol which also prevents moisture passing to inner leaf of cavity wall

Reinforced concrete lintol with internal insulation

Toe of metal lintol forming drip

DPC taken beneath metal lintol

Glass bedded in sealing strip

Preserved timber window frame

Rebates and drip to prevent passage of wind blown rain

Mastic seal

Mastic seal

Vertical damp proof course

Rebate

Durable hardwood timber cill and transome

Drip to shed water away from wall face

Cavity sealed by dpc material to prevent moisture from cavity affecting timber cill

Cavity wall tie designed to prevent passage of moisture from external leaf of cavity wall

6.5 *Construction method used to resist water and wind penetration through a window opening in a brick/block cavity wall*

ing into which a window specimen can be fitted and incorporates a means of controlling differential air pressures across the window, a means of controlling changes of differential air pressure within defined limits, a system of spraying water at a specific flow rate across the face of the window, and a means of measuring water flow, differential pressure and deflection. In essence, the apparatus tests the window for *air permeability*, *watertightness* and *wind resistance*, but it is left for specifiers to choose their own acceptable level of performance in these areas relative to the degree of exposure to be experienced by a proposed building.

The design of windows to provide weather resistance has received much attention and development linked closely with the need to conserve energy within buildings. Figure 6.6 indicates the change from the old type single rebated timber casement to the now common double rebated (lipped) casement. And this latter form has also undergone changes to make it even more weather resistant. The window casement must be fixed so as to give an efficient tight fit against the edge of the rebates on the frame to prevent water penetration and draughts. To facilitate this, *weather stripping* can be provided at this point and most windows sections, timber and metal, are now provided with effective seals in the form of compressible strips of chloroprene rubber, cured ethylene propylene diene monomer (epdm), polypropylene pile or plasticized PVC (figure 6.7). With timber, spring strips of metal alloy can be used also, but these are probably most effective in curing draughty old windows rather than for use in new windows. The most difficult window to weatherseal is an inward opening casement, and an example of a weather stripping technique using epdm is shown used in conjunction with an inward opening metal casement in figure 6.8.

(e) Thermal control

The need to conserve energy in buildings has resulted in careful consideration of the effect windows have on the *overall heat loss* from an external wall. Conversely, large amounts of glazing in an external wall can result in excessive solar *heat gains* causing an uncomfortable environment in a building which is difficult to rectify speedily

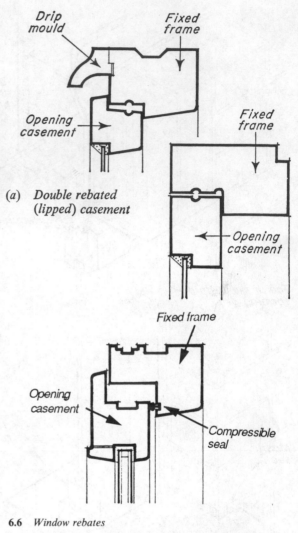

(a) **Double rebated (lipped) casement**

6.6 *Window rebates*

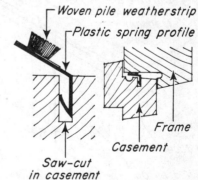

6.7 *Details of woven pile weatherstrip to casements*

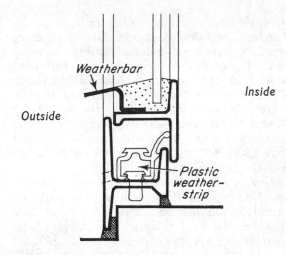

6.8 *Detail of inward opening casement at sill*

Purpose Group	Window(s) area as % of exposed wall	Roof light(s) area as % of roof
RESIDENTIAL GROUP Dwelling house	windows and roof lights together 12% of perimeter wall area	
Other residential	25%	20%
NON-RESIDENTIAL GROUP Places of assembly, offices and shops*	35%	20%
Industrial and storage	15%	20%

Areas which are double glazed may have up to TWICE the single glazed area.
Areas which are double glazed, with a low emissivity coating, or triple glazed, may have up to THREE TIMES the permitted single glazed area.

*Percentages shown not applicable to display windows in shops

6.9 *Maximum single glazed areas relative to Purpose Groups of Buildings when following* Procedures 1 and 2 of The Building Regulations 1985: Approved Document B, Section A. *For definition of Purpose Groups see page 289*

by opening windows or even the most sophisticated of artificial ventilation methods.

The *Building Regulations 1985: Approved Document L: Conservation of fuel and power* has four independent procedures of increasing complexity for meeting the thermal control requirements in dwellings (*L2*) and in buildings other than dwellings (*L3*); ie those having a floor area greater than 30 sq m which are residential buildings (hotels, etc), shops, offices, or used for recreational, educational, business, industrial or storage purposes.

Procedure 1 specifies thermal insulation material and construction thicknesses for external elements, whereas *Procedure 2* requires certain U-values to be met (0.6 W/m²K for exposed walls and floors in building types covered, except 0.7 for those used for industrial or storage purposes; and 0.6 for roofs, except 0.35 for dwellings and 0.7 in those buildings used for industrial or storage purposes). For both *Procedures*, maximum areas of single glazed windows and roof lights are specified and these are indicated in figure 6.9. Areas which are double glazed may have up to twice the single glazed area; those which are triple glazed, or are double glazed and incorporate a low emissivity coating, may have up to three times the permitted single glazed area. When calculating these percentages it may be necessary to include the surface area occupied by lintels, jambs

and sills as these often fall below the thermal insulation standards of the body of the wall. Furthermore, an external door with 2 sq m or more of glazed area should be counted as part of the percentage allowed for windows and roof lights. The U-values required for construction are obtainable from the *CIBSE* (Chartered Institute of Building Services Engineers) *Guide Section A3: 1981: Thermal properties of building structures.*

Procedure 3 and *Procedure 4* involve calculation methods for designing the exposed-building fabric without limiting the areas of windows and roof lights to maximum percentages. In calculating the rate of heat loss that would occur, the U-value of windows and roof lights is taken as 5.7 W/m²K if single glazed, 2.8 for double glazing, and 2.0 for triple glazing or for double glazing incorporating a low emissivity coating.

Procedure 3 allows 'trade off' between windows and roof lights and, independently, between exposed walls, roofs and floors. In the case of dwellings where the thermal insulation is better than the minimum allowed in the *Regulations*, larger glazed areas are permitted although no account is taken of heat gains. *Procedure 4* (not to

155

be used for dwellings) also allows 'trade-off' between glazed and solid areas, but account can be taken of useful heat gains as well, including solar gains and those resulting from artificial light, industrial processes, etc. Acceptance of this method of calculation relies on proof that sufficient heating controls can be provided in respect of the contribution of useful heat gains.

Condensation is a problem most obviously associated with windows and is a complex problem requiring a balance of ventilation, temperature, humidity and appropriate construction. Even frames with an excellent thermal performance, for example uPVC or timber frames glazed with sealed units, may still suffer from condensation. It is recommended that condensation channels should be provided in the window sections used in those areas of buildings where condensation commonly occurs, such as bathrooms, shower and washing rooms, kitchen, utility and laundry rooms. Indeed, where condensation cannot be controlled it may be wiser to use single glazing and to collect the condensation in drainage channels before directing it to the outside. Where the design of a building incorporates an energy management policy, such as could occur for offices, consideration can be given to the use of a sealed glazing system based on a low-emissivity gas-filled double glazing unit which reduces the 'U-value' to zero and virtually eliminates the risk of condensation.

Further information about thermal control and window design is given in 7.2(c) Thermal control (*Glazing*).

(f) Fire precautions

Another limitation set upon the size and amount of windows which can be placed in an external wall is that dictated by the need to ensure that fire will not readily spread from one building to another. In the *Building Regulations 1985*, both door and window openings (as well as other non-fire resisting components) are classified as **unprotected areas** when situated in an external wall because a fire *within* the building in which they are located could be spread rapidly through them to an adjoining property. Therefore, the permitted amount of 'unprotected areas' is again stipulated as a percentage of the remaining fire resisting part of an external wall construction. The precise

amount is determined by its distance from the site boundary, or a 'notional boundary' (imaginary boundary between buildings sharing common land). Generally, no windows are permitted within 1.0 m of a boundary unless less than 1 sq m in area, but an increasing percentage of window to fire resisting external wall (starting at 20%) is allowed the further a building is away from its site boundary. Further information can be obtained from BS 5588 Parts 1–5 *Fire precautions in the design and construction of buildings*.

Approved Document B of the *Building Regulations 1985* provides three methods for calculating permitted 'unprotected areas' and 5.2(e) Fire resistance and 5.8 Fire doors provide additional information about fire control in buildings.

(g) Sound control

A window may have to fulfil particular sound resistance requirements and these generally relate to aspects of glazing as indicated on page 221. See also comments on sound resistant doors, chapter 5 page 124. Aspects of window design which can help to reduce transference of noise include:

- elimination of air gaps at edges of opening lights by the use of draught excluders;
- using thicker glass – doubling glass thickness can provide an additional 4 dB sound reduction;
- providing double or multiple glazing in isolated frames – minimum gap of 100 mm between glass, and jambs lined with sound absorbent material;
- ensuring glass panels of sealed double glazed units (normally only 6 mm gap) are of different thickness to avoid sympathetic resonance between panels;
- specifying sealed glazed units with gap(s) filled with heavy inert gas;
- providing laminated glass since plastic interlayer will give a reduction of sound at different frequencies to glass

CP 153: *Windows and roof lights* Part 3: 1972 *sound insulation* deals with sound transmission through windows, roof lights and glazed curtain walling. It is an extension of the more basic information on the subject given in CP 3: chapter III and provides guidance on likely external noise levels and degrees of sound transmission afforded by various forms of glazing (see chapter 7 *Glazing*).

(h) Durability and maintenance

The durability of a window depends largely on the characteristics of the different materials used for manufacture, how they are prepared for the rigours encountered during their life, the construction techniques used for installation in a building, and subsequent maintenance.

CP 153: *Windows and roof lights* Part 2: 1970 *Durability and maintenance* deals with the durability and maintenance of wood and metal windows, including protection on site, pre-conditioning, type of glues, selection of species and preservative treatment for wood windows, environmental suitability, frequency of washing and other notes on the behaviour of individual metals.

Factors relating to the **durability of windows** arising from use of specific materials are covered later under each type of window.

The **maintenance of windows** can only be carried out with ease when consideration has been given during their initial design stage to all factors involved. Cleaning is a very important consideration requiring careful thought at the design stage of the window as every effort should be made to ensure building owners or maintenance personnel can carry out window cleaning in safety. For example, above the third storey of a building (and also where access for ladders is not convenient), windows should be designed so that they can be cleaned and reglazed from inside the building. Alternatively, balconies and special devices need to be incorporated. When windows are to be cleaned from inside the building, the choice of an inward opening type of window may be suitable. For the pivoted type window illustrated in figure 6.10, the design of the hinge allows the window to turn through 180 before locking in a reversed position. However, consideration must be then given to the effect of this swing on the design of the interior spaces of the building, not of least importance is the positioning of curtains. When not wanting to use this form of window, the designer must consider alternative arrangement for cleaning. By making the size and proportion of accessible glazing suitable to human reach (figure 6.11) and through the use of special hinges

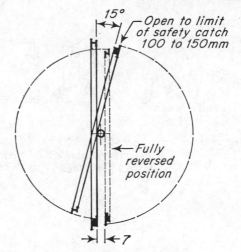

6.10 *Reversible window-space requirements*

(figure 6.12), cleaning can still be done without the aid of an external ladder.

The cleaning of windows in tall buildings can be solved by the incorporation of one of several items of specialist equipment, including cantilevered gantries, specially profiled curtain wall mullions to allow safety clips to be inserted for external cradles, or strategically positioned sparge pipes to allow water to be sprayed on the façade thereby eliminating the need for human access altogether. The appearance of the building will be influenced by such devices and it is important that the designer and the future window cleaning contractor work together during early design stages – see *MBS: Introduction to Building*, 15.8 *Maintenance Team*.

CP 153: *Windows and roof lights* Part 1: 1969 *Cleaning and safety* deals with cleaning of glazing relative to problems of safety. See also 7.2(h) Durability and maintenance.

6.3 Timber windows

Timber lends itself to the manufacture of profiled sections for purpose-made and mass-produced windows, but factors such as movement with variations in moisture content and the tendency to rot must be taken into consideration – see previous sections *Durability* and *MBS: Materials* chapter 2. Most of these problems arise from the inherent characteristic of timber and can now be

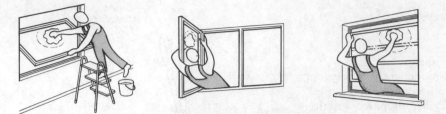

Dangerous practices in cleaning the outside of windows from inside building

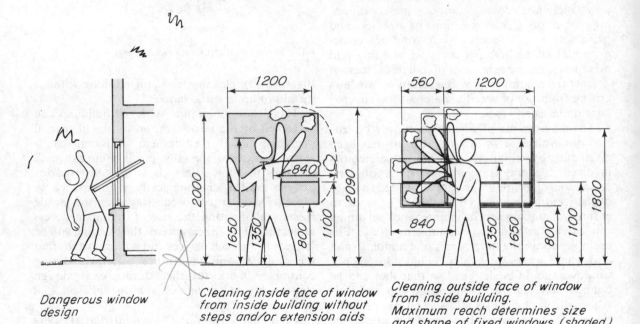

Dangerous window design

Cleaning inside face of window from inside building without steps and/or extension aids

Cleaning outside face of window from inside building.
Maximum reach determines size and shape of fixed windows (shaded)

6.11 *Design factors influencing safety of window design*

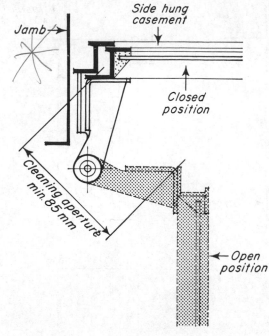

6.12 *Extending (easy-clean) hinge.
Space requirements*

adequately resolved through careful design of the sections themselves to eliminate danger zones, and then by pressure impregnation of the sections with anti-decay preservatives. Therefore, timber window sections are capable of providing a relatively cheap solution to window design which, when carefully installed in a building to ensure their continued protection from the hazards of moisture, provide satisfactory results for 50 to 60 years using readily available maintenance skills.

(a) Standard and high performance
Until recently the quality, design and construction of standard timber window sections was covered by BS 644: Part 1: 1951: *Wood casement windows.* However, the research and developments by manufacturers and other interested bodies has resulted in the production of windows with sections giving better performance than recommended in this BS and it has now been withdrawn pending a new universal standard.

The standardization of window sections contained in the BS 644 were based on the work undertaken by the English Joinery Manufacturers Association (*EJMA*) some 50 years ago when

timber was scarce. During 1976, amalgamation occurred between the British Woodwork Manufacturers Association and the Joinery and Timber Construction Association, and the British Woodworking Federation was formed. Since then, the BWF worked to improved *EJMA* sections in a number of ways, starting with the need to meet higher performance standards to embrace problems of wind and water penetration. Also, the *EJMA* sections were not by then as cheap to manufacture because of imperial/metric dimensional conversion discrepancies. Furthermore, although timber is not as scarce today, it must be used efficiently in terms of both the material and the labour required for its conversion from tree to window section. Owing to the high costs involved in this process, the finished window must provide a low cost-in-use ratio in competition with other materials, such as metals and plastics. Examples of a typical standard timber windows and the name of the various parts of the frame are shown in figure 4.38 page 87.

Figure 6.13 illustrates a typical window manufactured to BS 644 sections, and figure 6.14 provides a comparison with a typical higher performance window of today. In the BS window, both opening and fixed windows are rebated so that a double draught and weather check is provided. The twin *capillary groove* between head and casement prevent water gaining access by capillary attraction and the groove and chamfer between the bottom rail of the casement and the sill is designed to prevent driving rain being blown under the casement to the interior. For similar reasons, the half round anti-capillary grooves are also provided on the edges of opening members and the reveals of the frames These link with those in the top rail of the casement and allow water to be collected and run down and out on to the projecting sill.

The sill is *throated* to catch the water running down the face and blown under the sill, and to allow it to drip clear of the face of the wall. The sill is also *weathered*, that is to say, the sloping surface is angled away from the building to take away the water which runs down the face of the glass. The opening casement is also protected by means of a *weather mould* which projects over the opening. The casement itself must be fixed so as to give an efficient tight fit against the edge of the

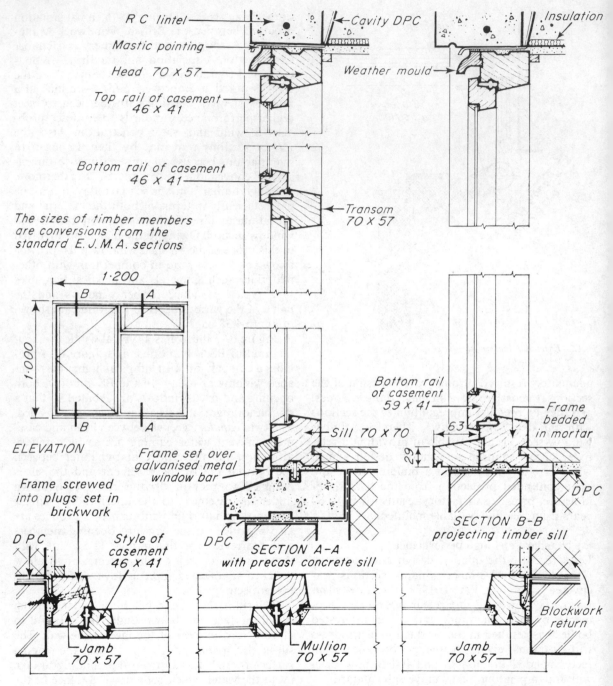

R C lintel

Mastic pointing

Head 70 x 57

Top rail of casement
46 x 41

Cavity DPC

Insulation

Weather mould

Bottom rail of casement
46 x 41

Transom
70 x 57

The sizes of timber members
are conversions from the
standard E.J.M.A. sections

1·200

B   A

1·000

B   A

ELEVATION

Frame set over
galvanised metal
window bar

Sill 70 x 70

Bottom rail
of casement
59 x 41

Frame
bedded
in mortar

63

29

DPC

SECTION A-A
with precast concrete sill

DPC

SECTION B-B
projecting timber sill

Frame screwed
into plugs set in
brickwork

DPC

Style of
casement
46 x 41

Jamb
70 x 57

Mullion
70 x 57

Jamb
70 x 57

Blockwork
return

PLAN

6.13 *Standard casement windows (EJMA section)*

160

rebates on the frame. However, after much use, gaps up to 3 mm may appear. Although providing some degree of protection against wind and water penetration from the outside, the *EJMA* sections used do not permit effective weatherstripping; nor will they readily accept double glazing to improve thermal performance.

Consideration of the high performance timber window sections currently recommended by the British Woodworking Federation and some manufacturers' details show the careful thought required to produce a window that successfully resists air and water penetration (figure 6.6).

Major features include the larger grooves to permit the collection of water penetrating from the outside and the measures taken to ensure that it is channelled back without progressing to interior surfaces. The provision of compressible type weather seals on the face of the head frame, jambs and sill against which the casements close provided not only a physical barrier against the possibility of penetrating water but also an air seal as well. The effect of this air seal is to create a *negative pressure* within the (larger) grooved parts of the frames which further helps to force the water back to the outside. An alternative form of frame section, based on the former BS section, to achieve this same purpose is shown in figure 6.7. Weatherstripping is often fitted within a groove around the rebate of the frame and is always jointed at the corners. It must be compatible

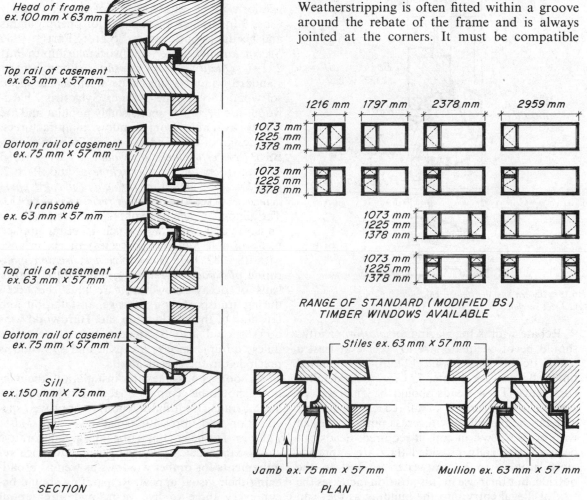

Head of frame
ex. 100 mm × 63 mm

Top rail of casement
ex. 63 mm × 57 mm

Bottom rail of casement
ex. 75 mm × 57 mm

Transome
ex. 63 mm × 57 mm

Top rail of casement
ex. 63 mm × 57 mm

Bottom rail of casement
ex. 75 mm × 57 mm

Sill
ex. 150 mm × 75 mm

SECTION

RANGE OF STANDARD (MODIFIED BS)
TIMBER WINDOWS AVAILABLE

Stiles ex. 63 mm × 57 mm

Jamb ex. 75 mm × 57 mm   Mullion ex. 63 mm × 57 mm

PLAN

6.14   *Modified BS windows for double glazing*

with all types of finishes to the window frame, including preservatives, stains and paints, and be easily wiped clean. Figure 6.15 shows an inward opening timber framed window using modified BS sections.

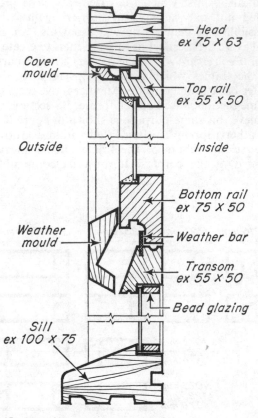

6.15 *Inward opening timber window (EJMA sections)*

Rebate widths for glazing, or *platform* widths should be of adequate size to receive at least a sealed double glazed unit (12 mm) plus internal timber beads – see chapter 7 : *Glazing* for detailed comments. These beads should be of preserved durable wood, scribed or mitred at the corners and can be pinned in with brass pins or screwed with brass screws, in cups if required. Beads can be used externally provided they are appropriately profiled to ensure water is shed to the outside, but their use in this position increases the risk of illegal entry into the building as they can be reasonably easily and quietly removed! In either position, the beads must be bedded in putty or sealing tape, and the glazing itself should have 'back and front' bedding of similar materials to allow for even support and adequate seal. Putty can be used externally and is cheaper than beads, but the area and thickness of glazing will limit its use to smaller sized windows. When used, the glazing is usually put in with putty formed to a triangular bead with a putty knife.

In Scandinavia it is common practice to finish and glaze timber windows in the factory and deliver them to site fully packaged for installation, and this approach is gradually being accepted by UK manufacturers.

Major manufacturers offer high performance windows using suitable types of timber (usually Class 3 for frames and Class 2 for opening lights and beads) as specified in BS 1186: Part 1: 1986 *Specification of timber*, and workmanship to Part 2: 1971 *Quality of workmanship*. Although most standard windows are made from a European softwood (Scots Pine – Pinus Sylvestris), hardwoods are becoming increasingly popular and are widely available from window manufacturers. The design of the windows normally accord with BS 6375: *Performance of windows*, Part 1: 1983 *Classification for weathertightness*, and Part 2: 1987 *Specification for operation and strength characteristics* – see also *Weather resistance* page 152. The almost universal use of *preservative treatment* on softwood windows (which is often applied using double vacuum processes) in accordance with BS 1282: 1975 *Guide to choice, use and application of wood preservatives*, has reduced problems of decay. However, care must be taken during transportation, storage, installation and finishing of the windows on site. Hardwood windows should also be treated with preservative unless durable species are used and sapwood is precluded in the specification.

As soon as possible after installation, the windows should be given an opaque finish (paint) or a semi-transparent finish (stain) to approved specification and application methods – see *MBS: Finishes*. The newer types of paints and decorative stains can considerably reduce maintenance requirements for timber windows as well as broadening their visual appeal. Re-painting should occur every three to five years, and after about twenty years it may be necessary to remove the thick layers and start again. Stain finishes normally require more frequent maintenance than good exterior quality paints, but the amount of maintenance can be reduced by careful preparation.

As an alternative to site finishing, timber windows can be supplied factory finished to a high standard, clad in a plastics or stainless steel covering, or faced with aluminium. These windows require special protection during their installation in prepared openings.

The lower members of windows are obviously subjected to more water than other parts because they are the final point of collection of rainwater before it is shed clear of the wall below. For this reason, the use of durable hardwoods is to be preferred for these timber sections. Figure 6.16 indicates devices recommended by the Norwegian BRE to limit water entering the bottom members of the window. These include:

- *bottom rebate* sloped 1:8 and protected, eg with PVC tape carried up the sides 40 mm at each end;
- *bottom bead* drainage notches in underside at least 6 mm square at 300 mm centres; generous drip to front edge; concealed surfaces protected, eg polyurethane varnish; upper surface sloped 1:6; ends cut square; aluminium bottom beads incorporating drips are often recommended instead of timber beads;
- *side beads* ends cut to leave gaps at least 6 mm above top of the bottom bead to prevent water entering the end grain.

Manufacturers of high performance windows have their product tested in accordance with the recommendations laid down in BS 5368 *Methods of testing windows* and meet the criteria laid down in BS 6367 *Performance of windows* (see *Weather resistance* page 152). Many manufacturers have also obtained British Board of Agrément test certificates and participate in the BSI Quality Assurance Scheme recommended in BS 5750 (see chapter 1 page 14).

A typical range of sizes for standard timber windows is as follows. Work sizes are 5 mm less than the co-ordinating sizes indicated. It is important to note that because of the flexibility of timber, manufactures are able to make purpose-

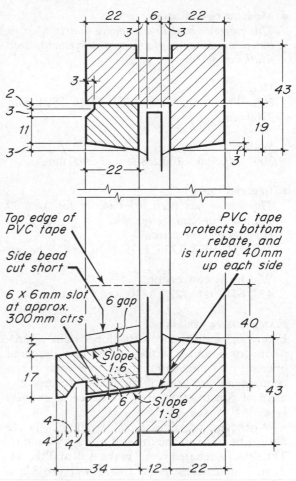

6.16 *Window with protected sill rebate*

made versions or special windows at little extra cost.

- **Metric dimensionally co-ordinated range**
  This is the most used range and encompasses the sizes suitable to most forms of construction, coupled with cost consciousness of a highly engineered mass-produced building component.

Heights in increments of 150 mm to enable alignment with brick courses of the outer skin of the building see figure 1.7 page 25:
450, 600, 750, 900, 1050, 1200, 1350, 1500, and 2100 mm

Widths based on multiples of standard sash sizes:
488, 631, 915, 1200, 1769, and 2338 mm

163

- **Modular co-ordinated range**
  This range is based on a simple matrix of sizes based on heights of 150 mm increments and widths of 300 mm.

  Heights:
  600, 900, 1050, 1200, 1350, 1500, 1800, and 2100 mm

  Widths:
  300, 600, 900, 1200, 1800, and 2400 mm

- **Imperial range**
  This range has been in existence for over 30 years and are still being made.
  Heights by conversion:
  768, 921, 1073, 1226, 1378, 1530, and 2394 mm

  Widths by conversion:
  438, 641, 921, 1226, 1810, and 2394 mm

Fixing timber windows

Figure 6.5 indicates construction details appropriate for a timber window fixed in a prepared opening of a conventional masonry wall. When components are fitted in an already formed element of construction, they are called *second fixings*.

Whenever possible, wood windows should always be fixed to the dry leaf of cavity walling. The use of a rebated reveal in the wall and the use of a flexible *damp proof course* will provide a suitable seal against the penetration of rainwater and moisture across the jamb to the interior. This dpc also serves as a water barrier between the wet and the dry leafs of the wall and should lap with the dpc over the lintel forming the opening, and with a dpc placed beneath the window sill to prevent detrimental effects from rising moisture. The sill must be *weathered* at a sufficient slope to throw off the water and *throated* with a groove near the front on its underside so that the water will drip off and not run back to the bed of the sill. Sills are usually pointed in mastic and, depending upon the form of wall construction, may have a water bar to locate the sill horizontally and act as an additional check against the penetration of moisture.

If timber windows are to be positioned as a masonry wall is being built, care must be taken to prevent their being damaged or any load being imposed on them during the 'building-in' process. Although this is not easy to ensure, this method of installation ensures a good fit for the window. Where the window is placed in position after the opening is formed there may be difficulties in ensuring correct tolerances or a good connection with the jamb dpc, but there is likely to be less damage to the frame. A suitable template can be used to assist the process, and it is recommended that a maximum manufacturing tolerance on the size of the actual frame to be installed should be 3 mm on all edges.

When the timber window is to be installed during the construction of the wall, it is easier to ensure a suitable seal between the wall and the frame. This is effectively accomplished by fixing a flexible dpc in a groove formed in the outside of the timber frames and then building the dpc into the wall – see figure 6.17. If the rebated jamb detail shown in figure 6.5 is not adopted for a window installed after the opening has been formed, the window must be carefully moved into the opening from the interior of the building so that the projecting dpc is collected by the groove in the side of the frame. Having accomplished this, the frame is fixed and a mastic seal applied to the outside, between the frame and the wall. The dpc beneath the sill can then be bent up behind the sill and the wall construction completed. In some cases, a sub-sill of tiles, stone, concrete, or metal on to which the timber window sill sits can be used. Again, the sub-sill must be provided with a *throating* or drip in order to shed water as far as practicable away from the wall face below.

Whatever the material used for their construction, sills are very subject to defects caused by dampness. Either the weathering is not sufficiently steep to shed the water, or water can get back to the bed joint of the sill because the drip does not function, or because the slope of the concrete, stone or brick sub-sill allows the water to run back instead of outwards. Paint must not be relied upon to protect timber at this critical point, and it is essential that only durable hardwood for timber sill and frames should be specified.

The head is not usually so troublesome when considering water penetration, but the dpc in the cavity above must catch water running down the inside surface of the outer leaf and conduct it properly to the outside of the head.

Window frames should be secured to walls by means of metal lugs (see figure 5.24 page 119) fixed in the dry leaf of the cavity wall, or alternatively, screwed in place into plastics or similar plugs cast or drilled into the surrounding masonry. Only non-ferrous metals should be used for these fixings. In general, timber windows should be secured at the jambs only. However, large windows must also be secured at the head and the sill is used to locate but *not* secure the window. The minimum number of fixing points recommended is four to a window up to 6000 mm square, and eight up to 1800 mm square.

The frames are bedded in cement mortar with the external joint sealed by the application of correct mastic, although this latter defence measure should only be considered as an initial stop to water penetration and not a substitute for adequate construction techniques.

Figure 6.17(a) to (e), illustrates various methods of locating timber windows in openings in the following types of construction:

● **Conventional cavity wall construction**
In figure 17(a) the head of the opening is supported by two reinforced concrete lintels, the inner one splayed to close the cavity over the frame. The exposed faces of the inner lintel have been lined with 12 mm polystyrene insulation to lessen the 'cold bridge' effect resulting in the differing thermal efficiency of concrete as compared with the *lightweight* concrete block it supports. In order to provide a good key to the subsequent plaster finish, this polystyrene skin is often lined with expanded metal lathing which may be extended to lap with the blockwork above to avoid the effects of differential cracking between the two materials (see also figure 6.21).

The *cavity tray* or *cavity flashing* can be of patented form consisting of a thin layer of metal (lead or copper) sandwiched both sides with bitumen impregnated felt.

The timber sill which should be of hardwood is projected over the external rendering. This projection should be a minimum 35 mm and preferably 50 mm in order to shed water clear of the face of the building. The cavity wall should always be sealed with a dpc below the window sill and board

to ensure that their undersides are protected from moist air within the cavity. This seal also counteracts possible damage to the wall below by water which may permeate around the sill's defences.

At the jamb the dpc is turned into the groove in the timber frame. The frame would be set in mortar by 'buttering' the opening as the brickwork is built. The frame is built in as the work proceeds. Note that the dpc projects into the cavity by about 40 mm to avoid any 'short circuiting' of water at the brick/block junction. At the jamb the cavity is closed by return of the inner leaf brickwork against a vertical dpc. This dpc will be the same material used as the horizontal damp-proof course or asbestos based bituminous felt.

In figure 6.17(b) both leaves of the cavity wall are supported by a reinforced concrete *boot* lintel. This is a neat detail which allows a more satisfactory placing of the cavity flashing than in figure 6.17(a). This detail also shows a concrete subsill, whereby the bottom sill member of the timber window frame has a drip mould which guides the water on to the concrete sill which protects the main structure. This is more expensive but more satisfactory construction than in figure 6.17(a) which relies on the timber sill being of first class quality and being regularly maintained by painting. The window frame will be set in cement mortar at the jamb and head whilst the metal water bar which seals the gap between the timber frame and the concrete sill, will be set in mastic. The outer edges of the frame will also be pointed in mastic. The plaster is returned on the soffit of the concrete lintel at the head of window and is 'tucked in' behind the frame. The frame may alternatively be grooved to receive the plaster and a small cover strip would prevent a view of the crack which will develop between the frame and plaster.

In figure 6.17(c) here the inner leaf of the walling is supported by a splayed or reinforced concrete lintel whilst the outer brickwork is reinforced by expanded metal strips for 3 or 4 courses over the opening. The reinforcing (which could also be done by small diameter – say 6 mm mild steel rods – should extend a minimum of 225 mm beyond the opening on each side. The technique is suitable for small spans say up to 3.000 m and

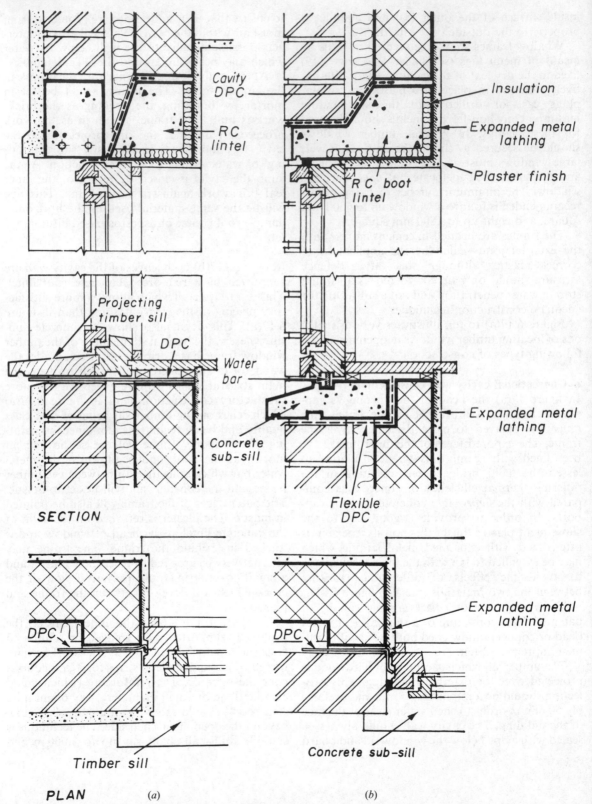

Cavity DPC

RC lintel

Insulation

Expanded metal lathing

Plaster finish

RC boot lintel

Projecting timber sill

DPC

Water bar

Expanded metal lathing

Concrete sub-sill

Flexible DPC

SECTION

DPC

Timber sill

DPC

Expanded metal lathing

Concrete sub-sill

PLAN   (a)   (b)

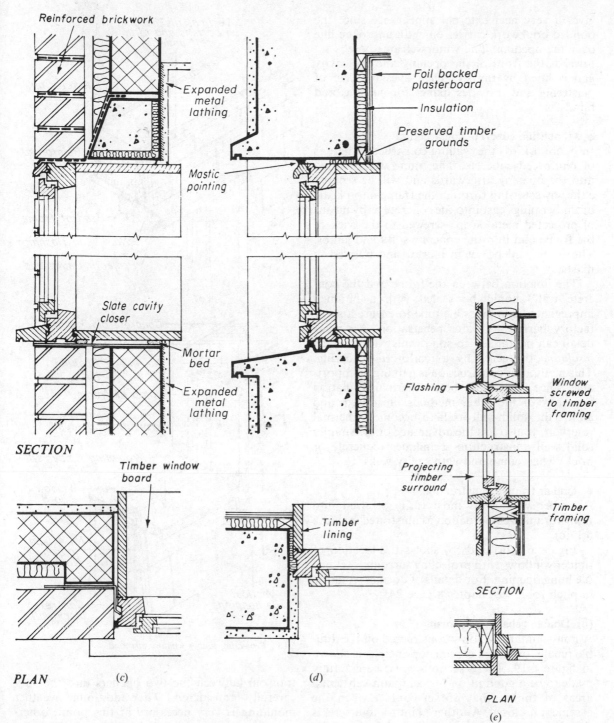

6.17 *(a) to (e) Methods of locating timber windows*

167

gives a very neat external appearance since the bonded brickwork carries on in an unbroken line over the opening. The window frame here is set towards the front of the opening and the cavity gap is lined by timber. This saves the cost of plastering and provides fixings for curtains and blinds.

● **Monolithic concrete construction**

In figure 6.17(d) the walling construction here is of reinforced concrete. The frame will be fitted into the opening afterwards and will be secured either by screwing through the frame into plastic or timber plugs cast into the concrete or by means of protected metal strips screwed to the back of the frame and into the concrete soffit and jambs. The frame will be set in mortar and pointed in mastic.

The junction between the frame and the concrete wall should be sealed with a bitumen impregnated compressible tube to ensure a satisfactory barrier to water penetration. A similar detail can be applied to solid walls with *external insulation* protected by a reinforced rendering. This method of construction is gaining in importance since it provides better thermal insulation than any of the other methods illustrated, and allows the solid wall itself to become a thermal reservoir. It also has the advantage of the simpler solid wall construction techniques (concrete or brick) when compared with cavity walls.

● **Timber framed construction**

A timber window is most easily screwed into timber framed construction as illustrated in figure 6.17(e).

Figure 6.18(a) and (b) shows the location of timber windows with projecting surrounds set in a tile hung opening. For details of dormer windows in pitch roof, see chapter 8 page 241.

(b) Double rebated casement

A non-standard window constructed on the double rebate, or lipped casement principle, is shown in figure 6.19. These sections must be carefully made to be a good fit on the comparatively small areas of timber that are in contact when the casement is closed. Another point to note here, is that the two top hung opening lights are one above the other which means that the detail at the

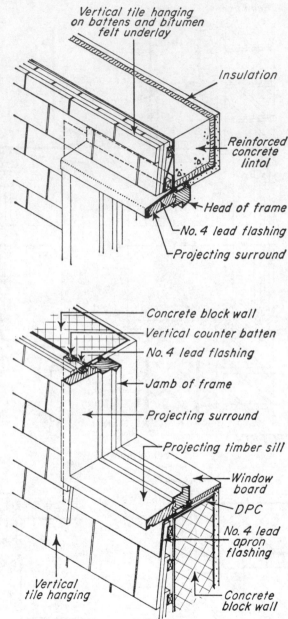

6.18 *Projecting timber window surround*

transom between the two openers must be very carefully considered. The additional weather moulding is very necessary at this point, otherwise the rain would run down the glass on the upper casement and be blown into the unpro-

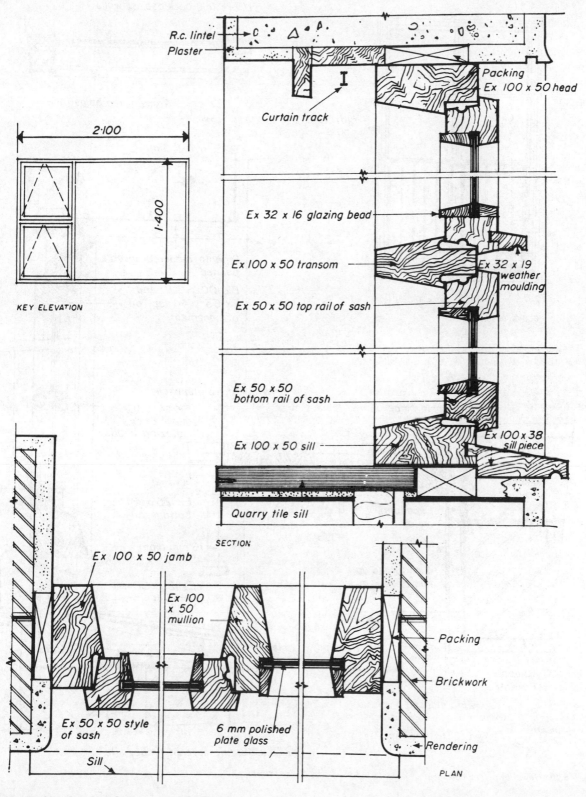

KEY ELEVATION

2·100

1·400

R.c. lintel

Plaster

Curtain track

Packing
Ex 100 x 50 head

Ex 32 x 16 glazing bead

Ex 100 x 50 transom

Ex 32 x 19
weather
moulding

Ex 50 x 50 top rail of sash

Ex 50 x 50
bottom rail of sash

Ex 100 x 50 sill

Ex 100 x 38
sill piece

Quarry tile sill

SECTION

Ex 100 x 50 jamb

Ex 100
x 50
mullion

Packing

Brickwork

Ex 50 x 50 style
of sash

6 mm polished
plate glass

Rendering

Sill

PLAN

6.19   *Double rebated top hung vents and deadlight*

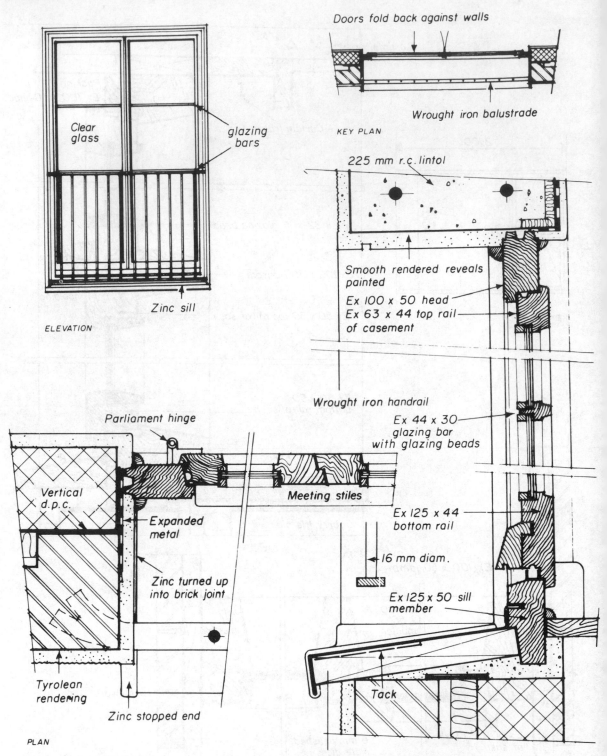

Clear glass

glazing bars

Zinc sill

ELEVATION

Doors fold back against walls

Wrought iron balustrade

KEY PLAN

225 mm r.c. lintol

Smooth rendered reveals painted

Ex 100 x 50 head

Ex 63 x 44 top rail of casement

Wrought iron handrail

Ex 44 x 30 glazing bar with glazing beads

Parliament hinge

Vertical d.p.c.

Expanded metal

Zinc turned up into brick joint

Meeting stiles

Ex 125 x 44 bottom rail

16 mm diam.

Ex 125 x 50 sill member

Tyrolean rendering

Zinc stopped end

PLAN

Tack

275 x 38 zinc covered timber sill

SECTION

6.20 *Inward opening casement*

tected top rebate of the lower casement. Another point to notice is that the window is fixed (by screwing) to timber packing pieces plugged to the brickwork, which is a technique suitable where the window is part of the *second fixing* operations, being placed and secured in position after the opening is formed. The frame is set well forward in the opening and this leaves space for the formation of a *blind box* on the soffit, so that curtains may be hung within the window opening.

(c) Inward opening casement
Figure 6.20 shows details of a lipped or double rebated casement window, inward opening and hung folding. This is to say, the two lock styles are rebated together and there is no centre mullion against which the casements would normally close. Inward opening is convenient for cleaning but inconvenient for conventional curtains. This type of window is much used on the continent and is meant to be either shut or fully open. The example is arranged on the inside of the wall thickness so that each casement can fold back, out of the way, against the wall. Note the zinc sheet covering dressed on a timber sill, also a continental detail which is quite satisfactory provided the ends are turned up against the brickwork and tucked in. The metal balustrade has a bottom rail so that the sill is not perforated by the fixing of the balusters. The sill details for an inward opening casement, always need special consideration because the rebate is reversed and rain will enter unless a water-bar or weather board is used. The channel water-bar shown gives double protection from driving rain and the outer flange is provided with draining holes at intervals.

(d) Horizontal pivot
Most manufacturers produce a 'standard' range for delivery from stock for this type of window. Other types of timber windows, eg inward opening casements, casements for double glazing and double casements, are also made to manufacturers' standard ranges.

Figure 6.21 shows a horizontal pivot hung timber window – the word *horizontal* refers to the placing of the hinges, which are opposed horizontally. The hinges of a vertical pivot hung window would be one above the other in a vertical line. The success of a pivot window depends upon the friction action of the hinge which should be strong enough to hold the window firmly in any open position. The pivot hung window is very much used because it gives a neat appearance to the façade of a building and provides good control of ventilation. There may be some difficulty in respect of hanging curtains or blinds on the inside of the window if the frame is set back into the window reveal. The example is shown fixed as far as possible towards the front of the brickwork opening and secured by rustproofed metal lugs. These lugs are screwed to the back of the frame and 'built in' as the brickwork is carried up when the opening is formed, as shown on the plan in figure 6.21. The opening casement is secured in this example by an espagnolette bolt which holds the casement to the frame at four points.

(e) Double sash pivot window
The horizontally pivoted double sash has for a long time been developed by window specialists on the continent and is now produced by several manufacturers for use in this country. Details of such a window are shown in figure 6.22. The outer sash is secured to the inner sash and hinged so that the space between can be cleaned. The joint between the two sashes is not airtight, in fact the simple locking device is also a spacer to ensure that external air can circulate through the space. The air circulation should be enough to evaporate any condensation within the space but not sufficient to have any serious overall cooling effect. To separate the two sashes they have to be rotated through 180 degrees. Accordian pleated, or venetian blinds can be fixed in the space and operated from the side with cords. These windows, being balanced, can be made to a large size, limiting factors being the distance the top swings into the room and the extra cost of plate glass. The window can be fastened with a mortice turn button into the sill, but larger windows need securing at all corners by an espagnolette bolt set in a groove on three sides and operated by one handle. The pivot mechanism holds the sash in any desired open position by friction. Note the traditional method of *weathering* the window opening, shown in figure 6.22, by means of a mild steel angle to support the outer leaf of brickwork and a sheet lead cavity *tray* dpc. The lead must be carried over the metal angle to catch any water

171

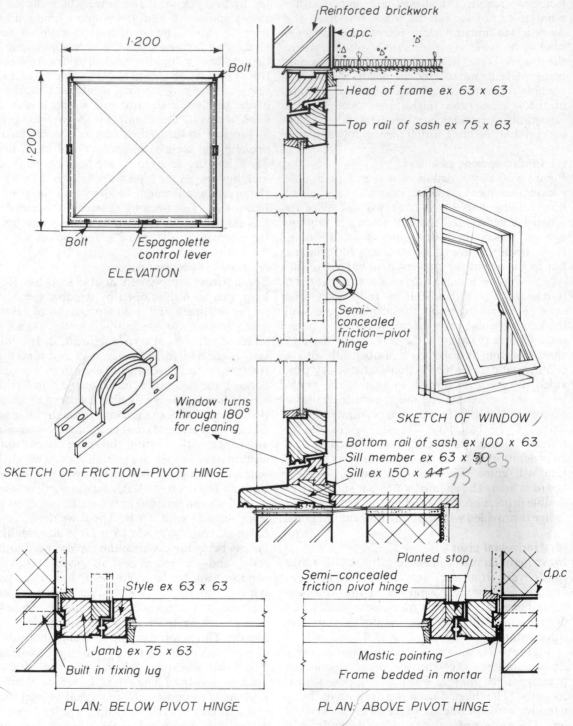

1·200

1·200

Bolt

Bolt   Espagnolette
control lever

ELEVATION

Reinforced brickwork
d.p.c.

Head of frame ex 63 x 63

Top rail of sash ex 75 x 63

Semi-
concealed
friction–pivot
hinge

SKETCH OF WINDOW

Window turns
through 180°
for cleaning

SKETCH OF FRICTION–PIVOT HINGE

Bottom rail of sash ex 100 x 63
Sill member ex 63 x 50
Sill ex 150 x 44

Style ex 63 x 63

Jamb ex 75 x 63

Built in fixing lug

PLAN: BELOW PIVOT HINGE

Planted stop

Semi-concealed
friction pivot hinge

d.p.c

Mastic pointing

Frame bedded in mortar

PLAN: ABOVE PIVOT HINGE

6.21   *Horizontal pivot window – single sash*

172

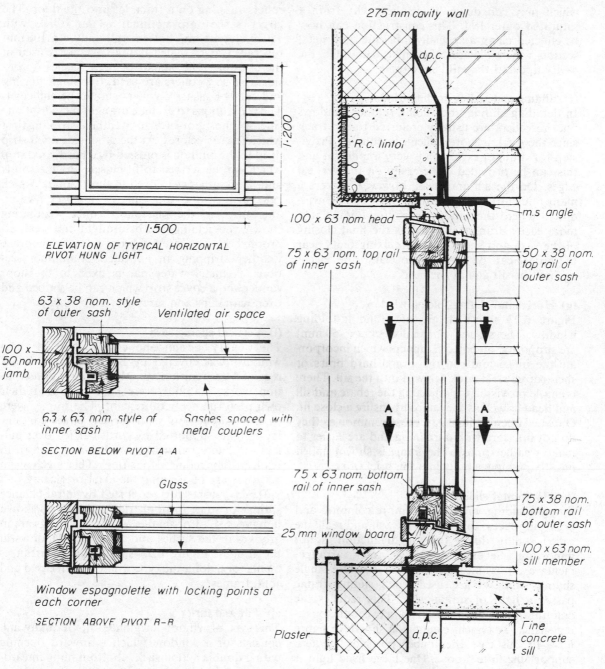

275 mm cavity wall

d.p.c.

R.c. lintol

100 x 63 nom. head

m.s angle

75 x 63 nom. top rail
of inner sash

50 x 38 nom.
top rail of
outer sash

B B

A A

75 x 63 nom. bottom
rail of inner sash

75 x 38 nom.
bottom rail
of outer sash

25 mm window board

100 x 63 nom.
sill member

Plaster

d.p.c.

Fine
concrete
sill

VERTICAL SECTION

ELEVATION OF TYPICAL HORIZONTAL
PIVOT HUNG LIGHT

1·200

1·500

63 x 38 nom. style
of outer sash

Ventilated air space

100 x
50 nom.
jamb

6.3 x 6.3 nom. style of
inner sash

Sashes spaced with
metal couplers

SECTION BELOW PIVOT A–A

Glass

Window espagnolette with locking points at
each corner

SECTION ABOVE PIVOT B–B

6.22 *Horizontal pivot window – double sash*

173

which may run down inside the cavity from a saturated outer leaf. This construction can now be effected using a specially fabricated all metal section which replaces the inner RC lintel, the cavity dpc and the mild steel angle.

(f) Sliding and sliding-folding windows
In detailing sliding and sliding-folding windows bottom rollers are usually preferred to top track since the track is more difficult to conceal. Provision for draught exclusion is very important and this can be provided quite easily on the vertical edges. On the sill and head, however, there are many difficulties in particular with sliding windows. Where the window is sliding-folding it is more easily draught-proofed as the final closing of the sash and shooting of the fixing bolts near the hinges can be arranged to clamp the sashes against the sill and at the head.

(g) Horizontal sliding-folding window
Figure 6.23 shows details of a sliding-folding window. The sashes (nominal thickness 50 mm) are supported on bottom runners which incorporate the hinge and run on special hard brass or sherardized steel track screwed into the sill. There is ample provision for adjusting the rebate and sill and head as well as the jambs to ensure a close fit. Outward opening lights are most common as they do not interfere with curtaining and are easier to make weather-proof. The frame is shown nailed into fixing blocks built into the brickwork.

(h) Horizontal sliding window
Straight sliding windows are more common and providing access to a terrace they should really be called sliding doors but the distinction is not important. Several alternative track arrangements are possible, the simplest is where single sliding windows are used, each sliding frame passes a light of similar size. This reduces the amount of track and the joints between the opening sashes. A typical example is shown in figure 6.24. In this case the timber posts or *mullions* support the lintel above. One large fixed light is fixed direct to the mullions in a rebate and the sliding window passes behind the mullion and fixed light. This simplifies the joint at the jambs and enables the top track to be fixed on a packing at the side of the lintel. The door is carried on

rollers running on a track let into the floor. The larger sashes are nominal 63 mm thick with 150 mm styles and bottom rail and with 100 mm top rail. Cavity sealed double glazing is used in the example. The weight of these sashes is considerable so 8 rollers are used. For single glazing and smaller sashes 2 rollers should be sufficient. The precautions to exclude draught include at one side a phosphor-bronze weather strip against which the sash closes. At the other side a felt strip fixed to the mullion is pressed by a hardwood stop which can be scribed to fit closely. At the top is another weather strip fixed to the head and which rubs against the top rail as it closes. As an alternative to the phosphor-bronze weathering shown, the detail could be draught and weather-proofed by the use of wool-pile or neoprene weather stripping in extruded aluminium sections. A metal water bar is fixed to the floor runner and a cover strip which can be scribed and fixed with cups and screws overlaps this.

(i) Vertical sliding sash
The quality, design and construction of these windows was covered by BS 644 and, as it has regained recognition mainly through conservation work, manufacturers have produced their own performance requirement. The frames were traditionally 'cased' with vertical boxes containing weights supported by cords carried over pulleys to counterbalance the sashes and hold them open in any required position. This mechanism allowed ease of cleaning the exterior glazing.

Today, sashes are supported by spiral balance springs or some form of friction device as shown in figure 6.42. For smaller windows springs are in grooves in the sashes and for larger windows in the frames. Figure 6.25 shows typical arrangements for a domestic type window with cased and solid frames.

(j) Tilt and turn
This type of window originated in Germany and consists of a window which is inward opening with a double action sash – bottom hung inward-opening (tilt) for draught free ventilation and side hung opening-in (turn) for cleaning. They are very sophisticated windows which are steadily increasing in popularity in the UK. Advances in tilt and turn fittings have improved safety: these

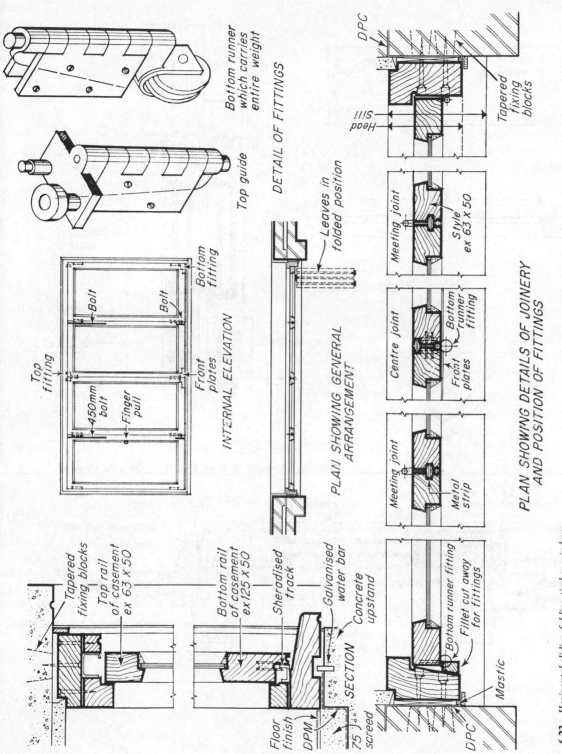

Bottom runner which carries entire weight

Top guide

DETAIL OF FITTINGS

Top fitting

Bolt

Bolt

Bottom fitting

Front plates

450mm bolt

Finger pull

INTERNAL ELEVATION

Leaves in folded position

PLAN SHOWING GENERAL ARRANGEMENT

DPC

Head Sill

Tapered fixing blocks

Meeting joint

Style ex 63 x 50

Centre joint

Bottom runner fitting

Front plates

Meeting joint

Metal strip

PLAN SHOWING DETAILS OF JOINERY AND POSITION OF FITTINGS

Tapered fixing blocks

Top rail of casement ex 63 x 50

Bottom rail of casement ex 125 x 50

Sheradised track

Galvanised water bar

Concrete upstand

SECTION

Floor finish

DPM

DPC

75

screed

Bottom runner fitting

Fillet cut away for fittings

Mastic

DPC

6.23 Horizontal sliding-folding timber windows

175

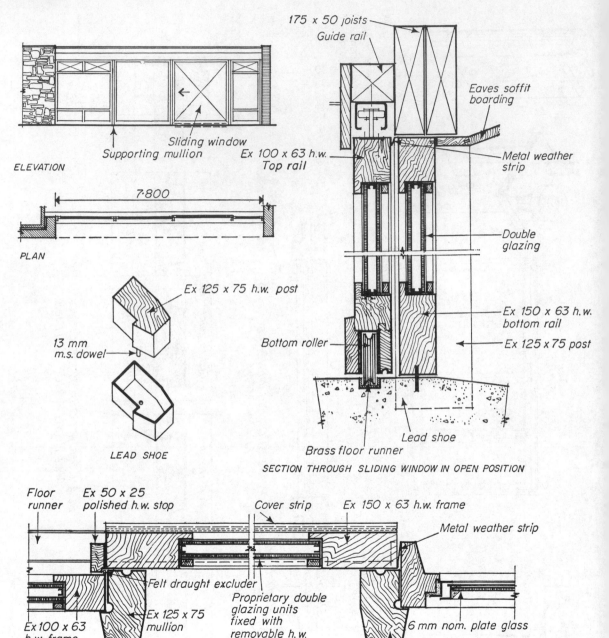

ELEVATION

Sliding window

Supporting mullion

175 x 50 joists

Guide rail

Eaves soffit boarding

Ex 100 x 63 h.w. Top rail

Metal weather strip

7·800

PLAN

Double glazing

Ex 125 x 75 h.w. post

13 mm m.s. dowel

Bottom roller

Ex 150 x 63 h.w. bottom rail

Ex 125 x 75 post

LEAD SHOE

Lead shoe

Brass floor runner

SECTION THROUGH SLIDING WINDOW IN OPEN POSITION

Floor runner

Ex 50 x 25 polished h.w. stop

Cover strip

Ex 150 x 63 h.w. frame

Metal weather strip

Felt draught excluder

Proprietary double glazing units fixed with removable h.w. beads

Ex 100 x 63 h.w. frame

Ex 125 x 75 mullion

6 mm nom. plate glass

Ex 115 x 63 h.w. frame

PLAN

6.24 *Sliding window*

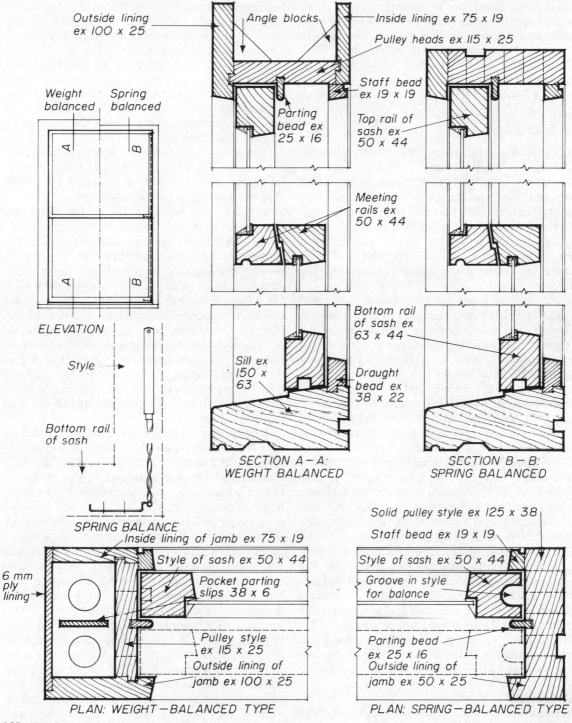

ELEVATION

Weight balanced   Spring balanced

Style

Bottom rail of sash

SPRING BALANCE

Outside lining ex 100 x 25

Angle blocks

Inside lining ex 75 x 19

Pulley heads ex 115 x 25

Staff bead ex 19 x 19

Parting bead ex 25 x 16

Top rail of sash ex 50 x 44

Meeting rails ex 50 x 44

Sill ex 150 x 63

Bottom rail of sash ex 63 x 44

Draught bead ex 38 x 22

SECTION A – A: WEIGHT BALANCED

SECTION B – B: SPRING BALANCED

6 mm ply lining

Inside lining of jamb ex 75 x 19

Style of sash ex 50 x 44

Pocket parting slips 38 x 6

Pulley style ex 115 x 25

Outside lining of jamb ex 100 x 25

PLAN: WEIGHT–BALANCED TYPE

Solid pulley style ex 125 x 38

Staff bead ex 19 x 19

Style of sash ex 50 x 44

Groove in style for balance

Parting bead ex 25 x 16

Outside lining of jamb ex 50 x 25

PLAN: SPRING–BALANCED TYPE

6.25 *Standard timber vertically sliding sash windows*

177

include the provision of security stays, crack (narrow gap) ventilation in either the tilt or turn mode, and the introduction of switch barriers to ensure the windows cannot be put into both modes at the same time. Roller shutters can be fitted in combination with this design of window to give added security and thermal insulation.

6.4 Steel windows

Steel and aluminium are the most common metals used in the manufacture of window sections. Where cost, in terms of permanency and freedom from maintenance can be justified, bronze is a material which can be used as an alternative. Stainless steel is a material which is eminently suitable for use as window frames and its rapid development as a building material for more general use make it the window material of the future.

Recommendations for steel windows are given in BS 6510: 1984 *Specification for steel windows, sills, window boards and doors*. Many manufacturers of steel windows have their product tested in accordance with the recommendations laid down in BS 5368 *Methods of testing windows* in order to meet the criteria laid down in BS 6367 *Performance of windows* (see *Weather resistance*, page 152). Some have also obtained British Board of Agrément test certificates and participate in the BSI Quality Assurance Scheme recommended in BS 5750 (see 1.4 Component Testing and Quality Assurance). There is no BS for stainless steel windows or windows made from pressed sections.

Steel window frames readily conduct heat, and condensation can occur along their relatively small surface area within a room where humid conditions exists without proper heating and ventilation. Timber sub-frames (see page 184) will help prevent staining of the adjacent wall surfaces and an insulating break between external/internal sections will reduce the cold-bridge causing the condensation. Double windows, separated by 75–200 mm can give very good sound reduction up to 49 dB, especially if the reveals between the two windows are lined with absorbent materials.

(a) Standard
Standard steel windows are manufactured from solid sections of hot rolled steel to specified profiles: the composition of the steel is specified in BS 6510. White hot steel ingots are passed through rollers to form a billet of steel about 50 mm square, 1200 mm long. The billet is then re-heated and 're-rolled' through a further series of rollers under very heavy pressure which produces the correct section profile from which the window frame is formed. Welding occurs at corners with internal sub-divisions either welded or tenoned and riveted.

The completed frames are then hot-dip galvanized to BS 729: 1971 *Hot-dip galvanized coatings on iron and steel articles*. Undecorated galvanized steel windows have a life of more than 15 years in an urban environment, but in-situ painting every five years or so will considerably increase this period. Alternatively, the galvanized window frames can be factory finished with a polyester powder coating (an organic stoved finish available in a fairly wide colour range) to BS 6497: 1984 *Powder organic coatings for application and stoving to hot-dip galvanized hot-rolled steel sections and preformed steel sheet for windows and associated external architectural purposes, and for the finish on galvanized steel sections and preformed sheet coating with powder organic coatings*. Regular washing of paint or polyester powder coating will further prolong the life of the steel window frame.

BS 510 does not contain preferred modular sizes for steel windows. However, many manufacturers offer standard size ranges: some of these are dimensionally co-ordinated but only as an indication of what is available, since most windows are made to order.

A range of basic spaces for the windows are shown in figure 1.5 page 22, and the single or multi-pane window units indicated in figure 6.26 will fit into these spaces. Figure 1.7 page 25 shows how these basic spaces can be adapted to suit non-modular brickwork. The use of timber sub-frames, as indicated in figure 6.27(a) and (b), to dimensionally co-ordinate sizes is not always economical in the use of timber but may be required for visual reasons, eg to provide a bolder outline to the window frame than is provided by the steel frame. The softwood or hardwood timber sub-frames should accord with the recommendations in BS 1285: 1980 *Specification for wood surrounds for steel windows and doors*. See page 184 for

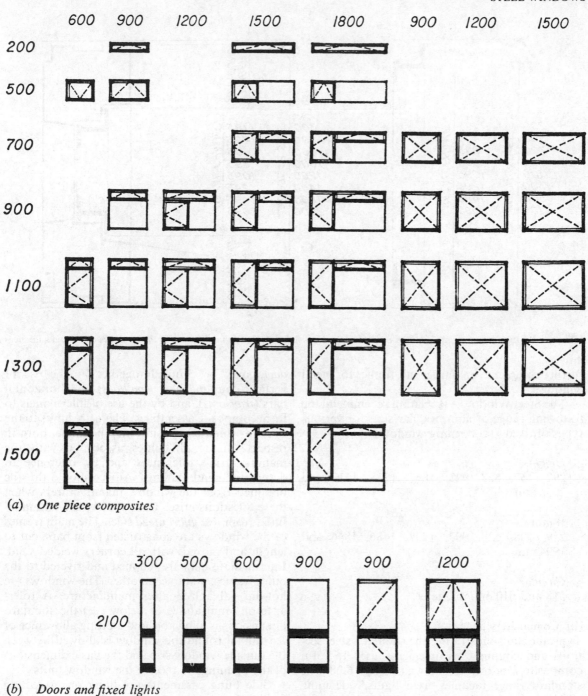

(a) **One piece composites**

(b) **Doors and fixed lights**

6.26 *Selection of module 100 steel windows*

179

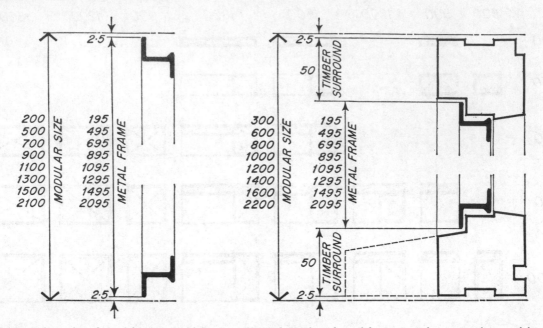

6.27 (*a*)   *Relationship of metal frames to modular sizes* (*b*)   *Relationship of metal frames in timber surrounds to modular sizes*

further comments on timber sub-frames for metal windows.

The Steel Window Association recommend the following range of non-modular sizes for various types of fixed and opening windows:

Heights
292, 457, 628, 923, 1067, 1218, 1513 and 2056 mm

Widths
279, 508, 628, 997, 1237, 1486, 1846 and 1994 mm

Circular
518 and 610 mm diameter

(b) Composite standard

Typical details illustrating the standard steel sections and coupling arrangements used to form composite windows are shown in figure 6.28. The standard range includes fixed lights, side hung casements opening outwards, horizontally pivoted reversible casements and top hung casements opening outwards, with a selection of casement *doors* opening outwards. Windows and *doors* may be coupled together by the use of vertical coupling bars (*mullions*) and horizontal bars (*transoms*), and by the use of filler panels to form composite assemblies. There are limits to the sizes to which composites may be made, both in respect of the difficulties associated with the manufacturing tolerances and by reference to designated wind loadings. Advice should thus be obtained from the window manufacturers when these questions arise. The windows are manufactured from *test guaranteed* steel. The main frames of the windows are constructed from bars, cut to length and mitred, with all corners welded solid. Intermediate bars are tenoned and riveted to the outer frames, and to each other. The windows are hot-dip galvanized after manufacture. A tolerance of 2 mm above or below (±) the standard dimensions is allowable and a fitting allowance of 2.5 mm all round the window is allowed between the outside window size and the basic dimensions of the openings to receive the window units.

Side hung casements are hung on projecting friction hinges without a stay. They are made of steel and are welded or riveted to the frames. The hinge pins are either rust proofed steel or aluminium alloy. The friction hinge is adjusted by the

180

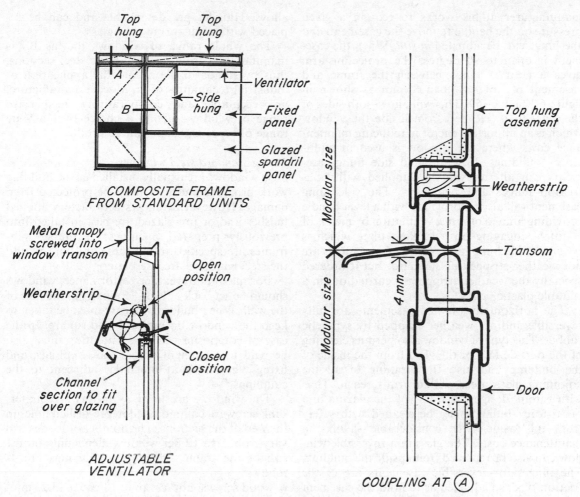

COMPOSITE FRAME
FROM STANDARD UNITS

Top hung · *Top hung*

A

B

Ventilator

Side hung

Fixed panel

Glazed spandril panel

ADJUSTABLE VENTILATOR

Metal canopy screwed into window transom

Weatherstrip

Open position

Closed position

Channel section to fit over glazing

COUPLING AT Ⓐ

Top hung casement

Weatherstrip

Transom

Door

Modular size

Modular size

4 mm

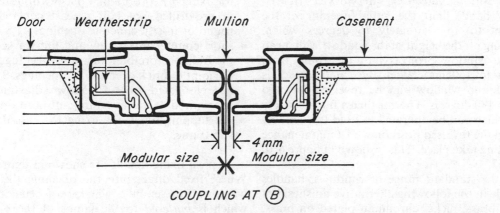

COUPLING AT Ⓑ

Door · Weatherstrip · Mullion · Casement

4 mm

Modular size · Modular size

6.28 *Coupling of standard steel sections*

manufacturer at his works to require a given pressure on the handle to move the casement, and the hinge can be adjusted *in situ*. When the casement is open to 90 degrees the projecting arm gives a clear distance between the frame and casement of not less than 85 mm as shown in figure 6.12 page 159. This will allow both sides of the glass to be cleaned from inside the window which is an important factor in reducing maintenance costs where the window is used in multistorey buildings. If so ordered side hung casements can alternatively be supplied with non-friction hinges and peg stays. The side hung casement will also be provided with a lever handle providing limited or *crack* ventilation by means of a notch, engaging on a striking plate which is bevelled. Side hung (and top hung) casements are not weather stripped as standard, but if ordered specially the weather stripping is carried out in a suitable plastic, ie PVC.

The horizontally pivoted casements are fully reversible and are weather stripped by synthetic rubber. This type of window also permits cleaning of the outside face of the glass from the inside of the building and also the cleaning of all the adjoining glass areas within arm's reach. Thus with careful design the whole of the glazing to a multistorey building can be cleaned with safety from the inside, with considerable savings in maintenance costs. The glass in a reversible window can also be replaced from inside the building. The hinges for reversible casements are of the friction type, so adjusted as to hold the casement in any position. Automatic safety devices (releasable by hand) limit the initial opening of the casement to approximately 15 degrees which, depending on the height of the window, will mean that the window projects into the room from 100 mm to 150 mm. When the safety device is released, the window can be reversed, pivoted through 180 degrees. There is then a further safety catch which can be operated to hold the window firmly in the reversed position whilst maintenance or cleaning take place. This is shown in figure 6.10 page 157.

For the standard range of windows, handles are made in the following alternative finishes: hot pressed brass; nickel chromium plated on brass, or on zinc based alloy; and various aluminium alloys. Handles are detachable and can be replaced without disturbing the glass.

The whole range of windows to this BS is manufactured from only 12 basic steel sections, thus by standardization, and the application of industrial techniques of large scale manufacture, an acceptable and comparatively inexpensive range of windows giving a choice over a wide range of types and sizes can be produced.

Fixing standard steel windows
Steel windows are usually installed as the building work proceeds and they must be protected from damage. However, windows with factory applied finishes and/or pre-glazed are best installed into previously prepared openings. If timber sub-frames are specified, often these are built-in and the steel windows are fixed later.

For maximum weather performance, windows should be set back at least 75 mm from the face of the wall. When building-in, care must be taken to keep the window both plumb and square. In the case of composite windows, attention must also be paid to alignment across the couplings, and fixings should be at the holes adjacent to the couplings.

The windows are fixed by means of countersunk screws accommodated in pre-drilled holes in the web of the sections. The number of fixings will vary from 2 to 12 per window, depending on the size of the frame. The types of fixings are as follows:

- wood screws, not less than 10 gauge (3.25 mm) for fixing into proprietary plastics or fibre plugs in pre-drilled holes in precast concrete surround or in-situ concrete openings;
- short countersunk screw and nut for securing the frame before building-in to steel lugs set in the joint of brick or masonry openings. The lug has elongated slots to allow adjustment to accommodate variation in joint position;
- self tapping screw for fixing to pressed metal sub-frame.

Typical fixing details are shown in figure 6.29. Where fixed direct into the opening, the metal windows are set in a waterproof cement fillet, which is *buttered* to the jambs of the opening before the window is offered into position and

182

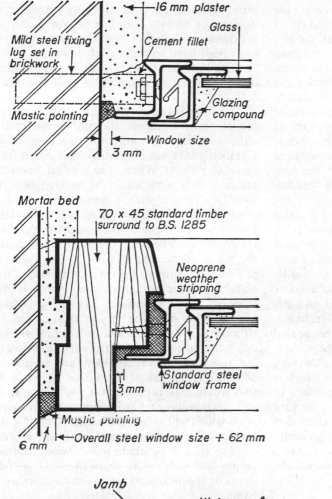

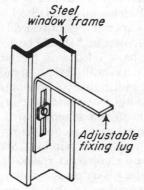

Steel window frame

Adjustable fixing lug

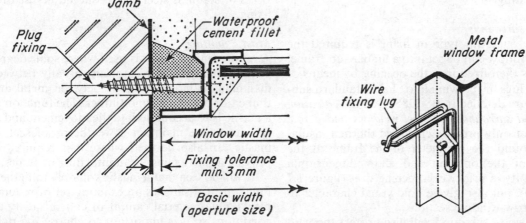

6.29 *Typical metal window fixing details*

Metal window frame

Wire fixing lug

Alternative types of adjustable fixing lug

183

connects with the wall dpc. The space between the frame and the opening is then pointed in a suitable mastic, and the inside reveal usually plastered. As the window height dimension may not always coincide with brick courses, the window should be positioned to fit close under the lintel, and the brickwork under the sill adjusted to suit. Sills should be positioned with the outside face of the upstand in line with the inner face of the outer leaf of brickwork so that the window will locate correctly at the jamb. The window should then be sealed to the sill with bedding compound and external pointing is recommended.

Three examples of the arrangement of a metal frame within a surround are shown in figure 6.30:

(a) shows the use of a pressed steel combined lintel and cavity flashing at the head, and a pressed metal surround. Steel sills should be fixed by special lugs provided by the window manufacturer and should be bedded on mortar, or back filled with mortar after fixing. The cavity wall below should be sealed against moist air by a horizontal dpc;

(b) shows a purpose made slate surround serving as sill, head and window board, into which is fixed small cross section hardwood fillets to receive the steel window. Slate is a very effective water barrier and no dpc is necessary under the sill unless there are joints to seal;

(c) an alternative to (b), where the slate is expressed only in the external face of the building.

Timber surrounds

Where a superior type of fixing is required the metal window can be set into a timber sub-frame, which is then fixed into the opening by means of built-in lugs or screwing into plugs. Standard sub-frames are detailed in BS 1285: 1980 *Specification for wood surrounds for steel windows and doors*. They not only provide enhanced thermal insulation around the perimeter of the frame at the jambs of the opening and allow dimensional conformity in brickwork opening sizes (figure 1.7 page 25), but also give a bold visual character to the narrow window sections.

The wood surround will also protect the window during transport to site or, when separate from the window, can be used as a permanent building-in template for a factory finished window to be installed at a later time. Damaged windows can be more easily replaced when they have been fixed within a timber frame.

Details of the arrangement of a steel window in a standard timber surround are shown in figure 6.31 page 186.

The joint between the head and the jamb, and the sill and the jamb in the timber surround will either be a mortice and tenon, or a combed joint. Combed joints will be pinned with a non-ferrous metal star dowel. Where mortice and tenon joints are used they must either be wedged or – more usually – pinned with a non-ferrous metal star dowel. Both combed joints and mortice and tenon joints are also glued. In order to produce a watertight joint between the timber surround and the metal frame, the rebates of the frame after pinning are spread with a continuous strip of suitable mastic and then the metal frame is screwed into position, 32 mm countersunk screws, being suitable. Very often standard metal windows are set in timber surrounds of similar construction to the standard surround described but using timber of non-standard section, very often in hardwood. It should be borne in mind that where teak is chosen for the surround, this, and certain other hardwoods contain harmful acids which will attack untreated steel. It is therefore particularly important that the protective coating should be made good, where damaged, before the window is screwed into the frame. Brass or stainless steel screws should be used for fixing.

Mastic jointing

A mastic seal to a joint is used where some degree of movement is likely to occur, usually between dissimilar materials, such as between metal and timber, or brickwork and timber. The function of a mastic is to accommodate the movement and at the same time maintain a weatherproof seal. A mastic can also be used where it is required to provide a seal against draughts, dust or fumes.

It will be seen that a mastic will only fulfil these functions if it satisfies an exacting set of requirements. One material cannot of course satisfy all conditions so it is important to choose the right material for the job. The various types of mastic and their uses are discussed in *MBS: Materials,*

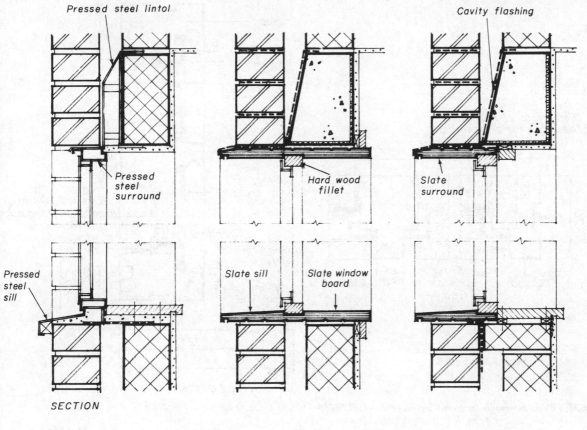

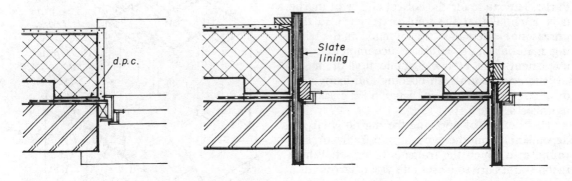

6.30 *Metal window in brick/block openings*

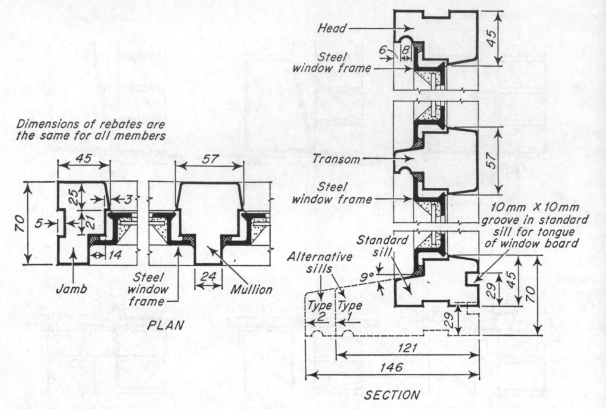

Dimensions of rebates are the same for all members

PLAN

SECTION

6.31 *Wood surrounds for steel windows or doors: BS 1285*

chapter 16 and for the use of mastics in curtain walling, etc, see *MBS: Structure and Fabric Part* 1. Having made the correct choice of mastic it is essential that the joint is designed so that unreasonable demands are not made on the jointing material in its effort to accommodate the movement. The practical application of mastic seals in connection with bedding and fixing window frames is shown in figure 6.32 – see also figure 6.14 page 161.

The method of applying the mastic is largely dependent upon the type of sub-frame or surround into which the frame is to be set. Where metal frames are to be set into wood surrounds a continuous ribbon of mastic applied in the external and internal rebate of the surround will ensure a perfect seal when the frame is placed in position. Any surplus mastic can be removed by a rag. soaked in mastic cleaner. The external vertical joint between the timber sub-frame or surround

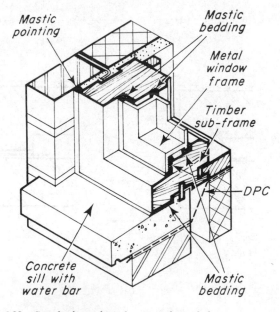

6.32 *Standard metal window in timber sub-frame*

186

and the brick or masonry jambs of the window opening are particularly subject to differential rates of expansion and contraction. It is therefore essential that these joints be pointed with a mastic which will accommodate this movement of the joint.

Water bars should be bedded in mastic and a ribbon of mastic applied to the rebate on the underside of the sill of the wood surround, before this is plated into position. Care should be taken that the two surfaces with which the mastic will be in contact are dry and free from dust. The vertical joints between sub-frame and window opening should be grouted in a weak cement mix, raked out to a depth of not less than 12 mm and, when dry, pointed with mastic. With old property where a mastic joint has not been used a deep, wide cavity may exist; in this case the joint should either be packed with hemp to within 12 mm of surface before pointing with mastic, or grouted with a weak cement, raked out and pointed.

Figure 6.33 shows the use of mastic for the joints between frames and loose mullions (or transom rails) in metal windows.

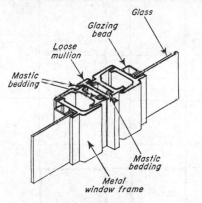

6.33 *Metal window with loose mullion*

With composite windows a certain amount of movement is inevitable at the junction of the fixed frames and the mullions and transoms. It is therefore essential, and is indeed now common practice, to seal these joints with mastic. It is recommended that a ribbon of mastic for the internal and external joint be applied either to the fixed frame or to the mullion or transom as convenient during assembly.

(c) Purpose-made

A range of universal steel sections is produced known as **W20** from which *purpose-made windows* can be manufactured. The hot-rolled sections are heavier than that normally used – see figure 6.34. The basic spaces allocated for W20 steel windows are indicated in figure 6.35 and maximum per-

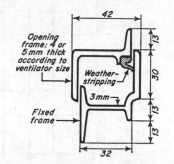

6.34 *W20 steel section for purpose made windows*

missible size of window to fill them are as indicated in figure 6.36.

Method of opening	Size of section	Height plus width	Height	Width
Side hung	Normal	2600	1900	700
	Heavy	3300	2600	900
Folding	Normal	3200	1900	1300
	Heavy	3900	2400	1800
Vertically	Normal	2900	1900	1100
Pivoted	Heavy	3900	2600	1400
Folding vertically	Normal	3600	1800	1800
Pivoted	Heavy	4700	2400	2300
Top hung	Normal	2600	1500	1500
	Heavy	3200	1800	1800
Horizontally	Normal	2600	1500	1500
Centre hung	Heavy	3200	1800	1800
Bottom hung	Normal	2600	1500	1500
	Heavy	3200	1800	1800

6.36 *Extreme sizes of ventilators made of steel W20 Universal Section (dimensions in mm)*

Basic units of purpose-made windows are coupled together by mullions and transoms in the same way as standard steel windows to form dimensionally co-ordinated composite units. Purpose-made windows are usually fitted with good quality handles and other furniture, possibly of bronze.

Where floor to ceiling glazing is required and

187

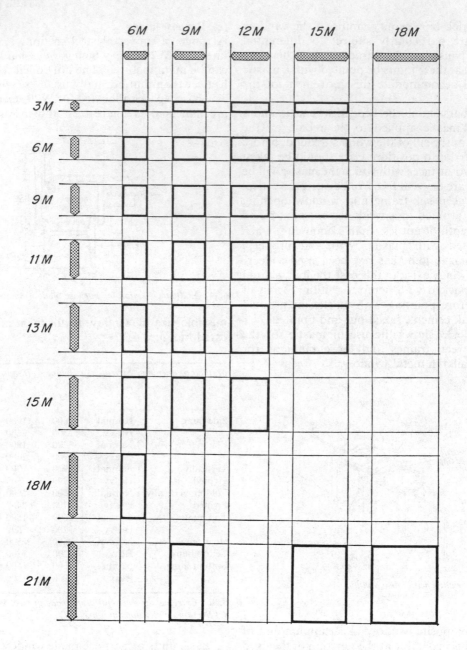

*M = 1 module of 100 mm and refers to the size
of opening into which the window fits*

6.35 *Basic spaces for purpose-made steel
windows*

188

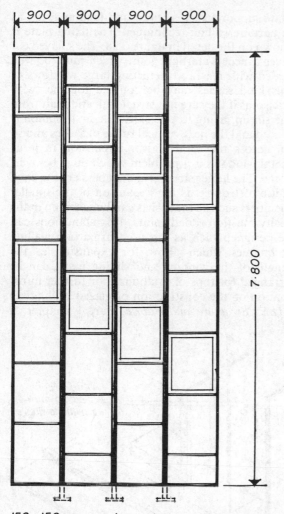

150 x 150 mm m.s. base plates welded on to mullions

KEY ELEVATION

6.37 *Large metal windows*

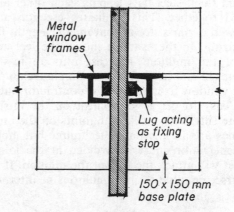

2 no. 175 x 10 m.s. flat section, drilled, tapped and secured by countersunk screws

Metal window frames

Lug acting as fixing stop

150 x 150 mm base plate

DETAIL OF MULLION: CONCEALED FIXING STOPS

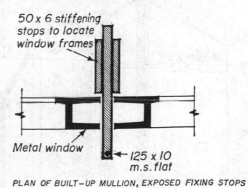

50 x 6 stiffening stops to locate window frames

Metal window

125 x 10 m.s. flat

PLAN OF BUILT-UP MULLION, EXPOSED FIXING STOPS

purpose-made metal steel windows are indicated the mullions are usually the primary members. Figure 6.37 shows such a window detailed to have substantial mullions. Each mullion is 175 mm deep with a total height of 7.800 m. The problems of jointing mullions of this kind can be solved in several ways. In the example the stops are concealed so that the mullion is built up of two lines of 9 mm thick steel flats lapping each other and screwed together. This facilitates erection and reduces the parts to a convenient length for galvanizing. In the example shown the feet and tops of the mullions are cast into an in-situ concrete sill and head. This is a simple technique for the window fixer and for the contractor but it is not easy to get a good finish on the in-situ concrete sill. Precast sills with joints on the mullion lines are an alternative technique but moisture penetration must be avoided at the joints where it will attack the foot of the mullion. It is, of course, possible to joint mullions at interme-

diate supports such as floor and landing levels as in curtain walling techniques. The fixing plate is shown on the detail in figure 6.38. The splayed cut gives a neat watertight joint which must be well sealed with mastic. In erecting large windows of this kind sashes may be coupled together with transoms if they are not structural, and built from the sill up, fixing to one side. The first mullion is placed and the next vertical range of sashes and so on across the total width. Expansion in large metal windows is a problem which must be overcome. The larger structural members are the chief cause of trouble as the expansion of the smaller members such as the sashes can be taken up in the many mastic bedded joints. Box stanchions can be designed such as are used in curtain walling techniques which allow for expansion in the length of the window and sliding fixing can be arranged for tops of mullions. For further information on the construction of glazed walling see *MBS: Structure and Fabric*, Part 1 chapter 5,

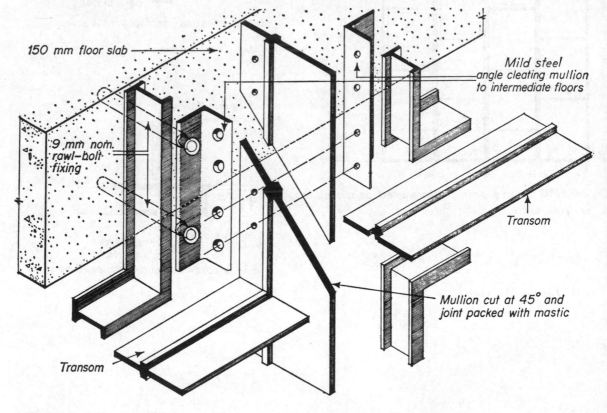

6.38 *Coupling of large metal windows*

Curtain walling. BS 5516: 1977 *Patent glazing* Appendix G: 1986 *Safety of vertical patent glazing* gives recommendation about the *risk areas associated with vertical glazing*, including door side panels that may be mistaken for doors or which contain more than one pane of glass; glass wholly or partially within 800 mm from floor level; and glass in bathing areas (see chapter 7 *Glazing*).

(c) Pressed steel

Metal pressings first came into the building industry in the use of standard door frames, which proved strong, quick to erect, and clean in outline.

Skirtings, stair treads, risers, window frames and shelving have been made of pressed sheet metal for some time. Now doors, particularly lift doors, large window frames, and many other elements are produced.

Mild steel sheet is used mostly in a range of gauges, 26 gauge for angle bead, 20 gauge for door frames, 12, 14 and 17 gauge for window frames and sometimes 10 gauge, approximately 3 mm thick, where greater strength and rigidity is required. Sheets up to 3.000 m × 1.300 m are used, depending on the size of the press or folder the manufacturer has.

Typical profiles of pressed steel sections are shown in figure 6.39. Folds can be made through any angle up to 105 degrees, that is forming an angle of not less than 75 degrees, but a stiffened edge can be made by pressing a fold down flat. This is called a *bar fold*. Surfaces of the member must be flat planes: sharp angles cannot be obtained, the minimum outside radius being usually 2 mm for 16 gauge and 5 mm for 10 gauge. Minimum width of any face is from 12 mm for 16 gauge sheet to 20 mm for 10 gauge. Sections are usually open for most of one side, this being necessary for connections, fixing stiffening cross-members, etc. If a member is to be formed with the fourth side mostly closed, it is necessary to form it with a false fold as shown.

Cutting is done by mechanical saws or by grinding wheels, or by burning. Sheet metal is also cut by knife in a guillotine. Burning is now precise enough to be used for cutting square mortices for a square member to pass through. Holes, including small mortices, are of course formed by drilling or punching. The latter may cause some deformation of the metal member which, if there are many holes, may accumulate to measurable increase in length and width. Running joints are made with sleeves, bedded in mastic and tapped and screwed with countersunk screws, as shown in the diagram. Junctions between members are formed by scribing the end of the stopping member to the profile of the continuing member, filling it with a shaped cleat and screwing it to the continuing member, with a good supply of mastic packed in the joint. It will be seen how the use of a simple rectangular profile simplifies the junction. Complicated profiles call for a complicated cleat and may present difficulties in screwing up. Similarly, the scribing can only be done against flat planes; but, most important of all, the stopping members should be smaller than the continuing member so that it is quite clear of the slightly rounded angles of the continuing member. This is shown in the same diagram. The joint of mullion to sill is made in the same way, the end of the mullion being filled with a cleat and being well filled with mastic before screwing up. It is essential that the cleat be solid behind the front edge of the mullion, so that the mastic is squeezed between the two metal faces and there is no cavity to hold moisture. In some cases it may be more convenient to make a joint in the sill at each mullion; the latter will then continue down with the sill scribed to it. Figure 6.39 shows typical sill and mullion sections. If the front or back face of a frame of pressed-steel members is to be in one plane, it is necessary to form the angles by mitring and welding, and forming site joints with sleeves in the lengths of the members as shown in figure 6.40. Large members can be built up out of several pressings. This is satisfactory if the joints can be masked by the sashes, or hidden on internal angles.

Where long members are used – tall mullion or a long sill – it is important to ensure that the arris is dead straight and the planes are true. What may look satisfactory in elevation may look very bad when seen from directly below or from one side, where it is easy to get 'an eye along the edge'. To get this trueness it is essential that the metal be thick enough to keep its folded shape and that it is carefully fixed. The architect can get the latter put right, but if the metal is too thin any remedy is rather expensive.

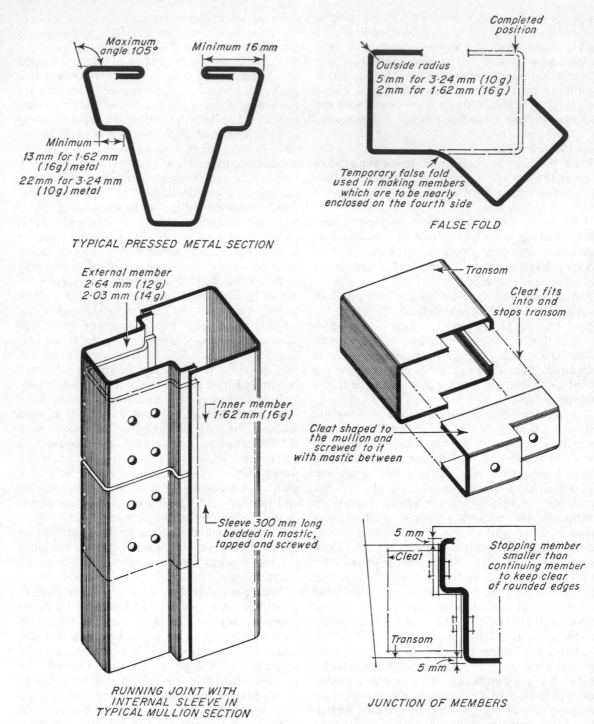

Maximum angle 105°

Minimum 16 mm

Minimum 13 mm for 1·62 mm (16 g) metal 22 mm for 3·24 mm (10 g) metal

TYPICAL PRESSED METAL SECTION

Completed position

Outside radius 5 mm for 3·24 mm (10 g) 2 mm for 1·62 mm (16 g)

Temporary false fold used in making members which are to be nearly enclosed on the fourth side

FALSE FOLD

External member 2·64 mm (12 g) 2·03 mm (14 g)

Inner member 1·62 mm (16 g)

Sleeve 300 mm long bedded in mastic, tapped and screwed

RUNNING JOINT WITH INTERNAL SLEEVE IN TYPICAL MULLION SECTION

Transom

Cleat fits into and stops transom

Cleat shaped to the mullion and screwed to it with mastic between

5 mm

Cleat

Stopping member smaller than continuing member to keep clear of rounded edges

Transom

5 mm

JUNCTION OF MEMBERS

6.39 *Pressed metal frames (1)*

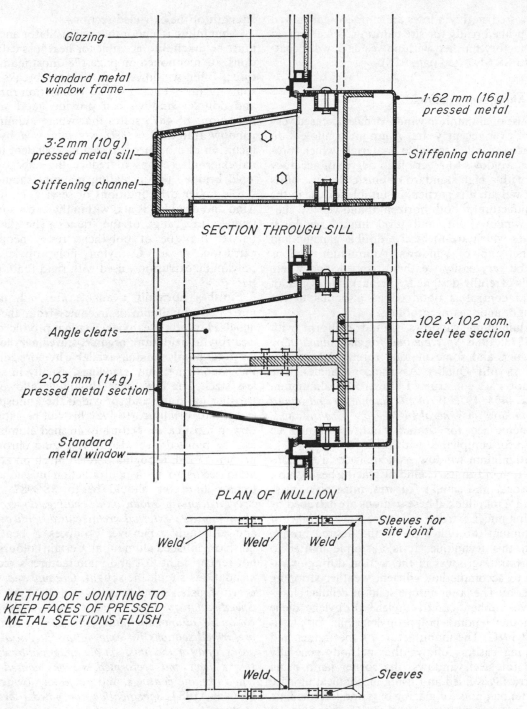

Glazing

Standard metal
window frame

1·62 mm (16 g)
pressed metal

3·2 mm (10 g)
pressed metal sill

Stiffening channel

Stiffening channel

SECTION THROUGH SILL

Angle cleats

102 X 102 nom.
steel tee section

2·03 mm (14 g)
pressed metal section

Standard
metal window

PLAN OF MULLION

Sleeves for
site joint

Weld   Weld   Weld

METHOD OF JOINTING TO
KEEP FACES OF PRESSED
METAL SECTIONS FLUSH

Weld   Sleeves

6.40 *Pressed metal frames (2)*

Pressed steel windows are supplied galvanized and primed ready for site painting, or galvanized and factory finished with polyester powder coating to BS 6497 (see page 178).

6.5 Aluminium windows

The use of aluminium windows has increased very much over recent years. Aluminium alloy is an attractive and adaptable material, which produces windows to a very high degree of accuracy and with a high standard of finish. Because of its light weight, it is particular suitable for use in the manufacture of both horizontal and vertical sliding windows; 'tilt and turn' hinged windows; frames which are to receive double glazing; and reversible pivot windows. Aluminium sections can be very easily weather stripped, and where this is carefully designed, a remarkable degree of sound control is obtained as a bonus to the draught and weatherproofing.

Aluminium windows should conform with BS 4873: 1986 *Specification for aluminium alloy windows*, and some manufacturers also participate in BSI Quality Assurance Schemes. The windows are constructed of extruded aluminium to BS 1474: 1972 *Wrought aluminium and aluminium alloys for general engineering purposes*, and, as mentioned for timber windows, should be tested for compliance with BS 6375.

Aluminium window sections used in the construction of frames, excluding glazing beads, nibs, interlocks and similar features, must be not less than 1.2 mm thick. These sections are extruded by forcing under extreme pressure, a heated billet of aluminium through a die of the desired profile. With this technique, it is a simple matter to incorporate grooves in the section during extrusion to accommodate efficient weather stripping material. The latter can be solid or cellular chloroprene rubber, cured ethylene propylene diene monomer (epdm), polypropylene pile, or plasticized PVC. The manufacture of the frames and opening sashes follows the methods generally used for steel windows, the corner jamb being electrically welded and using mechanical mortice and tenon joints for glazing bars and intermediate members and riveting or screwing for the fixing of the fittings. The maximum sizes for primary ventilators will depend upon the cross-sectional strength of the extruded sections.

Aluminium is a poor thermal insulator and this must be taken into account for heat loss calculations. As mentioned on page 178, most manufacturers offer windows with thermal breaks and some means of coping with condensation run-off; and double windows can provide good sound reduction. BS 4873 states that where aluminium window frames are *thermally improved* by the inclusion of a barrier between independent internal/external sections to reduce the effects of a 'cold bridge', the insulating material should be stable under the conditions of service, eg under wind and dead loads and within the likely surface temperature range of the frames. The thermal barrier may be of polythene resin, neoprene extrusion, or uPVC, nylon, polypropylene or polyamide extrusions, used with rigid foam plastics.

Finishes normally available are: **mill finish**, untreated aluminium as it comes from the die; **anodized protective oxide coating** produced by electrolytic oxidation; **organic, stoved acrylic** and **polyester powder coating** available in more colours than anodizing; and, **claddings,** usually in stainless steel. The *mill* finish should be allowed to weather naturally and, provided the atmosphere is not industrially corrosive, this will be satisfactory in most cases. Naturally finished aluminium can be painted provided that a zinc chromate primer is used, though a painted finish on aluminium seems to be a contradiction in economic terms. *Anodizing* should be to BS 3987: 1974 *Specification for anodic oxide coatings on wrought aluminium for external architectural applications*, and although expensive, produces a beautiful finish on polished aluminium. Certain colours will not remain light-fast and manufacturer's recommendations should be sought. *Organic and stove acrylic* finishes should comply with BS 4842: 1984 *Specification for liquid organic coatings for application to aluminium alloy extrusions, sheet and preformed sections for external architectural purposes, and for the finish on aluminium alloy extrusions, sheet and preformed sections coated with liquid organic coatings*, and polyester powders to BS 6496: 1984 *Specification for powder organic coatings for application and stoving to aluminium alloy extrusions, sheet and preformed sections for external architectural purposes, and for the finish* *on aluminium alloy extrusions, sheet and pre-formed sections coated with powder organic coatings*. These finishes are gaining in popularity, are proving to be very durable and are available in a wide range of colours. A few manufacturers produce aluminium window frames which are *clad* in stainless steel to produce relatively economic frames taking advantage of the properties of both materials, usually for shopfronts.

The aluminium alloys used in windows are very durable, and good quality anodizing or organic coatings will maintain appearance for 15 to 20 years. Aluminium can be attacked by atmospheric pollutants and cleaning should take place with mild detergent or soap and water every six months on rural sites, and every month on urban and marine sites. Mill finished aluminium windows should not be installed on marine sites.

Wheels, rollers and other devices fitted at the head or sill of horizontal sliding aluminium windows to support the weight of sash in order to facilitate movement, and the hardware (ironmongery) used on the window need special consideration in order to minimize wear and corrosion arising from electrolyte reaction. BS 4873 lists a range of suitable materials, including aluminium in compliance with BS 3987, or BS 5466: *Methods for corrosion testing of metallic coatings* Part 1 1977 *Neutral salt spray test (NSS test)*; and zinc die casting alloy complying with BS 1004: 1972 (1985) *Specification for zinc alloys for die casting and zinc alloy die castings*, or steel finished in accordance with BS 6338: 1982 *Specification for chromate conversion coatings on electroplated zinc and cadmium coatings*.

Mill finish windows will normally be despatched from the factory unprotected and must be cleaned down by the contractor just before the scaffolding is dismantled. When the windows are anodized, organic, stoved or powder coated, they should be temporarily covered by a film of wax and then protected by strong self-adhesive tape on all the visible and exposed surfaces. The contractor can then easily remove the tape and polish the wax away to give a finished surface. This should not be done, of course, until there is no risk of damage by following trades.

(a) Standard
BS 4873 does not contain preferred modular sizes

for aluminium windows. However, many manufacturers offer standard size ranges: some are dimensionally co-ordinated but only as an indication of what is available, since most windows are made to order.

The Aluminium Window Association have produced a chart of the basic spaces and ranges in which dimensionally co-ordinated windows should be made. Figure 6.41 shows these spaces: they indicate aperture sizes and not the *working size* of the window: the sizes of an assembled frame should be within a permissible deviation of + or − 1.5 mm from the work size and the maximum difference between the diagonals of the assembled frame should be 4 mm. In addition to the sizes shown there is a range 21 m high suitable for vertical sliding sashes, single or double doors and sliding doors. As explained on page 23, modular windows can be used in non-modular brickwork with the use of filler pieces and/or timber sub-frames.

Fixing aluminium windows
Aluminium windows are normally fixed into prepared openings as *second fixings*. Most manufacturers provide a fixing service so that the window and its installation are the responsibility of one company. All straps, clips, brackets, lugs, screws, bolts, rivets. metal washers and shims and other fixings must be of suitable strength and of materials which minimize corrosion arising from electrolyte reaction as previously described for bearing devices and hardware (zinc plated and hot dip galvanized steel or aluminium, etc). BS 4873 states that if timber surrounds are used, the timber should be specified to comply with BS 1186: Part 1 and the workmanship with BS 1186: Part 2. The materials used in their preservation treatment should have no harmful effects on aluminium in contact with the treated timber in accordance with advice given in CP 153: *Windows and roof lights* Part 2 1970 *Durability and maintenance*. There should be no direct contact between aluminium and oak, sweet chestnut or western red cedar.

It is necessary that great care is taken during handling and installation on site. The frames are not so strong as steel and will not support scaffold poles or boards etc, and aluminium will show immediate ill-effects. Preferably, they should not

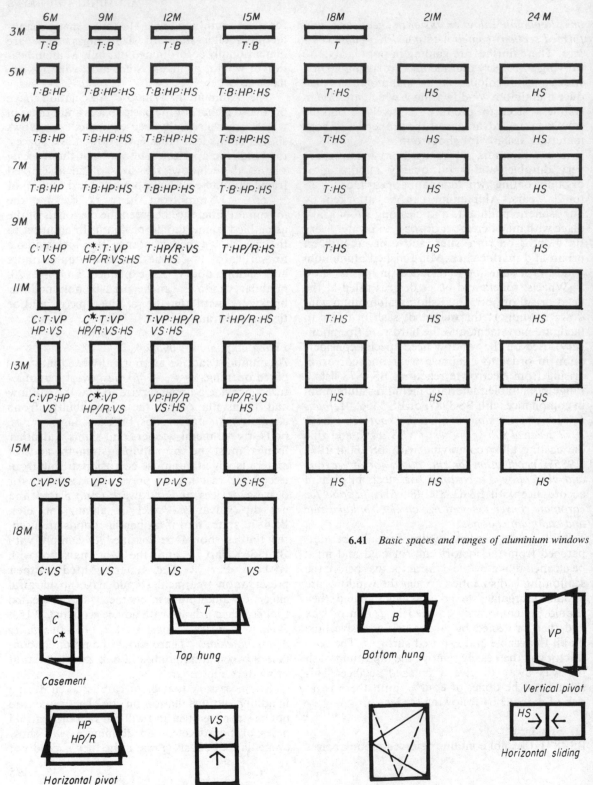

M = 1 module of 100 mm, and refers to size of opening into which the window fits

6.41 *Basic spaces and ranges of aluminium windows*

be fixed until all the structural work and wet finishes are completed and should be protectively wrapped before dispatch and carefully stored on the site. They must be kept very clean during the progress of the work as cement or plaster will adhere to the surface and will leave a mark on bright aluminium. Allowances for expansion of aluminium members are made roughly the same as for steel windows.

(b) Vertical sliding sash

A fully framed purpose-made aluminium double-hung sash window of sophisticated design is shown in figure 6.42.

The alloy used is the same as for the extrusions for the bottom hung sash illustrated previously. The corners for this window, however, are mechanically jointed by screw and spline since the box section cannot be satisfactorily welded. The sashes are controlled by special spring balances and are held by continuous extruded plastic guides which are designed to prevent any uneven response during movement. Note the very effective polypropylene weather stripping which is clipped into the fixed frame in such a way that it can be replaced after damage or wear during use. The meeting rails have a positive interlocking action which ensures good security by preventing the release of the catch from the outside.

The form of the extruded sash section is such that it will accommodate proprietary double glazing units up to 14 mm overall thickness. The glazing is *internal*, that is to say the glass is fixed from inside the building which is an important factor in cost and ease of maintenance. The front edges of the glass are bedded in polysulphide glazing compound; each sheet being located by small spacing blocks within the frame, to give the correct balance all round. The glass is secured by an extruded aluminium *clip-on* bead with a *push-in* vinyl glazing trim to complete the glazing procedure.

Two very neat design points incorporated in the extruded sections are the gap left to receive a window pole, and the continuous neat recess on the lower rail of the outer sash to act as a sash pull.

A window of this type could be made up to a maximum height of 2.440 m and a maximum width of 1.525 m with the limitation that the perimeter measurement must not exceed 7.625 m, which means that the maximum width and height cannot be used in the same window. The basic spaces relative to this type (VS) of window are shown in figure 6.41 page 196.

The following points should also be noted. The rain screen principle of design has been used to prevent water being blown under the bottom sash. The pressure created within the hollow inverted U section of the bottom rail in conditions of high wind and rain, has a screening effect which helps to prevent rain penetration – the higher the pressure, the more positive the screening effect. The sashes are factory glazed so that the helical spring balances can be adjusted to the correct tension by taking into account the variations in weight of glass. The nylon sash guides are to prevent crabbing – or sideways motion of the sash during opening. This is a fault which occurs with loosely fitted sashes and causes the sash to become jammed. The U-shaped tube outline seen on the sections is part of the continuous extrusion and receives long self tapping screws which connect the horizontal and vertical members of the frame. The timber frame is built into the opening and the complete factory glazed window fixed later.

(c) Bottom hung

A domestic scale bottom hung opening inwards aluminium window is shown in figure 6.43. This type of window is useful where draught-free ventilation at low level is desirable. The sections are extruded from aluminium alloys HE 9P and HV 9P in accordance with BS 1470: 1987 *Specification for wrought aluminium and aluminium alloys for general engineering purposes: plate, sheet and strip.* Note the dovetailed grooves to receive the neoprene insert to act as weather stripping. The lengths of weather stripping *clip in* and can be removed for replacement if they become damaged or worn over the life of the window. The hinges have nylon bushed stainless steel pins and the opening casement is returned on hinged side arms which can be released to allow the window to fall back for cleaning and maintenance.

The figure shows examples of both single and double glazing. The glass which is put into the frame from the inside is bedded in suitable glazing compound and in the case of the single glazing the

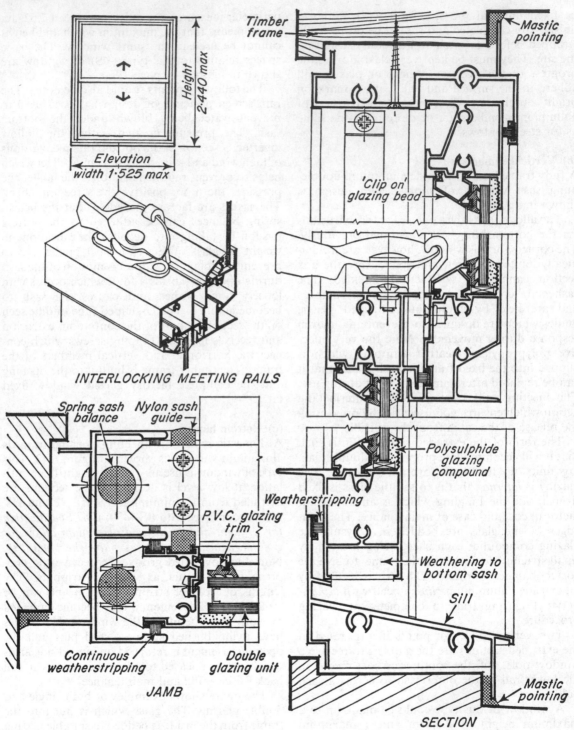

6.42 *Aluminium sliding sash window*

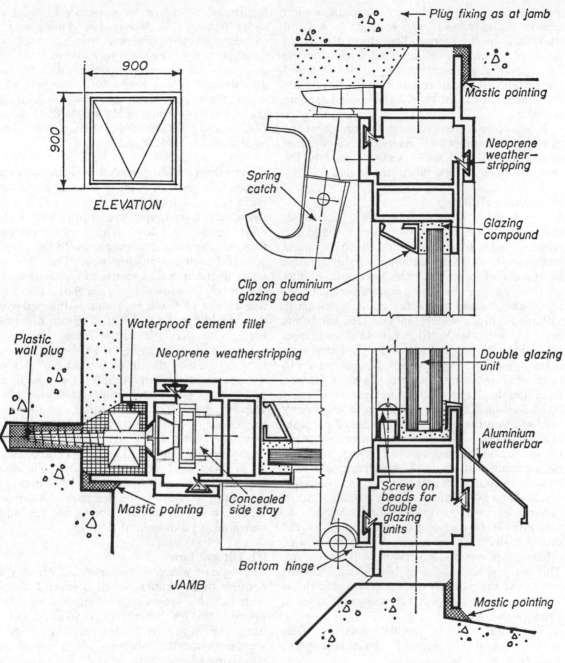

900

900

ELEVATION

Plug fixing as at jamb

Mastic pointing

Neoprene weather-stripping

Spring catch

Glazing compound

Clip on aluminium glazing bead

Plastic wall plug

Waterproof cement fillet

Neoprene weatherstripping

Double glazing unit

Aluminium weatherbar

Screw on beads for double glazing units

Mastic pointing

Concealed side stay

Bottom hinge

JAMB

Mastic pointing

SECTION

6.43 *Aluminium window: bottom hung, opening inwards*

inner glazing bead which is extruded aluminium section, is clipped over, and retained by a nylon stud fixed to the frame. The alternative is an extruded aluminium section bead screwed to the frame. Note the mastic pointing at the head and the sill and the weather bar which protects the vulnerable joint at the base of the inward opening casement.

It is interesting to compare the profile of the extruded aluminium sections used in this window with the mild steel rolled sections used in the standard steel window illustrated in figure 6.28.

(d) Horizontal sliding

Figure 6.44 shows a purpose-made horizontal sliding window in aluminium which is made in a range of sizes to comply with the basic space recommendations for aluminium windows shown in figure 6.41 page 196. The horizontal sliding window is a type much used in commercial buildings, schools, and hospitals, being particularly suitable for high rise development. The window is detailed so that both sashes can be cleaned from the inside without removal, and a feature to note is the nylon skids upon which the sashes run. In large windows using say 6 mm glass, or heavier, or in double glazed windows nylon rollers would be used as an alternative, as shown. The windows are fixed into the opening by the use of purpose-made brackets which *twist lock* into position in the frame and are then screwed or shot fired into the concrete or brickwork. The tracks are fixed into the opening first and then the pre-assembled window at a later date. Alternatively the window can be set in a timber surround. A point to remember in respect of fixing aluminium is that ordinary steel or brass screws should not be used otherwise bi-metallic corrosion will be set up. This window has a security bolt which locks the window in the partially open position, and this is a point that must be watched with all horizontal sliding windows.

The window will be factory glazed, the glass being sealed into the frames by reusable neoprene gaskets.

The problem of weather resistance is difficult to overcome with a horizontal sliding type of opening light and much careful thought has been given to this problem in the example shown, which is designed to conform with the forthcom-

ing British Standard on resistance to wind and water penetration. Woven pile double weather stripping is incorporated at the head, sill, and meeting style of the window panes and the PVC jamb sections ensure a good weather seal. Note also the use of the many PVC channels which isolate the weather stripping and nylon skids from the aluminium frame. This use of PVC reduces friction and resists the deteriorating action due to accumulation of dust and grit.

(e) Horizontal sliding window in timber surround

Figure 6.45 gives an example of a standard aluminium horizontal sliding window in a timber surround which is competitive in price with a standard timber window. The timber surround provides the basic construction with the opening part of the window in aluminium. This window is made in the standard metric range of sizes to fit the openings shown in figure 6.41. The figure illustrates a 1300 mm high window inserted over a deep middle rail to give a 2100 mm composite unit. Note that the actual frame size of the window will be 5 mm less than the aperture size subject to a manufacturing tolerance of $\pm$ 3 mm. The metric sizes are in multiples of a basic module of 100 mm. The timber frames, which should be vacuum treated with preservative, and afterwards primed, will be built into the opening in the usual way. Then when all the wet trades are completed the head and sill of the aluminium component are set in mastic and screwed in position. The sashes are factory glazed with 3 mm or 4 mm glass according to overall size. See page 184 for comments on which timbers not to use for timber surrounds to aluminium windows.

(f) Tilt and turn

This type of window originated in Germany and consists of a window which is inward opening with a double action sash – bottom hung inward opening (tilt) for draught free ventilation and side hung opening-in (turn) for cleaning. They are very sophisticated windows which are steadily increasing in popularity in the UK. Advances in tilt and turn fittings have improved their safety: these include the provision of security stays, crack (narrow gap) ventilation in either the tilt or turn mode, and the introduction of switch barriers to ensure the windows cannot be put into both

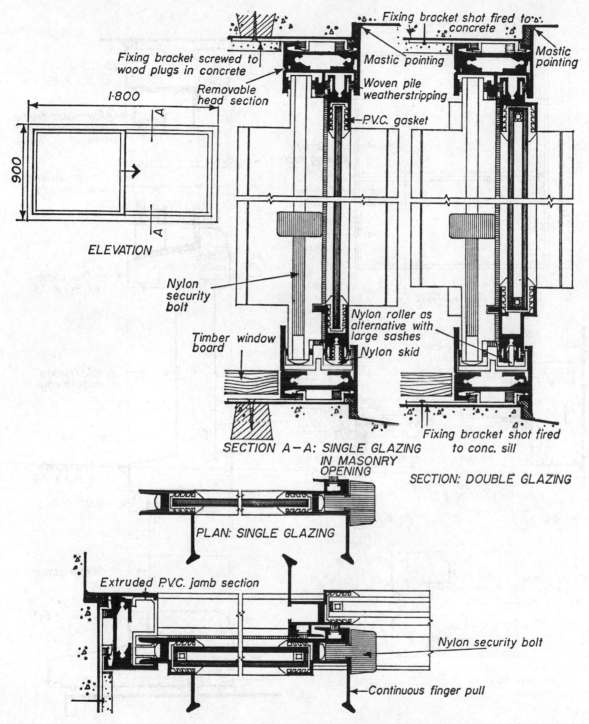

Fixing bracket shot fired to concrete

Fixing bracket screwed to wood plugs in concrete

Removable head section

Mastic pointing

Mastic pointing

Woven pile weatherstripping

P.V.C. gasket

1·800

900

ELEVATION

Nylon security bolt

Timber window board

Nylon roller as alternative with large sashes

Nylon skid

Fixing bracket shot fired to conc. sill

SECTION A – A: SINGLE GLAZING IN MASONRY OPENING

SECTION: DOUBLE GLAZING

PLAN: SINGLE GLAZING

Extruded P.V.C. jamb section

Nylon security bolt

Continuous finger pull

PLAN AT JAMB AND INTERLOCKING MEETING STYLE: DOUBLE GLAZING

6.44 *Purpose-made aluminium horizontal sliding window*

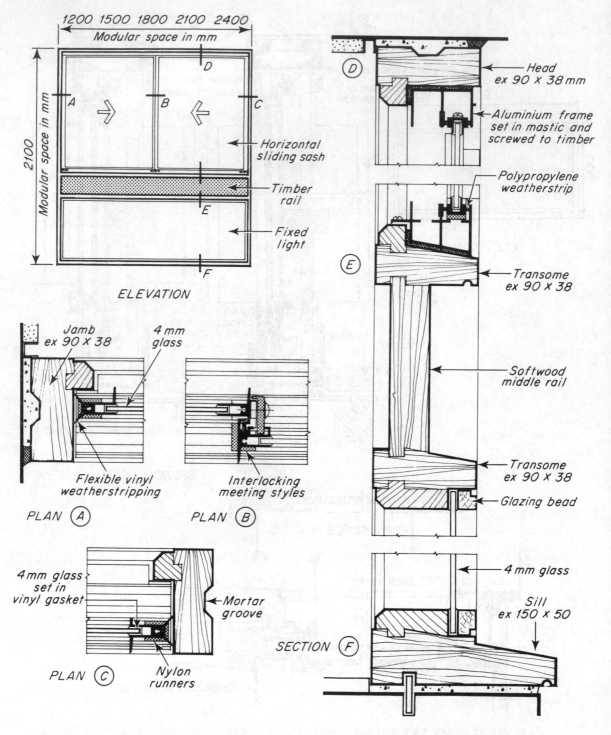

1200 1500 1800 2100 2400

Modular space in mm

D

A → *B* ← *C*

Horizontal sliding sash

2100

Modular space in mm

Timber rail

E

Fixed light

F

ELEVATION

Head ex 90 × 38 mm

Aluminium frame set in mastic and screwed to timber

Polypropylene weatherstrip

Transome ex 90 × 38

Softwood middle rail

Transome ex 90 × 38

Glazing bead

Jamb ex 90 × 38   4 mm glass

Flexible vinyl weatherstripping

Interlocking meeting styles

PLAN Ⓐ   PLAN Ⓑ

4 mm glass

4 mm glass set in vinyl gasket

Mortar groove

Sill ex 150 × 50

PLAN Ⓒ   Nylon runners

SECTION Ⓕ

6.45 *Aluminium sliding window in timber surround*

202

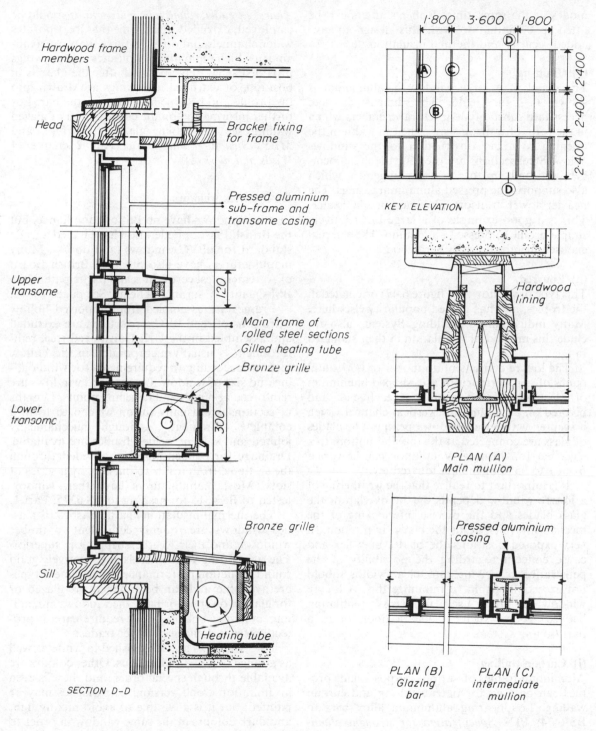

Hardwood frame members

Head

Bracket fixing for frame

Pressed aluminium sub-frame and transome casing

Upper transome

Main frame of rolled steel sections

Gilled heating tube

Bronze grille

120

Lower transomc

300

Bronze grille

Sill

Heating tube

SECTION D-D

6.46 *Large aluminium window*

1·800   3·600   1·800

D

A   C

B

2·400   2·400   2·400

D

KEY ELEVATION

Hardwood lining

PLAN (A)
Main mullion

Pressed aluminium casing

PLAN (B)
Glazing bar

PLAN (C)
intermediate mullion

modes at the same time. Roller shutters can be fitted in combination with this design to give added security and thermal insulation.

(g) 'Built-up'

The detail of a large window in aluminium is shown in figure 6.46. The dimensions here necessitate substantial structural members which in the form of transoms span the full width of the opening to avoid obstruction to the windows below. Steel sections are used for the main members and built up to give an arrangement which also supports the pressed aluminium casings. The heavier lower transom also supports a heater. This is a good example of a large but relatively simple profile in pressed aluminium. The external exposed members are in hardwood.

(h) Louvred

This type of window (see figure 6.47) originated in the tropics, and has gained popularity elsewhere. Many industrialized Building Systems also include this method of ventilation in their standard range.

The louvre consists of a number of horizontal panes of glass gripped in a U-shaped aluminium or plastics extruded section at each end, and pivoted on an aluminium vertical channel which is secured within the window opening. The blades of glass are connected at the top and bottom to a lever bar for opening. Ventilation can be varied from 1 to 95% of the net louvred area.

It is important to realize that the weathering of a louvre window depends on the overlap of the glass blades and the precise interlocking of the mechanism which holds the blades in position. In very exposed positions the blades may flex and cause concern regarding the possibility of the penetration of driving rain; clear widths should not exceed 1066 mm to minimize this. A louvre window is often used for cross ventilation between rooms such as over a door, or in a partitioning system.

(i) Curtain walling

Aluminium frames of various purpose-made profiles can be used for patent glazing and curtain walling. Loadbearing aluminium alloy bars to BS 1474: 1972 *Specification for wrought aluminium and aluminium alloys for general engineering*

– *bars, extruded round tube and sections* should be employed, extruded to a profile that incorporates water channels and other features. Bars are available in which aluminium or plastics caps or wings provided separately are fitted after the glass is in position, or extruded lead wings are drawn into the profile and become integral with the bar. For further information on the construction of glazed walling see 7.4 Patent glazing (*Glazing*), and *MBS: Structure and Fabric:* Part 2 chapter 4 *Walls and piers*.

6.6 Plastics windows

Plastics windows have no BS for compliance, but the British Plastics Federation have issued a trade standard for uPVC windows (and doors). Many manufacturers have also obtained British Board of Agrément test certificates and participate in the BSI Quality Assurance Scheme. See pages 16–19.

Frames are assembled from imported hollow extrusions of rigid PVC, or sections are extruded and assembled in the UK. Galvanized steel reinforcement is usually incorporated in the hollow sections according to requirements for windloading and size of window. Larger sized windows are reinforced at hinges and fastening points. Lengths of sections are usually fusion welded to form a complete casement, although mechanically jointed and solvent welded frames are available. Drainage for condensation is provided through the sections, from inside to outside, by a series of slots. Most manufacturers have their window tested to BS 4315 for grading to BS 6375: Part 1.

The thermal insulation characteristics of plastics windows are roughly equivalent to timber windows, and their weatherstripping is superior. The tight fitting weather seals give relatively good sound reduction performance. All casement types are available and can be supplied pre-glazed or for glazing on site: normally the windows are built into prepared openings and require careful protection from damage by other trades.

PVC windows are self finished in white as well as a range of greys and browns. Other colours are available through special order, and there is even an imitation wood version! The plastics may be painted, but it is advisable to avoid mixing light and dark colours in the same window in order to avoid differential expansion. As a result of acce-

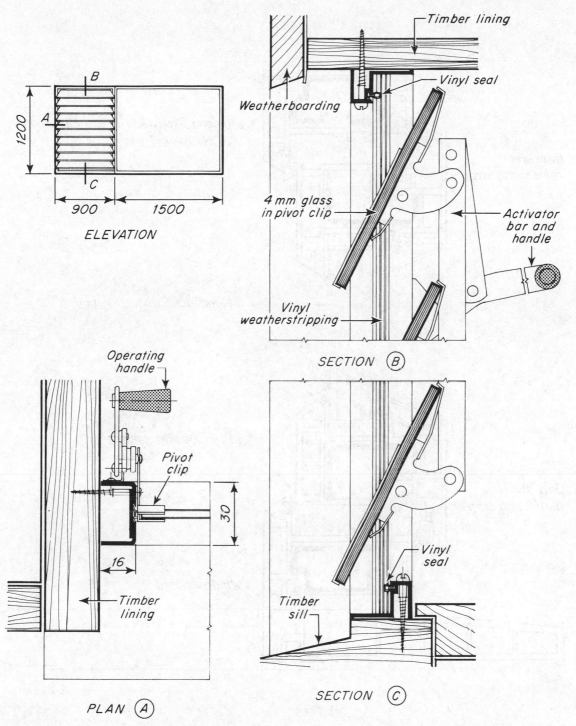

6.47 *Louvre window*

ELEVATION

1200

900   1500

B
A
C

SECTION B

Timber lining
Weatherboarding
Vinyl seal
4 mm glass
in pivot clip
Activator
bar and
handle
Vinyl
weatherstripping

SECTION C

Vinyl
seal
Timber
sill

PLAN A

Operating
handle
Pivot
clip
30
16
Timber
lining

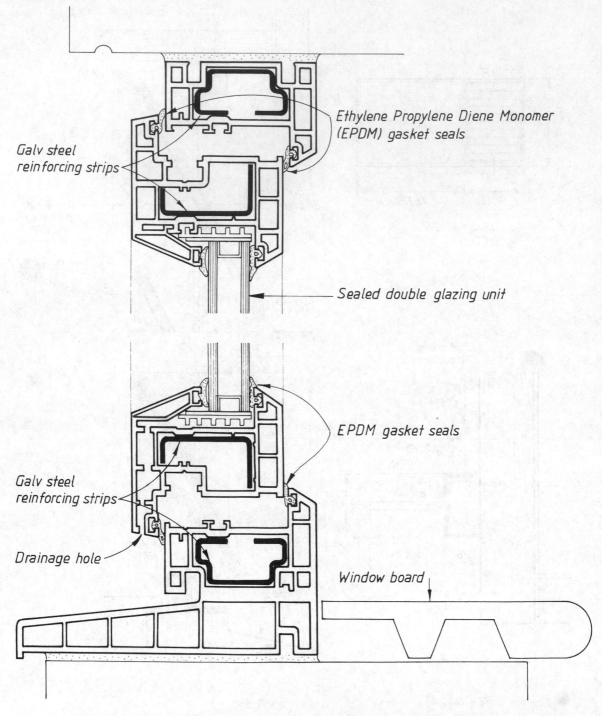

Ethylene Propylene Diene Monomer (EPDM) gasket seals

Galv steel reinforcing strips

Sealed double glazing unit

EPDM gasket seals

Galv steel reinforcing strips

Drainage hole

Window board

6.48   *Typical details of a side-hung window using plastic sections (Plastmo)*

lerated testing procedures, the anticipated life of plastics windows is stated to be more than 25 years. They should be cleaned regularly to maintain a bright appearance, and painting may be required after 20 years. Figure 6.48 indicates typical sections and details.

Plastics windows are purpose made and do not have a recommended modular range of sizes other than as stipulated by the manufacturers and/or designers. Combinations of window units can be used by incorporating mullions and transoms which are connected to the outer frame and, where relevant, to each other by means of welded joints.

PVC coated timber sections are also available and these have similar characteristics to the hollow sections described above. It is obviously important that the timber core is thoroughly kiln dried and protected against biological destruction, firstly by a preservative treatment against wood-attacking insects and all forms of fungi, and secondly, by the uPVC extrusions which should be adequately sealed around the whole of

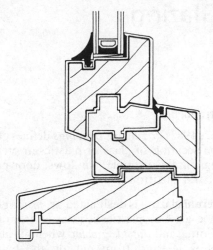

6.49 *Typical details of window using plastic coated timber sections (Blacknell Buildings Ltd)*

the timber. Figure 6.49 indicates typical details. These windows require very careful installation into prepared openings and must be carefully maintained thereafter.

7 Glazing

7.1 Introduction

BS 6262: 1982 *Glazing for buildings* defines **glazing** as, 'The securing of glass or plastics in prepared openings in, for example, windows, door panels, screens and partitions'.

External glazing is designated as, *inside glazing* when the glass or plastics is inserted from inside the building; and *outside glazing* when the glass or plastics is inserted from outside the building.

Internal glazing is designated as, glass or plastics where neither face is exposed outside the building.

MBS: Materials, chapter 12 gives details of the properties associated with each type of *glass* used in the construction of buildings. Most glass specified is soda/lime/silica-based, conforming with BS 952: *Glass for glazing* Part 1: 1978 *Classification*, and Part 2: 1980 *Terminology for work on glass*. After being formed to the shape required by various heat-based processes, ordinary glass must be cooled slowly (*annealed*) to relieve the strains which would otherwise result. Most glass is referred to as *annealed glass* to distinguish it from *toughened glass* which is suddenly cooled during manufacture, thereby putting the surfaces into compression and the interior into tension. For convenience, the descriptions of the different types of glass are summarized below.

Annealed flat glass:
(a) Clear float *for general use.*
(b) Solar control glass *tinted for solar absorption and reflection.*
(c) Roughcast glass *surface textured for obscuration.*
(d) Patterned glass *surface patterned for obscuration.*
(e) Opal glass *coloured or variegated for obscuration.*
(f) Wired glass *cast or polished wire reinforced for fire resistance.*

Those based on flat glass, *annealed* and/or *toughened*:
(g) Toughened glass (non-annealed) *strengthened for impact resistance.*
(h) Laminated glass *reinforced with sandwiched plastics sheet against impact.*
(i) Laminated solar control glass *tinted interlayer for solar reflection and absorption.*
(j) Laminated sound control glass *interlayer thickness combination for sound resistance.*
(k) Laminated ultra-violet light control glass *interlayer to reflect 98% of ultra-violet radiation.*
(l) Anti-bandit laminated glass *thicker interlayers to provide security/alarm devices.*
(m) Bullet-resistant laminated glass *as above but also resists bullets.*
(n) Blast-resistant laminated glass *combines safety, anti-bandit and bullet-resistance.*
(o) Insulating glass units *double or more glazing with hermetic seals.*
(p) Fire-resisting glass *softening, or intumescent interlayer, or copper glazing.*
(q) Lead X-ray glass *contains lead oxide for X-ray resistance.*

Those having applied surface treatment, *annealed*:
(r) Obscuring *obscuration by sandblasting, grinding or acid embossing.*
(s) Brilliant *surface cutting and polishing.*
(t) Engraving *cutting surface with small wheel.*
(u) Enamelling, staining or painting, and firing *coating with fusible pigment then firing.*
(v) Stoving *as above but fired at lower temperature.*
(w) Gilding *application of metal leaf to surface.*
(x) Silvering *deposition of silver on surface for 'one-way glass'.*
(y) Striped silvering or 'Venetian' stripe *alternate silver and clear bands ('one-way glass').*
(z) Applying metallic film *reduction in light transmission/increase in reflectance.*

All glass, except toughened glass, can be worked after manufacture, including cutting and shaping, hole cutting, notching, edge finishing, and bending for curved windows and domes. In addition to those listed above, hand-made antique, bullion (bulls-eye), glass blocks, channel section, stained and leaded light glass are available.

Bent and curved glass can be produced from most types of flat annealed glass by kiln heating until it is soft enough to allow formation over a mould. Although largely superseded by the use of plastics, curved glass is still employed for windows and roof light domes (see chapter 8: *Roof lights*), and for mirrors (convex or concave). Figure 7.1 shows standard curves for bent glass as given in BS 952: Part 2.

Various publications of the *Glass and Glazing Federation* are useful, including the *Glazing Manual* and booklet No 1 *Site glazing procedures for insulating glass*; No 8 *The use of laminated glass*; No 9 *Glass bending*; and No 10 *Toughened glass*.

MBS: Materials chapter 13 gives details of the properties associated with each type of *plastics* used in the construction of buildings. Plastics materials commonly used for glazing include: polycarbonate (PC), polymethyl methacrylate (PMMA) – commonly referred to as 'acrylic', unplasticized polyvinyl chloride (uPVC), glass reinforced plastics (GRP), hollow section extruded profiles in PMMA and PVC, cellulose acetate butyrate (CAB), and polystyrene (internal applications only). They are ideal for many situations where safety and security are important because of their relative high strength and impact resistance characteristics. When compared with thick glass, the significantly reduced weight gives other advantages relating to framing materials. Plastics for glazing are available wired, laminated, tinted, textured and with solar control. Composite glass and plastics forms are also available, as are anti-bandit and bullet-proof grades, and single, double and triple skinned PC sheet extrusions. However, they are all combustible (see page 236).

A useful publication by the *Glass and Glazing Federation* is their booklet No 7 *Glazing with plastics*.

7.2 Performance requirements

Developments in glazing have reached a high level of sophistication and Section 15 of BS 6262 places great emphasis on the need for designers to make their requirements clear at each stage of the design process. However, the *performance specification* for successful glazing obviously depends to a very large extent on characteristics of the glass or plastics used, including the selection of the appropriate type to fulfil specific function(s), and the correct thickness relative to size of opening. This criteria is fully covered in *MBS: Materials* chapter 12: *Glass*, and chapter 13: *Plastics*, and will only be covered in outline here except where a more detailed explanation is necessary to justify aspects of *glazing*, the securing of glass or plastics to its surround. This section on performance specification for glazing should be read in conjunction with 6.2 Performance specification (*Windows*).

(a) Appearance

The relationship of window and door openings to the remaining wall significantly contributes to the character of a building. Forms, shapes, patterns, textures and colours are partly provided by these openings and the materials and techniques used for their construction. Window frames can be expressed boldly by the use of large sections, or have minimal influence when thin sections are used. Glazing located towards the external face of the wall creates a feeling of 'flatness' in the appearance of the façade, whereas deeply recessed glazing leads to the casting of heavy shadows in the external reveals and a feeling of 'punctuation'. In this respect, the viewing distance away from the window plays an important role. The amount of external light passing through or reflected back by the glazing will also play an influential part in the appearance of a building, as can the reverse situation at night, when rooms and their occupants can either be concealed from or exposed to view from outside.

The performance specification should include factors relating to other aesthetic considerations, including psychological factors relating to the provision of a view, and a combination of physiological and psychological factor arising from the

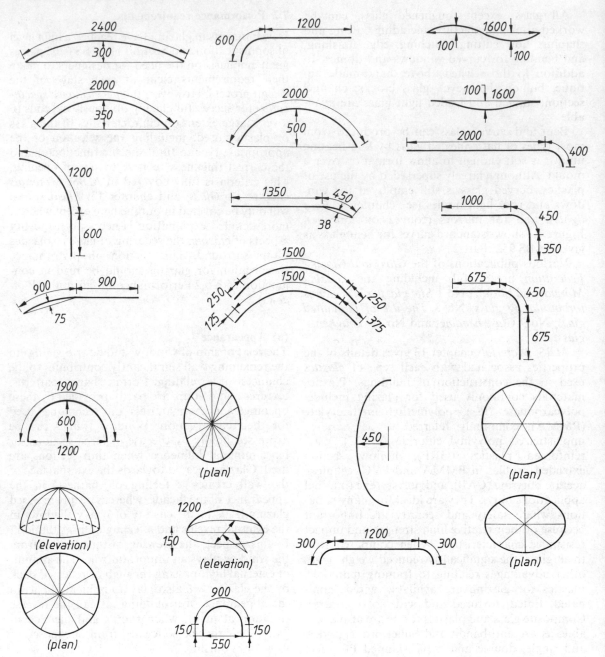

7.1 *Standard curves for bent glass in BS 952: Part 2: 1980*

provision of comfort, security, privacy, light, glare and colour rendition within the building.

(b) Strength

Glass Annealed glass, including wired glass, is easily broken in the thicknesses which are commonly used and the fragments are very dangerous: wire in glass holds fragments in position and fragments of laminated glass are held in position by plastics interlayers. Toughened glass is much stronger than annealed glass and the fragments are relatively harmless.

Glass must not only be sufficiently thick to resist stresses due to minor impact by persons and animals, but also pressures exerted by wind, the severity of which will vary with exposure conditions, the type of glass and method of fixing. Figures 7.2 and 7.3 provide a guide to the minimum safe thicknesses relative to wind loadings for the more common types of glass, glazed vertically and supported at four edges in panes of stated areas. The thick lines are for square panes and the extremities of the shaded bands are for length: width ratios of 3 to 1 and more. Proportional positions on the bands should be read for ratios between 1 to 1 and 3 to 1. The design wind loadings for *pressure and suction* should be determined from CP 3 *Code of basic data for the design of buildings* chapter V Part 2: 1972 *Wind loads*, or for low rise buildings only, an abbreviated method of determination contained in BS 6262.

Using the CP 3 method of calculation, basic *wind speeds* (in newtons per square metre) are converted to *design wind speed* (in metres per second) by applying a *topography factor* (usually 1.0), a *ground roughness factor* (0.56–1.27) for actual height and nature of terrain, and a *life factor* (usually 1.0). Using these criteria for appropriate wind force locations in the UK, 600 N/m basic wind speed brings the calculated design wind speed, in rounded figures, to 27 m/s; 800 N/m to 29 m/s; 1000 N/m to 31 m/s; 2000 N/m to 44 m/s; 3000 N/m to 60 m/s; 4000 N/m to 67 m/s; and 5000 N/m to 78 m/s. The design wind speeds in the UK range from 38 m/s in the south east of England to 56 m/s in the extreme north of Scotland and, according to the Meteorological Office, are likely to be exceeded on the average only once in 50 years at 10 m above the ground in open level country.

The BS 6262 abbreviated method is not suitable for any buildings higher than 10 m from ground level or where the basic wind speed is higher than 52 m/s, nor should it be used for buildings on cliff tops.

Plastics Figures 7.4 to 7.7 similarly provide a guide to minimum safe thickness and pane proportion/sizes for plastics. The wind loading should be derived from appropriate design wind speed given in CP 3: chapter V: Part 2. (see explanation under *Glass*). If the pane is situated where it may be subject to accidental breakage or is required to withstand vandal attack, the thickness should be increased or the glazing appropriately modified.

Glazing techniques In order to take full advantage of strength characteristics it is important that all edges of glass and plastics panes are adequately supported, normally within or against a frame of timber, metal or plastics. To effect this requirement, **glazing compounds or gaskets** are provided to produce a joint between the panes and the frame which, whilst holding the pane firmly in position, also allows for differential movement between the two components. Glazing can be executed in supporting frames with *rebates* and the glass or plastics is held by the glazing materials alone (figure 7.8(a) and 7.8(b) or, alternatively, a *bead* is provided for this purpose and the glazing material fulfils the other functions of sealing and allowance for movements only (figure 7.9).

Panes can also be held by gaskets located within *grooves* or over *nibs* of a supporting frame – see figure 7.8 and figure 7.10. Glazing is usually held clear of its framing when *structural gaskets* are used, or has no independent frame when glass is made structurally self sufficient by suspension or through its geometrical configeration (see page 228).

Glazing compounds and gaskets Materials used for glazing are described in detail in BS 6262, and briefly, the classifications are:

Continued on page 215

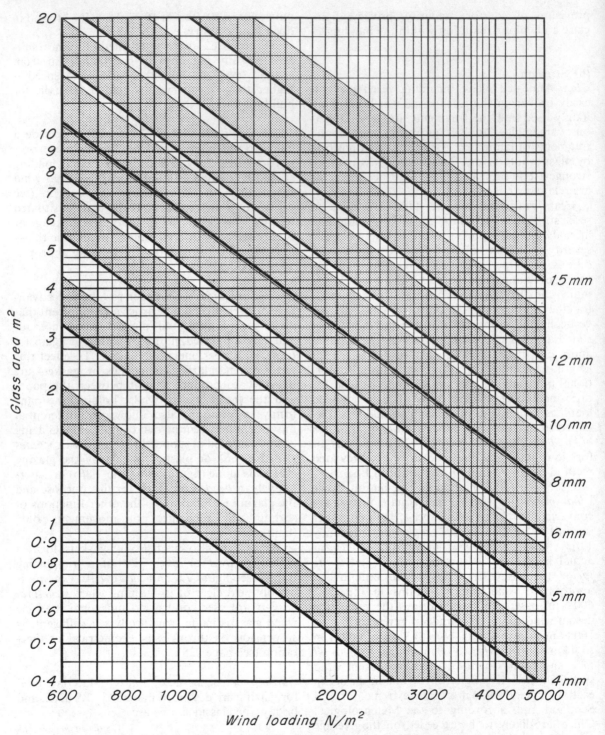

7.2 *Minimum thickness of clear glasses (except laminated) subject to three second mean wind loadings, glass held vertically and at four edges (Pilkington Glass Ltd)*

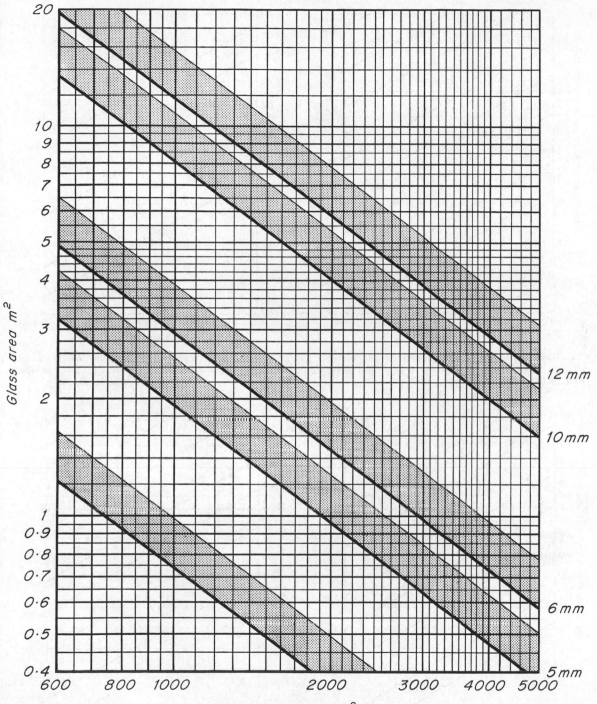

7.3 *Minimum thicknesses of wired, rough cast and patterned glasses, subject to three second mean wind loadings, glass held vertically and at four edges (Pilkington Glass Ltd)*

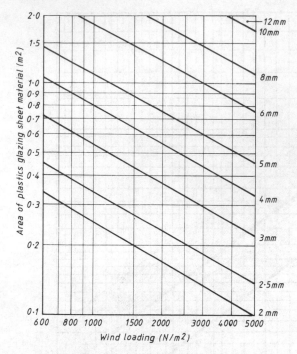

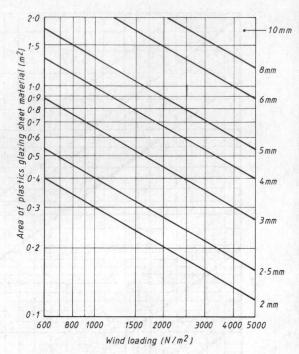

7.4 *Wind loading graph for plastics glazing sheet material, three second mean wind loading, 15 mm edge cover and aspect ratio of 1 : 1 to 1.5 : 1. (BS 6262: 1982)*

7.5 *Wind loading graph for plastics glazing sheet materials, three second mean wind loading, 15 mm edge cover and aspect ratio greater than 1.5 : 1 up to and including 2.5 : 1. (BS 6262: 1982)*

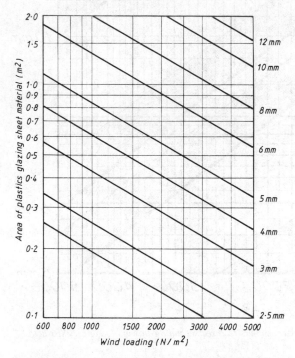

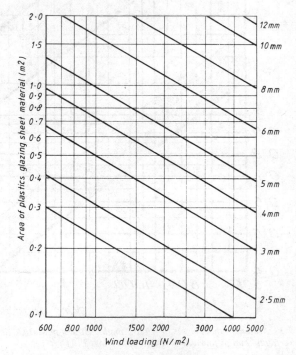

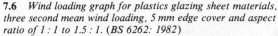

7.6 *Wind loading graph for plastics glazing sheet materials, three second mean wind loading, 5 mm edge cover and aspect ratio of 1 : 1 to 1.5 : 1. (BS 6262: 1982)*

7.7 *Wind loading graph for plastics glazing materials, three second mean wind loading, 5 mm edge cover and aspect ratio greater than 1.5 : 1 up to and including 2.5 : 1. (BS 6262: 1982)*

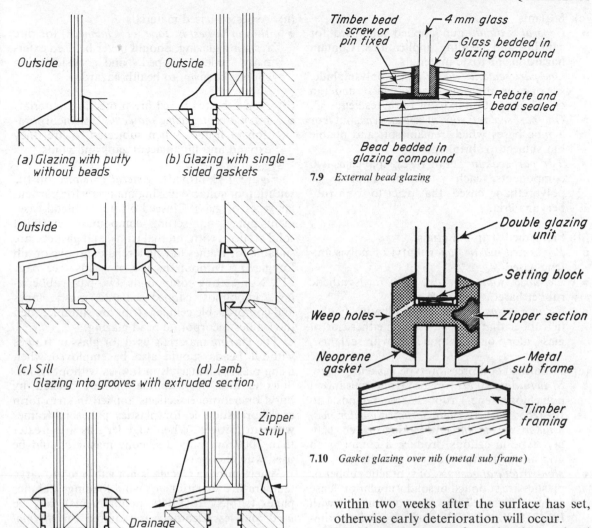

(a) Glazing with putty without beads

(b) Glazing with single-sided gaskets

(c) Sill
(d) Jamb
Glazing into grooves with extruded section

(e) Glazing into grooves with channel gaskets

(f) Glazing into grooves with structural gaskets

7.8 *Rebate and grooved glazing*

7.9 *External bead glazing*

Timber bead screw or pin fixed — 4 mm glass — Glass bedded in glazing compound — Rebate and bead sealed — Bead bedded in glazing compound

7.10 *Gasket glazing over nib (metal sub frame)*

Double glazing unit — Setting block — Weep holes — Zipper section — Neoprene gasket — Metal sub frame — Timber framing

Continued from page 211

(a) Putties
- *Linseed oil putty*, (BS 544: 1969 *Specification for linseed oil putty for use in wooden frames*) is used for glazing into softwood and absorbent hardwood frames. Needs to be painted within two weeks after the surface has set, otherwise early deterioration will occur.
- *Metal casement putty*, formulated to set hard and adhere to non-porous surfaces. Needs to be painted within 28 days.

(b) Flexible compounds
- *Non-setting glazing compounds*, used in conjunction with beads or in grooves where glass is subject to structural or thermal movement which cannot be accommodated by putties. Minimum thickness of 3 mm, maximum of 5 mm.
- *Two-part rubberized compounds*, hand or gun applied, flexible and used with beads in exposed situations and for frames subject to movement or distortion.

215

(c) Sealants
- *General sealant*, gun applied and used for capping and bedding applications. Contain hazardous or toxic materials.
- *One-part sealant*: *curing types*, polysulphide, silicone or urethane bases which undergo chemical reaction to form a firm resilient seal.
- *One-part sealant*: *solvent release type*, butyl or acrylic bases which remain soft and pliable but subject to shrinkage.
- *Two-part sealant*: *curing types*, applied as two components, each either polysulphide or polyurethane based, that react to form rubbery material.

(d) Preformed strip materials
- *Preformed mastic tapes*, butyl or polyisobutene based.
- *Extruded solid sections*, PVC or synthetic rubber based.
- *Cellular strips*, made of self-adhesive synthetic rubber that may be used on either side of glass, alone or in conjunction with sealants.

(e) Preformed compression type gaskets
- *Structural gaskets*, made from vulcanized polychloroprene rubber compounds to BS 4255: Part 1: 1986 *Specification for non-cellular gaskets*. *Integral locking strips* or 'zipper' type insertions produce a compression grip on the frame structure and the glass.
- *Non-structural gaskets*, of synthetic rubber or plastics are supplied in solid, tubular or dense sponge form. They should comply with BS 4255: Part 1: 1986, and are used as primary seals when maintained under positive pressure, or need to be mechanically retained in rebates and top sealed with one- or two-part sealant.

(f) Glazing materials for internal glazing
- *Self-adhesive glazing tapes*, of treated cotton-based tapes and black velvet ribbons treated with adhesive coating on one side.
- *Simulated washleather and black velvet tapes*.
- *Extruded mastic tapes*, of treated cotton-based tapes and black velvet ribbons treated with an adhesive coating on one side.

(g) Asbestos-based materials
- *Woven asbestos tape or channels*, for fire resisting glazing. Should never be used externally unless capped, and consideration should be given to health hazard.

(h) Non-asbestos based fire-protecting materials
- *Intumescent glazing materials*, for incorporation in frame. When subjected to fire, they expand and fill adjacent gaps and voids.

Figure 7.11 provides *general guidance* on the selection of suitable glazing materials for particular types of glass. Linseed oil putty, metal casement putty, non-setting compounds, extruded solid sections with internal trims, and gaskets, are suitable for frames having a rebate, groove or nib for glazing without the use of beads – see page 215. Non-setting compounds, two-part rubberizing compounds, capped sealants, mastic tapes and compressible cellular strips are suitable when the frames incorporate bead glazing.

The glazing materials used for glass in frames without beads should also be employed when using plastics materials in frames without beads. Silicone and polysulphide mastics backed by butyl or neoprene sections applied in strip form are more suitable for plastics panes in frames without grooves. When edge lengths are greater than 2000 mm only a silicone mastic should be used with the strips.

Where *interior glazing* is not subjected to large temperature variations or wind loadings, thinner panes (subject to safety requirements) may be used and less clearance is required for *thermal movements*. Exceptions, are when the glazing forms part of a fire barrier (see page 220) or when it is used as part of a bathroom wall or door. In all other cases also, a sealant or gasket need not be used if beads form the retaining rebates. However, in order to reduce vibration and noise, a small amount of permanently flexible sealant, usually in the convenient tape form, should be used in conjunction with the beads.

(c) Thermal control
The type of glazing can play a very important role in regulating the total annual energy consumption

Glass	Glazing material											
	Linseed oil putty	Metal casement putty	Non-setting glazing compounds	Two-part rubberizing compounds	One-part sealant: curing types	One-part sealant: solvent release types	Two-part sealent: curing types	Preformed mastic tapes	Extruded solid sections	Cellular strips	Structural gaskets	Non-structural gaskets
Transparent glass												
(a) Float glass												
1 Clear	X	X	X	X	X	X	X	X	X	X	X	X
2 Body tinted	C	C	X	X	X	X	X	X	X	X	X	X
3 Surface modified tinted	–	–	X	X	X	X	X	X	X	X	X	X
4 Surface coated	–	–	X	X	X	X	X	X	X	X	X	X
(b) Polished wired glass	X	X	X	X	X	X	X	X	X	X	X	X
(c) Sheet glass												
1 Clear	X	X	X	X	X	X	X	X	X	X	X	X
2 Body tinted	C	C	X	X	X	X	X	X	X	X	X	X
3 Flashed or pot coloured	C	C	X	X	X	X	X	X	X	X	X	X
Translucent rolled and cast glass												
(a) Patterned	X	X	X	X	X	X	X	X	X	X	X	X
(b) Tinted patterned	C	C	X	X	X	X	X	X	X	X	X	X
(c) Wired patterned	X	X	X	X	X	X	X	X	X	X	X	X
(d) Rough cast	X	X	X	X	X	X	X	X	X	X	X	X
(e) Tinted rough cast	C	C	X	X	X	X	X	X	X	X	X	X
(f) Rough cast wired	X	X	X	X	X	X	X	X	X	X	X	X
Toughened (tempered) glass												
Clear rolled, cast	X	X	X	X	X	X	X	X	X	X	X	X
Enamelled, tinted	–	–	X	X	X	X	X	X	X	X	X	X
Insulating infill panels	–	–	X	X	X	X	X	X	X	X	X	X
Laminated glass (all types)	–	–	C	C	C	C	X	C	C	X	X	X
Multiple glass units												
Hermetically sealed units	–	C	C	C	C	C	C	C	C	X	X	X
Stepped hermetically sealed units	C	C	C	C	C	C	C	C	C	X	X	X

Key

X denotes suitable

– denotes not suitable

C denotes consider, but dependent on precise details of compound constituents; consult the manufacturers involved

Figure 7.11: Summary of usage of glazing materials for various glass types (BS6262: 1982 Table 4)

217

of a building. The implications of solar gain and heat loss should be considered in relation to the total heat balance of the building and the glazed areas should be chosen accordingly. This process involves analysis of the natural light requirements, the use of special thermal control glasses and, apart from solar gains, the effects of ambient heat gains from artificial lighting, mechanical plant, etc, used in the building. The desire for natural and/or artificial ventilation is another important factor. Further reference should be made to 6.2(e) Thermal control and *MBS: Environment and Services*.

Double glazing Double glazing reduces thermal transmission, but not solar gain. In vertical glazing, a cavity width of about 20 mm halves the heat loss by a single pane, but a 3 mm gap provides about 70% of this optimum. The thickness of glass has no practical effect on thermal insulation.

Double glazing can be achieved using either hermetically sealed glazing units, coupled windows, or converted single glazing.

Hermetically sealed multiple glazing units
These consist of multiple (usually two or three) parallel panes sealed together so that there is a gap between each pane. The spacer may be a tube which contains a dessicant to absorb any moisture between the panes. They are produced in a factory and any range of glasses may be used in combination for their fabrication – annealed, toughened, laminated, solar control, etc. – as well as plastics. A range of sizes for the units is given in figure 7.12, and figure 7.13 shows glazing details (see also figure 7.21 page 223). A low emissivity coating to one of the surfaces of a double-glazed unit with a 12 mm air space can increase the insulation from about 2.8 to 2.0 W/mK in a sheltered zone; if the cavity is also filled with argon gas the U-value lowers still further to 0.0 W/mK. Manufacturers will produce purpose-made hermetically sealed triple-glazed units. Glass sealed units as indicated in figure 7.14 are also available.

The handling and fixing of double glazed units calls for considerable care and skill. Figures 7.15 and 7.16 show examples, and figure 7.17 shows a stepped unit in a small rebate. As site and exposure conditions vary widely it is important that

Nominal total thickness (mm)	Thickness of each pane (mm)	Air space (mm)	Square units (mm)	Rectangular units (mm)
11	3	5	1270	1780 × 1270
12		6	1270	1780 × 1270
14		8	1270	1780 × 1270
15		9	1270	1730 × 1270
16		10	1270	1780 × 1270
18		12	1270	1780 × 1270
12		6	1270	1780 × 1270
13	4	5	1300	2130 × 1300
14		6	1300	2130 × 1300
16		8	1300	2420 × 1300
17		9	1300	2300 × 1300
28		10	1300	2400 × 1300
15	5	5	1700	2600 × 1300
16		6	1700	3050 × 1300
18		8	1830	2600 × 1400
19		9	1930	3050 × 1450
20		10	2100	4270 × 1600
22		12	2130	3050 × 1600
17	6	5	2000	4270 × 1370
18		6	2000	4270 × 1370
20		8	2130	5000 × 1700
21		9	2240	4270 × 1680
22		10	2440	4270 × 2000
24		12	2440	4270 × 2000
32	10	12	3000	5000 × 3000
36	12	12	3250	5000 × 3180

7.12 *Maximum manufacturd sizes for symmetrical, hermetically sealed double-glazing units (source: Architects Journal, May 1985)*

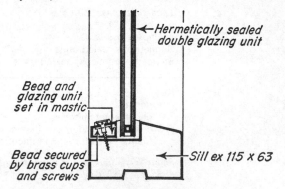

7.13 *Double glazing sealed fixed unit*

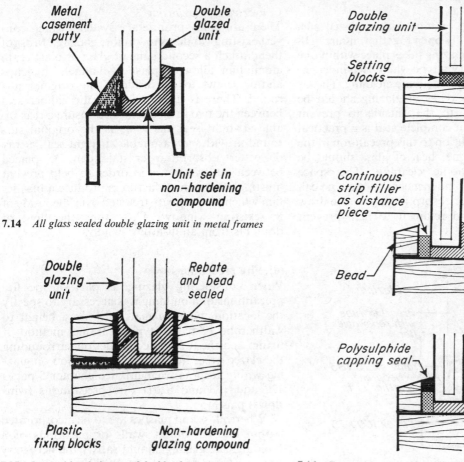

7.14 *All glass sealed double glazing unit in metal frames*

7.15 *Internal bead glazing of double glazing units*

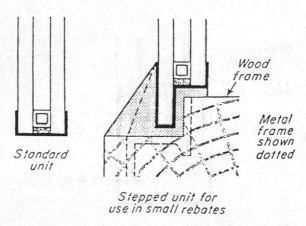

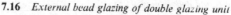

7.16 *External bead glazing of double glazing unit*

glazing compounds should be carefully chosen. Front 'puttying' is possible for units up to 2.3 square metres and not exceeding 11 mm thick, but a polysulphide sealant must be used – *not linseed oil putty*. Two or more bedding or weathering materials may have to be used in the glazing of a unit. Whichever method of glazing is used, the edges of non-glass seals must not be in continuous contact with trapped water, or there is a danger that the seal will be damaged.

The edge seal depth varies with the width of the air space and the area of the unit, from 11 mm with a unit having a 5 mm air space to 29 mm for units having a 12 mm air space. Clearances and rebate depths for bead fixing have been discussed under those headings. More detailed information should be sought from manufacturers.

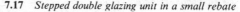

7.17 *Stepped double glazing unit in a small rebate*

Coupled windows

These comprise two or more single glazed surrounds which normally open together: figure 7.18 shows a type where glazing takes place within one frame, and figure 7.19 a type where two independent frames are used to facilitate cleaning. The air space between both types of glazing should be allowed to 'breath' to the outside to prevent condensation, since a complete seal is a practical impossibility. In addition to this precaution in the single frame type, one sheet of glass should be removable for periodic cleaning. The space between panes of the independent frame type can contain trays of water absorption crystals to draw in water vapour and retain it to help prevent 'misting'.

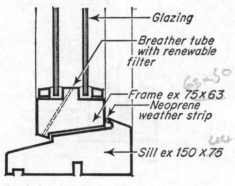

7.18 *Single frame double glazed*

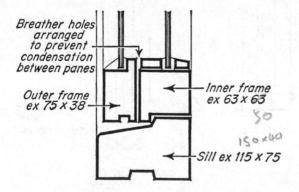

7.19 *Coupled surrounds separately glazed*

Converted single glazing

There are many proprietary systems which convert existing windows to 'double glazing'. Most of them attach a second pane of glass or plastics, in aluminium alloy or plastics channels, by clips and/or screws to the inside of the original surround. There is usually a synthetic rubber seal between the two in an attempt to ensure a reasonable air-tight seal. As long as the original surround provides a reasonable air-tight seal, a tray of water absorption crystals can be placed between the two panes in order to help prevent 'misting'. Some manufacturers produce a plastics film which can be heat-stretched over the inside of an existing window. This stops the flow of draughts from an ill-fitting window.

(d) Fire precautions

When considering glazing as part of the fire precautions of a building it is necessary to specify the location, types of materials, sizes, height to width ratio of panes, type of frame, method of fixing, and the form of construction surrounding the glazed area. For further information on glazing within external elements see chapter 5 pages 122 and 123 and 6.2(f) Fire precautions (windows) page 156.

Where glass and plastics are to be incorporated within internal doors, walls or partitions of a building, the glazing should satisfy the necessary fire resistance in terms of BS 476 *Fire tests on building materials and structures* Part 20: 1987 *Methods for determination of the fire resistance of elements of construction (general principles)*, and Part 22: 1987 *Methods for determination of the fire resistance of non-loadbearing elements of construction*. For further information on glazing within internal elements see 5.8 Fire doors, page 120.

Annealed glass cracks in fires, but wired glass and plastics interlayers in laminated glass hold broken particles for a time. *Georgian wired glass* can produce fire resistance of up to 90 minutes when 6 mm thick in panes not exceeding 1.6 m², depending on the materials and design of frames – see 5.8 Fire doors, page 120. *Laminated glass* can also be used to provide fire resistance provided one lamina is a wired glass at least 6 mm thick to the same maximum size of 1.6 m². *Copper-light* *glazing* is a method of providing fire resistance using unwired annealed glass set in copper glazing cams. The panes should not be less than 6 mm thick and no larger than 0.015 m², placed in panels not more than 0.4 m² overall. Larger panels may be provided by using metal dividing bars (not aluminium) and can give up to 1 hour fire resistance.

Plain fire-resisting glass is available in three forms:

- *Prestressed borosilicate glass* which softens at high temperatures without cracking and, although it can only be cut at the works, is manufactured in sheet sizes up to 2 × 1.2 m;
- *Laminated with a special intumescent gel interlayer* which foams under heat to give the glass integrity, stability and insulation from radiant heat (see page 120);
- *Toughened calcium/silica flat glass*, a relatively new product produced by an abnormal re-heat and cooling process which enables the finished product to satisfy the requirement of BS 476: Parts 20 and 22.

Plastics are combustible and polymethylmethacrylate (acrylic) materials are not self extinguishing. Unplasticized PVC has inherent self-extinguishing properties. Therefore most plastics used for glazing, although often having good surface spread of flame characteristics when tested to BS 476: Part 7 1987, are considered combustible and have little fire resistance.

(e) Sound control

All aspects of glazing in windows and doors can help reduce the transmission of sound – see 5.2(d) Thermal control and sound control (doors), and 6.2(g) Sound control (windows).

The basic principles to be observed are:

- eliminate gaps around frames by the use of weatherstripping;
- the thicker the glass the better, and double glazing will increase sound reduction by 4 db – more if panes are of different thicknesses;
- and air space of 100–200 mm between two panes and absorbent linings to reveals will substantially increase sound reduction (see page 156);

- sealed unit double glazing can also give significant reduction, even with a 6 mm cavity, provided the glass panels differ in thickness from each other by at least 30% and/or the cavity is filled with inert gas;
- laminated glass can resist noise considerably as the plastics interlayer will give sound reduction at different frequencies to the glass.

Double windows

These comprise two single glazed surrounds, fitted separately into window openings as shown in figure 7.20. This construction is suitable where sound reduction is a main consideration and for this the space between panes should be at least 100 mm and preferably 200 mm. The surrounds should be separated.

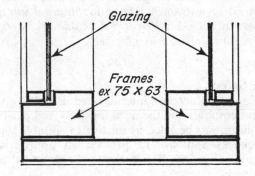

7.20 *Double window*

The glass should be as thick as possible, and sound reduction is further improved by lining the reveals with sound absorbent material. The surrounds must be sealed at their edges as tightly as possible, but one of them should be hung to give access for occasional cleaning within the cavity.

(f) Security

Security glazing systems are available to provide a high degree of protection to persons or property subject to malicious attack. The main areas of concern involve protection against manual attack, the use of firearms, and the effect of explosions – see *Mitchell's: Introduction to Building* chapter 12.

Materials suitable for security glazing in these

221

areas include toughened glass, anti-bandit laminated glass, bullet-resistant laminated glass and blast-resistant laminated glass, as well as certain single plastics sheets and laminated plastics. Laminated glass and plastics can incorporate an alarm sounding interlayer which activates when attacked. The selection of an appropriate material depends on the precise nature and severity of the violence likely to be encountered. The proposed application and performance should, therefore, always be discussed between the client and the manufacturer.

Further reference on this subject should be made to BS 5051 *Security glazing* Part 1: 1973 *Bullet-resistant glazing for interior use*, and Part 2: 1979: *Specification for bullet-resistant glazing for exterior use*. Recommendations for installing anti-bandit framed glazing, and bullet-resistant framed or unframed glazing for internal use are given in BS 5357: 1976 (1985) *Code of practice. Installation of security glazing*.

(g) Safety
Taking into account intended use, BS 6262 gives great emphasis on the need for glass and plastics in glazing to be selected relative to suitable type, thickness and size to provide an appropriate degree of safety. The following '**risk areas**' are defined:

- doors and side panels, fully or partially glazed and side panels that may be mistaken for doors;
- low level glazing, glass or plastics within 800 mm of floor level – especially in public places
- balustrades – see chapter 10;
- bathing areas and swimming pools;
- areas of special risk, where only proposed activity may cause a special risk.

Performance requirements and test method in respect of energy absorption (impact) for flat safety glass and safety plastics which are intended to reduce the risk of cutting and piercing injuries are given in BS 6206: 1981 *Specification for impact performance requirements for flat safety glass and safety plastics for use in buildings*. This BS requires all safety glazing to be marked permanently in a position that is visible after installa-

tion. The marking must indicate the BS number, the class of glazing listed in its clauses (A, B, or C), the type of material (ie 'T' for toughened), and the trade mark or name of the company who last cut the material if the original manufacturer's mark has been removed. The Glass and Federation has compiled a register of marks to assist identification.

(h) Durability and maintenance
The designer must always take account of the potential durability of glass, plastic and glazing materials when selecting and an appropriate glazing system. This concern extends beyond the system itself and involves consideration of various interactions which can take place between adjacent surfaces and components.

Before installation, glass and plastics should be adequately protected on site and during building work may require special protection both externally and internally from the effects of plastering, welding spatter, adhesives, alkaline paint removers, stone cleaning chemicals, etc. The durability, scratch and abrasion resistance of plastics will depend on their chemical nature, added constituents or surface coating.

Once installed, the building owner should be given precise guidance of appropriate methods of inspection, maintenance, cautionery action, specialist work and replacement instructions. For comment on maintenance, including cleaning, see chapter 6 *Windows* under each framing material and general points given in 6.2(h) Durability and maintenance.

7.3 Window and doors

(a) Rebated surrounds
Rebates are provided in the window or door frame to receive the glass or plastics and they should be true, rigid, dry and unobstructed before glazing. Figure 7.21 indicates the terminology for the various aspects needing consideration in the design of rebates.

BS 6262 lays down precise recommendations for the procedures to be followed when glazing with glass or plastics. The minimum *width* will vary according to the thickness of glass or plastics

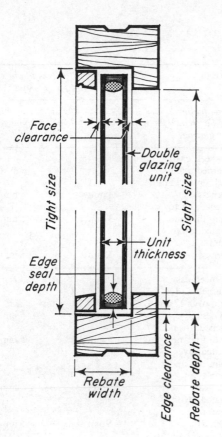

$$Glazing\ size\ (actual\ size) = tight\ size - clearance$$

7.21 *Terminology used in glazing*

and the type of fixing to be accommodated (glazing compound or gasket) which, to some extent, is influenced by the framing material (wood, metal or plastics). The minimum *depth* is also determined by these factors as well as the severity of the exposure conditions. Rebates for glass should not be less than 8 mm deep, except for very small panes up to 0.1 m², when 6 mm depth is adequate. For panes over 1.0 m², bead glazing should be used and the depth of rebate will range from 9 mm to 18 mm, depending on the precise area and thickness of the glass, and the wind loading conditions. The minimum rebate depth for different plastics sheet materials depends on the allowances rquired for their thermal expansion as well as the severity of exposure conditions. Manu-

facturer's advice should always be taken on this matter.

It is always necessary for edge and back clearances between the glass or plastics in order to provide an adequate seal which also allows for differential movements. Panes over, say 0.2 m², must be horizontally located on **setting blocks** to provide **edge clearance**, and these should be of resilient material such as lead, sealed hardwood or rigid nylon. Unplasticised PVC is suitable only for light single panes of clear glass. The setting blocks need to be thicker than the pane(s), and generally from 25 mm to 75 mm long. The exception is a vertical pivoted window, in which case the blocks should be no less than 150 mm long. **Location blocks**, which are used at the sides and top of the window to ensure correct edge tolerances, are usually about 25 mm long. They should be of plasticized PVC or an equivalent softer material than used for setting blocks. The positions of setting and location blocks are shown in figure 7.22, and figure 7.23 indicates the recommended minimum edge clearances for glass and plastics. However, more generous clearances may be needed for clear, particularly wired glass, and for dark coloured glass, solar control glass and double glazed units which have a dark background (ie a backed spandril infill). Such glasses can reach 90°C in temperate climates and as little as possible of their surfaces should be shaded by beads which cause stresses in them by keeping the edges cooler than the exposed parts. It is important also to note that plastics glazing materials need larger clearances to accommodate the greater thermal movements when compared with glass. Ensuring that the edges of the glass are not damaged will help reduce the possible effects of thermal stresses.

In addition to the use of setting and location blocks, where non-setting glazing compounds may be displaced by wind pressure **distance pieces** should be placed between the back edge of glass and the rebate – as shown in figure 7.16 page 219. Distance pieces are usually 25 mm long and a depth to give a 3 mm cover of mastic. They should be under slight compression when beads are fixed. Distance pieces must not coincide with setting blocks or location blocks but they should be of a softer material than setting blocks, usually plasticized PVC.

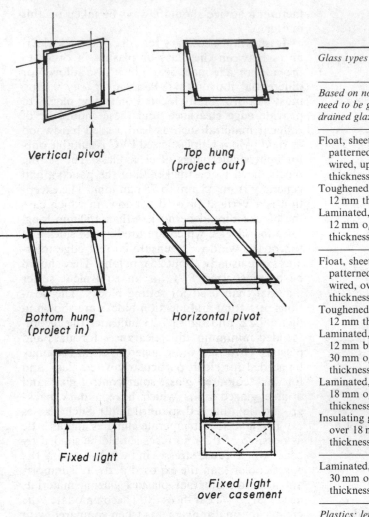

Vertical pivot

Top hung
(project out)

Bottom hung
(project in)

Horizontal pivot

Fixed light

Fixed light
over casement

(min. 75 mm from corner of frame)

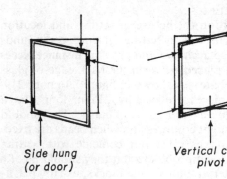

Side hung
(or door)

Vertical centre
pivot

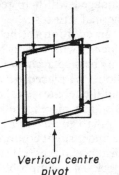

Glass types	Edge clearance for a length or breadth	
	up to 2 m	over 2 m

Based on nominal glass cutting sizes. Edge clearance may need to be greater for some glazing systems, eg some gaskets, drained glazing.

Float, sheet, cast, patterned and wired, up to 12 mm thickness	3 mm	5 mm
Toughened, up to 12 mm thickness	3 mm	5 mm
Laminated, up to 12 mm o/a thickness	3 mm	5 mm
Float, sheet, cast, patterned and wired, over 12 mm thickness	5 mm	5 mm
Toughened, over 12 mm thickness	5 mm	5 mm
Laminated, over 12 mm but under 30 mm o/a thickness	5 mm	5 mm
Laminated, over 18 mm o/a thickness	5 mm	5 mm
Insulating glass units, over 18 mm o/a thickness	5 mm	5 mm
Laminated, exceeding 30 mm o/a thickness	10 mm	10 mm

Plastics: length of side	Reduction on tight rebate size to allow for thermal movements

For cutting at 18°C to 20°C and use in ambient temperatures up to 35°C

Up to 1000 mm	3 mm
1000 to 2000 mm	5 mm
2000 to 3000 mm	7 mm

7.23 *Minimum frame edge clearance for glasses and plastics (BS 6262: 1982, tables 20 and 23)*

◄ **7.22** *Positions of setting and location blocks*

Putty in wood frames with rebates
Putty is a commonly used method of fixing glass (figure 7.8(a)), and is associated with ordinary quality painted joinery in small pane sizes, but rarely for internal glazing. Putty embrittles with age: it must be regularly painted and it is difficult to remove without damaging sashes or frames. It is too rigid to accommodate large differential movements and for wind loadings up to 1900–2300 N/m², the *combined lengths and heights* of panes should not exceed 2700 and 2300 mm respectively.

Linseed oil putty to BS 544: 1969 (1987) *Specification for linseed oil putty for use in wooden frames* sets partly by absorption of the oil in wood surrounds, and partly by oxidation. For this reason, linseed oil putty should not be used on dense, non-absorbent hardwood, such as teak, because initial setting will be considerably delayed. To prevent excessive and premature absorption of oil into more absorbent woods, it is necessary to prime the rebates. The primer should be one coat to conform with BS 2523: 1966 (1983) *Specification for lead-based priming paints*, or be an aluminium based wood primer to BS 4756: 1971 (1983) *Specification for ready mixed aluminium priming paints for woodwork*.

Setting blocks are placed in position for the glass and the rebates are puttied with bedding putty. The glass is then pressed into position and secured with glaziers' sprigs spaced at about 450 mm apart around the perimeter of the frame. On pressing in the glass, the remaining *back putty* should be not less than 2 mm thick between the glass and the rebate. Some putty will be squeezed out and this should be stripped inside at an angle, to prevent shrinkage causing a groove in which condensation and dirt would accumulate.

The glass is then *front puttied* and formed with a putty knife at about 45 degrees to throw off water at this vulnerable point. The putty should be stopped about 2 mm from the sight line of the rebate so that when paint is applied it is carried over the glass up to the sight line and so seals the edge of the putty to the glass. The putty must be protected with paint as soon after the initial hardening of the surface, to prevent long-term shrinkage and cracking.

As an alternative to linseed oil putty, flexible glazing compounds in strip form can be used.

This type also needs protection by paint after initial setting.

Putty in metal frames with rebates
Metal casement putty is formulated to set hard and adhere to non-porous surfaces. The putty needs to be painted as soon as it has hardened (normally 7–14 days) otherwise loss of adhesion or cracking can occur.

Rebates in galvanized steel windows, unless suitably treated or painted 'at works', should be primed with calcium plumbate or self-etching primers. Aluminium surrounds should be primed with zinc chromate, or an etch primer where putty glazing materials are used – see page 215.

This method is similar to that described for wood frames, but, as no absorption of the oil in the putty can take place, a special type of glazing compound is used containing a hardening agent. The glazing compound should be left for about 14 days in order to harden before painting commences. A wire clip, used to retain the glass before the front putty is applied, is shown in figure 7.24.

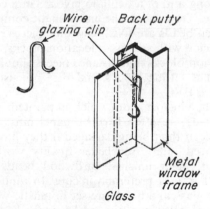

7.24   *Wire glazing clip*

Single glazing and a small double glazing unit in metal frames are shown in figures 7.25 and 7.14.

Beads in wood frames with rebates
Beads are neater than putty fillets, more easily removed and they are necessary to retain large panes. However, as replacement beads cannot always be guaranteed to be waterproof, and the possibility of unauthorized removal must be con-

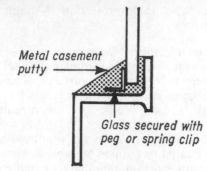

Metal casement putty

Glass secured with peg or spring clip

7.25 *Single glazing in metal frames (see also figure 7.14 Double glazing unit in metal frames)*

sidered, beads are better fixed inside windows and doors.

In addition to setting and location blocks, where non-setting compounds may be displaced by wind pressure, *distance pieces* should be placed between the back edge of glass and the rebate – as shown in figure 7.15, page 219 – in this case for a double glazing unit. Distance pieces are usually 25 mm long and of a depth to give a 3 mm cover of mastic. They should be under slight compression when beads are fixed. Distance pieces must not coincide with setting or location blocks.

Location blocks and distance pieces should be softer than setting blocks, and they are usually plasticized PVC.

For the cheaper work which is painted, softwood beads are often fixed by panel pins, with some risk to their being damaged if they have to be removed later. For better quality work in particular, clear finished hardwood beads are fixed with screws, preferably in cups. In windows, both the glass and beads are set in mastic which must be of good quality, and be applied generously so water will not penetrate. Wood beads should be primed on the back to prevent initial absorption of binder from the mastic. Glass set into doors, is cushioned by binding the edges with a resilient tape, which in external doors, must be water resistant.

Beads which provide fire-resistance are described on pages 123–4.

Figure 7.9 shows an example of single glazing with external beads. The rebate and beads are first sealed with a proprietary sealing compound applied by brush, the glass is then set into the

opening using setting blocks at quarter points and distance pieces to restrain movement.

The glass is then bedded in glazing compound and the bead screwed or pinned in position on a fillet of sealant, usually applied by gun. For internal bead glazing, the bedding for the bead can be omitted. The fixing of a solid infill panel such as plywood is shown in figure 7.26. Figure 7.27 shows bead glazing for an internal door or screen.

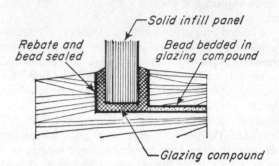

Solid infill panel

Rebate and bead sealed

Bead bedded in glazing compound

Glazing compound

7.26 *Fixing a solid infill panel*

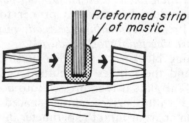

Preformed strip of mastic

25 mm x 2 mm preformed strip of 'reinforced' mastic wrapped around edge of glass

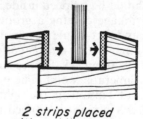

2 strips placed either side of glass and secured by bead

7.27 *Glazing to internal doors or screens*

Figures 7.15 and 7.16 show examples of bead glazing of double glazed units.

Beads in metal frames with rebates

Pressed metal beads are either fixed by screws into threaded holes or they are clipped over studs. Wood beads can be used, but solid steel beads improve the fire resistance of metal frames. A sealant, preformed strip or gasket glazing compound (see page 216) is used in conjunction with bead glazing in metal frames. A typical technique is illustrated in figures 7.28 and 7.29.

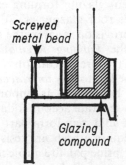

7.28 *Metal beads fixed by screws*

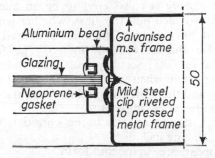

7.29 *Metal beads fixed by clipping over protruding studs*

(b) Grooved surrounds

With this method of securing glass or plastics, the frame usually has a groove at the head and jambs and a bead at the sill – see figure 7.8 (c) to (f). The grooves need to be of sufficient depth to allow the positioning of the pane, and extruded seals or channel gaskets are normally used for glazing. Non-setting compounds, with the use of setting and location blocks, can also be employed. Sometimes the glass or plastic is located clear of the frame and structural gaskets are used to connect the two, rather like a window in a car – see figure 7.30. Therefore, structural gaskets not only have

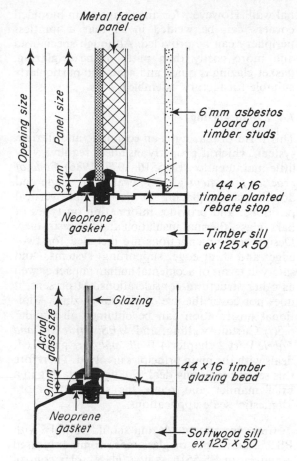

7.30 *Infill panel and glazing with gasket seal into groove*

to provide an effective seal against the weather but also have to support the glass. The sealing pressure on the periphery of the glass and on the surround is derived from a 'zipper' strip of a harder synthetic rubber than that used for the main gasket. The strip is inserted and removed (for re-glazing) with the use of a special tool.

(c) Nibbed surrounds

Instead of having a rebate or groove, a frame can incorporate a projecting nib for glazing. In this case a structural gasket is also used – see figure 7.10. page 215.

Being resilient, the use of structural gaskets over nibs allows curved surrounds and is ideal for building using GRP, GRC or metals as an external wall. However, for angles, injection moulded corners can be welded in so that a jointless periphery can be provided. Although specialized and more costly than putty or bead glazing, gasket glazing is quick and neat, and particularly suitable for factory assembled units.

7.4 Patent glazing

This form of glazing is an economic and flexible system, which if properly installed, requires very little maintenance. BS 5516: 1977 (1986) *Code of practice for patent glazing*, deals with single and double patent glazing in sloping and vertical positions, and provides information on types of bars, glass, thermal insulation and fire resistance. Design recommendations are included for two-edge and four-edge supporting systems, and safety in terms of accidental human impact as well as other structural considerations. At present, it does not cover the use of plastics glazing. Additional information can be obtained also under 6.5(i) Curtain walling, and *MBS: Structure and Fabric* Part 2 chapter 4 *Walls and piers* page 167, deals with the main principles involved. Therefore this section will only deal with patent glazing in a brief manner and relate the subject to more 'domestic' scale applications.

Glass for patent glazing should comply with BS 952 and types of glass more commonly used are given in BS 5516 as float glass, solar control glass, wired glass, patterned and rough cast glass, laminated glass, toughened glass, enamelled toughened glass, insulating glass units, and double glazing systems. *Plastics* in various types and formulations in single, double and triple skin forms are available. They have higher impact strengths and are less rigid than glass, but require more positive edge restraint to prevent 'spring-out' or displacement under load due to excessive deflection. *Opaque infill panels*, including metal-faced composite panels and opaque glass or plastics with or without insulation, can be incorporated with clear patent glazing.

Bars for supporting the glazing can be of aluminium or mild steel; and of preserved timber machined from European Redwood or Whitewood, Western Hemlock or Douglas Fir – defects limited as specified in BS 1186: Part 1: *Specifica-*

tion for timber. *Cappings and wings* designed to fit over the bar to form a barrier against water penetration and to restrain the glass from moving away from the bar under wind suction forces, should be of aluminium, copper, zinc or plastics, having various forms of fixing (snap, bolted, etc). Alternatively, the supporting bars can have *wings* which are dressed down to form a barrier against water penetration. These should be integral with the bars and made from either lead or plastics.

Vertical patent glazing forming external walls (which includes roof glazing at 70° or more) is subject to the provisions against the spread of fire contained in the *Building Regulations 1985* as described in 6.2(f) Fire precautions (Windows) as they are classified as totally *unprotected areas* and distance from boundaries is important. Patent glazing used to separate accommodation from an internal atrium void may form part of a *separating wall* and require a high fire resistance rating. For roofs, the principal fire protection requirement is that the roof deck and its covering shall prevent fire from *entering* the building. Roof patent glazing is considered to be an adequate barrier provided that the glass, whether wired or unwired, has a nominal thickness of at least 4 mm (see also chapter 8 Roof lights). The factors outlined in 7.2(f) Security and 7.2(g) Safety are also important when considering the use of patent glazing and the advice of specialist manufacturers should always be adhered to.

Other design aspects to be considered with patent glazing include:
- appearance, shape and form;
- strength and stiffness of glazing bars
- span between points of attachment to structure;
- span between glazing bars for glass or plastics sheets;
- points of connection with ground, wall or roof;
- weathertightness;
- thermal insulation requirements;
- condensation and the need for ventilation;
- doors, windows and roof lights;
- points of penetration (service pipes, etc)
- method of drainage (if any).

Figure 7.31 shows an example of small scale

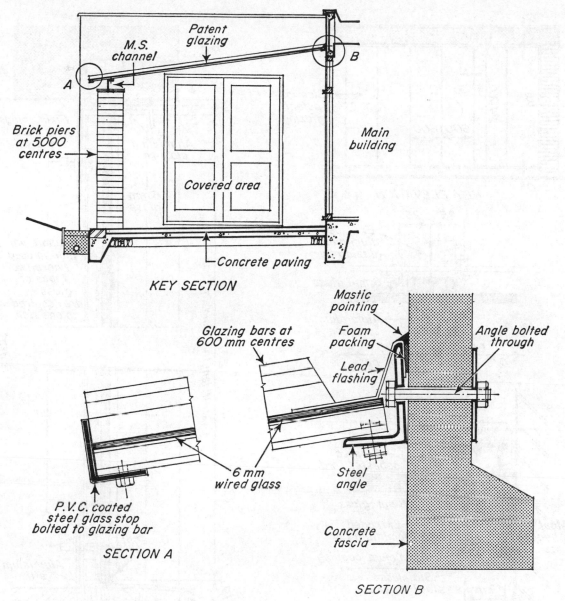

Patent glazing
M.S. channel
A
B
Brick piers at 5000 centres
Main building
Covered area
Concrete paving

KEY SECTION

Glazing bars at 600 mm centres
Mastic pointing
Foam packing
Lead flashing
Angle bolted through
6 mm wired glass
Steel angle
P.V.C. coated steel glass stop bolted to glazing bar
Concrete fascia

SECTION A

SECTION B

7.31 *Glazed covered area*

roof patent glazing, and figure 7.32 of small scale vertical patent glazing. The bars can be of mild steel or aluminium alloy suitably formed for either single or double glazing as indicated in the typical details shown in figure 7.33. The steel is galvanized and protected by a jointless lead or

PVC sheath. The inverted T-section bars support the glass on greased resilient cords. Bars are made in different depths for varying spans between purlins or other supports.

Figure 7.33 also indicates the alternative use of aluminium or lead wings to provide an external

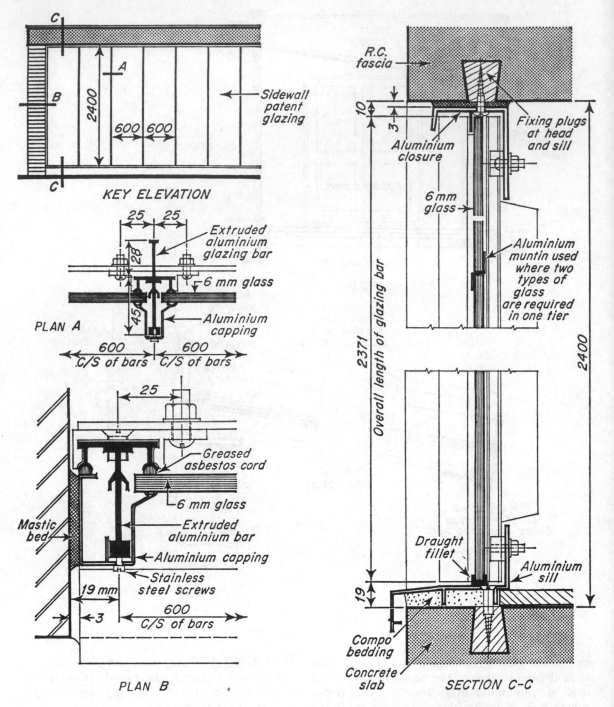

KEY ELEVATION

2400

600 600

C

C

B

A

Sidewall patent glazing

PLAN A

25 25

28

450

Extruded aluminium glazing bar

6 mm glass

Aluminium capping

600 600
C/S of bars C/S of bars

PLAN B

25

Mastic bed

19 mm

3

600
C/S of bars

Greased asbestos cord

6 mm glass

Extruded aluminium bar

Aluminium capping

Stainless steel screws

SECTION C-C

R.C. fascia

10

3

Aluminium closure

6 mm glass

Overall length of glazing bar

2371

Fixing plugs at head and sill

Aluminium muntin used where two types of glass are required in one tier

2400

Draught fillet

19

Compo bedding

Concrete slab

Aluminium sill

7.32 *Vertical patent glazing*

230

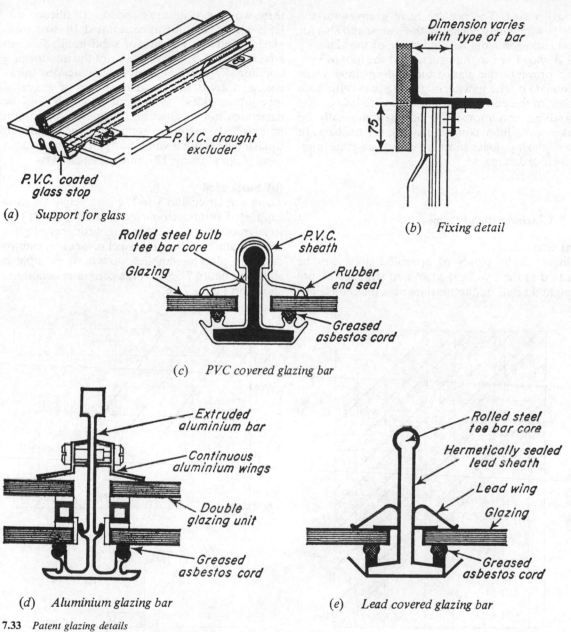

(a)   Support for glass

P.V.C. draught excluder

P.V.C. coated glass stop

Dimension varies with type of bar

75

(b)   Fixing detail

Rolled steel bulb tee bar core

P.V.C. sheath

Glazing

Rubber end seal

Greased asbestos cord

(c)   PVC covered glazing bar

Extruded aluminium bar

Continuous aluminium wings

Double glazing unit

Greased asbestos cord

(d)   Aluminium glazing bar

Rolled steel tee bar core

Hermetically sealed lead sheath

Lead wing

Glazing

Greased asbestos cord

(e)   Lead covered glazing bar

7.33   *Patent glazing details*

weather seal. The profiles have grooves for the water which may penetrate the wings, and also for condensation from the underside of the glass.

A shoe fixed to the structure at the foot of each bar prevents the glass from sliding downwards (detail (a)). The spacing of glazing bars is the 'safe span' of the glass (typically 6 mm wired glass) and handling conditions. 600 mm can normally be taken as 'safe' maximum spacing for the bars. In roof glazing, glass must be wired, or even toughened or laminated.

7.5 Glazing without frames

(a) Structural
Single height plates of annealed glass can be butted at their vertical edges and stiffened by full height 12 mm minimum thickness glass fins. The three-way junctions are bonded with silicone sealant. Doors can be incorporated in structural glazing and the absence of solid mullions is an advantage for effective display of the interior of a building. Figure 7.34 shows recommended thickness and areas for the main panes of annealed monolithic glass, as well as a graph for the determination of glass fin thickness. In addition to external glazing systems, the back walls to squash courts are a valuable application of structural glazing, using 12 mm toughened glass.

(b) Suspended
There are strict limits to the safe height of glass supported at its bottom edge, whereas a height up to 20 m of (usually 12 mm thick) toughened glass can be hung by adjustable steel suspension clamps and grip plate assemblies. A typical example is shown in figure 7.35, and the perimeter details are shown in figure 7.36.

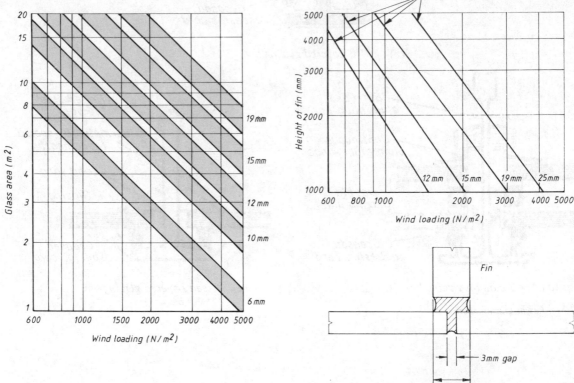

7.34 *Recommended thickness and areas for structural glazing, including glass fin thickness (BS 6262: 1982)*

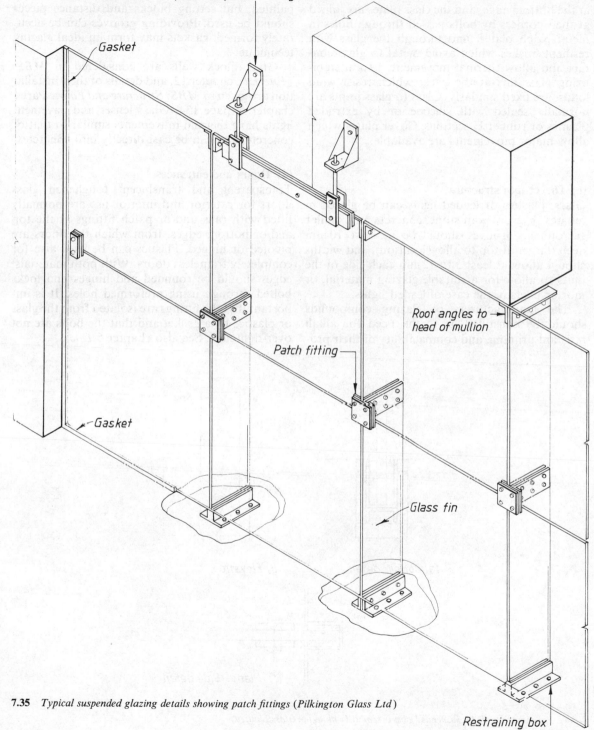

Standard two-point suspension hanger

Gasket

Gasket

Root angles to head of mullion

Patch fitting

Glass fin

Restraining box

7.35 *Typical suspended glazing details showing patch fittings (Pilkington Glass Ltd)*

Within a structural opening there is clearance at the bottom edge, and the glass plates are joined at their corners by bolts passed through holes in metal patch plates, and through the glass with resilient bushes which avoid metal to glass contact and allow thermal movement. 19 mm stabilizing glass fins at the back, which resist wind loads, are fixed similarly. Glass to glass joints are normally sealed with silicone or by extruded plastics or rubber H sections. Cover plates which allow major movements are available.

(c) Direct into structure

Glass, plastics or leaded lights can be glazed in rebates or grooves in stone, concrete and similar surrounds. Grooves should be at least 10 mm deep (larger at top to allow location), and widths should allow at least 3 to 12 mm each side of the units to allow for a suitable glazing material, or mortar fillets in the case of leaded lights.

The manufacturers of glazing compounds should be consulted as to the need for alkali resistant priming, and compatability of their pro-duct. Non-setting compounds need not be painted, but setting blocks and distance pieces should be used. Providing grooves can be accurately formed, gaskets may form an ideal glazing technique.

Glass block walls are considered in *MBS*: *Materials*, chapter 12, and details of their installation are given in *MBS*: *Structure and Fabric* Part 1 chapter 5, page 134. Glass lenses and pavement lights have thermal movements similar to that of concrete, and can be cast directly into concrete.

(d) Doors and entrances

Transparent and translucent toughened glass doors for exterior and interior use are normally fitted with rails and/or patch fittings at the top and/or bottom edges, from which the doors are pivoted or hinged. Plastics can be used also for completely frameless doors. With both materials, edges should be rounded and hinges and locks bolted through using preformed holes. It is important that the fittings are isolated from the glass or plastics by a gasket and that the bolts are not over-tightened. See also chapter 5 *Doors*.

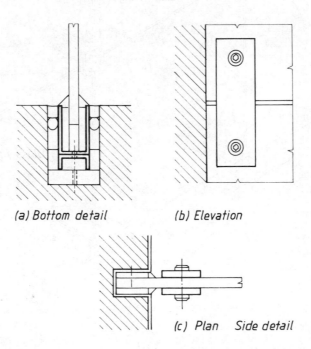

(a) Bottom detail   (b) Elevation

(c) Plan   Side detail

7.36   *Perimeter details for suspended glass assembly (Pilkington Glass Limited)*

8 Roof Lights

CI/SfB (37.4)

8.1 Introduction

Trends towards deep plans in buildings to maximize site usage and the desire to keep perimeter accommodation for primary activities result in the need for natural light and ventilation from windows to be supplemented by a roof light system. They are particularly useful in internal circulation spaces as well as internal rooms, including those used for storage, washing or detention, where privacy or even protection is required. The need for the control of sunlight and glare in certain types of display galleries may also be resolved by the use of roof lights. Nevertheless, apart from purely practical reasons, the use of roof lights can considerably enhance the quality of spaces in buildings by providing subtle natural lighting affects.

8.2 Performance requirements

The provision of natural lighting units for roofs, usually by dry glazing techniques in the form of dome lights, monitors, skylights and lantern lights, has become a specialist matter.

Apart from some general guidance on performance given in CP 153: *Windows and roof lights* Part 1 *Cleaning and safety*, Part 2 *Durability and maintenance*, and Part 3 *Sound insulation*, at present there is no British Standard covering the detailed requirements of roof lights. However, the comments given under 7.2 Performance requirements (*Glazing*) are applicable to roof lights. Guidance is available also from publications of the *Glass and Glazing Federation*, including one covering overhead glazing.

Since the roof light is situated on the most vulnerable and exposed part of a building and usually has joints within its construction and/or requires integration with different roof finishes, formidable problems of *weather resistance* have to be overcome. In addition to being completely weatherproof, a system of roof lights must be strong enough to withstand wind and dead loads;

act as a defence against the external penetration of fire, be able to resist thermal losses and solar heat gains; perhaps provide ventilation and escape for smoke and humans in the event of a fire whilst not causing condensation and draughts; and be burglar-proof as well as easily maintained or replaced.

Comments about the contribution roof lights make towards the *overall heat loss* from a building and the associated requirements of the *Building Regulations 1985* are given in 6.2(e) Thermal control (Windows). Solar control glass, insulating glass and plastics double skinned roof lights are available, complete with upstand kerbs in insulated metal or plastics to avoid cold bridging. Also, electronically operated blinds, either externally or internally, are sometimes incorporated in their construction. They can be automatically activated according to the environmental conditions, so that solar heat gains or glare from sunlight can be reduced. Manually or electrically operated louvres for ventilation are also available.

The principles involved in a roof construction providing *resistance to fire* are covered in 14.2(f) Fire precautions (Roofings). By reference to the size/use of a building and the proximity of its roof to the site boundary, the *Building Regulations 1985: Document B* classifies the performance of various roof coverings (including glazing) according to their ability to withstand *external fire penetration*, as well as resistance to *surface spread of flame*. The covering is designated by the letters A, B, C and D in *each area of performance*, according to the levels of ability achieved in tests to BS 476: Part 3: 1975 *External fire exposure fire test* – AA being the best result for resisting external fire penetration and in resisting surface spread of flame. Roof coverings designated AA, AB or AC are allowed to be placed close to a *boundary*, which is defined as the line of the land belonging to the building, including up the centre of an abutting street, railway, canal or river.

Glass is designated as AA. Therefore, both

235

framed (mild steel, aluminium or plastics) and frameless forms of roof lights using wired annealed glass, toughened glass, or fire resisting glass of a nominal thickness not less than 4 mm are acceptable for most applications.

The basic types of plastics glazing sheet materials used for roof lights have varying surface spread of flame classifications when tested to BS 476: Part 7: 1987 *Method for classification of the surface spread of flame of products*; and, although some are self extinguishing, they are combustible at different temperatures. Therefore, although glass fibre reinforced polyester and wired PVC are rated also AA to BS 476: Part 3, their use is restricted by the *Regulations* to a distance of at least 6 m from the boundary, unless they form part of a roof of a balcony, verandah, open car port, covered way, or detached swimming pool; or are for a garage, conservatory or outbuilding with a floor area not greater than 40 m².

Nevertheless, the *Building Regulations 1985*: *Document B*, *Appendix B* allows concessions for other plastic materials used for roof lights which do not achieve appropriate, or any, 'external roof covering' classification. Those made of unwired rigid PVC (*Class 1 – very low spread of flame and self extinguishing*) are allowed at a minimum distance of 6 m from a boundary, whereas acrylic roof lights (for example) must be at least 22 m away because of their DD classification. This 'proximity to boundary' concession is given on the understanding that the height of the interior face of the vertical upstand to the roof light is at least one-quarter the greatest width of the roof light, and the surfaces are lined with materials having very low (*Class 1*) surface spread of flame characteristics. In offices, shops and other public buildings there is also a limit on the size (5 m²) and distance apart (3.5 m, or 2.8 m when Class 1 interior lining to kerb) for plastics roof lights having medium (*Class 3*) surface spread of flame characteristics. In order for the designer to ensure compliance with these concessions, it is essential that fire test information is obtained from manufacturers in the form required by the *Regulations*. Figure 8.1 indicate the fire performance characteristics of thermoplastics roof light glazing. BS 2782 *Methods of testing plastics* has eleven Parts with 143 main sub-divisions which provide

information for testing the thermal, electrical, mechanical, chemical, optical and colour, dimensional, rheological, and other properties of plastics.

Figure 12.3, page 306 indicates the minimum *internal* surface spread of flame classifications for roof lights when they form part of a ceiling. See figure 8.1 on facing page.

8.3 Metal framed wired glass

Figure 8.2 shows a basic form of roof light constructed from a rolled steel, hot-dip galvanized frame into which is set wired glass in non-hardening glazing compound using setting blocks to allow thermal movement. The roof light is either fixed or openable. The latter is illustrated, having a pressed steel hood to protect the opening. It is always difficult to guarantee that rain will not be blown into a building when an open type roof light is used and for this reason the opening end of the light should always be placed with its back to the direction of the prevailing wind.

Many manufacturers have a detail which incorporates a louvre flap or 'hit and miss' ventilator in the upstand, which means that the top of the roof light can remain fixed, whilst ventilation can be obtained from the side. This is a slightly easier weathering problem. Some manufacturers also incorporate a temperature operated catch on the opening section which provides an automatic vent in case of fire.

Similar forms of framing are available in aluminium alloy for glass and plastics roof lights.

8.4 Plastics domes

Although domes can be made of glass, circular or rectangular on plan (see page 239), today most are made less expensively in plastics. They are available in clear and opaque polycarbonate (PC), polymethyl methacrylate acrylic (PMMA), glass fibre reinforced polyester resin (GRP), and unplasticised polyvinyl chloride (uPVC). When making a selection, it is very important to check the performance characteristics of each material to ensure compliance with design, technical and

Test	Polycarbonate	Standard acrylic	uPVC	Reinforced uPVC	10 mm Twin-wall Polycarbonate
BS 2782: 1970 Method 508A	Flame retardant	Not flame retardant	Flame retardant	Flame retardant	Flame retardant
BS 2782: 1970 Method 508 D	Very low flammability	Flammable	Very low flammability	Very low flammability	Very low flammability
BS 476: Part 4: 1970 Non-combustibility	†Combustible	†Combustible	†Combustible	†Combustible	†Combustible
BS 476: Part 6: 1981 Fire propagation test for products	Index of performance I = less than 12 i_1 = less than 6	Not applicable	Not applicable	Not applicable	I = 9 i_1 = 4.5 i_2 = 2.7 i_3 = 1.74
BS 476: Part 7: 1971 Surface spread of flame	Class 1	Class 3	*Class 1	*Class 1	Class 1
BS 476: Part 8: 1972 Fire resistance of elements of building construction	†Less than ½ hour	† Less than ½ hour	†Less than ½ hour	†Less than ½ hour	†Less than ½ hour
BS 476: Part 3: 1958 External fire exposure roof test	Not applicable	DDX	Not applicable	F.AA	Not applicable

*When tested in 3 mm thickness and over.
† Assumed results.

8.1 *Thermoplastic glazing materials for rooflights tested in accordance with relevant British Standards (William Cox Ltd)*

legislative requirements. With regard to the latter, a fire test certificate should be obtained.

Figure 8.3 gives a selection from a range of 300 mm modular co-ordinated dome light forms, and shows a typical upstand kerb component in GRP. Figure 8.4 illustrates a method of fixing a dome light to the kerb. The foam strip and clamp fixing detail provides a good weather seal and allows thermal movement to take place without damaging the dome light or surrounding structure. Condensation falls into the gutter formed by the upstand and the moisture then drains away through the plastics edge strip. Insulation can be improved by the placing of the roof lights one over the other to make a double-skin construction. Insurance companies are demanding high standards of security for constructions. Manufacturers are aware of this concern and are able to provide appropriate fixings for their products according to the likely risk involved. The L clamps shown are easily fixed, but once in position, they are permanently locked and should it be required to release the top component it will be necessary to cut through the clamps above the base.

Figure 8.5 indicates a double-skin plastics dome light fixed to a galvanized steel upstand. This is the type used by the *CLASP* building system (*3.5 Consortium of Local Authorities Special Programme (CLASP): (b) Construction*) and two dimensionally co-ordinated sizes, 900 mm and 1800 mm square to suit the planning grid of the system. The roof lights are available in clear, opal and solar control PVC, or in GRP with an expanded aluminium ventilation screen and a projecting aluminium weather baffle fixed to the upstand. Additional ventilation can be provided by simply adding more screens and baffles, or they

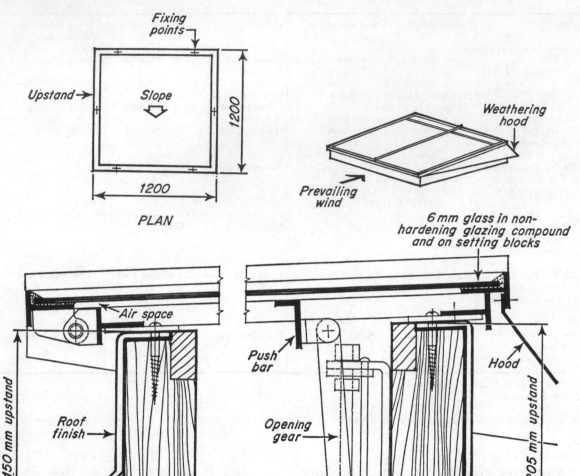

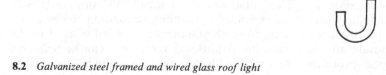

8.2 *Galvanized steel framed and wired glass roof light*

238

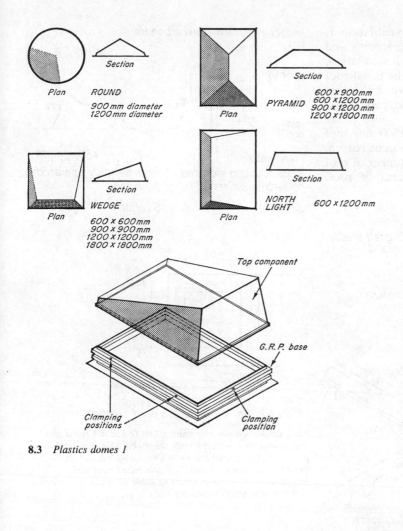

Plan
Section
ROUND
900 mm diameter
1200 mm diameter

Plan
Section
PYRAMID
600 × 900mm
600 × 1200mm
900 × 1200mm
1200 × 1800mm

Plan
Section
WEDGE
600 × 600mm
900 × 900mm
1200 × 1200mm
1800 × 1800mm

Plan
Section
NORTH
LIGHT
600 × 1200mm

Top component

G.R.P. base

Clamping
positions

Clamping
position

8.3 *Plastics domes 1*

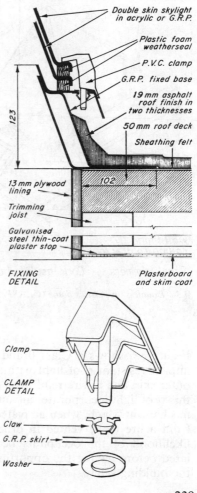

Double skin skylight
in acrylic or G.R.P.

Plastic foam
weatherseal

P.V.C. clamp

G.R.P. fixed base

19 mm asphalt
roof finish in
two thicknesses

50 mm roof deck

Sheathing felt

123

102

13 mm plywood
lining

Trimming
joist

Galvanised
steel thin-coat
plaster stop

FIXING
DETAIL

Plasterboard
and skim coat

Clamp

CLAMP
DETAIL

Claw

G.R.P. skirt

Washer

8.4 *Plastics domes 2*

can be omitted altogether if no ventilation is required. 'Hit and miss' ventilating screens and baffles can be used for controlled ventilation. Note that the upstand is bolted to the metal roof deck. As openings for roof lights have an effect on the structural performance of the roof deck, 900 mm roof lights may not be positioned closer to each other than 900 mm and 1800 mm roof lights closer than 1800 mm. For the same reason, there are some limitations on the number of roof lights occurring within a given area of roof.

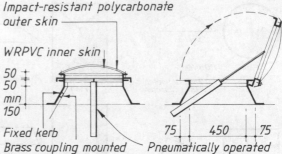

Impact-resistant polycarbonate outer skin

WRPVC inner skin

50 / 50 / min / 150

Fixed kerb
Brass coupling mounted on kerb by others

Pneumatically operated push rod

75 / 450 / 75

Section   Section

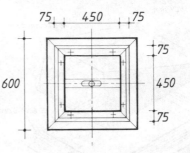

75 / 450 / 75

600   450

75 / 75 / 75

Plan
600 x 600 mm Rooflight in closed position

8.6 *Smoke venting roof light: Class O and AA rated high impact resistant polycarbonate outer skin plus wire-reinforced pvc inner skin. Pneumatic cylinder opening mechanism, mounted between roof light and galvanized steel curb, operated by smoke/heat sensor or other alarm system which activates airline (Transplastix Ltd)*

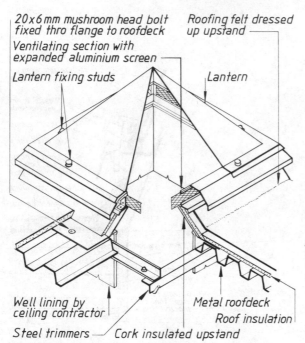

20x6mm mushroom head bolt fixed thro flange to roofdeck

Roofing felt dressed up upstand

Ventilating section with expanded aluminium screen

Lantern fixing studs

Lantern

Well lining by ceiling contractor

Metal roofdeck

Roof insulation

Steel trimmers   *Cork insulated upstand*

8.5 *Double-skin plastics dome (CLASP)*

Figure 8.6 shows a Class 0 and AA rated high impact resistant roof light with a polycarbonate outer skin and a wire-reinforced PVC inner skin: this roof light incorporates an automatic opening mechanism which, when activated, allows smoke from a fire to be vented in order to reduce the likelihood of the occupants becoming asphyxiated before having the opportunity to evacuate the building safely.

8.5 Traditional timber skylight and lantern light

Traditional forms of a fixed skylight and a timber lantern light are shown. These forms of construction are now largely superseded by the other dome lights and lantern lights illustrated, but the traditional form will be found in large numbers on existing buildings and a knowledge of its construction will help in determining the maintenance required. Figures 8.7 and 8.8 show a fixed skylight suitable for a pitched roof. The roof members have to be trimmed to the requisite size opening to take the 50 mm frame members, which would be housed together at the angles and secured to the trims. It is essential that this frame is wide enough to stand up well above the roof finish and to form an adequate gutter at the top or back edge of the light. If not, water or snow, particularly, may penetrate at the junction between the skylight and the frame. If the light is hinged to open, penetration of rain is highly likely and opening lights of this type are to be avoided. In the detail the thickness of the roof is not great and it has been possible, using 300 × 50 mm framing, to make the lower edge coincide with the ceiling so that the frame acts as a lining as well; it is so marked on the drawing. The light itself is 50 mm softwood with 150 mm nom. styles and top rail and 175 × 38 mm nom. bottom rail. Note the condensation groove to the bottom rail.

The roof lantern light shown in figure 8.9 takes the form of 4 inclined skylights basically similar to the skylight shown in figures 8.7 and 8.8 but is constructed out of styles and rails, these being cut angular or truncated on plan. These separate lights are tongued together and the joints protected by lead secured with a wood roll. They are supported on a framework of 100 × 100 mm timbers which themselves form the heads and corner posts with 100 × 75 mm mullions. This frames a set of vertical casements, some fixed and some horizontally pivoted with planted stops. The opening casements would be operated by cords or other remote control. The whole skylight stands on a 125 mm timber curb. This is the minimum height of curb to avoid the sill being saturated by rain splashing. The opening is trimmed by 75 mm wide trimmer and this and the firings and curb are masked by a lining of hardboard. There is 100 × 20 mm condensation gutter lined with lead formed around the base of the glazing.

It should be remembered that the details shown in figures 8.7 to 8.9 are applicable to traditional design criteria and do not indicate the thermal insulation which would be necessary today for compliance with mandatory requirements and the need to conserve heat in buildings.

8.6 Dormer windows and skylights in pitched roofs

Figure 8.10 and 8.11 indicate typical details for a dormer window. Although their use is not currently common in new dwellings in the UK, the need to economize on building costs and space heating could result in their increased adoption. By making the roof space a usable habitable space, the conventional upper floor construction can be combined with the roof construction – particularly now that prefabricated trussed rafter configurations are available which easily allow this to happen. The practice of providing the upper floor accommodation within a roof space is common today in Sweden. For further details of dormer window construction see *MBS: Structure and Fabric*, Part 1 chapter 7 pages 193–196. Figure 8.12 indicates a proprietary GRP dormer window unit which is currently available.

An alternative to the *dormer window* is the *skylight* which is indicated in figures 8.13 and 8.14.

Under the *Building Regulations 1985: Mandatory rules for means of escape in case of fire*, loft conversions with habitable rooms require a window or skylight with the bottom line of opening to be a maximum of 1100 mm high from the floor. The window or skylight must be at least 500 mm wide and 850 mm high to allow people to escape and be positioned for ease of rescue by ladder from the ground. The external roof slope from eaves to opening should be not more than 1500 mm.

Continued overleaf

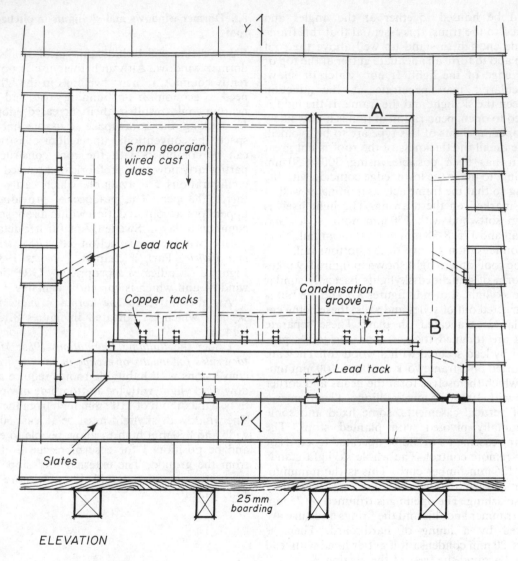

6 mm georgian
wired cast
glass

A

B

Lead tack

Copper tacks

Condensation
groove

Lead tack

Slates

Y

25 mm
boarding

ELEVATION

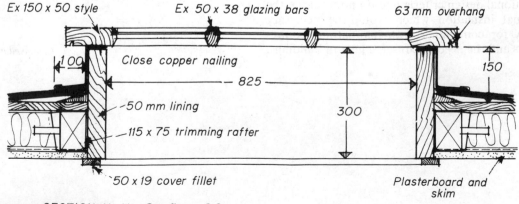

Ex 150 x 50 style

Ex 50 x 38 glazing bars

63 mm overhang

Close copper nailing

100

825

150

50 mm lining

115 x 75 trimming rafter

300

50 x 19 cover fillet

Plasterboard and
skim

SECTION X–X   See figure 8.8

8.7 *Traditional timber framed skylight 1*

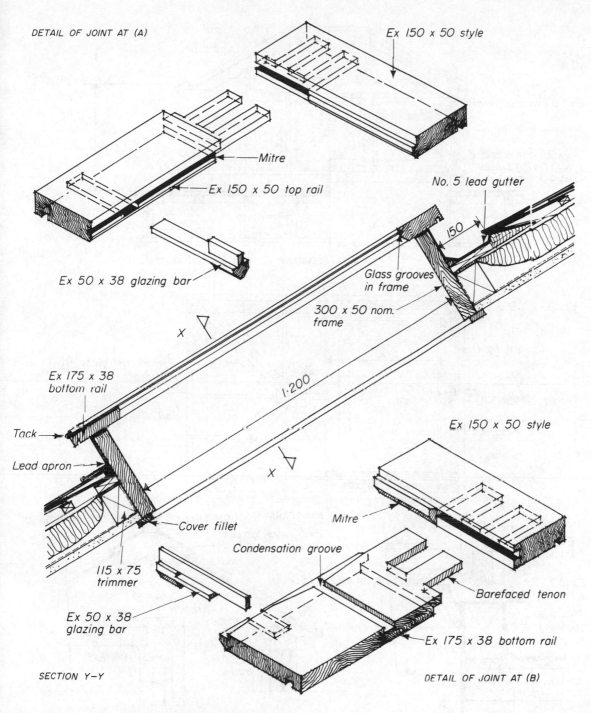

DETAIL OF JOINT AT (A)

Ex 150 x 50 style

Mitre

Ex 150 x 50 top rail

Ex 50 x 38 glazing bar

No. 5 lead gutter

150

Glass grooves
in frame

300 x 50 nom.
frame

Ex 150 x 50 style

X

1·200

X

Ex 175 x 38
bottom rail

Tack

Lead apron

Cover fillet

Mitre

Condensation groove

Barefaced tenon

115 x 75
trimmer

Ex 50 x 38
glazing bar

Ex 175 x 38 bottom rail

SECTION Y–Y

DETAIL OF JOINT AT (B)

8.8 *Traditional timber framed skylight 2*

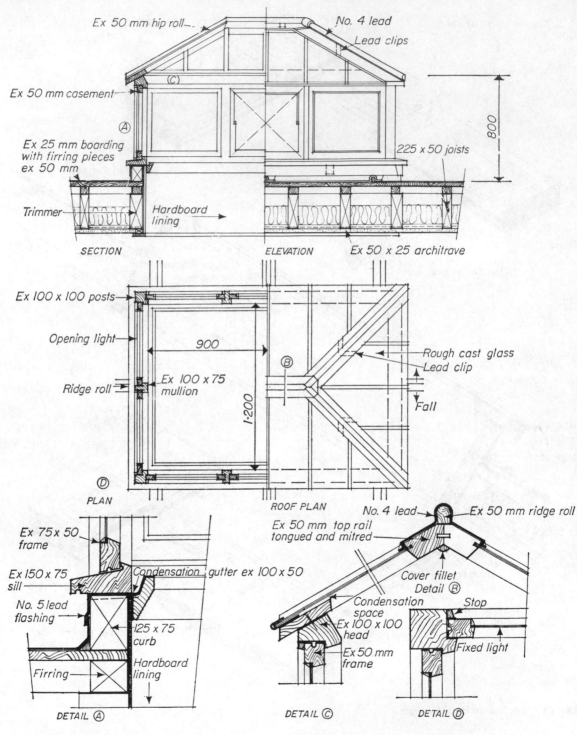

Ex 50 mm hip roll

No. 4 lead

Lead clips

Ex 50 mm casement

Ex 25 mm boarding
with firring pieces
ex 50 mm

Ⓐ

Ⓒ

225 x 50 joists

800

Trimmer

Hardboard
lining

SECTION

ELEVATION

Ex 50 x 25 architrave

Ex 100 x 100 posts

Opening light

Ridge roll

900

Ex 100 x 75
mullion

1·200

Ⓑ

Rough cast glass
Lead clip

Fall

Ⓓ

PLAN

ROOF PLAN

No. 4 lead

Ex 50 mm ridge roll

Ex 50 mm top rail
tongued and mitred

Ex 75 x 50
frame

Ex 150 x 75
sill

Condensation gutter ex 100 x 50

Cover fillet
Detail Ⓑ

No. 5 lead
flashing

125 x 75
curb

Hardboard
lining

Firring

Condensation
space

Ex 100 x 100
head

Ex 50 mm
frame

Stop

Fixed light

DETAIL Ⓐ

DETAIL Ⓒ

DETAIL Ⓓ

8.9 *Traditional timber framed lantern light*

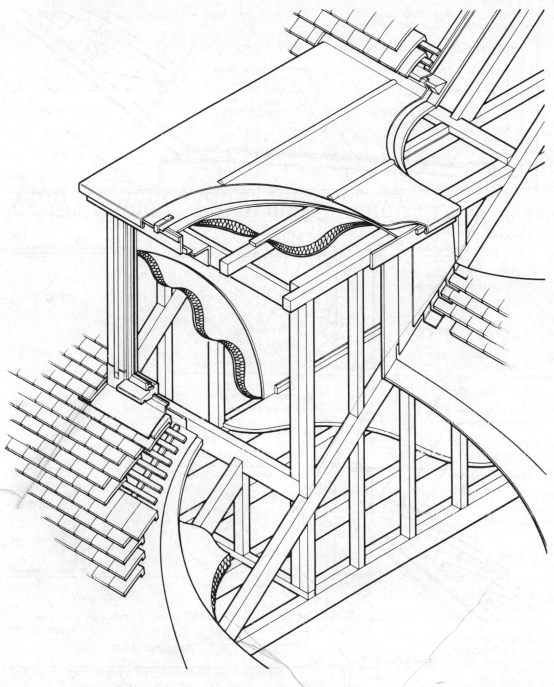

8.10 *Dormer window*

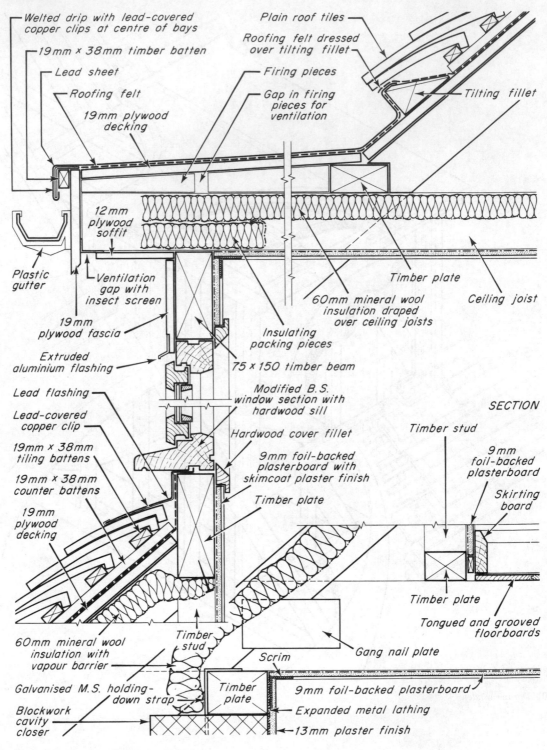

Welted drip with lead-covered copper clips at centre of bays

19mm × 38mm timber batten

Lead sheet

Roofing felt

19mm plywood decking

Plain roof tiles

Roofing felt dressed over tilting fillet

Firing pieces

Gap in firing pieces for ventilation

Tilting fillet

12mm plywood soffit

Plastic gutter

Ventilation gap with insect screen

19mm plywood fascia

Extruded aluminium flashing

Insulating packing pieces

75 × 150 timber beam

Modified B.S. window section with hardwood sill

Lead flashing

Lead-covered copper clip

19mm × 38mm tiling battens

19mm × 38mm counter battens

19mm plywood decking

Hardwood cover fillet

9mm foil-backed plasterboard with skimcoat plaster finish

Timber plate

60mm mineral wool insulation draped over ceiling joists

Timber plate

Ceiling joist

SECTION

Timber stud

9mm foil-backed plasterboard

Skirting board

Timber plate

Tongued and grooved floorboards

60mm mineral wool insulation with vapour barrier

Timber stud

Galvanised M.S. holding-down strap

Blockwork cavity closer

Scrim

Timber plate

Gang nail plate

9mm foil-backed plasterboard

Expanded metal lathing

13mm plaster finish

8.11 *Typical section through dormer window*

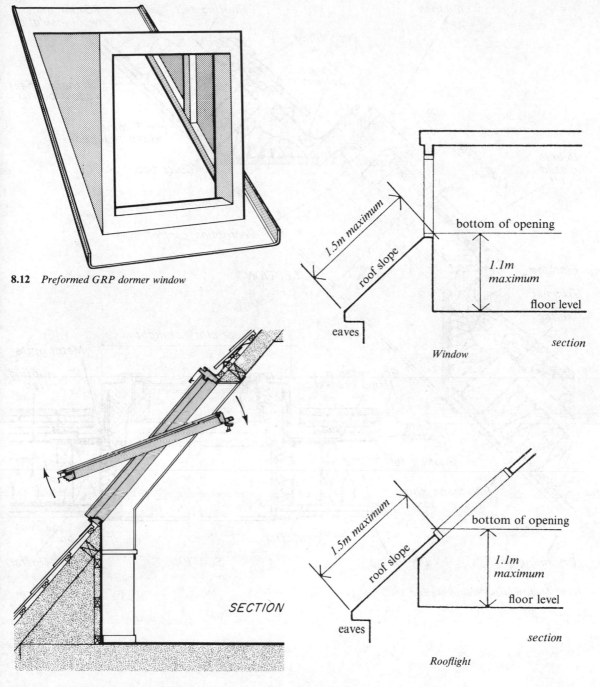

8.12 *Preformed GRP dormer window*

1.5m maximum

roof slope

bottom of opening

1.1m maximum

floor level

eaves

Window

section

8.13 (a) *Modern timber framed skylight 1*

SECTION

1.5m maximum

roof slope

bottom of opening

1.1m maximum

floor level

eaves

section

Rooflight

8.13 (b) *Position of window or rooflight*
(*Building Regulations 1988*)

247

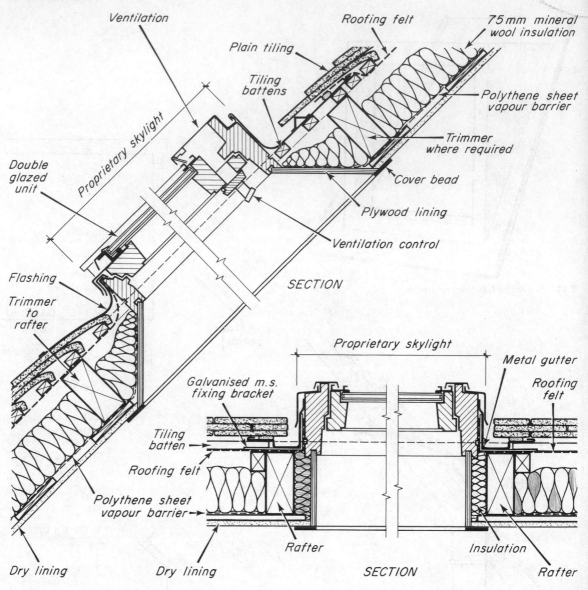

Ventilation

Roofing felt

Plain tiling

75 mm mineral wool insulation

Tiling battens

Polythene sheet vapour barrier

Proprietary skylight

Double glazed unit

Trimmer where required

Cover bead

Plywood lining

Ventilation control

SECTION

Flashing

Trimmer to rafter

Proprietary skylight

Metal gutter

Roofing felt

Galvanised m.s. fixing bracket

Tiling batten

Roofing felt

Polythene sheet vapour barrier

Rafter

Insulation

Rafter

Dry lining

Dry lining

SECTION

8.14 *Modern timber framed skylight 2*

248

9 Ironmongery

8.1 Introduction

Many components forming essential 'working parts' of a building, such as windows, doors and hatches, are required to pivot, fold and/or slide open by means of mechanisms which are collectively referred to as *ironmongery*. This includes the methods of support such as hinges and pivots; methods of closing such as springs, hydraulic and other devices; methods of securing such as locks, latches, bolts and clasps; and methods of activating opening or closing such as knobs, levers and other accessories.

The choice of the correct type and quality of ironmongery is very important since, no matter how good are the windows, doors and hatches, they will fail to function and cause annoyance if the working mechanisms controlling their movement are not durable and efficient.

9.2 Performance requirements

The performance requirements which ironmongery has to fulfil are formidable. For instance, the self-closing device of a door into a shop may operate hundreds of times every day and, in a department store, perhaps a million times a year. The door must be easy for a child or disabled person to push open, but must be capable of holding the door closed and not allowing it to be opened by the wind. During its working life there should be no breakage, it should be maintenance free and not susceptible to corrosion, and should be easily replaced when necessary. Working against these criteria lies the fact that ironmongery is one of the easiest and, therefore, the most likely item of expenditure to be cut back if building construction costs rise on a project (see chapter 2). Nevertheless, cost-in-use is important, and specifiers need to satisfy their clients' increased awareness of financial outlay for the continual maintenance of buildings, particularly in the commercial sector.

Further comments on performance requirements will be included under each item of ironmongery considered.

9.3 Materials and finishes

Ironmongery is generally manufactured from aluminium, brass, cast-iron, stainless steel or plastics in a range of appropriate finishes as follows:

Aluminium In alloy form, this is probably the most commonly used material since its properties lead to ease of manufacture of appropriate profiles and sections. It is also a reasonable cheap material. Finishes include satin anodized or polishes.

Brass More expensive than aluminium alloy and is mainly used today for refurbishment and conservation work. It is available in a matt or highly polished finish, usually protected against discolouration (oxidation) by lacquer. This lacquer should be treated carefully, particularly when repainting the component on which the item of ironmongery is fixed. Relacquering may be required after several years, although the naturally worn polishing finish may be preferred.

Cast iron Used for garden gate furniture as well as rustic hardware, and has a black beaten finish. Products are very durable.

Stainless steel Various grades available for inside and outside use. Costly, but becoming popular and finished as matt or polished. Products are highly durable.

Plastics Available in self-finished solid nylon or as nylon capping to a steel or aluminium core.

Metals and finishes on metals are dealt with in *MBS: Materials* chapter 9 *Metals*.

The less costly aluminium alloys are widely

used because of their relative freedom from corrosion. Anodizing on aluminium alloy ironmongery is an electrical process in which an anti-corrosive film is produced. Although the alloy can be stained with colour before sealing, natural anodizing is a 'silver' finish.

Applied finishes such as chromium or nickle plating can be electroplated, or the finish can be an enamel or a lacquer. A black japanned lacquer finish is common for inexpensive ironmongery. An applied finish will not last so long as regularly cleaned matt finish, satin or bright polishes on durable metals like nickle-silver, brass, bronze, stainless steel or aluminium.

Real BMA (Bronze Metal Antique) is a finish for bronze and gunmetal produced by heating after polishing to give an iridescent finish. This is an expensive process and is sometimes imitated by other means, but imitation BMA is visually inferior to the real thing.

It is vital for durability, as well as appearance that ironmongery is fixed with the correct screws, wherever possible, of the same metal as the body of the fitting.

Plastics are dealt with in *MBS: Materials* chapter 13 *Plastics*.

Plastics are used in ironmongery, currently mostly as a finish on a metal base, eg plastics door handles and furniture on to a metal core. Some fittings which receive much wear, such as sliding stays and fasteners for casements, door knobs and some hinges are made in nylon. Items not subject to stress, such as finger plates, can also be of nylon but are more often manufactured from unreinforced plastics sheet.

9.4 Hinges

(a) Types
Butt The *butt hinge* is the most common hinge screwed to the edge of a door. They are recessed into the frame as well as the door. Normally, one pair of 75 mm or 100 mm butts suits a standard internal door: external and other heavier doors (FDs) might require 1.5 pairs, ie three 100 mm butts. Butt hinges are made in steel, brass with steel pins, brass with brass pins, or in nylon (figure 9.1).

Rising butts Rising butts lift the door as it opens so as to clear a carpeted floor, and this type of hinge is in some degree self closing. Rising butts must be 'handed' (see 9.11). A falling butt hinge is also available and this will keep a door in the open position (figure 9.1).

Tee Tee hinges of cross-garnets are used for heavy doors of the ledged type (figure 9.2).

Pin With pin hinges or lift-off butts, the door can be taken down without unscrewing the hinge and this type is, therefore, always used for doors that are pre-hung and assembled in the factory (figure 9.3).

Back-flap Back-flap hinges are for screwing on the face of the work where the timber is too thin to screw into the edge, or where appearance is not important. They make a strong job when used on internal joinery fittings (figure 9.3).

Parliament The parliament hinge is used to enable a door to fold back. It projects from the face of the frame (figure 9.4).

Centre The centre hinge is used where it can be fixed to the top or to the side of a fitting (figure 9.4).

Cranked The cranked hinge is necessary for lipped or rebated casements and is usually made with the two halves separate so that a pin fixing can be used in assembling the casement in factory production of windows (figure 9.5).

Offset The offset or *easy-clean* hinge (see page 159) is used to allow the outside of the window to be cleaned when open at 90 degrees (figure 9.5).

Counter flap and strap The counterflap hinge is set in flush with the face of the work – its name being indicative of its use. The strap hinge is similarly used, but has a projecting knuckle (figure 9.6).

Friction Figure 6.21 page 172 shows typical friction-type hinges used for pivot windows which are a convenient form of hanging very heavy or large sashes so that they can be operated easily.

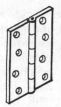
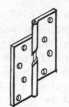

9.1 *Butt hinge and rising butt*

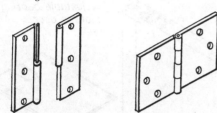

9.2 *Tee hinge*

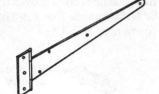

9.3 *Lift-off hinge and back-flap hinge*

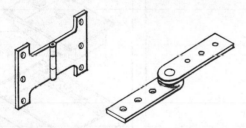

9.4 *Parliament hinge and centre hinge*

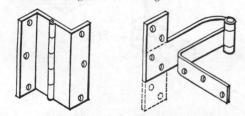

9.5 *Cranked hinge and offset hinge (easy-clean)*

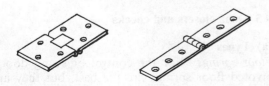

◄ **9.6** *Counter flap and strap hinge*

Complete reversibility on some types allow for internal cleaning of the glass external face.

Spring See next section 9.5 Door closers and checks.

(b) Application

BS 1227 *Hinges* Part 1A: 1967 *Hinges for general building purposes* gives classifications according to metals as well as dimensions and weights. The Guild of Architectural Ironmongers' publication on *Hinges*, Parts 1 and 2 also provide useful references.

Doors and hatches Selection of an appropriate type of hinge for a door or hatch in a particular location is determined by:
- the weight of door or hatch, including other ironmongery;
- action or other loads, eg floor springs and door closers;
- frequency of use;
- exposure to elements;
- fire resistance requirements.
- burglar resistance requirements.

Typically, the weight of a 1950 mm high by 750 mm wide by 45 mm thickness door can vary between 36 and 54 kg according to whether it is half or fully glazed, or solid. When manufacturers recommend the use of a third hinge to support the weight of a door it should be positioned immediately below the top hinge (see figure 9.7 and figure 5.26 page 121). However, it may sometimes be stipulated that the third hinge should be fitted centrally to stop warping in doors of certain constructions or, in the case of external doors, to prevent twisting. Sheradised steel hinges provide good service in sheltered external locations but, ideally, steel or hinges with steel washers should not be used externally. In all cases, the size and construction of door and frame should ensure that a secure fixing can be obtained.

Hinges on fire doors must have a melting point above 800°C and suitable materials include steel, stainless steel, cast iron, phosphor bronze and brass. The Guild of Architectural Ironmongers' publication, *Fire and escape door hardware*, further recommends that the hinges should be at least 100 mm long, should not extend across the full thickness of the door, and should leave enough room for intumescent plugs or a strip of intumescent material to be placed between the hinge leaf and the door to insulate the hinges. For practical reasons, rising butts should not be used on fire-doors.

Windows Good quality timber windows and those manufactured from metal and plastics are supplied from the factory complete with hinges and other furniture, including sophisticated friction pivot hinges, espagnolette bolting systems and locking handles (see page 266). However, some of the cheaper window types still employ the stormproof hinges which were developed for side and top hung sashes rebated over the frame using BS 644 *EJMA* sections (see 6.3(a) Standard and high performance, and 9.8).

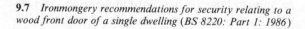

Securely fixed frame and threshold
Frame and 44mm solid door of recommended timber
1 pair of hinge bolts set between the hinges

Door viewer

Rim night latch

Door chain or limiter

Mortice deadlock

1 ½ pairs of steel hinges

Viewed from inside

9.7 *Ironmongery recommendations for security relating to a wood front door of a single dwelling (BS 8220: Part 1: 1986)*

The need for increased security to combat the rise in crime and the need to reduce insurance premiums also means that the choice of hinges must fulfil more than just a straight working role. The recommendations relating to appropriate quality and number of hinges on external doors needed to provide protection against burglars are covered in BS 8220 *Security of buildings against crime*, Part 1: 1986 *Dwellings*, and Part 2: 1987 *Offices and shops*. Figure 9.7 shows some of the recommendations relating to a wood front door of a single dwelling. As hinges can be forced, it is necessary to incorporate additional reinforcement or bolts to back-up ordinary hinges and/or use hinge bolts (see figure 9.39).

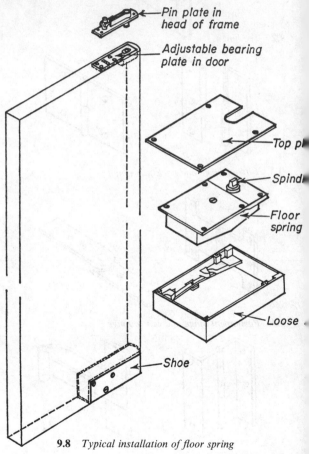

Pin plate in head of frame

Adjustable bearing plate in door

Top pl

Spind

Floor spring

Loose

Shoe

9.8 *Typical installation of floor spring*

9.5 Door closers and checks

(a) Types
Floor springs For the control of swing doors, pivoted floor springs are the best, but they are

252

expensive. The component consists of a strong spring contained in a metal box; a *shoe* which is attached to the base of the door; and a top pivot. The assembly is shown in figure 9.8. The box is fitted into the floor thickness so that the cover plate is flush with the finished floor level. For this reason the use of a floor spring is somewhat restricted, since many types of floor and threshold construction do not permit easy cutting away to receive the box. The adjustable pivot plate or top centre is fixed to the head of the frame and top of the door, and is adjusted up and down by a screw. The lower pivot is connected to the shoe, which is in turn firmly fixed to the bottom of the door and to the side of the door at the base. The spring should have an hydraulic check which slows down the door at a point where it still has, say, 150 mm to travel before closing. This avoids banging or injury to a person following behind.

Floor springs are illustrated in figure 9.9. The hydraulic check mechanism is seen in the figure as a cylinder attached by a lever arm to the strong metal springs. Double action (swinging both ways) and single action (swinging one way only) floor springs are shown.

The cover plates which are available in a variety of finishes to match the general ironmongery specification, have been omitted for clarity. To ensure the smooth working of a double swing door in conjunction with a floor spring, it is important that both the closing and fixed edges of the door are profiled to the correct radius. The recommended dimensions are given in figure 9.10.

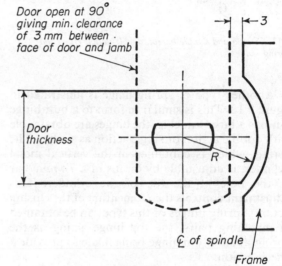

Door heels and their radii for standard applications

Door thickness	40	44	50	64
Heel radius R	32	35	38	48

9.10   *Door heels and their radii*

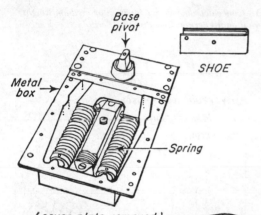

(cover plate removed)

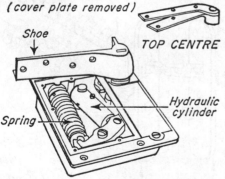

(cover plate removed)

9.9   *Double and single action floor springs*

Spring hinges   There are also various types of spring hinges. Figure 9.11 illustrates a patented type of hinge controlled by a small but powerful horizontal spring held in a metal cylinder at the back of the face plate. The cylinder or cylinders have to be housed into mortices cut into the frame and are covered by the face plate. The moving part of the hinge clips round both sides of the door in a shallow housing and is screwed firmly into position so that there are no projecting knuckles or plates. Both double and single action hinges are illustrated, the form controlled by two springs, the latter by one. This type of hinge is not made with a check action.

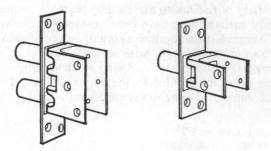

9.11 *Single and double barrel, double action Hawgood spring hinges*

Another type of spring hinge is illustrated in figure 9.12. This is similar in form to a butt hinge but has a large knuckle, the hinges are obtainable with double action or single action as shown. The spring, which is contained in the vertical metal cylinder, is adjustable by means of a *Tommy* bar in the hole at the top of the cylinder. This adjustment controls the momentum of the closing action. Spring hinges of this type can be obtained in matching pairs, the top hinge acting as the spring, the bottom hinge being made to provide a check action.

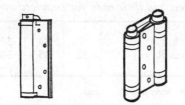

9.12 *Single and double action spring hinges*

Figures 9.13 and 9.14 indicate forms of door spring closure which are recessed into the door and frame, and are independent of the hinges.

9.14 *Concealed door closer incorporating combined hydraulic mechanism and spring assembly for use on fire doors (Pertkins and Powell: 'Perkomatic')* ▶

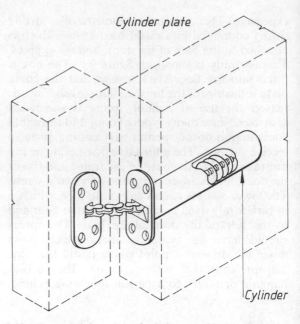

9.13 *Concealed door closer for light or medium weight internal door (Perkins and Powell: 'Perko')*

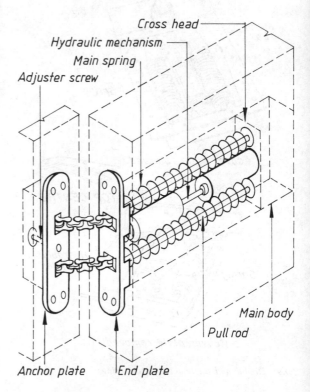

254

Overhead The closing action of doors hung on ordinary butt hinges can be controlled by the fixing of check mechanisms on the top of the face of the door and the door frame head. There is a very wide range of this type of overhead door closer which provides a combined closing and check action control. This type of closer is adjustable to balance the weight of the door and is much less expensive than the pivot floor spring control. The overhead closer is available in double and single action patterns; handed and reversible. Three alternative methods of fixing are shown. Figure 9.15 shows an example of a closer in a pleasantly designed case, for surface fixing to the opening face of the door. Figure 9.16 shows the same spring, but for fixing to the closing face of the door, and figure 9.17 shows a closer which fits into the thickness of the door at the top and is thus concealed with the exception of the projection arm.

Door checks The door closer fittings so far described control the whole of the movement of the door, but perhaps a more universal requirement is to prevent the slamming of the door. Figure 9.18 shows such a device which by engaging a wheel attached to a cantilevered arm, causes the movement of the door to be checked. This type of check would be used in conjunction with a spring hinge which works in conjunction with the check to achieve final and positive closing.

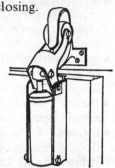

9.18 *Door holder to prevent door slamming*

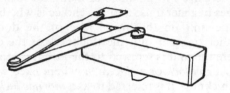

9.15 *Hydraulic check, single action door check, surface fixing to opening face*

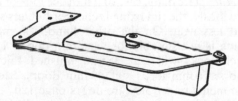

9.16 *Hydraulic check, single action door check, surface fixing to closing face*

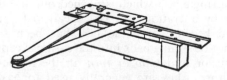

9.17 *Concealed fixing door check (fits into thickness of door)*

Where pairs of doors which have rebated meeting styles are fitted with closing devices it is necessary to arrange that the leaves close in the correct order. To do this, a *selector* is fitted to the head of the door frame. This is a device consisting of two lever arms of unequal lengths which engage both leaves of the swing doors and can control the doors so that the rebates engage on closing. This action is shown in figure 9.19.

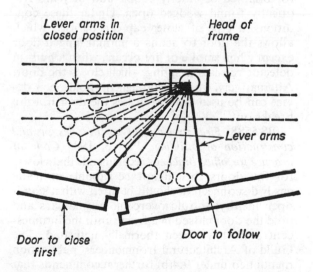

Lever arms in closed position

Head of frame

Lever arms

Door to close first

Door to follow

9.19 *Door selector*

(b) Application

Selection of an appropriate closer involves the following considerations:

- whether exposed or concealed type required;
- ease and type of fixing possible;
- need for tamper or vandal-proof device;
- need for adjustable device to check closing speed according to weight of door;
- incorporation of snap action which releases extra pressure during the last few degrees of closing to overcome the resistance provided by door latch;
- incorporation of a back check which brings resistance into action at predetermined angle of opening to prevent the door opening further;
- the need for a hold-open device to allow door to remain open (not for fire doors);
- the need for a delay action which allows the door to remain open for a predetermined period before closing to allow the passage of people and goods.

Door closers must ensure the door comes to rest in a closed position. The *Building Regulations 1985*: *Approved Document B, Appendix F3* requires that all fire resisting doors should be fitted with an automatic self-closing device which is capable of closing the door from any angle *and against any latch to the door*. However, self-closing doors usually form formidable obstacles for disabled or elderly people and they are frequently found wedged open. Under these conditions, a type of closer cap can be used which allows the door to act as a normal hinged door except when smoke or fire occurs, when a built-in detector releases a spring which closes the door. Alternatively, an electromagnetic hold-open device can be used which releases the door if a fire breaks out.

BS 5588 *Fire precautions in the design and construction of buildings* Part 3: 1983 *Code of practice for office buildings* recommends that closers for fire doors should not be capable of being easily disconnected; should be fitted with a stand-open facility; should overcome any latches and hold the door closed in a frame until the intumescent seals have been thermally activated. The Guild of Architectural Ironmongers' publication mentioned under 9.4(b) further recommends that concealed overhead hydraulic check-action closers should not be used for fire doors because their installation requires too much removal of timber in the head member of a door; springs should only be employed for FD30 doors to cupboards; and then only certain forms of floor springs should be used, ie those with strap shoes.

BS 6459 *Door closers* Part 1: 1984 *Specification for mechanical performance of crank and rack and pinion overhead closers*, covers mechanical back-check but not requirements specific to door closers for fire doors or other special requirements. The Guild of Architectural Ironmongers have also produced a publication on door closers.

9.6 Locks and latches

(a) Types

Both a lock and a latch can be supplied as separate units of ironmongery, or in combination to form a lock and latch unit.

There are two methods of fixing for locks and latches in general use and the choice is whether to fix the unit on the inside face of the door or whether to set it into the thickness of the door. Where the unit is screwed to the face it is referred to as a *rim lock* or a *rim latch*; where fixed within the thickness, it is referred to as a *mortice lock* or a *mortice latch*. The projecting bolt of a rim lock or latch is retained by a *keep* fixed to the adjoining door frame, whereas it is retained by a recessed *striking* plate in the case of a mortice lock or latch. Obviously, the rim fixing is cheaper but less secure and less neat. On the other hand, the mortice fixing is not suitable for very thin doors: 13 mm thick locks will suit 35 mm finished thickness doors, 16 mm locks suit 40 mm doors. See also comments under 5.8 Fire doors page 120.

There are four basic types from which other variations derive:

Dead lock   The version illustrated in figure 9.20 has a single bolt which is pushed out and drawn back by operation of a key. Dead locks are so-called because once the bolt has been shot it cannot be sprung back into the casing except with a *key*, or by a *snib* or *turn* on the inside door furniture. They are generally used for securing rooms where continual free access is not a criterion. Dead bolts are sometimes designed to have *double throw*, which means that the bolt goes further into the staple or keep when the key is turned a second time. This action provides added security.

Latch These are the simplest way to hold a door in the shut position. The latch illustrated in figure 9.21 has a bolt held in the extended position by a spring, which can be drawn back to allow the door to open by the turning of a handle or knob only.

9.20 *Mortice dead lock*

9.21 *Upright mortice latch*

Lock and latch The two-bolt lock illustrated in figure 9.22 combines the mechanisms of a dead bolt and a latch bolt. The spring latch operated by a handle serves for all general free access purposes; the dead bolt is operated by a key from one or both sides of the door for locking purposes. A dead lock suitable for a sliding door requires a claw or hook bolt to engage over an engaging

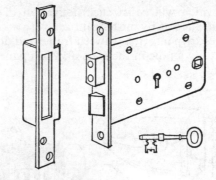

(b) *Horizontal mortice lock*

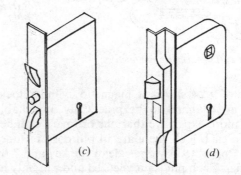

(c) *Double hook bolt for sliding doors*
(d) *Rebated mortice lock*

9.22 (a) to (d) *Horizontal mortice locks*

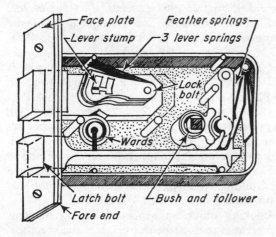

(a) *Horizontal mortice lock showing component parts*

device in the frame. Where pairs of doors with rebated meeting stiles are used, it is necessary to fit a rebated mortice lock. Here the fore-end of the lock case is cranked to fit the rebate on the stiles.

Cylinder night latch The *rim pattern* night latch illustrated in figure 9.23 has a spring bolt operated by a handle on the inside and a key on the outside of the door. When going out the door can be pulled shut behind the user, but a key is necessary for re-entering the premises. A knob or thumb slide, operated from the inside, will hold the bolt open or shut when needed and the key will then not opeate. Other versions incorporting all these features are available, including a *mortice pattern* which is concealed within the door but weakens its structure, and a *narrow-style pattern* which is suitable for use on framed doors with narrow styles. Another version is the *dead-locking*

257

pattern which will resist elicit activation of the latch bolt, such as by pushing it back with a knife or plastics strip inserted between frame and door, or by cutting a hole in the glass or wood panel of the door.

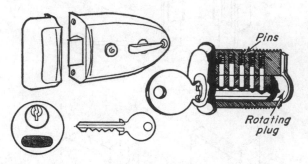

9.23 (a) to (b) *Cylinder rim latches*

Figure 9.24 shows a magnetic cylinder lock. These are claimed to be practically unpickable and is more expensive than the ordinary cylinder lock. In each lock there are 14 pin positions (see later), 7 operated by one side of the key and 7 by the other. Each pin is magnetized and can only be repelled from the locked position by a magnetic force of the correct polarity, as supplied by the key.

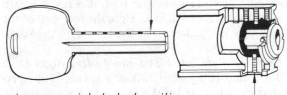

9.24 *Magnetic cylinder lock*

Special Most lock manufacturers now produce microswitches and electric strikers for remote release. When connected with telephonic inter-

communication systems, these are particularly useful for multi-storey dwellings because visitors can announce their arrival from a distance.

Time release locks are also available. Locking units that can be opened by a push-button code or a pass-card are shown in figure 9.25.

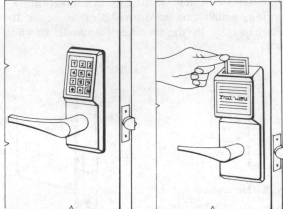

Keypad controlled dead-locking latch   Keycard controlled dead-locking latch

9.25 *Push-button code and pass-card locking units*

(b) Application

BS 3621: 1980 *Thief resistant locks* specifies design requirements, test methods and performance requirements for thief resistant locks; BS 3827 *Glossary of terms relating to builders' hardware* Part 1: 1964 *Locks* (*including locks and latches in one case*), Part 2: 1967 *Latches*, Part 3: *Catches*, and Part 4: 1967 *Door, drawer, cupboard and gate furniture*, describes general concepts; BS 4951: 1973 *Specification for builders' hardware: locks and latch furniture* (*doors*) gives performance tests and criteria for lever and knob furniture; and BS 8220: *Security of buildings against crime* Part 1: 1986 *Dwellings*, and Part 2: 1987 *Offices and shops*, contains guidance on security measures aimed at deterring burglars from entering dwellings and includes recommendations for windows and external doors. Reference can be made to the Guild of Architectural Ironmongers' publication on locks and latches, Parts 1 and 2.

Locking units contain complex mechanisms and great care must be exercised in the specification of appropriate quality. The specifier must be quite clear as to the precise requirements since, in general terms, cost is proportionate to security achieved. It is important to realize that, apart from the convenience of the user, the insurance company requested to cover the contents of the building will be concerned with security whilst the designer must be additionally concerned with providing easy means of escape in case of fire. These two conditions are not always easy to reconcile.

The strongest lock fittings are made of steel with wearing parts of special bronzes.

A lock, with latch mechanism, is shown in figure 9.22. This illustrates most of the essential features. A measure of security is given by the number and complexity of the wards. If the cuts on the key bit do not correspond to the wards the key cannot be turned. The bolt is released by tumblers, or a system of levers. When the key turns, the levers have to be lifted to a certain position before the bolt will pass and so a larger number of levers gives greater security. The tumbler mechanism (pin tumblers) is applied in the normal cylinder lock as shown in figure 9.23(b). The V-cuts on the key have to lift the pins the exact amount so that their tops become flush with the surface of the rotatable plug to enable the latter to be turned and the latch to operate. There are many thousands of combinations of pin positions, which gives many thousands of 'differs' or locks requiring different keys. It is important when writing the specification for the locks to be clear as to what differs are needed. In a house there is usually no point in having different room locks; in fact it is convenient, in the event of a room key being lost, to be able to use another from an adjoining room. However, on the other hand, in a building such as an hotel all room keys must differ. For this type of building locks which differ can be opened by a master key, or a number of locks, perhaps all on one floor, can be opened by a sub-master key. There is a large range of mastering 'possibles' to suit all requirements and the technique of arranging the mastering of the keys in the most convenient way is known as *suiteing*. Each group of keys being called a *suite*.

Figure 9.26 shows a typical suiteing arrangement and hierarchy of keyholders for a small factory. Some manufacturers offer a registered key system whereby the owner is registered with the merchant or supplier, and further keys are only issued to that person on receipt of his/her signature. BS 3621 describes a series of performance requirements for dead locks which, however, result in the locks not being able to have master keys.

Comments on the provision of locks and latches in connection with the need to provide effective means of escape from a building are given in 5.8 Fire doors, page 120. The Guild of Architectural Ironmongers' recommendations for locks and latches incorporated on fire doors include: the maximum dimensions for upright mortice units should be 225 × 32 mm for faceplate with a 160 × 19 mm case; care should be taken when fitting a mortice lock and all gaps filled with intumescent material to delay the effects of thermal bridging and fire; locks containing materials which melt at fairly low temperatures (nylon and aluminium) should be avoided in fire doors because they need to be retained in a closed position during a fire; and as locking sets designed for the rebated meeting stile of double doors may affect the integrity of the door during a fire, only square-edge meeting stiles with intumescent seals should be used. Special devices used in conjunction with locks and latches help to solve the problem of allowing ease of escape for occupants while providing security against intruders from outside. Although this can be achieved by the use of *panic bolts* (see page 266), locks can incorporate a protective glass panel on the internal face of a door which, when broken, allows access to the opening handle. Alternatively, a unit is available which allows the bolt to be automatically released when the glass is broken.

The normal mortice lock is made 'horizontal', ie suitable for a deep mortice into the middle rail of the door, and this type of lock is illustrated in figure 9.22. Where a lock must fit into a narrow style it is made 'upright'. This type of lock, which is illustrated in figure 9.21, has a comparatively narrow case. In a lock (lock and latch) set, the keyhole and spindle mortice are in line vertically in a vertical mortice lock, and the keyhole and spindle mortice are in line horizontally in a horizontal mortice lock. The horizontal set is usually used in conjunction with knob furniture, and the vertical set with lever handle furniture. Drawer and cupboard locks are usually for a flush fixing.

259

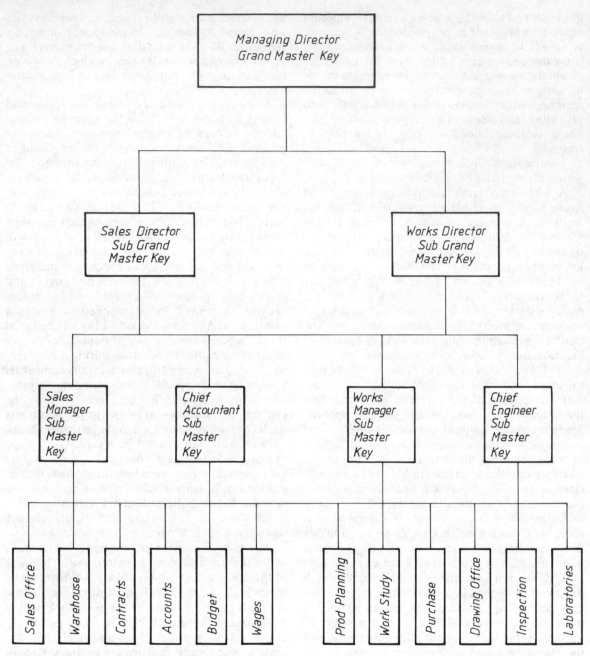

9.26 *Typical suiteing arrangements and hierarchy of key holders for a small factory*

This means that they are let into the inside face of the work, so that the outside of the lock is flush with the inside face of the timber. The cover plate is usually extended round the side to give a neat finish. Figure 9.27 shows a typical cupboard lock. Simplification of the fixing is an attractive proposition as mortice cutting takes a long time. A combined lock-latch set which needs only two holes to be drilled has been produced. This type of lock, which is now in common use, has the locking mechanism in the knob, and is usually referred to as a *knob set*. A typical example is shown in figure 9.28.

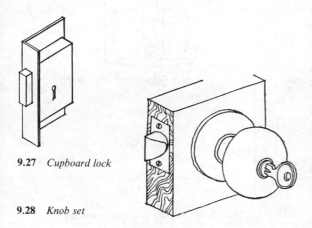

9.27 *Cupboard lock*

9.28 *Knob set*

Ball catches and roller catches are used for cupboards and because they are inexpensive they have also been used for the doors to living rooms in place of a latch. They are, however, very noisy and tend to give trouble in adjustment unless the projection can be easily altered to suit any change in the gap between door and frame.

9.7 Knob, lever and pull handles

(a) Types

The words 'knob' and 'lever' adequately describe the mechanisms used to operate locks and levers. They are both available in a wide range of shapes and finishes. Although style and fashion are matters of personal taste, some products will perform better in specific locations. Round-knob furniture can be difficult for some people to operate, particularly very young children and the disabled.

Lever furniture is much easier to operate, and some have an end turned into the face to further assist the grip of a disabled person as well as to prevent clothing catching. It is important that all furniture on doors and windows in the same building should be co-ordinated and most manufacturers offer complete ranges of matching ironmongery.

Two main types of pull handles are available. Those which are *D-shaped* allow a door or window to be pulled open or closed and, for doors, are often used in conjunction with push-plates on the opposite side to the pull handle (see figure 5.33 and 5.34 pages 128 and 129). The handle can be screwed to the face of a solid door, but should be bolted through glass doors or doors which are heavy. The push plate on the opposite side of the door will conceal the bolt fixing. A *cylinder pull* is located behind external key-plate of a night latch to facilitate pulling a door to a closed position. This is necessary when a knob or lever handle is not specified for entrance doors.

(b) Application

Knobs should not be used where the backset of the lock is less than, say, 60 mm. The backset is the distance from the outer face of the fore-end of the lock to the centre of the key hole. The reason for this is if a knob-set is fixed too near the door frame the user will suffer damaged knuckles when operating the knob. The question of the fixing of the knob in relation to the spindle and rose requires some special consideration.

There are many methods of fixing knob furniture, several of which were patterned. The two basic variants are:
- a spindle which is 'fixed' to the knob by a grub screw or patented fixing so that the pull of the knob is resisted directly by the spindle. This is a strong and most satisfactory method but requires exact and careful fitting;
- 'floating' or free spindle which slides on to the knob and which relies for its fixing by screwing the rose to the face of the door. This type is easily fitted but a disadvantage is that when used with mortice locks only short screws can be used to secure the rose because of the thickness of the lock case. These screws may work loose even in the best quality doors.

An 'exploded' drawing of a knob and spindle fixing is shown in figure 9.29.

Knob furniture provides a neat, unobtrusive and strong specification well suited to resist rough usage. Knob furniture is available in various alloys. Bronze is the most expensive but most hard wearing, but aluminum, because of its pleasant appearance and relatively low cost, is very popular.

Lever furniture must be well designed and strongly constructed since the lever arm produces considerable strain on the lock or latch mechanism (figure 9.30).

Where upright mortice locks are specified, lever furniture is essential because the distance of the spindle from the edge of the door is small. Most British lever furniture is of the floating spindle type in which the handles take the pull of the door through the handle plates or roses. Lever handles sometimes have, in place of a rose, a handle plate which allows the screws to be fixed beyond the mortice and so ensures that the fixing screws will not foul the lock case. This, of course, makes a stronger fixing. British lever handles often embody a spring to counterbalance the weight of the handle as British locks do not

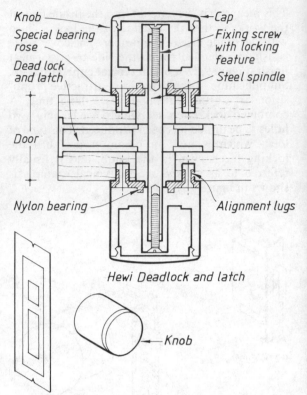

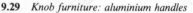

Hewi Deadlock and latch

9.29 *Knob furniture: aluminium handles*

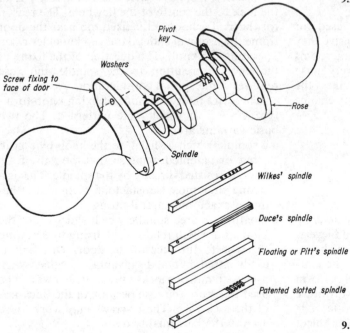

9.30 *Knob furniture: plastics handles (Hewi)*

normally have strong springs on the latch. Continental locks have a strong latch spring and so their handles also operate on this. This point should be borne in mind when considering using continental lever handles on British locks. In a vertical mortice lock the spindle for the lever handle or knob is vertically above the key hole. This means that a specifier can choose between lever furniture which has a long handle plate incorporating a key hole and a lever handle with a small handle plate and a separate key escutcheon plate. The key escutcheon plate is used as a cover plate for the key hole. In order to hide the large number of screws which are necessary for fixing door furniture of this kind, several different types of cover plate have been produced. The cover plate will either clip over or be screwed over the fixing plates. The screw type are usually better but can only be used where circular roses are specified since the clip on types tend to give trouble in use unless very well designed. A drawing of a lever handle showing the fixing is given in figure 9.31.

open in high winds. They are also used to hold the window in a limited opening position to provide ventilation. Conventional sash fasteners for top hung windows are shown in figure 9.32; folding cam openers, sliding, shadbolt friction and roller stays are shown in figure 9.33. Of particular note is the roller stay for use on bottom hung casements which open inwards; and on horizontal centre pivot windows to control the projection of the top part of the window into the room. Another form is *quadrant stays*, the traditional method used for limiting the opening of bottom-hung windows. Most stays can be supplied with an independent locking device to provide additional security to that provided by the fastener (see figure 9.39(d) and (g). Some insurance companies give reduced premiums when locks are incorporated with window stays.

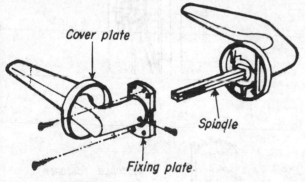

9.31 *Lever furniture*

Lever furniture is available in a very wide range of materials. The choice of stainless steel, bronze, aluminium alloy, plastic covered metal, or nylon, will depend on considerations of first cost, appearance, type of use and subsequent maintenance costs.

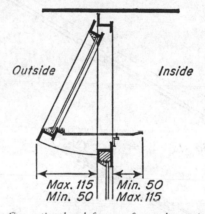

9.32 *Conventional sash fastener for top hung window*

Fasteners These are required to draw the casement or sash to a tightly closed position against the frame. Figure 9.34 indicates typical forms. Casement fasteners are available in wedge or cross-tongued types and some incorporate a night ventilation slot to allow enough ventilation while maintaining security.

Espagnolette bolts (see figure 6.20, page 170) are used on high performance windows and consist of a multi-point locking system activated from a single handle which secure the sash firmly and evenly against the seals. *Sash fasteners* (see figure 6.41, page 196) are available in several types, and

9.8 Window stays and fasteners

(a) Types
Stays These are required on windows to prevent people falling out, or to prevent casements flying

263

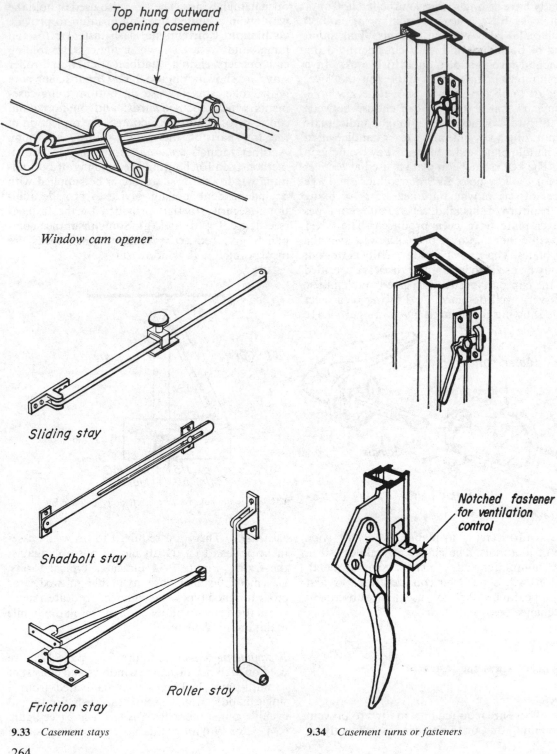

Top hung outward
opening casement

Window cam opener

Sliding stay

Shadbolt stay

Friction stay

Roller stay

Notched fastener
for ventilation
control

9.33 *Casement stays*

9.34 *Casement turns or fasteners*

are fixed to the meeting rails of double-hung sash windows in order to secure both sashes in the closed position. Forms are available which incorporate locks (see figure 9.39(e), (f), (h) and (i).

(b) Application

BS Code of Practice 153: *Windows and roof lights* Part 1: 1969 *Cleaning and safety* recommends the following for tall buildings:

● fittings for windows above third storey, and preferably above the ground floor, should limit the initial opening to 100 mm by means which cannot be tampered with by children;

● the window should be prevented from swinging and slamming in high winds beyond the initial opening of 100 mm and friction hinges may not be adequate for this purpose;

● large side-hung opening lights may require stays at both top and bottom to prevent distortion in high winds;

● safety bolts or catches used for locking pivoted windows in their reversed position should be positive in action and not liable to give way under pressure.

9.9 Bolts

(a) Types

Bolts form additional locking devices which can only be operated from the inside of a building

Barrel This is the most common type and has a round or barrel-like shoot on the back plate for surface fixing, as shown in figure 9.35. The shoot runs in a guide and is slid home into a metal keep. This type of bolt is inexpensive and easy to fix.

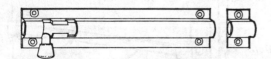

9.35 *Barrel bolt*

Flush lever This is shown in figure 9.36. It is recessed into a shallow housing in the component to be secured until the face plate is flush with the

surface of the timber. The bolt is operated by a thumb slide or lever action. Flush lever bolts are more expensive than barrel bolts and take more time to fix.

Cremorne This is a particular type of bolt used for minimizing the twisting of a door or window (see figure 9.37). It extends the full height of the door or window so that when the handle is turned, the top bolt slides upwards and the bottom bolt slides downwards to give top and bottom fixing.

9.36 *Lever bolt*

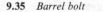

9.37 *Cremorne bolt*

Espagnolette This type of bolt provides centre fixing as well as fixing at the top and bottom. The centre fixing is commonly also a lock. Espagnolettes may be surface or flush fitting as required – see figure 6.20 page 170.

Panic Ordinary bolts must not be fixed on doors which are used as means of escape in case of fire. To overcome the problem of security, a *panic latch* or a *panic bolt* is employed (see figure 9.38). Panic latches are used on single doors, and consist of a cross bar which is pushed against a latch to release it. A locking knob is often fixed to the outside of the door to enable two-way traffic to operate. Panic bolts are used on single and double doors, and have a striking plate at the top and bottom so that the door is held in three places, thus giving a greater degree of security. A mortice panic bolt is let into the face of the door for neatness.

Security This is the name given to those bolts which are usually morticed into the construction of a door or window or are fixed to their stays and fasteners in order to provide greater security. Figure 9.39 shows a typical range.

(b) Application
The principles involved in the application of bolts to windows and doors are mostly self evident. They are usually fixed at the top and bottom of doors and should always have a socket to receive the shoot of the bolt. This is particularly important at the threshold. The diameter of the shoot, the type of metal used and the method of fixing of the bolt are an indication of its strength. For double doors it is normally necessary to secure the first closing leaf with bolts to enable the doors to be locked.

There are various designs of panic latches and panic bolts to suit different degrees of security. The height of the push-bar is important since in an emergency it must operate when people fall against it – the generally accepted height being 1050 mm above floor level. BS 5725: *Emergency exit devices* Part 1: 1981 *Specification for panic bolts and panic latches mechanically operated by horizontal push-bar*, gives maximum acceptable forces needed to operate them as well as specify-

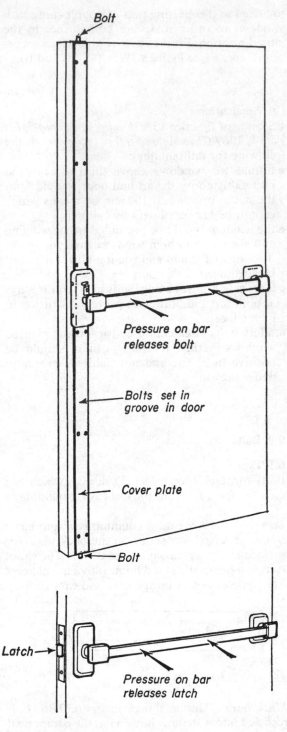

9.38 *Mortice panic bolt*

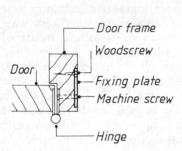

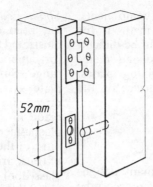

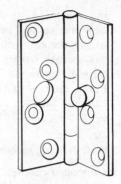

(a) Hinge plates

Doors

(b) Hinge bolt

(c) Hinge with bolt

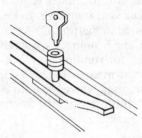

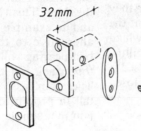

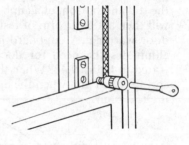

(d) Stay lock

(e) Sash lock

(f) Sliding sash lock

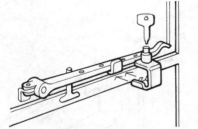

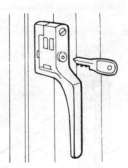

(g) Stay lock

Windows

(h) Patio lock

(i) Lockable window latch

9.39 *Typical range of security bolts and locks*

267

ing the strength and durability of components, heat resistance of materials, and methods for fitting the equipment. Panic bolts can be difficult to operate unless regularly cleaned and maintained, particularly the lower striking plates. Panic latches can have a locking device on the external face for routine access.

9.10 Miscellaneous items

Cupboard catches   There are very many designs and types of cupboard catches as reference to the manufacturers' catalogues will indicate. The specifier must decide on the exact requirements before choosing the most suitable catch, depending for instance, on whether or not the catch is used in conjunction with some form of handle. Catches should be arranged, if possible, both at the top and bottom of a cupboard door since they will then act as a form of restraint to prevent the door warping. A cupboard interior catch which eliminates the need for door furniture is illustrated in figure 9.40. When the door is pressed it springs open and when the door is pushed closed it clicks shut.

9.40   *Cupboard catch*

Sliding gear   Sliding gear for doors and windows has been described separately with the fittings illustrated in the appropriate chapter. Sliding gear for cupboard doors is available in a very wide range. Small cupboard or bookcase fronts of plate glass with polished edges can be fitted directly into the channels of fibre, metal or plastic made in single, double or triple section. Thin plastic-faced sheet, or ply-wood, can also run in most of these tracks. Typical sections of this type of track are shown in figure 9.41. For larger plate glass doors a metal section track is provided in aluminium or brass which incorporates small wheels or ball bearings that run on a bottom track to take the extra weight of glass.

For larger plywood or blockwood, or framed cupboard doors, a fibre track with sliders is manufactured. The track is grooved into the sill, the sliders being morticed into the under edge of the door. This type of track is also made in nylon and an example is illustrated in figure 9.42. As an alternative to this there are a number of small ball-bearing roller fittings, for running on a bottom track, which are illustrated in figure 9.43. These run easily and so are used where the door is tall in proportion to its width and which might jam in a simple channel track.

Window opening gear   The rod and worm gear type of control has been traditional for large and heavy windows – it is suitable where cost is the main consideration and a neat appearance is not

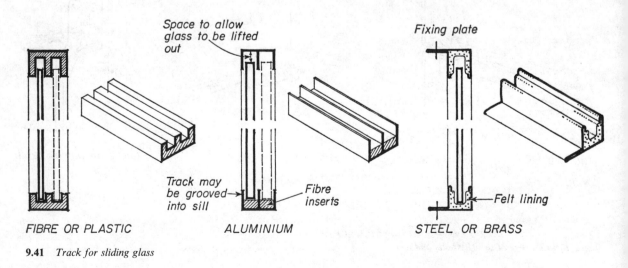

9.41   *Track for sliding glass*

268

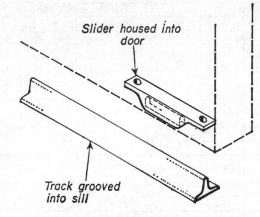

Slider housed into door

Track grooved into sill

9.42 *Door sliders and track*

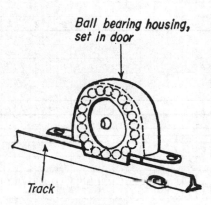

Ball bearing housing, set in door

Track

9.43 *Cupboard ball bearing roller track*

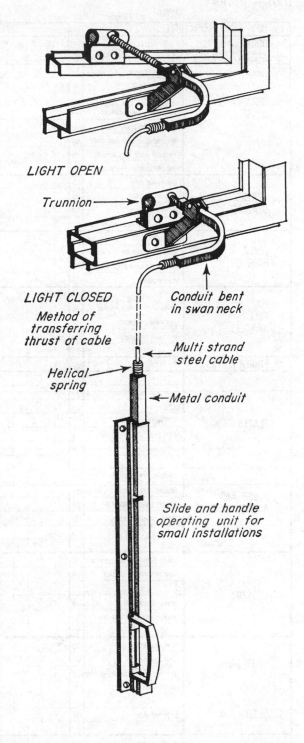

LIGHT OPEN

Trunnion

LIGHT CLOSED

Method of transferring thrust of cable

Conduit bent in swan neck

Multi strand steel cable

Helical spring

Metal conduit

Slide and handle operating unit for small installations

9.44 *Remote control device for high level opening windows*

essential. Regular maintenance must be organized since the working parts must be kept clean and well oiled. If they seize up, the fixings will be wrenched from the wall by forcing the gearing. Alternative systems in common use comprise a special wire cable sliding in a metal tube. A system in which the cable is wired to serve efficiently both in compression and in tension is shown in figure 9.44. The wire operates directly on the window and is in turn worked either by a slide for small installations or, in the case of heavier windows, by a geared regulator. There is a limit to the range of windows which can be controlled by mechanical means and for very large installations travelling over long distances electrical or hydraulic systems must be used. This type of system is, however, uneconomical for small installations.

DOOR GROUP PREFIX LETTERS			INTERNAL DOORS													EXTERNAL DOORS coded XD												
DOOR NUMBERS			1.	2	3	4	5	6	7	8	9	10	11	12	13	1	2	3	4	5	6	7	8	9	10	11	12	13
COMMON SUITING MASTER KEYING.	REFERENCE NUMBERS	AZA								DOUBLE						DOUBLE				DOUBLE		DOUBLE		DOUBLE				
UPRIGHT LOCKS	WITH ONE KEY	100																										
	LOCKS TO PASS	101	1	1	1		1					1	1	1														
	WITH TWO KEYS	102																										
	REBATED COMPONENTS	103																										
	ROLLER BOLT, ONE KEY	104																										
	ROLLER BOLT, LOCKS TO PASS	105																										
	ROLLER BOLT, TWO KEYS	106																										
	ROLLER BOLT REBATED COMP'S	107																										
UPRIGHT DEADLOCK	WITH ONE KEY	112																										
	LOCKS TO PASS	113								1.						1.		1	1	1		1		1		1	1	1
	WITH TWO KEYS	114																										
	REBATED COMPONENTS	115														1		1	1	1		1		1		1	1	1
LEVER HANDLES	PAIR ON ROSE	130																										
	PAIR ON BACKPLATE, KEYHOLE	131	1	1	1		1					1	1	1														
	PAIR ON BACKPLATE, NO KEYHOLE	132																										
	ESCUTCHEONS	133								2						2		2	2	2		2		2		2	2	2
PULL HANDLES	150 mm CENTRES FIXING	134																										
	225 mm CENTRES	135						1	1	1	1				1	1	1	1	1	1	1	1	1	1	1	1	1	1
	300 mm CENTRES	136																										
FINGER PLATES	300 x 75	140				1		1	1	1	1				1	1	1	1	1	1	1	1	1	1	1	1	1	1
KICKING PLATES	625 mm WIDE	141													1.													
	725 mm	142				1	1	1	1	2	2		1															
	775 mm	143	1	1	2							2		2						1	1					1	1	
	825 mm	144														1	1	1	1			1	1	1	1			1
	875 mm.	145																										
FLUSH AND BARREL BOLTS	PAIR FLUSH BOLTS	150								1						1				1		1		1				
	SOCKET FOR WOOD	151																										
	SOCKET FOR CONCRETE	152																										
	PAIR BARREL BOLTS	153																										
OVERHEAD CLOSERS	FOR EXTERNAL DOORS OPEN OUT	160																										
	FOR INTERNAL DOORS	161				1		1	1					1	1													
	DOOR SELECTOR	162																										
	OVERHEAD LIMITING STAY	163														1	1	1	1	1	1	1	1	1	1	1	1	
DOOR STOPS	FOR TIMBER	170																										
	FOR CONCRETE	171				1						1	1	1	1													
	POST MOUNTED DOOR HOLDER	172																										
	CABIN HOOK	173																										
LETTER BOX	LETTER BOX.	174																									1	
HAT AND COAT HOOKS	ALUMINIUM	180																										
	NYLON COATED SECRET FIX.	181																										
	PAIR NYLON COATED SECRET FIX	182																										
	NYLON COATED SCREW FIX.	183																										

9.45 *Ironmongery schedule*

For this type of control a motor is installed at the receiving end which will drive a local installation of cable gear. The main push-button control can be situated in a convenient central position and is coupled to a forward and reverse contactor. The switching off of the current in both directions is by micro-switches at the receiving end.

Hydraulic control is achieved by a small bore copper nylon tubing filled with oil. A pump, either hand or electrically operated, delivers the requisite pressure to small hydraulic rams positioned in the actual opening gear. In this system a single operating position can be used to control a large number of opening lights remotely situated both from the operating position and from each other. Because of their neat appearance both electric and hydraulic systems are preferable provided that their initial cost can be justified.

Door viewers These are small telescope devices fitted through solid doors to allow the occupier to identify visitors without opening the door.

Door chains These chains are fitted to a door to prevent unauthorized forced entry when the visitor cannot be seen without opening the door. Their success depends on the adequacy of the screw fixing plates and the quality of the metal used for the chain.

9.11 Scheduling ironmongery

The usual method for specifying ironmongery involves the production of a schedule which locates the door or window by number, and then by type, fire resistance, frame details before listing the required ironmongery or code for an ironmongery package (figure 9.45). Alternatively, individual data sheets are produced for each door or window. These schedules are now frequently produced with the aid of computer software programmes.

Many fittings, such as locks and handles, are handed. This means that they are specifically for a door hung either on the left side or the right side of an opening. Therefore, it is essential to have a standard way of describing on which side the door is hung. It is usual to describe the direction of opening as *clockwise* or *anti-clockwise* when viewed from the outward opening position. The clockwise part is self evident, but the 'outside' is generally agreed as:

- for external doors – the 'open-air' side;
- for internal doors – the corridor side of a room;
- for cupboards – the room side.

When describing locks, the door is viewed from the outside and a lock on the left side will be a left-hand lock.

10 Balustrades and barriers

10.1 Introduction

Balustrades form the protective barriers to the otherwise open side(s) of staircases and landings. They are designed and positioned to protect persons from various hazards, and also usually provide support for handrails to assist people in using the stairs, particularly in the event of a fire when smoke may cause confusion and/or a temporary loss of vision. Balustrades and handrails can be manufactured from a range of materials and can take various forms. This chapter is primarily concerned with metal framed balustrades and should be read in conjunction with *MBS: Structure and Fabric* Part 1, chapter 10 *Stairs*, and *MBS: Structure and Fabric* Part 2, chapter 8 *Stairs, ramps and ladders*.

Barriers are similarly designed to protect persons from hazards associated with height and means of escape in the event of fire, but may be additionally required to restrict or control the movements of persons and/or vehicles, and to indicate routes or provide defence against impact.

10.2 Performance requirements

(a) Balustrades
There is no British Standard which covers specific requirements of balustrades for staircases and landings. Recommendations for the design and construction of stairs are given in BS 585 *Wood stairs* Part 1: 1984 *Specification for straight flight stairs and stairs with quarter or half landings for domestic use*, and Part 2: 1985 *Specification for performance requirements for domestic stairs constructed of wood-based materials*: BS 5395 *Stairs, ladders and walkways* Part 1: 1977 (1984) *Code of practice for design of straight stairs*, Part 2: 1984 *Code of practice for the design of helical and spiral stairs*, and Part 3: 1985 *Code of practice for the design of industrial type stairs, permanent ladders and walkways*; BS 5578 *Building construction – stairs* Part 1: 1978 *Vocabulary*, and Part 2: 1978

Modular co-ordination: Specification for co-ordinating dimensions for stairs and stair openings: and BS 5588 *Residential buildings* Part 5: 1986 *Code of practice for firefighting stairways and lifts*: and, BS 5619: 1978 *Code of practice for design of housing for the convenience of disabled people*.

Although the *Building Regulations 1985* do not require buildings to have stairs or ramps, certain rules apply when they are incorporated in the design as part of a means of escape, or form a rise of more than 600 mm, or a drop at the side of more than 600 mm. These rules are contained in *Approved Document K: Stairways, ramps and guards* and those relating to dimensional requirements are summarized in figures 10.1 to 10.4. Different requirements are given for treads, risers, balustrades and handrails according to the type of building (*Purpose Group*) in which they are located; ie, private stairways (used for one dwelling), common stairways (used for two or more dwellings), institutional building stairways, assembly building stairways, and all other building use stairways. These requirements have an affect on the design of balustrades and barriers, with or without separate handrails.

The number of risers in a flight should be limited to 16 if a stairway serves an area used for a shop or assembly purpose, and stairways of more than 36 risers in consecutive flights should make at least one change in direction between flights of at least 30. Landings should be provided at the top and bottom of every flight and the width and depth of landing must be at least as great as the smallest width of the stairway. Part of the floor of the building can count as a landing providing it is firm and not sloping at more than 1 in 12. In order to allow safe passage, the landing has to be clear of any permanent obstruction, although a door may swing across it at the *bottom of a flight* providing it leaves a clear space of at least 400 mm along the full width of the stairs.

Stairways which form part of a means of escape in case of fire, or which are part of the only means of access for disabled, may need to meet additional requirements, eg construction to have appropriate period of fire resistance and within protected shaft.

A *balustrade* or *guard* is required at the open sides of stairways and landings where there is a drop of more than 600 mm. In private, common and other residential buildings, as well as relevant institutional buildings it is necessary to ensure that it is constructed so that a 100 mm diameter sphere cannot pass through any part in order to stop children under five from being held fast by the construction. In these building types it is also required that the balustrading should not allow children readily to climb up it. The required height of the balustrading is indicated in figure 10.3 and should be designed to resist a horizontal force of 0.35 kN for each metre length if it guards a private or common stairway, or 0.75 kN if it guards any other stairway. Any glazing below the required height of balustrading should be of glass blocks, toughened glass or laminated safety glass: annealed wire glass should not be used.

The provision of a *handrail* on one side of a stairway is always necessary. A handrail must be provided on *each side* if the stairway is over 1000 mm wide, and any stairway of balcony (and certain other areas above ground level which are likely to be used for other than just maintenance) must be also have a balustrade or *guard*. Horizontal dimensions refer to clear unobstructed width, ie between wall faces, between wall face and internal face of handrail on one side, or between internal faces of handrails fixed both sides.

The *Regulations* stipulate that the width of ramps should be as given for stairways (figure 10.2) and that the rules regarding landings for stairways should also apply. Where a ramp and a flight of stairs are combined to form a stepped ramp, the length of ramps between the steps should be between 1.0 m and 2.0 m. Barriers for ramps and their landings for different building use are also equivalent to those for stairways (figure 10.3): for private and common use a horizontal force of 0.36 kN/m must be resisted at the appropriate height of barrier, and 0.74 kN/m for any other use.

Handrails must be provided on at least one side if the ramp is less than 1.0 m wide (or 1.0 m between inside face(s) of handrail) and both sides if wider: none are required if the total rise of the ramp is not more than 600 mm. Handrails should

Type of stairway	Max. rise (mm) See figure 10.4	Min. going (mm)
Private stair	220	220
Common stair	190	240
Stairway in: institutional building, unless used by staff only	180	280
assembly building and serving area used for assembly purposes, unless area less than 100 m²	180	280
All other stairways	190	250

For private stair, any rise between 155 and 220 mm used with any going between 245 and 260 mm; and any rise between 165 and 200 mm used with any going between 220 and 305 mm.

For common stair, any rise between 155 and 190 mm used with any going between 240 and 320 mm

10.1 Rise and going dimensions for stairways: any goings and rises (see figure 10.4) within the ranges given for private and common stairs will meet the limitation of permitted angle of pitch and lie within the limits of (2 rise + going). (Building Regulations 1985: Approved Document K, table 1)

Type of stairway	Unobstructed width (mm) clear of handrails
Private stair providing access only to one room (not being a kitchen or living room) or to a bathroom or closet	600
All other private stairs	800
Common stair	900
Stairway in: institutional building, unless used by stall only	1000
assembly building serving area used for assembly purposes, unless area less than 100 m²	1000
any other building serving area which can be occupied by more than 50 people	1000
All other stairways	800

10.2 *Widths of stairways (Building Regulations 1985: Approved Document K, table 2)*

273

be between 840 and 1000 mm and can form the top of the ramp barrier providing the heights coincide.

Type of stairway		Height (mm)
Private stair	flights	840
	landings	900
Common stair	flights	900
	landings	1000
All other stairs	flights	900
	landings	1100

10.3 *Height of balustrading (guarding): heights indicated may not necessarily be the same as heights for handrails, see figure 10.4 (Building Regulations 1985: Approved Document K, table 3)*

(b) Barriers

BS 6180: 1982 *Protective barriers in and about buildings* gives recommendations for the general design and construction of temporary and permanent protective barriers to prevent people from falling and to stop persons or vehicles. BS 1722 *Specification for fences* Parts 1–13 deals comprehensively with design criteria for wood and metal fences and gates.

Protective barriers should be designed to resist the most unfavourable combination of imposed loads and wind loads without unacceptable deflection or distortion and with an adequate margin of safety against collapse. Materials commonly used for this purpose include reinforced concrete; brick, block and stone; steel and aluminium framework; and timber.

For most situations except those involving vehicles, laminated or toughened glass can be suitable, as can wired glass providing it is adequately framed in panes with no dimension exceeding 300 mm. The glass can be used as an infill to metal frames which have rebates for normal glazing, or profiled for clip fixings at a maximum spacing of 600 mm, or the glass can have point bolted supports and patch plates (see 7.5(a) Structural glazing). Alternatively, the glass can form a freestanding protective barrier where glass plates are clamped to the structure along their bottom edge and, as there are no balustrades, the handrail is attached to the top edge of the glass.

Various plastics materials can also be used, either as structural framing members or as infill panels, and are particularly suitable for barriers subjected to corrosive environments. Safety plastics materials for infill panels should comply with the impact performance requirements of BS 6206 (see 7.1(g) Safety (*Glazing*)) and include, acrylic, polycarbonate and rigid PVC, as well as glass fibre reinforced plastics (GRP). Fixing should be in grooves of not less than 20 mm depth per metre length and neoprene, butyl or similar rubber gasket.

BS 6180 recommends minimum heights for barriers used in different building types, an acceptable maximum design loading applied at a height of 1.1 m (height assumed for centre of gravity of the human body), a UDL (uniformally distributed load) on the barrier infill, and a point-load on the barrier infill. It further recommends that the height of barriers for theatres, cinemas and concert halls should also take account of viewing site lines, particularly when seats are placed within 530 mm of the barrier.

The *Building Regulations 1985* require that pedestrian barriers or *guarding* should be capable of preventing people from being injured by falling from a height of more than 600 mm, and vehicle barriers should be capable of resisting or deflecting impact from cars, lorries, etc. In dwellings, barriers against people falling from floors should be at least 900 mm high and be capable of resisting a horizontal force at that height of 0.36 kN/m. In other types of buildings as well as dwellings, balcony and roof barriers should be at least 1100 mm high and resist a horizontal force at that height of 0.74 kN/m: the height may be reduced to 790 mm for assembly building balconies in front of fixed seats.

If vehicles have access to a floor, roof or ramp which forms part of a building, the *Regulations* require barriers to be provided to any edges which are level with or above the floor or ground, or any other route for vehicles. In any building, the barriers for floors or roof edges should be at least 375 mm high and be capable of resisting a horizontal force at that height of 150 kN/m; at ramp edges they should be not less than 610 mm high and be capable of resisting the same horizontal force at that height. The vehicles covered by the horizontal force requirement are those weighing less than 2.5 tonnes (cars and light vans), and for appropriate forces for the range of heavier

274

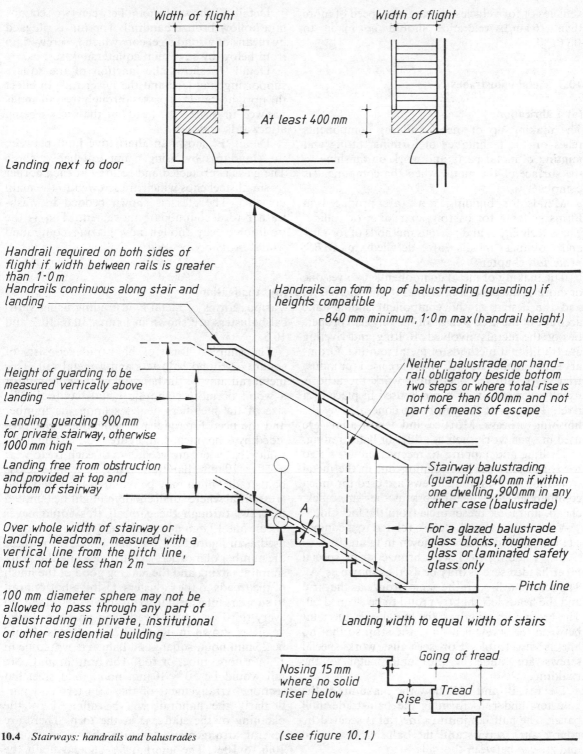

Width of flight

Width of flight

At least 400 mm

Landing next to door

Handrail required on both sides of flight if width between rails is greater than 1·0 m
Handrails continuous along stair and landing

Handrails can form top of balustrading (guarding) if heights compatible
840 mm minimum, 1·0 m max (handrail height)

Height of guarding to be measured vertically above landing

Landing guarding 900 mm for private stairway, otherwise 1000 mm high

Landing free from obstruction and provided at top and bottom of stairway

Neither balustrade nor hand-rail obligatory beside bottom two steps or where total rise is not more than 600 mm and not part of means of escape

Stairway balustrading (guarding) 840 mm if within one dwelling, 900 mm in any other case (balustrade)

Over whole width of stairway or landing headroom, measured with a vertical line from the pitch line, must not be less than 2 m

For a glazed balustrade glass blocks, toughened glass or laminated safety glass only

Pitch line

100 mm diameter sphere may not be allowed to pass through any part of balustrading in private, institutional or other residential building

Landing width to equal width of stairs

A

Nosing 15 mm where no solid riser below

Going of tread

Tread

Rise

10.4 *Stairways: handrails and balustrades*

(see figure 10.1)

vehicles or for vehicles moving at a speed of more than 16 km/h reference should be made to BS 6180.

10.3 Metal balustrades

(a) Fabrication

The making up of metal building components relies on the techniques of forming, fitting and jointing of metal parts and work on finishing to the surface of the metal when the component is complete.

Metals for building work are produced in forms suitable for casting, extruding or rolling. These techniques and various methods of forming and jointing metals are detailed in *MBS: Materials* chapter 9.

The making of metal components involves one or more of the processes or operations referred to, and the design of the component should take account of these as well as of the physical properties of the metals involved. Bolting and riveting are traditional methods of metal jointing. Ordinary semi-circular headed rivets are used for industrial work, but for decorative work the head is usually cleaned off or a pin is used in place of a rivet. The top of the pin being concealed by the finishing process. Mortice and tenon joints are used in open work such as grilles or balustrading.

Drilling and tapping to receive screws is also used, not only for site jointing but in the metal workshop. Self-tapping screws are used for much commercial sheet metal work as they are quick, cheap, and look presentable from the face side.

Various metalwork details related to a composite metal balustrade are shown in figure 10.5.

For cladding steel with bronze strips special taper headed screws may be used as shown as 'A'. The screws will be in the same bronze as the strip and the heads left slightly proud to be cleaned off. The buffing up will drag the metal over the joint between the screw head and the strip so that no line is discernible. For specialist work special screws are made in the same metal as the cladding.

Details 'B' and 'D' show the make up of the balusters and rails forming the balustrade infill panel. The half lap joint in the rail is secured by countersunk screws and the baluster is screwed and *riveted* between the rails.

Detail 'C' shows the joint between two sections in a hollow bronze handrail. The rail is plugged by means of a solid steel core which is screwed up from below by say 9 mm countersunk screws.

Detail 'E' shows the junction of the square supporting standard and the lower rail. In effect the upright standard passes through the rail and is screwed in place – the heads of the screws being afterwards removed.

Detail 'F' shows an alternative infill between the standards by using 6 mm toughened glass. The glass is protected and secured at each corner by small steel clips which are screwed to the main uprights. The glass is shown bedded in wash-leather to accommodate movement. This is the traditional way though now glazing compound would probably be used.

(b) Application

Various forms of metal balustrading using vertical balusters are shown in figures 10.6, 10.7 and 10.8.

The simplest form of balustrade consists of square or round balusters and a metal rail. This metal rail may be the handrail or the core rail for a wood or more elaborate metal handrail. The size of the members depends upon the number and the need for rigidity if stiffening is not provided by other means. In figure 10.4, 16 mm nom. square balusters are used, two of each tread with a 50 × 19 mm handrail. This is a very close balustrade which may be required for safety and is essential where small children might be tempted to crawl through the gaps. If this could never occur, one 19 mm nom. baluster per tread may be used as in figure 10.6, 10.7 and 10.8. This reduces the number of mortices in the treads and therefore simplifies fixing and the making good of the finish of the treads to the balusters. Using a bottom rail to support intermediate balusters with a standard every third or fourth tread gives an easier fixing detail as shown in figure 10.7. Standards should be 25 mm nom. square and balusters would be in 13 mm nom. tube, or rod. The bottom and core rail would be 50 × 10 mm nom. mild steel flat section. Arrangement of the balusters and particularly the handrail will be affected by the planning of the staircase at the turn. There are several arrangements of turn shown in figures 10.6 to 10.9. The alternatives depend upon the

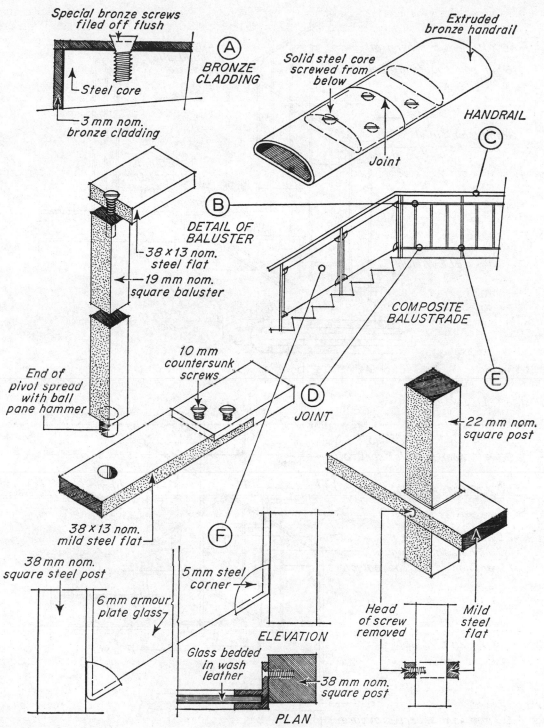

Special bronze screws
filed off flush

Ⓐ BRONZE CLADDING

Steel core

3 mm nom.
bronze cladding

Extruded
bronze handrail

Solid steel core
screwed from
below

HANDRAIL

Joint

Ⓒ

Ⓑ DETAIL OF
BALUSTER

38 × 13 nom.
steel flat

19 mm nom.
square baluster

End of
pivot spread
with ball
pane hammer

10 mm
countersunk
screws

Ⓓ JOINT

COMPOSITE
BALUSTRADE

Ⓔ

22 mm nom.
square post

38 × 13 nom.
mild steel flat

Ⓕ

38 mm nom.
square steel post

6 mm armour
plate glass

5 mm steel
corner

ELEVATION

Glass bedded
in wash
leather

38 mm nom.
square post

PLAN

Head
of screw
removed

Mild
steel
flat

10.5 *Metal balustrade details: fabrication of joints*

277

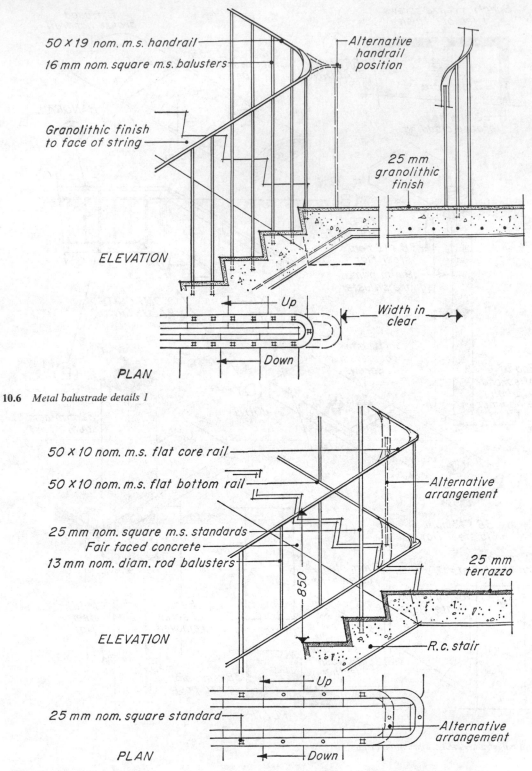

50 × 19 nom. m.s. handrail

16 mm nom. square m.s. balusters

Alternative handrail position

Granolithic finish to face of string

25 mm granolithic finish

ELEVATION

Up

Down

Width in clear

PLAN

10.6　*Metal balustrade details 1*

50 × 10 nom. m.s. flat core rail

50 × 10 nom. m.s. flat bottom rail

Alternative arrangement

25 mm nom. square m.s. standards
Fair faced concrete
13 mm nom. diam. rod balusters

25 mm terrazzo

850

ELEVATION

R.c. stair

Up

25 mm nom. square standard

Alternative arrangement

PLAN

Down

10.7　*Metal blaustrade details 2*

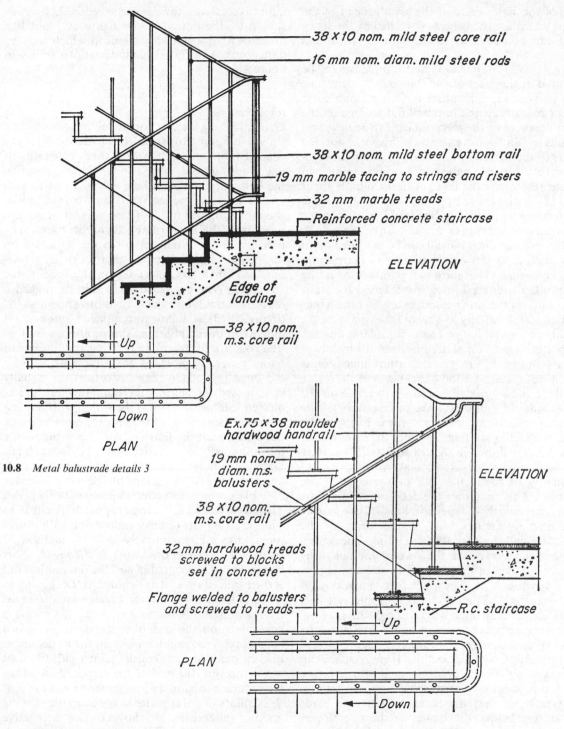

38 × 10 nom. mild steel core rail

16 mm nom. diam. mild steel rods

38 × 10 nom. mild steel bottom rail

19 mm marble facing to strings and risers

32 mm marble treads

Reinforced concrete staircase

ELEVATION

Edge of landing

38 × 10 nom. m.s. core rail

Up

Down

PLAN

10.8 *Metal balustrade details 3*

Ex. 75 × 38 moulded hardwood handrail

19 mm nom. diam. m.s. balusters

38 × 10 nom. m.s. core rail

32 mm hardwood treads screwed to blocks set in concrete

Flange welded to balusters and screwed to treads

ELEVATION

R.c. staircase

Up

PLAN

Down

10.9 *Metal balustrade details 4*

279

size of the stair well and the arrangement of the steps which are themselves governed by the space that can be allocated to the stair at the design stage.

It is very important that ample space be allowed at this part of the staircase. A tight turn not only makes difficulties for the manufacturer of the balustrade and handrail but also makes the neat detailing of the steps difficult to achieve and results in an inconvenient arrangement for the users of the staircase. The most common arrangement for a turn is a half space landing as shown in figure 10.6 where the faces of risers in both upper and lower flights are opposite or almost opposite each other on plan. The handrail has to drop the equivalent of one riser at the turn so unless the well is wide or the handrail can be extended on to the landing, as shown dotted, a very sharp ramp will be needed. There are two points to be borne in mind, a wide well loses space across the staircase but, on the other hand, extending the handrail on to the landing as shown loses space on the width of the landing. These considerations are important, since on staircases used for means of escape in case of fire, the important dimension is the measurement 'in the clear' between the inside of the handrail and the wall or handrail on the other side. In figure 10.6 the intersections of the sloping soffit of the stairs are not in line with the junction of the landing. A better arrangement of this detail is shown in figures 10.7 and 10.8. Here the soffits coincide at a point which can conveniently be made the face of the edge of the landing. This simplifies the detailing of the staircase, particularly if expensive finishes like marble are used as facings both to the string of the staircase and the edge of the landing. The setting back of the top riser in the lower flight makes the staircase much more pleasant to use and it permits a pause in descending before embarking on the next flight. The handrails also intersect at a level to suit a proper height above the landing. The arrangement shown in figure 10.7 also permits an easy ramp at the turn and one well suited to forming in a metal section. If more space can be taken up on the landing, as shown in figure 10.8, it is possible to arrange the handrail without a wreath, so that the turns on plan are made separately before the bends to the two slopes. This arrangement is also shown by dotted line in

figure 10.6. Space can also be saved in this way as shown by the dotted line in figure 10.7 but this involves a very considerable drop which may be dangerous. A further balustrade detail is shown in figure 10.9.

(c) Fixing

General fixing details for metal balustrading is shown in figures 10.10 and 10.11. Balustrades are usually fabricated in the workshop in lengths of one flight and one turn. The turn helps to stiffen the balustrade. Where there are no turns to give lateral bracing special stays may be needed as shown in figure 10.11. These special stays are fixed into the edge of the flight of stairs. The balustrates are usually fixed to the structure by setting the standards into a mortice or by screwing through a base plate set on the face of the structure. Where a standard is split or ragged a mortice should have the dimensions shown as 'A' (figure 10.10). It is, however, more common to cut indents in the standard as shown alternatively at 'B'. To allow for tolerance in fixing and for ease of fixing generally mortices are preferably wide in the direction of the flight. Mortices are usually run in with cement grout though fixers prefer molten lead as the joint is then rigid within a few minutes. The mouth of the mortice must be made good to match the finish of the treads unless the technique allows the treads to be faced later. Detail 'C' shows a method which permits a little adjustment in all directions by the use of a cover base plate which also covers up any making good. This plate can be drilled and tapped in position to suit the base plate of the standard and with power tools this is comparatively easy. A method of fixing a stay rail to brickwork is shown. A short length of rail is grouted in and the flat section rail is then spliced on to it as detailed at 'D'. Fixing to wood is simpler but a large bearing area to resist lateral pressure is necessary. Detail 'E' shows a base plate on the end of a standard let into a hardwood tread and the plate on the underside is held in place and makes the joint rigid, by a set screw, up into the end of the standard. A detail for securing a baluster into concrete is shown at 'F'. Collars or cover plates to cover up the making good of the mortice are shown in two alternative constructions in detail 'G'.

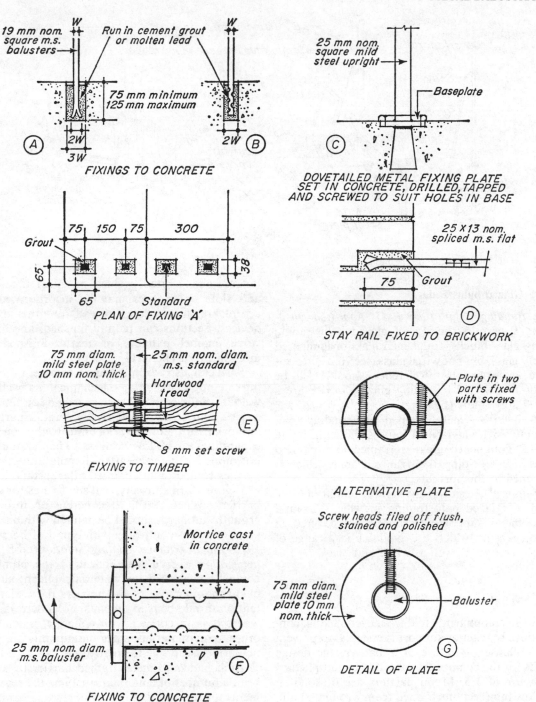

10.10 *Metal balustrade details: fixings 1*

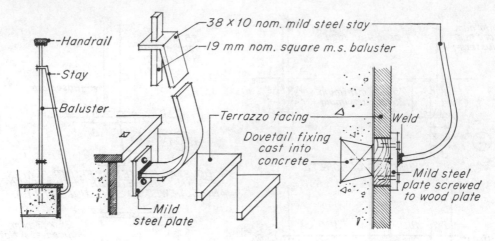

10.11 *Metal balustrade details: fixings 2*

10.4 Glazed balustrades

The *Building Regulations 1985: Approved Document K* permits the use of glazed balustrading using glass blocks, toughened glass or laminated safety glass, but not wired glass (see 10.2 Performance requirements). Reference should also be made to BS 6262 regarding glazing in risk areas (see 7.2(g) Safety (*Glazing*).

A detail of metal framed balustrading to a balcony with glass panel infill is shown in figure 10.12. Toughened glass is framed in a painted mild steel hot-dipped galvanized angle which is attached to the uprights.

Figure 10.13 shows an example of a 'frameless' form of glazed balustrading in which the mild steel metal supporting sections are covered in nylon plastics which are available in a range of bright colours as well as white and black.

10.5 Metal barriers

BS 6180 recommends that whenever a fixing, connection, bracket or support is essential to prevent the collapse or failure of a barrier, the design loads for the components should be multiplied by a factor of 1.5. Metal barriers are of solid or hollow tube sections formed from wrought aluminium alloys or aluminum casting alloys; or from carbon/low alloy steels or stainless steel.

Aluminium components may be clipped, hinged, slid, slotted, welded or glued together, and slots or grooves may be incorporated to accept bolt heads, screw threads or other fixing devices. Sections can be mill finished, anodized, stove enamel painted, or texture-finished by mechanical or chemical processes.

Steel can also accommodate a number of jointing methods, including mechanical as well as welding. Solid sections, such as rounds or flat bar, can be bent readily to fairly tight radii, particularly when hot, but there are limits to the bending capabilities of hollow sections. They should be hot-dipped galvanized after shaping and can be plastics coated or site painted after installation.

Figure 10.14 shows typical site fixings for steel barriers. Where set into concrete or into the ground, standards should be painted with bituminous solutions complying with type 1 of BS 3416: 1975 *Black bitumen coating solutions for cold application* over a length around the point of contact between the two materials. During subsequent maintenance of the barriers particular attention should be paid to joints, bolts, screws, etc, where it is in contact with concrete, mortar or other fixing materials, since these points are particularly susceptible to corrosive attack.

Infill panels to metal framed barrier rails can be of a number of materials satisfying the requirements for resistance to impact, including bars and hollow sections of aluminium and steel, and hollow section plastics. In certain situations plastics and glass could also be used, as mentioned earlier.

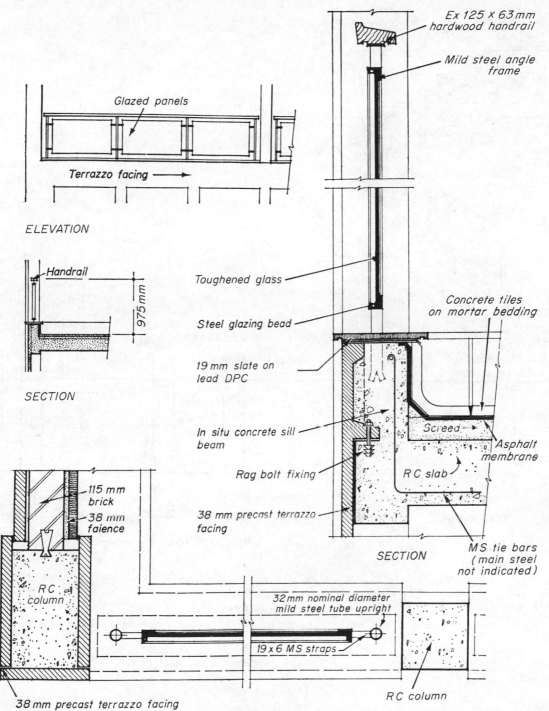

Ex 125 x 63 mm
hardwood handrail

Mild steel angle
frame

Glazed panels

Terrazzo facing →

ELEVATION

Handrail

975 mm

SECTION

Toughened glass

Steel glazing bead

19 mm slate on
lead DPC

Concrete tiles
on mortar bedding

Screed →

In situ concrete sill
beam

Asphalt
membrane

R C slab

Rag bolt fixing

38 mm precast terrazzo
facing

115 mm
brick

38 mm
faience

MS tie bars
(main steel
not indicated)

R C
column

SECTION

32 mm nominal diameter
mild steel tube upright

19 x 6 MS straps

R C column

38 mm precast terrazzo facing

DETAIL PLAN

10.12 *Glazed balustrades: framed glass panels used externally*

283

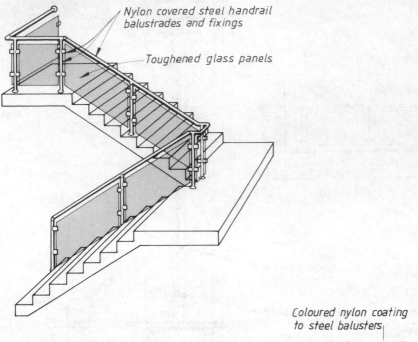

Nylon covered steel handrail balustrades and fixings

Toughened glass panels

Coloured nylon coating to steel balusters

Expansion bolt fixings

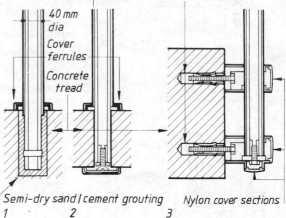

40 mm dia

Cover ferrules

Concrete tread

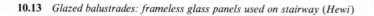

Semi-dry sand|cement grouting

Nylon cover sections

1   2   3

10.13   *Glazed balustrades: frameless glass panels used on stairway (Hewi)*

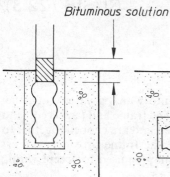

Bituminous solution

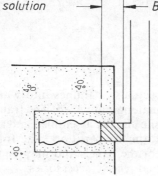

Bituminous solution

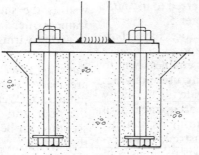

Standard set into
preformed or cut
mortice

Standard set into preformed
or cut mortice in side
(pocket should be suitably
reinforced)

Preset bolts normally require slotted holes, or
similar tolerance in fixing plates

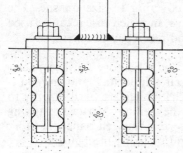

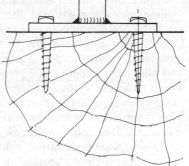

Expansion bolts in drilled holes

Caged foundation bolts in prepared
holes

Coach bolts or suitable screws
for fixing to timber

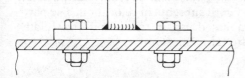

Standard bolted (or alternatively,
welded) to steelwork

10.14 *Metal barriers: fixing detail (BS 6180: 1982)*

285

11 Demountable partitions

11.1 Introduction

A partition is an internal wall used to divide space within a building in order to form separated rooms, circulation spaces, service walls, etc. It may be loadbearing or non-loadbearing and *fixed in position*, or non-loadbearing and *relocatable*. This chapter is concerned with the latter form. They are generally referred to as **demountable partitions**, and their installation, removal and subsequent relocation in a building do not materially affect the surrounding structure. The other forms of partition systems are referred to in *MBS: Structure and Fabric* Part 1 chapter 5.

Demountable partitions, therefore, have characteristics of *lightness in weight* and *independence* from the building structure. This enables them to be moved around to suit changing user activities and plan requirements, and provide the flexibility which is often essential when occupancy of a building is expected to change during its lifetime. This is particularly true for Industrial, Commercial and Educational buildings where changes in processes, plant installation, working methods, or sociological factors affecting space utilization are likely to occur.

The construction principles used to fulfil the requirement for demountability of partitions are closely related to those adopted for suspended ceilings and raised floors. They rely on factory based prefabrication of components, including not only the panels or sheets used in forming divisions, but also the interlocking mechanisms and other fixing devices used for installing the partition in a building. Therefore, they involve 'dry construction' techniques and, in order to meet reasonable cost targets, the number of components must be kept to an economic minimum and the erection techniques should not be too specialized.

There are numerous propriety systems available which can be divided into four broad constructional categories:

Frame and panel systems This consists of metal sections or frames into which a variety of panel materials are fixed. The frame and panels come to site already assembled and are clipped together to form the partition. The frame provides support for the panels and may be used to accept wiring and receive accessories.

Frame and sheet systems This has an exposed vertical frame and horizontal and vertical studs which are concealed by sheet materials forming the division. Where required, partition sizes can be adjusted by cutting frame and stud members as well as the sheet covering to size on site. The frame is often hollow, in which case it can be used to accept wiring and receive fixed accessories.

Panel to panel systems Factory finished panels are made to be self supporting and are butt-jointed together. The panels are fixed directly to the floor and to the ceiling. Vertical trunking sections can be inserted between panels in order to carry services and/or fixing mechanisms.

Folding and sliding systems The partition can be retracted instantaneously by folding panels concertina fashion to occupy a much reduced space. Sometimes the panels can be removed completely and stored until subsequent relocation. The partition is mounted on a track and the folding sections are fairly short.

11.2 Performance requirements

BS 5234: 1975 *Code of practice for internal non-loadbearing partitioning* lists properties that may be required and recommends good practice to follow during design, manufacture, erection and maintenance. Reference should also be made to the Property Services Agency (PSA) publication Method of Building 08.101: 1983 *Partitions – technical guidance*.

The increasing desire for flexible use of spaces within buildings results in a highly competitive market for manufacturers of demountable partitions in which satisfaction of consumer and legislative requirements play a large role. Precise information about appropriate use of partition systems must be supplied: products are tested to British Standard recommendations, and normally have British Board of Agrément certificates. Many manufacturers also participate in the BSI Quality Assurance Scheme recommended in BS 5750 (see 1.4 Component testing and Quality Assurance).

(a) Appearance

Appearance can be a major factor in the selection of a system, and the visual expression provided by frames or joints as well as the surface finishes of the partitioning itself are the main areas of consideration.

Frames are generally of extruded aluminium with anodized or polyester paint finish in a wide colour range, or painted galvanized steel. Moulded PVC can be used for preformed skirtings, cover strips, trunking and panel edges. The appearance of 'make-up' pieces and junction details should be carefully considered.

Finishes of the partition wall are usually of two categories:

- *self finish* (factory applied on preformed panel) which is permanent and requires no maintenance in respect of re-decoration and includes vinyl, timber veneer, plastic laminates, hardboard, steel sheet, fabric, glass and acrylic sheet; and,
- *base finish*, such as plasterboard, which will be ready to receive a painted finish and will thus require normal maintenance.

Part of the selection process must be consideration of the preservation of surface characteristics and their resistance to damage by impact or abrasion. Permanent disfiguration can be caused by scorching or chemical action, and finishes can be made unsightly by stains and graffiti. Care must be taken to select finishes appropriate to their relative ease or difficulty in cleaning, redecorating, repairing or replacing.

(b) Demountability

The option of demountabily is a most significant factor in respect of initial cost and the effect it will

have on the fulfilment of other performance requirements, including appearance. Also, taking down a demountable partition and re-erecting in a new position may involve adaptation to the lighting and heating – although, when the building has been specifically designed with flexible arrangements of accommodation in mind, the services will also allow adjustment without significant alteration of the building fabric. For these reasons, demountable partitions are usually employed in conjunction with suspended ceilings and, for maximum flexibility, with raised floors. When considered together, they can provide a grid-based planning flexibility employing compatible construction methods.

The need for cost effectiveness and efficiency requires analysis of the frequency of change in partition position to be established, because this will determine to a great extent the complexity of the installation and the type of personnel required to carry out the alterations. For example, day-to-day adaptation will require the ease of a sliding/folding partition which can be carried out by the building users themselves; adaptation every few months will allow the use of a more sophisticated partitioning system capable of being manoeuvred by maintenance staff, whereas adaptation after a period of a few years will require the employment of an outside contractor. Properties of sound reduction are significantly reduced in direct proportion to ease of demountability because it will be harder to provide acoustic sealing around edges. A demountable partition system which provides a high degree of sound control will be expensive, both in first cost and cost of re-assembly, since the jointing technique will be complex. However, a system which gives demountability only at the junction points, such as doors, abutments and intersections, will be less expensive than a partition which, by reason of more sophisticated jointing techniques, can be demounted at each panel on the planning module.

Figure 11.1 shows examples of the two alternative methods of obtaining flexibility in demounting:

- by the use of an H section vertical member into which the partition panel fits. The sequence of erection with this type of partition is to fix the wall channel at the abutment and then continue, panel-post-panel, the panels being fitted from the side;

- by the use of a 'breakdown' member which is in three sections so that the panels can be fitted from the front or rear. Demountability can occur at each module.

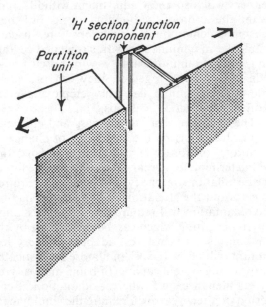

(a) '*H' sections at abutments and intersections*

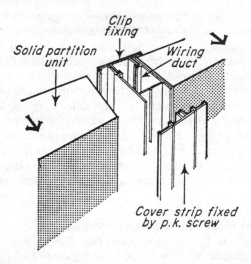

11.1 *Two methods of obtaining demountability*

288

(c) Strength

Although demountable partitions are non-load-bearing they must be capable of lateral stability, and of withstanding temporary sideways point loads as well as soft body impact of prescribed magnitude without deflection. Factors to be considered include the head and base fixings, joints between panels and the strength of the partition construction. Head details are generally most critical since they can be fixed directly to the framework of suspended ceilings. In addition to a rigid head fixing, a framed form of partition, or the insertion of frames in a panel-to-panel form, may be necessary where partition panels are required to carry shelving or other fixtures, including furniture and wash basins.

Manufacturer's recommendations should be taken even when deciding on methods of providing fixings for small items, such as coat hooks or fire extinguishers. Reference should be made to *A J Handbook* of fixings and fastenings: suitable methods must support without loosening or damaging the partition and include, back-clamping to the inside of the panel skin (*toggles and cavity fixings*); threading into fibres or core materials (*screws*); expansion into the face or core material (*nails or screws* into *plugs, bolts in anchors and expansion bolts*); pressure on the face or core material (*nails*); mechanical clamping through the partition (*bolts with washers or back-plates on opposite side*); and adhesion (*glues*).

BS 6262: 1982 *Code of practice for glazing for building* covers the design and performance criteria for vertical glazing within buildings. It is particularly concerned with safety and includes the recommendations of BS 6206: 1981 *Impact performance requirements for flat safety glass and safety plastics for use in buildings*. See also chapter 7 *Glazing*.

(d) Fire precautions

When a fire occurs, the danger arises both from within the building and in the risk of the spread of fire from one building to another. The various fire regulations state requirements to limit this spread, the risk of which is related to the use of the building. Factors to be considered include the resistance provided by the constructional elements, the resistance of the surface finishes to the spread of flame, the size of the building, the degree of isolation between the various parts of the building, the provision of fire fighting facilities, and the incorporation of appropriate means of escape for the occupants. Therefore, since demountable partitions are normally associated with building types having a high occupancy factor, they may have an important role in protecting the people and contents within a building as well as in preventing the spread of fire.

The *Building Regulations 1985: Approved Document B* classify partitions as *internal walls*, but do not specifically mention demountable partitions. This particular form of partition system is installed within the structural envelope of a building and will not normally be used to provide the fire resistance to the standard of compartment walls (see 5.8 Fire Doors for definitions). Their 'temporary' nature also makes them unsuitable for use in protecting escape routes. Nevertheless, they must not contribute towards the fire or allow it to spread.

Fire resistance Most systems will give a notional period of fire resistance of between half and one hour (stability, integrity and insulation – see 5.8). In certain situations, demountable partitions may be used to temporarily divide a large fire compartment of a building into smaller areas while certain functions are carried out, eg a series of separately controlled group meetings within a large hall. In these circumstances, particular care in selection is required in order to make sure that the junctions between panels, and between the partition and adjoining room surfaces, provide the integrity required.

Other factors concerning the ability or otherwise of a demountable partition to contribute towards the fire relates to material *combustibility*. BS 476 *Fire tests on building materials and structures*, Part 4: 1970 (1984) *Non-combustibility test for materials* is an important reference and the significance is explained in *MBS: Materials* chapter 1 page 35.

Surface spread of flame Figure 11.2 provides a summary of the surface spread of flame requirements for different building types as stipulated by the *Building Regulations 1985: Approved Document B*. A similar description of spread of flame classification applicable to ceilings is given in 12.2(d) Fire precautions.

Purpose Groups	Small rooms less than 30 m²	Other rooms	Circulation space and protected shaft
RESIDENTIAL GROUP			
Dwelling house			
One or 2 storey house, basement not counted	3	1*	1
Three storeys or more, basement not counted	3	1*	0
Flat or maisonette	3	1*	0
Institutional	1*	0*	0
Other residential	3	1*	0
NON-RESIDENTIAL GROUP			
Assembly	3	1*	0
Office	3	1*	0
Shop	3	1*	0
Industrial	3	1*	0
Other non-residential	3	1*	0

* *Part of wall surface may be lower class (Class 3 minimum), but the area of the part (or total area if there is more than one part) should not be more than one-half of the floor area of the room and not more than 60 m².*

11.2 *Minimum surface spread of flame classifications for walls relative to Purpose Groups Building Regulations 1988: Approved Document B)*

The Regulations consider buildings under the following two main *Purpose Groups*, and ascribe surface spread of flame classifications according to potential fire risk:

Residential group Includes dwelling houses; flats; maisonettes; institutional buildings, such as hospitals, homes, schools or other similar establishments used as living accommodation; and other residential buildings such as hotels, boarding houses and hostels.

Non-residential group Includes buildings used for assembly, offices, and shops; industrial purposes (factories as defined by Factories Act 1961); and for other non-residential purposes, such as storage, deposit or parking.

The classifications according to BS 476 *Fire tests on building materials and structures*, Part 7:

289

1971 *Surface spread of flame tests for materials are*:

Class 1 a surface of very low flame spread;
Class 2 a surface of low flame spread;
Class 3 a surface of medium flame spread;
Class 4 a surface of rapid flame spread.

These four BS classifications were not considered adequate in all cases and the Building Regulations stipulate a *Class 0*, defined as being:

- non-combustible throughout;
- with a surface (or if bonded to a substrate, the surface and substrate) having an index of *Performance* (I) not exceeding 12, and a sub-index (i) not exceeding 6 when tested in accordance with BS 476 Part 6: 1981 (1983) *Method of test for fire propagation for products*. If the face is of a plastics material with a softening point below 120°C when tested to BS 2782 *Methods of testing plastics* it *must either*:

be bonded to a substrate which is not a plastics material and the material in conjunction with the substrate satisfies the BS 476 Part 6 test; *or* satisfy the BS 476 Part 6 test and be so used that if the lining were not present, the exposed surface satisfies the test criteria and the exposed surface would not be a plastics material with a softening point below 120°C.

High surface spread of flame characteristics are particularly dangerous when occurring within concealed situations, such as in the cavities of partitions, and wherever possible hollow constructions should be avoided in potential fire risk situations. Alternatively, the internal voids must be limited by the provision of *fire stops*. Manufacturers must always provide enough performance data for an accurate assessment to be made and to allow facts to be presented to the Fire Control Officer.

(e) Sound control

A demountable partition by its nature is vulnerable to the passage of sound, and to expect a lightweight site-assembled structure to provide a very high standard of sound control is, to some extent, contradictory.

The matter of sound control should be considered at the design stage of a building so that noise producing rooms and rooms requiring quiet can be planned remote from each other. In order to solve the problem of protecting the occupants of a room against unwanted noise, both air and structure (impact and flanking) borne sound must be considered as well as external noise (see *Mitchell's Introduction to Building* chapter 7 *Sound Control*, and *MBS Environment and Services* chapter 6).

Airborne sound is created by fluctuations or waves in air pressure which are perceived by the ear as sound. These waves strike the surface of a partition and cause it to vibrate. In turn this causes the air on the opposite side of the partition also to vibrate and thus the sound is transmitted. The sound resistant properties afforded by the partition is a measure of the degree to which these vibrations can be reduced or absorbed.

The empirical mass law means that the heavier the material used for a component the greater is its resistance to sound transmission, and implies that demountable partitions are less effective in providing sound resistance than the other forms of partition. However, using lightweight cavity construction, sound reduction values better than those predicted by the mass law can be obtained. For example, a partition constructed of metal studs incorporating a flexible mounting for a plasterboard facing on both sides, results in up to a 10 dB better reduction. The air in the cavity can be considered as a spring between the facings which has inherent damping properties. The effects of this isolation between the facing and the stud can be further enhanced by the introduction of a sound absorbent material into the cavity.

Nevertheless, good sound performance in demountable partitions mostly relies on a number of very practical considerations relating to their construction. This must attempt to provide the maximum achievable sound reduction value throughout, including through doors and any infill panels. The design must not permit air leaks caused by joints, gaps, cracks or holes through which sound waves can travel, and in this respect, initial workmanship and subsequent handling are of major importance. Potential points of sound leakage can occur around partition edge seals, as well as poorly fitting doors. In some systems, sophisticated constructions, such as resilient air seals at abutments to walls and ceilings, are incorporated to assist in sound reduction as well as to take up possible dimensional inaccuracies in the structure. One irritating source of noise, that of door slamming, can easily be prevented by the fitting of automatic door closers, checks and rubber seals.

Sound waves will also travel over or under the demountable partitions when they are used in conjunction with suspended ceilings and raised floors, especially those incorporating ventilators, heating ducts or continuous lighting troughs. In fact when sound reduction is considered critical and demountable partitions *must* be used, measures need to be taken that ensure any voids forming part of the construction of the floor, ceiling and flanking walls contain absorbent baffles in positions likely to coincide with a future location of the partition. Alternatively, purpose-made panels must be placed in the cavities every time the partition is moved. This is more difficult for the wall construction than for the suspended ceilings and raised floors.

All sounds differ in pitch and intensity, and BS 2750 *Methods of measurement of sound insulation in buildings and building elements*, Parts 1 to 8: 1980, has been established for comparative acoustic testing. It provides the arithmetical average decibel reduction over the range of 100 to 3150 Hz (cycles per second) and all partition systems should be tested to this standard. It is possible to produce enhanced performance data by testing over a more limited frequency range, or by testing single panels in isolation rather than a panel and its framing components. In such cases, an apparent gain of 4 to 5 dB can be incorrectly claimed. Site conditions are very much more difficult than the controlled conditions of the laboratory and, although measured figures are useful for comparison, a poorer acoustic performance on the site is almost inevitable.

In designing for sound resistance, it is important to set targets which are correct in terms of the uses of the spaces separated by partitions. The following list (taken from the British Gypsum *White Book*) indicates the effect of decibel reduction levels on human speech which are useful when selecting a partition system:

20 dB Normal conversation can be easily overhead.

25 dB Loud conversation can be heard clearly.

30 dB Loud speech can be distinguished under normal conditions.

35 dB Loud speech can be heard but not distinguished

40 dB Loud speech can be heard faintly but not distinguished.

More than

40 dB Loud speech or shouting can be heard with great difficulty.

Where the background noise level is low, it is generally accepted that an insulation of 40 dB will give a tolerable amount of privacy between two adjacent offices. However, actual performance prediction is dependent on layout, the arrangement of adjacent elements, and the presence of absorptive materials. Whenever possible advice should be given by the partition manufacturer.

(f) Integration of services

In partition systems where flexibility is required, service integration is usually restricted to electrical power and communication wiring. Service channels are usually incorporated in suspended ceilings and raised floors, and connection can be made into demountable partitions (other than folding/sliding) by means of special vertical hollow frame units located between panels, or to hollow horizontal dado sections and skirtings. Socket outlets can be fixed in both these vertical and horizontal sub-components.

Split panel systems are also available which allow one side to be removed independently of the other. These give easy and complete access to wiring for both initial installation and for future maintenance and alteration, and provide greater flexibility for routing cables and positioning outlets. Metal trunking should be earthed and emerging cables should always be secured and protected by flexible bellows at movable junctions.

(g) Durability and maintenance

Whichever systems of demountable partitioning are employed in a building it is necessary to take great care during the moving processes in order not to destroy edges or scratch surfaces.

Where fairly frequent relocation is necessary a system should be chosen which enables all parts, skirtings, cover strips, moulding, etc, to be reused. Alternatively, it will be necessary to ensure these parts are readily available before relocation is proposed. Most sliding/folding systems can be manoeuvred without damage provided care is taken and the tracks and channels are kept in good working order.

Building maintenance manuals should include very precise information about cleaning, including the removal of graffiti, as well as a list of suppliers of replacement components (see *Mitchell's Introduction to Building* chapter 15: 15.8 *Maintenance Team*.

11.3 Frame and panel systems

Figure 11.3 shows an example of a simple frame and panel system. The frame is of aluminium alloy, anodized to BS 1615: 1972 *Anodic oxidation coatings on aluminium*, and the panels are designed to fit any module using standard sheets. The infill panels are sandwich construction with a core of polystyrene, mineral fibre or similar material according to the required performance specification. This core material is faced both sides with hardboard and finished with decorative PVC sheet, decorative laminated plastics or hardwood veneers. More complex panel construction may incorporate a single or double skin of pressed steel or aluminium sheet. This type of double skin panel may be filled with glass fibre or mineral wool.

The total nominal thickness of the panel illustrated is 50 mm. As with most partition systems, the doors are pre-hung, in this case on nylon washered aluminium butt hinges, and have a rubber strip air seal around the perimeter of the frame. Note the use of PVC glazing beads which fit neatly into the 'I' section frame and the clip-on cornice and skirting trim. The junction at floor and ceiling is most important, particularly in respect of partitions which must have high sound reduction. In the example illustrated, foam rubber sealing strip is used. Electric and communication wiring can be run in the vertical hollow junction frames as well as along the skirting sections.

A more sophisticated system is shown in figure 11.4. This is a *modular ceiling and partitioning* system with integrated storage and accessories. The ceiling grid has a dimensional relationship with the partitioning, thereby providing complete flexibility within the discipline of a modular layout. The framework to the ceiling is of extruded aluminium alloy channels suspended from the structure by rod or strap hangers attached to the main span members of the ceiling. Notched and turned aluminium connecting members are fixed to the spine framework at modular points. The junction of the spine and intermediate members is concealed by a plastics boss.

The grid is designed to receive any proprietary acoustic board or tile ceiling. Ceiling and partition modules are standard at 1220 mm. The partition system has a maximum height of 3050 mm, with a 51 mm overall thickness. Panel cores are of mineral fibre, chipboard or expanded polystyrene faced with 3 mm hardboard finished in PVC, laminate or hardwood veneer. The glazing uses extruded plastics beads with glass up to 6 mm thick. Storey height (or normal height) doors are supplied prehung and complete with furniture.

One feature of this system is the design of various special brackets which screw or clip into the cruciform framing to provide anchorage for such items as shelves, coat hooks, pinboards, the chalkboards. Storage cabinets can also be clipped and hung from the framing, provided that the rigidity of the supports to the ceiling is checked.

Figure 11.5 shows a type of frame and panel partition system where the frame is a solid timber post (sometimes referred to as post and panel system). The partition illustrated used glazed hardboard faced, timber lipped, compressed straw slab panels of 58 mm total overall thickness. There is a dry tongued joint between the edges of the panels and posts, and the units are housed at floor and ceiling positions by means of timber plates. The partition uses a standard 900 mm wide panel and a 100 mm post. It can be built to heights of 2400 mm and 3600 mm. The faced hardboard has a Class 3 surface spread of flame rating and the panel a half-hour fire resistance.

Other post and panel partition systems use panels of plasterboard 'egg box' construction, wood wool slabs, chipboard or medium density fibreboard (MDF).

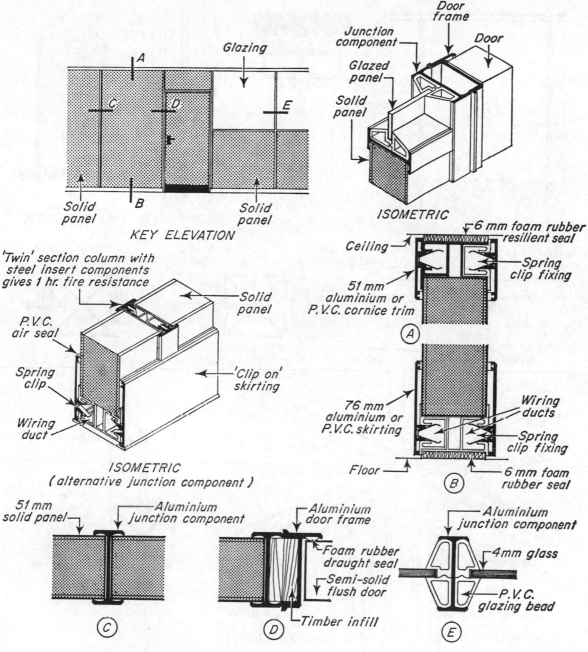

KEY ELEVATION

Glazing

Solid panel

A

B

C D E

Solid panel

ISOMETRIC

Door frame

Junction component

Door

Glazed panel

Solid panel

'Twin' section column with steel insert components gives 1 hr. fire resistance

P.V.C. air seal

Spring clip

Wiring duct

Solid panel

'Clip on' skirting

ISOMETRIC
(alternative junction component)

6 mm foam rubber resilient seal

Ceiling

Spring clip fixing

51 mm aluminium or P.V.C. cornice trim

(A)

76 mm aluminium or P.V.C. skirting

Wiring ducts

Spring clip fixing

Floor

6 mm foam rubber seal

(B)

51 mm solid panel

Aluminium junction component

(C)

Aluminium door frame

Foam rubber draught seal

Semi-solid flush door

Timber infill

(D)

Aluminium junction component

4mm glass

P.V.C. glazing bead

(E)

11.3 *Frame and panel system details 1*

293

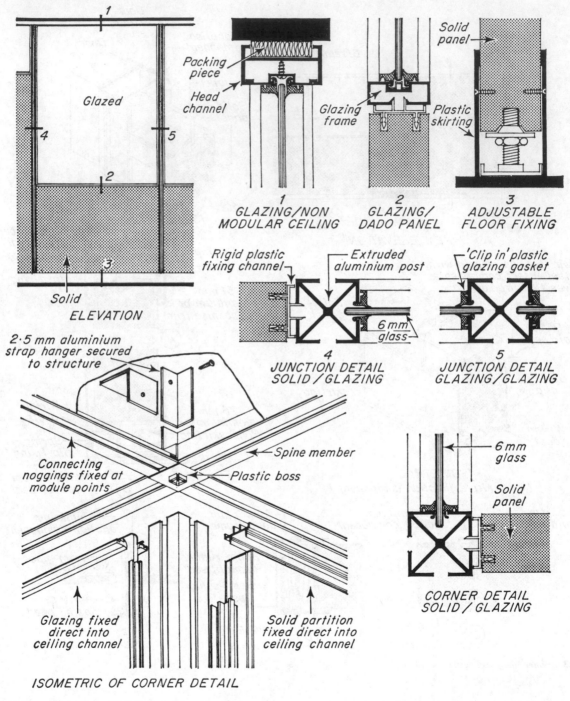

ELEVATION

1 GLAZING/NON MODULAR CEILING

Packing piece

Head channel

2 GLAZING/ DADO PANEL

Glazing frame

3 ADJUSTABLE FLOOR FIXING

Solid panel

Plastic skirting

4 JUNCTION DETAIL SOLID/GLAZING

Rigid plastic fixing channel

Extruded aluminium post

6 mm glass

5 JUNCTION DETAIL GLAZING/GLAZING

'Clip in' plastic glazing gasket

2·5 mm aluminium strap hanger secured to structure

Spine member

Plastic boss

Connecting noggings fixed at module points

Glazing fixed direct into ceiling channel

Solid partition fixed direct into ceiling channel

ISOMETRIC OF CORNER DETAIL

6 mm glass

Solid panel

CORNER DETAIL SOLID/GLAZING

11.4 *Frame and panel system details 2*

294

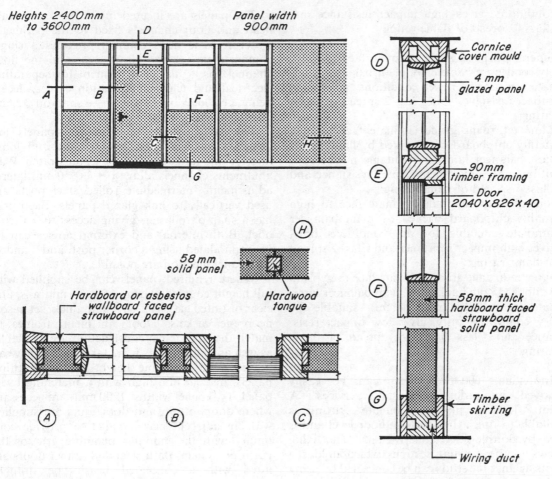

Heights 2400mm to 3600mm

Panel width 900mm

Cornice cover mould

4 mm glazed panel

90mm timber framing

Door 2040 × 826 × 40

58mm solid panel

Hardwood tongue

Hardboard or asbestos wallboard faced strawboard panel

58mm thick hardboard faced strawboard solid panel

Timber skirting

Wiring duct

11.5 *Frame and panel system details 3*

11.4 Frame and sheet systems

Figure 11.6 shows an example of a frame and sheet system consisting of a framework of galvanized steel studs faced both sides by sheets of plasterboard, chipboard or plywood. The frame is constructed of 50 mm wide floor and ceiling channel section studs into which the vertical studs are inserted at 600 mm centres to coincide with panel joints. Additional studs of steel channels or of timber may be required to provide anchor points for heavy fixtures. The 15 mm thick facing sheets are usually available in 600 and 1200 mm widths and span from floor to ceiling up to the standard sheet maximum height of 3030 mm. Smaller sizes can be made available to order. The sheets are held into position using predecorated galvanized

steel 'top-hat' sections which are secured to the studs by 15 mm × No 6 self-tapping screws at 600 mm maximum centres. 1200 mm wide sheets are fixed to the intermediate vertical studs by a gap-filling panel adhesive, gun applied before screwing the sheet to the studs at the edges.

The sheets forming the partition are supplied with a decorative plastics laminate finish to the core with a balancing laminate on the back to prevent bowing (total thickness 15 mm). They are supplied in various permutations of facing quality and core material, including the following:

● flame retardant grade laminate face to impregnated WBP plywood core backed by flame retardant balancer laminate – suitable for dry

295

conditions, gives high impact resistance and Class 0 spread of flame rating;

- general purpose grade laminate face to WBP plywood core backed by plain balancer laminate – suitable for wet conditions, gives high impact resistance and Class 2 spread of flame rating;
- flame retardant grade laminate face to high quality chipboard core backed by flame retardant balancer laminate – suitable in dry conditions only, gives high impact resistance and Class 1 spread of flame rating;
- general purpose grade laminate face to high quality chipboard backed by plain balancer laminate – suitable for dry conditions only, gives high impact resistance and Class 2 spread of flame rating;
- flame retardant grade laminate face to gypsum wallboard core backed by plain balancer laminate (overall thickness 14 mm) – suitable for dry conditions only, gives low impact resistance and Class 0 surface spread of flame rating.

Individual 600 mm sheets can be easily removed in order to install services. A 3 mm × 150 mm plastics laminate skirting is available to finish the sheets at floor level and is fixed by double-sided adhesive tape. The fixing screws in the top-hat sections which hold the sheets against the studs can be concealed by using a 12 mm width plastics laminate strip. If desired, the top-hat sections can be in extruded aluminium in the form of a shelving upright so that brackets can be clipped-on to provide a range of supports, or can be recessed into the edge of the sheets so that no face fixing can be seen.

11.5 Panel to panel systems

Figure 11.7 shows a panel to panel partition system which is based on a 600 mm modular horizontal planning grid. The preformed mono-block panels are of sandwich construction having two skins of 0.125 mm gauge galvanized steel finished externally with an epoxy polyester powder coat, and have an infill between skins of mineral wool. The overall thickness is 60 mm and the panels can be supplied to suit requirement up to a maximum of 4.5 m high.

The panels are located into rolled steel wall, head and floor channels fixed to the perimeter structure. The head channel provides a single compartment service wiring duct and the floor channel has a dual compartment for separating electrical and telecommunication cables, access being provided by means of a snap-on 72 mm high PVC skirting.

The vertical junctions between panels are achieved by a grooved edge profile and loose interlocking tongue technique as illustrated. Wall abutments channels allow a +/− 10 mm lateral adjustment. Intermediate rolled steel posts are used vertically to link glazed panels. Each post has a snap-on pilaster, giving access to a wiring duct. Both internal and external angles can be accommodated using a corner post, and 3 and 4-way panel junction are possible.

Where required, panels can be supplied with full height coupled glazing without midrails, and clear or tinted glass is used, 8 mm thick, set in soft neoprene gaskets. Doors in metal frames to match the solid panel construction are available, as well as timber doors in metal frames. They can be either to the same height as the partition panels, or 2048 mm high with a matching over-panel. Two panel widths (1200 mm) are necessary where doors occur, and door units are supplied with an adjacent glazed panel to provide continuity with the modular planning grid of the partition system. Both steel and timber doors are fitted with a concealed brush-type draught excluder.

Figure 11.8 shows another type of panel to panel system used for the construction of cubicles for wcs, showers, changing rooms and clothes lockers.

11.6 Folding and sliding systems

(a) Folding

Figure 11.9 shows a centre hung sliding folding partition used in the construction of a room divider. A half leaf is necessary against the frame on one side. The particular example illustrates the use of bottom track and rollers with a top guide. The requirement for a bottom track are, however, contradictory since the track giving the least break in the floor surface is least likely to restrain the door properly.

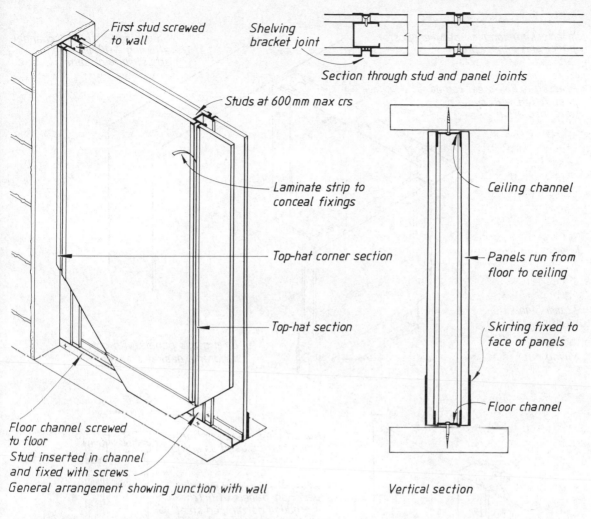

First stud screwed to wall

Shelving bracket joint

Section through stud and panel joints

Studs at 600 mm max crs

Laminate strip to conceal fixings

Top-hat corner section

Top-hat section

Ceiling channel

Panels run from floor to ceiling

Skirting fixed to face of panels

Floor channel

Floor channel screwed to floor

Stud inserted in channel and fixed with screws

General arrangement showing junction with wall

Vertical section

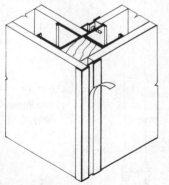

50mm square timber corner post

Floor channel screwed to floor

Studs secured with self-tapping screws

Corner details

11.6 *Frame and sheet system details*

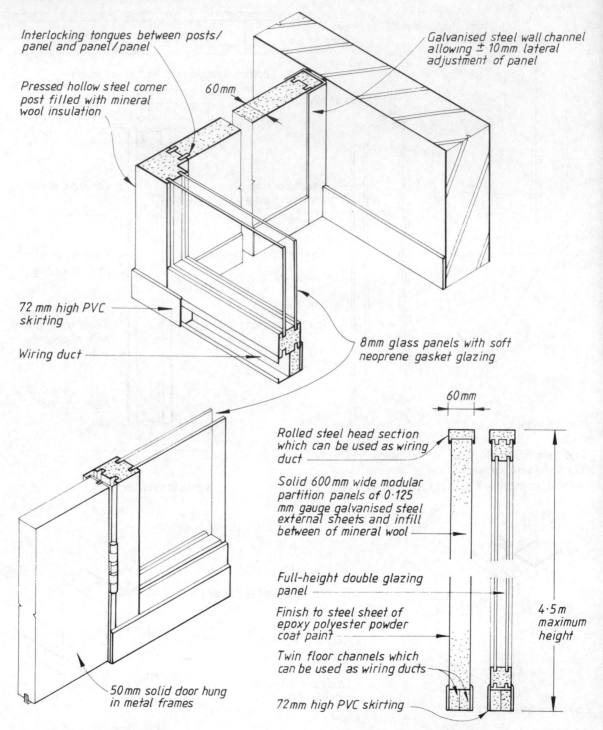

Interlocking tongues between posts/panel and panel/panel

Pressed hollow steel corner post filled with mineral wool insulation

60mm

Galvanised steel wall channel allowing ± 10mm lateral adjustment of panel

72 mm high PVC skirting

Wiring duct

8mm glass panels with soft neoprene gasket glazing

50mm solid door hung in metal frames

60mm

Rolled steel head section which can be used as wiring duct

Solid 600mm wide modular partition panels of 0·125 mm gauge galvanised steel external sheets and infill between of mineral wool

Full-height double glazing panel

Finish to steel sheet of epoxy polyester powder coat paint

Twin floor channels which can be used as wiring ducts

72mm high PVC skirting

4·5m maximum height

11.7 *Panel to panel system details*

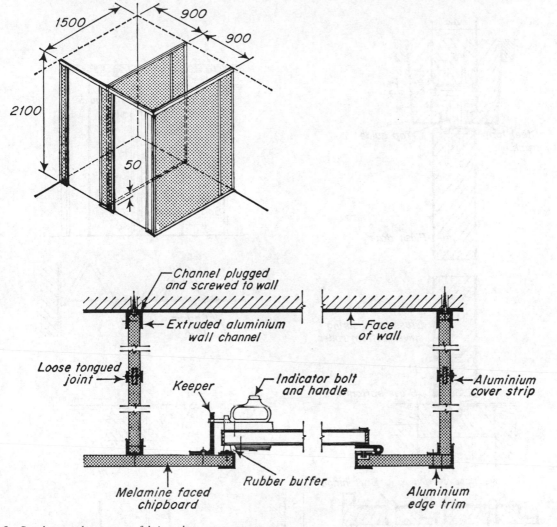

11.8 *Panel to panel system: prefabricated wc compartment*

299

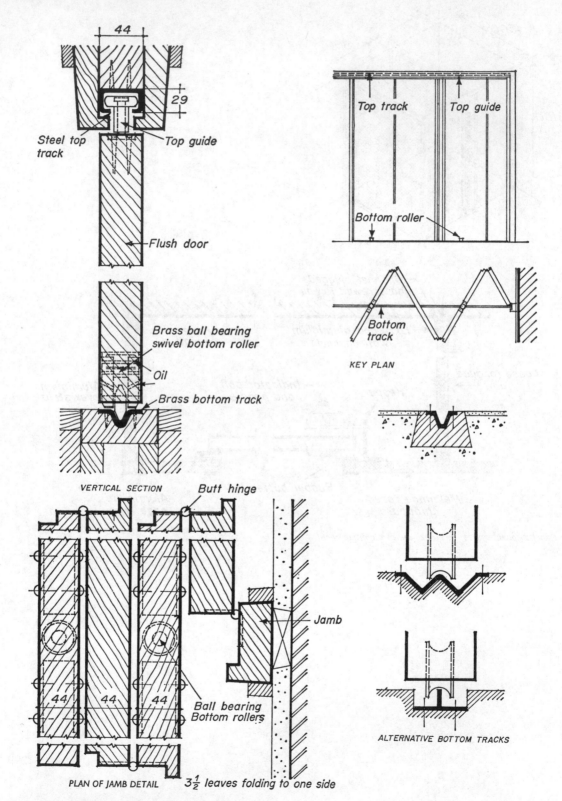

44

29

Steel top
track

Top guide

Flush door

Brass ball bearing
swivel bottom roller

Oil

Brass bottom track

VERTICAL SECTION

Butt hinge

Jamb

44   44   44

Ball bearing
Bottom rollers

PLAN OF JAMB DETAIL

$3\frac{1}{2}$ leaves folding to one side

Top track   Top guide

Bottom roller

Bottom
track

KEY PLAN

ALTERNATIVE BOTTOM TRACKS

11.9 *Folding and sliding systems: folding partition*

(b) Louvred folding

This type of partition, shown in figure 11.10, is also used as a room divider or decorative screen. Many manufacturers produce this type as standard at much less cost than purpose-made versions. Decorative timbers such as North American clear pine or Luan mahogany are used. The rails are dowelled and the louvre slats notched into the styles. This type is also suitable for built-in storage units and wardrobes where maximum access is required.

The use of top and bottom pivots leaves the threshold completely clear, and a spring loaded roller guide is fixed to the top leading corner of each pair of doors to ensure smooth running in the track. Special back flap hinges are used and the door alignment plates guide the doors together on the closing style of each pair of doors. If the four panels shown were hung to fold one way, then a different type of track would be required.

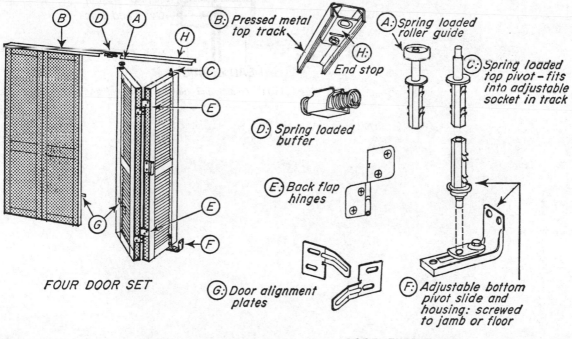

FOUR DOOR SET

B: Pressed metal top track

H: End stop

A: Spring loaded roller guide

C: Spring loaded top pivot – fits into adjustable socket in track

D: Spring loaded buffer

E: Back flap hinges

G: Door alignment plates

F: Adjustable bottom pivot slide and housing: screwed to jamb or floor

DOOR FURNITURE

11.10 *Folding and sliding systems: louvred folding partition*

(c) Collapsible

This type of partition has almost become standard construction for use as a space divider in houses, and in small community buildings. The partition illustrated in figure 11.11 is made up of an aluminium alloy collapsible frame over which is stretched leathercloth, PVC or similar material. These partitions are top hung and do not require a floor fixing or channel, and an important point to note is the minimum amount of space taken up when the doors are folded back.

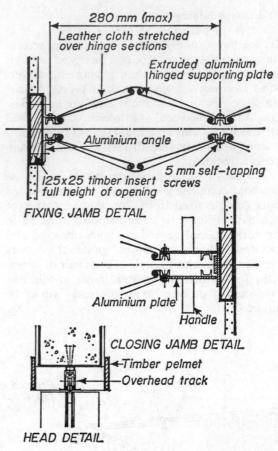

11.11 *Folding and sliding systems: collapsible partition*

12 Suspended ceilings

12.1 Introduction

A suspended ceiling is defined in BS 6100: *Glossary of building and civil engineering terms*, Part 1: *General and miscellaneous*. Subsection 1.3.3: 1984 *Floors and ceilings*, as 'a ceiling hung at a distance from the floor or roof above, and not bearing on the walls.' These ceilings serve a number of aesthetic functions involving the reduction of room height and provision of decorative planes; as well as practical functions, including the concealment of services, protection of structure against fire, thermal insulation, illumination, heating and ventilation, and contribution of sound control.

The methods of construction may vary widely, but can be grouped under the following systems:

Jointless systems These can be 'wet' or 'dry' methods of construction, and provide a joint-free ceiling soffit. They can incorporate removable or hinged panels for access to services located in the space above;

Frame and panel systems These consist of tiles or planks laid into a framework suspended from the structural floor or roof above. Access is easily obtainable by removing the tiles or planks;

Linear strip systems Similar to the frame and panel systems except much fewer joints owing to the use of long lengths of planks, which may or may not interlock;

Louvre and open strip systems These are formed by open panel or tile units in a suspension framework, and are used to provide a visual 'cut-off' from the soffit and services above;

Integrated service systems These consist of a ceiling which forms a service unit for the room below and incorporates heating, lighting, ventilation and sound absorption units.

All except 'wet' jointless ceilings are proprietary products. Manufacturers generally work to a 300 or 600 mm module, unless constructional detailing or visual preference makes a 100 mm module (or a 50 mm sub-module) more acceptable, such as in the linear strip system. For modular ceilings, the setting out should be carefully considered because angular perimeter cut-off can be unsightly. Special perimeter infill tiles or strips are usually available so that irregularities in structure can be taken into account, as well as possible movement due to expansion and contraction within the ceiling itself. Trims of painted, coated or capped steel can be used to camouflage ceiling perimeters and junctions. Timber cover moulds or fillets can be applied as a last resort to hide dimensional irregularities at perimeter junctions.

12.2 Performance requirements

CP 290: 1973 *Suspended ceilings and linings of dry construction using metal fixing systems* deals with the design of certain types of suspended ceilings and establishes criteria relating to their technical aspects of construction. A *Method of Building Note, Suspended ceilings: 1986*, published by the Property Service Agency (PSA) in their series *Current performance specification* is also a useful reference. Publications of the Suspended Ceilings Association include; Guide 1: 1982 *Good practice for the installation of suspended ceilings*; Guide 2: 1982 *Recommendations for suspended ceiling grid systems*; and Guide 3: 1984 *Recommendations for the selection of suspended ceiling materials*.

It is important to consider the ceiling in relation to any partitioning system that may be used in the building. In some cases the use of a raised floor system can also have an influence on the type of suspended ceiling, particularly when the building incorporates a large amount of mechanical services (see figure 13.1 page 315).

(a) Appearance

Suspended ceilings are often used for the sole

purpose of improving the appearance of the underside of the floor or roof above. They may be required to conceal service pipes or the visual results of certain construction techniques, such as composite reinforced concrete, which are not considered compatible with the functions to be carried out in the space below.

A lowered ceiling can be used to improve the function and quality of interior spaces by altering the height proportion in relation to the width and length. In this respect the positioning and size of access and lighting panels and/or ventilation grills play an important role in the overall pattern effect created by the ceiling in relation to other features in the room. The ceiling itself could be translucent and lit from behind, or be solid with a smooth surface or a range of textured surfaces. Auditoria and other spaces can be given directional emphasis by a sloping or profiled soffit through the use of suspended ceilings. Fibrous plaster is used for decorative ceiling work where moulded profiles are required, and sections up to 6 m square are possible using a suspension system similar to that employed for wet plaster construction.

The setting out of modular ceilings and the junction detail between ceiling and wall are particularly important, as is the quality and accuracy of workmanship used during their installation. See also comments above regarding the use of perimeter trims.

(b) Weight

As, by definition, the ceiling is suspended from the main structure, it is important to keep the weight of construction to a minimum. The jointless ceilings using traditional techniques of plasterboard finished by a skim coat of plaster is the heaviest form of suspended ceiling, weighing between 20 and 50 kg/m². The *panel and frame* system is much lighter and most proprietary systems weigh between 4 and 15 kg/m² (see figure 12.1) A linear strip ceiling is also a very light form of construction, weighing between 3 and 5 kg/m².

However, the construction must always be designed to be strong enough to support the weight of lighting and ventilation units incorporated in the ceiling, and this loading should always be calculated for each individual scheme.

(c) Accessibility

Accessibility is essential where the space between

Material	Thickness (mm)	Approx weight (kg/m²)
OPAQUE		
Wood or other organic fibre insulation board	12.7	3.7
Mineral fibre and wool insulation board	12.7–15.9	4.9–6.1
Perforated steel tray with insulation	30 o/a	7.3–14.6
Perforated aluminium tray with insulation	30 o/a	3.7
Gypsum plasterboard	12.7	10.25
Gypsum insulating plasterboard	9.56	7.5
Gypsum fibrous plaster tiles	15.9–31.8	14.7–17.0
Glass fibre tiles and boards	19.0	3.7
LUMINOUS		
Louvred polystyrene		4.9
rigid PVC		4.9
metal		0.5–5
Closed diffuser		
PVC sheet		2.3
acrylic/PVC		2.3
polystyrene		3.7
PVC film		4.9
glass fibre		4.9

12.1 *Typical examples of opaque and luminous suspended ceiling materials and their weights (BSCP 290: 1973, Tables 1 and 2A)*

the suspended ceiling and roof or floor space over is used as a horizontal service duct for heating pipes, water and waste pipes and all types of wiring and cable work can be easily and freely run. Thus, the question of easy access to the duct for maintenance purposes is of primary importance. It is important that the design of the suspended ceiling not only takes into account the provision of an adequate number and size of access points, but also ensures that the suspension points do not conflict with those required for the services above. A system of overlay sheets at design stage will ensure that pipework, ventilation ductwork, electrical trunking, fire barriers, acoustic barriers, loudspeakers, signs and recessed light fittings are fully co-ordinated with the ceiling suspension in the ceiling void. Adequate space allowance must be provided within this void for installation as well as future maintenance of services and, for example, when air-conditioning must be incorporated a 1 m or more *service zone* is required.

A modular panel, which can be removed over the whole area of the ceiling, becomes the easiest and most complete means of access. The consideration of the direction of the services, and the amount of connection required to the vertical ducts of partitions, etc, determine the amount of access required and will help to decide the type of suspended ceiling most suitable. Narrow strips which can be removed over certain areas will give access to parallel service runs, if necessary right up to the partition, whilst jointless ceilings will be satisfactory where one or two pre-determined access points are acceptable.

A ceiling system which gives full access may lead to an uneconomic design of the service runs. There is also the risk that the ceiling may be damaged if too many panels are removed. Where very extensive or frequent access is needed, a proprietary hinged access panel should be used, or a washable panel from which finger marks can be removed.

(d) Fire precautions

The requirements for suspended ceilings in the context of fire precautions are divided into two areas of consideration: fire resistance of construction and surface spread of flame characteristics.

Fire resistance If it is intended that a suspended ceiling shall contribute to the overall fire resistance of the *floor construction* of which it may be considered to form a part, the ceiling construction must fulfil the criteria set down in figure 12.2, based on the *Building Regulations 1985: Approved Document B*, table A2. Consideration must be taken of the height of the building, whether or not the floor is a *compartment floor* see 5.8, page 120), and the total period of fire resistance required.

The inference from these requirements is that the type of suspended ceiling relying on separate tiles within a framework of metal angles or 'T' sections is not allowed as contributing to the fire resistance of the total floor construction in buildings more than 15 m high where the period required is 1 hour, or in buildings of any type where the period required is more than 1 hour. In

TYPE OF SUSPENDED CEILING

A Surface of ceiling exposed to the cavity should be Class 0 or Class 1 spread of flame classification.

B Surface of ceiling exposed to cavity should be Class 0.

C Surface of ceiling exposed to cavity should be Class 0. Ceiling should be jointless.
Supports and fixings should be non-combustible.

D Ceiling should be of material of limited combustibility and be jointless, ie not contain access panels.
Supports and fixings should be non-combustible.
Any insulation above the ceiling should be of a material of limited combustibility.

Height of building (m)	Type of floor	Fire resistance of floor (hours)	Type of suspended ceiling
Less than 15	Not compartment	1 or less	A, B, C or D
	Compartment	Less than 1	A, B, C or D
	Compartment	1	B, C or D
15 or more	Any	1 or less	C or D
No limit	Any	More than 1	D

12.2 *The contribution to fire resistance by suspended ceilings (Building Regulations 1985: Approved Document B, Table A2)*

the latter circumstances, the ceiling must be of jointless construction.

Where a ceiling does not have to be fire resistant, combustible materials can be used. However, panels of combustible material falling to the floor or on to furniture can increase the spread of fire. Certainly, all ceiling fixings must be non-combustible.

Notwithstanding the above requirements, once penetrated by fire the ceiling void can become a horizontal flue and assist the spread of fire and smoke to another area of the building, either on the same floor or to the floor above should gaps occur in the floor construction, eg around ducting and pipework. The ceiling void must, therefore, be adequately compartmented by the use of fire resisting barriers, and compartment walls should be taken up through the ceiling to the level of the structural soffit.

Appendix G of the *Building Regulations 1985: Approved Document B* gives requirements for fire barriers in suspended ceilings. None are required in non-demountable jointless fire resisting ceilings provided that the surface facing the cavity has Class 1 spread of flame rating, the exposed surface has surface performance similar to Class 0 (see page 289), and the ceiling itself is of half-hour fire resisting construction enclosed by fire resisting walls. However, when the cavity voids are extensive, the Regulations require that they should be divided by fire barriers according to the fire risk involved. Cavities between a roof and a ceiling require barriers every 15 m in any direction (with area limited to 100 m²) for institutional buildings, or hotels, boarding houses and hostels; and every 20 m in any direction in buildings used for assembly, office, shop, industrial, and all other non-residential purposes. Cavities between a floor and a ceiling also require fire barriers every 20 m in any direction for any type of building: but when the ceiling has less than a Class 0 surface spread of flame weighting, the barriers must be placed every 8 m.

It may be difficult to construct an effective fire barrier where the void is congested with services, and it is often necessary to group ducting and pipework to reduce the need for cutting and packing. Access panels in fire rated suspended ceilings must be treated in the same way as fire doors (see 5.8 Fire doors), and for proprietary systems the manufacturers' recommended details should be closely followed.

It must be borne in mind that the Regulations are concerned only with the contribution made by suspended ceilings to the fire resistance of the total floor construction. The question of the protection afforded by suspended ceilings to structure steelwork is a separate consideration: the floor and ceilings combine together in providing the required fire resistance and form an element of construction tested to BS 476 Part 8: 1972 Test methods and criteria for the fire resistance of elements of building construction.

Surface spread of flame The ceilings can constitute a considerable fire hazard in respect of their surface spread of flame characteristics. Therefore, the Building Regulation 1985: Approved Document B places controls on the type of surface use for a ceiling, depending on their precise location within a particular Purpose Group of buildings. Figure 12.3 provides a summary of these controls: an explanation of the Purpose Groups and the BS 476 classifications for

surface spread of flame are given in 11.2(d) Fire precautions (Demountable partitions). For the purposes of fire risks relative to the surfaces of internal walls and ceilings, the space inside a building is divided into three categories: small rooms; other rooms; and circulation spaces.

The Regulations allow concessions for plastics materials used for suspended ceilings which do not meet the required surface spread of flame characteristic indicated in figure 12.3. Rooms and circulation spaces may have 1 mm maximum thickness PVC panels, each having a maximum area of 4 m², provided the material has been satisfactorily tested by certain specific methods laid down in BS 2782 Methods of testing plastics. Other thermoplastic materials satisfying tests in BS 2782 can also be used, but there are greater limitations on size as well as limitations on distance between panels and the percentage of total ceiling they can occupy. Reference should be

Purpose Groups	Small rooms less than 30 m²	Other rooms	Circulation space and protected shaft
RESIDENTIAL GROUP			
Dwelling house			
One or 2 storey house, basement not counted	3	3	3
Three storeys or more, basement not counted	3	1*	0*
Flat or maisonette	3	1*	0*
Institutional	1*	1*	0*
Other residential	3	1*	0*
NON-RESIDENTIAL GROUP			
Assembly	3	1*	0*
Office	3	1*	0*
Shop	3	1*	0*
Industrial	3	1*	0*
Other non-residential	3	1*	0*

* Plastics roof lights in rooms and circulation spaces may be of a lower class (Class 3 minimum), see page 289

12.3 Minimum surface spread of flame classifications for ceilings relative to Purpose Groups (for definitions see page 289) Building Regulations 1988: Approved Document B)

made to Appendix B of *Approved Document B* for precise information, and manufacturers' advice should be taken.

(e) Sound control
Suspended ceilings can contribute to the sound resistance between floors and adjoining rooms, and also correct acoustics by absorbing or reflecting sound. Whereas the former relies on mass and airtightness, the latter is a property of the construction or surfaces of the materials employed.

Although the structural floor is the main sound barrier, the ceiling can be used to contribute towards the overall resistance provided. The weight of the supporting structure, depth of cavity between floor and ceiling and the weight of tiles or panels are significant factors. When heavy construction is used for the supporting structure, say reinforced concrete of 200–220 kg/m², the effect of a relatively lightweight suspended ceiling (see 12.2(a)) will be insignificant when considering sound transmission between floors. It follows that, if the supporting structure is lightweight, the suspended ceiling can make an effective contribution to the overall sound resistance provided it is as heavy as practicable, dense in composition, imperforate, not too stiff and isolated from the structure above by flexible supports.

The resistance to sound provided by the ceiling is critically important when considering transmission between adjoining rooms. Sound will travel through tiles or boards via joints in the suspension system or through pores in the material. For this reason an acoustic tile ceiling can have a sound resistance as low as 12 dB. This figure can be vastly increased by using a jointless ceiling (12 mm plasterboard ceiling gives 28 dB, a double layer system 33 dB); or by laying an absorbent quilt over the tiles.

Suspended ceilings are commonly used to provide the correct acoustic requirements in a room. The machinery used in an open plan office, such as printers, computers and photocopiers, require the use of acoustic absorbent material which can only be conveniently placed at ceiling level. CP 290 specifies four types of acoustic absorbent:
- *resonant panels* to absorb sound near their resonance frequency, normally between 50 and 200 Hz – they include materials such as plywood and hardboard, although lighter-weight

panels have a resonance frequency of up to 500 Hz;
- *porous surface panels* to absorb frequencies of 500–4000 Hz – they include material such as mineral fibre;
- *semi-perforate and perforated composite panels* having a porous surface material which is fissured, textured, perforated drilled or slotted to increase acoustic efficiency and improve appearance;
- *perforated panels backed with independent acoustic* absorbent materials *used over an airspace combine* the advantages of porous absorbents with resonant panels.

From the above, it will be seen that frame and tile and linear strip systems with 'open' joints and perforations with overlay quilts provide the best acoustic absorbers. Acoustic control can be provided over selected areas of the room to suit particular conditions. Painting mineral fibre tiles and perforated metal tiles will impair their acoustic performance.

The acoustics of the space must be considered as a whole, taking into account wall finishes, carpets and furniture. Whenever possible, partitions should be continued up into the suspended ceiling void (see 11.2(e) Sound resistance (*Demountable partitions*)). Where sound absorption is not a requirement, open grid or strip ceilings can be used as these are acoustically transparent and allow the full volume of a space to be used to increase reverberation time. This could improve the acoustics for speech or avoid the room becoming acoustically 'dead'.

(f) Durability and maintenance
Many of the problems associated with suspended ceilings occur because insufficient consideration was given to their subsequent maintenance. Access panels or the simple removal of modular tiles can be a major source of client complaint unless the design of the ceiling takes into account the realities of service maintenance, some of which may occur in an emergency situation.

Building maintenance manuals should include very precise information about cleaning, as well as a list of suppliers of replacement components (see *MBS: Introduction to Building* chapter 15: 15.8 *Maintenance Team*).

12.3 Jointless systems

With the exception of the PVC membrane type, jointless suspended ceilings are usually non-proprietary, rely on conventional materials and methods of construction and give good fire resistance. They are also relatively cheaper than the other systems, although the slowness of the wet construction where plastering is used is a disadvantage.

The ceiling shown in figure 12.4 is a jointless suspended ceiling consisting of plaster applied to metal lathing. Two methods of securing the hangers to support the lathing are shown, and figure 12.5 indicates the construction of an access panel. This construction method can be used to provide ceilings to almost any moulded shape according to design requirements, limitations only being provided by practical considerations relating to the bending of the lathing and space for the application of the plaster. Lightfittings, ventilation ducts, etc, can be easily accommodated provided they are planned in advance of construction.

Using 15 mm thickness lightweight vermiculite plaster, a jointless ceiling system of this type will weigh 20 kg/m² , including the suspension. It will have a fire resistance of between 2 hours, or more when a greater thickness of plaster is used, and a Class 0 surface spread of flame classification. A similar construction using plasterboard finished with a coat of plaster will give similar ratings, depending on the form of supporting structure.

Figure 12.6 shows details of the use of a PVC foil membrane, stretched to form a jointless suspended ceiling. This type of ceiling can be installed in one sheet 0.2 mm thick, forming a panel up to 7.5 × 6.0 m. The method of construction is adaptable to any shape of room, and will accommodate any size of access panel or light fitting. The finish of the PVC foil is semi-matt, and does not require decoration. Where a higher degree of sound absorption is required, a special perforated foil with a loose backing of absorbent quilt is used.

Membrane ceilings are comparatively cheap but give no fire protection (see 12.2(d) for comments about fire resistance and the use of plastics materials for suspended ceilings).

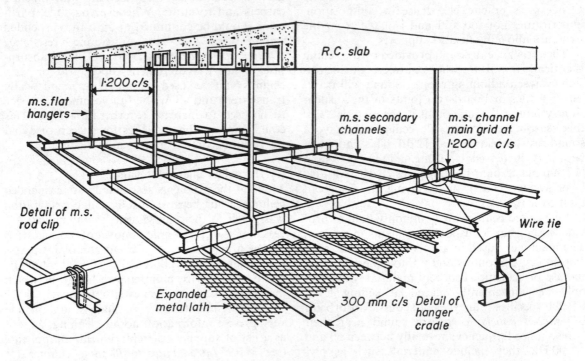

12.4 *Jointless ceiling system: plaster on expanded metal lathe*

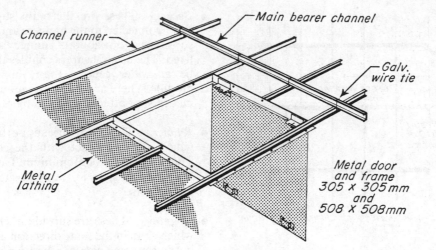

12.5 *Jointless ceiling system: prefabricated access door*

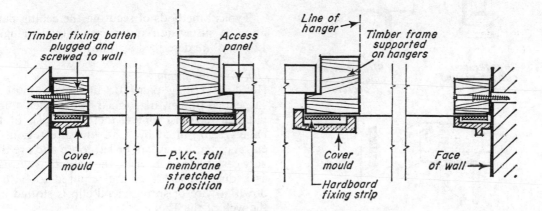

12.6 *Jointless ceiling system: PVC membrane*

12.4 Frame and panel systems

This is the most common type of suspended ceiling, comprising a light structural frame of metal angle or tees supporting infill panels or tiles of plasterboard, plywood, fibre building board or mineral wool or, alternatively, metal trays or plastics sections. For details of the sheet sizes and physical properties of these materials, see *MBS: Materials* and *MBS: Finishes*. Proprietary panels

are usually modular co-ordinated to 300, 600, 900 or 1200 mm.

There are various components used for securing the framing for the infill units (see figure 12.7):

- *Hangars* Metal straps, rods or angles which hang verticaly from the main floor or roof construction to support and 'level-up' the suspension system. Various methods of securing the hangers to the main floor construction are shown in figure 12.8.

309

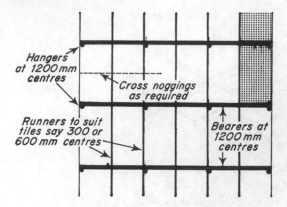

12.7 *Frame and panel systems: plan layout of suspension system*

Hanger rod clipped around joist

Strap hanger plugged to concrete

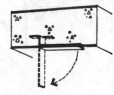

Fishtail strap hanger cast in concrete

Strap hanger screwed to side of wood beam

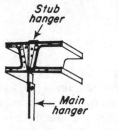

Stub hanger

Main hanger

Stub hanger fixed between pre-cast units

Strap hanger clipped to B.S.B.

12.8 *Frame and panel systems: hangers*

● *Bearers* These are the main supporting sections connected to the hangers and to which the subsidiary horizontal runner supports are fixed. The use of bearers enables the hangers to be at wider centres than the basic ceiling module. There are many ingenious proprietary methods of attaching the runners and hangers.

● *Runners* These are the supporting members which are in contact with the ceiling panels. They are usully of aluminium T or Z sections. The runners span in the opposite direction to the bearers.

● *Noggings* These are subsidiary cross members which span in the same direction as the bearers, but in the same plane as the runners in order to complete the framework. Runners and noggings can be concealed or exposed.

Typical methods of securing the ceiling panel into the suspension system are shown in figure 12.9 and are described as follows:

(a) Exposed fixing
Here the ceiling panel or tile drops into the suspended framework formed by extruded aluminium T sections. Unless there is a risk of the panels being lifted by wind pressure (eg, in an entrance hall), they can be left loose and are thus very easy to remove where the void above is used as a duct. Where they are required to be held down, a wire or spring metal clip is slotted into the web of the T.

(b) Concealed fixing
This is a concealed type of fixing since the method of support is not visible from below. The figure shows the grooved tiles slotted into the Z section runner. An alternative form of concealed fixing using a tongued and grooved tile is illustrated in figure 12.10. Concealed framework makes access more difficult, particularly at the head of partitions.

(c) Clip fixing
In this detail a special runner is used which holds a metal tray in position. The tray will be perforated and will probably have an infill of mineral wool or similar inert, non-combustible sound absorbent material.

(d) Screw fixing

This detail shows two alternative forms of securing the ceiling panels by direct screw fixing.

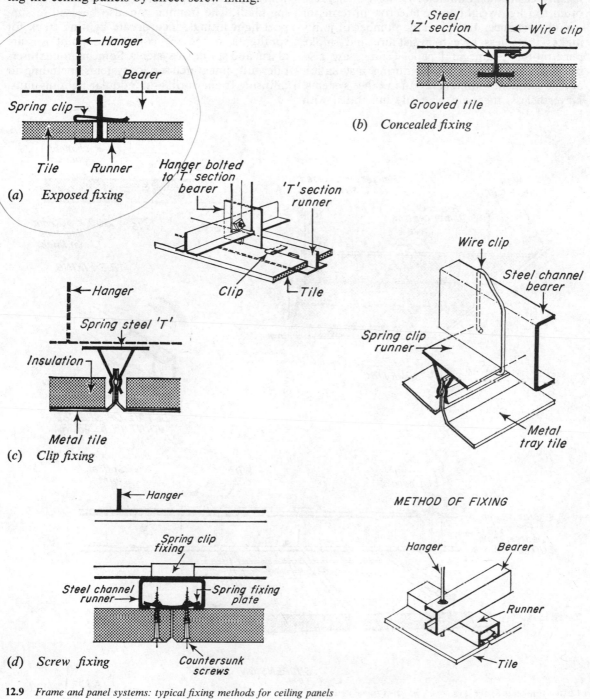

(a)   Exposed fixing

(b)   Concealed fixing

(c)   Clip fixing

(d)   Screw fixing

METHOD OF FIXING

12.9   *Frame and panel systems: typical fixing methods for ceiling panels*

311

SUSPENDED CEILINGS

The erection of a frame and panel ceiling is speedy and clean, and this type of ceiling is usually easily demountable. However, they are often too lightweight to be effective in terms of sound resistance, and the large number of joints makes them less able to resist fire and smoke penetration. Frame and panel ceilings are also more vulnerable to damage during installation and subsequent maintenance than other systems. Nevertheless, they can be easily integrated with overhead services, and parts of the supporting frame may be constructed of larger metal sections which act as air intakes/extracts for air-conditioning plant. The framing can also be used to support light fittings, incorporate lighting track for spotlights, or be the connection point for fire alarm and sprinkler systems. Some manufacturers offer fully integrated service systems, including air diffusing framework, and modular lighting units.

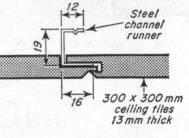

TILE FIXING

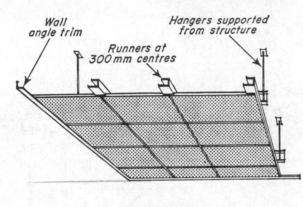

ISOMETRIC

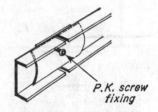

DETAIL OF SPLICED JOINT IN BEARER

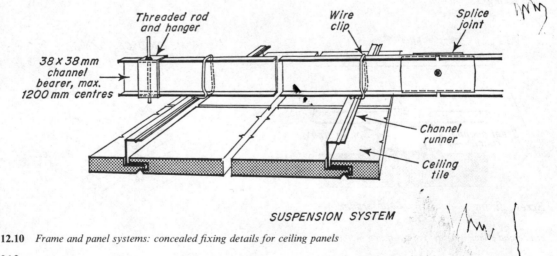

SUSPENSION SYSTEM

12.10   *Frame and panel systems: concealed fixing details for ceiling panels*

12.5 Linear strip systems

This type of ceiling uses material in long lengths in order to minimize the points of suspension and provide a linear visual effect. By using the inherent rigidity of metal and timber in strip form, the ceiling need only be supported in one direction. For example, fixing points can be as much as 6 m apart for deeply profiled metal sheets using a suspension system hung at 1.8 m centres. However, most linear strip systems have support grid modules of up to 1200 × 1500 mm, and the width of exposed metal strips vary upwards from 100 mm. The strips are available in a range of polyester coating colours as well as a mirror finish.

In all other respects, this system fulfils similar performance criteria to those of the frame and panel system. Little fire resistance is provided unless the strips interlock, and access is obtained by removal of several strips, which can be inconvenient because of their length.

12.6 Louvre and open strip systems

This type of ceiling consists of a series of strips or louvre panels made from timber or metal which are supported by the structural floor or roof above. They provide a visual cut-off when seen from below and conceal service pipes, unsightly construction details, etc. They can be lit from above and there is a wide range of fittings available to fit into various cell sizes.

Sound absorption is not good, but it can be improved by using deep louvres of perforated metal with a quilted core. However, the reverberation time of a space can be increased by allowing the full volume of the room to be used despite its partial division by the suspended ceiling.

Although this system provides no fire resistance, the open ceiling can be useful where smoke extraction is needed. The best advantage for this type of ceiling lies where there are a large number of services to which access is frequently required, but whose appearance is considered unacceptable.

12.7 Integrated service systems

Suspended ceilings in which the services form an integral part of the construction fall into the following categories:
- *fully illuminated ceilings*, having infill panels of translucent plastics which form the diffusers for the light fittings suspended above them. The diffusers may be plain faced, three dimensional, corrugated, embossed or 'eggbox' construction. This type of ceiling should not be confused with the use of modular light fittings, which fit into the grid spacing of the panel and frame suspended ceiling system;
- *ceiling panels incorporating low temperature heating*, using electrical elements or small bore hot water circuits, normally in conjunction with sound absorbing panels;
- *plenum chamber ceilings* in which the whole of the space between the ceiling and floor or roof soffit is used for the circulation and direction of hot or cold air;
- *fully 'service' integrated ceiling* which gives an element of construction providing heat and light, as well as sound absorption. This arrangement, though expensive, permits the ultimate in flexibility of use for the space below.

Integrated service system ceilings have a much larger grid layout than the other ceiling systems, ranging from 900 × 900 mm to 1800 × 1800 mm.

13 Raised floors

13.1 Introduction

Modular floors which are constructed above the level of the structural floors *on which they rest* are known as **raised floors**. They differ from *suspended floors* which are structural elements used to span between loadbearing walls for the purposes of achieving a higher floor level than is possible for the normal structural floor of a building. This form of floor construction is described in *MBS: Structure and Fabric* Part 1 chapter 3 page 204.

Raised floors were originally developed as a response to the design requirements for rooms accommodating mainframe computers, where cooling systems and festoons of cables could be conveniently located in a floor void and ready access for their maintenance was required. Since this development, there has been an increasing need for raised access floors in general office areas, as well as other spaces where services play a vital role in their function (figure 13.1). The heat released into an office by business machinery, known as 'wild heat', cannot always economically be controlled by air conditioning located at high level. Also, when large quantities of fresh air are needed from the direction of a ceiling, uncomfortable down-draughts can be caused. Instead, local cooling can be provided by recirculating air-conditioning cabinets; and the servicing for these, including pipework, etc, can easily be accommodated in the void of a raised floor system.

The use of a raised floor system will also reduce the construction period and give earlier occupation of a building. There is less need to plan the distribution routes for services at an early stage of construction, and a power-floated structural concrete floor slab can be left ready to receive the building users cabling system.

There are two categories of raised floor construction:

Shallow systems These comprise of panels laid over timber battens, or of a metal decking fixed to the subfloor and provide a cavity below of less than 100 mm;

Deep systems These comprise of panels supported by adjustable metal jacks which provide a cavity below of at least 100 mm, and are particularly useful for the accommodation of an extensive amount of services as well as when the structural floor surface is not level.

For shallow raised floor systems, the panels are made from steel, steel faced particle board, or plywood; and for deep raised floors the same material can be used as well as fibre reinforced inorganic materials, cast aluminum and glass reinforced cement (GRC). Non-rigid floor panels can give a springy, hollow sensation when being walked across. The panels can be self finished if appropriate, or finished in a range of sheet materials, including carpet and PVC. In a computer room, a material must be chosen which will not store static electricity, and metal framed raised floors should provide a simple earthing mechanism.

Common modular sizes for the panels are:

> 600 × 600 mm,
> 750 × 750 mm
> and 1200 × 1200 mm.

13.2 Performance requirements

As yet there is no BS which gives recommendations about raised floor systems. However, the Property Services Agency (PSA) have produced *Technical guidance: Platform floors* 1982, and *Performance specification: Platform floors* 1985.

(a) Appearance

The two factors affecting the appearance of raised floors are the visibility or non-visibility of the modular grid of the panels used for its construction, and the type of material used for the surface of the floor.

Whereas the modular grid of a suspended ceiling and, perhaps, of a demountable partition, will not necessarily influence the desirable positioning and size of furniture, etc in a room, a strongly emphasized floor grid could give aesthetic problems relative to the degree of dimensional incompatibility. If this is likely to be considered a problem, then the designer must ensure that the

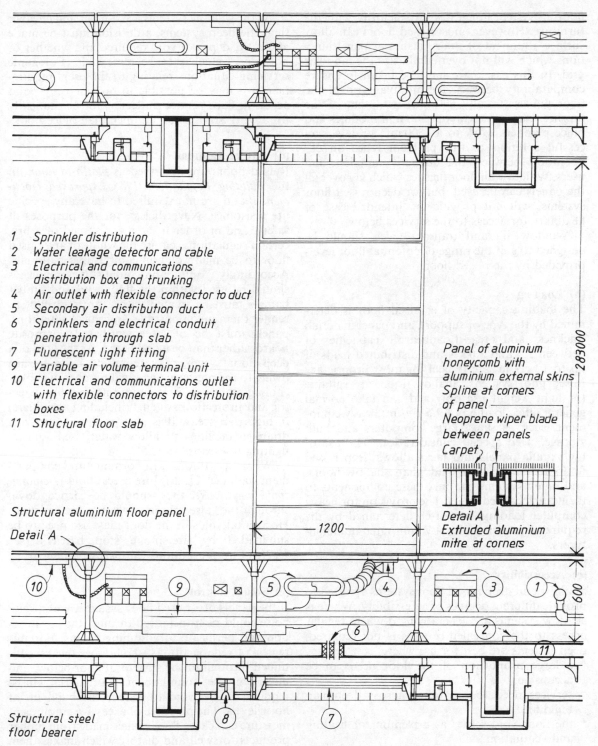

1   Sprinkler distribution
2   Water leakage detector and cable
3   Electrical and communications
    distribution box and trunking
4   Air outlet with flexible connector to duct
5   Secondary air distribution duct
6   Sprinklers and electrical conduit
    penetration through slab
7   Fluorescent light fitting
9   Variable air volume terminal unit
10 Electrical and communications outlet
    with flexible connectors to distribution
    boxes
11 Structural floor slab

Panel of aluminium
honeycomb with
aluminium external skins
Spline at corners
of panel
Neoprene wiper blade
between panels
Carpet

Detail A
Extruded aluminium
mitre at corners

Structural aluminium floor panel

Detail A

1200

283000

600

Structural steel
floor bearer

13.1   *Section through typical raised floor based on Hong Kong Bank (architect Richard Rogers).*
The raised floor void contains all service runs

315

flooring system integrates satisfactorily with the furniture. However, most raised floors can allow surface abutment of floor finishes at panel junctions which will not over-emphasize the modular grid. In this case, care must be taken to ensure compatability between the modular grid of the floor panels (usually 600 mm) with that of the finishes: carpet tiles favour 500 mm modules and office planners work to a 1500 mm grid. A successful solution to this problem relies on co-operation between the different suppliers and users. Wall to wall floor finishes which lay over all the panels can be used, but for deep raised floor systems, will not provide the intended ease of flexibility for access to the services below.

Window sill and transom levels should be designed to suit the range of potential floor levels provided by the raised floor.

(b) Loading

The loading capacity of a raised floor is determined by the type of support, and panel material, thickness and area. Loadbearing capacities of between 1.5 and 3.0 kN and distributed loads of up to 12 kN/m^2 are typical for most proprietary raised floor systems. Shallow floors are suitable for light weight use only and can take normal general office loading of 2.5 kN/m^2: heavy equipment, such as safes, large computers and bulk storage, need special consideration. The use of high grade panels and jacks allows deep raised floors to take greater loads than shallow floors, and many systems can mix these components to facilitate localized loads. The provision for heavy computer loadings are often determined by the requirements demanded by computer manufacturers.

(c) Accessibility

Shallow and deep raised floor systems are used to provide different degrees of accessibility. Whereas shallow systems are generally used where regular access to the concealed services is not required, deep systems are best for use where:
* a large proportion of the floor needs to be accessible;
* services need to be routed across deep-plan buildings;
* the floor void serves as a plenum for heating and ventilation.

As the shallow systems are simpler and cheaper than the deep systems, a decision must be made about the depth of void required and whether or not every panel is to be removable. For some servicing situations relating to the users requirements, it may be possible to provide only point access at fixed service outlets, ie for permanently fixed work stations on an open plan office floor.

(d) Fire precautions

Raised floors are described as *platform floors* in the *Building Regulations 1985: Approved Document B* and are not required to have any specific fire resistance. Nevertheless, for the purposes of safety, and in order to limit the spread of a fire, certain regulations require the whole of any raised floor to be made of non-combustible materials. Accordingly, only non-combustible materials should be used within the floor void and timber battens must be treated with a fire retardant to render them incombustible. In critical situations, panels must be of a cement-based composite board rather than be wood based. As the void of a deep floor system may represent a fire hazard owing to the presence of a great number of cables, cooling plant, etc, it may need its own fire detector and protection systems (including sprinklers) in high risk areas. It is also prudent to provide drainage facilities to allow water used for fire fighting to escape.

Where partitions are forming fire compartment walls (see 11.2(d) Fire precautions (*Demountable partitions*)) they should be carried down through the raised floor if it is not fire resistant. Horizontal voids in the floor may also need to be subdivided by fire/smoke stop barriers (see 12.2(d) Fire precautions (*Suspended ceilings*)).

(e) Sound control

If the panels of a raised floor system are not rigid, noise could be transmitted through the construction and permeate to adjoining rooms. For this reason, fixed partitions should be always continued through to the structural floor below, and in certain cases sound absorbent material will be required in the void to reduce the build up of noise levels. The presence of excessive amounts of moisture can cause floor panels made from timber products to swell and distort which makes them creak when walked across or vibrated by machines. For this reason ground floor slabs must be adequately water and vapour proofed, and in doubtful situations only panels unaffected by moisture should be specified.

(f) Durability and maintenance

Like most components, the materials employed and skill of installation as well as subsequent usage all affect the durability and maintenance of a raised floor system. Frequency of access is an important factor as panels can become damaged and, in extreme cases, subject to wear. Some manufacturers provide purpose-designed carpet lifting tools, and also double suction lifting tools for ease in removing panels for access (see figure 13.3). One of the advantages of using modular carpet or PVC tiles is that they can easily be replaced.

13.3 Shallow systems

Shallow raised access floor systems generally have a small cavity, not exceeding 100 mm, which is capable of accepting electrical, communication and data cables. There is little provision for adjustment, and a very smooth structural floor is needed. Removable covers are provided at prescribed intervals, so access is limited. These systems are not suitable for high floor loadings and when of timber construction, have no fire resistance.

Figure 13.2 shows a typical example, comprising of 65 mm deep galvanized steel fluted trough decking fixed to the structural floor. The ducts are overlaid with 600 mm wide × 2400 mm long × 22 mm thick flooring grade tongued and grooved chipboard, riveted to the steel troughs and giving an overall raised floor depth of 87 mm. Cables lie in the troughs of the steel decking, with occasional cross-ducts inserted to allow cables to run against the normal direction of the troughs. Access to the floor void is usually provided at this point by 600 mm square removable panels. The system provides built-in electrical screening between power and signal cables.

The floor construction can take a maximum uniformly distributed load of 5.0 kN/m², a maximum concentrated load of 2.7 kN applied over an

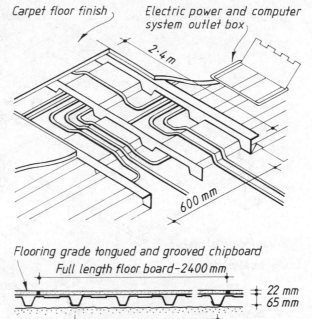

13.2 *Shallow raised floor system in galvanized steel fluted trough decking*
(*H H Robertson Buroplan 300*)

area of 300 × 300 mm, and a partition line load of 2.0 kN/m.

13.4 Deep systems

Deep raised access floor systems are used for very highly serviced areas, such as those requiring air-conditioning plant or computer room cables. The void may be totally accessible by the removal of all panels, or have point access only. The degree of fire resistance relates mainly to the panel material and finish. The supports, or *pedestals*, allow for adjustability against an uneven structural floor, or one which has been formed at different levels. Floor panels are available which are capable of taking high floor loads, and different strengths of jacks can be incorporated in the system where there is a need to consider heavily concentrated loads. Except where there are special requirement, such as the need for an anti-static finish in computer rooms, the range of finishes for the panels is limited only by the size of panel.

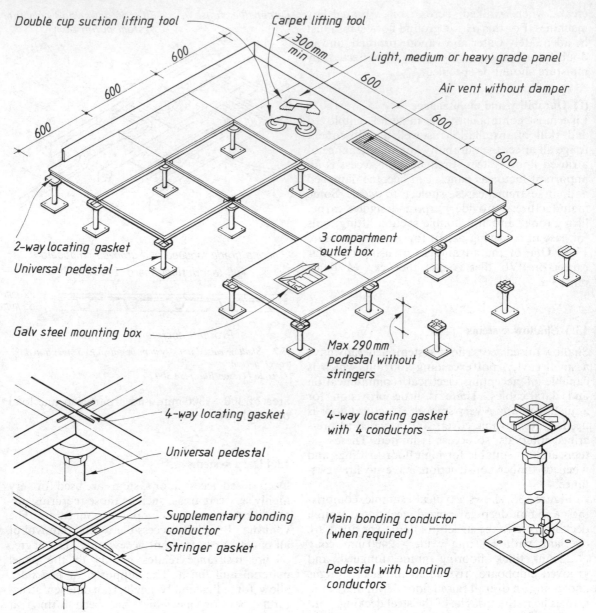

13.3 *Deep raised floor system in hot dipped galvanized trays incorporating high density particle board (Donn Products (UK) Ltd BMA Series)*

318

Figure 13.3 shows a typical example, comprising of 600 mm modular panels of hot dipped galvanized top and bottom trays in which is glued a 30 mm thick high density particle board. Service outlet boxes can be incorporated in panel cutouts, but require extra supports to maintain the integrity of the structure. The panels are supported by *stringers*, which in turn are supported by *pedestals* fixed to the structural floor.

The stringers are made from zinc plated steel hollow section, 35 mm × 35 mm and are bolted to the specially profiled top plate of the pedestals: accurate location between the stringers being achieved by inserting a four-way gasket. The stringers have sound deadening gaskets fixed to their topside to isolate the floor panels. Earth bonding conductors can be incorporated with the stringers and, when required, there can also be a main bonding conductor on the pedestals. For panels with edge trims, an internal electrical connection is made between the top and bottom metal trays: earth bonding conductors also can be supplied.

The pedestals are of mild steel, coated with a corrosion resistant finish, and incorporate a sliding tube arrangement with a tightening nut so that the floor can be made level when the horizontal surface of the structural floor is untrue.

The system illustrated complies with the requirements of the PSA's *Performance specification: Platform floors*: 1985 (Method of Building 01-801), regarding structural performance and deflection test data. Three loading grades of panels are available: *light grade*, maximum UDL of 2.5 kN/m², and maximum concentrated load over an area of 300 × 300 mm of 2.7 kN; *medium grade*, maximum of 5.0 kN/m² and 4.5 kN respectively; and for *heavy grade*, a maximum UDL of 12 kN/m². The use of particle board floor panels means that the floor has no fire resistance rating, and a Class 1 surface spread of flame classification. However, the system satisfies PSA's *Small scale fire test*.

319

14 Roofings

14.1 Introduction

Resolution of the aesthetic and technical criteria associated with *roofs* (the supporting structure), and with *roofings* (roof finishes), are essential to the satisfactory performance of the whole building. Structural behaviour and roof structure are considered in *MBS: Structure and Fabric*, Parts 1 and 2.

Some of the more common terms used in connection with roofing are illustrated in figure 14.1. Selection of a shape for a roof will be determined by consideration of the inter-relationship between the visual expression desired and the adoption of an appropriate structural support system. These two factors then allow a range of materials to be identified from which a choice can be made for the roof finish.

The basic forms for a roof are:

flat (which technically means a roof sloping less than 10 degrees), where the roof finishes consist of waterproof membranes that are continuously supported by a *decking*;

pitched, where roof finishes consist of either dry jointed overlapping units that are supported by a sloping framework or decking; or of waterproof membranes supported by a continuous sloping decking;

curved, where waterproof membranes are contin-

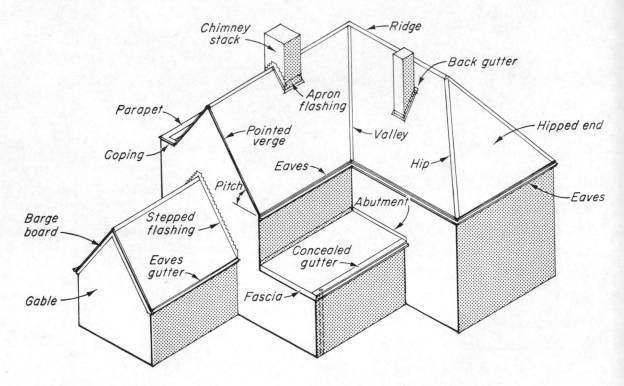

14.1 *Terms used in connection with roofing*

uously supported by decking; or, if large three-dimensional curves are required they are supported by cables or other suspension mechanisms.

Figure 14.2 gives the more commonly used roof finishes related to the minimum *falls* and *pitches* for flat and pitched roofs. A roof finish which is satisfactory on a flat roof or shallow pitch can also be adequate on a steeper pitch. Furthermore, a flat and sloping roof covering technique used in a modified form can also be employed as a *cladding* for vertical surfaces, eg metal sheeting, tiling or slating.

The roof *fall* is usually expressed as the rise in a stated horizontal distance or run – see figure 14.3. For example, a flat roof finish laid at an angle of 3/4 degree would have a fall expressed as 1:80, or 12:1000.

The roof *pitch* is the angle of slope to the horizontal. For the form of roof pitch shown in figure 14.3 (symmetrical two slope) the pitch used to be expressed as the fraction *rise/span* because this relationship of the rise to span was more expressive of the setting out techniques of traditional pitched roof construction using site-cut

Roof finish	Minimum pitch in degrees
FLAT AND SINGLE CURVED	
Asphalt; lead with drips; multi-layer bitumen felt; single-layer plastics	3/4 (1:80)
Aluminium, copper, zinc with drips	1 (1:60)
Steel, aluminium, fibre cement, or plastics profiled sheets with sealed laps	1 to 10
PITCHED	
Glass fibre reinforced bitumen slates	12
Metal multi-tiles	12
Copper and zinc with welted end seams	13.75
Timber shingles	14
Concrete interlocking tiles; flats	17.5
Concrete interlocking tiles: troughed and Roman	30
Fibre cement slates	20
Fibre cement and plastics profiled sheeting with 150 mm end laps	22.5
Slates: min 300 mm wide	30
Slates: min 225 mm wide	33.3
Clay tile: interlocking on four edges	25
Clay tile: interlocking on two edges	30
Clay tile: concrete	35
Clay tile: clay	40
Thatch	45

14.2 *Minimum pitches for various types of roof finishes. Variation will occur according to precise exposure conditions, methods of fixing and the type of access required to the roof: manufacturers recommendations must be taken.*

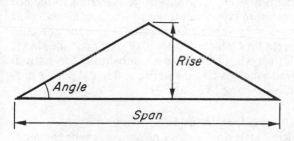

Pitched roof

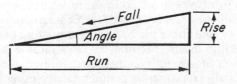

Flat roof

14.3 *'Pitch' and 'fall'*

timber or metal structural sections. For example, a roof finish laid at an angle of 33 1/3 degrees would have a rise/span = 1/3. However, as not all roofs have symmetrical slopes and preformed truss constructions are more normal today, most manufacturers of pitched roof finishes indicate the suitability of their product according to the *angle of slope*.

14.2 Performance requirements

*UP TO PAGE 328 ?
PERHAPS
FURTHER*

BS 6229: 1982 *Code of practice for flat roofs with continuously supported coverings* deals with the design, performance requirements and construction of the flat roof as a whole. This, together with other design guides, such as those produced by the Building Research Establishment (BRE), the Property Services Association (PSA) and the British Flat Roofing Council (BFRC), as well as other associations concerned with roofing provide greater understanding of flat roofing design. Nevertheless, it is important to note that this area of construction still provides a major source of building failure, and is the subject of much research and debate. Recommended design procedures must always be carefully followed.

BS 5534: *Code of practice for slating and tiling* Part 1: 1978 *Design*, and Part 2: 1986 *Design charts for fixing roof slating and tiling against wind uplift* deals with design factors for pitched roofs using dry jointed lapped units as a covering. The construction methods adopted for pitched roofs generally give less cause for concern than those for flat roofs, perhaps because they use natural gravity to shed water and mostly rely on a multi-defence system against the penetration of moisture. Certainly, the pitched roof has gained in importance as a roofing element in the UK over recent years.

Other BSs are also available for specific materials used as roof finishes, and these will be referred to at appropriate points in this chapter.

(a) Appearance

Apart from the purely technical factors, the choice between flat or pitched roof forms involves consideration of aesthetic appeal. To a large extent the choice is determined by a currently prevailing *fashion*, although in districts where it is important to maintain the overall character of existing buildings, precedent may have an over-riding influence, eg conservation areas. The requirements of the local Town Planning Office may also place limitations on choice, and in some cases very precise guidelines are provided.

When a flat roof is chosen, the building may have a 'cut-off', or 'block' appearance: this provided the neutral affect which was the hallmark of the Modern Movement. The appearance of a flat roof surface is unlikely to be of great importance as it is normally concealed from direct view by a parapet upstand, or an eaves overhang. The exception would be where the flat roof is overlooked from higher levels, or is used as a terrace or for vehicular traffic.

The more recent revival of interest in 'decorative' building façades has led to the increased use of the pitched roof. The degree of pitch is a primary design decision since it will effect the area of roof made visible which, in turn, will influence the choice of character of the surface finishes. The aesthetic objectives will involve consideration of preferred form, shape, pattern, texture and colour of the different roof coverings available. The selection process may also involve analysis of position and specific shape of the pitched roof, as well as the viewing distance and angle of vision. Much effort is now taking place in the development of acceptable substitute materials to replace the more costly natural and traditional materials used for pitched roof finishes. These include concrete tiles which imitate clay tiles or stone slates; fibre composite slates to substitute for natural and asbestos-cement slates; and metal panels profiled to look like pantiles.

(b) Weather exclusion

Roof coverings are required to prevent the entry of rain, snow and dust, as well as resist the effects of wind – both wind pressure and wind suction.

Water and dust penetration Figure 14.4 shows the principles involved in the movement of water for the two basic forms of roof construction. Flat roofs, and those pitched roofs consisting of interlocking sheets, provide an **impermeable barrier** which, if correctly constructed to give adequate falls, diverts water on contact. On the other hand, conventional pitched roof constructions provide a **semi-permeable barrier** which permit a certain amount of water to penetrate until reaching a

322

final barrier. In this case, the construction consists of an outer surface of lapped tiles or slates which provide the initial *water check*, backed by an impervious *water barrier* of sarking felt. The minimum pitch at which the outer roof covering can be laid depends on many factors, such as exposure to wind and weather, workmanship, design and type of joints in the roofing, porosity of the material and its tendency to laminate in frost, and the size of the unit.

For details of rainwater collection, including rainwater gutters, pipes and gullies, see *MBS: Environment and Services*. With flat roof construction, it is vitally important that adequate falls are provided so that rainwater is not allowed to collect on the surface and cause '*ponding*'. Large isolated areas of water lying on a flat roof covering can cause excessive differential movements in the membrane because the surface below the water is liable to be at a much cooler temperature than the surrounding dry surfaces, particularly on a sunny day. Differences in expansion and contraction in the roof covering material are liable to cause stresses resulting in cracking, and the penetration of water. For this reason, it is a wise precaution *not* to lay flat roof coverings at the recommended minimum fall of 1:80 where workmanship or the quality of the support decking will not guarantee against excessive deflection, which could cause pockets on the surface where water will collect. If in any doubt, the minimum fall for a flat roof should be 1:60.

It has been shown that rain penetration through the pitched roof outer coverings of slate or tiles depends both on amount of rain and wind speed, and is governed more by maximum rain intensity rather than total duration or total quantity. This form of outer covering depends upon the adequacy of the overlap of the units, and the pitch of the roof which sheds the water by gravity. Careful selection procedures must be adopted, therefore, to ensure that an appropriate roof covering is provided which is capable of providing maximum resistance to the prevailing climatic conditions, including wind driven rainfall.

In the United Kingdom, initial assessment of climatic conditions can be obtained by reference to the Driving Rain Index (DRI) for a particular location, as described in the published maps of the Building Research Establishment. Values are obtained by taking the mean annual wind speed in metres per second (m/s) and multiplying by the mean annual rainfall in millimetres. The product is then divided by one thousand, and the result used to produce contour lines linking areas of similar annual driving rain index in m^2/s throughout the country. Figure 14.5(a) and (b) shows a simplified diagrammatic analysis as follows:

- sheltered exposure zone refers to districts where the DRI is 3 or less;
- moderate exposure zone refers to districts where the DRI is between 3 and 7;
- severe exposure zone refers to districts where the DRI is 7 or more.

The value for a particular location within 8 km of the sea coast, or a large estuary, must be modified to the next zone above (Sheltered to Moderate, and Moderate to Severe), to take account of unusual exposure conditions. Furthermore, modifications may be necessary to allow for local topography, special features which shel-

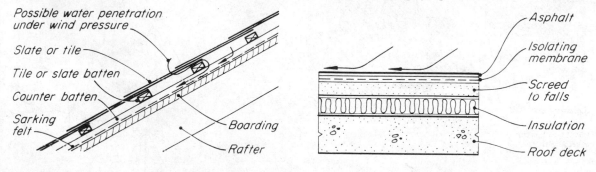

14.4 *Movement of water for roofs of different construction methods*

ter the site or make it more exposed, roughness of terrain, height of proposed building, and altitude of the site above sea level. The proportion of driving rain from various directions within one particular location can be obtained by reference to *Driving rain rose diagrams*, an example of which is also shown in figure 14.5(b). In conjunction with the DRI, the use of these 'roses' permits the approximate amount of driving rain to be calculated which can be expected to affect the exposed face(s) of a roof construction. DD 93: 1984 *Method for assessing exposure to wind driven rain*, describes two uses of the DRI: the *local spell index method* which measures the maximum intensity in a given period, and the *local annual index method* which measures the total rainfall in a year.

One of the most important lessons to be learnt from driving rain indexes and roses is that roof design and construction details, of necessity, may vary from one exposure zone to another: details applicable in sheltered conditions would probably leak if simply transferred to areas where severe or even moderate conditions prevail. In addition, there can exist a danger in using only meteorological climatic data of this nature for the final selection of appropriate materials and construction detailing.

This data may reveal only the general conditions, or *macro-climate*. There exists also a *micro-climate* surrounding the immediate outer face of a building, not more than 1 m from the surface, which arises from its precise form, location, juxtapositions, and surface geometry. Where there is no past experience to rely upon, it may be necessary to produce models of a building and its surroundings so that simulated environmental testing can be carried out.

Wind pressure and suction The design wind loadings for wind pressure and suction can be determined from CP 3 *Code of basic data for the design of buildings*, chapter V Part 2: 1972 *Wind loads*. The principles underlying the procedures in this document are explained in 7.2(b) Strength (*Glazing*), page 211.

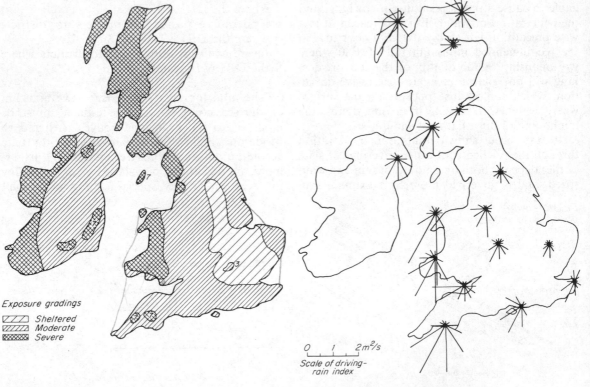

Exposure gradings
Sheltered
Moderate
Severe

0   1   2 m²/s
Scale of driving-
rain index

14.5(a)   *Driving Rain Index*

14.5(b)   *Driving rain rose diagram*

The effect of **wind pressure** upon a roof depends upon the angle of pitch and the degree of exposure of the roof slope, and detrimental effects can be avoided by use of roof finishes of appropriate strength and correct fixing details.

For a symmetrically pitched roof of between 20 degrees and 30 degrees, the **wind suction** will more or less be equally balanced on both roof slopes. On steeper pitches the negative pressure (the suction) is higher on the leeward side, and for shallower pitches (including 'flat') a suction also occurs on the windward side. The lower pitched roofs, therefore, may present a serious problem, particularly when lightweight sheet coverings are used on lightweight timber decking. With this form of construction, the roof deck should be securely anchored by firmly fixing to the roof framing and then securing to a wall plate by means of galvanized steel straps built into the wall below – see *MBS: Structure and Fabric*, Parts 1 and 2, and *Mitchell's Introduction to Building* pages 233 and 238/9. Severe air pressure tends to occur at the eaves of a roof, particularly in the case of projecting eaves used in conjunction with a low pitch. It is also especially important to seal the edges of flat roof coverings against their structural support to prevent wind entering beneath and lifting them. This sealing must be done in such a way so as not to restrict differential movements which may damage the flat roof coverings.

(c) Sub-structure

Whereas slats or tiles used on pitched roofs need to be supported at intervals by means of battens, the materials like bituminous felts and copper, or jointless systems such as asphalt, normally used on flat roofs require *continuous overall support*. The sub-structure which provides this support is generally referred to as **decking**, and there are two basic forms:

- *in situ monolithic*, such as a reinforced concrete slab;
- *prefabricated units*, ranging from thin pre-cast concrete slabs and metal panels, to timber and pre-formed boards, eg plywood, particle board, compressed straw or wood-wool.

In situ monolithic decking   An in situ monolithic deck should be designed and constructed so that

it does not break-up or crack in a manner which will affect the roof covering. This may be achieved by providing suitable joints. Precise specification and careful site supervision is essential. Screeds which are used to provide falls or insulation should have adequate strength so that they do not cause stresses which will affect the roof covering. It is advisable not to place a vapour barrier underneath water based *insulating* screeds as this will seal any residual moisture content against the impermeable roof covering. The provision of temporary weep holes through the supporting slab will allow this residual moisture to drain away during the remaining construction period, and the provision of strategically placed roof ventilators will avoid the dangers of subsequent interstitial condensation which would otherwise be avoided by the vapour barrier. As an alternative, bitumen coated insulating screed can be used *with* a vapour barrier as these do not use water in their formation.

In situ or reinforced concrete must be well cured and dry. The surface should be hard and smooth and clean without irregularities and preferably wood floated. Where it would otherwise be of open texture, it must be floated or screeded. Adequate crack control methods including movement joints must be provided in the sub-structure.

Lightweight aggregates may be used in in situ concrete. The types generally in use are either prepared from manufactured materials such as foamed slag, expanded vermiculite, or expanded clay. Lightweight concrete should comply with requirements for ordinary concrete in respect of condition of surface. The water content should be kept to a minimum and sufficient time must be allowed for any water to dry out or disperse. The porous nature and high residual water content of lightweight concrete make it essential to take special precautions to disperse this trapped water so that it does not disrupt the roof finish.

Pre-cast (including pre-stressed) concrete beams or slabs   Where this type of structural unit is used for a flat roof deck, a 1:4 cement and sand screed of at least 25 mm thick is required. Drainage holes should be provided to prevent water being trapped in the construction after laying. It is important to establish the maximum amount of deflection likely to take place in the units after all

325

dead loads have been applied, including that provided by the screed which, when the units are not laid at a slight incline, will provide the necessary falls for the roof covering.

Lightweight concrete slabs Where this type of deck is laid carefully, a cement and sand screed may not be required and the construction is totally 'dry', except for the possible need of grouting between units. A bitumen emulsion primer should be applied to the top surface of the slabs as soon as possible after installation to prevent absorption of rainwater.

Profiled metal panels This form of construction is suitable for both flat and pitched roofs, and is usually laid complete with thermal insulation and built-up felt waterproofing as a *composite roof construction* installed by specialist sub-contractors. The decking may be of galvanized steel or of aluminium formed by a continuous rolled process in a variety of profiles and gauges to suit most spans and loading requirements. Fibre insulation board, polystyrene, cork, or other flexible materials are used in sheet form to provide thermal insulation. This insulation is protected by bituminous felt vapour check where necessary. The decking units are fixed by hook bolts or by shot-firing to the steel supporting structure. The vapour check is bonded to the top surface of the metal decking followed by the insulation board and the outer roof finish. Alternatively, the insulation can be incorporated in a sandwich construction with outer and inner skins of metal sheets. The outer sheet can have a polyester powder-coating in a range of attractive colours and forms the outer waterproof covering. This form of roofing system uses profiled metal sheets, the edges of which form upstands to interlock and seal with the adjoining panel and provide an impermeable joint.

Timber boarding The whole of the timber substructure should be constructed in accordance with BS 5268 *Structural use of timber*, Part 2: 1984 *Code of practice for permissible stress design, materials and workmanship*, which provides guidance on the structural use of timber, plywood, glue laminated timber and tempered hardboard in load bearing members. See also the *Building*

Regulations 1985: *Approved Document A*, and *MBS:Materials* chapter 2.

The construction should minimize the effects of shrinkage, warping and displacement, or relative movement of the timber. All timber used in roof construction must have a preservative treatment in accordance with BS 1282: 1975 *Guide to choice, use and application of wood preservatives*, and the *Building Regulations 1985*: *Approved Document* to support Regulation 7 *Materials and workmanship* require that in certain geographical areas, softwood used for roof construction or fixed in the roof space should be adequately treated with a suitable preservative to prevent infestation by the House Longhorn Beetle.

Care should be taken to guard against all conditions which might allow decay through moisture already present in unseasoned timber or resulting from the ingress of water from other parts of the structure, or from condensation. To avoid dry rot, ventilation should also be provided between roof boarding and the ceiling (see page 329). Roof boarding should be well seasoned to avoid the tendency to shrink and cup. It should not be less than 25 mm thick and 100 mm wide, and should be tongued and grooved. Arrises should be rounded, upstanding edges planed flat and nail heads well sunk. The supporting roof construction should be rigid with joists at maximum 450 mm centres and the board fixed by nails at each edge to minimize the risk of curling. Boarding should be laid either in the direction of the fall of the roof or diagonally, and the roof surface should be protected as far as possible from rain during the course of construction.

Plywood BS 5268 also deals with plywood, and BS 6566 *Plywood*, Parts 1 to 8 specifies characteristics in great detail. Tongued and grooved sheets should be used for roof decking to provide perfect alignment at joints and it is essential to supply sufficient support between the supporting joists at sheet edges. Nailing, or preferably, screwing should be at 150 mm centres and at all edges as well as at intermediate supports. Rafter centres and nail lengths, according to plywood thickness are as follows:

Plywood thickness 8 mm, 12 mm, 16 mm, 19 mm.
Rafter centres 400 mm, 600 mm, 800 mm, 1200 mm.

Nail length 38 mm, 38 mm, 50 mm, 50 mm.

Particle boards   These are described in BS 5669: 1979 *Specification for wood chipboard and methods of test for particle board.* Tongued and grooved sheets should be used for roof decking for the reasons stated above, and the type used must be restricted to those whose binders are either MF/UF (Melamine Formaldehyde/Urea Formaldehyde) or PF (Phenol Formaldehyde) in order to comply with the recommendations of BS 5669, Types II/III. They should also incorporate a fungicide and care must be taken to eliminate the risk of condensation in the roof construction. For pitched roof construction, pre-felted and wax or bitumen coated boards can be used under tiles or slates to act in conjunction with counterbattens to provide the final water barrier in a similar fashion to sarking felt. However, improved loft insulation is likely to increase the moisture content in the boards, and in such cases a moisture resistant chipboard incorporating a fungicide is essential.

Compressed straw slabs   These must be of roofing quality which means that they are covered on the external face with an impregnated liner making the unit shower proof for short periods. Each edge of all the units must be fully supported and fixed in accordance with the manufacturer's instructions. Strawboard slabs should not be laid unless they can be covered (eg with built-up felt roofing) the same day. A sand and cement screed is not required but instead the joints are taped with strips of roofing felt bonded with hot bitumen compound before the first layer of felt is applied. Thus close co-ordination is essential during the fixing of the deck units and the application of the weather-proofing and for this reason it is good practice to allow the deck and built-up roofing to be supplied and fixed by the specialist roofing sub-contractor.

Wood-wool slabs   These should be the heavy duty type of slab fixed according to the manufacturers' instructions by clips or screwing to timber joists or steel purlins. The joints between the slabs should be filled with sand and cement and the slab should be topped with a 1:4 sand and cement screed 12 mm thick in bays not exceeding 9 m². On roof slopes of more than 20 degrees the screed

may be omitted and a sand and cement slurry used instead. Where wood-wool units are fixed direct to roof support the span should not exceed 600 mm and the bearing surface at the edge of each unit should not be less than 50 mm and fixed securely at every bearing point. Wood-wool slab units of this nature are usually 50 mm thick and it is important that once fixed, they are temporarily protected by crawling boards to avoid the danger of fracture or collapse under point-loads which could occur during subsequent operations involved in providing the roof covering. To avoid the use of crawling boards, a wood-wool slab unit is available which incorporates a plastic 'safety-net' reinforcement.

Galvanized mild steel channel reinforced wood-wool units must be used for increased loading and/or span requirements. These vary in thickness from 50 mm to 100 mm and span up to 4000 mm: trough section reinforced units capable of spanning 6000 mm are also available.

Note should be taken of the risk of condensation due to the direct conductivity of the steel reinforcing channels, and in order to counteract this, thick slabs are available rebated at the joints to receive inserts to achieve continuity of insulation at each joint. Pre-screeded and pre-felted wood-wool slabs are also available. The felt is a protective layer only and does not form part of a built-up felt system. The joints of this type of wood-wool slab should be taped immediately the slabs are laid to prevent moisture infiltration.

In general terms, it is advisable that where moisture sensitive materials are used for roof decking they should be sealed on all surfaces if they are to maintain stability in cases where condensation is likely.

Most forms of structural decking require an intermediate layer of material between its top surface and the outer roof covering in order to provide: a suitably smooth surface; isolation between decking and roof covering to allow for differential movements; a fall for drainage purposes; additional thermal insulation; sound control; or to provide any combination of these factors. The use of appropriate materials to fulfil the requirement for thermal insulation is covered under 14.2(d). For just isolation purposes, vegetable fibre boards can be used, and include those made from wood or cane fibres of natural or regranulated cork. Care should be taken to guard against the decay of the boards, particularly through moisture. Where this type of board is laid on concrete or similar materials, and where there will be moisture vapour diffusion from within the building, a *vapour check* is essential as described under 14.2(e). Alternatively, mineral fibre and granular boards can be used which are made from glass, mica or similar granules compressed and bonded with bitumen, synthetic resin, or other material. In theory, a vapour check can be omitted when using these materials except in conditions of very high humidity, eg as found in laundries. Extruded polystyrene is also a commonly used non-structural board and for most practical purposes, is vapour proof when the joints are sealed. When placed on metal decking, joints in the insulating boards must not be made over the trough of the deck or the board will collapse under normal maintenance traffic.

The provision of a *screed* may be necessary on certain flat roof decks, including those of in situ or pre-cast concrete and wood-wool slabs. This screed provides the falls and a smooth surface upon which to lay the roof waterproofing, and the selection of a suitable mix and thickness is very important. Whilst the mix must be related to that of the sub-structure, a cement/sand screed should not be richer than 1 part cement to 4 parts sand by volume. There should be a low water to cement ratio and the screed should be laid in areas not exceeding $9\,m^2$, even if they are reinforced. The minimum thickness should be 25 mm except where they are laid as topping on wood-wool slabs, when the minimum thickness can be reduced to 13 mm. Additional thermal insulation to that already provided can be achieved when using a *lightweight concrete screed*. In such cases entrapped water is always a problem, and if allowed to remain, it will seriously reduce the thermal insulation value of the screed and may cause blistering of the roof finish where built-up felt, asphalt or single layer roofing is used. It is customary to provide a topping of 12 mm sand/cement screed immediately after the lightweight concrete screed has been laid. This topping provides a surface which will shed water to pre-arranged temporary drainage holes passing through the screed and roof decking at the lowest part of the roof. The problems that may arise where water is trapped in a screed are more fully discussed on page 325. As an alternative to a water-mixed lightweight concrete screed, a *bitumen-mixed screed* can be used which has a dry exfoliated vermiculite aggregate. This screed does not present the same problems as the sand/cement screed.

Whatever type of screed is employed to provide falls and a smooth surface, the roof covering will still require to be isolated from it in order to allow for differential movements. A layer of underfelt may be all that is necessary where thermal insulation is provided by other means.

(d) Thermal control

The *Building Regulations 1985*: *Approved Document L: Conservation of fuel and power stipulates that the maximum thermal transmittance value* ('U'-value) for the roofs of dwellings should be $0.35\,W/m^2K$; for other residential buildings, shops, offices or assembly buildings, $0.6\,W/m^2K$; and for buildings used for industrial, storage or other purposes so far not described, $0.7\,W/m^2K$. These values are applicable to a roof of *less than* 70 degrees pitch. Above this angle, a roof is classified as a wall and the required U-value is $0.6\,W/m^2K$, except for the purpose group of building designated as 'industrial, storage or other purposes', for which the value remains at $0.7\,W/m^2K$.

Roof and wall constructions having the U-values stated in the *Regulations* are considered to provide an acceptable limit on the *overall heat loss* from a building and, therefore, help in the overall conservation of energy. As roof lights and windows (which lose more heat than the solid parts of roofs and walls) are liable to cause greater overall heat loss from a building, their combined areas are limited in proportion to the amount of solid construction of roof or wall construction for a building. Where the permitted area of roof lights and windows requires to be increased for other reasons, the permitted *overall heat loss* from a building can be maintained by a corresponding increase in the thermal insulation properties of the roof and walls. Further information about the procedures to be followed when regulating the areas of roof lights and windows relative to the *overall heat loss* from a building is given in 6.2(e) Thermal control (*Windows*) and 8.2 Performance requirements (*Roof lights*).

Thermal control, from the aspects of both heat loss and heat gain, may be provided as part of the roof construction so as to provide either a *cold roof construction*, or a *warm roof construction*:

Cold roof construction

● A layer of thermal insulation material is provided within or at the lowest level of the roof structure. This is an economical method of providing insulation since the space occupied by the roof construction above the insulation is not heated. It also has advantages where rapid changes of interior temperature are expected and no heat is wasted in warming the structure. In both flat and pitched roofs the insulation is placed between joists and immediately above the ceiling. Alternatively, the insulation can form an integral part of a flat roof decking (lightweight concrete blocks or insulated sandwich metal panels), or can form part of the ceiling construction.

Warm roof construction

● A layer of thermal insulating material is located *immediately below the roof covering*, but external to the roof structure. This method insulates the roof structure and thus reduces stress due to temperature change, can be fully continuous and eliminates cold spots in the construction, and the insulation is conveniently supported by the structure without additional suspension. In flat roof construction, the insulation can be placed immediately beneath the waterproof covering. In pitched roof construction, it can be placed over or between the rafters.

● Slabs of weighted thermal insulation material are placed *externally* to the whole roof construction, including the roof covering. This is known as an '*inverted roof*' construction, and has the advantage of ensuring that minimal thermal stresses develop in the roof covering and the structure below. Used in conjunction with masonry wall and externally applied wall insulation, the whole structure is kept warm and can be used as a thermal reservoir.

There are numerous materials which can be used to provide thermal insulation (see *MBS: Materials*): the merits of each must be established relative to the exact location in the roof construction and to any other performance requirements which need to be fulfilled. They are available as quilts, foams and rigid batts, as well as loose granules. Polyurethane foams are used under built-up bituminous felt or single layer systems; polyisocyanurate foams under asphalt, built-up bituminous or single layer systems; polystyrene, protected with fibre board or similar, under built-up bituminous felt systems; and foamed glass or cork under any roof covering. Extruded cellular polystyrene slabs, weighted down with paving slabs, are used over the roof covering in inverted roofs having to take heavy traffic, including cars, and this material as well as mineral fibre batts is used where normal foot traffic loading is required. Mineral fibre or glass fibre are used in friction-fit batt form between joists and rafters, or in quilt form over rafters.

A large proportion of the insulating materials are combustible, so the type included in a roof construction can effect the spread of fire from one building to another. Some cannot be used at all when roof coverings are heat applied to the decking. Only mineral wool and foamed glass can be said to be truly non-combustible. Ideally, the insulant should also be highly permeable to water vapour so that it does not retain moisture, *and* resistant to the detrimental effects of dampness. Most insulation materials, therefore, require some form of *vapour control* on their 'warm' side (see 14.2(e)) to prevent deterioration by water diffusion; the exceptions being, perhaps, mineral fibre, polystyrene and foamed glass when not used in highly humid conditions. Nevertheless, for most circumstances, it is always wise to provide vapour control material with the insulant in order to prevent the formation of condensation in cold roof voids, even when these voids are thoroughly ventilated.

(e) Vapour control

The atmosphere contains water in the form of water vapour but the amount varies according to the temperature and the humidity. The temperature at which air is saturated is called *dew point*, and warm air is able to contain more water vapour than cold air before it becomes saturated. Thus, if air containing a given amount of water vapour is cooled there will be a temperature at which condensation of the water vapour into water droplets will occur, either as *surface condensation* or as *interstitial condensation*.

Surface condensation occurs when moisture laden air comes into contact with a surface which is at a temperature below the dew point of the air. In respect of roof construction, surface condensation can be avoided quite simply by keeping the internal surface at a temperature above the dew point of the internal air. This is done by thermal insulation.

Where internal environments are warm and humid, the difference in the *vapour pressure* of the internal atmosphere and the cold external atmosphere may be such that the warm water vapour will move into and through the roof towards the colder side and condense within the roof construction. This form of condensation is known as **interstitial condensation**. Where this type of condensation occurs, the water will most likely cause the roof structure and insulation to deteriorate, and also some of the moisture may drip back into the building. In such cases, a *vapour barrier* (or *vapour check*) is necessary to prevent this moisture movement.

As no material can be regarded as impermeable and joints, etc, can provide easy paths for water vapour, a more accurate term for the 'barrier' is *vapour check*. This term helps in placing emphasis on the need for additional defences to reduce the amount of moist air within a building, or within the roof space. A vapour control layer with even a small hole in it is useless if sole reliance is placed on it as a barrier against the passage of vapour. The possibility of allowing vapour to escape harmlessly by means of adequate *ventilation* is a factor of importance in reducing condensation.

A *vapour check* consists of an impermeable material, such as polythene sheet, aluminium foil or bitumen felt, which is positioned at a point where the temperature remains above the dew point of the vapour. For practical reasons, the vapour check is placed on the warmer side of the insulation since it is easier to fix at this point and it will also stop the insulation from becoming saturated by condensation and losing its effectiveness. This is illustrated in figure 14.6. It is import-

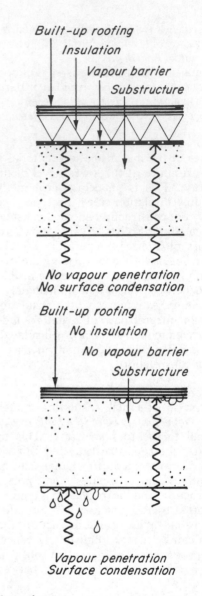

14.6 *Vapour barrier*

ant that the vapour check is continuous across the insulation and, if sheet material is used, care is taken to seal all joints and to guard against the likelihood of perforations, such as may be caused by installing lightfittings in the ceiling.

The *Building Regulations 1985: Approved Document F*, requires that for roofs with insulation below the roof covering (a 'cold roof'), a certain amount of ventilation openings must be provided, as shown in figure 14.7.

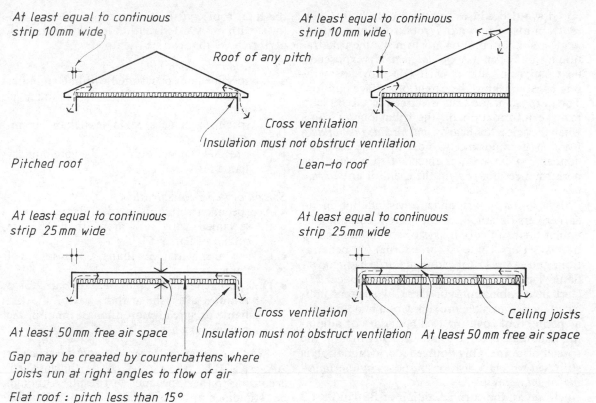

At least equal to continuous
strip 10 mm wide

Roof of any pitch

At least equal to continuous
strip 10 mm wide

Cross ventilation

Insulation must not obstruct ventilation

Pitched roof

Lean–to roof

At least equal to continuous
strip 25 mm wide

At least equal to continuous
strip 25 mm wide

Cross ventilation

Ceiling joists

At least 50 mm free air space

Insulation must not obstruct ventilation

At least 50 mm free air space

Gap may be created by counterbattens where
joists run at right angles to flow of air

Flat roof : pitch less than 15°

14.7 *Ventilation requirements for 'cold roof' coverings (Building Regulations 1985)*

These requirements apply only to dwellings. Roofs with a pitch of 15 degrees or more must have ventilation openings at eaves level on opposite sides of the roof, equivalent to a 10 mm slot running the full length of the eaves. In the case of a monolithic roof, equivalent ventilation should be provided as near as possible to the top of the roof, as well as at the eaves. These rules do not apply to roofs in which the ceiling follows the pitch of the roof, as they are treated as having a pitch of less than 15 degrees.

The ventilation openings in roofs with a pitch of less than 15 degrees should be equivalent to a slot 25 mm wide, running the length of the eaves. The void between the roof deck and the top of the insulation should be 50 mm deep. If joists run at right-angles to the flow of air, the space between the tops of the joists and the underside of the deck should be maintained by means of counter-battens.

The *Regulations* allow an alternative approach to the rules contained in the *Approved Document F*, whereby the ventilation provision should conform to the recommendations of BS 5250: 1975 *Code of basic data for the design of buildings: the control of condensation in dwellings*. These recommendations are similar to those of the *Regulations* except that the ventilation openings at the eaves of roofs with pitches of less than 15 degrees are required to be equivalent to a slot of only *10 mm width*, and that when the pitch of a roof is over 20 degrees (or the span is greater than 10 m) ridge ventilators should be incorporated which provide ventilation equivalent to a 3 mm continuous slot for a duopitch roof, or a 5 mm slot for a monopitch roof.

(f) Fire precautions

BS 476 *Fire tests on building materials and structures* Part 3: 1975 *External fire exposure roof test,* lays down procedures to measure the ability of a representative section of a roof, roof light, domelight or similar components to resist the penetration by fire, when its *external surface* is exposed to heat radiation and flame. It also provides methods of establishing the extent of surface ignition. The purpose of the tests described in the BS is to provide information on the behaviour of roofs when there is a fire nearby, *but outside the building itself*. It is important to note that the tests are neither capable of, nor intended to, predict the performance of a roof in the event of an *internal fire*.

BS 476 Part 3 is under revision, but in an earlier version (1958) of the current edition, particular forms of roofing systems were designated by two letters – A to D for external fire penetration, and A to D for external surface spread of flame (see 11.2(d) Fire precautions page 28). Certain combinations of these two letters indicated the permissible proximity of a building with a specific roof covering to a boundary or adjoining buildings, relative to the necessity to limit the spread of a fire. This double-letter designation is still used for classification purposes by the *Building Regulations 1985*.

However, the current edition of BS 476 Part 3 contains different but related designations for roof coverings, firstly to avoid confusion with the surface spread of flame test characteristics associated with wall and ceiling linings, and secondly to give reference to actual performance data. Accordingly, these designations are P60, P30, P15, and P5: they relate to precise *groups* of the two letter designations, and reference should be made directly to the BS for clarification as well as *MBS*: *Materials* page 36.

In the test procedures laid down in the 1958 version of BS 476: Part 3, samples of the roof construction are subjected to radiant heat on the upper surface and measurements are made of the possibility of fire penetration during one hour. A test flame is applied after 5 minutes to simulate the fall of a burning brand and the spread of flame is observed. A preliminary test is also made in which the specimen is subjected to a flame in the absence of radiant heat to identify highly flammable coverings. The two criteria of performance are **penetration time** and distance of external **surface spread of flame**, and the performance of

the total roof construction is represented as follows, with an AA designation indicating the best performance that can be obtained:

Penetration classification
- A   specimen not penetrated within 60 minutes
- B   specimen penetrated in not less than 30 minutes
- C   specimen penetrated in less than 30 minutes
- D   specimen penetrated in the preliminary flame test

Spread of flame classification
- A   specimen with no spread of flame
- B   specimen with not more than 533 mm spread of flame
- C   specimen with more than 533 mm spread of flame
- D   specimen which continues to burn for 5 minutes after the withdrawal of the test flame or spread more than 381 mm in the preliminary test.

Roof coverings are given designations such as AA, AC, BA, BB, CA, CD, or 'unclassified' according to their specimen test result. Although not stipulated as a requirement for consideration in the *Building Regulations 1985*, the BS also gives an additional designation (suffix 'x' to the two letters) which indicates the likelihood of dripping from the underside of the specimen during test and of mechanical failure or the development of any hole.

The two letter designations achieved during specimen tests are used in *Approved Document B*: Appendix A3 of the *Regulations* to define acceptable *roof constructions*, including coverings, relative to their distance from a possible external fire source. For example, mastic asphalt provides AA designation over deckings of timber, wood-wool, plywood, particle board, concrete, steel, or aluminium; and natural slates achieve this designation when used with timber rafters with or without underfelt, sarking, boarding, wood-wool slabs, compressed straw slabs, plywood, wood or particle board, or fibre insulating board. Nevertheless, the provisions for roof constructions and coverings are made by reference to the size and use of the building and the proximity of the roof to the site boundary. Reference must be made to the

Building Regulations 1985: *Approved Document B* for precise requirements, which not only include required designations for roof coverings for Purpose Groups of building, but also state the area limitations imposed on coverings with less than an AA rating. Generally, those roof coverings designated AA, AB or AC are allowed to be placed close to a boundary for all Purpose Groups; whereas those designated BA, BB and BC need to be at least 6 m from a boundary, and DA, DB, DC or DD at least 22 m from a boundary. A boundary is defined as a line of land belonging to the building, including up the centre of an abutting street, railway, canal or river.

The *Regulations* allow concessions for certain plastics materials used in roofing, see 8.2 Performance requirements (*Roof lights*).

(g) Durability and maintenance

In general terms a roof is more vulnerable to the effects of rain, snow, solar radiation and atmospheric pollution, than any other part of a building. Traditional pitched roof coverings such as tiles, slates, lead sheet and even thatch remain serviceable for many years but flat roof coverings often have a shorter life. The question of the rate at which water will 'run off' a roof is of fundamental importance. Pitched roofing has a high rate of 'run off' and, provided that the detailing of overlaps or jointing is satisfactory, the materials used to cover pitched roofs will be expected to have a long life. The 'run off' from a truly flat roof is very slow indeed and in practice most materials used for flat roof covering do not remain perfectly level and true after laying. As a result, water is very often retained in shallow pools on the finished roof surface. This is known as *ponding*. It is a prime cause of deterioration because local variations in temperature between the wet and dry area of the roof cause differential thermal movement, which together with accumulations of acid left by evaporating rain cause a breakdown in the roof surface. It is, of course, possible to design roofs to retain a considerable depth of water to protect and insulate the roof surface so that the roof benefits from freedom from diurnal temperature changes. The depth of water must however be sufficient to withstand evaporation and it must not be allowed to stagnate. Because this is difficult in practice, the most

satisfactory method is to construct the roof deck so that it slopes or falls towards the roof outlet to a sufficient degree to shed the surface water. The outline of the roof can still retain its flat appearance by the use of a horizontal fascia. A fall of 1 in 80, say 12 mm in 1000 mm, is required for sheet metal covering and mastic asphalt although a greater fall is desirable where possible. Skirtings at all abutments must be at least 150 mm high.

Apart from the care needed in detailing roofs to ensure adequate performance, the quality of workmanship is another obviously important factor. The National Federation of Roofing Contractors (NFRC) has made training a major issue in order to raise standards of work on site. In addition, many roofing companies participate in the BSI Quality Assurance Scheme recommended in BS 5750 (see 1.4 *Component testing and Quality Assurance*). Insurance companies have played a large role in up-grading flat roof construction, including their covering systems, by insisting on appropriate standards: the serviceable life of the roof is reflected by the amount of annual premiums payable by the building owner. Designers are increasingly being forced to take this factor into account when considering performance requirements.

Following its construction, the roof requires regular maintenance inspections by a roofing contractor or other person familiar with roof coverings. Should any repairs be found necessary, it is important to put that work in hand immediately to avoid deterioration of the roof. These repairs should always be carried out by skilled operatives using similar materials and techniques to those used on the original roofing. It is very important that the designers of a roofing system prepare guidelines for building users as part of a *Building Maintenance Manual* (see *Mitchell's Introduction to Building* section 16.8).

In calculating the 'cost-in-use' of a roof covering, the cost of maintenance and periodical renewal must be taken into account. Although roof coverings can be replaced and repaired with less disturbance than for most other parts of the fabric, failure to do so will usually involve very costly damage to the structure as well as to the building contents. From a study cost analysis on various projects, the waterproofing element of a flat roofed building represents 1.5% of the total cost per unit area. This figure applies to water-proofing in respect of built-up felt roofings or similar materials.

14.3 Flat roofing materials

Flat roofing materials provide an *impermeable barrier* to weather penetration (see 14.2(d) Weather resistance) and consist of *continuously supported* coverings of mastic asphalt, bitumen felt, single-ply plastics sheeting, liquid coatings, and dry jointed flat sheets of lead, copper, zinc, aluminium, and stainless steel; or *intermittently supported* profiled sheets or units. The installed weight of these flat roof coverings are as indicated below: it is important to check with manufacturers and/or suppliers to obtain precise weights according to specification of materials used.

Material	Approx installed weight (kg/m²)
Mastic asphalt	46.0
Bitumen felt	9.6 –12.0 (no chippings)
Single-ply sheeting	1.9 – 4.7
Liquid coatings	0.5 – 1.5
Flat metal sheets	
lead	24.4 –40.2
copper	2.82– 6.3
zinc	4.32– 7.2
aluminium	1.92– 3.4
stainless steel	3.0
pre-bonded panels	17.0 –29.3
Corrugated fibre cement sheets	
single	15.0 –19.2
sandwich	22.0 –32.0
Profiled metal sheets	
aluminium	
single	2.5 – 5.2
sandwich	6.0 –10.0
steel	
single	4.9 –21.9
sandwich	12.0 –15.5

(a) Mastic asphalt

Mastic asphalt is a mixture of several materials and is prescribed for various purposes, such as roofing, flooring and tanking by a series of British Standards. Those relevant to asphalt for roofing are BS 6577: 1985 *Specification for mastic asphalt for building (natural rock asphalt aggregate)*; BS 988, 1076, 1097, 1451: 1973 *Mastic asphalt for building (limestone aggregate)*; and CP 144 *Roof coverings*, Part 4: 1970 *Mastic asphalt*. Where the roof is liable to be used by vehicular traffic, for example as a car park, the relevant British Standards are BS 1446: 1973 *Mastic asphalt (natural rock asphalt) for roads and footways*; and BS 1447: 1973 *Mastic asphalt (limestone fine aggregate) for roads and footways*. A specially formulated polymer modified material has been developed which has properties of high temperature stability, thereby reducing its tendency to flow when used on slopes, as well as increasing its low temperature flexibility (see page 342). Good general references on the subject of asphalt flat roofing includes *Flat roofing: a guide to good practice*, which is a trade publication sponsored by Tarmac Building Products Limited (1982); and the technical information sheets published by the British Flat Roofing Council (BFRC).

As will be seen from the British Standards, asphalt consists of an asphaltic cement and an aggregate. The asphaltic cement will consist of bitumen from petroleum distillation or a blend of this bitumen with Trinidad Lake Asphalt. The choice is then between rock asphalt from Switzerland, France or Sicily which is a limestone naturally impregnated with about 6% bitumen or a natural ordinary crushed limestone. Mastic asphalt produced from the natural rock asphalt is lighter in colour but is about one-third more expensive than the crushed limestone material. The British Standards permit alternative percentages of Trinidad Lake asphalt which may be incorporated in the asphaltic cement. The specifier should thus indicate which composition of asphaltic cement is required in accordance with the British Standards. CP 144 requires the use of black sheathing felt to BS 747: 1977 *Specification for roofing felts*, BS 747 type 4A (i) as an isolating membrane under the asphalt. *Black sheathing felt* is available with either a bitumen or a pitch saturant. On wet construction decks the bitumen impregnated type must be employed whilst on decks of dry construction either the bitumen or the pitch impregnated type may be used.

Roofing asphalt can be used either to form a continuous waterproof covering over either, flat, pitched or curved surfaces and can be easily worked round pipes, roof lights and other roof projections. It can be laid on most types of rigid sub-structure such as concrete either precast or in situ, timber boarding or a variety of proprietary structural deck units.

Durability Mastic asphalt when laid by a good specialist roofing sub-contractor on a sound base will not require major repairs for at least 60 years. When repairs are required they should always be carried out by a specialist. Eventually, exposed mastic asphalt is broken down by acids in the atmosphere and by ultra-violet radiation. So a special surfacing such as stone chippings, greatly increase the durability of the covering. Special surfacing is also necessary where there will be pedestrian or vehicular traffic.

Mastic asphalt is a dense material and being a very dark colour the uncovered material absorbs the heat very readily and especially where insulation is laid below the alphalt. To counteract this, a wide range of chippings is available for applying to the surface of asphalt roofing to give a high degree of reflection. Various coloured granites, white limestone, calcined flint and white spar usually in sizes up to 13 mm are the most widely used. Reflective chippings are suitable for use on roofs up to 10 degree pitch. They are embedded in a layer of bitumen dressing compound to form a textured surface.

Thermal insulation For general comments on thermal insulation standards for roofs see page 328. Figure 14.8 indicates forms of construction and thicknesses of various insulation boards which each give a U-value within the Building Regulations 1985. Figure 14.8 allows for top surface chippings on 20 mm mastic asphalt and black sheathing felt – the effects of a vapour beneath the insulation quoted has also been allowed for but *not* the effects of an applied ceiling.

It should be remembered that insulation within the roof construction leads to a reduction in temperature variations in the roof structure, thereby minimizing thermal movement.

Vapour control It is necessary to provide a vapour check on the warmest side of the insula-

Sub-structure	Insulation	0.6 W/m²K	0.3 W/m²K
		thickness (mm)	
150 mm in situ concrete slab and screen	Polyisocyanurate	30	67
	Glass fibre board	46	103
	Mineral wool slab	46	103
	Cork board	57	127
	Foamed glass	61	136
100 mm precast concrete lightweight concrete	Polyisocyanurate	19	55
	Glass fibre board	29	85
	Mineral wool slab	29	85
	Cork board	35	105
	Foamed glass	38	113
Plywood or particle board deck	Polyisocyanurate	30	66
	Glass fibre board	45	102
	Mineral wool slab	45	102
	Cork board	56	126
	Foamed glass	60	135
Metal deck	Polyisocyanurate	32	68
	Glass fibre board	48	105
	Mineral wool slab	48	105
	Cork board	60	130
	Foamed glass	64	139

14.8 *Typical examples of materials used for thermal insulation under mastic asphalt (warm roof) relative to sub-structure. The insulation materials must be overlaid with loose laid separating felt: mineral wool and glass fibre must also be overlaid with firm heat resistant board (cork, perlite or wood-fibre) before applying separating felt. Foamed glass requires mopping with hot bitumen and then two layers of non-bituminized paper to avoid adhesion to separating belt.*
(Flat roofing—guide to good practice, *produced by Tarmac Building Products Limited*)

tion. The vapour check may consist of a layer of roofing felt with sealed laps but the best type incorporates an impermeable metal foil. A good example of a proprietary vapour check supplied by specialist asphalt contractors consists of a sheet of aluminium foil protected by a coating of bitumen on both sides and reinforced with a sheet of glass fibre tissue. The vapour check should be folded back at least 225 mm over the outer edges of the insulating layer and the asphalt roofing bonded to the overlap as shown in figure 14.9. See page 329 for general comments.

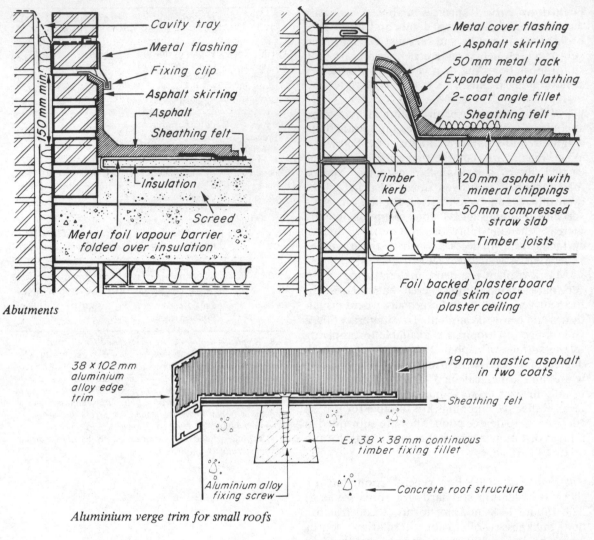

Abutments

Aluminium verge trim for small roofs

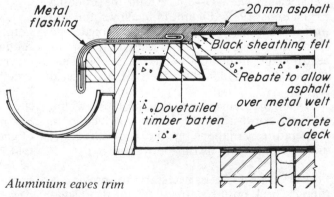

Aluminium eaves trim

14.9 *Asphalt details: abutments, eaves and verge*

Fire precautions Asphalt for roofing achieves the designation AA under the test requirements of BS 476 Part 3 *External fire exposure roof tests*. See also page 331 for general comments.

Application In situ concrete, precast concrete beams and slabs, wood-wool slabs, timber construction, compressed strawboard and metal decking are all suitable methods of construction for the sub-structure upon which asphalt may be laid.

In all cases the sub-structure must be strong enough to prevent excessive deflection. And in particular, where metal decking is used the deflection limit must be reduced 1/325 of the span instead of the more normal 1/240. For timber, particle board, plywood, strawboard or metal decking a timber kerb on which expanded metal is fixed as a key for asphalt, is required at walls. An air space between the wall and kerb allows for movement as shown in figure 14.9.

Timber rolls, similar to those shown in figure 14.26 are required to prevent water being blown over verges. With a sub-structure formed of wood-wool, strawboard, timber or plywood, provision must be made for ventilation between the roof deck and the ceiling. The sub-structure on which the asphalt is to be laid should ensure the rapid dispersal of rainwater, and so provide falls not less that 1 in 80. Any change in the direction of the roof surface in buildings shaped as letter T or L indicates the need for movement joints. They should be continuous through the entire structure, including roof, walls and upstands, as shown in figure 14.14, which is similar in one of those illustrated for built-up felt roofing in figure 14.30.

To assist in drying out screeds used in connection with concrete decks and to release trapped moisture, it is good practice to install drying vents. A proprietary example is shown in figure 14.10.

On flat roofs and roofs up to 30 degrees pitch the roofing asphalt is applied with a wooden float in two coats laid to a minimum thickness of 20 mm on an underlay of black *sheathing felt* laid loose with 50 mm lapped joints. The asphalt surface should be dressed with reflective mineral chippings to reduce the temperature induced by solar heat and to protect it from ultra-violet radiation and fire. On flat roofs having foot traffic, the asphalt should be laid in two coats to a

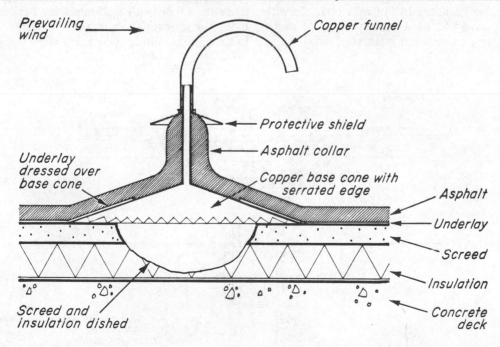

14.10 *'Parovent' copper ventilator*

minimum total thickness of 25 mm. On slopes of over 30 degrees the asphalt is applied without sheathing felt in three coats, the first coat being applied very thinly with a steel trowel. The second and third coats are then applied breaking joint to give a total thickness of not less than 20 mm. Where the asphalt is laid on vertical or sloping surfaces of more than 30 degrees a positive key is required. In the case of sloping surfaces over 10 degrees formed in timber boarding a layer of black sheathing felt is nailed to the timber boards and bitumen coated expanded metal lathing is then fixed at 150 mm centres with galvanized clout nails or staples to form the key for the asphalt which is then applied in three coats. In all cases where the asphalt is laid on flat or slightly sloping roofs, clean sharp sand is rubbed evenly over the surface of the asphalt whilst it is still hot. This breaks up the skin of the bitumen brought to the surface by the wooden float at the time of application. The object of this is to minimize the gradual crazing of the surface due to the action of the sun.

Details at abutments and edges are shown in the drawings as follows: figure 14.9 Abutments, eaves and verge; figure 14.11 Cast iron outlet with grille; figure 14.12 an alternative type of outlet made from gun metal or spun steel which has a domed grating and a clamping device which allows the grating to be tightened against the waterproofing; figure 14.13 Projections through roof; figure 14.14 Movement joint.

Where there is continuous foot traffic, mastic asphalt can be protected with concrete or fibre-cement tiles or with a jointed screed.

Tiles Concrete tiles are approximately 300 mm × 300 mm × 25 mm thick. The tiles are laid in bays of maximum 9 m² with 25 mm joints between the bays which are filled with bitumen compound. The tiles are set 25 mm back from the base of angle fillets and the margin is completed with bitumen compound. A bitumen primer is applied to the surface of the mastic asphalt roof covering and to the backs of the tiles and allowed to dry. The tiles are then bedded in hot bitumen bonding compound, taking care not to squeeze the compound upwards between the individual tiles.

Jointed screed A cement and sand screed 25 mm thick is laid on a separating membrane of building paper and grooved into a 600 mm square tiled pattern. The screed should be laid in bays of not more than 9 m² with a 25 mm joint between the bays. The grooves and joints can be filled with hot bitumen compound on completion.

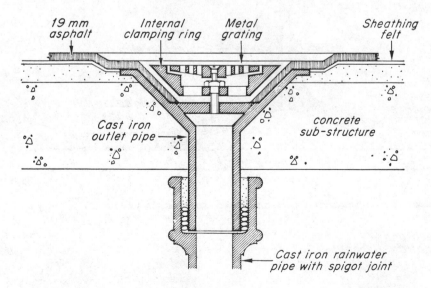

14.11 *Asphalt details: cast iron rainwater outlet for balcony*

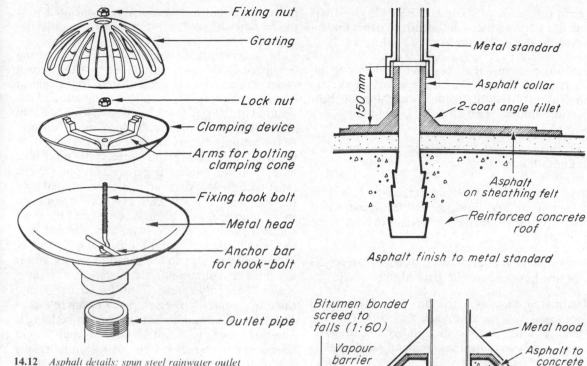

14.12 *Asphalt details: spun steel rainwater outlet*

Asphalt finish to metal standard

Projection through roof with upstand

14.13 *Asphalt: projections through roof*

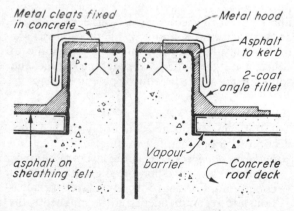

Twin kerb expansion joint

14.14 *Asphalt: movement joint*

The following are examples of typical mastic asphalt roofing specifications:

Timber decking (cold roof)
Decking of prefelted 19 mm tongued and grooved chipboard panels of type II/III or type III to BS 5669 well nailed to 50 × 200 mm timber joists and noggings, laid to falls. Any deck joints not closed off by the support system should be taped 102 mm mineral wool boards with vapour check incorporated above 9 mm plaster board ceiling finished with skim coat plaster (giving combined $U = 0.3 \text{ W/m}^2 \text{ K}$). Cavity above insulation vented to outside (see 14,2(e) Vapour control).

339

Separating layer of loose-laid BS 747 type 4A(i) sheathing felt with non-bitumenized paper underlay to prevent adhesion to pre-felted deck.

Roof covering of 20 mm two/coat mastic asphalt to BS 988T (75% bitumen, 25% Lake asphalt) finished with 10 mm stone chippings bedded in bitumen based adhesive compound.

Concrete decking (warm roof)
150 mm in situ cast deck incorporating temporary drainage holes.

40 mm minimum thickness screed to falls 1:60 with top surface finished smooth using wood float: apply a bitumen based primer to bind damp or dusty surfaces.

Single layer vapour check of BS 747 type 2B asbestos base or type 3B glass fibre base felt.

Thermal insulation of 67 mm polyisocyanurate roofboard (giving combined $U = 0.3 \text{ W/m}^2\text{ K}$). Heat sensitive boards such as expanded polystyrene, polyurethane foam mineral wool or glass fibre must be overlaid with a firm heat resistant board, such as wood fibre board, perlite board or cork.

Separating layer of loose-laid BS 747 type 4A(i) sheathing felt to allow for differential movements.

20 mm two coat mastic asphalt to BS 988T (75% bitumen, 25% lake asphalt), finished with 10 mm stone chippings bedded in bitumen based adhesive compound.

Figure 14.15 shows an alternative form of flat roof construction where the thermal insulation is placed *external* to the mastic asphalt (or built-up bituminous felt, or butyl rubber sheet – see page 342). This method of construction creates a 'warm roof' (see 14.2(d) Thermal control), and is referred to as a 'protected membrane roof', 'inverted roof', 'upside-down roof', 'inside-out roof' or simply, as an 'externally insulated roof'. Non-absorbent insulation is placed over the mastic asphalt (or felt) and is held down by gravel, or by paving slabs. In this way, the waterproof layer is protected from rapid extremes of temperature. ultra-violet light and impact damage; and it also serves as an effective vapour barrier, avoiding the problems of entrapped moisture associated with the 'sandwich' roof construction previously described.

In the example shown the waterproof covering is applied in the normal manner to a dry screed which has been laid to a fall of 1:60. In the case of mastic asphalt, it is laid on sheathing felt and the upstand at the wall is taken up to at least 150 mm above the level of the finished roof surface. Extruded polystyrene foam boards are placed on the asphalt: they are laid loose, with tight butt joints and all joints staggered. The polystyrene must be 20% thicker than in a conventional roof to overcome the external exposure conditions (wind, rain and frost), and is considered the most suitable material in this situation because it is water and vapour resistant, dimensionally stable, tough and resistant to temperature cycles, and is available in a flame retardant, self-extinguising grade. The polystyrene is protected by 50 mm thick hydraulically pressed precast concrete paving slabs, laid dry with butt joints. No bedding is necessary, but they must be laid on small blocks or spacers at corners (eg 80 × 100 mm inorganic felt pads) to avoid water retention between the underside of the slabs and the insulation, as well as to facilitate drainage. A 38 mm minimum gap must be left between perimeter abutments and the insulation/paving to allow for differential movements, and this gap can be filled with bitumen impregnated fibre board, a compressible plastics strip or loose gravel.

No gutter is formed in the roof as the screed falls to a lowest line and the rainwater runs to this line before being collected by outlets located to ensure each serves about 35 m² of roofing. The outlets may be required at two levels: some to collect water from the waterproof membrane, and some for the water flowing at paving level.

(b) Bitumen felt
The following terms are commonly used in connection with bitumen felt roofing:
- *built-up roofing* – two or more layers of bitumen roofing fused together on site with bitumen compound. For flat roofs, three layer specifications are recommended, and for pitched roofs two layers are usual;
- *layer* – a single thickness of membrane roofing. The word *ply* is often synonymous with layer,

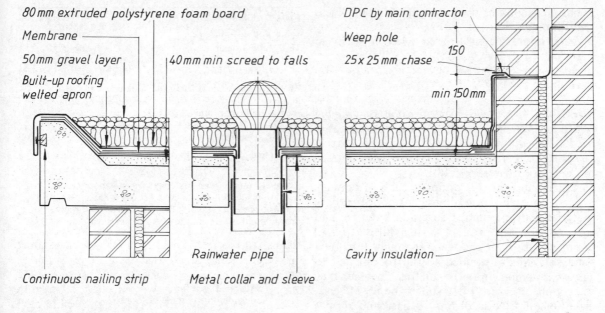

80 mm extruded polystyrene foam board

Membrane

50 mm gravel layer

Built-up roofing welted apron

40 mm min screed to falls

Continuous nailing strip

Rainwater pipe

Metal collar and sleeve

DPC by main contractor

Weep hole

25 x 25 mm chase

150

min 150 mm

Cavity insulation

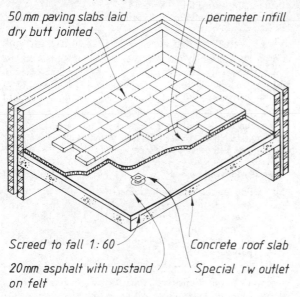

80 mm extruded polystyrene board

50 mm paving slabs laid dry butt jointed

perimeter infill

Screed to fall 1:60

20 mm asphalt with upstand on felt

Concrete roof slab

Special rw outlet

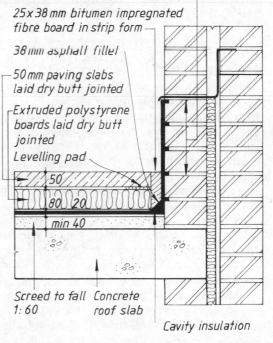

Asphalt taken up 150 mm min and tucked into 25 x 25 mm chase, mortar pointing

25 x 38 mm bitumen impregnated fibre board in strip form

38 mm asphalt fillet

50 mm paving slabs laid dry butt jointed

Extruded polystyrene boards laid dry butt jointed

Levelling pad

50

80 20

min 40

Screed to fall 1:60

Concrete roof slab

Cavity insulation

2 coat roof asphalt with felt underlay

14.15 *Flat 'warm roof' construction details*

341

but is sometimes used to denote the thickness of bitumen sheet;

- *under-layer* – an unexposed layer in built-up roofing;
- *cap-sheet* – an exposed or final layer in built-up roofing.

BS 747: 1977(1986) *Specification for roofing felts* describes different types of bituminous based roof felts, and CP 144 *Roof coverings*, Part 3: 1970(1978) *Built-up bitumen felt* gives suitable methods for their application.

The manuacture of roofing felt is a continuous process involving the impregnation of a base material with a penetration grade bitumen, and then coating the product with a filled *oxidized bitumen* to provide the waterproofing. Finally, a sand surfacing is applied to the roofing felt to prevent sticking within the roll form in which they are supplied. Figure 14.16 shows the BS 747 classification of felts according to base and *surface finish*. Each type of felt is further subdivided according to its weight per length and width of roll. The heavier felts are normally used as a top layer and taking into account the different types, finishes and weights available, the specifier has a wide choice.

The ageing and weathering characteristics of bitumen over a period of time approximating to 15 years are well known. The addition of a polymer to the bitumen improves its properties as a roofing material in almost all respects, and in particular, the flexibility, strength and fatigue resistance. The most commonly used modifying additives are styrene butadiene styrene (SBS) and atactic polypropylene (APP). Roofings with SBS additives have the greatest elasticity and elongation and generally involve conventional hot bitumen bonding techniques. Those with SBS additives have improved high temperature performance, and can have better weathering characteristics. But they are not suitable for bonding with ordinary oxidized bitumens and are generally bonded by torching.

Polymer modified bitumens are usually applied to a base of polyester or glass and form part of a range of **High Performance Roofings** recom-

14.16 *BS 747: 1977 (1986) classification of bitumen felts* ▶

Class 1	Fibre based	Weight/roll
1B	fine granule surfaced	36 kg/20 × 1 m
1E	mineral surfaced	38 kg/10 × 1 m
1F	hessian reinforced base with fine grandule surfaced	22 kg/15 × 1 m

These are the original felts used in industry, the cheapest, and have failings which suggest they should no longer be used in built-up roofing.

Class 2	Asbestos based	Weight/roll
2B	fine granule surfaced	36 kg/20 × 1 m
2E	mineral surfaced	38 kjg/10 × 1 m

These are useful as an underlay or as a vapour check beneath insulation on concrete or screed decks. Some authorities require them for improved fire performance as they maintain their integrity better than most other felts.

Class 3	Glass based	Weight/roll
3B	fine granule surfaced	36 kg/20 × 1 m
3E	mineral surfaced	28 kg/10 × 1 m
3G	(perforated) grit finished underside, fine granule surfaced topside	32 kg/15 × 1 m

These give the best waterproof performance and should give many years of service. They are not suitable for nailing as they do not have enough strength. Type 3G is used for the first layer in partially bonded systems.

Class 4	Sheathing felts	Weight/roll
4A (i)	black sheating felt (bitumen)	17 kg/25 × 0.81 m
4A (ii)	brown sheathing felt	17–21 kg/25 × 0.81 m
4B (i)	black hair felt	41 kg/25 × 0.81 m
4B (ii)	brown hair felt	41 kg/25 × 0.81 m

These are used under mastic asphalt roofing because they are dimensionally stable, and as sarking felts under metal roofing. Hair felts are used for heat insulation, sound absorption and other purposes.

Class 5	Polyester based	Weight/roll
5B	fine granule surfaced bitumen polyester top layer	34 kg/8 × 1 m
5E	mineral surfaced bitumen polyester cap sheet	38 kg/8 × 1 m
5U	fine granule surfaced bitumen polyester underlayer	14 kg/8 × 1 m

Development work on built-up roofing felts has led to the recent inclusion of this type in the BS. Two main areas of deficiency in the other types had to be addressed: age hardening of bitumen, and long-term strength of elongation properties of the felt base. Polyester bases appear to be stable and strong for a long life, and to be compatible with bitumen. It provides a non-rotting base, with greater strength than glass and greater elongation before breaking. See also main text regarding the use of polymer modified bitumen.

mended by the British Flat Roofing Council (BFRC). Others in the range are *calendered polymeric roofings* which do not contain a base as they are formed from proprietary compounds of polymers and bitumen which are calendered to form sheets of high flexibility and elasticity; and *metal foil surfaced felts* which achieve high strength with a polyester or woven glass base and have a facing of aluminium or copper. The metal facing provides an effective protection to the membrane as it excludes ultra-violet light, oxygen and ozone which are the chief factors causing ageing and hardening of bitumen. Aluminium also has good reflective properties and effectively reduces the temperature of the bitumen, but these roofings should not be used where there are alkaline atmospheres.

It is usual to use a protective finish on the top layer of built-up felt roofing to give a reflective finish and protect the bitumen from sunlight or to provide a wearing surface. Stone chippings 10 mm to 13 mm size are often used bedded in bitumen and there is a wide range of types, Derbyshire, White Spar and Leicester Red granite being examples. If the roof is to withstand foot traffic the spar finish will not be suitable because of the danger of the sharp granules cutting the felt. Thus for promenade roofs concrete GRC or fibre-cement tiles should be used.

In general, for roofs not taking foot traffic (except for maintenance) the main area will be stone chippings; edges and upstands will be in mineral surfaced felt and gutters in self finished felt.

Durability Successful built-up felt roofing is dependent on the correct specification for each situation. Good materials, careful detailing and correct application are all necessary and so since supervision is difficult the contract should be carried out by a specialist contractor experienced in this type of work.

Thermal insulation For general comments on thermal insulation standards for roofs see page 328. Figure 14.17 indicates forms of construction and thicknesses of various insulation boards which each give a U-value within the *Building Regulation 1985*. The figure allows for top surface chippings on three layers of built-up felt – the

Sub-structure	Insulation	0.6 W/m²K thickness (mm)	0.3 W/m²K thickness (mm)
150 mm in situ concrete slab and screen	Expanded polystyrene*	38	94
	Glass fibre board	46	103
	Mineral wool slab	46	103
	Cork board	57	127
	Foamed glass	61	136
100 mm precast concrete lightweight concrete	Expanded polystyrene*	20	77
	Glass fibre board	29	85
	Mineral wool slab	29	85
	Cork board	35	105
	Foamed glass	38	113
Plywood or particle board deck	Expanded polystyrene*	37	93
	Glass fibre board	45	102
	Mineral wool slab	45	102
	Cork board	56	126
	Foamed glass	60	135
Metal deck	Expanded polystyrene*	40	96
	Glass fibre board	48	105
	Mineral wool slab	48	105
	Cork board	60	130
	Foamed glass	64	139

* The U-value for expanded polystyrene allows for additional 13 mm wood fibreboard overlay.

14.17 *Typical examples of materials used for thermal insulation under built-up felt (warm roof) relative to substructure. (Flat roofing—guide to good practice, produced by Tarmac Building Products Limited)*

effects of a vapour shock beneath the insulation quoted has also been allowed for but *not* the effects of an applied ceiling.

Vapour control Condensation is liable to occur on the internal surfaces of a roof construction within a building if the temperature and humidity of the air inside is appreciably higher than the outside temperature and humidity. Thus a vapour check will be required on the underside of the insulating layer below the built-up roofing. The check should incorporate an impermeable metal foil, and the type and application detailed in the notes on asphalt, page 335, is suitable for use with built-up felt roofing.

Fire precautions Where stone chippings are used

as topping all felt flat roofs have the highest AA BS 476 Part 3 fire rating. On pitched roofs the rating varies according to the type of felt in each layer and the combustibility of the roof deck. Asbestos felt has the best fire resistance and most Local Authorities require its use.

Application   Hollow precast concrete beams or slabs, in situ concrete, aerated concrete, wood-wool slabs, compressed straw slabs, timber construction or asbestos cement or metal decking are all suitable roof decking for built-up felt roofing. The use of these materials is more fully discussed on page 325. All built-up felt roofing should be carried out in accordance with the requirements of CP 144 Part 3 1970(1978) *Built-up bitumen felt*. It is necessary to provide falls to clear the water from a flat roof and a minimum of 17 mm in 1000 mm is recommended (1 degree slope). The first layer of roofing felt is fixed by nailing, or by full bonding or by partial bonding according to the nature of the sub-structure. Partial bonding to the deck prevents the formation of blisters in the waterproof due to vapour pressure, and gives a measure of freedom of movement between the roof deck and covering.

BRE Digest 51 *Developments in roofing* discusses at length the problem of water vapour in the roof deck, particularly in connection with lightweight screeds. The sources of screed moisture are as follows:

(i) mixing water

(ii) rain water during the drying out period and

(iii) condensation formed within the building.

The effect of a saturated screed is as follows

(i) diminished thermal insulation

(ii) blistering and damage to waterproofing by vapour pressure

(iii) staining of internal decoration.

Experiments at the Building Research Establishment with an exposed aerated screed found that after four wet days and with subsequent shielding from further rain complete drying out needed 36 good summer days or 180 winter days. Research and long observation has revealed that nearly all roof blisters are caused by the entrapping of constructional moisture in the roof deck. Solar heat vapourizes this moisture and causes considerable pressure which weakens the bond between the roofing layers and the roof sub-

structure. Ventilation of the roof deck, below built-up felt roofing, can be obtained in several ways:

(i) *deliberately isolating the first layer of felt* by means of uniform granules on the underside. This first layer is of perforated glass fibre felt laid dry on the sub-structure and the bonding bitumen of the upper layer penetrates the perforations automatically to give 10% bonding. Precautions must be taken to release pressure through special vents at eaves and abutments as shown in figure 14.18. The specially prepared base sheet is known as a *vented underlay* or *venting base layer*.

(ii) *partial bonding* or *frame bonding* where provision must be made for the release of pressure by the installation of special perimeter details. Figure 14.19 shows typical patterns of partial bonding. Partial bonding, or vented underlay must always be used on a screeded finish; a vented underlay is in fact recommended for most roof decks (except timber boarding) due to the possibility of moisture being trapped during construction.

(iii) *installing proprietary plastics* or *metal breather vents* spaced in accordance with the manufacturers' instructions with various types specially designed to dry out wet screeds and/or to act as pressure release vents. Note that this type of ventilation is also suitable for asphalt roofing.

Where roofs of timber joists with timber boards, compressed straw slabs, flax board, particle board or plywood decks are constructed so that there is a space between ceiling and deck, it is wise for this space to be ventilated to the open air to avoid fungal growth. Minimum ventilation is given by 300 mm^2 opening per 300 mm run on two opposite sides of the building. Provision must be made for a free air path from one side to the other. Where the width of the roof between openings is greater than 12 m the size of the openings should be doubled. Vents should be preferably located in the walls rather than roof. The ceiling below a ventilated roof space should be free from gaps and holes and have no vapour permeability.

BS 6229: 1982 *Flat roofs with continuously supported coverings* recommends that all timbers used for the structure of a flat roof should have preservative treatment to BS 5268: Part 5 (see 14.2(e) Vapour control).

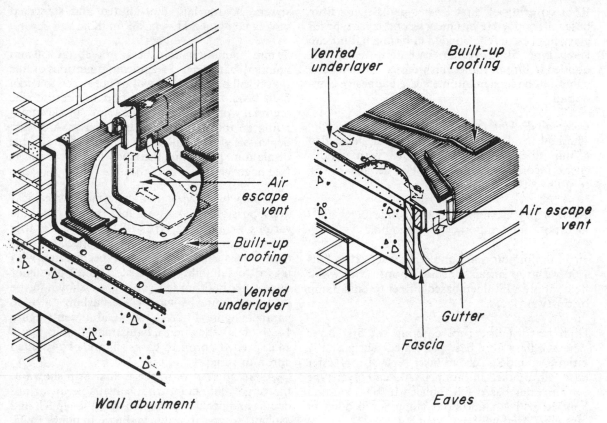

14.18 *Bitumen felt details: water vapour release by vented underlay*

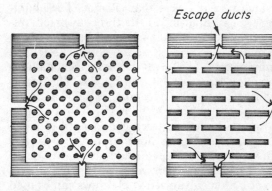

14.19 *Bitumen felt details: water vapour release by frame bonding*

The following are typical examples of built-up felt roofing specifications:

Timber decking (warm roof)
Decking of exterior grade WBP 19 mm tongued and grooved plywood panels to BS 1455 well nailed to 50 × 200 mm timber joists and noggings, laid to falls. Any deck joints not closed off by the support system should be taped.

Single layer vapour check of type 2B asbestos base or type 3B glass fibre base felt bonded in bitumen.

Thermal insulation of 102 mm thick mineral wool slab bonded in hot bitumen (giving combined U = 0.3 W/m² K).

345

Roof covering of: first layer type 3B glass fibre base felt, bonded in bitumen; second layer type 3B glass fibre base felt, bonded in bitumen; and cap layer type 5B polyester base felt or similar, bonded in bitumen and finished with 10 mm stone chippings bedded in bitumen based adhesive compound.

Concrete decking (cold roof)
Thermal insulation below decking of suspended 55 mm thick polyurethane board with vapour check incorporated in suspended ceiling (giving combined U = 0.3 W/m^2 K).

100 mm precast lightweight concrete deck units incorporating temporary drainage holes.

40 mm minimum sand and cement screed to falls 1:60 with top surface finished smooth with wood float: apply a bitumen based primer to bind damp or dusty surfaces.

High performance roof covering of: first layer type 3G glass fibre base perforated felt, partially bitumen bonded; second layer type 3B polyester base felt, bonded in bitumen; and cap layer type 3B polyester based felt, bonded in bitumen and finished with 10 mm stone chippings bedded in bitumen based adhesive compound.

Concrete decking (protected membrane warm roof – see figure 14.15)
175 mm in situ cast dense concrete slab deck with wood float finish to falls and incorporating temporary drainage holes. Apply a bitumen based primer to bind damp or dusty surfaces.

High performance roof covering of: first layer type 3G glass fibre base perforated felt, partially bonded in bitumen; second layer type 3B glass fibre base felt, bonded in bitumen; and cap layer of bitumen polymer or pitch polymer roofing bonded in bitumen (pour or roll method), *or*, an APP modified bitumen roofing (torch applied).

Underlay sheet (if required) to insulation manufacturer's specification laid loose to even out cap layer surface irregularities.

Thermal insulation of 80 mm extruded poly-styrene boards laid butt-jointed and staggered (giving combined U = 0.3 W/m^2 K).

50 mm minimum thickness gravel (20–30 mm nominal diameter). If significant quantities of fine gravel will be present, it will be necessary to add a filter layer above the insulation to prevent fine material working through the joints and accumulating on the underside of the boards. A 50 mm depth of gravel will prevent floatation of the insulation, providing there is efficient drainage (see page 340).

In view of the very many alternative specifications possible in built-up felt roofing and the various weights and types of felt available, it is advisable to take advice from the specialist contractor regarding the intended specification with regard to suitability and cost. Typical details of three-layer built-up felt roofing are shown in the following figures. Figure 14.20 flashing to brick parapet; figure 14.22 detail at abutment: figure 14.21 detail showing a balustrade fixing; figure 14.23 welted apron to eaves; figure 14.24 welted apron to verge.

As an alternative to the welted drip shown at the verge, aluminium trim is available in various depths and profiles to receive the built-up felt and asphalt. A typical profile is shown in figure 14.25. The welted drip (figure 14.24) is formed by nailing the felt to a timber strip and returning the felt over the roof surface lapping with the roof covering according to the direction of the fall. The depth of the apron can be varied but will not be satisfactory if it is less than 50 mm. The aluminium trim is 'built-in' to the three-layer felt system as shown in figure 14.25, and because of the possibility of electrolytic action between steel and aluminium, it is fixed with stainless steel or aluminium alloy screws at 450 mm centres. The trim is produced in standard lengths of 3.050 mm, the longer pieces are jointed by a spigot and a 3 mm gap should be left between each length to allow for expansion. A glass fibre reinforced polyester resin verge trim is shown as an alternative detail figure 14.26. Since there is no possibility of electrolytic action galvanized steel screws can be used for fixing. Because of the lower thermal expansion of this material, it is not necessary to leave a gap between the lengths of trim. Built-up felt roofing

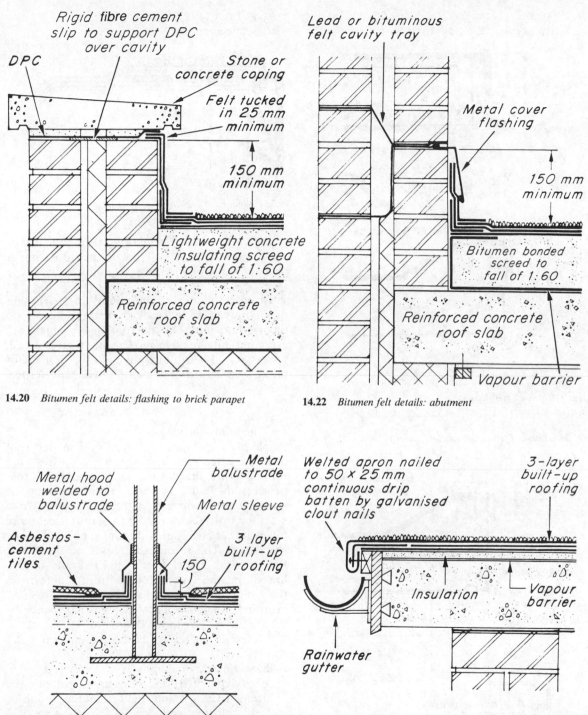

14.20 *Bitumen felt details: flashing to brick parapet*

14.22 *Bitumen felt details: abutment*

14.21 *Bitumen felt details: balustrade fixing*

14.23 *Bitumen felt details: welted apron to eaves*

347

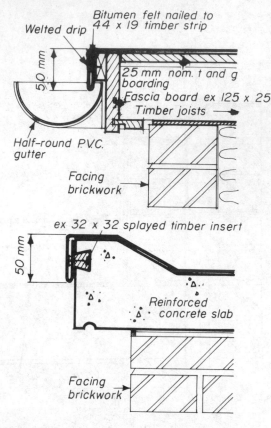

14.24　*Bitumen felt details: welted apron to verge*

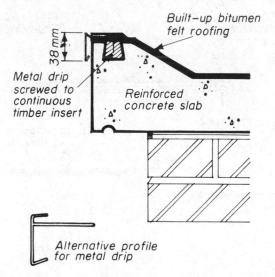

14.25　*Bitumen felt details: aluminium verge trim*

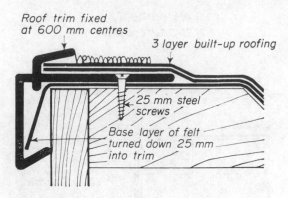

14.26　*Bitumen felt details: grp verge trim*

will often be detailed to incorporate an internal or *secret gutter*. A typical detail incorporating a plastics outlet component is shown in figure 14.27.

In order to prevent the failure of the roofing due to movement in the structure it is necessary to incorporate joints in the roof finish which will accommodate relative movement, figures 14,28, 14.29 and 14.30 illustrate suitable joints for minor, moderate and major movement respectively.

(c) Single ply sheeting
Single ply membrane laid over an insulated roof deck are often seen by designers as an ideal flat roof covering: they form a seamless umbrella that protects the building from rainfall without the risk of water penetration through joints. However, for satisfactory results to permit acceptance by insurance companies, they must be installed by specialists. The recommendations of the Single Ply Roofing Association (SPRF) should be followed and the system adopted must conform to the requirements of published standards, or have been independently assessed for performance by the British or European Boards of Agrément.

Materials currently used for single ply flat roofing are:
- **thermoplastic**: including black coloured polyisobutylene (PIB) and ethylene copolymerised bitumen (ECB); and, light coloured, white or grey, chloropolyethylene (CPE), polyvinylchloride (PVC), and chlorosulphonated polyethylene (CSPE) *Hypalon*;

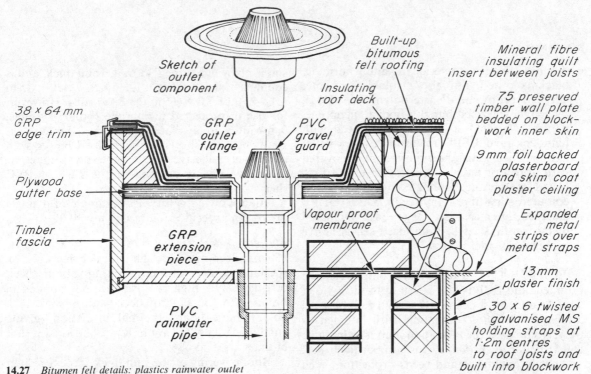

Sketch of outlet component

Built-up bitumous felt roofing

Insulating roof deck

Mineral fibre insulating quilt insert between joists

38 × 64 mm GRP edge trim

GRP outlet flange

PVC gravel guard

75 preserved timber wall plate bedded on block-work inner skin

Plywood gutter base

9mm foil backed plasterboard and skim coat plaster ceiling

Timber fascia

GRP extension piece

Vapour proof membrane

Expanded metal strips over metal straps

13mm plaster finish

PVC rainwater pipe

30 × 6 twisted galvanised MS holding straps at 1·2m centres to roof joists and built into blockwork

14.27 *Bitumen felt details: plastics rainwater outlet*

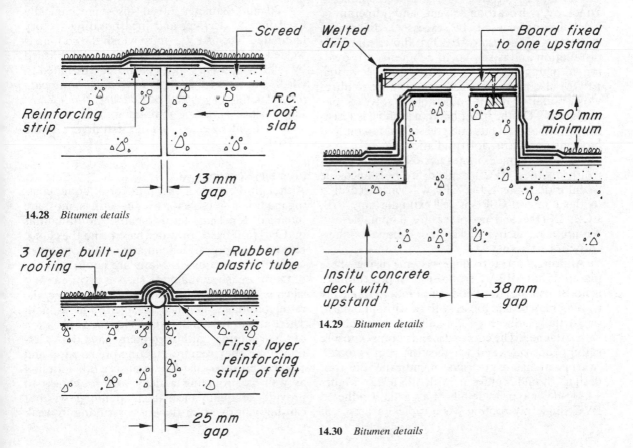

Screed

Reinforcing strip

R.C. roof slab

13 mm gap

14.28 *Bitumen details*

Welted drip

Board fixed to one upstand

150 mm minimum

Insitu concrete deck with upstand

38 mm gap

14.29 *Bitumen details*

3 layer built-up roofing

Rubber or plastic tube

First layer reinforcing strip of felt

25 mm gap

14.30 *Bitumen details*

- **thermosetting** (elastomeric): including normally black coloured, but also available in white, ethylene propylene dieneterpolymer (EPDM); reflective white coloured silicone; neoprene, naturally black but sometimes surfaced with light coloured CSPE to improve ultra-violet and chemical resistance; butyl rubber covered with gravel or paving slabs to serve as a protected membrane roofing system; and light coloured glass fibre reinforced plastics (GRP);
- **modified bitumen**: (see page 342) including metal foil finished or sand-faced self adhesive bitumen polymer felts.

ECB, PIB, CSPE and CPE are compatible with bitumen, and ECB is also resistant to ultra-violet light, ozone, most chemicals as well as biological attack. PVC is *not* compatible with bitumen or polystyrene used for insulation, and is vulnerable to *plasticiser migration*. PIB is comparitively soft and easily punctured and needs protection, even for normal foot-traffic. It is also susceptible to attack by hydrocarbon solvents and intolerant of local flexing caused by excessive differential movements. The use of EPDM allows rapid site installation and is similar to neoprene in providing a highly elastic, ozone resistant covering. EPDM also provides excellent resistance to ultra-violet radiation, but is vulnerable to solvents, oils and grease. On the other hand, neoprene is resistant to oils, animal fats and grease, but is damaged by acids and ultra-violet radiation.

Each of the membranes has different fire control properties: PVC has good fire resistance due to chloride content, but CPE will vary according to this content; CSPE is self extinguishing; PIB, ECB, EPDM and neoprene are flammable and require a protective finish; and silicone is inherently fire resistant.

Although most roofing systems using these materials have BBA Certification, at present there is no British Standard code of practice. Single ply roofing may be laid loose, with or without ballast, or partially adhered, fully adhered or mechanically attached. The choice depends upon exposure rating, substrate, and whether the roof is 'cold', 'warm', or has a protected membrane: the roof design should conform with BS 6229. Figure 14.31 shows typical details of a partially adhered PVC single ply roofing. As a typical example of

single ply roofing, the PVC is 1.5 mm thick, and is supplied 0.6 × 25 m (28.5 kg), 1.1 × 15 m (31.4 kg), or 1.8 × 15 m (51.3 kg) rolls. However, for use in protected membrane roofing systems, 3 m widths are available which are 2.5 mm thick. Joints between sheets are normally achieved with a contact adhesive and double-sided tape, or often by solvent welding in the case of PVC sheets.

The following is a typical example of a single ply roofing specification (see figure 14.32):

Metal roof deck (warm roof)
150 mm deep metal trough roof decking fixed by specialist contractor incorporating vapour check of single layer high performance felt bonded in bitumen to top flats of deck; and 68 mm thick polyurethane board thermal insulation (giving combined $U = 0.3 \, W/m^2 \, K$) bonded in hot bitumen.

Roof covering of: 1.5 mm thick 'Trocal S' light grey plasticised PVC held against wind uplift with 1 × 80 mm diameter metal discs mechanically fixed first to decking and incorporating factory laminated face of PVC on to which the roofing is welded. The number of disc fixings are established by reference to the wind uplift force calculated to CP 3: chapter V: Part 2: 1972 *Code of basic data for the design of buildings – Loading: Wind loads*. Laps in sheets must be a minimum of 50 mm wide and solvent welded using tetrahydrofurane (THF).

(d) Liquid coatings
Although there are a vast number of liquid coating materials suitable for roof coverings, most are intended for short-term repairs. Formulations may be spirit based or water based, and the choice relies on the prevailing climatic conditions when application is required. Many are liquid versions of thermoset sheet material, such as neoprene and silicone, and others include polyurethane, acrylic resin, bitumen, modified bitumen, and asphalt. There are no British Standards for the application of these coatings, although many have BBA Certification. They require exacting preparation and surfaces must be dust free to ensure full adhesion as well as providing a degree of roughness to provide adequate mechanical bonding without causing variable film thickness resulting in weak spots.

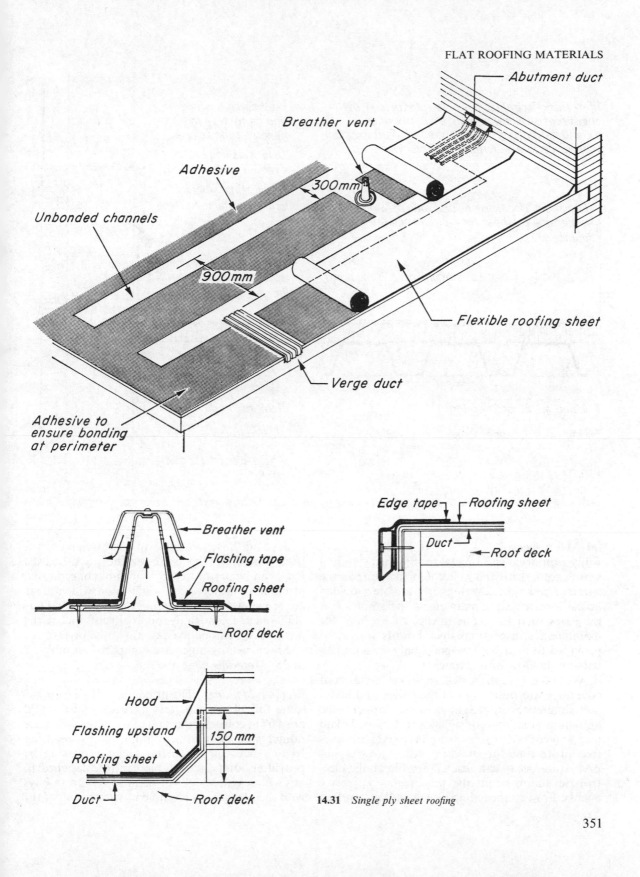

Abutment duct

Breather vent

Adhesive

Unbonded channels

300mm

900mm

Flexible roofing sheet

Verge duct

Adhesive to
ensure bonding
at perimeter

Breather vent

Flashing tape

Roofing sheet

Roof deck

Edge tape — Roofing sheet

Duct

Roof deck

Hood

Flashing upstand

150 mm

Roofing sheet

Duct — Roof deck

14.31 *Single ply sheet roofing*

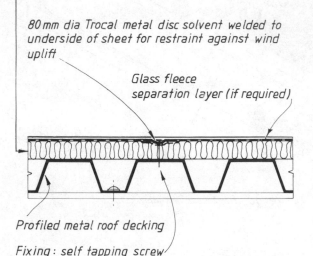

1·5m thick Trocal 'S' light grey plasticised pvc
sheet roof membrane, high flexibility and
extendability, high tensile strength, and excellent
resistance to air-borne pollutants

80 mm dia Trocal metal disc solvent welded to
underside of sheet for restraint against wind
uplift

Glass fleece
separation layer (if required)

Profiled metal roof decking

Fixing: self tapping screw

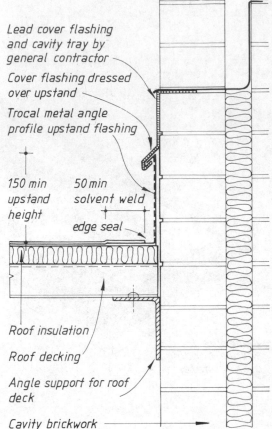

Lead cover flashing
and cavity tray by
general contractor

Cover flashing dressed
over upstand

Trocal metal angle
profile upstand flashing

150 min   50 min
upstand   solvent weld
height

edge seal

Roof insulation

Roof decking

Angle support for roof
deck

Cavity brickwork

14.32 *Single ply sheeting details: Trocal 'S' PVC roofing system*

(e) Metal sheets

Fully supported sheet metal roofing has standing
seams, rolls, drips and welted joints to connect the
sheets. These roof coverings are suitable provided
access is restricted to maintenance personnel. For
purposes such as escape in case of fire and for
maintenance inspections duck boards should be
provided to distribute weight evenly without restricting the flow of rainwater.

With the exception of lead, sheet metal roof
coverings are much lighter than tiles and slates
and differences in weight between copper, zinc
and aluminium are not significant. Correctly laid
lead and copper roof covering have given trouble-
free protection for buildings for centuries but
premature decay can result from bimetallic electrolytic action or in the presence of corrosive
agents. For instance, timber such as Western Red

Cedar and those treated with corrosive preservatives should not be used for the duck boards.
Lead can be perforated by constant concentrated
dripping of water from roofs upon which algae
are growing. See *MBS*: *Materials* chapter 9. Durability increases with the pitch of roofs and all the
metal sheets can be fixed at any pitch or vertical.

Sheet metal gauges are compared in table 78
MBS: *Materials* page 195.

Methods of fixing The principles of fixing are the
same for all sheet metals. Stresses which could
arise from constant thermal movements will cause
fatigue and should be minimized by reducing
friction between the metal and the decking by
providing joints at suitable centres, designed to
absorb movement. Sheet metals are laid in bays
with their lengths in alignment with the fall of the

roof. The sheets are turned up to form upstands against abutments and these are protected by cover flashing being taken into a raked joint in the case of brickwork or a raglet groove in the case of masonry or concrete. The cover flashing is retained by wedges and afterwards pointed. Joints in the direction of the fall are formed into rolls. Rolls with solid cores are preferable where there may be foot traffic and also on flat roofs since their greater height is an advantage. An alternative to the roll is a standing seam. Differences between the properties of the metal determine the techniques for laying, thus lead is malleable but roofing grades of copper and aluminium are less so and zinc is relatively stiff. In consequence lead can be formed into complex shapes by bossing, copper and aluminium can be formed into standing seams and welts while details in zinc roof covering are generally restricted to simple folds, the sheets being preformed before being placed in position. Joints across the fall are formed as follows:

- in pitches up to 5 degrees, as steps called *drips* – these are at least 50 mm high;
- pitches over 5 degrees, as welts;
- for very steep pitches in lead, laps are satisfactory. Where the longitudinal joints are standing seams welts across the fall must be staggered to avoid the problem which arises if the corners of four sheets coincide.

Underlays Underlays are required: to allow free movement of metal; to prevent corrosion by screeds or timbers; and for sound deadening. Rain and hail can be very noisy on copper, aluminium and zinc sheets.

Lead, copper and zinc sheets should be laid on an inodorous felt (BS 747 Type 4A(ii) Brown no. 1 inodorous felt) butt jointed and fixed with clout nails. The same felt is suitable for aluminium which is laid over timber boarding but on other bases, 2000 gauge polyethylene sheets (0.508 mm thick) should be used. The underlay in this case should be laid with 50 mm sealed laps. Underlays should be dry when the roof coverings are laid, and this is particularly important in the case of inodorous felt.

Lead
This form of roofing is described in CP 143 *Sheet roof and wall coverings*, Part 11: 1970 *Lead*. The metal is discussed in *MBS: Materials* chapter 9, and should conform to BS 1178: 1982 *Specification for milled lead sheet and strip for building purposes*. The use of this extremely durable roof covering is limited by its weight and high initial cost. It is, however, still widely valued for its malleability and consequent suitability for items such as flashings which require to be bossed into complex shapes. The use of lead for vertical cladding has been revived recently and the use of thin gauge metal premounted on panels is likely to increase. Fully supported lead sheet for roofing has an AA fire rating in respect of BS 476 Part 3 (see page 332) except where laid on plain edge boards when the rating is reduced to BA. The following table is a guide to the thicknesses of lead sheet suitable for various uses, and the appropriate code number.

Code No	Thickness mm	Use
5	2.24	Roofing and gutter lining
6	2.64	
7	3.15	
4	1.80	Flashings and lead 'slates'
5	2.24	
3	1.32	Soakers
4	1.80	

A typical small lead flat roof is shown in figure 14.33. The upstand flashing at each abutment is protected by a cover flashing secured by means of lead tacks and wedges, illustrated at A and B. The cover flashing is tucked at least 25 mm into the brickwork joint. The object of the cover flashing is to seal the joint between upstand and wall and at the same time, allow the covered sheet freedom to contract or expand.

The joints shown in figure 14.34 are:

A An enlargement of the drip shown in figure 14.33. The flat roof consists of plane surfaces slightly inclined and separated by low steps or *drips* to facilitate the run off at the joints where the ends of the lead sheets overlap.

B A drip with a groove to resist capillary attraction.

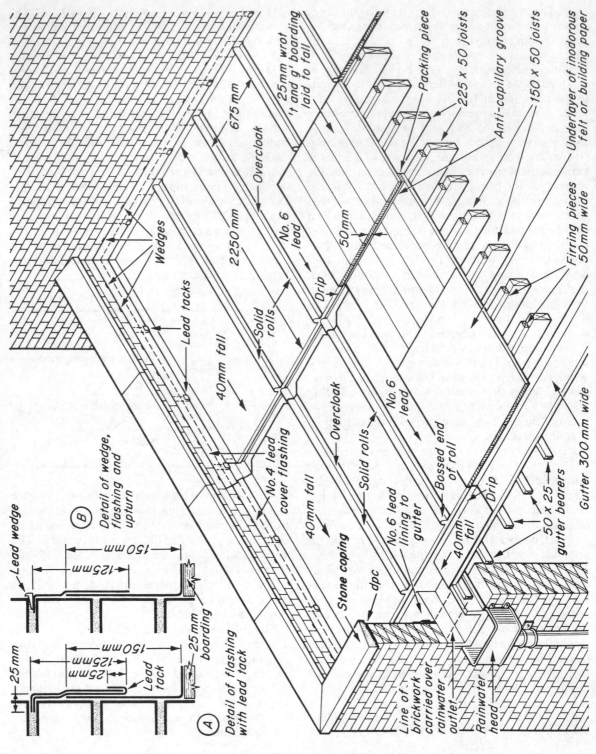

25mm wrot 't and g' boarding laid to fall

Packing piece

225 x 50 joists

Anti-capillary groove

150 x 50 joists

Underlayer of inodorous felt or building paper

675 mm

Overcloak

No. 6 lead

50 mm

Drip

Firring pieces 50mm wide

Wedges

2250 mm

Lead tacks

40mm fall

Solid rolls

No. 4 lead cover flashing

Overcloak

No. 6 lead

Solid rolls

Bossed end of roll

Gutter 300 mm wide

Stone coping

40mm fall

No. 6 lead lining to gutter

Drip

dpc

40mm fall

50 x 25 gutter bearers

Line of brickwork carried over rainwater outlet

Rainwater head

B Detail of wedge, flashing and upturn

Lead wedge

150mm

125mm

25mm boarding

A Detail of flashing with lead tack

25mm

150mm

125mm

25mm

Lead tack

25mm boarding

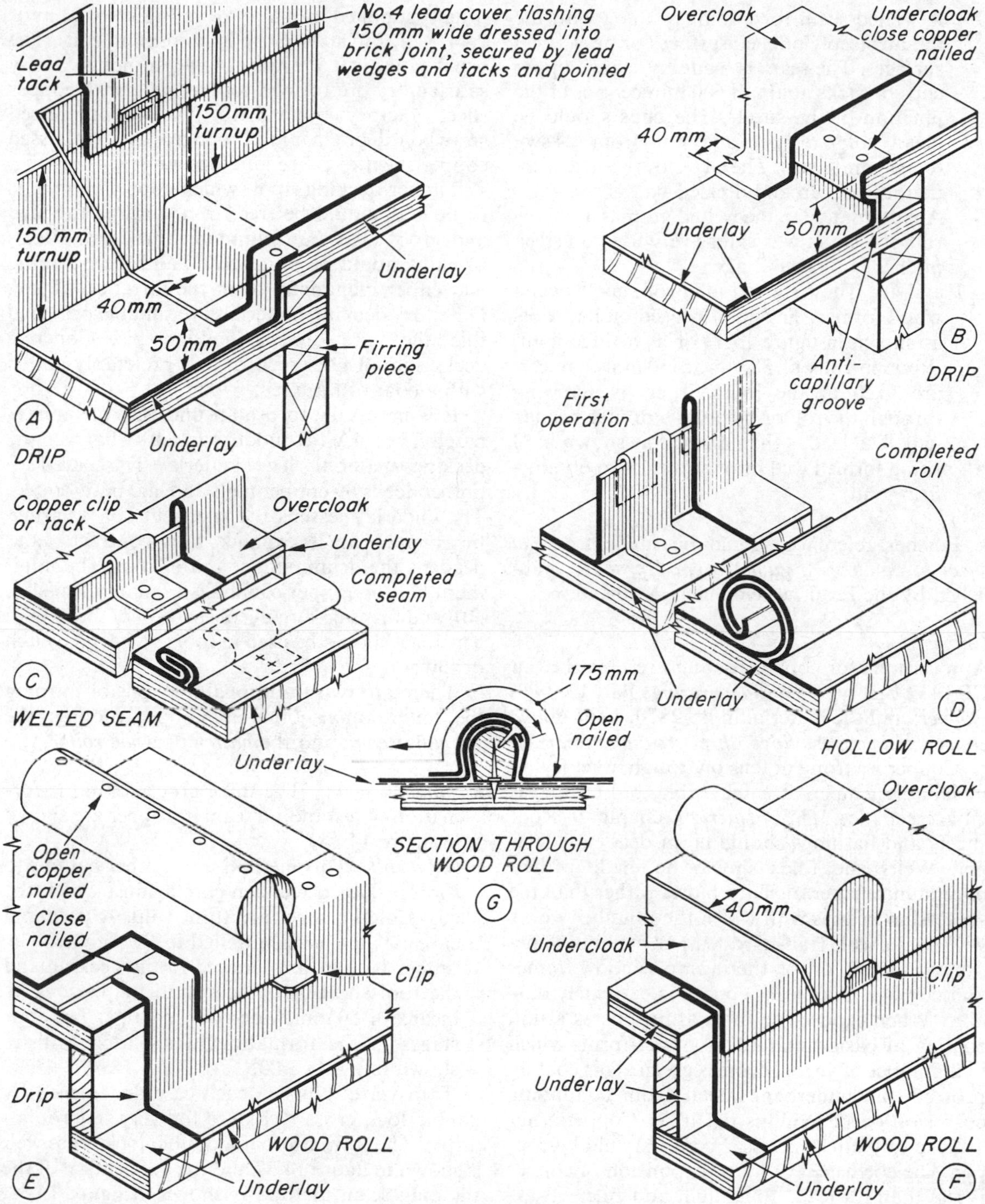
No.4 lead cover flashing
150 mm wide dressed into
brick joint, secured by lead
wedges and tacks and pointed
Lead
tack
150 mm
turnup
150 mm
turnup
Underlay
40 mm
50 mm
Firring
piece
Underlay
A
DRIP
Overcloak
Undercloak
close copper
nailed
40 mm
Underlay
50 mm
B
Anti-
capillary
groove
DRIP
First
operation
Completed
roll
Copper clip
or tack
Overcloak
Underlay
Completed
seam
C
WELTED SEAM
175 mm
Open
nailed
Underlay
Underlay
D
HOLLOW ROLL
SECTION THROUGH
WOOD ROLL
G
Open
copper
nailed
Close
nailed
Clip
Drip
WOOD ROLL
Underlay
E
Overcloak
40 mm
Undercloak
Clip
Underlay
WOOD ROLL
Underlay
F

14.34 *Lead sheeting details: joints*

C   A welted seam for a joint running with the fall on steeply pitched surfaces or on vertical surfaces. The seam is made by fixing copper clips or tacks at about 600 mm centres at the junction of the sheets. The clips should be 'dead soft' temper and cut from 24 swg (0.559 mm sheet). The edges of the sheets are then turned up and dressed flat as shown.

D   An alternative to the welted seam is a hollow roll of lead. It was extensively used on steep pitches in old buildings.

E, F and G   These show a solid roll, made over a wood former. This joint is used on flat roofs as shown in figure 14.33 or as a ridge joint. Wooden rolls of 38 mm to 50 mm diameter are fixed at the joint either by screwing through the roll or by using a double headed nail. The lead is then dressed as shown in G being formed well into the angles to obtain a firm joint.

Further reference should be made to *Lead sheet in building: a guide to good practice*, published by the Lead Development Association.

Copper

Applications for copper roofing are described in CP 143 *Sheet roof and wall coverings* Part 12: 1970 *Copper*; and the material in BS 2870: 1980 *Rolled copper and copper alloys: sheet strip and foil*.

Copper is strong in tension, tough, ductile and in suitable tempers it is malleable, but has negligible creep. See *MBS: Materials*, chapter 9. Roof sheets and flashings should be in dead soft temper. Welts and folds should be made with a minimum number of sharp blows rather than the succession of taps with which the plumber works with lead sheet. Half-hard temper metal is sometimes required for weatherings to window frames and copings. Like lead, copper is extremely durable. When exposed to most atmospheres a thin coating of basic sulphate of copper forms which in a number of years becomes green. This coating protects the underlying metal from continuing corrosion – even in industrial areas. Copper is not attacked by other metals. Fixings should be copper. The coefficient of linear expansion of copper is less than for lead, aluminium and zinc.

Fully supported copper sheet for roofing has a fire rating of AA in respect of BS 476. Sheets are usually supplied in 1.22×61 m, 1.83×0.91 m or 2.44×1.22 m sizes. Strip is supplied in coils. The usual gauge is 0.559 mm (24 swg) although a very satisfactory pre-formed roofing unit, with copper sheet, factory bonded to 50 mm compressed strawboard or 25 mm chipboard uses embossed copper sheet of 0.315 mm (30 swg).

Timber decking upon which copper roofing is to be laid should be free from 'spring', tongued and grooved 25 mm minimum thickness. Heads of nails should be punched in, and the boarding laid either diagonally or in the direction of fall. Other dry decking materials are suitable provided that they are dimensionally stable. Concrete decks should be screeded, and preferably sealed with a coat of bitumen.

It is necessary to use an underlay of impregnated Type 4A (ii) inodorous felt, whatever the decking material. The underlay is secured to timber decks by copper nails and laid butt jointed. The underlay lessens the possibility of 'wearing' the copper as it expands and contracts, and deadens the drumming sound of rain. The minimum fall for copper roofing is 12 mm in 1 m (1 in 60), and drips 63 mm deep, spaced not more than 3 m apart should be used in roofs of 5 degree pitch or lower.

There are two traditional methods of forming the longitudinal joints in copper roofing: the *standing seam*, and the *batten* or *wood roll*:

● *standing seam*   The three processes in the formation of a standing seam in copper are shown in figure 14.35

● *wood roll*   This method uses timber battens to form a shaped wooden core against which the edges of the sheet are turned up. A prepared capping strip is then welted to the flanges. The timber battens are screwed to the decking and the roof sheeting is secured to the battens by means of 50 mm wide copper strips. The four stages in the formation of a batten roll are shown in figure 14.35.

Transverse joints in each case are formed by double lock cross welts (or for very flat roofs – drips). The formation of a double-lock cross welt is shown in figure 14.37 and the application of the standing seam method is shown in figure 14.38. *Long strip 'economy' roofing* can be used where the total distance between eaves and ridge does

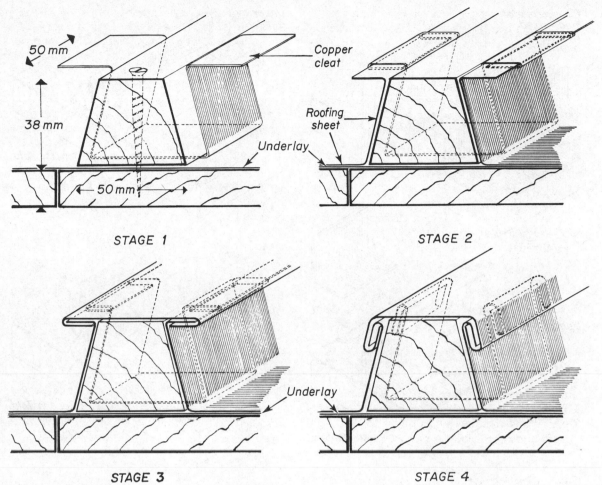

14.35 *Copper sheeting details: batten roll*

not exceed 8.5 m. Expansion cleats in the standing seam joint allow movement over this length.

A proprietary roofing material utilizes an indented copper sheet (42 gauge) backed with bitumen and laid as a top layer of built-up felt roofing on an underlayer of asbestos or glass fibre based bitumen felt. This copper/bitumen roofing gives the appearance of traditional copper at less cost.

Further details should be obtained from the Copper Development Association.

Zinc
Applications for zinc roofing are described in CP 143 *Roof and Wall Coverings* Part 5: 1964 *Zinc Sheet*. The metal is considered in *Materials* chapter 9 and is described in BS 6561: 1985 *Specification for zinc alloy sheet and strip for building*.

The minimum thickness of zinc sheet for roofing should not be less than 0.3 mm. In average urban conditions the maintenance-free life of zinc roofing conforming to the CP should not be less than 40 years for a roof laid to the minimum fall of 1 in 60 (approx. 1 degree). In rural areas or by the sea, and with steeper pitches, the life will be longer. Zinc is attacked by acids and water must not be allowed to drain from Western Red Cedar shingles on to a zinc roof, nor should drainage

357

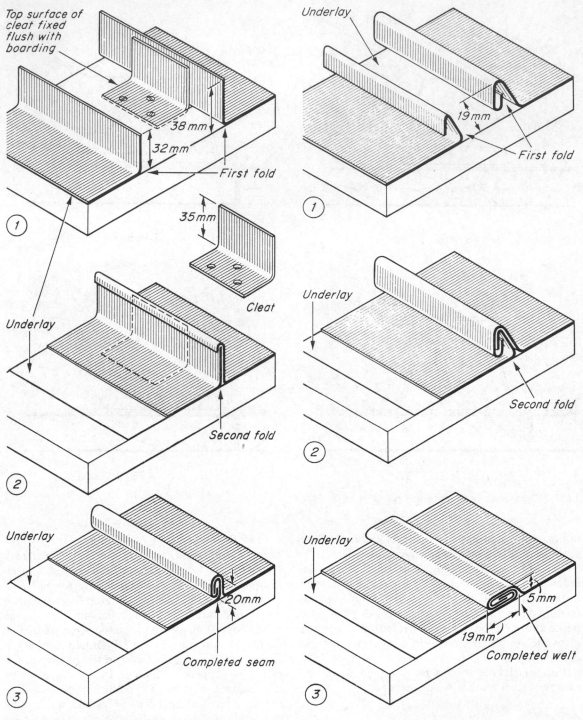

14.36 *Copper sheeting details: formation of a standing seam*

14.37 *Copper sheeting details: formation of a welted joint*

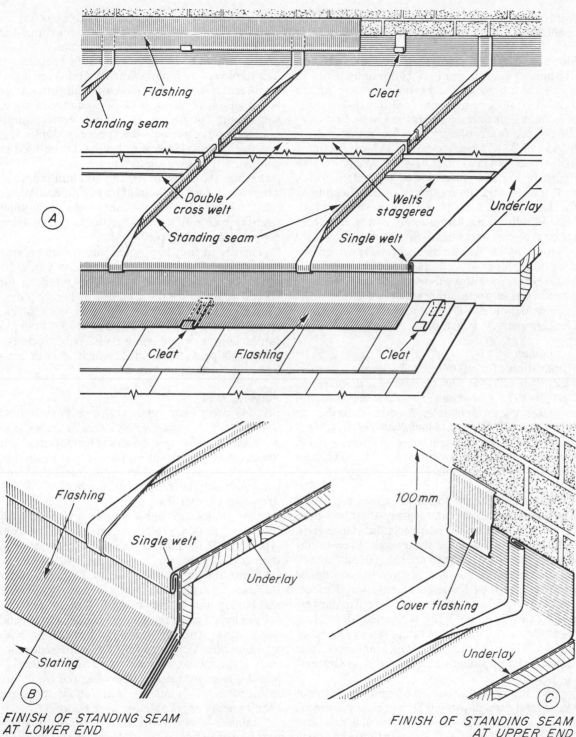

14.38 *Copper sheeting details: application of standing seam method*

359

from copper pipes discharge on to zinc. The coefficient of thermal expansion of zinc is greater than that of copper, but slightly less than lead. Standard sizes of zinc sheet are 2400 mm and 210 mm × 920 mm and as continuous strip in widths of up to 1 m. Zinc provides one of the lightest roof coverings which although less durable than lead or copper has the lowest first cost. Zinc sheet for roofing has a fire rating AA in respect of BS 476 (see page 332). Typical details of a flat roof covered in zinc sheet are shown in figure 14.39. The formation of the batten roll is shown at A and the treatment of the sheeting at the junction of a drip and roll is shown at B. Detail C shows the formation of a 'dog ear' at an internal corner and a detail of a holding down clip is shown at D. Saddle pieces are formed on the ends of cappings at walls and drips as shown at E and where a roof abuts the wall at a drip, a corner piece is welted to the upper sheet as shown at F. Further details should be obtained from the Zinc Development Association.

Aluminium

Applications for aluminium flat roofing are described in CP 143: *Sheet roof and wall coverings* Part 15: 1973 *Aluminium*. The metal is considered in *MBS: Materials* chapter 9, and is described in BS 1470: 1972 *Wrought aluminium and aluminium alloys for general engineering purposes – plate, sheet and strip*. Grades S1, S1A, S1B, S1C, NS3 and NS4 are all suitable for fully supported roof coverings.

Since aluminium forms a protective oxide when exposed to the atmosphere the alloy used for roofing is normally extremely durable even in industrial and marine atmospheres. Precautions must however be taken to avoid a galvanic attack with other materials and aluminium should be protected from wet concrete and mortar. Timbers containing acid and preservatives are also dangerous to the sheeting. Fully supported aluminium sheet for roofing has a fire rating AA in respect of BS 476. The techniques of laying aluminium fully supported roof coverings are similar to those of copper.

The minimum fall for an aluminium flat roof system is 1.60 and using 0.7 mm thickness sheets. Bay width should be between 450 mm and 600 mm with lengths of between 2.5 and 2.0 m

respectively. For a longer bay length of 3.0 m, the width should be restricted to 450 mm and the thickness of metal increased to 0.9 mm.

Aluminium is the lightest of roofing metals – it has ample strength and ductivity and creep is not significant. Hand forming is easiest in soft temper and high purity metal. It has a high reflectivity to solar heat. The durability of high purity aluminium is good in normal atmospheres provided it is washed by rain. However, it must not be used in contact with copper or copper alloys.

Fixings should be preferably of aluminium but where steel is used it should be galvanized. Water must not be allowed to drain on to aluminium from copper roofing and particularly not from copper expansion pipes.

The use of fully supported aluminium roofing has increased in popularity in recent years. Its initial bright appearance can be retained for several years in rural areas, but in highly industrial regions the surface will turn matt black. Aluminium to BS 1470 (S1C, 0-grade 99% purity) can be colour coated using PVF2 paint formulations: this provides a finish which is both malleable in working and durable.

Stainless steel

BS 1449 *Steel plate, sheet and strip* Part 2: 1983 *Specification for stainless and heat resisting steel plate, sheet and strip* provides information about the chemical composition, mechanical properties and dimensional tolerances for stainless steel, and the material is described further in *MBS: Materials* chapter 9.

Two grades are manufactured specifically for roofing: type 304 S16 for normal situations and type 316 S31 for more aggressive atmospheres in industrial and marine conditions. Although the standard thickness is 0.376 mm (28 swg), other thicknesses are available to order. Widths of sheets vary and lengths of up to 9 m are possible for pitches of more than 5 degrees. Sheets are laid using long strip or traditional methods with standing seams or batten rolls at centres depending on the gauge, exposure and roll width; 375 and 435 mm are usual. Otherwise, the sheets are installed on an underlay and follow the same requirements applicable to copper roofing.

Stainless steel is inherently resistant to corrosion and even has an invisible self-repairing oxide

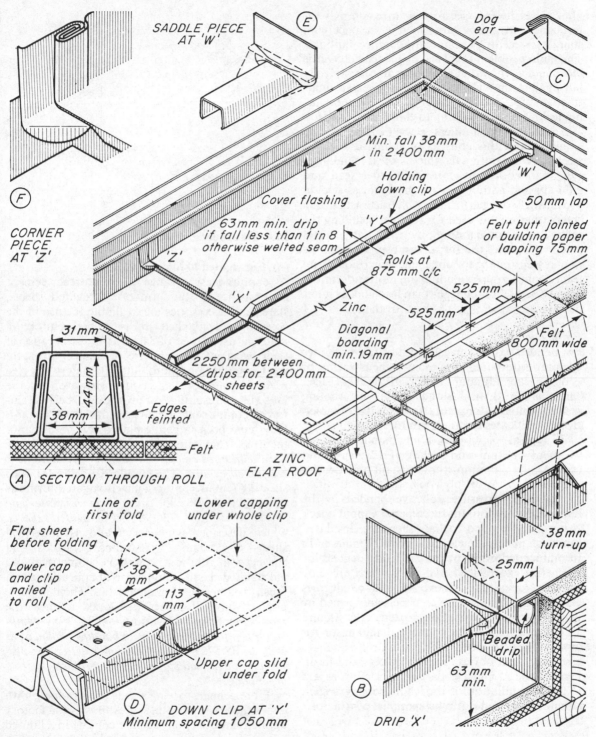

SADDLE PIECE AT 'W' (E)

Dog ear (C)

(F)

CORNER PIECE AT 'Z'

Min. fall 38mm in 2400mm

Cover flashing

Holding down clip

'W'

50 mm lap

63mm min. drip if fall less than 1 in 8 otherwise welted seam

'Y'

Felt butt jointed or building paper lapping 75mm

'Z'

Rolls at 875 mm c/c

'X'

525 mm

525 mm

Zinc

Diagonal boarding min.19mm

Felt 800mm wide

2250mm between drips for 2400mm sheets

31mm

44mm

38mm

Edges feinted

Felt

(A) SECTION THROUGH ROLL

ZINC FLAT ROOF

Line of first fold

Lower capping under whole clip

Flat sheet before folding

Lower cap and clip nailed to roll

38 mm

113 mm

Upper cap slid under fold

(D) DOWN CLIP AT 'Y' Minimum spacing 1050mm

38mm turn-up

25mm

Beaded drip

63mm min.

(B) DRIP 'X'

14.39 *Zinc sheeting details*

film. Nevertheless, electrolytic corrosion may affect zinc and aluminium when in contact with stainless steel in permanently damp conditions. The main problem involves the tendency towards *oil-canning*, where the sheet does not lie perfectly flat against the substrate, as this gives an unattractive appearance. However, new manufacturing techniques are helping to eliminate this affect.

Terne-coated stainless steel (TCSS) is now available and this consists of standard stainless steel used for roofing to which *terne* is metallurgically bonded. Terne consists of 80% lead and 20% tin and combines with the stainless steel in providing better performance characteristics than some other metals used for roofing: including the reduction of 'oil-canning'; increased fatigue and creep resistance, use for all atmospheres; and its non-susceptibility to bimetallic corrosion from lead, copper, zinc or aluminium, mortar or timber preservatives. It is cheaper than lead and, as it has little scrap value, is not subject to theft.

Pre-bonded panels
Pre-bonded panels consist of a substrate of timber or composite panel which has a metal facing of copper, lead, aluminium zinc or stainless steel. There is no British Standard for this roofing system, but most manufacturers have obtained BBA Certificates for their product.

A typical panel has a maximum standard width of 600 mm and length of 1219 mm, and consists of 18 mm moisture resistant high density chipboard, or WBP plywood substrate to which the metal is pressure adhesive bonded in the factory. An aluminium-faced paper vapour check is normally bonded to the other face. Insulated sandwich panels are also available. The minimum recommended pitch for the panels is 6 degrees for all metals except lead and zinc, which are only suitable for pitches above 45 and 65 degrees respectively. Joints between panels are formed by using standing seams or batten rolls (figure 14.40); but for lengths of more than 9 m, or for areas subject to foot traffic, batten roll joints are essential. Accessories, such as gutters and flashings, can be supplied as part of the roofing system and the installation of the whole roofing system should be carried out by a specialist contractor.

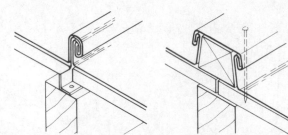

Welted seam   Capped wood–rolls

14.40 *Pre-bonded panel details*

14.4 Flat roofing sheets

(a) Corrugated fibre cement sheets

A comprehensive range of reinforced cement components in the form of corrugated sheets, slates and accessories are available for use in the covering of pitched roofs. The reinforcing material used to be of asbestos fibres because of their excellent inherent fire resistance, strength, weatherability and durability characteristics (see *MBS*: *Materials* chapter 10). However, as the loose fibres resulting from working asbestos reinforced components are an extreme health hazard, they have been largely replaced by those manufactured from safer materials, such as *cellulose fibre reinforced calcium-silicate* or *polymeric fibre reinforced cement*. The standard profile for roof sheeting remains in the same corrugated forms as those given in BS 690 *Asbestos cement slates and sheets* Part 3: 1973(1981) *Corrugated sheets*, which describes symmetrical and asymmetrical sheets of straight, longitudinal cranked and curved configuration, as well as geometrical and mechanical classification, general appearance and finish, and physical characteristics. The new components have also been developed to meet the requirements laid down in CP 4624: 1981 *Methods of test for asbestos cement building products*, as well as BS 5427: 1976 *Code of practice for performance and loading criteria for profiled sheeting in building*.

Fibre cement roofing sheets are available with either the textured natural grey finish, or a factory applied smooth epoxy surface coating in a limited range of colours.

362

Although complex shapes can be covered by fibre cement sheets, maximum economy is achieved where the roof is simple in plan shape. The roof should also be planned so that the purlin spacing allows the use of standard sheets without cutting to waste. Figure 14.41 gives an idea of the range of accessories available for use with standard profile sheets. Note that certain of the roof ventilators have integral soaker flanges and so dispense with the need of separate flashings.

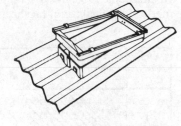

Adjustable close-fitting ridge

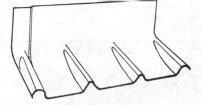

Cranked crown sheet

Ridge soaker with extractor ventilator

Roof light – opening type

Apron flashing piece

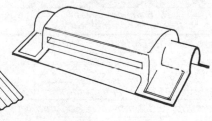

Dormer ventilator

Ridge ventilator

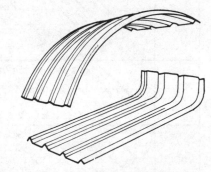

Curved and curved-end tiles

14.41 *Corrugated fibre cement sheeting details: accessories*

BS 690: Part 3 separates the sheeting for roofing and vertical cladding into five profile classes according to depth and minimum loadbearing capacity. Fittings are detailed in BS 690 Part 6: 1976. Figure 14.42 gives a range of the more commonly used profiles for roof sheeting. Metal fixing accessories are covered by BS 1494 *Fixing accessories for building purposes* Part 1: 1964. *Fixings for sheet, roof and wall coverings.* Sheets may be coloured by factory applied processing in a range of subdued colours giving a high resistance to fading. Profiled translucent sheeting made from glass fibre reinforced polyester-resin, and transparent sheets from rigid PVC are manufactured for use with the various sheet sections to give a natural diffused daylighting, and are available clear, or in a range of colours. The thermal transmittance (U) through a single layer of unlined roof sheeting is approximately 6.1 W/ m^2 K, so it is not acceptable under the *Building Regulations 1985* for dwellings. See page 328. A method of insulating the sheets which satisfies the Regulations, and which does not require the use of additional supporting members, is to incorporate a top corrugated sheet with an associated lining panel. BS 690 Part 5: 1975 is relevant to lining sheets and panels. The cavity between the two sheet layers accommodates an additional insulant in the form of a glass fibre or mineral wool mat 60 mm thick which improves the insulation value of the structure and at the same time restricts the flow of free air circulating within the cavity. This sytem of construction thus improves insulation and helps to provide a reasonable dust tight covering. Several types of sandwich construction are available and two typical profiles are illustrated in figure 14.43. However, insulated double cladding can also be arranged with timber spacer pieces fixed between the lining panels and corrugated sheets as indicated in figure 14.44. This method avoids compression of the insulation infill by the superimposed weight of the top sheeting and thereby provides a further improved U value. The mandatory U-values of 0.6 or

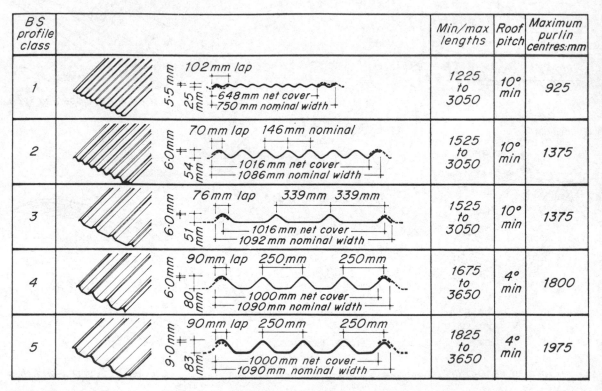

BS profile class		Min/max lengths	Roof pitch	Maximum purlin centres:mm
1	5·5 mm, 25 mm · 102 mm lap · 648 mm net cover · 750 mm nominal width	1225 to 3050	10° min	925
2	6·0mm, 54 mm · 70 mm lap 146 mm nominal · 1016 mm net cover · 1086 mm nominal width	1525 to 3050	10° min	1375
3	6·0mm, 51 mm · 76 mm lap 339mm 339mm · 1016 mm net cover · 1092 mm nominal width	1525 to 3050	10° min	1375
4	6·0mm, 80 mm · 90mm lap 250 mm 250mm · 1000mm net cover · 1090mm nominal width	1675 to 3650	4° min	1800
5	9·0mm, 83 mm · 90mm lap 250mm 250mm · 1000mm net cover · 1090mm nominal width	1825 to 3650	4° min	1975

14.42 *Corrugated fibre cement sheeting details: profiles*

0.7 W/m² K for roofs of non-domestic buildings (see page 328), makes it essential to use spacers in sandwich construction. The internal lining sheet can be of profiled sheet steel finished with an acrylic coating which is available in a wide range of colours as specified in BS 4904: 1978(1985) *Specification for external cladding colours for building purposes*, or BS 4903: 1979 *Specifications for external colours for farm buildings.*

Where it is considered necessary to provide

BS profile class		Thermal insulation 'U' approx.	
		Sandwich (25mm glass fibre insulant)	Single skin
2		1·00 W/m² K	6·1 W/m² K
3		1·00 W/m² K	6·1 W/m² K

14.43 *Corrugated fibre cement sheeting details: insulated double cladding profiles*

Thermal insulation ('U' valve) for quilt thickness

60mm	80mm	100mm
0·55	0·46	0·41

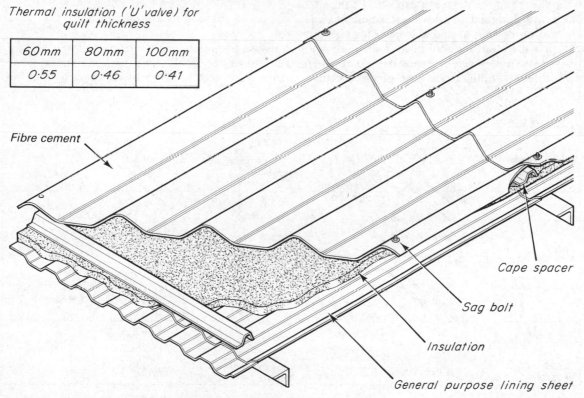

Fibre cement

Cape spacer

Sag bolt

Insulation

General purpose lining sheet

14.44 *Corrugated fibre cement sheeting details: insulated double cladding profile*

insulated natural lighting panels in conjunction with the insulated roofing, hermetically sealed insulated roof lights or translucent lining panels are available. As an alternative to sandwich construction satisfactory thermal insulation can be obtained by 'under drawing' or lining the roof above or below the purlin by suitable rigid sheet of insulation material such as fibre building board or plasterboard which incorporates insulation.

Fixing for fibre reinforced cement sheeting should not be rigid since allowance must be made for slight movement. Usual fixings are various types of hook bolts which pass through the asbestos sheet and clip round steel or concrete purlins, or drive screws into timber purlins or timber plugs in concrete purlins as shown in figure 14.45. In order to accommodate movement and render the detail weathertight a plastic washer with a separate dome shaped cap-seal is used, as shown in figure 14.46. Alternatively galvanized steel or bitumen washers are available. The minimum pitch of the roof will vary according to the profile of the sheet and the degree of exposure of the site. Sheets are designed to provide resistance to the penetration of rain at end and side laps without seals provided that the roof pitch is adequate and the site is not severely exposed. Where such conditions are fulfilled the base of the corruga-

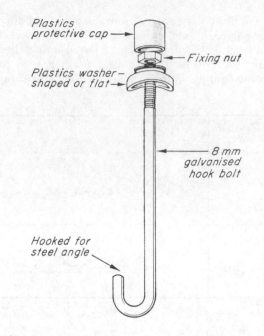

14.46 *Corrugated fibre cement sheeting details: hook bolt*

tions act as gutters and the rainwater will usually run down the roof slope without the risk of penetration into the interior. A shallow pitch or

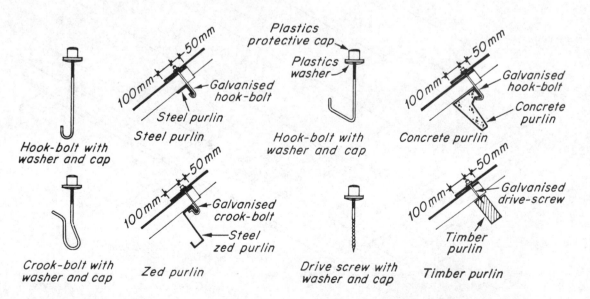

14.45 *Corrugated fibre cement sheeting details: purlin fixings*

wind blowing at the slope of the roof may reduce the velocity of flow sufficient to cause a build-up of water which may then be forced under the joints in the sheets. In such conditions, or to prevent dust penetration, it is necessary to seal the laps. Figure 14.47, taken from BS 5247: *Code of practice for sheet roof and wall coverings* Part 14 1973, *Corrugated asbestos cement* may be used as a guide.

The 4 degree pitch is recommended only for a limited number of profiles and the manufacturers should be consulted to check suitability. Where it is necessary to use a mastic seal 8 mm extruded mastic strip should be used. The type and method of laying should be as directed by the manufacturers. It should be borne in mind, however, that the efficiency of the seal can be affected by the temperature at which it is laid and it is recommended that a routine check be made on the compression of mastic laid during winter months.

Laying procedure Sheets should be fixed in accordance with the recommendations made in BS 5427: 1976 *Code of Practice of performance and loading criteria for profiled sheeting in building*. Fixing holes should never be punched, they should always be drilled through the crown of the corrugations. Always use roof ladders to avoid damaging the roof sheets when fixing and provide properly constructed walkways or roof boards where it is necessary to give regular access to roof lights, or other places likely to need periodical attention, and maintenance.

Sheets are designed to be laid smooth side to the weather with a side lap of one corrugation. They are fastened through the crowns of corrugations on each side of the side laps except at each intermediate purlin where one fixing only on the overlapping side is adequate. The laying procedure is shown in figure 14.48. Working upwards from the eaves sheets may be laid either from left to right, or right to left, but it is advisable to commence at the end away from the prevailing wind. The starter sheet and the last sheet to be fixed are laid unmitred, all other sheets require mitring where the overlap occurs as shown.

Lap treatment*	Minimum sheet pitch†	
	Profile class 3 and 4 BS 690 : Part 3	Profile class 1 and 2 BS 690 : Part 3
	Degrees	Degrees
(a) Sheltered and normal sites‡		
150 mm end laps unsealed	22½	22½
300 mm end laps unsealed	15	15
150 mm end laps with end laps sealed	15	10
150 mm end laps with side end laps sealed	20	4
(b) Exposed sites		
150 mm end laps unsealed	25	25
150 mm end laps with end laps sealed	17½	15
150 mm end laps with side and end laps sealed	15	10
300 mm end laps with side and end laps sealed	10	4

* The table should be used as a guide for roof slopes up to 32 m in length. For recommendations for roof slopes over 32 in length, the manufacturer's advice should be sought.

† Pitches detailed above are the minimum for the sheeting as laid, therefore it is important that the pitch of the rafter is designed to take into account the lapping of the sheeting including mastic (which reduces the pitch by ½ degree for unsealed laps and by 1 degree for sealed laps) and the deflection of the supporting structure due to live and dead loads.

‡ The degree of exposure to be taken for design purposes is a matter of experience coupled with local knowledge, and the above table should be regarded as a guide. In case of doubt the advice of the manufacturer should be sought.

For the purpose of this table, an exposed site is one where the wind suction on any part of the roof cladding exceeds 1200 N/m² when calculated in accordance with CP 3 chapter V: Part 2.

14.47 *Minimum sheet pitches and corresponding lap treatments*

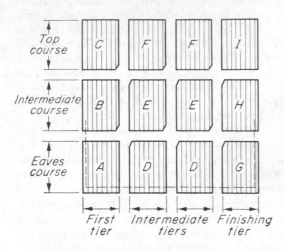

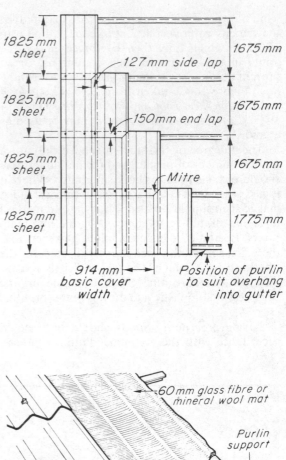

14.48 *Corrugated fibre cement sheeting details: laying procedure*

With insulated double cladding the fixing procedure is similar. The lining panels are first laid mitred as for the roofing sheets except that they are laid smooth side to the underside. The sheets are secured with a short bolt through the intermediate corrugation. Lining panels are then overlaid with a glass fibre or mineral wool insulating mat which should have a minimum 100 mm lap to all joints. The laying of the final covering sheet then proceeds as before. A typical double cladding unit is shown in figure 14.49. Figure 14.50 shows a typical roof sheeting arrangement using single skin construction suitable for a storage building where space heating is not required. Detail A shows the finish at the eaves. The sheets should not have an unsupported overhang of more than 300 mm beyond the eaves purlin and the detail is completed by an eaves filler component. Details B and C show the method of construction where a translucent roof light is used. The translucent sheet is unmitred, and 13 mm diameter sealing strips are used at the end laps. Detail D shows a close fitting ridge. Because it is in two parts, it is adjustable to suit various degrees of slope. An alternative apex detail is shown using a cranked crown sheet. The correct positioning of the top purlin is important and

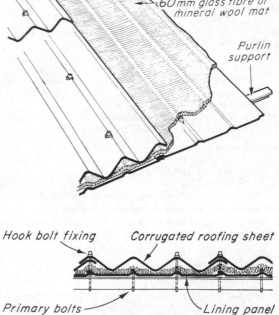

14.49 *Corrugated fibre cement sheeting details: laying procedure*

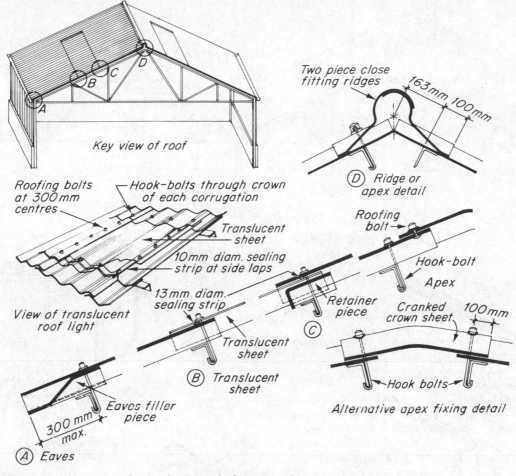

14.50 *Corrugated fibre cement sheeting details: single skin construction*

should be arranged so that the hook bolt fixing is not less than 100 mm from the end of the crown sheet.

Figure 14.51 illustrates the use of insulated double cladding. The eaves detail at A indicates the use of eaves filler pieces and a method of fixing an asbestos gutter by means of front and back plates. B shows a typical end lap detail at an intermediate purlin. Detail D is a section through the roof verge and illustrates the barge board component which provides a neat finish between the vertical cladding and roof sheeting. Details E, F and G show the method of detailing the translucent roof sheeting. Note the use of the closure piece on the underside of the roof. H shows the use of a valley gutter and the method of flashing the sheets into the gutter. J gives the fixing of the cranked crown sheet and lining panel at the apex of the roof.

Fibre cement sheets for roofing have P60 (Ext S AA) fire rating to BS 476: Part 3, and are non-combustible to BS 476: Part 4 (see page 332). When an insulated sandwich roof system incorporating a metal internal lining is used, the combined construction achieves an *internal* fire resistance of up to 4 hours (fibre cement itself has no fire resistance). The internal lining has a Class 1 surface spread of flame classification to BS 476: Part 7, or Class 0 classification in accordance with the *Building Regulations 1985*.

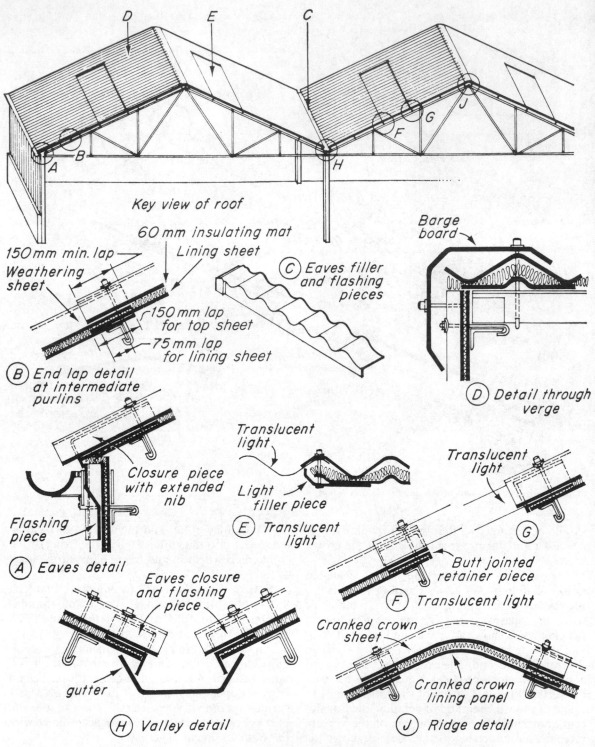

Key view of roof

150 mm min. lap

Weathering
sheet

60 mm insulating mat

Lining sheet

150 mm lap
for top sheet

75 mm lap
for lining sheet

B End lap detail
at intermediate
purlins

C Eaves filler
and flashing
pieces

Barge
board

D Detail through
verge

Closure piece
with extended
nib

Flashing
piece

A Eaves detail

Translucent
light

Light
filler piece

E Translucent
light

Translucent
light

Butt jointed
retainer piece

F Translucent light

G

Eaves closure
and flashing
piece

gutter

H Valley detail

Cranked crown
sheet

Cranked crown
lining panel

J Ridge detail

14.51 *Corrugated fibre cement sheeting details: insulated double cladding fixings*

(b) Profiled aluminium sheeting

BSCP 143 *Sheet roof and wall coverings*, Part 1: 1958 *Aluminium, corrugated and troughed*, describes the main types of roof sheeting and gives information on fixing accessories, contact with other materials, weathering, thermal insulation, fire resistance and condensation, as well as recommendations about minimum pitch, methods of fixing, side and end laps. BS 4868: 1972 *Profiled aluminium sheet for building* specifies two suitable alloys: NS3–H8 to BS 1470, and NS 31–H6 to BS 4300/6.

The behaviour of aluminium when exposed to the atmosphere is discussed on page 360. Profiled sheets are available with a plain mill finish which darkens as it weathers, or with an organic coating (see page 360) in a range of bright colours. There are also alkyd-amino coatings which can be stoved on in the factory after forming as well as a range of PVF2/acrylic paints.

Figure 14.52 shows the BS 4868 profiles and specialist manufacturers produce a more extended range. Some include an interlocking edge profile which reduces the number of visible fixings, and a sandwich roofing system which incorporates thermal insulation between two skins of aluminium sheeting (a single aluminium sheet has a U value of 2.6 W/m^2 K). Single and double glazed translucent plastics sheets to match the aluminium profiles are available. The minimum recommended gauges of aluminium for durability related to the use of sheeting are as follows:

Use	SWG
Heavy and marine industrial	18
Industrial	20
Light industrial	22
Agricultural	24

Fixing techniques for the ordinary profiled sheets shown in figure 14.52 follow the principles used for fibre cement sheeting. Hook bolts are used to secure the sheets to purlins, but in addition, the side laps should be secured by bolts or rivets passing through the crown of the profile. A comprehensive range of accessories is available in 20 and 22 swg, and aluminium alloy fixings are preferable although galvanized fittings may be acceptable in a non-polluted atmosphere. Flashings for aluminium roofing are preferably preformed and of $\frac{1}{2}$ H or $\frac{3}{4}$ H temper aluminium.

Figure 14.53 indicates methods of fixing interlocking profiled sheets to the roof sub-structure by special clips fixed by mechanical fasteners to the purlins. With this method no through-fixing of the roof sheeting is required. The linear panels are positioned first with all joints lapped and fixed to the roof purlins. All joints are sealed with PVC tape or mastic, and any swarf or debris is removed from the panels before covering the whole instal-

Type	Profile with nominal pitch	Gauge	Available sizes (max. and min.)	
			Width	Length
Corrugated sheet BS 4868 type S	76.2mm 76.2mm / 19 mm	1.00 mm to 0.5 mm	1118 to 508mm	Any length to 1.22 m
Trough sheet BS 4868 type A	127 mm / 38.1mm	0.9 mm to 0.7 mm	1187 to 579mm	Any length to 7.62 m
Heavy trough sheet BS 4868 type B	130.2mm / 44.5 mm	1.2 mm to 1.00 mm	1229 to 705mm	Any length to 7.62 m

14.52 *Profiled aluminium sheeting details: profiles*

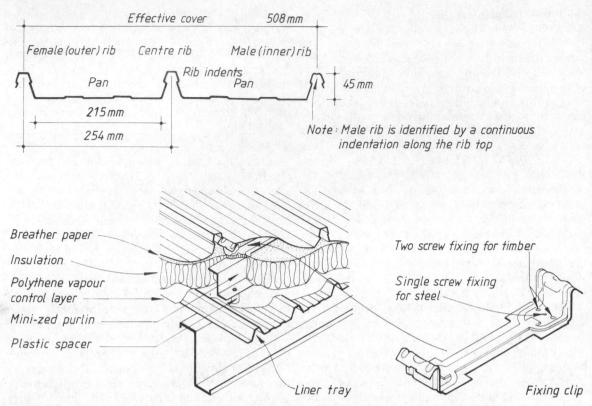

14.53 *Profiled aluminium sheeting details: insulated double cladding (a) profile of 'SpeedDeck' sheet; (b) typical fixing details; (c) detail of fixing clip located immediately below outer sheet*

lation with vapour control sheets made continuous by lapping all joints and sealing with PVC tape. The mini-zed purlins are then fixed through nylon spacers and liner panel to the roof purlins. A mineral wool blanket is placed over the mini-zed purlins and pushed tightly around each of them. The breather paper is then placed over the insulation and the mini-zed purlins so that any moisture vapour getting into the insulation from below can ventilate to the outside. Finally, secret fixing clips are fixed by self-tapping screws into the mini-zed purlins and the top sheet is secured by pushing down firmly to engage profiles.

Fire ratings for profiled aluminium sheeting are as described for the fibre reinforced cement construction on page 369.

(c) Profiled steel

BSCP 143 *Sheet roof and wall coverings*, Part 10: *Galvanized corrugated steel* deals with materials,

appliances, components, design considerations, application and maintenance, together with information on weather tightness, durability, thermal insulation, fire-hazard, rain water drainage and other characteristics. Steel for profiling should comply with BS 2989: 1982 *Specification for continuously hot dip zinc coated and iron-zinc alloy coated steel*. Profiles are available in both rounded and sharp profiles, and in 6 m × 1.2 m maximum size panels or 13 m maximum lengths, 1.0 m wide. Thickness gauges are from 0.3 mm (30 swg) to 1.6 mm (16 swg).

Unprotected steel would have a very short life, but zinc coating (galvanizing) affords substantial protection at relatively low cost (*MBS: Materials* chapter 9). Finish can be natural hot dipped galvanized or hot dipped zinc/aluminized steel; or with an addition to galvanizing of PVC Plastisol factory applied as a liquid to provide a textured surface, silicone polyester stoving, polyvinylidene fluorides (PVF) coating, or acrylic modified polyester coating.

Fixing methods for profiled steel roofing, single sheets U = 0.3 W/m² K) or sandwich construction, are similar to aluminium profiled roofing, and also have the same fire ratings.

14.5 Suspended and air supported roofing membranes

In certain situations, thin fabric membranes are either suspended by external tension cables or supported by internal air pressure to form the walls and roof of a building. Since the 1950s, this form of building has developed in use from temporary pavilions for festivals and exhibitions to more permanent structures of every description, including factories and laboratories. During this period, the design of the structures has been reflected by progress made in the development of fabric membranes materials. Early versions consisted of cotton, cotton polyester, and simple PVC coated nylons and polyesters as well as Neoprene or Hypalon coated nylons. These were either short lasting or expensive.

The most commonly employed fabric membrane used for this purpose today consists of Teflon coated glass fibre. This woven glass fabric is immensely strong and has the advantage of being inert and rot proof. The waterproofing is provided by Teflon, which is a fluorocarbon resin providing additional characteristics of durability and translucence (15% daylight transmission). An alternative waterproof coating with similar properties is silicon, and it is transparent (80% daylight transmission).

Teflon or silicon coated glass fibre fabric membranes in themselves provide virtually no thermal control and their application must, therefore, be limited. It is technically possible to add insulation by using two layers of fabric between which is a quilt of mineral wool, but daylight transmission will be neglible.

There is no British Standard on fabric membranes, and when compared with conventional fully supported roof coverings, their use is still considered to be experimental and insurance warranties may be difficult to obtain. Nevertheless, there are an every increasing number of applications to be studied and the resulting visual forms are exciting. Their use allows relatively large areas to be covered which are free from internal supports: when used with a structural suspension system, the frequency of fixings must be determined by calculation using three-dimensional models and special computer programs which allow the development of a satisfactory shape for the building.

14.6 Pitched roofing coverings

Pitched roof coverings may consist of the membranes or the large sheets and units already considered under 14.4 Flat roof coverings, or more usually, of the small dry-jointed units described as slates and tiles. Slates and tiles provide a *semi-permeable barrier* to weather penetration, and need to be used in conjunction with a backing *water barrier* of impervious felt or plastics sheet in order to provide a complete weather seal (see 14.2(b) Weather exclusion). Another system of pitched roof covering involves the traditional method of *thatching*.

Roofing slates are made from stone and fibre cement; tiles from clay, concrete, fibre cement, reinforced bitumen strip, metal, and wood (shingles). It is important to distinguish between those units which *overlap*, such as plain tile, pantiles and slates; and those which *interlock* (see figure 14.54). Of those which overlap, plain tiles and slates are laid to a **double lap**, whereas pantiles are laid to a **single lap**. Tiles which **interlock** may do so on two sides or on all four sides.

BS 5534 *Code of practice for slating and tiling*: Part 1: 1978 *Design* deals with the design and application of both slating and tiling, including the provision of underlay, boarding, counter battens, battens and their fixing; Part 2: 1986 *Design charts for fixing roof slating and tiling against wind uplift*, describes methods for determining the deadweight and nailing resistances against wind uplift in roofs of ridge height not exceeding 30 m above ground. Another useful reference source is *The Redland Roofing Manual: A guide to good practice and Redland roofing system* published by Redland Roof Tiles Limited.

The pitched roof construction is required to meet the thermal insulation standards of the

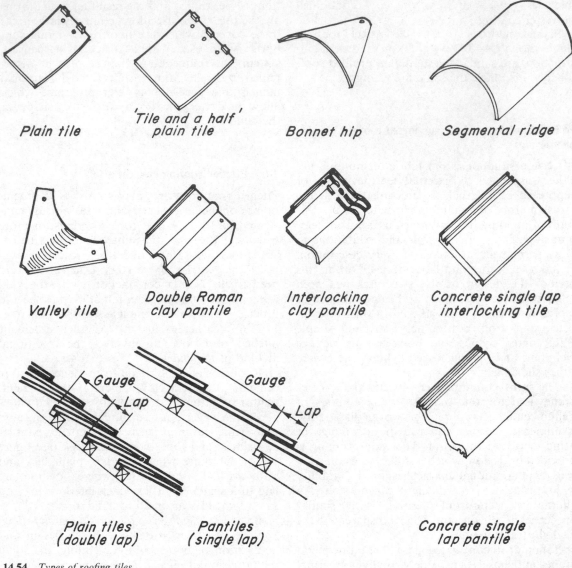

Plain tile

'Tile and a half' plain tile

Bonnet hip

Segmental ridge

Valley tile

Double Roman clay pantile

Interlocking clay pantile

Concrete single lap interlocking tile

Gauge

Lap

Gauge

Lap

Plain tiles (double lap)

Pantiles (single lap)

Concrete single lap pantile

14.54   *Types of roofing tiles*

Building Regulations 1985 and this is discussed in some detail under 14.2(d) Thermal control. For dwellings the required thermal transmittance (U) of 0.35 W/m² K is most simply achieved through the use of an 100 mm minimum thickness mineral wool (or similar material) insulation quilt. An alternative is to follow *Approved Document L: Procedure 2* as explained under 6.2(e) Thermal control: if the effect of the rest of the construction is taken into account, the insulation thickness can be reduced. The provision of thermal insulation must go hand-in-hand with the provision of effective vapour control mechanisms, as explained under 14.2(e). A vapour check is necessary on the 'warm' side of the insulation, and ventilation slots are required along the eaves to ensure adequate dispersal of moisture vapour, as shown in figures 14.55 and 14.58.

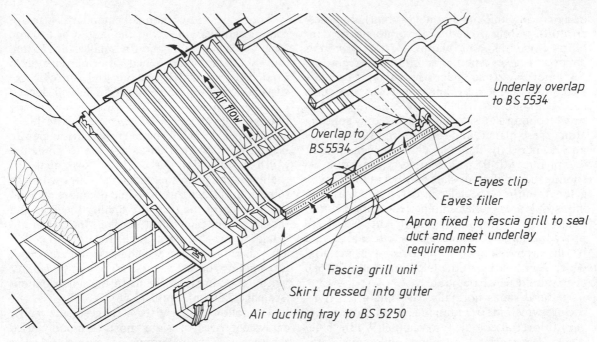

14.55 *Proprietary plastics airduct tray to BS 5250*

When correctly installed on timber rafters, with or without underfelt or boarding, slates and tiles have an AA external fire designation in the *Building Regulations 1985*: *Approved Document B* (see 14.2(f) Fire precautions). Slates and tiles with a backing of battens, counterbattens, underfelt and boarding (or plywood) provide a defence against burglars as well as better wind resistance when compared with a backing of battens, underfelt and open rafters.

The approximate installed weight of pitched roof coverings are as indicated below. It is important to check with manufacturers and/or suppliers to obtain precise weights according to specification of materials used.

Material	Approx installed weight (kg/m²)
Natural slates	28.0– 38.0
Fibre cement slates	20.3– 23.1
Plain tiles (double lap)	
clay	67.1– 76.2
concrete	80.0–104.0
Interlocking tiles	
clay	39.0– 50.0
concrete	43.9– 50.6
Bitumen strip	10.0
Metal multi-tiles	7.7
Wood shingles	7.5

(a) Slates

There are two forms of roofing slates: those made from natural stone, and those made from a composition of factory produced materials (fibre cement). They are classified as *double lap units*.

Natural slates

Natural roofing slates are obtained from the rock beds of Wales, North Lancashire, Westmorland and Cornwall. The slates should comply with BS 680 *Roofing slates* Part 2: 1971 *Metric units* which describes those from the Cambrian, Ordovician, Silurian, Devonian, and Dalradian formations; and describes characteristics, standard

375

designations, thickness gradings, marketing descriptons, testing procedure for atmospheric conditions, lengths and widths. *MBS: Materials* chapter 4 gives specific information regarding Metamorphic stone under which slate is categorized; it is formed by immense earth pressures acting upon clays which produce *planes of cleavage*. Roofing slates are manufactured by splitting along these planes, and the resulting surface may not be perfectly flat. Good slate, such as that complying with BS 680, provides a most durable roofing material: poor slate may begin to decay in a few months, especially in damp conditions in industrial areas. Slates imported from France, Spain and Portugal for use in the UK have proved to be of excellent quality, but care should be taken by designers when using a material which is not native to the UK climate and BS 680 tests should be carried out.

Natural slates normally have fine grain riven texture which may contain ingrained stripes, and vary in overall colour, for example: Welsh, blue/black; Westmorland, blue/grey, olive green, light green; Cornish, blue/grey to grey/green; and French, black.

There are more than 20 'standard' sizes of roofing slate varying from the largest at 610 mm long × 355 mm wide, and the smallest at 255 mm long × 150 mm wide. When rainwater falls on to a pitched roof it will fan out and run over the surface at a given angle. This angle will depend upon the pitch of the roof and is commonly referred to as the *angle of creep*, see figure 14.56. The steeper the pitch the narrower the angle will be and this can be used as a guide to minimum width of the slate used. It follows that the shallower the pitch the wider the slates will have to be and as a general principle the more exposed the position of the roof the smaller the slate and the steeper the pitch must be. Thus the larger unit is laid on the shallower pitch. In order to collect any wind blown water which passes the *rain check* provided by the slates, an underlay of *untearable felt* must be provided beneath the fixing battens (see page 322 and figure 14.58).

The following list gives a range of the metric equivalent sizes of slate most commonly used together with the recommended minimum rafter pitch.

Sizes of slates: length × width (mm)	Minimum pitch
305 × 205	45 degrees
330 × 180	40 degrees
405 × 205	35 degrees
510 × 255	30 degrees
610 × 305	25 degrees
610 × 355	22½ degrees

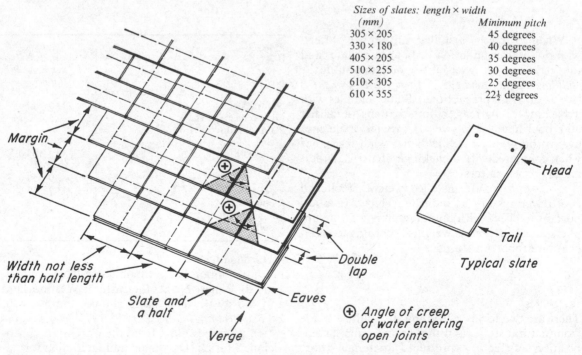

Margin

Width not less than half length

Slate and a half

Verge

Eaves

Double lap

Head

Tail

Typical slate

⊕ Angle of creep of water entering open joints

14.56 *Slating details: angle of creep*

The thickness of slates varies according to the source, those from Westmorland and North Lancashire being relatively thick and coarser in surface texture. The thickest slates from any quarry are called *Bests* or *Firsts*, and the thinner slates, *Seconds* and *Thirds*. Thus, this description does not refer to quality, but is an indication of thickness. Where slates supplied vary in thickness the thinner slates should be used at the ridge and the thicker slates at lower courses.

Each row of slates is laid starting from the eaves, and is butt jointed at the side and overlapped at the head (see figure 14.56). Slates are laid *double lap* with special slates at the eaves and verge. This means that there are two thicknesses of slate *over* each nail hole as protection, making in all, three thicknesses of material at the overlaps[1]. The side joint should be left very slightly open so that water will drain quickly. Each slate is nailed twice. The slate should be holed so that the 'spoiling' will form a counter sinking for the nail heads. The slates are best holed by machine on the site so that the holes can be correctly positioned by the fixers. The nails should be of yellow metal, aluminium alloy, copper or zinc. They are 32 mm long for the lighter and smaller slates up to 63 mm long for the heavier slates. Galvanized nails are not recommended. The slates may be either centre nailed or head nailed. For centre nailing, the nail

[1]See figures 14.54 and 14.66.

holes are positioned by reference to the gauge and lap so that the nails just clear the head of the slates in the course below. Centre nailed slates on battens and counter battens on felt are illustrated in figure 14.57. For head nailed slates the holes will be positioned about 25 mm from the upper edge of the slate. Head nailed slates on battens and counterbattens on felt are illustrated in 14.58. The holes should not be nearer than 25 mm to the side of the slate. Centre nailing gives more protection against lifting in the wind or chattering. The technique of head nailing should therefore only be used on smaller sizes of slate. Because of the angle of creep the width of slate is chosen having in mind the pitch of the roof, the shallower the pitch the larger the unit required. The headlap is chosen according to the degree of exposure, and in relation to the pitch, since the steeper the pitch the quicker the run off. The following minimum laps can be taken as a guide for moderate exposure:

Rafter	Head laps
22¼ degrees	100 mm
25 degrees	90 mm
30 degrees	75 mm
40 degrees	65 mm

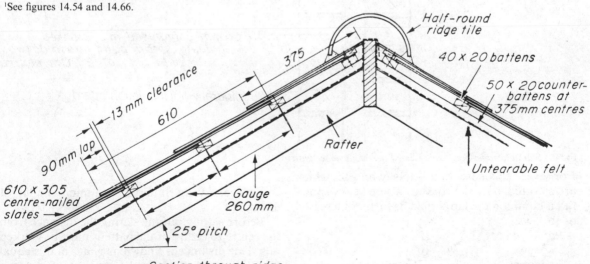

14.57 *Slating details: centre nailed slates showing counterbattens*

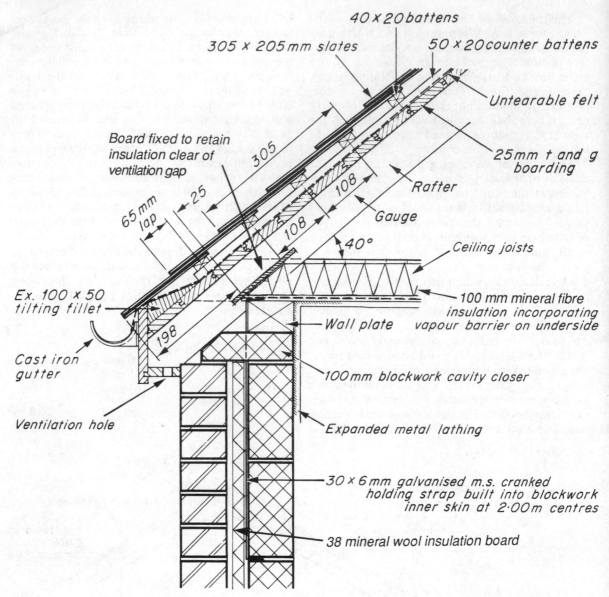

14.58 *Slating details: head nailed slated showing counter battens*

For severe exposure, that is to say on sites which are elevated, near the coast or where heavy snow-fall is common the lap should be further increased as follows:

Rafter pitches	Head laps
25 degrees	100 mm
30 degrees	75 mm

(See BS 5534: Part 1: 1978 and BRE Digest 23.)

Vertical slating should have a minimum lap of 30 mm.

Before setting out the slating the distance from the centre to centre of the battens must be worked out. This distance is known as *gauge* and is equal to the *margin* which is the amount of exposed slate measured up the slope of the roof. The gauge may be worked out as follows:

378

First decide on the head lap required with regard to the degree of exposure, say for example 90 mm at 25 degree pitch, using 610 mm × 305 mm slates. Then for centre nailed slates:

$$\text{gauge} = \frac{\text{length of slate} - \text{lap}}{2}$$

$$= \frac{610 - 90}{2}$$

$$= 260 \text{ mm (see figure 14.57)}.$$

If the slates are head nailed allowance must be made for the fact that the nail holes are positioned 25 mm from the top of the slates. For example, 65 mm lap for 305 mm × 205 mm slates at 40 degree pitch:

$$\text{gauge} = \frac{\text{length of slate} - (\text{lap} + 25 \text{ mm})}{2}$$

$$= \frac{305 - (65 + 25)}{2}$$

$$= 108 \text{ mm (see figure 14.58)}.$$

The preserved timber battens upon which the slates are fixed should not be less than 40 mm wide and of sufficient thickness to prevent undue springing back as the slates are being nailed through them. Thus the thickness of the battens will depend upon the spacing of the rafters and for rafters at say 400 mm to 460 mm centres and battens should be 20 mm thick.

Eaves courses of slates must always be head nailed and the length of the eaves slate is thus worked out as follows:

Length of slate at eaves
    = gauge × lap × 25 mm
Therefore previous example
    = 108 + 65 + 25 = 198 mm

In order that the maximum width of lateral cover is maintained the slates are laid half-bond so that the joints occur as near as possible over the centre of slates in the course below. This means that in each alternate course the slate at the verge will be '*slate and a half*' in width. Slating can be laid so that the gauge diminishes towards the ridge and this is known as laying in '*diminish-*

ing courses'. This technique gives an attractive appearance, particularly where slates of *random widths* are used.

It requires skilled craftsmanship to ensure correct bonding, and minimum lap should be specified which can be increased by the slates as required to maintain the diminishing margins. The technique is shown in figure 14.59 in which random width slates are illustrated.

Slating should overhang slightly at the verge in order to protect the structure below. The average overhang of the slate is 50 mm and the edge of the slate is supported by using an undercloak of slate or fibre cement sheeting bedded on the walling. The verge should have an inward tilt and the bedding mortar is usually 1:5 cement/sand by volume. The detail is shown in figure 14.60. Alternatively, the roof structure, supported on sprockets built into the brickwork may overhang the wall and be finished off with a timber *barge board*. The verge slating will then project slightly beyond the barge board.

Hips can be finished with lead rolls or with tiles but for the steeper pitches the neatest solution is to cut the slates and mitre them along the head using metal soakers lapped and bonded with each course and nailed at the top edges. Specially wide slates should be used so that the side bond is maintained when the slate is cut. Valleys are usually formed by having a dressed metal valley gutter and raking cut slates. As with hips specially wide slates are required so that they are sufficiently wide at their tails when cut. The slates are not bedded and do not have an undercloak. The traditional techniques for the *swept valley* formed by cutting slates to special shapes, and the *laced valley* require skilled craftsmen. Details are shown in figure 14.61. The flashing details where a chimney projects through a tiled roof are illustrated in figure 14.66.

Fibre cement slates

As already mentioned under 14.4(a) Corrugated fibre cement sheets, the manufacture of slate substitutes using asbestos fibre cement has declined and this material has been replaced by less hazardous materials. Accordingly, portland cement is now reinforced with a blend of natural and synthetic fibres (cellulose or glass fibre) to form slates in a range of colours (blue/black, grey,

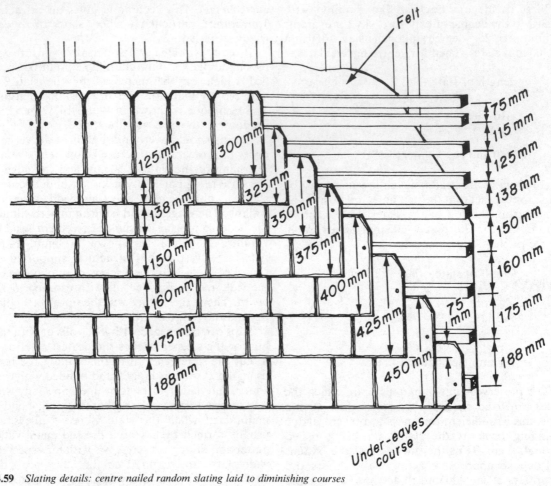

14.59 *Slating details: centre nailed random slating laid to diminishing courses*

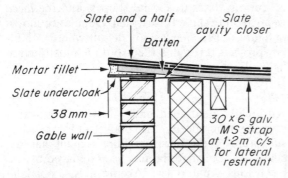

14.60 *Slating details: verge*

russet and brown), shapes and sizes – see figure 14.62. There is no British Standard at present for fibre cement slates, but the recommendations contained in BS 690: *Asbestos cement slates and sheets* Part 4: 1971 *Slates* are useful when considering these new products. Typical details at eaves, verge, ridge and valley positions are shown in figures 14.63 and 14.64.

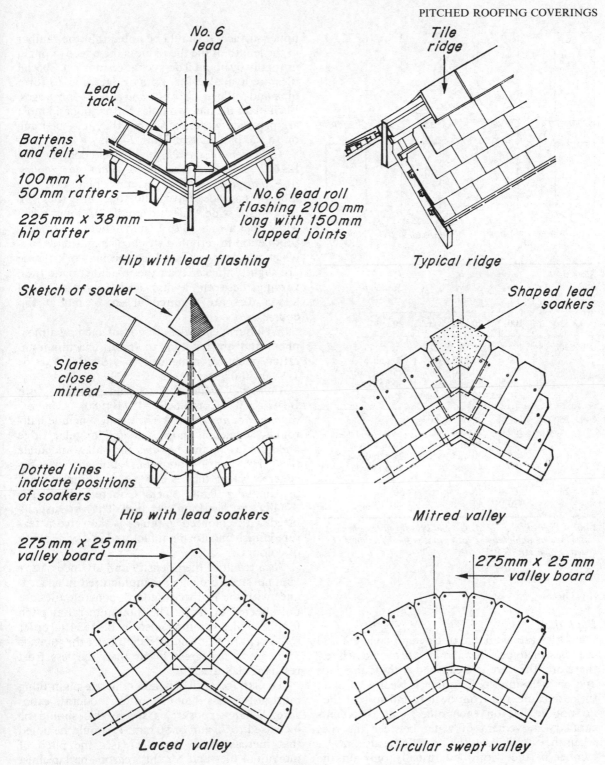

No. 6
lead

Lead
tack

Battens
and felt

100mm x
50mm rafters

225mm x 38mm
hip rafter

No.6 lead roll
flashing 2100 mm
long with 150 mm
lapped joints

Hip with lead flashing

Tile
ridge

Typical ridge

Sketch of soaker

Slates
close
mitred

Dotted lines
indicate positions
of soakers

Hip with lead soakers

Shaped lead
soakers

Mitred valley

275 mm x 25 mm
valley board

Laced valley

275mm x 25 mm
valley board

Circular swept valley

14.61 *Slating details: hips, ridge and valleys*

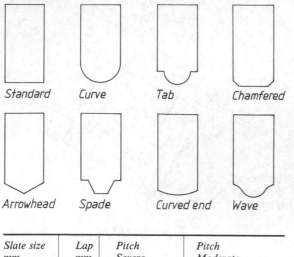

Standard   Curve   Tab   Chamfered

Arrowhead   Spade   Curved end   Wave

Slate size mm	Lap mm	Pitch Severe exposure	Pitch Moderate exposure
600 × 350	100	20 and over	20
600 × 300	106	20 to 25	—
	100	25 and over	20 and over
	90	30 and over	25 and over
	80	35 and over	30 and over
	70	40 and over	35 and over
500 × 250	106	25 to 30	—
	100	25 and over	22.5 and over
	90	30 and over	25 and over
	80	30 and over	27.5 and over
	70	45 and over	40 and over
400 × 240	80	45	30
	70	45	40

14.62 *Typical range of shapes and sizes for fibre cement slates, and minimum laps relative to exposure conditions (by courtesy of Eternit TAC Ltd)*

(b) Tiles

Plain tiles

Plain tiles are available in clay and concrete and are classified as *double lap units*. Like slates, therefore, they are laid in bond with double laps and have no interlocking joints. Nearly all plain tiles are cambered from head to tail so that they do not lie flat on each other, which prevents capillary movement of water between the tiles when they are laid on the roof. Some also have a camber in the width, but usually only on the

upper surface. It should be noted that the camber in the length of the tile reduces the effective pitch, normally by about 9 degrees at 65 mm lap. Special tiles are available for use as ridges and to form hips and valleys; also '*tile and a half*' for verges. Each plain tile has two holes for nailing and most are provided with nibs so that they may be hung on to the battens, see figure 14.54.

Clay plain tiles and fittings should comply with BS 402: 1979 *Specification for plain clay roofing tiles and fittings*. Sizes in mm: plain tile 265 long × 165 wide: Eaves and topcourse tiles 190 long × 165 wide: 'Tile and a half' 265 long × 248 wide; thickness is 10 to 15 mm. There is a limited production in certain districts of hand-made tiles which are now only used for special work. These are slightly thicker than the machine-made tiles, varying between 13 mm and 16 mm. Special length tiles are required at eaves and at top course.

Well burnt clay tiles are not affected by atmosphere and are resistant to frost. The minimum rafter pitch recommended in BS 5534: Part 1: 1978 is 40 degrees.

Concrete plain tiles should comply with BS 473/550 (Combined) 1971(1980) *Concrete roofing tiles and fittings*. The fittings include half-round, segmental, hogsback and angular ridge and hip tiles, bonnet hip tiles and valley and angle tiles. The metric equivalent standard size for concrete plain tiles is 265 mm × 165 mm × approximately 10 mm thick. Concrete plain tiles usually cost less than clay tiles. They are usually faced with coloured granules which give a textured finish and are manufactured in a wide range of colours.

As a result of their density and absence of any laminar structure when manufactured in accordance with the British Standard, concrete tiles are not affected by frost. The minimum rafter pitch for these tiles recommended in BS 5534 in order to prevent rain and snow penetrating the joints is 35 degrees, 5 degrees lower than the less frost resistant clay tiles.

The lap for both clay and concrete plain tiling must not be less than 65 mm for moderate exposure. Where exposure is severe this should be increased to 75 mm or 90 mm. It should be noted that increasing the lap decreases the pitch of individual tiles and for this reason the lap must

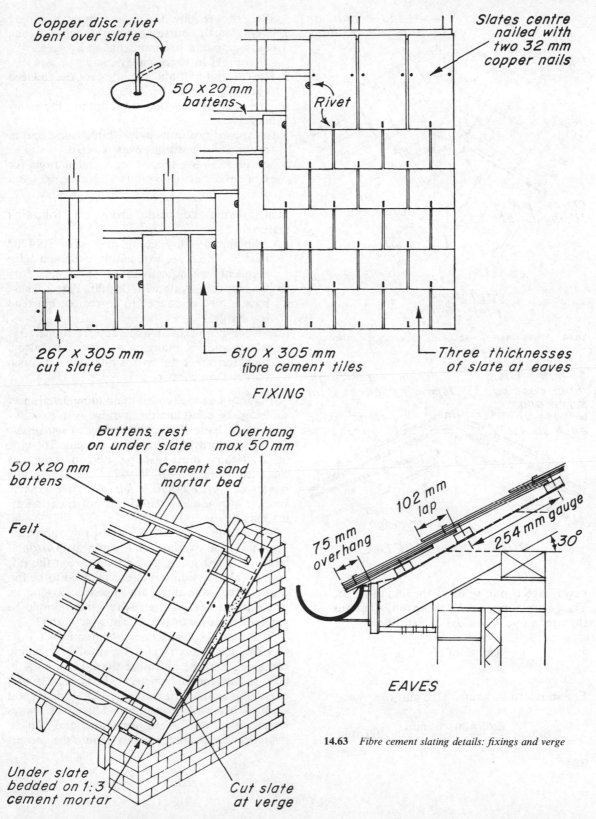

Copper disc rivet bent over slate

50 × 20 mm battens

Rivet

Slates centre nailed with two 32 mm copper nails

267 × 305 mm cut slate

610 × 305 mm fibre cement tiles

Three thicknesses of slate at eaves

FIXING

Buttens rest on under slate

Overhang max 50 mm

50 × 20 mm battens

Cement sand mortar bed

Felt

Under slate bedded on 1:3 cement mortar

Cut slate at verge

VERGE

102 mm lap

75 mm overhang

254 mm gauge

30°

EAVES

14.63 *Fibre cement slating details: fixings and verge*

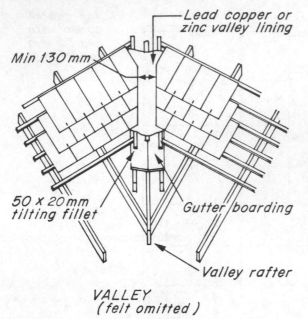

VALLEY
(felt omitted)

14.64 *Fibre cement slating details: ridge, hip and valley*

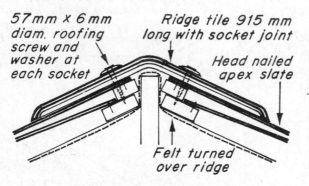

RIDGE OR HIP DETAIL

never exceed one third of the length of the tile. The gauge – or normal spacing of the battens – on the roof slope is worked out as follows:

$$gauge = \frac{length\ of\ tile - lap}{2}$$

For standard 265 mm × 165 mm tiles the

$$gauge = \frac{265\ mm - 65\ mm}{2} = 100\ mm$$

Plain tiles require nailing as follows:
1 Every fourth course and at the ends of each course adjacent to abutments and verges.
2 All cut tiles in swept valleys.
3 The tile and half and the adjacent tile in laced valleys.
4 Tiles adjacent to valley tiles, but not the valley tile itself.
5 In exposed positions every third course and in very exposed positions every course.
6 See BS 5534 for special recommendations for extra nailing at steep pitches of 50 degrees and over.

Nails should be made from the following materials:
(a) Aluminium alloy complying with BS 1202 Part 3. These are extensively used and have excellent resistance to corrosion.
(b) Copper complying with BS 1002 Part 2. These have a high resistance to corrosion, but tend to be soft.
(c) Silicon-bronze of an alloy of 96% copper, 3% silicon and 1% manganese. These have also a high resistance to corrosion, and are much harder than copper.

Figure 14.65 is a typical plain tiling detail sheet showing the construction at ridge, verge, valley and eaves. Note that an underlay of *untearable felt* must be provided under the battens. The type of felt (which must also be used in slating) is classified in BS 747: 1977(1987) Class IF *Hessian reinforced based bitumen felt with fine granule surface*; alternatively reinforced polythene sheeting may be used.

The felting is laid parallel to the ridge and each tier should be overlapped 150 mm at horizontal joints. The felt will sag slightly between the rafters, which, providing it is not allowed to be too pronounced, will allow any moisture to find its way into the eaves gutter, where there should be ample turn down of the felt into the gutter.

The *Building Regulations 1985* require that the thermal insulation (U) of the roof and ceiling combined shall be not more than 0.6 W/m² K in houses, flats and maisonettes. The U value of tiles over felt including the ceiling is 2.22 W/m² K, and so insulation will be required. This must always be provided with a vapour check and can be installed either immediately over the rafters

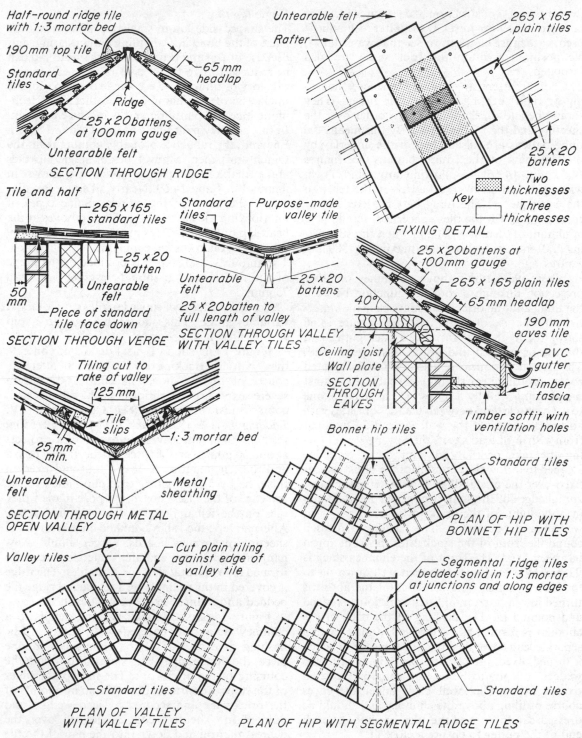

Half-round ridge tile with 1:3 mortar bed
190 mm top tile
Standard tiles
Ridge
65 mm headlap
25 x 20 battens at 100 mm gauge
Untearable felt

SECTION THROUGH RIDGE

Untearable felt
Rafter
265 x 165 plain tiles
25 x 20 battens
Two thicknesses
Key
Three thicknesses

FIXING DETAIL

Tile and half
265 x 165 standard tiles
25 x 20 batten
Untearable felt
50 mm
Piece of standard tile face down

SECTION THROUGH VERGE

Standard tiles
Purpose-made valley tile
Untearable felt
25 x 20 battens
25 x 20 batten to full length of valley

SECTION THROUGH VALLEY WITH VALLEY TILES

25 x 20 battens at 100 mm gauge
265 x 165 plain tiles
65 mm headlap
40°
190 mm eaves tile
PVC gutter
Ceiling joist
Wall plate
SECTION THROUGH EAVES
Timber fascia
Timber soffit with ventilation holes

Tiling cut to rake of valley
125 mm
Tile slips
1:3 mortar bed
25 mm min.
Untearable felt
Metal sheathing

SECTION THROUGH METAL OPEN VALLEY

Bonnet hip tiles
Standard tiles

PLAN OF HIP WITH BONNET HIP TILES

Valley tiles
Cut plain tiling against edge of valley tile
Standard tiles

PLAN OF VALLEY WITH VALLEY TILES

Segmental ridge tiles bedded solid in 1:3 mortar at junctions and along edges
Standard tiles

PLAN OF HIP WITH SEGMENTAL RIDGE TILES

14.65 *Plain tiling (double lap) details*

385

('warm' roof construction – see figure 14.5) or between the ceiling joists. If the latter technique is used, care must be taken to see that water tanks, etc positioned within the roof space are also insulated.

Counterbattens are required whenever boarding or rigid sheeting is used over rafters. They should be laid on the line of each rafter over the sheeting and the felt underlay. By this means the tiling battens are raised clear of the underlay by the thickness of the counterbattens (see figures 14.57 and 14.66) so allowing any wind-blown water penetration to drain away on the felt into the eaves gutter. The tiling battens, fixed to the correct gauge for the tiles concerned, should be a minimum of 25 mm × 20 mm when the supporting rafters are spaced at maximum 380 mm centres.

Where plain tiling abuts a chimney or other projection through a roof, the junction between the tiling and the brickwork must be made watertight by the use of metal flashings. Figure 14.66 shows the method of forming a back gutter and the use of stepped and apron flashings in lead. The same techniques are also applicable to slated roofs. The tiling (or slating) is weathered against the abutting wall by a series of lead soakers, one to each course, laid between the tiles or slates with an upstand against the wall. A lead flashing cut from a strip of lead sheet, the lower edge following the rake of the roof and the upper edge stepped to follow the coursing of the brickwork, is fixed over the upstands of the soakers. The horizontal edges of the steps are turned about 25 mm into the joints of the brickwork, secured by lead wedges and pointed in. The flashing is dressed round the front of the stack after the front apron has been fixed. The front of the chimney stack is flashed by a lead apron carried well down on to the tiles or slates. The top edge of the apron is turned into a horizontal brickwork joint, wedged and pointed in. The flashing to the back of the chimney is formed as a short valley gutter with a separate lead cover flashing, the top edge of which is turned, fixed into the brickwork joint with lead wedges and pointed. The lead should be carried over a tilting fillet well back under the eaves course of tiling above the chimney and should be dressed carefully over the tiles or slates at each end of the gutter to ensure a close fit.

Single lap tiles

The shaped side lap in single lap tiling takes the place of the bond in plain tiling and in slating, and because of this the protection at the head lap can be reduced to two thicknesses of material. In this category of tiling there is a single overlap (double thickness) of one tile upon the other. This technique includes pantiling and is of ancient origin. In this country pantiling was first used in Eastern England, the influence probably coming from the Dutch craftsmen. Many types of single lap tiles are available, examples of which are shown in figures 14.67 and 14.69. Nearly all single lap tiles are of the inter-locking pattern. Some types of interlocking tile have anti-capillary grooves at the head-lap of the tiles. This makes it possible to lay these tiles on roofs of comparatively flat pitch. The amount of side lap is determined by the shape of the tile. Head lap should never be less than 75 mm.

Certain patterns of single lap tiles can be laid at variable gauge. This should be used to avoid cutting tiles at top courses.

Figure 14.69 shows typical details of concrete tiles with interlocking side lap. Each alternate course of tiles is shown nailed but, in certain severe exposure conditions, each tile in each course must be nailed. (See CP 3 chapter V: *Loading* Part 2 1972 *Wind loads*) and BS 5534: Part 2: 1986. The eaves course of tiles projects about 50 mm over the edge of the fascia board and the felt underlay is drawn taut and fixed in this case by a proprietary eave clip nailed to the top edge of the fascia board. Purpose-made valley tiles on the felt underlay form the valley detail. Alternatively, the valley could be lined with metal sheeting over valley boards. Verges should overhang about 50 mm and the undercloak can be formed from natural slate, or plain tiles. The ridge is covered in the example by a segmental ridge tile bedded and pointed in 1:3 cement/sand mortar.

Figure 14.68 shows lead flashing details to a chimney in a roof covered with pantiles. The flashing at each side of the chimney is in one piece, the upper edge being stepped to follow the coursing of the brickwork. The horizontal edges of the steps are turned about 25 mm into joints of the brickwork and secured by lead wedges and pointed in. The free edge is dressed over the nearest tile roll and down into the pan of the tile

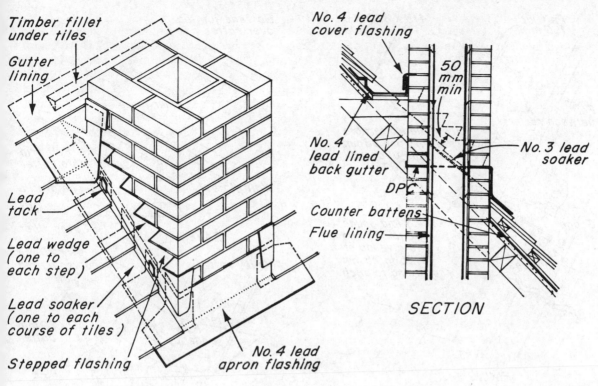

Timber fillet under tiles

Gutter lining

Lead tack

Lead wedge (one to each step)

Lead soaker (one to each course of tiles)

Stepped flashing

No. 4 lead apron flashing

FIXING

No. 4 lead cover flashing

50 mm min

No. 4 lead lined back gutter

DPC

Counter battens

Flue lining

No. 3 lead soaker

SECTION

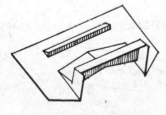

DETAIL OF BACK GUTTER FLASHING

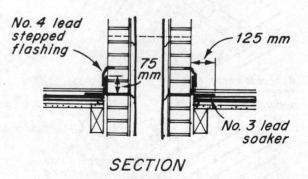

No. 4 lead stepped flashing

125 mm

75 mm

No. 3 lead soaker

SECTION

14.66 *Plain tiling (double lap) – or slating – details: lead flashings to chimney*

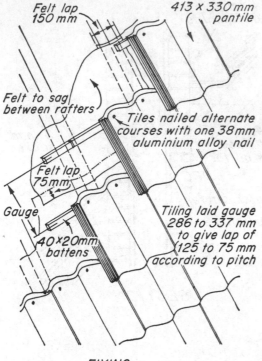

Felt lap 150 mm

413 × 330 mm pantile

Felt to sag between rafters

Tiles nailed alternate courses with one 38 mm aluminium alloy nail

Felt lap 75 mm

Gauge

40×20 mm battens

Tiling laid gauge 286 to 337 mm to give lap of 125 to 75 mm according to pitch

FIXING

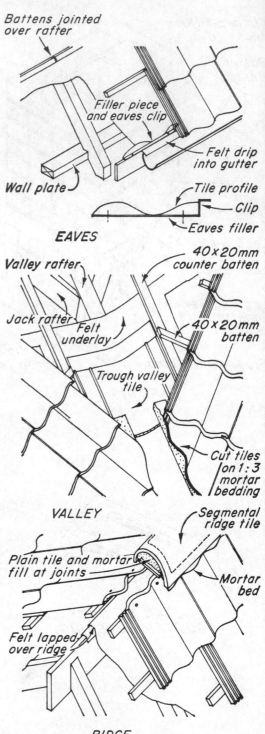

Battens jointed over rafter

Filler piece and eaves clip

Felt drip into gutter

Wall plate

Tile profile
Clip
Eaves filler

EAVES

Valley rafter

40×20 mm counter batten

Jack rafter

Felt underlay

40×20 mm batten

Trough valley tile

Cut tiles on 1:3 mortar bedding

VALLEY

Segmental ridge tile

Plain tile and mortar fill at joints

Mortar bed

Felt lapped over ridge

RIDGE

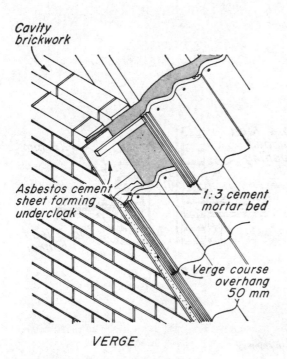

Cavity brickwork

Asbestos cement sheet forming undercloak

1:3 cement mortar bed

Verge course overhang 50 mm

VERGE

14.67 *Pantile roofing (single lap) details*

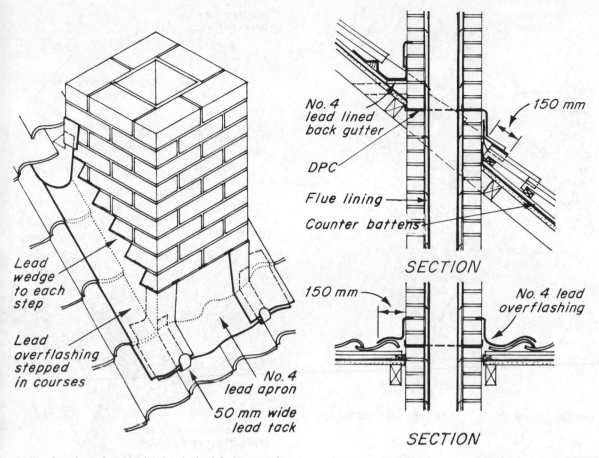

14.68 *Pantile roofing (single) details: lead flashings to chimney*

beyond the roll. The front of the chimney stack is flashed with a lead apron which is carried down on to the tiles at least 125 mm and dressed to a close fit. Where the exposure is severe, the front edge should preferably be secured with lead tacks as shown. The top edge of the apron is turned into a brickwork joint, wedged and pointed in.

Figure 14.69 shows the details using a single lap interlocking tile of simple profile. The neat interlocking detail at the side of the tile allows the adjacent units to lie in the same plane, giving an appearance of slating. Tiles of this and similar pattern on sites of moderate exposure can be laid on pitches down to between 22½ degrees and 15 degrees. The tiles can be laid to a variable gauge, so that the head lap can be increased to avoid cut tiles at the ridge. The minimum headlap is 75 mm.

The tiles are shown laid with broken joint and this is advisable on roofs of less than 30 degrees pitch. Where tiles are laid on roofs of lower pitch, the wind uplift increases. In consequence, the need for fixing becomes more important. On exposed sites, at lower pitches therefore, each tile is secured by a special clip nailed to the back of the batten carrying the course below. See CP 3 chapter V *Loading* Part 2 1972 *Wind loads* and BS 5534: Part 2: 1986. Under these conditions special verge clips are also used as shown on the detail. A special valley tile designed for use at low pitches is used in this example to form the valley gutter as an alternative to a metal open valley. The ridge tile is fixed by means of a special wire twisted around a nail driven into the ridge board. In addition, the ridge tiles are bedded solid at

389

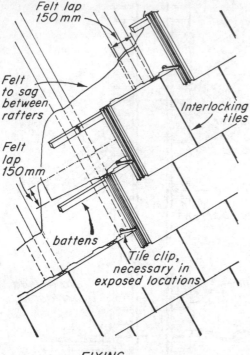

Felt lap 150 mm

Felt to sag between rafters

Felt lap 150 mm

battens

Interlocking tiles

Tile clip, necessary in exposed locations

FIXING

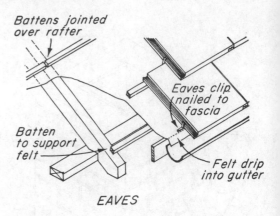

Battens jointed over rafter

Batten to support felt

Eaves clip nailed to fascia

Felt drip into gutter

EAVES

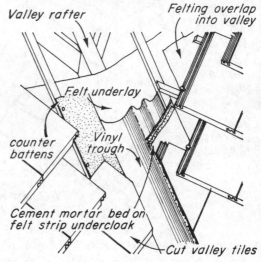

Valley rafter

Felting overlap into valley

Felt underlay

counter battens

Vinyl trough

Cement mortar bed on felt strip undercloak

Cut valley tiles

VALLEY

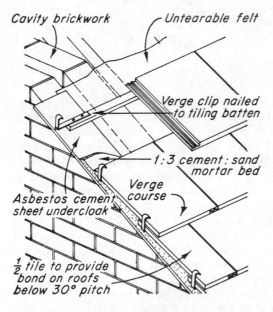

Cavity brickwork

Untearable felt

Verge clip nailed to tiling batten

1:3 cement: sand mortar bed

Verge course

Asbestos cement sheet undercloak

½ tile to provide bond on roofs below 30° pitch

VERGE DETAIL

Twisted wire anchor

Ridge tiles bedded solid at joints

1:3 mortar edge bedding

Felt lapped over ridge

RIDGE DETAIL

Continued . . .

390

Continued . . .

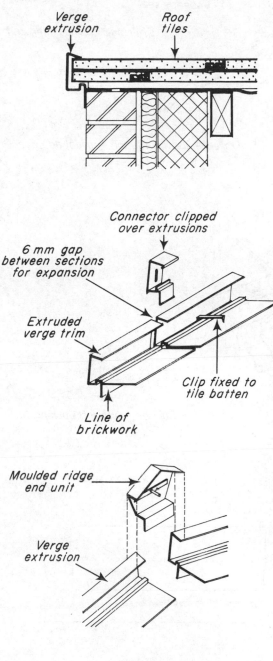

14.69 *Interlocking concrete tiling details*

joints in 1:3 sand and cement mortar and edge bedded along both sides.

For details of dormer windows and skylights in pitched roofs see *8.6 Dormer windows and skylights in pitched roofs.*

Figure 14.70 shows a typical detail of a proprietary ridge ventilator which is connected to a flexible pipe in the pitched roof-space. The half round ridge ventilation terminal provides a visually acceptable method of ventilating a wc located within a building without the need of external soil and vent pipework, or for terminating the ductwork from a mechanical extract system.

Reinforced bitumen strip
1000×336 mm bitumen tiles are made from roofing felts to BS 747, reinforced with glass fibre and surfaced with mineral granules, in shades of red, green, grey and brown (figure 14.71). They should not be used below 12 degrees pitch, have no inherent strength and must be fully supported and nailed to a preserved tongued and grooved boarded or WBP plywood roof deck. They are classified as either BB (at least 6 m from boundary) or CC according to the type of felt, and it is important to obtain a fire test certificate. There is no British Standard which describes their use.

Metal multi-tiles
1330×415 mm zinc coated galvanized steel units are profiled to resemble several tiles and are called *metal multi-tiles* (figure 14.71). They can be finished with a bituminous emulsion incorporating a mineral granule surface (charcoal grey, terracotta and sea green), or with a smooth plastics or aluminium pigment surface (blue/black, black and red). They should not be installed below a pitch of 12 degrees, have adequate strength characteristics when tested to BS 5534, are classified as AA for fire control purposes, are unaffected by frost, require little maintenance, and have an anticipated life of twenty years. There is no British Standard for metal multi-tiles.

Wood shingles
Shingles are cut from the blocks of Western red cedar in a tapered cross-section, with edges trimmed square and parallel to uniform length of 405 mm. Widths are random from 100 mm to

391

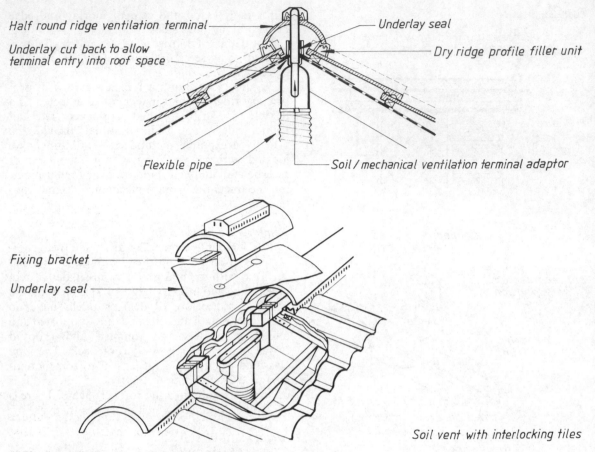

Half round ridge ventilation terminal

Underlay cut back to allow terminal entry into roof space

Underlay seal

Dry ridge profile filler unit

Flexible pipe

Soil / mechanical ventilation terminal adaptor

Fixing bracket

Underlay seal

Soil vent with interlocking tiles

14.70 *Interlocking concrete tiling details: proprietary ridge ventilator for wc*

350 mm. They must be pressure impregnated with copper chrome arsenate preservative to BS 4072.

Shingles should be installed at 14 degrees pitch, according to lap, using conventional pitched roof construction techniques or by nailing through an under felt into a continuous deck of WBP plywood. They have no classification for fire control and may not be used on roofs less than 22 m from a boundary. Properly preserved and installed, they have a life expectancy of more than 50 years. There is no British Standard for shingles, but they are normally specified in the UK to Canadian standards.

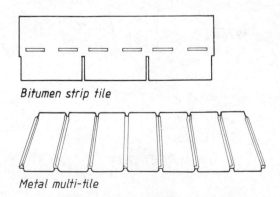

Bitumen strip tile

Metal multi-tile

14.71 *Bitumen strip tile and metal multi-tile*

14.7 Thatch

Thatch is a traditional form of roof covering which has gained in popularity in recent years due to the revival of interest in craft based construction skills and the publicity provided by the Thatching Advisory Service Ltd. There is no British Standard for thatching.

There are six basic types of thatch:

- *Norfolk reed*, which is the common water reed Phragmites Australis and the most durable natural thatching material;
- *long straw*, which is threshed winter straw in common use through the country, but generally has the shortest life expectancy;
- *combed wheat reed (Devon reed)*, which is winter wheat straw that is 'combed' rather than threshed but is less readily available owing to modern farming methods;
- *sedge*, which is similar to, but more pliable and less durable than reed, and is used to form ridges on reed thatching;
- *heather*, which comes in much shorter lengths than straw or reed;
- *bark*, which comes from chestnut fencing stakes and can be used as thatching;
- *synthetic*, which is made from polypropylene oil based yarn, tufted into a woven polypropylene base with a rubber latex backing.

Thatch of conventional materials is laid in bundles, termed *bunches* or *shoves* for Norfolk reed, or *nitches* for combed wheat reed. Roofing commences at the eaves and the first course is tied in place to preserved timber battens with tarred hemp twine. Subsequent courses are held in position with hazel or elm rods (*sways*) laid across the thatch and held to the rafters or boarded deck by wrought iron hooks. The eaves should tilt upwards, and the pitch of the roof should be a minimum of 45 degrees. In order to protect the thatch from birds, the roof should be covered with a netting of galvanized wire or plastics. A felt underlay to the thatch reduces the accumulation of debris in the roof spaces when rafters are not boarded.

Thatching has the advantage of being adaptable to different plan forms, lightweight, and providing good thermal insulation (300 mm thickness gives $U = 0.35 \, \text{W/m}^2\text{K}$ as well as good sound control. In addition, gutters and downpipes are not required, and the materials make use of a renewable resource (unless synthetic). The main disadvantages relate to fire control and thatch has no classification in the *Building Regulations 1985* which means that the roof must be more than 22 m from the boundary. For this reason, insurance companies are reluctant to provide a fire policy for a thatch roof covering. The Thatching Advisory Service Ltd recommended the use of a fire retardant treatment consisting of a chemical water-based solution which is injected by means of a multi-headed spray lance into the thatch. When the chemical dries, the individual straws or reeds of the thatch remain coated with a deposit of the fire resistant material. However, weathering causes this deposit to wear off at the top of the ridge and the outer surface of the roof, and a better method involves dipping the bundles in the retardant prior to thatching. It is also possible to install external sparge pipes at the ridge position which will cause the roof to be sprayed with water in the event of a fire. Other precautions can also be taken, such as providing an underlining of a material having a Class 0 spread of flame rating, running electric wiring in conduit to BS 31/4568 or MICC to BS 6207 within roof spaces, locating television aerials and cables on masonry, and ensuring properly constructed and maintained chimneys.

SI units

Quantities in this volume are given in SI units which have been adopted by the construction industry in the United Kingdom. Twenty-five other countries (not including the USA or Canada) have also adopted the SI system although several of them retain the old metric system as an alternative. There are six SI basic units. Other units derived from these basic units are rationally related to them and to each other. The international adoption of the SI will remove the present necessity for conversions between national systems. The introduction of metric units gives an opportunity for the adoption of modular sizes.

Full details of SI Units and conversion factors are contained in the current edition of the *AJ Metric Handbook*.

British Standards, Codes of Practice and other documents are being progressively re-issued in metric units. In addition, it should be noted that new Codes of Practice are now being issued as ordinary BSs and not as formerly BCPSs.

Multiples and sub-multiples of SI units likely to be used in the construction industry are as follows:

Multiplication factor	Prefix		Symbol
1 000 000	10^6	mega	M
1 000	10^3	kilo	k
100	10^2	hecto	h
10	10^1	deca	da
0·1	10^{-1}	deci	d
0·01	10^{-2}	centi	c
0·001	10^{-3}	milli	m
0·000 001	10^{-6}	micro	µ

Further information concerning metrication is contained in BS PD 6031 *A Guide for the use of the Metric System in the Construction Industry,* and BS 5555:1976 *SI units and recommendations for the use of their multiples and of certain other units.*

Quantity	Unit	Symbol	Imperial unit × Conversion factor = SI value		
LENGTH	kilometre	km	1 mile	=	1·609 km
	metre	m	1 yard	=	0·914 m
	millimetre	mm	1 foot	=	0·305 m
			1 inch	=	25·4 mm
AREA	square kilometre	km²	1 mile²	=	2·590 km²
	hectare	ha	1 acre	=	0.405 ha
			1 yard²	=	0·836 m²
	square metre	m²	1 foot²	=	0·093 m²
	square millimetre	mm²	1 inch²	=	645·16 mm²
VOLUME	cubic metre	m³	1 yard³	=	0·765 m³
	cubic millimetre	mm³	1 foot³	=	0·028 m³
			1 inch³	=	1 638·7 mm³
CAPACITY	litre	l	1 UKgallon	=	4·546 litres

continued...

Quantity	Unit	Symbol	Imperial unit × Conversion factor = SI value		
MASS	kilogramme gramme	kg g	1 lb 1 oz 1 lb/ft (run) 1 lb/ft²	= = = =	0·454 kg 28·350 g 1·488 kg/m 4·882 kg/m²
DENSITY	kilogramme per cubic metre	kg/m³	1 lb/ft³	=	16·019 kg/m³
FORCE	newton	N	1 lbf 1 tonf 	= = =	4·488 N 9 964·02 N 9·964 kN
PRESSURE, STRESS	newton per square metre	N/m²	1 lbf/in.²	=	6 894·8 N/m²
	meganewton per square metre	MN/m²† or N/mm²	1 tonf/ft² 1 tonf/in.² 1 lb/ft run 1 lbf/ft² 1 ton/ft run	= = = = =	107·3 kN/m² 15·444 MN/m² 14·593 N/m 47·880 N/m² 32 682 kN/m
	*bar (0·1 MN/m²) *hectobar (10 MN/m²) *millibar (100 MN/m²)	bar hbar m bar			
VELOCITY	metre per second	m/s	1 mile/h	=	0·447 m/s
FREQUENCY	cycle per second	Hz	1 cycle/sec	=	1 Hz
ENERGY, HEAT	joule	J	1 Btu	=	1 055·06 J
POWER, HEAT FLOW RATE	watts newtons metres per second joules per second	W Nm/s J/s	1 Btu/h 1 hp 1 ft/lbf	= = =	0·293 W 746 W 1·356 J
THERMAL CONDUCTIVITY (K)	watts per metre degree Celsius	W/m K	1 Btu in./ft²h deg F	=	0·144 W/m K
THERMAL TRANS- MITTANCE (U)	watts per square metre degree Celsius	W/m² K	1 Btu/ft²h deg F	=	5·678 W/m² K
TEMPERATURE	degree Celsius (difference)	deg C	1 deg F	=	$\frac{5}{9}$ deg C
	degree Celsius (level)	°C	°F	=	$\frac{9}{5}$ °C + 32

* Alternative units, allied to the SI, which will be encountered in certain industries

† BSI preferred symbol

A guide to the SI metric system

395

Appendix A

The following information from the *Construction Indexing Manual 1976* is reproduced by courtesy of RIBA Publications Ltd.

Used sensibly and in appropriate detail, as explained in the manual, the CI/SfB system of classification facilitates filing and retrieval of information. It is useful in technical libraries, in specifications and on working drawings. *The National Building Specification* is based on the system, and BRE Digest 172 describes its use for working drawings.

The CI/SfB system comprises tables 0 to 4, tables 1 and 2/3 being the codes in most common use. For libraries, classifications are built up from:

Table 0	Table 1	Tables 2/3	Table 4
-a number code	-a number code in brackets	-upper and lower case letter codes	-upper case letter code in brackets
eg 6	eg (6)	eg Fg	eg (F)

An example for clay brickwork in walls is: (21) Fg2, which for trade literature, would be shown in a reference box as:

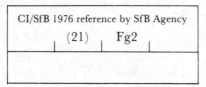

```
CI/SfB 1976 reference by SfB Agency
        (21)   |  Fg2
```

The lower space is intended for UDC (Universal decimal classification) codes – see BS 100A 1961. Advice in classification can be obtained from the SfB Agency UK Ltd at 66 Portland Place, London W1N 4AD.

In the following summaries of the five tables, chapter references are made to the seven related volumes and chapters of *Mitchell's Building Series* in which aspects of the classifications are dealt with. The following abbreviations are used:

Introduction to Building	IB
Environment and Services	ES
Materials	M

Structure and Fabric, Part 1	*SF (1)*
Structure and Fabric, Part 2	*SF (2)*
Components	*C*
Finishes	*F*

Table 0 **Physical Environment**
(main headings only)

Scope: End results of the construction process

0 Planning areas
1 Utilities, civil engineering facilities
2 Industrial facilities
3 Administrative, commercial, protective service facilities
4 Health, welfare facilities
5 Recreational facilities
6 Religious facilities
7 Educational, scientific, information facilities
8 Residential facilities
9 Common facilities, other facilities

Table 1 **Elements**

Scope: Parts with particular functions which combine to make the facilities in table 0

(0-) Sites, projects
Building plus external works
Building systems *C* 11

(1-) Ground, substructure
(11) Ground *SF (1)* 4, 8, 11; *SF (2)* 2, 3, 11; *IB* 17.3
(12) Vacant
(13) Floor beds *SF (1)* 4, 8; *SF (2)* 3
(14), (15) Vacant
(16) Retaining walls, foundations *SF (1)* 4; *SF (2)* 3, 4; *IB* 17.4, 17.5
(17) Pile foundations *SF (1)* 4; *SF (2)* 3, 11
(18) Other substructure elements
(19) Parts, accessories, cost summary, etc

(2-) Structure, primary elements, carcass
(21) Walls, external walls *SF (1)* 1, 5; *SF (2)* 4, 5, 10; *IB* 17.6

(22) Internal walls, partitions *SF (1)* 5; *SF (2)* 4, 10; *C* 9; *IB* 17.7

(23) Floors, galleries *SF (1)* 8; *SF (2)* 6, 10; *IB* 17.8

(24) Stairs, ramps *SF (1)* 10; *SF (2)* 8, 10

(25), (26) Vacant

(27) Roofs *SF (1)* 1, 7; *SF (2)* 9, 10; *IB* 17.9

(28) Building frames, other primary elements *SF (1)* 1, 6; *SF (2)* 5, 10; Chimneys *SF (1)* 9

(29) Parts, accessories, cost summary, etc

(3-) Secondary elements, completion of structure

(31) Secondary elements to external walls, including windows, doors *SF (1)* 5; *SF (2)* 10; *C* 3, 4, 5, 7; *IB* 17.6

(32) Secondary elements to internal walls, partitions including borrowed lights and doors *SF (2)* 10; *C* 3, 7; *IB* 17.7

(33) Secondary elements to floors *SF (2)* 10; *IB* 17.8

(34) Secondary elements to stairs including balustrades *C* 8

(35) Suspended ceilings *C* 10

(36) Vacant

(37) Secondary elements to roofs, including roof lights, dormers *SF (1)* 7; *SF (2)* 10; *C* 6

(38) Other secondary elements

(39) Parts, accessories, cost summary, etc.

(4-) Finishes to structure

(41) Wall finishes, external *SF (2)* 4, 10; *F* 3, 4, 5; *IB* 17.6, 17.11

(42) Wall finishes, internal *F* 2, 4, 5; *IB* 17.7, 17.11

(43) Floor finishes *F* 1; *IB* 17.5, 17.8, 17.11

(44) Stair finishes *F* 1; *IB* 17.11

(45) Ceiling finishes *F* 2; *IB* 17.11

(46) Vacant

(47) Roof finishes *SF (2)* 10; *F* 7; *IB* 17.9, 17.11

(48) Other finishes; *IB* 17.11

(49) Parts, accessories, cost summary, etc; *IB* 17.11

(5-) Services (mainly piped and ducted)

(51) Vacant

(52) Waste disposal, drainage *ES* 11, 12, 13; *IB* 17.10

(53) Liquids supply *ES* 9, 10; *SF (1)* 9; *SF (2)* 6, 10; *IB* 17.10

(54) Gases supply; *IB* 17.10

(55) Space cooling; *IB* 17.10

(56) Space heating *ES* 7; *SF (1)* 9; *SF (2)* 6, 10; *IB* 17.10

(57) Air conditioning, ventilation *ES* 7; *SF (2)* 10; *IB* 17.10

(58) Other piped, ducted services; *IB* 17.10

(59) Parts, accessories, cost summary, etc Chimney, shafts, flues, ducts independent *SF (2)* 7; *IB* 17.10

(6-) Services (mainly electrical)

(61) Electrical supply; *IB* 17.10

(62) Power *ES* 14; *IB* 17.10

(63) Lighting *ES* 8; *IB* 17.10

(64) Communications *ES* 14; *IB* 17.10

(65) Vacant

(66) Transport *ES* 15

(67) Vacant

(68) Security, control, other services; *IB* 17.10

(69) Parts, accessories, cost summary, etc; *IB* 17.10

(7-) Fittings with subdivisions (71) to (79)

(74) Sanitary, hygiene fittings *ES* 10

(8-) Loose furniture, equipment with subdivisions (81) to (89)
Used where the distinction between loose and fixed fittings, furniture and equipment is important.

(9-) External elements, other elements

(90) External works, with subdivisions (90.1) to (90.8); *IB* 17.12

(98) Other elements

(99) Parts, accessories etc. common to two or more main element divisions (1-) to (7-) Cost summary

Note: The SfB Agency UK do not use table 1 in classifying manufacturers' literature

---

Table 2 **Constructions, Forms**

Scope: Parts of particular forms which combine to make the elements in table 1. Each is characterised by the main product of which it is made.

A Constructions, forms – used in specification applications for Preliminaries and General conditions

B Vacant – used in specification applications for demolition, underpinning and shoring work

C Excavation and loose fill work

D Vacant

E Cast *in situ* work *M* 8; *SF (1)* 4, 7, 8; *SF (2)* 3, 4, 5, 6, 8, 9

397

Blocks

F Blockwork, brickwork
Blocks, bricks *M* 6, 12; *SF (1)* 5, 9
SF (2) 4, 6, 7

G Large block, panel work
Large blocks, panels *SF (2)* 4

Sections

H Section work
Sections *M* 9; *SF (1)* 5, 6, 7, 8; *SF (2)* 5, 6

I Pipework
Pipes *SF (1)* 9; *SF (2)* 7

J Wire work, mesh work
Wires, meshes

K Quilt work
Quilts

L Flexible sheet work (proofing)
Flexible sheets (proofing) *M* 9, 11

M Malleable sheet work
Malleable sheets *M* 9

N Rigid sheet overlap work
Rigid sheets for overlappings *SF (2)* 4; *F* 7

P Thick coating work *M* 10, 11; *SF (2)* 4;
F 1, 2, 3, 7

Q Vacant

R Rigid sheet work
Rigid sheets *M* 3, 12, 13, *SF (2)* 4; *C* 5

S Rigid tile work
Rigid tiles *M* 4, 12, 13; *F* 1, 4

T Flexible sheet and tile work
Flexible sheets eg carpets, veneers, papers,
tiles cut from them *M* 3, 9; *F* 1, 6

U Vacant

V Film coating and impregnation work *F* 6;
M 2

W Planting work
Plants

X Work with components
Components *SF (1)* 5, 6, 7, 8, 10; *SF (2)* 4;
C 2, 3, 4, 5, 6, 7, 8

Y Formless work
Products

Z Joints, where described separately

Table 3 **Materials**

Scope: Materials which combine to form the products in table 2

---

a **Materials**

b, c, d Vacant

Formed materials e to o

e **Natural stone** *M* 4; *SF (1)* 5, 10; *SF (2)* 4

e1 Granite, basalt, other igneous

e2 Marble

e3 Limestone (other than marble)

e4 Sandstone, gritstone

e5 Slate

e9 Other natural stone

f **Precast with binder** *M* 8; *SF (1)* 5, 7, 8, 9, 10; *SF (2)* 4 to 9; *F* 1

f1 Sand-lime concrete (precast)
Glass fibre reinforced calcium silicate (gres)

f2 All-in aggregate concrete (precast) *M* 8
Heavy concrete (precast) *M* 8
Glass fibre reinforced cement (gre) *M* 10

f3 Terrazzo (precast) *F* 1
Granolithic (precast)
Cast/artificial/reconstructed stone

f4 Lightweight cellular concrete (precast) *M* 8

f5 Lightweight aggregate concrete (precast) *M* 8

f6 Asbestos based materials (preformed) *M* 10

f7 Gypsum (preformed) *C* 2
Glass fibre reinforced gypsum *M* 10

f8 Magnesia materials (preformed)

f9 Other materials precast with binder

g **Clay (Dried, Fired)** *M* 5; *SF (1)* 5, 9, 10; *SF (2)* 4, 6, 7

g1 Dried clay eg pisé de terre

g2 Fired clay, vitrified clay, ceramics
Unglazed fired clay eg terra cotta

g3 Glazed fired clay eg vitreous china

g6 Refractory materials eg fireclay

g9 Other dried or fired clays

h **Metal** *M* 9; *SF (1)* 6, 7, *SF (2)* 4, 5, 7

h1 Cast iron
Wrought iron, malleable iron

h2 Steel, mild steel

h3 Steel alloys eg stainless steel

h4 Aluminium, aluminium alloys

h5 Copper

h6 Copper alloys

h7 Zinc

h8 Lead, white metal

h9 Chromium, nickel, gold, other metals, metal alloys

i   **Wood** including wood laminates *M* 2, 3; *SF (1)* 5 to 8, 10; *SF (2)* 4, 9; *C* 2
i1   timber (unwrot)
i2   Softwood (in general, and wrot)
i3   Hardwood (in general, and wrot)
i4   Wood laminates eg plywood
i5   Wood veneers
i9   Other wood materials, except wood fibre boards, chipboards and wood-wool cement

j   **Vegetable and animal materials** – including fibres and particles and materials made from these
j1   Wood fibres eg building board *M* 3
j2   Paper *M* 9, 13
j3   Vegetable fibres other than wood eg flaxboard *M* 3
j5   Bark, cork
j6   Animal fibres eg hair
j7   Wood particles eg chipboard *M* 3
j8   Wood-wool cement *M* 3
j9   Other vegetable and animal materials

k, 1   Vacant

m   **Inorganic fibres**
m1   Mineral wool fibres *M* 10; *SF (2)* 4, 7
     Glass wool fibres *M* 10, 12
     Ceramic wool fibres
m2   Asbestos wool fibres *M* 10
m9   Other inorganic fibrous materials eg carbon fibres *M* 10

n   **Rubber, plastics, etc**
n1   Asphalt (preformed) *M* 11; *F* 1
n2   Impregnated fibre and felt eg bituminous felt *M* 11; *F* 7
n4   Linoleum *F* 1

Synthetic resins n5, n6
n5   Rubbers (elastomers) *M* 13
n6   Plastics, including synthetic fibres *M* 13
     Thermoplastics
     Thermosets
n7   Cellular plastics
n8   Reinforced plastics eg grp, plastics laminates

o   **Glass** *M* 12; *SF (1)* 5; *C* 5
o1   Clear, transparent, plain glass
o2   Translucent glass

o3   Opaque, opal glass
o4   Wired glass
o5   Multiple glazing
06   Heat absorbing/rejecting glass
     X-ray absorbing/rejecting glass
     Solar control glass
o7   Mirrored glass, 'one-way' glass
     Anti-glare glass
o8   Safety glass, toughened glass
     Laminated glass, security glass, alarm glass
o9   Other glass, including cellular glass

Formless materials p to s
p   **Aggregates, loose fills** *M* 8
p1   Natural fills, aggregates
p2   Artificial aggregates in general
p3   Artificial granular aggregates (light) eg foamed blast furnace slag
p4   Ash eg pulverised fuel ash
p5   Shavings
p6   Powder
p7   Fibres
p9   Other aggregates, loose fills

q   **Lime and cement binders, mortars, concretes**
q1   Lime (calcined limestones), hydrated lime, lime putty, *M* 7
     Lime-sand mix (coarse stuff)
q2   Cement, hydraulic cement eg Portland cement *M* 7
q3   Lime-cement binders *M* 15
q4   Lime-cement-aggregate mixes
     Mortars (ie with fine aggregates) *M* 15; *SF (2)* 4
     Concretes (ie with fine and/or coarse aggregates) *M* 8
q5   Terrazzo mixes and in general *F* 1
q6   Lightweight, cellular, concrete mixes and in general *M* 8
q9   Other lime-cement-aggregate mixes eg asbestos cement mixes *M* 10

r   **Clay, gypsum, magnesia and plastics binders, mortars**
r1   Clay mortar mixes, refractory mortar
r2   Gypsum, gypsum plaster mixes
r3   Magnesia, magnesia mixes *F* 1
r4   Plastics binders
     Plastics mortar mixes
r9   Other binders and mortar mixes

s   **Bituminous materials** *M* 11; *SF (2)* 4
s1   Bitumen including natural and petroleum bitumens, tar, pitch, asphalt, lake asphalt
s4   Mastic asphalt (fine or no aggregate), pitch mastic
s5   Clay-bitumen mixes, stone bitumen mixes (coarse aggregate)
Rolled asphalt, macadams
s9   Other bituminous materials

Functional materials t to w
t   **Fixing and jointing materials**
t1   Welding materials *M* 9; *SF (2)* 5
t2   Soldering materials *M* 9
t3   Adhesives, bonding materials *M* 14
t4   Joint fillers eg mastics, gaskets *M* 16 *SF (1)* 2
t6   Fasteners, 'builders ironmongery'
Anchoring devices eg plugs
Attachment devices eg connectors *SF (1)* 6, 7
Fixing devices eg bolts, *SF (1)* 5
t7   'Architectural ironmongery' *C* 7
t9   Other fixing and jointing agents

u   **Protective and Process/property modifying materials**
u1   Anti-corrosive materials, treatments *F* 6
Metallic coatings applied by eg electro-plating *M* 9
Non-metallic coatings applied by eg chemical conversion
u2   Modifying agents, admixtures eg curing agents *M* 8
Workability aids *M* 8
u3   Materials resisting specials forms of attack such as fungus, insects, condensation *M* 2
u4   Flame retardants if described separately *M* 1
u5   Polishes, seals, surface hardeners *F* 1; *M* 8
u6   Water repellants, if described separately
u9   Other protective and process/property modifying agents eg ultra-violet absorbers

v   **Paints** *F* 6
v1   Stopping, fillers, knotting, paint preparation materials including primers
v2   Pigments, dyes, stains
v3   Binders, media eg drying oils
v4   Varnishes, lacquers eg resins
Enamels, glazes

v5   Oil paints, oil-resin paints
Synthetic resin paints
Complete systems including primers
v6   Emulsion paints, where described separately
Synthetic resin-based emulsions
Complete systems including primers
v8   Water paints eg cement paints
v9   Other paints eg metallic paints, paints with aggregates

w   **Ancillary materials**
w1   Rust removing agents
w3   Fuels
w4   Water
w5   Acids, alkalis
w6   Fertilisers
w7   Cleaning materials *F* 1
Abrasives
w8   Explosives
w9   Other ancillary materials eg fungicides

x   **Vacant**

y   **Composite materials**
Composite materials generally *M* 11
See p. 63 *Construction Indexing Manual*

z   **Substances**
z1   By state eg fluids
z2   By chemical composition eg organic
z3   By origin eg naturally occuring or manufactured materials
z9   Other substances

Table 4   **Activities, Requirements** (main headings only)

Scope: Table 4 identifies objects which assist or affect construction but are not incorporated in it, and factors such as activities, requirements, properties, and processes.

Activities, aids
(A) Administration and management activities, aids *C* 11; *M* Introduction, *SF (1)* 2; *SF (2)* 1, 2, 3; *IB* 14, 17.13
(B) Construction plant, tools *SF (1)* 2; *SF (2)* 2, 11
(C) Vacant
(D) Construction operations *SF (1)* 2, 11; *SF (2)* 2, 11

Requirements, properties, building science, construction technology
Factors describing buildings, elements, materials, etc

(**E**) Composition, etc *SF (1)* 1, 2; *SF (2)* 1, 2; *IB* 1
(**F**) Shape, size, etc *SF (1)* 2; *IB* 4
(**G**) Appearance, etc *M* 1; *F* 6; *IB* 1

Factors relating to surroundings, occupancy

(**H**) Context, environment *IB* 6

Performance factors

(**J**) Mechanics *M* 9; *SF (1)* 3, 4; *SF (2)* 3, 4; *IB* 5
(**K**) Fire, explosion *M* 1; *SF (2)* 10; *IB* 9
(**L**) Matter *IB* 10
(**M**) Heat, cold *ES* 1; *IB* 8
(**N**) Light, dark *ES* 1; *IB* 10

(**P**) Sound, quiet *ES* 1; *IB* 7
(**Q**) Electricity, magnetism, radiation *ES* 14
(**R**) Energy, other physical factors *ES* 7; *IB* 3
(**T**) Application

Other factors

(**U**) Users, resources *IB* 11, 12
(**V**) Working factors
(**W**) Operation, maintenance factors
(**X**) Change, movement, stability factors
(**Y**) Economic, commercial factors *M* Introduction; *SF (1)* 2; *SF (2)* 3, 4, 5, 6, 9; *IB* 1, 13
(**Z**) Peripheral subjects, form of presentation, time, place – may be used for subjects taken from the UDC (*Universal decimal classification*), see BS1000A 1961

Subdivision: All table 4 codes are subdivided mainly by numbers

Acknowledgment to the 1971 edition

Figure and page numbers refer to the 1971 edition

The authors and publishers thank the many individuals and firms who have given help and advice in the preparation of this book and those who have given permission to quote from technical literature and other material.

The author of *Components* chapters 1 to 11 and *Roofings* chapter 18 thank the following for the use of drawings on which various figures are based:

Abbey Hanson Rowe and Partners for figure 76
D. Anderson and Son Limited for figures 268, 269 and part of 255
Boulton and Paul (Joinery) Limited for figure 111
The British Woodwork Manufacturers Association (EMJA Certification Trademark) for figures 45, 107, 110 and 119
Cape Universal for corrugated asbestos cement sheet roofing pages 401 to 410
Copper Development Association for copper roofing figures 280 and 281
Crittal Hope Limited for figures 121, 122, 164 and 167
Crosby and Company Limited for figures 10 and 56

Dixon Components (Building) Limited for figure 223
Expamet Contracts Limited for figures 228, 229 and 230
Fulbora Limited for figure 258
Gardiner Architectural Engineering Limited for figures 94, 135, 136 and 138
Grahams (Seacroft) Limited for figure 102
Aldam Coburn Limited for figures 86, 87, 88 and 92
Hill Brothers Glass Company Limited for figure 166
F. Hills and Sons Limited for figure 75
Louvre (Windows) Limited for figure 140
Lead Development Association for figures 120, 305 and 307
The Marley Tile Company Limited for figures 274, 275, 276, 277, 306 and 308
Mandor Engineering Lmited for figure 80
The Nuralite Company Limited for page 393
Paramount Asphalte Limited for figure 256
Permanite Limited for figure 255
Robin Architectural Products for figure 169
The Ruberoid Company Limited for figures 261, 263, 264, 265, 266, 267, 271, 272 and 273
Stramit Limited for figure 225
Tenon Contracts Limited for figures 137, 222 and 224

CIP Tentest Limited for figure 233
Venesta International Construction Materials Limited for figure 226
The author is also indebted to the following:
Arnold Ashton for practical advice regarding joinery manufacture and timber jointing
R. Baker of F. and E. V. Linford Limited for advice on joiner's shop production in chapter 2
R. H. Burford of Crosby and Company Limited for advice in chapter 3 on doors
R. E. Hale of Crittal-Hope Limited for help and advice on the metal windows section in chapter 4 and the SCOLA window-walling in chapter 11
Geoffrey Hamlyn Dip Arch FRIBA for making available the material relevant to the SCOLA system of Industrialized Building in chapter 11 and figures 234 to 247 inclusive
Peter Martin ARICS for reading and commenting on Component Design, chapter 1

A. Morris and T. Temple of Boulton and Paul (Joinery) Limited for information on the factory production of joinery components in chapter 2
Tenon Contracts Limited for information and advice on demountable partitions, chapter 9
G. E. Till and H. A. Bolton of The Ruberoid Company Limited for advice on built-up bitumen felt roofing in chapter 18
Mr Turley of MAC Engineering for advice on Ironmongery, chapter 7

Grateful thanks are due, in addition, to Robert Humphreys for his invaluable work in drawing diagrams and to G. W. Dilks for assisting. To E. M. Thomas for ably translating tape to typescript and to Thelma M. Nye for her most helpful and patient editorial advice.

Hexham 1971   H K

Acknowledgment to the 1979 edition

The publisher's desire to bring about this new edition of *Components* (as a separate volume from *Components and Finishes*) coincided with the tragic death of its original author, Harold King. Most of his excellent work remains, but I have made necessary alterations to bring it in line with current practice and attitudes.

I am grateful to the Director General and Clerk of Greater London Council for permission to quote from the London Building Acts 1930–39 and the Constructional By-laws made under these Acts, to the Controller of Her Majesty's Stationery Office for permission to quote from the Building Regulations 1976, and to the Directors of the following organisations for their kind permission for quotations to be made from their publications:

The Building Research Establishment
The British Standards Institution
The Fire Research Station
The Princes Risborough Laboratory
The British Woodworking Federation
Research and Development Associations of the construction industry

My gratitude also goes to those already listed under Harold King's acknowledgement who responded to my request for current information regarding their original contribution, the Velox Company Limited for their window details in figures 177 and 178, Hodkin and Jones (Sheffield Limited) for figure 166, and Timber Research and Development Association for their information on page 132 regarding the work of the Norwegian BRE.

David Clegg of the RIBA Services Limited gave invaluable guidance on the CI/SfB classification codings, and George Dilks proved very tolerant in producing new drawings and altering existing drawings.

I am indebted to my friend and colleague, Alan Everett, who not only redrafted the 'Joinery' chapter, but up-dated the 'Glazing' chapter and also helped me so willingly throughout. Leslie Coburn, senior lecturer in carpentry and joinery at the Polytechnic of North London, also gave valuable guidance during the preparation of the 'Joinery' chapter. Lastly, sincere thanks are given to Thelma M. Nye for patience and helpful editorial advice.

London 1979   D O

Index

Figures in *italics* refer to drawings